INVESTIGATING ARGUMENTS

ARGUMENTS

Readings for College Writing

JEFFREY WALKER

Pennsylvania State University

GLEN McCLISH

Southwestern University

HOUGHTON MIFFLIN COMPANY   BOSTON

Dallas   Geneva, Illinois   Palo Alto   Princeton, New Jersey

ACKNOWLEDGMENTS

SAPPHO
From Mary Barnard, tr., *Sappho: A New Translation*, Fragments 39, 40, 41, 42, 43, 87, 93, 82, and 60. Copyright © 1958 The Regents of the University of California; © renewed 1984 Mary Barnard.

GORGIAS OF LEONTINI
Extract adapted from George Kennedy, tr., "Gorgias' Encomium of Helen," in *The Older Sophists*, by Rosamund Kent Sprague. University of South Carolina Press, 1972. Used by permission of the publisher. Under license from Weidmann, Hagentorwall 7, D-3200, Hildesheim, West Germany.

LYSIAS
Reprinted by permission of The Loeb Classical Library from *Lysias*, W. R. M. Lamb, translator, Cambridge, Mass.: Harvard University Press, 1930.

PLATO
Reprinted with permission of Macmillan Publishing Company from Plato: *Phaedrus* translated by William C. Helmbold and Wilson Rabinowitz. © 1956 The Bobbs-Merrill Company, renewed 1984 by William C. Helmbold and Wilson Rabinowitz.

RENÉ DESCARTES
Excerpts from René Descartes, *Selected Philosophical Writings*, tr. by John Cottingham, Robert Stoothoff and Dugald Murdoch. Copyright © Cambridge University Press, 1988. Reprinted with the permission of Cambridge University Press.

Acknowledgments continue on page 625

CONTENTS

PREFACE
vii

INTRODUCTION

READINGS

CONTENTS

CONTENTS

PREFACE

Investigating Arguments treats rhetoric as a fundamentally dialogic art of critical thought and reasoned discourse—and rhetorical education as a process of gaining informed experience in rhetoric by engaging, in the context of a community discussion, with significant and challenging issues and arguments, and by inventing argumentation of one's own. In addition to the pragmatic goal of cultivating skill in discourse, a rhetorical education aims at the greater goal of helping students better exercise their freedom (and their responsibility) in the realm of ideas, a freedom (and responsibility) they all too frequently don't know they have. Rhetoric, after all, is the realm of thought in which things may always be otherwise.

What we offer, then, is a set of occasions for rhetorical experience in which students can exercise and develop their powers as critical readers and as writers of argumentative prose. In selecting these forty-one readings, at various levels of challenge and ranging over a broad historical spectrum from pre-Socratics to contemporaries, we have sought to enable students to examine issues and arguments in their intellectual-historical contexts; to examine a writer's argumentation critically, without being excessively reverential or thoughtlessly dismissive; to see the ways in which the argumentation of bygone writers still has (or can have) relevance today; to see relationships between different arguments, or the ways that differing arguments construct a conversation (or a set of conversations) among themselves; and, finally, to begin to take responsibility for their own place in the forum that has shaped, for better or for worse, the thinking of the civilization in which we live.

Though constrained by the number of readings we could realistically include, a part of our intent was to embody, or at least partially reflect, an intellectual history centered on the ancient and ongoing conflict between Sophistic and Platonic approaches to knowledge and discourse. This history includes some of the major shifts in Western thought, such as the emergence of scientific method, "natural reason," and the "rights of man"; Darwinism and the "death of God"; and the twentieth-century return to something like a Sophistic skepticism (but also an optimism) concerning the nature of "truth" and human belief. An important part of this history, moreover, is the emergence of strong critiques—from women, from Marxists, from African-Americans, and others—of the dominant culture and its values, and the increasing (though still limited) presence in the literary forum of voices formerly excluded from it. Though constrained by numbers, again, we have sought to represent this aspect of the story in our book. To represent the whole story fully would require, of course, an enormous volume; and to study it fully takes years, not weeks. Here, it functions as the background narrative in the choice and chronological arrangement of our readings—and, as represented by the readings themselves, as an introductory overview or sketch, and the beginnings of a full rhetorical education.

FEATURES

Besides offering a collection of readings as occasions for critical reading, discussion, and argumentative writing, *Investigating Arguments* also includes a number of features meant to inform the student's experience and help the instructor guide it.

- The *Introduction* presents, in dialogue format, an informal but concise discussion of the main rhetorical principles to be applied throughout the book, with major emphases on critical reading and inventing and developing written argumentation.
- *Headnotes* provide background information for each reading, such as discussion of the writer's historical context and rhetorical situation, and explanation of key terms and concepts that are presupposed but unexplained in the text itself. Headnotes are meant to frame the student's reading and rhetorical analysis but not to constrain or predetermine it.
- *Questions for Discussion and Writing* appear in both the Introduction and the readings. Those in the Introduction are meant to reinforce its basic concerns, while those in the readings supplement and extend those concerns by focusing attention on particular aspects of a writer's rhetoric and particular issues the writer's argument may raise.
- *Extensions* ask students to work with groups of readings that raise alternative perspectives on a given issue or on a rhetorical principle; they are, in effect, "extended" Questions for Discussion and Writing. Extensions can be used as a way of pulling together readings that have been studied individually or as the basis for a course syllabus.
- The *Glossary* provides an easily accessible, cross-referenced review of all the key rhetorical terms and concepts in *Investigating Arguments*, in some cases giving further detail; it also includes selected terms and concepts that we have not used in the book but that students may encounter or instructors may want to introduce.
- The *Instructor's Resource Manual* (bound separately) provides detailed suggestions for using the materials in this book and includes discussions of the Introduction and each of the readings, and of ways to set up and conduct a course.

ACKNOWLEDGMENTS

Rhetoricians will recognize that our approach owes much to the version of classical rhetoric rooted in Isocrates' *Antidosis*, Aristotle's *Rhetoric*, Cicero's *De Oratore*, and the counterarguments of Plato, from whom we have borrowed the speakers in our Introduction (though they have changed a lot since Plato's time)—and much as well to the modern work of Kenneth Burke, Chaim Perelman, and Stephen Toulmin. Beyond these major presences, particular debts become too numerous to list. We should, however, mention the professors and students of the Department of Rhetoric at the University of California, Berkeley, to whom we owe special gratitude. Among the friends and colleagues from whom we have learned we should at least mention John T. Gage and Marie Secor. For their assistance and encouragement, Jeffrey Walker thanks the English Department of Pennsylvania State University, which granted leave time when this book was in the early stages of development, and Yoko and Eliot, for being who they are. Glen McClish wishes to thank Stephanie Tyler, David Gaines, Edward Weismiller, Jackie Bacon, and, of course, Oscar. Thanks go to the students we have worked with at Penn State and Southwestern, for giving us reasons to believe in what we do. And we thank the editors at Houghton Mifflin who worked closely with this project for their intelligence and reasonability.

Finally, we are grateful to the following reviewers for their comments and suggestions:

Julia M. Allen, Sonoma State University, CA

Lynn Z. Bloom, The University of Connecticut

James V. Catano, Louisiana State University

Jean Chimsky, University of Cincinnati

Keith V. Comer, University of Oregon

Michael Daher, Henry Ford Community College, MI

Neil Daniel, Texas Christian University

Muriel Davis, San Diego Mesa College

Vivian I. Davis, Eastfield College, TX

Joan Graham, University of Washington

Miriam Dow, George Washington University, Washington, DC

David Foster, Drake University, IA

Susan J. Hanna, Mary Washington College, VA

Carolyn Hares-Stryker, University of California, Davis

Keith Hjortshog, Cornell University

Michael L. Keene, University of Tennessee

Dennis A. Lynch, University of California, Los Angeles

Mary A. McCay, Loyola University, LA

Kathy McClelland, University of California, Santa Barbara

George Miller, University of Delaware

Frank G. Novak, Jr., Pepperdine University, CA

Donovan J. Ochs, The University of Iowa

Louise Z. Smith, The University of Massachusetts-Boston

Donald C. Stewart, Kansas State University

George Y. Trail, University of Houston

J. D. Williams, The University of North Carolina at Chapel Hill

Robert Wiltenberg, Washington University in St. Louis

J.W. AND G.M.

INTRODUCTION

A GENERAL PROLOGUE

For reasons they themselves should make apparent, we have put our introduction into the mouths of Socrates and Phaedrus, speakers from a dialogue by Plato, though they are not quite the characters Plato portrays. Nor is this introduction really a Platonic dialogue. More than twenty centuries have passed since Plato wrote, and much has changed. Both speakers are aware of all that rhetoric has been between Plato's time and this. Both do, in fact, have modern minds. They represent the main positions in the debate about what rhetoric is or should be, a debate that extends from deep antiquity to now and that probably will never end, though from time to time one side or the other gets the upper hand.

The essence of our rationale, however, is this: Such doubleness of view is basic to rhetorical thought itself. Rhetoric, as we see it (and as others have said before us), is the realm in which things may always be otherwise, the realm in which belief stands open to change. It is, in fact, the realm in which virtually all the ideas we live by have been made. To learn to better exercise your freedom in this realm is the entire purpose of education. This book asks you to read, think, and write rhetorically—to read critically, examine arguments, and develop arguments of your own in the context of a "community" or group discussion—beginning with this introduction.

The dialogue from which our speakers come is Phaedrus, *a portion of which appears in this book (pp. 75–99).*

RHETORIC AND/OR PHILOSOPHY

SOCRATES   Phaedrus, remember how we lay that time, in the heat of a summer afternoon, in cool wild grass and tree-cast shade outside the city wall, listening to crickets and the gentle stream that ran nearby? And how we discussed your favorite subjects, love and rhetoric? And how I tried to save you from the wiles of clever Sophists? Or so they were called, back then, the ones who first codified and taught the art of rhetoric—the art, as they declared, by which opinions and beliefs are shaped, ignorance instructed, minds and hearts persuaded, persons changed, careers advanced, communities joined, and the fates of cities and nations guided.

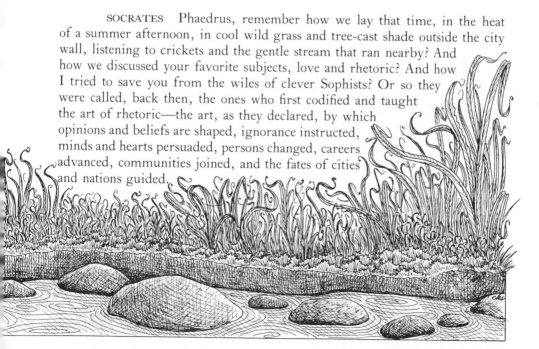

PHAEDRUS   I remember it all quite well. And a great art rhetoric is indeed, just as you say: the art by which societies decide the things that matter to them most—and without which there is only violence, coercion, and war. But you were much too hard on them—the Sophists, I mean—and on me.

SOCRATES   That may be so; but remember where we started from. You thought, as many did then and still do now, that rhetoric was simply a technique, or a collection of techniques, for composing "effective" discourse. Worse, you thought the practitioner didn't need to know the truth about the subject under discussion, and didn't need to be concerned about the truth, but needed only to know what his or her audience believed. The idea, it seemed, was to manipulate a crowd by playing on its preconceptions and emotions merely for personal gain, without caring much about the actual ideas one promoted. All that seemed to matter was personal success!

PHAEDRUS   I'm not quite sure that's how it was; but have it as you will.

SOCRATES   Those beliefs disturbed me greatly, just as they disturb me now, for they seemed to me not only foolish but immoral, irresponsible, and even dangerous. Shouldn't we care, for example, what justice is? Or should we care only about getting our way? Shouldn't the persuaders care if their persuasion helps or hurts the community? Or is the persuader just an isolated, disconnected, self-serving individual, a kind of privateer? And be-sides—can the superficial manipulator I'm describing really be successful with intelligent, well-informed, and thoughtful persons, those who care about the subject and have spent some time inquiring into it?

PHAEDRUS   I doubt it.

SOCRATES   Is rhetoric, then, merely a technique for preying on the ignorant and foolish? Is the rhetorician just a quack?

PHAEDRUS   Socrates—

SOCRATES   I tried to convince you, Phaedrus, that the rhetoric your teachers taught had little value. In fact, I tried to make you see that any genuine art of rhetoric must be philosophical, and that its best practitioner would also be a philosopher, by which I meant a "lover of wisdom"[1]—someone who knew the truth, or at least desired it, and could "cure" the "sickness" of false opinion with the "medicine" of knowledge. And didn't you agree with me?

PHAEDRUS   Yes, I did, but only because I was young and inexperi-enced, and so easily manipulated. Had I been more skilled in rhetoric (I was just a beginner), I would have better exercised that skill the Sophists were so famous for: arguing both (or many) sides of a question with equal vigor and persuasiveness. And that, my friend, is really the heart of rhetoric. So, Socrates, let's first of all admit that you were less than fair to the Sophists.

---

[1] In Greek, *philo* means "friend" or "lover"; *sophia* means "wisdom."

You loved to satirize them, exaggerate their positions, and present them at their worst for the sake of effect.

SOCRATES   Didn't everyone?

PHAEDRUS   But what happened to your "truth" and "medicine of knowledge"? All you really did was play with *my conception* of the Sophists' teachings, and not with the actual teachings themselves. In other words, you based your rhetoric on what I happened to believe, and manipulated those beliefs to produce persuasion—I mean, to lead me to conclusions you desired. You were, in short, following the very principles you seemed to be refuting!

And you could not have done otherwise, in truth; for whenever anyone persuades (or even teaches) anyone else, that's just what happens. There is no other way. So the Sophists were quite right. As you yourself said at one point, Socrates, a speech must be adapted to the "soul" of its listener, or to the thinking of its audience.

SOCRATES   Yes, but only to a point. It's not the speaker's job, for example, to make everything so easy that the audience must make no effort whatsoever. Speaker and audience must meet halfway; their meeting must be active, like a conversation. And further: There will be people we cannot persuade, no matter what we do; and there are limits to how much we can adjust or compromise the things we strongly believe! To adapt a speech *completely* to the soul of its listeners would be to tell them only what they already thought, and in the language most familiar to them. But the point of rhetoric is not to merely repeat what's obvious already, or to flatter people's prejudices (or even their thoughtless habits), or to betray ourselves. The point is to transform minds. And I don't see how anyone can do that, if they don't care about what's true. And I did, Phaedrus, care about what was true, even if I did manipulate your thinking.

PHAEDRUS   But the Sophists weren't indifferent to the truth! Rather, they were skeptical about the human ability to know it. Indeed, some of them were skeptical about the existence of any permanent "truth" at all. The world, the universe itself, might be in endless flux—we know the surface of the earth has changed over millions of years, and we know there is change among the stars—and even the laws of nature may not be permanent, but instead may change with time, though perhaps too slowly for us to tell. The upshot, Socrates, is that nobody can claim an absolute or certain knowledge of what's true.

SOCRATES   Well, who's to say? I myself did not reject this picture of an uncertain world, and I was always conscious of my ignorance and said so. But I wanted to believe in a truer, more permanent heaven of pure ideas that lay beyond this world, or behind it, or above it, somewhere. "Justice," for example, might be an actual eternal thing, with a permanent changeless nature: a thing confusedly, imperfectly reflected in the material world, but possibly seen and known by the reasoning power implanted in our souls. Sounds good, doesn't it?

PHAEDRUS   It's quite a seductive, beautiful idea. But the Sophists weren't seduced. On one hand, what reason is there to believe that any such heaven of truth exists? On the other, even if it does exist, how can we know that we perceive it, and not just a figment of our own imagination?

SOCRATES   Well, Phaedrus, I think I hear a sophistical line of thought advancing. Suppose we give it voice and say as follows: "Whatever the ultimate nature of reality may be, O Socrates, all we can ever know is *our experience of it,* and *our opinions or beliefs about that experience.* No human being ever directly knows the truth itself (if truth exists), and will never, in fact, know anything at all with certainty. All knowledge, all belief, is inescapably and thoroughly subjective, personal. And yet beliefs have consequences. Belief determines choice, and what we choose can bring us life or death, happiness or misery, wealth or poverty, success or failure, honor or shame. So we look for the best beliefs—the best opinions—by testing ideas through discussion, debate, and dialogue; by using our skill to find or make good arguments on every side of a question; and by constantly renewing and revising the possibilities of thought. What we call 'objectivity,' you truth-obsessed philosopher, is simply the result of all this comparing, testing, and revising of many subjectivities, many opinions. As we deem and declare, many eyes are better than two; diversity and difference of opinion improve our chance of judging well. Eventually we come, together, to some belief we find believeable enough, *persuasive enough,* to give the name of 'truth,' though temporarily. Accept this, Socrates. For if the world can change, as it assuredly does, and if our experience of it can change as well, then we never can afford to close our minds. Human beings, in sum, cannot have truth, but can achieve a flexible kind of wisdom, by considering the diverse arguments possible in any given case." How's that? Is that what your Sophists would have us say?

PHAEDRUS   I like it, Socrates. That's just what they do say, or at least the better ones.

SOCRATES   Yes, they do. And perhaps they would argue this way, too: "What if we did believe there was a fixed truth somewhere, and that some people knew it better, whereas others didn't? Don't you see the consequence, idealistic Socrates? We would end democracy. For only those who supposedly knew—the 'experts'—would be qualified to speak, or to have opinions, whereas the rest would be obliged to believe and do what experts told them. We would replace democratic dialogue with authoritarian monologue (although, of course, the authorities might have a dialogue among themselves). Freedom of speech would be curtailed. But what if we believe that *everyone is ignorant,* in varying degrees? And that's precisely what we ask you to believe. In this case, everyone (at least potentially) must have an equal right to speak in the public forum— and to be listened to—and everyone must have an equal right to judge." Would the Sophists argue this way, Phaedrus?

PHAEDRUS   Very probably. You've put it well.

SOCRATES   Then, it seems, the sophistical point of view is really democratic, whereas mine isn't—or wasn't, back then.

PHAEDRUS   Yes, so it seems.

SOCRATES   Yes . . . but I don't think we should give up yet on this philosophical rhetorician I propose.

PHAEDRUS   Why not? It seems to me you've rendered such a creature quite improbable, or undesirable.

SOCRATES   Because, Phaedrus, even if the Sophists are right about the nonexistence of certain or permanent truth, shouldn't we still desire the best possible opinions? Shouldn't we still care about what "justice" is—or about what people think it is—and about a thousand other things? And doesn't it still seem reasonable to say that no one can speak or write persuasively and well without also thinking well?

PHAEDRUS   Of course, Socrates. In fact, that's what the Sophists point to when they talk about finding, or inventing, the argument most worthy of belief in a given situation by imagining the possibilities and by considering different, even opposing, points of view. If that's what you call "philosophical," perhaps we have a point of agreement here.

SOCRATES   Yes, I think so. Indeed, Phaedrus, it seems to me that a person skilled merely in verbal technique and yet incapable of inventing arguments—a person whose skill amounted to dressing up what others had thought and said before—would be little more than a trained parrot. Such a person might impress the foolish, but could hardly persuade the wise, or contribute to the thought of the community, or even exercise good judgment. And so, my friend, I think we still can say that any worthwhile art of rhetoric must be philosophical, in one way or another, whether ultimate truth is reachable or not. I mean, Phaedrus, we must at least *desire* the best belief, if we are to gain real skill in rhetoric. And so we have come full circle, back to this crucial point, although we have modified it in the process.

PHAEDRUS   Yes, it seems that way.

SOCRATES   Then, Phaedrus, I think we will not be unjustified if we conclude, as many have done before us, that "rhetoric" must be defined as follows: the use of reason and critical thought to search for, or *invent,* the most persuasive argument, the one most worthy of belief, in a given set of circumstances. Agreed?

PHAEDRUS   Yes, but only if we add: *And to present it with grace and power.*

SOCRATES   Why so? You've lost me here.

RHETORICAL EDUCATION

PHAEDRUS   As I was listening to you talk, it struck me that scarcely any rhetorician shares your lack of interest in technique—even the ones that you might label "philosophical." For even if we do discover the best available belief (or even truth!), nothing guarantees that we can make this good belief prevail: Simply telling people what we think is best is not enough. Nor, for that matter, is crudely imposing our will on them by force. The agreement of others must, after all, be fairly earned. So merely knowing what is best is not enough. Even the truth is not enough. Truth is not self-evident, and doesn't speak for itself; indeed, the worse argument can (and sometimes does) defeat the better. It matters not only what you think and say, but *how* you say it to your audience. Our good, philosophical rhetorician must therefore also find or invent the most effective *strategy* for guiding the thoughts and feelings of readers and listeners. And here we come to matters of technique.

SOCRATES   So! It seems the Muse of Rhetoric has spoken; I've heard this argument before. I won't dispute it, but instead I'll recall another. For how does one acquire skill in these matters of technique? And, moreover, how does one acquire the deeper skill of inventing arguments? What the rhetoricians say, as I recall, goes something like the following: "Although technique is important, merely following a manual of technique—rules and formulas for inventing, structuring, and styling arguments—is of little use."

PHAEDRUS   Well, so some of them say. But why believe it?

SOCRATES   Because what makes the invention and presentation of an argument successful is its suitability to its *situation*, that is, to the issue, audience, and purpose for which it is designed. As you've reminded me, a speech must be adapted to the soul of its listener. Or a written discourse to the soul of its reader. (Up to a point!) Now, admitting we can generalize about some types of situations and can propose some general guidelines—I'll grant you this much, Phaedrus—we still can't avoid the fact that the *actual specific situations* one might face are endlessly variable. In short, we can't prescribe mechanical routines for inventing and presenting arguments in all possible situations, because all the possible situations are impossible to predict. Isn't this what Sophists say?

PHAEDRUS   Well, yes; some of them. But if that's right, how *does* one acquire skill in rhetoric? By talent? Don't you think you've made it seem entirely mysterious?

SOCRATES   Do I? Then I think we might say this: First, everyone has a certain amount (and I suspect the same amount) of natural, inborn talent. Rhetoric, the use of language to induce the agreement or cooperation of others, is a basic human activity, something all of us engage in every day. Human beings are rhetorical animals, by nature, by instinct, just as they are speaking animals. And all of us cultivate our natural capacity for rhetoric, just as we cultivate our natural capacity for language, through practical experience. So— depending on the sort of experience we get, and depending on the level of challenge at which we get it, some of us eventually become more "talented" than others. Or in other words, and truer ones, more skilled.

In the *art* of rhetoric, which applies to the somewhat more formal, artificial activities of oratory and writing, the relevant experience is participation in public discourse, either spoken or written (or both). This does not only mean practice in writing or speaking. Indeed, an essential form of experience is participation *as a member of an audience,* as a reader or listener. Of course, I don't mean the passive participation of the person who merely consumes or receives ideas, like a couch potato watching television. I mean an *active* reader or listener, one who carefully and critically interprets the arguments given in debate or in a single text, observing what the grounds of persuasion are and exercising judgment. Through such experience, one begins to cultivate the analytical, philosophical abilities essential for finding or inventing good arguments, as well as an awareness of techniques for effective presentation, varieties and effects of verbal style, and so forth.

PHAEDRUS   What all this seems to amount to, if I may say so, is a doctrine of *natural talent plus practical experience makes perfect*—though by talent you mean a fundamental human capacity with which all persons are endowed, and by practical experience you mean participating in discourse as a reader or listener as well as a writer or speaker. Is that your position, Socrates?

SOCRATES   Well, this is how we can explain the fact that some people have acquired great powers of reasoning and eloquence without any formal training in rhetoric (or philosophy or logic) at all.

PHAEDRUS   Yes, maybe, but this doctrine of yours, persuasive as it seems, has certain limitations, and it's insufficient as you've stated it.

SOCRATES   I thought you might say that—but please explain.

PHAEDRUS   First, let's note that even if we call experience the great and natural school of rhetoric, it is also the school of hard knocks, and a school of uneven quality. In nature, after all, for every seed that blooms a thousand come to nothing. Likewise, for every distinguished graduate of experience's school of rhetoric—the eloquent, well-reasoning person who has had no formal training—there are many more whose talents have scarcely developed at all. Perhaps it's obvious why this is so. Not all experiences are good or helpful. But there's another reason, too. Even good experience is useless, or of little use, if it is unclearly understood. We can't learn much from what we haven't noticed. We need some analytical knowledge, a knowledge of principles, to help us illuminate our experience and perceive it more richly.

Discussions of technique, Socrates, aren't meant as how-to-do-it recipes, or as rules of "correct" procedures that must be followed, or as "prescriptions" for fixing up our speech or writing, as you seem to think. Instead, they are meant as *descriptions* or *explanations* of the elements and principles of persuasive discourse. They don't tell us what to do in every single situation, but they give us a means of analyzing how rhetoric works—and, thus, of enriching the quality of our own experience, and of developing our competence more fully. So let's at least amend your doctrine, and say, "Natural talent plus practical experience *informed by theoretical knowledge* makes perfect," or at least improves the chances for development.

SOCRATES   That's fine with me—but doesn't it make a difference, too, what we have an experience *of*?

PHAEDRUS   I don't know. It seems to me we might start anywhere. We could, for example, start with the rhetoric of television commercials. In some ways, I'll admit, it's trivial and crude. But in other ways it's often very

9

skillful, and sometimes technically ingenious—and revealing, too, about the values, dreams, and fantasies our society seems to live on.

SOCRATES   That's true, but we're forgetting something. We have already agreed, I think, that rhetoric is not an art of mindless technique; it is, essentially, an art of reasoning. I don't say that we would waste our time by studying such things as television commercials, and indeed they may serve quite well as elementary illustrations. But let's remember that the *level of challenge* at which we gain experience has something to do with the level and quality of competence we cultivate, and that we are aiming primarily at competence in reasoning, or that kind of inquiry the rhetoricians call invention. For this we need experience with discourse in which significant ideas are at stake, and in which the argumentation is richly developed.

PHAEDRUS   You mean a study of "great ideas"? We should fill our heads with "great ideas" and imitate "great arguments"?

SOCRATES   No, you miss the point. And you're being unfair. The point, as I said before, is not to be a mere receiver of ideas, but to play an active role as audience member and respondent. Not all the so-called "great ideas" we meet in famous books are good ones, and none is entirely good. After all, as your Sophist friends point out, for every idea, and for every argument, there will always be some counteridea, some counterargument, that can be equally (or more) persuasive . . . under the right circumstances. And not all "significant ideas" are necessarily the ones considered "great" by people who like to make up lists of such things. No, Phaedrus, the point is not at all to fill up one's head—mindlessly—with somebody's collection of the "right" ideas to have. The point is to read critically, to exercise judgment, and to develop our own position (at a given moment) in relation to the arguments we meet. The point, I might even say, is to exercise our freedom, and powers, of thought—and to prepare ourselves to live in the public forum, in a free society.

And so the rhetorical education I have in mind requires the study of what your Sophist friends called literature. Of course (and you needn't remind me, Phaedrus, I know this perfectly well), by literature they simply meant all sorts of written discourse—including written versions of orations, poems, essays, histories, and so forth—that dealt with culturally or humanly significant issues. In fact, some of them thought the best literature to study was what they sometimes called "political" discourse, meaning written arguments concerning how the life of the city (*polis*, in Greek) should be conducted. Such political discourse dealt with ethics, economics, law, art, social customs, and many other things, as well as matters of governmental policy. Ultimately, it dealt with what some called the "philosophy of life." It spoke to the forum of community beliefs and values, and tried to build consensus through persuasion.

PHAEDRUS   Surely this isn't *you* I hear talking now, Socrates, or is it? Or perhaps the Sophist Isocrates, whom you once praised for being philosophical? Or is it Aristotle? Or that Roman orator, statesman and philosopher Cicero?

SOCRATES   Well, possibly. Suppose, Phaedrus, that we join them, and say: This literature we have in mind is generally the domain of highest eloquence, from which the writer or speaker draws the greatest persuasive power—*because* it is the domain of fundamental values and beliefs about which audiences most deeply care. With such literature, then, we can most fully exercise our powers of reasoning and judgment, and cultivate most fully our competence in rhetoric. As you yourself said, Phaedrus, rhetoric's the "art by which societies decide the things that matter to them most."

PHAEDRUS   So I did.

SOCRATES   Shall we, then, amend our notion of rhetorical education just once more, and then be done? Suppose we take your words and say, "Natural talent plus theoretical knowledge and practical experience *with challenging, significant discourse* (or literature)—through critical reading, and through the invention and presentation of arguments to audiences—is the best way to cultivate our skill in rhetoric." Will this be sufficient and acceptable, Phaedrus?

PHAEDRUS   It seems that way, at least right now—and in a general sense. But I think we need to talk about specifics . . .

*H*ere *we interrupt. Let's note, before Socrates and Phaedrus turn to these "specifics," that what they're discussing is, in fact, the model of rhetorical education that has generally prevailed from ancient to modern times—and that has evolved, from its early beginnings in the fifth century* B.C., *to become the varieties of "liberal education" we find at work in colleges and universities today.*

No single book, no single course in college, can possibly give you a complete rhetorical education of this kind. Indeed, this sort of education is never really finished, since there will always be new situations and new challenges from which to learn, an endless and infinite number. All one book or course can do is offer part of such an education, or the beginnings of one. What you will encounter in this book are many voices, embodied in written texts—some from the deep past, some more recent— offering various arguments, persuading (or trying to persuade) in various ways, and creating various opinions. Many of these arguments and voices have, for better or for worse, deeply affected the thinking of the civilization in which we live. Others have had more limited impact. But all of them are worth examining. The point, however (and as Socrates has argued), is not to treat what has been thought and said by distinguished writers as "great ideas" we cannot question. Likewise, we must not assume our task is merely to imitate these writers. The point is to read them critically and carefully, neither rejecting them out of hand nor paying thoughtless or excessive reverence, in an effort to assess the methods, grounds, and implications of their discourse. The point is to exercise responsible and reasoned judgment, to exercise our skill in argument. So that's what this book in your hand is for. It asks you to examine these texts, discuss them, and develop written arguments about their rhetoric—and about the issues that they raise.

Questions for Discussion and Writing

1. The word *rhetoric* is used in many ways, with many different meanings. Make a list of all the *negative* meanings commonly given it. Give an example of rhetoric that seems to fit each meaning. Then describe how you typically respond to these kinds of rhetoric, or at least one of them, and why. (Or discuss the characteristics these kinds of rhetoric seem to have in common.)

2. Socrates argues that a "superficial manipulator," skilled in technique but shallow in thought (or uninterested in truth or "wisdom"), can't be very successful. We wonder about this judgment. Are you persuaded? List examples that, in your opinion, do and do not support his claim. Then, explain how successful you think a "superficial manipulator" can really be, and why.

3. Is the Sophistic approach to knowledge and rhetoric (as presented here) really more democratic than what Socrates prefers? Are there dangers in a Sophistic approach? List examples that illustrate the advantages and problems you can see in this approach. Then discuss the ways in which you would defend, adjust, revise, or oppose the position Socrates has taken here.

CRITICAL READING

PHAEDRUS   Well, Socrates, it seems we've agreed, in a general sort of way, that rhetorical competence is cultivated by practical experience—that is, by the critical reading of what we might call rhetorical literature, and by the development and presentation of arguments to audiences—informed by "theoretical knowledge" of rhetorical principles. And, that being the case, I have a suggestion to make.

SOCRATES   What is it?

PHAEDRUS   Suppose we look at an actual text and consider what some of the principles involved in critical reading are.

SOCRATES   That's fine with me. But, in one way, it seems to me the principles are fairly simple. First of all, we need to think about the *intention* revealed in the design of a text—I mean, the effect the writer has tried to have on a certain audience—and about *the means of persuasion* the writer has employed. Basically, we can ask, *What has the writer tried to do, and how has the writer tried to do it?*

And further, we can ask questions like, *How much am I persuaded?* or, *What's my position?* as we try to formulate our own relation to the text and develop a reasoned response.

PHAEDRUS   Well, yes—but again, suppose we consider what this general description means, in practice, looking at an actual text.

SOCRATES   What text, Phaedrus?

PHAEDRUS   I have it right here with me, in my coat. It's an essay—an extract from a book, really—called "Shakespeare's Sister," by Virginia Woolf.

SOCRATES   All right. Please go right ahead—read it through, and we can talk about what a critical reader might be looking at, and looking for.

But first, since "Shakespeare's Sister" is really just one part of a larger discourse, a book, tell me a little about that book, to help me frame the text. Are you familiar with it?

PHAEDRUS   Reasonably. The book's called *A Room of One's Own,* and it's based on two lectures Woolf delivered in 1928, at Newnham and Girton—two women's colleges at Oxford and Cambridge, in England—on the general subject of "women and fiction," and more specifically on the question (which she raises in the opening paragraph of the first chapter) why "a woman must have money and a room of her own if she is to write fiction." The book itself is written as an imaginary lecture to a group of women at an imaginary college—"Oxbridge"—in which Woolf speaks partly as herself and partly as a fictional character: "Call me Mary Beton, Mary Seton, Mary Carmichael or by any name you please," she says in her introduction. The names are taken, by the way, from an old folk ballad that tells a tragic tale: "Last night there were four Maries, / Tonight there'll be but three; / There was Mary Seton, and Mary Beton, / and Mary Carmichael, and me." The "me" in the balled is a servant girl, Mary Hamilton, who's about to be executed for killing the illegitimate infant fathered on her by the master of her house, her king.

I guess that's enough of a frame, for now. "Shakespeare's Sister" is actually part of the third chapter. Woolf is discussing the time of Queen Elizabeth, when Shakespeare lived and wrote; and, as her previous chapter has shown, she—or Mary Seton/Beton/Carmichael—has been doing some research in the library. Now listen carefully, Socrates. What is Woolf trying to do, and how is she trying to do it? It starts like this:[1]

SHAKESPEARE'S SISTER

It is a perennial puzzle why no woman wrote a word of that extraordinary literature   1
when every other man, it seemed, was capable of song or sonnet. What were the conditions in which women lived, I asked myself; for fiction, imaginative work that is, is not dropped like a pebble upon the ground, as science may be; fiction is like a spider's web, attached ever so lightly perhaps, but still attached to life at all four corners. Often the attachment is scarcely perceptible; Shakespeare's plays, for instance, seem to hang there complete by themselves. But when the web is pulled askew, hooked up at the edge, torn in the middle, one remembers that these webs are not spun in midair by incorporeal creatures, but are the work of suffering human beings, and are attached to grossly material things, like health and money and the houses we live in.

I went, therefore, to the shelf where the histories stand and took down one of   2
the latest, Professor Trevelyan's *History of England*. Once more I looked up Women, found "position of," and turned to the pages indicated. . . .

I'm going to skip a little here. Basically, she finds Trevelyan reviewing a few facts about the lives of Elizabethan women, facts that contrast strangely with the images one finds in literature:

It was certainly an odd monster that one made up by reading the historians first   3
and the poets afterwards—a worm winged like an eagle; the spirit of life and beauty in a kitchen chopping up suet. But these monsters, however amusing to the imagination, have no existence in fact. What one wants, I thought—and why does not some brilliant student at Newnham or Girton supply it?—is a mass of

---

[1] For additional information on Woolf, and for the second chapter of *A Room of One's Own*, see pp. 365–376.

information; at what age did she marry; how many children had she as a rule; what was her house like; had she a room to herself; did she do the cooking; would she be likely to have a servant? All these facts lie somewhere, presumably, in parish registers and account books; the life of the average Elizabethan woman must be scattered about somewhere, could one collect it and make a book of it.

But what I find deplorable is that nothing is known about women before the 4 eighteenth century. I have no model in my mind to turn this way and that. Here am I asking why women did not write poetry in the Elizabethan age, and I am not sure how they were educated; whether they were taught to write; whether they had sitting-rooms to themselves; how many women had children before they were twenty-one; what, in short, they did from eight in the morning until eight at night. They had no money evidently; according to Professor Trevelyan they were married whether they liked it or not before they were out of the nursery, at fifteen or sixteen very likely. It would have been extremely odd, even upon this showing, had one of them suddenly written the plays of Shakespeare, I concluded, and I thought of that old gentleman, who is dead now, but was a bishop, I think, who declared that it was impossible for any woman, past, present, or to come, to have the genius of Shakespeare. He wrote to the papers about it. He also told a lady who applied to him for information that cats do not go to heaven, though they have, he added, souls of a sort. How much thinking those old gentlemen used to save one! How the borders of ignorance shrank back at their approach! Cats do not go to heaven. Women cannot write the plays of Shakespeare.

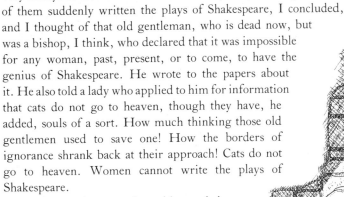

Be that as it may, I could not help thinking, as I looked at the plays of Shake- 5 speare on the shelf, that the bishop was right at least in this; it would have been impossible, completely and en- tirely, for any woman to have writ- ten the plays of Shakespeare in the age of Shakespeare. Let me

imagine, since facts are so hard to come by, what would have happened had Shakespeare had a wonderfully gifted sister, called Judith, let us say. Shakespeare himself went, very probably—his mother was an heiress—to the grammar school, where he may have learnt Latin—Ovid, Virgil and Horace—and the elements of grammar and logic. He was, it is well known, a wild boy who poached rabbits, perhaps shot a deer, and had, rather sooner than he should have done, to marry a woman in the neighborhood, who bore him a child rather quicker than was right. That escapade sent him to seek his fortune in London. He had, it seemed, a taste for the theatre; he began by holding horses at the stage door. Very soon he got work in the theatre, became a successful actor, and lived at the hub of the universe, meeting everybody, knowing everybody, practising his art on the boards, exercising his wits in the street, and even getting access to the palace of the queen. Meanwhile, his extraordinarily gifted sister, let us suppose, remained at home. She was as adventurous, as imaginative, as agog to see the world as he was. But she was not sent to school. She had no chance of learning grammar and logic, let alone of reading Horace and Virgil. She picked up a book now and then, one of her brother's perhaps, and read a few pages. But then her parents came in and told her to mend the stockings or mind the stew and not moon about with books and papers. They would have spoken sharply but kindly, for they were substantial people who knew the conditions of life for a woman and loved their daughter—indeed, more likely than not she was the apple of her father's eye. Perhaps she scribbled some pages up in an apple loft on the sly, but was careful to hide them or set fire to them. Soon, however, before she was out of her teens, she was betrothed to the son of a neighbouring wool-stapler. She cried out that marriage was hateful to her, and for that she was severely beaten by her father. Then he ceased to scold her. He begged her instead not to hurt him, not to shame him in this matter of her marriage. He would give her a chain of beads or a fine petticoat, he said; and there were tears in his eyes. How could she disobey him? How could she break his heart? The force of her own gift alone drove her to it. She made up a small parcel of her belongings, let herself down by a rope one summer's night and took the road to London. She was not seventeen. The birds that sang in the hedge were not more musical than she was. She had the quickest fancy, a gift like her brother's, for the tune of words. Like him, she had a taste for the theatre. She stood at the stage door; she wanted to act, she said. Men laughed in her face. The manager—a fat, loose-lipped man—guffawed. He bellowed something about poodles dancing and women acting—no woman, he said, could possibly be an actress. He hinted—you can imagine what. She could get no training in her craft. Could she even seek her dinner in a tavern or roam the streets at midnight? Yet her genius was for fiction and lusted to feed abundantly upon the lives of men and women and the study of their ways. At last—for she was very young, oddly like Shakespeare the poet in her face, with the same grey eyes and rounded brows—at last Nick Greene the actor-manager took pity on her; she found herself with child by that gentleman and so—who shall measure the heat and violence of the poet's heart when caught and tangled in a woman's body?—killed herself one winter's night and lies buried at some cross-roads where the omnibuses now stop outside the Elephant and Castle.

That, more or less, is how the story would run, I think, if a woman in Shakespeare's day had had Shakespeare's genius. But for my part, I agree with the deceased bishop, if such he was—it is unthinkable that any woman in Shakespeare's day would have had Shakespeare's genius. For genius like Shakespeare's is not born among labouring, uneducated, servile people. It was not born in England among the Saxons and the Britons. It is not born today among the working classes. How, then, could it have been born among women whose work began, according to Professor Trevelyan, almost before they were out of the nursery, who were forced to it by their parents and held to it by all the power of law and custom? Yet genius of a sort must have existed among women as it must have existed among the working classes. But certainly it never got itself on to paper. When however, one reads of a witch being ducked, of a woman possessed by devils, of a wise woman selling herbs, or even of a very remarkable man who had a mother, then I think we are on the track of a lost novelist, a suppressed poet who dashed her brains out on the moor or mopped and mowed about the highways crazed with the torture that her gift had put her to. Indeed, I would venture to guess that Anon,[2] who wrote so many poems without signing them, was often a woman. It was a woman, I think, who made the ballads and folk-songs, crooning them to her children, beguiling her spinning with them, or the length of the winter's night.

Well, Socrates, what do you think of that?

    SOCRATES   It's certainly well written, and generally persuasive, I think, though some parts puzzle me. But first, let's consider the various aspects of its rhetoric.

    PHAEDRUS   Starting where?

    SOCRATES   We might start anywhere that seems appropriate. There's no particular procedure we must follow, no mechanical routine. But suppose, for now, we start with the general question of *intention*.

    PHAEDRUS   Fine; but tell me what you mean by that.

INTENTION

    SOCRATES   The basic point, I think, is to remember what's obvious in spoken discourse—and especially in oratory—but easily forgotten in writing. Discourse always happens in a situation involving at least two people: it is always directed *to someone*, and for some purpose. In writing this is easily forgotten, because the reader isn't present to the writer, except as a mental image of an *intended audience* the writer hopes to connect with. And the writer

---

[2] *Anon:* an abbreviation for "anonymous" that typically appears in literature anthologies. [Editors' note.]

isn't present to the reader, except (again) as a mental image of an *implied author* that the reader infers, mainly, from the ideas and attitudes reflected in the text. Likewise, the speaker in the text may or may not be a direct representation of the author—and may be an entirely or partly fictional character, or what is sometimes called a "persona"—and may be speaking not directly to the intended audience, but to a fictional audience within the text— just as we see, it seems, in this book of Woolf's.

PHAEDRUS   But what does all this have to do with intention? It seems to me you're drifting.

SOCRATES   My point is this: We need to keep in mind the actual situation of the text we read, as well as we can understand it, so we can be reasonably clear about our own relation, as readers, to the writer's rhetoric. We need to be clear about *what the writer is trying to do*—and to whom, and why.

PHAEDRUS   So, what *is* the writer trying to do?

SOCRATES   The writer, basically, is trying to *persuade an audience to answer a certain question (or questions) in a certain way*. This question is, in fact, what creates the situation in the first place—insofar, at least, as it is a question about which people might reasonably argue, and that seems to be worth answering. It's what creates the writer's urge to write in the first place, and the reader's urge to read.

PHAEDRUS   Show me what this means, Socrates, in "Shakespeare's Sister." How do we recognize the writer's intentions, or the writer's intended audience?

SOCRATES   The simplest way to identify intention is to look at *introductions* and *conclusions*. One basic function of an introduction, after all, is to bring the issue into focus, to help the audience perceive the relevance of what follows. The issue may be focused by stating it as a question of some kind, or by stating the *thesis* the writer intends to prove—in which case, the question at issue becomes, "Why so?" And, of course, we typically find a focused statement of the thesis in conclusions also, as the writer brings the argument to closure.

We see this clearly in "Shakespeare's Sister." Woolf focuses the issue, in her introductory paragraph, by stating, "It is a perennial puzzle why no woman wrote a word of that extraordinary literature," and so on—and then she asks, focusing further, "What were the conditions in which women lived?" The answer to the second question is the basis for an answer to the first one, as we see in Woolf's concluding paragraph: "It is unthinkable that any woman in Shakespeare's day would have had Shakespeare's genius," she says, because such genius "is not born among labouring, uneducated, servile people." So, Phaedrus, I would say that Woolf's basic intention is to persuade her audience to believe this thesis, and its supporting "because."

PHAEDRUS   Yes, I see that, but it seems to me not every text will offer such clearly focused statements of the questions at issue, or of the writer's thesis. Even here, in fact, I'm not sure that all of Woolf's intention has been directly stated.

SOCRATES   Well—that's so. In some cases, when the writer thinks the issue is obvious already to the audience, the introduction may not give it any focused statement at all; and, likewise, writers won't always state the thesis either, in a conclusion or anywhere, if they feel their argument has made it obvious enough. Some things will simply be *implied*. In such cases, we have to infer the writer's intention from the overall design of the text itself. This is frequently the case, in fact, with "poetic" kinds of discourse—including not only poems, but also fictional narratives, plays, and movies.

But even in more direct kinds of argument (and Woolf's is reasonably direct, even though she frames it in a semifictional situation), the writer aims not only at the proof or explication of a thesis, but at a total *effect on the reader's mind* (and heart). Woolf, it seems to me, intends her audience not only to believe that Elizabethan women could not have had Shakespeare's "genius" because of the "labouring, uneducated, servile" condition in which they lived— but also to believe, or feel, that women were unjustly, tragically oppressed, and to feel that such oppression shouldn't be permitted. And we can infer this, as I say, from the overall design of the text: from the story of Judith Shakespeare, in particular, and from the general attitude Woolf seems to adopt.

PHAEDRUS   That seems reasonable enough. So tell me—who's the audience for "Shakespeare's Sister"?

SOCRATES   We can talk about this on several levels, if we wish. For example, we can talk about Woolf's original audience, the audience of her lectures in 1928—upper-class, well-educated British women at elite colleges, who have an interest in the arts. Or we can talk about the broader reading audience (including, probably, men as well as women) the published book was aimed at, when it first appeared.

But we can talk about a still more generalized audience, one distributed over time, up to and including the audience the text may have today. This audience corresponds to the original audience only in approximate ways, and in varying degrees. This audience, basically, consists of *those who care about the issues* the writer is dealing with—anyone, in short, able to feel the text is "talking to" them. Or anyone who can imagine the audience of the text and play its role.

Woolf's audience today, for example, can include not only those who find the "perennial puzzle" she mentions a question worth exploring, but also those who care about a number of related questions—about the nature of social justice; about the historical place of women in a male-dominated society, and what their place should be in a just society; or about the nature of oppression and its effect on people's capacity for cultural achievement; or about what people need to overcome oppression; or about the nature of artistic "genius," or "genius" generally; and so on. Insofar as we care about these things, and feel that "Shakespeare's Sister" speaks to such concerns, we become members of the audience—in one way or another.

PHAEDRUS   So then, it seems we now can say that Woolf is trying to persuade an audience that cares about such things (or some of them) that women in Shakespeare's time could not have achieved "genius" because of the conditions in which they lived—and this constituted tragic and unjust oppression.

SOCRATES   Right. Of course, different readers may interpret Woolf's intentions somewhat differently; but for now, I think, we can agree that such a statement is more or less adequate.

PHAEDRUS   Then, since we agree about *what* Woolf is trying to do, let's consider *how* she tries to do it. How should we describe her methods?

MEANS OF PERSUASION

SOCRATES   We need, Phaedrus, to consider the basic *means of persuasion* writers have available. I mean the processes of *argumentation*, by which the writer can establish *relationships between ideas*—that is, relationships among:

1.   The *inferences* or *judgments* the writer asks the audience to make
2.   The *reasons* for those inferences and judgments
3.   *Assumptions*—ideas the writer doesn't try to prove but expects the audience to share, or to take on faith—ideas that make the jump from reason to inference "reasonable"

Argumentation, really, is a reasoning process—unfolding paragraph by paragraph, page by page—by which the writer connects ideas that readers may not believe in yet with ideas they definitely do believe in, to make them feel the writer's judgments are consistent with the judgments they themselves would also make. And every idea that is established then becomes part of the pool of available "assumptions" on which further reasoning can build.

PHAEDRUS   According to the rhetoricians, Socrates, reasons come from three main sources: *logos*, by which we mean the statements actually given in the text; *ethos*, the character of the writer or person speaking; and *pathos*, the feelings of the audience. Reasons from these sources are sometimes called "appeals," or "proofs."

SOCRATES   Yes, but I prefer to think of writers presenting "reasons," rather than "proofs," for the relative *probability* of some claim (compared, that is, to other claims that might be made). But now, since you're so well informed, suppose you tell me about Woolf's logos.

LOGOS

PHAEDRUS   Well, according to the rhetoricians, proofs from logos— or "logical" proofs, or reasons—consist of things like explanations that tell why or how a certain state of affairs (past, present, or future) is likely to be true; or examples that seem to confirm or illustrate a point; or statistics; or testimony from authorities or witnesses; or citations of various kinds of factual evidence; and so forth.

SOCRATES   Yes, but "logical proof" can be a misleading name. Again, *logos* simply means "statement," or "word." So when we say a proof is logical, that's all we really mean: one statement is made persuasive by being connected to some other statement that gives a reason (or reasons) for believing it. And, to say a proof is logical does *not* necessarily mean it's right, or automatically persuasive or true. The persuasiveness of logos comes not from the mere fact of being logical, but from the strength of the reasons given and the assumptions they depend on—as judged, that is, by the audience.

PHAEDRUS   Yes, I know that. Anyway—if you'll let me use the word—Woolf's logical reasons consist partly of the facts she cites, but mainly of one long example, namely, the story of Judith Shakespeare. The facts, which she takes from Trevelyan's *History of England*, seem to support a general impression that women in Shakespeare's time were "labouring, uneducated, servile people," as she later says. This leads her, in the fourth paragraph, to offer the tentative conclusion that "it would have been extremely odd, even on this showing, had one of them suddenly written the plays of Shakespeare." Here she asks her audience to assume that, in general, "labouring, uneducated, servile people" are unlikely to produce great literature—it's an assumption about probability, about the way things tend to happen. If the audience believes that assumption, Woolf's conclusion will seem to make rational sense; otherwise, her conclusion will seem nonsensical or unpersuasive.

SOCRATES   Yes, but there's another assumption Woolf's audience must accept for this reasoning to be really persuasive—namely, that the few facts she's collected are sufficient evidence for believing her general picture of Elizabethan women's lives. I'm not so sure they are. Also, all her facts seem to come from just one book, Trevelyan's *History*. Is that a sufficient basis for making factual claims?

PHAEDRUS   Much depends, I think, on whether the audience considers Trevelyan an authority; perhaps the few facts he reports are all that is available. And besides, remember that Woolf (or her speaker) is talking to an audience that is reasonably well educated, and British, and that probably has some knowledge about Elizabethan life already. What Woolf says may be reasonably consistent with what they know already—or consistent enough for them to find it *plausible*, at least.

That's why Woolf includes, I think, the hypothetical example of Judith Shakespeare. It serves to make her tenatative conclusion seem more *probable*, and persuasive, by illustrating it in concrete detail. Again, if this story fits the audience's sense of what Elizabethan life was like, and of how things probably would have happened for a woman who tried to live a life like Shakespeare's, it will seem believable. And, insofar as it does seem believable, it works to *confirm* the reasoning that preceded it.

SOCRATES   Yes, and there's another sort of assumption working in this story, too—namely, that Shakespeare could have had a sister as "gifted" as himself. If the audience won't accept the premise that a woman could really be that gifted, the whole story falls apart and becomes merely an unrealistic, unbelievable fantasy. (This is just how it would look to someone like the bigoted old bishop she mentioned in the fourth paragraph.) Woolf requires her audience to assume the basic premise of her story as an actual possibility.

PHAEDRUS   Yes—but notice that she does give this assumption, and the story itself, a certain amount of confirmation in her concluding paragraph, when she says, "When . . . one reads of a witch being ducked, of a woman possessed by devils, of a wise woman selling herbs . . . then I think we are on the track of a . . . suppressed poet," and so on. Here the facts seem to fit the pattern of Woolf's hypothetical story, and thus enhance its probability.

SOCRATES   That's good, Phaedrus; I like that. But that's enough, for now, about Woolf's logos. Tell me about her use of ethos, as you see it.

ETHOS

PHAEDRUS   *Ethos* means "character," or *apparent character*. In "ethical" proof, the writer's or speaker's character—as the audience sees it—functions as a reason for trusting (or not trusting) or believing (or not believing) what is said. The main ways in which an ethos can be made persuasive are three:

1. "Credentials" or qualifications the writer presents or reveals, plus whatever reputation the writer may have already (does the writer seem knowledgeable about the subject under discussion?)
2. Attitudes and values communicated by direct statement (does the writer declare belief in certain values, or explicitly praise or blame certain kinds of things?)
3. Attitudes and values indirectly communicated by the writer's "tone of voice," or style (does the writer indirectly praise or blame certain things by adopting tones of scorn, admiration, reverence, outrage, humor, and the like?)

SOCRATES   In "Shakespeare's Sister," the question of ethos is a little complex, isn't it? How much is Woolf's fictive or semifictive speaker, "Mary Seton/Beton/Carmichael," a direct representation of herself? If they are different, then we really have two layers of ethos to think about: the ethos of Woolf's persona and the ethos of the author behind the text, "Woolf herself," as we imagine her.

PHAEDRUS   For now, let's assume they're more or less the same; I think they are, in fact. "Mary Seton/Beton/Carmichael" is a version of Woolf, a kind of self-portrait.

Some of Woolf's "credentials" include, first of all, the fact that she is herself a prominent female writer, and (on that account) has been invited to speak on the subject of "women and fiction" at an elite university. In addition, she shows herself doing research on the subject, not only in "Shakespeare's Sister" but throughout the book, and generally displays wide knowledge of both literature and history. These facts make it apparent that she's highly qualified to talk about the issues she brings up.

Among the many attitudes and values Woolf communicates, directly and indirectly, we might point to her commitment to "being reasonable"—the way she looks for factual evidence, her skeptical but fair treatment of authorities like Trevelyan (whose account of Elizabethan women Woolf partly accepts, and partly rejects) and her dismissive treatment of irrational prejudices like the bishop's. Further, she seems committed to "being reasonable" in a specifically female way, one that is consistent with her general picture of women's (traditional) exclusion from the male world of scholarship and literature: Her argument is not conducted in the language of academic treatises (like Trevelyan's), but in a more personal, lively, nonauthoritative style, and with a definite feminine perspective on history—pointing out, for example, areas of research neglected by male scholars that the women at Newnham and Girton might pursue.

In general, Woolf presents an ethos that is well qualified, appropriate to the sort of person she claims to be and to the speaking situation of a woman lecturing to women, fair in her opinions, and personally engaging. All this makes the reader more inclined to be receptive to her arguments.

SOCRATES   Yes, but that's not "proof." I don't think her ethos gives the reader sufficient reason to *believe* her arguments, all by itself.

PHAEDRUS   It's not supposed to. That would, in fact, be inconsistent with the skeptical attitude toward authority she herself presents. The main function of ethos, generally, is not to make the audience yield its freedom of opinion to the demands of some authority, but to make the writer's statements seem *reliable*. But even if it isn't a decisive proof, ethos is essential. After all, no amount of "logic," however "logical" it sounds, is likely to persuade an audience that feels distrustful, suspicious, and resistant. Don't you agree?

SOCRATES   Well, yes—

PHAEDRUS   And likewise for the so-called "pathetic" or "emotional" proof. Who can persuade an audience that doesn't care, or has no feelings at all about the subject?

SOCRATES   So tell me about Woolf's use of pathos, then.

PATHOS

PHAEDRUS   *Pathos* means "feeling," or more specifically *the feelings of the audience*. Feelings of anger, admiration, pity, sadness, charity, outrage, duty, or whatever can be provoked and used as reasons for believing (or doing) what the writer says.

The ways of rousing and guiding a reader's feelings are, perhaps, even more various than the ways of establishing ethos. But again we might summarize. The main ways seem to be:

1. Presenting "images" or scenes that make strong impact on the reader's imagination and that arouse feelings (of sadness, fright, amusement, desire, or whatever)
2. Placing strong emphasis on ideas or concepts (such as "freedom") that have deep emotional resonance for the reader, either through the use of memorable figures of speech or simply by dwelling on the concept at some length
3. Using emotive language to intensify the feelings aroused by concepts and/ or images

And, of course, all three ways of generating pathos may combine, in various ways.

In "Shakespeare's Sister," clearly, the main means of arousing pathos is the story of Judith, with its "images and scenes." Instead of discussing her fate in general, abstract terms, Woolf brings her before the reader's imagination. We see her scribbling "some pages up in an apple loft on the sly," we see her father beating her and begging her "not to hurt him," we see her climbing down a rope with her "small parcel" of belongings, we see her on the road to London, in summer, with the birds singing—and so on. All this makes her seem more like an actual person, and makes it easier to sympathize and to respond emotionally to what she suffers: We feel, not just think, how unjust it is, and how tragic, for such a "gifted" young woman (or any young woman) to come to such a fate. So it is the audience's emotional response, as provoked by this story, that becomes the main reason, in Woolf's concluding paragraph, for feeling that the conditions of Elizabethan women's lives, in general, were oppressive and wrong—and, in the final lines, for attaching feelings of sympathy for the oppressed to the "witch being ducked," the "woman possessed by devils," the "wise woman selling herbs," and so on, down to the woman "beguiling her spinning, or the length of the winter's night," by "crooning" ballads to her children.

SOCRATES   Yes, that is certainly Woolf's central use of pathos, but there are numerous other uses as well. For example, she makes the bishop (in the fourth paragraph) seem laughable by putting his ideas about women next to his ideas about cats going to heaven, and she emphasizes that feeling with an ironic or sarcastic tone of voice: "How much thinking those old gentlemen used to save one!" and so on. Or, in the first paragraph, her poetic description of imaginative literature connected to life "like a spider's web" helps to make the idea seem not only realistic, but also beautiful—whereas her description of it as the work of "suffering human beings" adds an appeal to the audience's sense of sympathy. And so on. We could talk in great detail, if we wanted to, about how Woolf connects with the reader's feelings and uses those feelings as reasons for making certain kinds of judgments, or for responding in certain ways to the ideas she presents. But now there's another point I wish to make.

PHAEDRUS   Which is?

THE "LOGIC" OF LOGOS, ETHOS, AND PATHOS

SOCRATES   I fear we're on the verge of a typical mistake—if we suppose that calling one mode of proof "logical" means the other kinds are therefore "not logical," or "irrational" somehow.

All three kinds are logical, or rational, because in every case persuasion comes from the reader's intuitive perception of relationships among ideas. The logic of logos inheres, as we have said, in the perceived relationships between actual statements, with one statement standing as the evidence or explanation for another. The logic of ethos and pathos is less explicit, but it inheres, similarly, in the connection between unspoken, subconscious ideas and the information that enters consciousness. If, for example, the reader's impression of the writer's ethos fits the reader's sense of what a trustworthy person is, then the reader will probably consider that writer trustworthy also, and place some trust in what the writer says. Pathos is basically the same. If certain things that enter the reader's mind fit the reader's deep, gut-level ideas about, say, what is frightening, laughable or beautiful, then that is how these things will seem—and, accordingly, the reader will feel frightened, or will laugh, or will admire. And, of course, these feelings will then affect any further judgment the reader makes about the things in question.

Most readers will make these kinds of responses without awareness of the complex mental processes involved, or even the deep ideas on which their inferences and "feelings" have been based. Indeed, it's quite possible that they have never directly thought about or verbalized those deep ideas, and that, even if they tried, they would find it quite difficult to do so. It's possible, too, that those unexamined ideas may be extremely bad. Or good, or somewhere in between. They may be not so relevant to the point in question, or they may be quite relevant. Let's say that all three kinds of proof are logical in some sense, and can be right or wrong, reasonable or unreasonable, and may or may not justifiably earn belief. And that is just what we, as critical readers, have to judge.

Isn't this argument consistent, Phaedrus, with what we've said about persuasion as a process of establishing relationships between ideas?

PHAEDRUS   Yes; but I would add, as well, that all three modes of proof—ethos, logos, and pathos—are present in any effective argument, and that their function is interdependent. None works well, alone, without the support of the others. Of course, one type may predominate over the others; and, in some kinds of discourse, the only feelings aroused are very, very sober ones. Still, they're feelings all the same.

EVALUATION AND RESPONSE

SOCRATES   We've said enough, I think, about argument—or about Woolf's argument. By now, we have a pretty good sense of what she has tried to do and how she has tried to do it. But we can also go further. As critical readers, after all, our goal is not only to understand what a text is doing, but also to assess our own relationship to it, and to recognize what further issues it raises for us. These are matters of evaluation and response.

We need to consider, among other things, the stated or unstated *assumptions* on which the writer's effort to persuade depends—the knowledge, beliefs, and values the writer doesn't try to prove, but expects the audience to share—and the *implications* that follow from the various ideas the writer has asked the audience to believe and from connections with our own ideas and concerns. The point, Phaedrus, is to consider how much we are willing to accept the writer's overall argument, and how much we find it, or particular points within it, questionable or potentially arguable. Do we think a reasonable person ought to be persuaded by the writer's argument? Do we think it's fair? How does the writer's argument apply today? Are there points that we might argue differently?

PHAEDRUS   It seems to me we've identified a number of assumptions already while analyzing Woolf's argument. We noted, for example, that she asks her audience to assume that "genius" does not appear among "labouring, uneducated, servile" people—and that it's possible for a woman to have a "gift" like Shakespeare's. Likewise, she asks us to assume that oppression is unjust, and that the destruction or suppression of a "gifted" person is a tragedy.

SOCRATES   Yes; and we identify all such assumptions, when they are not stated (and they usually aren't) by asking *what must one also believe, for this reasoning to be persuasive?* So—do you accept those assumptions?

PHAEDRUS   Yes, I think so, but several things bother me. I'm not so sure, for example, *how much* I believe in "giftedness." It seems to me that "giftedness" is largely a matter, as we were saying earlier, of experience. And, if that is so, I'm not sure Shakespeare could have had a sister with the same "gift"—if their experiences were so different (and if the sister's was so restricted). I suspect, after all, that Woolf's "Judith" is a modern woman in a world that couldn't have produced her. On the other hand, I'm not so sure that "genius" doesn't appear among "servile people," or "among the working classes," as Woolf says in her closing paragraph—or that every "Judith" dies or goes crazy—especially when I think of the art produced, for example, by African-American slaves, or those ballads Woolf mentions. Are the plays of Shakespeare inherently better than the poems of "Anon"? Woolf seems to think so; should she? I guess it all depends on what "genius" means, or on what counts as cultural achievement.[3]

---

[3] For a perspective on this issue, see "In Search of Our Mothers' Gardens," by Alice Walker (pp. 581–589).

And here's another problem: It seems to me that Woolf's more interested in the "gifted" person, whatever that may be, than in the ordinary one. She seems, for example, to want us to think that "Judith's" fate is tragic, but on the other hand she seems to feel (in the third paragraph) that a woman needs a servant. So is it acceptable for some people to lead "labouring, uneducated, servile" lives, as long as "gifted" people lead creative lives? I'm not sure how I feel about this idea. It may have seemed more "natural" to a product of the British class system in 1928, and yet I think it's still with us today, in various forms—for example, in the practice of "streaming" students in public schools, in "fast" (college-bound), "slow" (probably not college-bound), and "medium" (maybe college-bound) classes, according to "intelligence" tests. What are the consequences of such ideas, and such practices?[4]

I'm not at all sure how these questions should be answered, and yet they seem to me important.

SOCRATES   It seems to me, Phaedrus, that all these questions are connected to the more general questions of what "giftedness" is, how it is developed, what its relation is to things like social class and education—and how one overcomes oppression. It seems to me we could explore these questions in many ways by focusing on particular cases, and we might argue them differently than Woolf has done.

And we might raise different issues, too. For example: How does Woolf's argument apply to the condition of women now? Does the modern woman pursuing a career experience problems comparable to Judith Shakespeare's? In what ways is she hemmed in by family needs, and by the "power of law and custom"? What is it like, for example, to be a woman in engineering school? Or a woman with an interest in politics or law?

But notice that, at this point, whatever issues we take up, we're moving beyond critical reading and toward the formulation of new arguments. This movement brings us, eventually, to consider the community of minds for whom the issues we're raising might be issues—and the *ways* in which those issues might be issues—and to examine the grounds on which a sharable opinion might be based. We move, in sum, from the privacy of our personal judgments toward the publicity of a reasoned response, one that can be judged and responded to by others, tested and revised. We become, in other words, practitioners of the very art we've been observing.

PHAEDRUS   Which brings us back, I think, to the question of how we do that.

*T*his book asks you to formulate two main kinds of arguments about the readings it contains, and to do this in the context of class discussion. First, you can take up issues concerning how the rhetoric of a text, or some aspect of its rhetoric, seems

---

[4] For a discussion of the early history of intelligence testing, see "Measuring Heads," by Stephen Jay Gould (pp. 509–545).

meant to work. How, for example, does the writer's use of ethos serve an overall persuasive intention? How does the step-by-step unfolding of the writer's argument guide the reader's judgments and responses? Who the audience is may be an issue for discussion and debate; so may the question of what the writer's intentions are. And so forth. And second, beyond such analytical or "descriptive" kinds of issues, you may take up matters of evaluation and response. You may, for example, develop a critique of the rhetoric a text employs, or an argument about the further issues it has raised for you and for the participants in your class discussion.

You can approach the readings in this book in either way. For each, however, the starting point is critical reading, focused on the basic concerns that Socrates and Phaedrus have discussed. Those concerns might be summarized with questions such as these:

What has the writer tried to do?
(intention, issue, audience)

How has the writer tried to do it?
(means of persuasion: ethos, logos, pathos, argumentational "unfolding")

How much am I persuaded? What's my position?
(evaluation and response: assumptions, implications, further issues)

In addition to these basic questions, each reading is followed by additional Questions for Discussion and Writing, which supplement and extend the basic concerns by focusing on particular matters that might be further explored. Each question is meant as a starting point for group discussion, leading eventually to the development of written arguments—and to the concerns that Socrates and Phaedrus will take up in the following chapter.

Questions for Discussion and Writing

1. Select, for class discussion, one of the shorter essays in this book.[5] Before class, read the essay carefully and write a brief analysis of the rhetoric you find at work: Identify what you consider the writer's issue, audience, main intention, and chief means of persuasion; then explain *how* that means of persuasion works (or is meant to work) to guide the thinking of the audience toward acceptance of the writer's thesis. After your class has met and fully discussed the text, rewrite your analysis—carefully explaining the evidence and reasoning on which it is based.

2. Go further. Evaluate and/or respond to the rhetoric you have analyzed. List the assumptions, implications, assertions, and the like that you feel raise genuine

---

[5] Suggestions: Richard Rodriguez, "Aria" (pp. 560–577); Alice Walker, "In Search of Our Mothers' Gardens" (pp. 581–589); Joan Didion, "Some Dreamers of the Golden Dream" (pp. 480–494); and Gorgias of Leontini "Encomium of Helen" (pp. 61–64).

issues and that you would be willing to propose to your classmates for debate. In class discussion, list and examine possible issues and various positions that might be taken. If possible, select and focus on a single issue. Then, taking the issue you (and/or your classmates) have found most interesting, write a brief description of the argument you feel would be persuasive for the group, outlining the reasoning (and the assumptions) on which your thesis would be based.

3. Examine the rhetoric of the three speeches in the extract from Plato's *Phaedrus* (pp. 75–99). How would you describe the rhetoric of each? Would you agree with the evaluations (of the speeches, that is) made by Plato's speakers in the dialogue? Be ready to discuss in class your answers to these questions and to explain the basis for your position. After class, write a brief analysis and/or evaluation of each speech.

DEVELOPING AN ARGUMENT

SOCRATES   Well, Phaedrus! We've covered the principles of rhetoric, haven't we?

PHAEDRUS   What? How's that again? Done? Of course, I think that what we've said is useful, and perhaps even informative. But all we've talked about is reading. What about writing? What is this critical reader we've been imagining going to do, having discovered an issue to write about—or having the beginnings of an intention—and having begun to formulate an argument?

SOCRATES   That seems simple enough to me. First, you figure out what you want to say to your audience; then you say it, or write it down.

PHAEDRUS   Don't be ridiculous! You know perfectly well, I'm sure, that there's more to it than that. Writing is a process of planning, drafting, and revising, and the writer constantly shifts back and forth among these three activities. We don't just "write it down." Our sense of what we want to say, and how we want to say it, *evolves* during the whole time we work on a piece of writing. It's seldom possible to do an adequate job in just one sitting, or just one draft.

SOCRATES   Yes, I know that. Or at least, I've heard it before. Still, it seems likely to me that the writing process must necessarily begin with mainly "planning" activities, as you call them, and end with mainly "drafting and revising" activities. This will be true, I think, even for the writer who begins by writing down ideas and sentences with no plan in mind, just to see where they might lead; such exploratory writing is a "planning" activity one does on paper, instead of in one's head. For some, of course, it's quite productive. Still, the writer can't start really focused, efficient drafting—drafting, I mean, of what will eventually be the finished essay—until a fairly definite sense of "plan" has been developed. The writer needs, in short, to be fairly clear about what his or her argument is and how it can be most effectively unfolded for its audience.

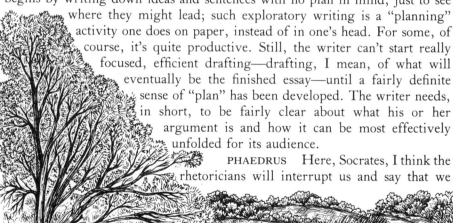

PHAEDRUS   Here, Socrates, I think the rhetoricians will interrupt us and say that we can talk about these things in much more specific terms. And so, for now, suppose you let me speak for them; perhaps I can even instruct you, for a change. After all, I had been with them already, that day when you and I first sat and conversed, in the shade by the banks of the Ilissus, and near that rustic shrine inscribed with sacred images, including images of Hermes, the messenger of gods to mortals, and the patron of travelers, merchants, thieves, and orators—of which I am one, as is nearly everyone, as far as I can see. For who is not a daughter or son of the people Hermes is patron to, the ones to whom he brings his messages from heaven? Perhaps I know the rhetoricians' lore better and more fully than even you.

SOCRATES   Go right ahead, Phaedrus; I'm all ears.

PHAEDRUS   Then listen carefully as I deliver the discourse of the rhetoricians. This time we'll approach matters more from the perspective of the writer, rather than the reader, although I think that much of this discourse will be relevant for each. For we shall have much to say about the *invention* of an argument, and something to say as well about its *structure* and its *style*. And this is what we should say first:

INVENTION

Beginning from a sense of the question at issue, and of the intended audience, the writer investigates and tests the possible kinds of arguments that might be made. Further, the writer will often begin as well from a general sense of the thesis he or she wants to argue for: One's interest in a given issue typically arises, after all, from the fact that one has an opinion about it. In any case, it's from the initial, rough conception of a possible thesis that the writer's invention process really begins in earnest.

Basically, invention is a process of considering, or imagining, the various possible reasons for believing the thesis, and *how the audience would probably respond to those reasons*. This means considering, on one level, what assumptions those reasons depend on, and the degree to which the audience would be likely to accept them. On another level, even if the assumptions seem acceptable, the writer must try to judge the strength of the reasons themselves—for the audience, I mean—compared to other reasons (and counterarguments) that might be given. The consequences of this "reason-testing" process is very frequently—normally, in fact—*revision of the thesis itself*. The writer may actually end up with a thesis utterly different from the rough, initial thesis that the invention process started with! The point, in sum, is to discover *how far the audience can be persuaded* toward the kind of position the writer prefers, and to find a place where writer and audience can meet: the conclusion, in other words, they both can accept, and the grounds on which that conclusion can be based.

SOCRATES   How does the writer do this? By writing down lists of reasons?

PHAEDRUS   Possibly; but the most direct way is actual dialogue with members of the intended audience—I mean informal conversations, group discussions, and the like—or with a friend willing to represent the audience or play its role. If dialogue partners play their roles with energy and skill, I can hardly think of a better way to explore and generate new arguments. The pooled knowledge and perspectives of a group of people provides the richest of all possible sources for invention.

SOCRATES   The world, however, is imperfect. Dialogue partners aren't always as energetic, skillful, or helpful as one would like. Nor are they always available.

PHAEDRUS   That's true; one solution, of course, is to go to the library and search for dialogue partners in the published texts that bear on one's issue. That, after all, is what "research" is: a critical reading of diverse arguments, both friendly and opposed, leading to a fuller perception of the inventional possibilities. In this case, the voices confronted in this reading become part of the writer's audience, as they enter into the writer's thought.

But eventually, the writer must go solo—constructing a mental image of the audience and creating an *imaginary dialogue* with the arguments and voices incorporated in that image. But here the writer needs a warning. This imagined audience will be productive for invention only if the writer makes it a worthy (energetic, skillful) dialogue partner: a reasonable person whose agreement must be earned, and an intellectual equal who is capable of arguing for the opposite side of the case.

TYPES OF ISSUES

SOCRATES   At this point, Phaedrus, I suspect those rhetoricians you're speaking for will step forward and remind you that, aside from this general picture of invention, you promised to speak "in more specific terms"—such as, if I remember the rhetoricians correctly, the *type of issue* or *type of question* one is dealing with, and what it requires.

PHAEDRUS   They will remind us also, I think, that the types of issues can be (and have been) divided up in different ways, depending on the purposes one's theory is meant to serve. I think, however, they won't denounce us if we recognize three main types of question that people argue about:

1.   *What is the case?*
2.   *How should we judge it?*
3.   *What should we do?*

The point of dividing issues up this way is to identify the place in a discussion where agreement stops and where arguments have to be made before it can be reestablished. People might, for example, agree about what the case is in a given situation but disagree about how it should be judged. Or they might agree about how it should be judged but disagree about what we should do about it. And, of course, they might disagree about what the case is.[1]

With each of these basic issue types, the writer has a wide range of inventional possibilities, and there is no single formula for the arguments that will be most effective in each case. Still, each type of issue does have certain general characteristics, or tendencies, that the writer should probably keep in mind.

WHAT IS THE CASE?

Questions of "what is the case" involve what might be called *descriptive* or *analytic* issues—that is, issues in which we try to determine what "the facts" are and how they fit together.

SOCRATES   Isn't that what we were doing before, when we discussed the rhetoric of "Shakespeare's Sister?"

PHAEDRUS   Exactly. A descriptive issue might be, "What are the characteristics of Woolf's ethos?" or even, 'What sort of audience did Woolf originally write for?" And an analytic issue might be, "How does Woolf's ethos work to make the argument of 'Shakespeare's Sister' more persuasive for its original audience?" Before, Socrates, we answered these kinds of questions rather quickly, because our aim was merely to note the sort of thing a critical reader might observe. In fact, however, in a given discussion such questions could very well be at issue, and we could develop arguments to answer them.

SOCRATES   Yes, that's so. Also, it seems to me that some of the further issues we thought Woolf's argument might raise were likewise descriptive or analytic. For example, a question like, "What is the nature of 'genius'?" could be seen as a descriptive question about what the characteristics of "genius" are—or, perhaps, about what most people think they are. Likewise, a question like, "What it's like to be a woman in engineering school," which was really a very vague and general sort of question, could become much more precise if we bring it into focus as an analytic question: "Do gender stereotypes make it more difficult for women to get through engineering school?"

PHAEDRUS   Well, the better we can focus the question, the more clearly we can see what's going to be required to answer it persuasively. Most analytic questions will be, I think, about *cause-and-effect* relationships, or what we might call *consequentiality*, as in your questions about the effect of Woolf's

---

[1] Some examples of the three issue types in this text: *What is the case:* Stephen Jay Gould, "The Mismeasure of Man" (pp. 509–545); Alexis de Tocqueville, "In What Way Americans Cultivate the Arts" (pp. 205–208). *How should we judge it:* Roland Barthes, "The World of Wrestling" (pp. 385–393); Susan B. Anthony, "On Women's Right to Suffrage" (pp. 252–253). *What should we do:* E. D. Hirsch, Jr., "Literacy and Cultural Literacy" (pp. 437–463); Thomas Paine, "Common Sense" (pp. 150–181).

ethos on her audience, and about the effect of gender stereotypes on women who want to become engineers. Likewise, we can start from a known effect and ask about its cause: We can ask, for example, why so few women become engineers or corporate managers. Or, as Woolf asked, why women in Elizabethan England produced so little literature.

But we can also ask about matters of *comparability*. In general, these are questions about how much we can infer the characteristics of one thing from the characteristics of another. If, for example, test scores show that first-year students at a "top" university are weak in math, can we infer that first-year students at "average" universities, or at "most" universities, are probably weak in math also?[2]

SOCRATES   Yes, I see all that, but—whether we ask descriptive questions about the characteristics of a thing, or analytic questions about consequential or comparative relationships—what *is* required to answer them?

PHAEDRUS   That's a question about the kinds of evidence required for different kinds of questions. Actually, we've discussed this already, at least in a general way, when we talked about the means of persuasion in Woolf's argument. But here we can add a few more remarks.

Establishing the facts in a descriptive argument is largely a matter of *documentary evidence:* statistics, for example, or testimony from reliable sources. Such evidence is, as we have seen, the basis of Woolf's description of the conditions in which Elizabethan women lived. Likewise, if we want to establish a factual claim that, for example, American women have not been very successful in reaching "top" levels in various professional careers—even after a supposed half-century of liberation—we may cite studies that show the percentage of women at "top" levels is low (or has not increased), or quote prominent professional women who talk about the barriers they have faced.

But as soon as we step beyond claims about the raw facts to more analytic claims about how they fit together, or about what other "facts" the established facts make probable, we need other kinds of evidence to make our claims persuasive. The premier kind is *reasoning*—explanatory statements that respond to questions like "Why?" or "How?" In arguments about "what is the case," such reasons ultimately depend on assumptions about the structure of reality. Suppose, for example, that our claim is, "Gender stereotyping impedes the progress of women in engineering schools," and that our audience doesn't find this claim immediately persuasive, and says "Well, maybe, but *why?*" We might back our claim this way:

Gender stereotyping impedes the progress of women in engineering schools
   because

---

[2] There are many kinds of comparative relationships, such as: similarity (whatever is true for X is true for Y); relative degree (whatever is true for X is *more* true for Y); and opposition or antithesis (whatever is true for X, the opposite is true for Y). Phaedrus' example involves relative degree.

34

images of women as "illogical" or "unscientific" make it difficult for female engineering students to be taken seriously by male professors and fellow students.

Our audience may dispute our "because," in which case we would have to think of ways to back it up: Perhaps we can find some documentary evidence, or perhaps we can offer further reasons to make our statement probable. (Or we may need to revise our claims.) Even if the audience does accept our "because," once we have explained it, we still may need to explain or defend the general assumption it appeals to—namely, that students who are not taken seriously by their teachers have less chance of prospering, which is an assumption about the structure of reality.

Examples are the other great means of making claims persuasive. Examples can be real or hypothetical; either way, their function is to represent or *illustrate* a typical pattern in the "way things happen." They can be brief or extended— by which I mean that a single example can be "extended" as a complete, detailed story. In "Shakespeare's Sister," as we noted before, Woolf uses an example that is hypothetical and somewhat extended. Long or short, however, examples gain persuasiveness from the reader's feeling of their typicality, the feeling that the writer's illustration of the "way things happen" is indeed realistic and probable.

SOCRATES   Yes, but examples have a problem. What if we tell a story (even a true story) about a female student having trouble in engineering school, and our audience says, "Well, yes, the story seems quite believable, but it doesn't necessarily prove the same thing always happens"; and what if our audience points to some examples where it *didn't* happen? And, as every arguer learns by hard experience, *there is always a counterexample*, or nearly always. Examples are, in truth, a relatively weak form of proof.

PHAEDRUS   That's so; but when *coupled with reasoning*, they can be much stronger. If reasoning shows why or how a certain state of affairs is probable, then examples can *confirm* that probability. In effect, the example then says, "See, I have explained that it's probable, and here it really is!" In this case, counterexamples have less force. If our explanation has made our example appear to be the more probable fact, then the counterexample can be dismissed as an "exception to the rule."

But enough about evidence, Socrates; we still have two more kinds of issues to consider.

HOW SHOULD WE JUDGE IT?

Beyond questions about "what is the case," we come to questions about "how it should be judged." Here we really have two closely related kinds of issues: *definitional* questions about what something should be called, and *evaluative* questions about its goodness or badness. In practice, these two kinds of issues tend to overlap, or blend together. Most definitions, after all, imply an evaluation, because virtually every term we use to define or name a thing has an evaluative aspect, *compared to* the other possible terms that might be used: calling a university's change in requirements a "raising of standards" or "elitism," for example, are positively and negatively shaded ways of naming the same raw facts. But we can also separate definition and evaluation. We might, for example, admit that the university's requirements are "elitist," but then argue that, in this case, elitism is good or justifiable.

SOCRATES   How do we make these kinds of arguments, Phaedrus?

PHAEDRUS   In definitional arguments, where we are making disputable claims, we assert that something belongs to a certain class of things it doesn't obviously belong to, at least from the audience's point of view—or, in other words, that X is an instance of Y.

SOCRATES   You mean we argue that an apple is an orange?

PHAEDRUS   Well, in a way. The argument depends on what we mean by "orange." To make our claim persuasive, we would have to set up, or appeal to, a particular description of "orange" that our audience accepts, and then show that apples have certain qualities that match the description, or at least enough of them to let us say that apples are, in a certain sense, a kind of orange. Likewise, if we wanted to argue that women in certain professional careers experience "oppression," we would need to follow the same general strategy. Definitional arguments are, in essence, matters of explanatory reasoning, backed up by evidence, or by examples, in which the ultimate appeal is to assumptions about the *criteria* by which we identify things—the criteria that define such things as "elitism," "raising of standards," "oppression," and so forth.

SOCRATES   And what about evaluative arguments?

PHAEDRUS   Much the same thing happens, but here we appeal to assumptions about the criteria by which we value things, or decide they're desirable or undesirable.

SOCRATES   Well, I've heard it said, somewhere, that "for pleasure or gain or honor all do all they do."[3] Those are the three reasons why anyone desires or does anything.

PHAEDRUS   Yes, and if that's so, we can identify three main types of value criteria, which we might name as follows:

1.   *The ethical*
2.   *The aesthetic*
3.   *The pragmatic*

By *the ethical*, I mean ideas about moral rightness (and wrongness): We might decide that something is "good" because it's ethically praiseworthy, or honorable.

---

[3] Socrates quotes the Sophist Isocrates (*Antidosis* 217).

36

By *the aesthetic*, I mean ideas about what gives pleasure: We might decide that something is "good" because it is pleasant, or because it is beautiful, or "bad" because it is ugly or displeasing in some way. And by *the pragmatic*, I mean ideas about practical advantage or benefit: We might, for example, decide that something is "good" because it brings us money, power, or security, or "bad" because it causes us to lose these things (or reduces our chances of possessing them). Moreover, these three types of criteria may compete or overrule each other in various ways. We might, for example, reject something that is profitable because it is dishonorable; or choose something that is unprofitable because it is beautiful. And so on.

SOCRATES   Evaluative arguments have a special problem, Phaedrus.

PHAEDRUS   What's that?

SOCRATES   I mean, we can't just argue that something is "good" because it's praiseworthy, pleasant or profitable.

PHAEDRUS   Why not?

SOCRATES   Suppose, for example, that we wish to argue that an ad campaign for cigarettes is "unethical."

PHAEDRUS   Okay, I'll take the bait. Why is it unethical?

SOCRATES   Well, suppose we say "because it encourages adolescents to take up smoking."

PHAEDRUS   Does it?

SOCRATES   There! You see? Our "because" is a claim about "what is the case," and your question shows that it needs to be backed up with further evidence. Indeed, this is very typically the case in value arguments: we must push our invention to a deeper level, at which we confront again descriptive and analytic questions. Consider the argument again:

The ad campaign for cigarette X is unethical   [value claim]

because it encourages adolescents to take up smoking   [analytic claim]

because . . . (reasons, examples, documentary evidence)

Notice, Phaedrus, that "encouraging adolescents to take up smoking" *is* the "unethical thing" that makes the ad campaign "unethical" (according to this argument). And supporting that first "because" with various kinds of evidence is likely to be our main activity when we present this argument to its audience—whereas declarations that the ad campaign is "bad" or "unethical" will occupy a relatively small portion of our actual discourse. We might, for example, make that declaration in the introduction, or in the conclusion (or in both places). But we could hardly spend all our time saying, "It's unethical," over and over, even if we could think of lots of different ways to say it. My point, then, is that our value claim is mainly a declaration of *stance* or *attitude* that doesn't really provide us with a lot to talk about, whereas our first "because" provides the main subject matter of the argument, its substance. A value thesis, in sum, will tend to rest on a substantive claim about "what is the case," or perhaps a definitional claim—requiring us to push our invention to a deeper level of argument, as we explore the evidence required to make that substantive claim persuasive.

PHAEDRUS   Well said, Socrates—I'm impressed. So much, then, for questions of definition or evaluation.

WHAT SHOULD WE DO?

Next come *policy issues*. These arise whenever a community comes to recognize a problem requiring a solution, and the question becomes, "What should we do?" Policy questions are, in essence, *questions about the future*—whereas definitional and evaluative issues are mainly concerned with the present and the past, with observed "facts" we wish to judge. So, when we argue for (or against) a particular policy, the argument we develop must focus mainly on the *benefit* or *harm* likely to follow from the policy in question, its *probable outcomes or consequences*. If we do what is proposed, what will happen and why?

Here, the invention process turns again to value criteria. After all, the audience must be persuaded not only that the claimed outcomes of the proposed policy are probable, but also that they are desirable enough to be worth pursuing. (Otherwise, why bother?) Will the policy bring honor, pleasure, or profit, or their opposites, or nothing? But policy arguments must consider other criteria too: A "good" policy must also be *feasible* or *realistic*. It must be something that can actually be done *by the people we are trying to persuade*. (I guess this is really a specialized sort of "pragmatic" criterion that typically comes up in policy arguments.)

Now—as I'm sure you'll say—policy issues contain within themselves the other types of issues: first, because they rest on agreements about "what is the case" and whether it constitutes a problem (value question); second, because they must propose realistic, feasible policies and demonstrate probable outcomes, and these, again, are basically matters of "what is the case," or will be; and third, because those outcomes must be seen by the audience as desirable enough to make the action we propose worth doing (value question again). In a very long and complex policy argument, moreover, it's possible that all these issues could be dealt with.

SOCRATES   We come to the same point again, don't we? Clearly, a policy thesis like, "This community should ban the ad campaign for cigarette X," rests on more substantive arguments that tend to lead our invention process back to deeper descriptive and analytic issues—just as a value thesis does. For again, we can't spend all our time declaring, "We should ban it." We might advance such a stance declaration in an introduction, or conclude with it, but in between the actual substance of our discourse will consist of arguments—reasonings, supplemented with examples and documentary kinds of evidence—showing what the policy will do, and why.

REFUTATION

PHAEDRUS   We should at least mention one other source of invention: namely, the types of arguments we develop when trying to make opposed arguments seem less persuasive. Of these, the basic type is *logical refutation*— demonstrating weaknesses in the opposition's reasoning. Do they make statements that contradict or undermine their main position? Are there aspects of the issue they've neglected to consider, such as the feasibility of their proposal or potential consequences besides the ones they mention? Is there important evidence they overlook? Do they offer reasons that are not really relevant to the claim they're trying to make, such as saying University X should "raise its standards" because "America's a great country"? Do they make "sweeping" or overgeneralized claims that their reasoning does not sufficiently support, as in, "Raising the university's standards will improve the national economy because our graduates will be more highly qualified"? And so on.

There are two other basic types, namely *refutation from pathos* and *refutation from ethos,* both of which are somewhat risky. The first, refutation from pathos, works by arguing that an opponent's argument is morally offensive, even if probable. The second, refutation from ethos, works by undermining an opponent's argument by arguing that he can't be trusted. The danger of such refutation is that it can degenerate into mere name-calling and slander— the kinds of smear techniques sometimes employed in political campaigns. Ultimately, in general, the best procedure is logical refutation.

But I have said enough, I think, about inventing and refuting arguments.

STRUCTURE

SOCRATES   Well then—what shall we say about the structure of an argument, Phaedrus? How should it unfold? In what order, in what sequence, should the writer place and present the reasonings invention has devised?

PHAEDRUS   As usual, there is no fixed rule, but the basic principle is very simple: What comes first will influence the reader's response to what comes after. Beyond this point, however, we might mention some particulars. Certainly, the rhetoricians will remind us that a well-constructed discourse does not just start, continue along for a while and then stop, but that it will tend, like a piece of music, to consist of definite parts or "movements," each with a function of its own and with a sense of progression in the whole. They would, in short, have us at least discuss the principles of *introductions, middles,* and *conclusions.*

SOCRATES   What about *introductions,* then? As you know, Phaedrus, inexperienced writers (and some experienced ones, too) often try to begin by blurting out the entire substance of their argument—a kind of summary— and sometimes even in the very first sentence!

39

PHAEDRUS   There is no absolute rule against doing that, of course, but it's seldom necessary, and it may in fact be very bad strategy. Why summarize what hasn't been explained or proven yet? Why begin by asking for rejection?

An introduction's basic job is simply to focus the reader's sense of what question is at issue. It must also earn the reader's willingness to read, which means, on one hand, establishing some sense of the issue's importance *for the reader* and, on the other hand, establishing a "good" or appropriate ethos, in order to make the reader feel receptive and open minded. These functions can, of course, be performed in any number of ways. The introduction can be short and simple—just a paragraph—or long and elaborate, running to several pages. It can begin with a statement of the issue, or end with it. And so on. In general, however, all the introduction has to do is prepare the reader's mind for what will follow.

It is the *middle* of the discourse, or what some have called the "body," that should unfold the writer's actual argument.

SOCRATES   And how should this proceed?

PHAEDRUS   Again, there's no fixed formula, but the main procedures—the parts or "movements"—tend to be as follows:

First, *setting up:* This is a preliminary sort of movement, in which the writer establishes the information or ideas that must be shared—factual knowledge, assumptions, definitions—in order for the audience to understand and accept the writer's main line or lines of argument. Also, the writer might divide the issue into parts, and announce (or "forecast") the main lines of proof that will be taken up.

Next comes the *proof* itself, or the proofs. By this, I mean presentation and discussion of the evidence for the writer's thesis—reasonings, examples, documentary evidence—plus response to whatever questions or objections the argument seems likely to provoke (if any). This responding can be taken up in a separate section or, better, wherever a question would arise.

Finally, the writer may include a *summation* of the basic argument, in which the thesis and the main reasons for it are briefly and concisely pulled together.

SOCRATES   So the urge we feel when beginning a discourse—that urge to blurt out the "whole thing"—is generally postponed until the argument has reached its final stages.

PHAEDRUS   Yes; but there is still one more structural "movement" to consider—namely, the *conclusion*. Conclusions, like introductions, do not serve primarily to summarize the argument, although they often do include a statement (or restatement) of the thesis. Basically, conclusions function to create a sense of completion, or what is sometimes called *closure*, by allowing the reader to reflect a while on the argument that has now been made persuasive and by adding whatever final remarks seem appropriate.

SOCRATES   You mean, I take it, things like *calls to action* (in policy arguments), declarations or presentation of the writer's attitudes or *stance* (in evaluative arguments), or reflections on *further implications* of the argument (in descriptive or analytic arguments).

PHAEDRUS   Yes—or any combination thereof, depending on what the issue, argument, and audience make possible, and depending on what our intentions are.

SOCRATES   It seems to me, Phaedrus, that we can see these sorts of introductory, middle, and concluding "movements" in that essay of Virginia Woolf's we discussed before. But tell me: How does a writer *plan a structure?* Suppose we take one of those arguments we were considering before, about gender stereotypes and women in engineering school, or the ad campaign for cigarette X. What structural plans might we lay out for an actual presentation of the argument?

PHAEDRUS   Well, it's largely a matter of *tactics,* that is, a matter of setting up each point so that it seems to follow logically from what precedes, and of considering what each point needs to be successful. Let's take the argument about women in engineering school—which was, as I recall, "Gender stereotyping impedes the progress of women in engineering school *because* images of women as 'illogical' or 'unscientific' make it difficult for female students to be taken seriously by male professors and fellow students." This may or may not be a good argument; for now, however, let's simply consider its structural possibilities.

In my introduction, I might set the issue up by first discussing the relatively low numbers of women who graduate from engineering school (if that is the case); here, of course, I would need some factual information to present. Having established that factual point, I would then be able to raise the question *why* it is so, and thereby focus the issue; and I might also establish my stance, by declaring that I suspect gender stereotyping to be the cause. Of course, I can't yet assume that my declaration is persuasive; I can only present it, at this point, as a claim that has to be proved.

SOCRATES   What then? What about the middle of the argument? What would you say next?

PHAEDRUS   I have several options. The argument depends, as we noted before, on an assumption that students who are not taken seriously by professors and fellow students are less likely to do well; so I might want to set the argument up by discussing this idea, getting it firmly established in the reader's mind.

SOCRATES   But it seems to me the reader wouldn't yet know why you were discussing that particular point. Would it be clear that you were still focusing on the problems women face in engineering school?

PHAEDRUS   Maybe not. Another option, and perhaps the better one, would be to set up the argument by discussing gender stereotyping, and its presence in engineering school: I would need, in short, to show a high incidence of images of women as "illogical" and "unscientific" among professors and students. To make this point, of course, I would need some evidence: a survey of attitudes, or interviews with students and professors, or testimony from reliable sources (such as an engineering professor or administrator declaring that the attitudes in question are prevalent in their department).

Having made that point, I would then be in a position to discuss my "because." That is, my next step would be to talk about how male professors and students who have those stereotyped ideas would be less likely to treat a woman student seriously; and I might be able to back this reasoning up with some examples, either hypothetical illustrations or (better) some actual incidents. My next step, at this point, might be a discussion of the assumption that I thought of bringing up earlier—but only if I thought it needed emphasizing, or if the audience might question it. Otherwise, I would just proceed directly to my conclusion.

In the conclusion, and if I have made my previous points successfully, I should be in a position to declare my basic thesis persuasively: "It seems, then, that gender stereotyping impedes the progress of women in engineering school." And, having made that point, I would probably close with some reflections on the unacceptability of such a situation, and the need for a change in attitudes.

So, Socrates—in brief, that's how I might unfold the argument about women in engineering school.

SOCRATES   One question: would you *draft* the argument in just the order you have planned it? Would you start by writing the introduction, and go straight through to the conclusion?

PHAEDRUS   Possibly, but not necessarily. While working out the structural plan, in actual drafting, we often make new discoveries—or discover new problems—that require some revision in the plan, or in the argument itself. Some writers, in consequence, like to draft the middle first, the conclusion next, and the introduction last; some need to write a "rough" introduction first, to get themselves started. Even if we do the introduction first, it's generally a good idea to go back and revise it or redo it, as the last step in drafting. It's hard to write a good introduction for an essay that doesn't exist yet, and much easier for one that does.

Once we have developed a basic draft of the argument, we can then *test* it by finding a dialogue partner willing to play the role of audience and willing to offer comments and responses (either orally or in writing) to each segment of the argument—giving us, in effect, a play-by-play account of how each step in the sequence has affected them. Testing out our structure in this way can (and frequently does) lead us to revise our plans; and it can also lead us to revise, once more, the argument itself, or it can prompt new phases of invention as we develop our reasonings and illustrations of specific points. Basically, developing the structure of an argument means extending the invention process from a sense of the overall argument to working out the details of its parts.

STYLE

SOCRATES   Speaking of detail, Phaedrus, what about style? Isn't that the ultimate level of detail? I mean, as we move from mostly planning activities to drafting and revising activities, the focus of our attention shifts from the overall argument down to the "movements" or segments of its structural unfolding, and finally down to sentences and even individual words. After all, we do the actual writing more or less one sentence at a time.

PHAEDRUS   Yes; that's so. And, because it is so much a matter of detail, style is also a seemingly inexhaustible and endless subject, one about which volumes can be (and have been) written.

SOCRATES   Yes, but I think we might capture the basic idea. *Style*—the writer's actual language, with its particular choice of words, its sentence structures, its rhythms, and its general tone—is a kind of microargument, in which the writer can make linkages between ideas. Consider these two sentences (the first is by Karl Marx),[4] which express the same general idea, more or less, but with very different effects:

A specter is haunting Europe—the specter of communism.

All over Europe, people fear what they imagine the rise of communism to be.

Any idea can be expressed with a variety of different words, in a variety of different ways. Any word that may be chosen carries with it a particular set of associations—connections to other words, ideas, memories, and so forth—so that no two words ever mean quite the same thing, even though their "basic" meaning may be the same. And different rhythms convey different emotional tones, different moods. So, depending on which stylistic choices a writer makes, those choices connect with particular ideas, attitudes, and moods in the reader—producing an impression of the writer's attitudes, and also of the ideas or things being discussed. Clearly, the "communism" in Karl Marx's sentence is a much more threatening presence than it is in the second sentence, which is much blander. Likewise, Marx himself seems to take an aggressive stance toward those who fear the "specter," an impression communicated partly by our knowledge that he is himself the voice of the "specter," and partly by the rhythm of the sentence itself.

PHAEDRUS   Yes, it seems almost to have a stalking movement, though I can't explain exactly why I think so. Likewise, it seems much easier to remember than the blander sentence, and again I don't know why, though it clearly has something to do with the rhythm and the repetition of "specter."

SOCRATES   I think it has to do with deep, perhaps subconscious associations in your mind, with the mingled effects of word meanings and

---

[4] The opening sentence of *Manifesto of the Communist Party*, pp. 212–238.

rhythms, and with the musical "charm" (I don't know what else to call it) of things like rhythm and melody; we would need a sophisticated psychological theory to untangle it all. Anyway, Phaedrus, without going into all that, you can see what a difference word choices and rhythms can make. The writer's style is the filter through which things are seen, and the embodiment of the writer's ethos.

PHAEDRUS   Yes; but we still might ask what that idea means for the writer who must *invent a style*.

SOCRATES   Shouldn't we say, as the rhetoricians surely would, that a style must be both *clear* and *appropriate?* By clarity, I mean only that the writer's style should be reasonably accessible for the audience, or that it be no more confusing, distracting, or difficult to read than necessary. And by appropriateness, I mean only that the writer's tone be neither emotionally excessive, nor mechanical and lifeless. And further, the writer's style should be *original*—avoiding the unreflective, automatic use of cliché expressions. For cliché expressions are the language of vague and superficial thought, creating an impression that the writer isn't really thinking much or doesn't really care. Ultimately, being clear, appropriate, and original are matters of ethos. For to have these qualities is to be credible, to seem to be an articulate, thoughtful person who cares. And to lack them is to seem the opposite. Or so the rhetoricians say.

PHAEDRUS   Yes, Socrates, but beyond these standard generalities, there are some basic principles we should consider—or that a writer should keep in mind.

VOICE

The first is this: As an embodiment of ethos, style is likewise an embodiment of *voice*, the voice of a speaking person. And to the degree that a writer's style is credible as voice, as the voice of a speaking person, it will tend to be more effective.

SOCRATES   Why?

PHAEDRUS   Two reasons: First, because the more the writer's ethos comes across, through voice, as an actual human being, the more the reader can identify with it and be open, sympathetic, and responsive to what is said. A speaker who sounds like a machine, and some do, is far less likely to inspire such feelings (unless, perhaps, the audience consists of people who want to be machines). The writer's voice, of course, may be "erudite" or "scientific," or whatever; a style may be quite elaborate, with convoluted, complex sentences. But insofar as that style continues to embody a literate, educated *voice* that is still a believable human voice, that style will generally be more effective.

Second, a believably voicelike style tends to be more effective because it has *ear appeal*. Such language "goes in" more effectively, makes a deeper impression, and is more easily remembered. Language with *no* ear appeal, on the other hand, is generally much harder to read and remember, and may even be soporific, as its featureless droning gradually brings on an attack of drowsiness.

SOCRATES   So how do we develop a sense of voice?

PHAEDRUS   Well, we might find a dialogue partner again and test our style by reading it aloud. (We can also do this alone, if necessary, or with a tape recorder.) Are there sentences that don't seem "speakable," or that are difficult to get your mouth (and breath) around? Are there places where the style loses energy, or begins to sound like a featureless, rhythmless hum? And where does the style work well, creating interest, emphasis, and memorability?

To help develop our sensitivity to voice, we can also take passages that we admire and read *them* aloud—with a tape recorder, or a dialogue partner who will offer criticisms—in an effort to discover the specific quality of voice, the specific rhythms, emphases, and shifts of tone that seem embodied in the language. We could even try copying the passage, writing it out word by word and phrase by phrase, with careful attention to its vocal possibilities.

SOCRATES   And should we mention poetry, Phaedrus? I mean, that is, the poetry of major poets, the poetry that endures, the memorable and eloquent poetry. For nothing, generally speaking, has been composed with greater care for style and voice.

PHAEDRUS   I didn't know you liked the poets, Socrates.

RHYTHM, VARIETY, AND EMPHASIS

But now I think we ought to pause and explicate, at least briefly, what we mean by voicelike qualities, or qualities with ear appeal. I suggest we summarize them with the words *rhythm*, *variety*, and *emphasis*.

Effective prose style has rhythm, just as poetry does, though the rhythm is looser and more flexible. We can analyze it in some detail, if we wish, but for now a rough-and-ready kind of analysis will do. That is, we can just count words, words per sentence, to see the rhythmic pattern in a given passage. Consider, for example, the first paragraph of Joan Didion's "Some Dreamers of the Golden Dream,"[5] which seems quite effective to me:

> This is a story about love and death in the golden land, and begins with the country. The San Bernadino Valley lies only an hour east of Los Angeles by the San Bernardino Freeway but is in certain ways an alien place: not the coastal California of the subtropical twilights and the soft westerlies off the Pacific but a harsher California, haunted by the Mojave just beyond the mountains, devastated by the hot dry Santa Ana wind that comes down through the passes at 100 miles an hour and whines through the eucalyptus windbreaks and works on the nerves. October is the bad month for the wind, the month when breathing is difficult and the hills blaze up spontaneously. There has been no rain since April. Every voice

---

[5] The paragraph appears on pages 480–481 of this text.

seems a scream. It is the season of suicide and divorce and prickly dread,
wherever the wind blows.

This paragraph consists of six sentences, with these word lengths:

17

81 (25 + 56, if we count the parts before and after the colon separately)

20

7

5

15

What we see, then, is this: Didion works with a "basic" sentence length (of
about fifteen to twenty words), and uses variations on that length to create a
fluctuating yet balanced rhythm. After establishing the basic length in her first
sentence, Didion expands it, then doubles it, in the two parts of the second
sentence; then she reestablishes the basic length in her third sentence; the short
fourth and fifth sentences are each about half the basic length; and the final
sentence, which is roughly equal to the two before it, restores the basic length
(and rebalances the rhythm).

My point is that the variations in a rhythmic pattern work to create subtle
kinds of *emphasis*. Variations create contrasts, and the contrast highlights
whatever seems to stand out against the background. Note, for example, the
way those two short sentences stand out. Or how the long sentence emphasizes
the "panoramic" feel of what it describes.

In addition to this rhythmic variation, and closely related to it, a style must
also vary the *forms* of its sentences. A series of sentences that all have more or
less the same basic form is going to sound mechanical, unnatural, and dull,
as in this example:

> Style is a fascinating subject. Style is a large subject. Many writers have
> discussed it. One part of style is rhythm. Rhythm is important. Variation
> is important, too. Variation creates emphasis.

We could do this also with longer, more complex sentences of equivalent or
similar form, and the effect would still be just as dull—although, perhaps,
less "elementary" sounding. Not incidentally, and as our example illustrates,
sentences repetitive in form are usually repetitive in length as well.

SOCRATES   It seems, then, that for an effective, voicelike style the
writer must have various sentence forms available, and be able to modify them
in various ways.

PHAEDRUS   That's so. And, if the writer's ability to vary sentence
shapes is limited, then he or she should visit the grammarians. In general,
however, and as far as style goes, the advice I would rather prescribe is this:
Let writers pay close attention to the languge they encounter in their reading,

and especially to the language that impresses them, the striking and distinctive. Let them read such language aloud, and carefully, until they feel its shape and movement, until they feel the way it works with tone, until they can live and speak within it. Let them copy such language in their notebooks, and imitate and play with it, and try it out on dialogue partners, and, when it is integral to their thought, take advantage of it in the style they invent.

SOCRATES   Well! All this seems highly satisfactory, Phaedrus. Should we go on, do you think, and take up the figures of speech? Should we discuss *synechdoche, chiasmus, epenthesis, zeugma,* and all the other myriad flowers of language, domestic and exotic? What about *tmesis?*

PHAEDRUS   About that, I have only two words to say: im possible.[6]

SOCRATES   Why so?

PHAEDRUS   The figures are an endless subject, Socrates. It's getting late. Let's save them for another day.

SOCRATES   Then, perhaps, we've said enough. We've spoken about what rhetoric is, and rhetorical education; about critical reading; and about the basic principles of invention, structure, and style. We now can rest. Send my greetings to those skeptical friends of yours, the Sophists, whom I would make my friends. Peitho, wise Persuasion, muse of Rhetoric, accept what I have said, and what Phaedrus has said as well. May Hermes continue to visit us also. And may that writer we've been imagining find true eloquence.

PHAEDRUS   Come on, Socrates, let's go.

*F*inally, *we wish to emphasize a point implicit in what Socrates and Phaedrus have been saying. Invention, structure, and style are not "steps" in the process of developing a written argument. Rather, they are aspects of rhetoric with which the writer may be concerned—sometimes separately, sometimes all at once, as the writer's attention shifts back and forth from one aspect to another—during the process of planning, drafting, and revising. Further, the principles of invention, structure, and style are just that: principles, not rules. Bend them and distort them; abandon them, when necessary. What is best in any given argument is always a function of the situation, and of the opportunities and problems it provides.*

As you develop arguments in response to the readings in this book and to class discussion, you can proceed in two main ways. First, you can develop arguments directly about the readings themselves; here you will be dealing mainly with questions about "what is the case" in the rhetoric of the text, or with questions about how that rhetoric should be judged. And second, you can develop arguments in response to the issues that the readings raise for you (and for your class); here you will have the full range of issues open to you, up to and including policy questions. As you do this, you will be entering a conversation that has been going on since antiquity, a conversation in which the ultimate question is (and will always be), "How should we live?" This question has no final answer, of course; but it has to be answered all the time.

---

[6] "im possible" is *tmesis*—breaking one word, ungrammatically, into two.

Questions for Discussion and Writing

1. Invent an argument. (You can work with the argument you outlined in question 2 of the previous chapter, or with any issue that has emerged from reading and class discussion.) Identify the question at issue and write out an initial thesis; outline the reasons (plus examples and/or documentary evidence) on which the thesis might be based. Then test this sketch for an argument in group discussion. What further questions and problems does the argument seem to raise? Are you depending on assumptions your audience will accept? Which reasons seem strongest for your audience? Which seem weak or not especially effective? In what ways do you think you need to revise or change the argument?

2. Go further. Develop a structure for the argument you have invented and revised. In class, you can write and/or discuss structural plans for introductions, middles, and conclusions with dialogue partners; afterwards, consider what revisions (or additions) you would make in your plan and in the argument itself. Then write a rough draft, working out the argument in greater detail. At the next class meeting, have dialogue partners (a) *identify* the main steps in your sequence (by writing a brief structural description), and (b) *respond* (or "talk back") to each step, in writing, playing the role of audience. Did your readers respond in unexpected ways? Were there places where they got confused or questioned the point being made? What revisions do you probably need to make?

3. Go further still. Prepare a prefinal draft of the argument you have worked on in the previous two questions, incorporating revisions you have decided to make and paying closer attention to your style. Test the style by reading it aloud. In class, have dialogue partners (again, playing the role of audience) respond in writing to your style. Is the style clear and appropriate? Does it give the reader a clear sense of the writer's voice? Does it make good use of rhythm, variety, and emphasis? Are there places where these qualities break down or where the tone seems inconsistent? Do some word choices or phrasings seem especially effective or ineffective? When you have had a chance to review the comments of your readers and to consider what stylistic revisions you probably need to make, prepare a final version of your essay.

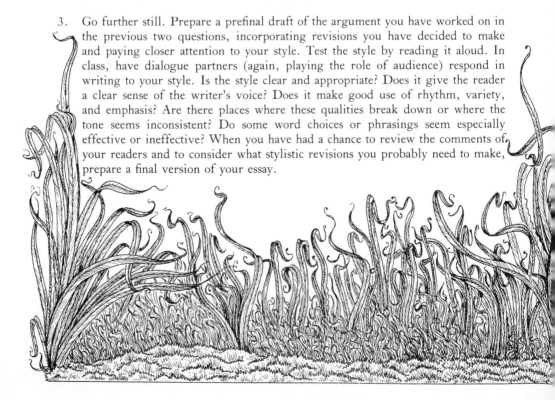

READINGS

SAPPHO

(c. 612–? b.c.)

Sappho lived between the seventh and sixth centuries B.C. on the Greek island of Lesbos (from which derives our word "Lesbian"). She was a composer of lyrics, specializing mainly in epithalamia— marriage songs that were probably performed at public ceremonies—and in more personal lyrics that were written (and perhaps performed) for her friends, lovers, and enemies.

Today, very few hard facts are known about Sappho's life. Many ancient rumors and legends, however, surround this remarkable woman: She is said to have been beautiful; to have been a witch, or a prostitute; to have lived a scandalous life (she may have committed suicide over a failed love affair with a ferryman); to have been a priestess of Aphrodite (the goddess of love); to have been the mistress of the poet Alcaeus, who wrote an "indecent" poem to her (and that she answered with a poem of reproof); to have surrounded herself with young women, who may have been her students, her fellow devotees of Aphrodite, or her lovers (or all three things combined); and so on.

Ever since her own time, Sappho has been regarded as one of the foremost lyric poets of the ancient world—in the eyes of some critics, the greatest of them all. After more than two and a half millennia, her writing still seems vivid and alive today. In fact, as a woman writing boldly and passionately about women, Sappho has received special attention with the rise of women's studies and her poetry has experienced a resurgence in popularity in the last twenty years.

—What little of it now remains, that is. All the collections in which Sappho's poetry was recorded were lost after the collapse of the ancient world (in roughly the fifth century A.D.). Her surviving poems and fragments of poems come to us from indirect sources: quotations in works of ancient literary criticism that happened to be preserved, copies of poems written on the backs of documents, and so forth. Oddly, much has been recovered from the sands of Egypt. Strips of material used to wrap some mummies were cut from scrolls containing Sappho's poems; and so, here and there, mummy windings yield us Sapphic lines and phrases. Altogether, of Sappho's works we now have slightly more than 100 fragments, some consisting only of a few words, others possibly complete lyrics.

The selections that follow include some of Sappho's major fragments and a few minor ones as well. It is important to remember that Sappho is speaking to a specific person in each fragment, and that the person she addresses changes from fragment to fragment. Each poem is thus grounded in a human situation that prompts what Sappho has to say. Note also that the names you will encounter— Atthis, Anactoria, Praxinoa, Gongyla—are all women's names. To a certain

52

extent, we are "overhearing" parts of different conversations, and from what we overhear we can form an intuitive picture of what Sappho's world was like; each fragmentary bit of Sappho's voice comes surrounded with its context, and that context is indirectly present in everything that is said. But as readers we are more than simply eavesdroppers here. To the degree that we can identify with Sappho and the people to whom she is talking, and with the world of ideas and concerns that she inhabits, she speaks to us as well.

FRAGMENTS

He is a god in my eyes—[1]
the man who is allowed
to sit beside you—he

who listens intimately
to the sweet murmur of   5
your voice, the enticing

laughter that makes my own
heart beat fast. If I meet
you suddenly, I can't

speak—my tongue is broken;   10
a thin flame runs under
my skin; seeing nothing,

hearing only my own ears
drumming, I drip with sweat;
trembling shakes my body   15

and I turn paler than
dry grass. At such times
death isn't far from me

---

[1] In this poem, Sappho is speaking to a woman; the man "who is allowed to sit beside you" is probably the woman's husband or betrothed. The only social male/female relationships sanctioned by ancient Greek culture were husband/wife, brother/sister, and parent/child. Homosexual relationships were not unusual; such connections were considered "naughty" but normal. [Editors' note.]

Even in Sardis[2]
Anactoria will think often of us

of the life we shared here, when you seemed
the Goddess[3] incarnate
to her and your singing pleased her best   5

Now among Lydian[4] women she in her
turn stands first as the red-
fingered moon rising at sunset takes

precedence over stars around her;
her light spreads equally   10
on the salt sea and fields thick with bloom

Delicious dew pours down to freshen
roses, delicate thyme
and blossoming sweet clover; she wanders

aimlessly, thinking of gentle   15
Atthis, her heart hanging
heavy with longing in her little breast

She shouts aloud, Come! we know it;
thousand-eared night repeats that cry
across the sea shining between us   20

Some say a cavalry corps,
some infantry, some, again,
will maintain that the swift oars

of our fleet are the finest
sight on dark earth; but I say   5
that whatever one loves, is.

---

[2] *Sardis:* the capital of Lydia, an ancient country of western Asia Minor bordering on the Aegean Sea. [Editors' note.]

[3] *the Goddess:* probably Aphrodite, the goddess of love. [Editors' note.]

[4] *Lydian:* of Lydia. [Editors' note.]

This is easily proved: did
not Helen[5]—she who had scanned
the flower of the world's manhood—

choose as first among men one 10
who laid Troy's honor in ruin?
warped to his will, forgetting

love due her own blood, her own
child, she wandered far with him.
So Anactoria, although you 15

being far away forget us,
the dear sound of your footstep
and light glancing in your eyes

would move me more than glitter
of Lydian horse or armored 20
tread of mainland infantry

Frankly I wish I were dead.[6]
When she left, she wept

a great deal; she said to
me, "This parting must be
endured, Sappho. I go unwillingly." 5

I said, "Go, and be happy
but remember (you know
well) whom you leave shackled by love

"If you forget me, think
of our gifts to Aphrodite 10
and all the loveliness that we shared

---

[5] *Helen:* Helen of Troy. Legend had it that the beautiful Helen abandoned her husband, King Menelaus, to run away with her Trojan lover, Paris. This act brought on the Trojan War and the eventual destruction of Troy by the Greeks. For further explanation, see the Gorgias headnote, page 61. [Editors' note.]

[6] The poem is possibly incomplete. [Editors' note.]

"all the violet tiaras,
braided rosebuds, dill and
crocus twined around your young neck

"myrrh poured on your head   15
and on soft mats girls with
all that they most wished for beside them

"while no voices chanted
choruses without ours,
no woodlot bloomed in spring without song . . ."   20

"Sappho, if you will not get
up and let us look at you
I shall never love you again!

"Get up, unleash your suppleness,
lift off your Chian[7] nightdress   5
and, like a lily leaning into

"a spring, bathe in the water.
Cleis is bringing your best
purple frock and the yellow

"tunic down from the clothes chest;   10
you will have a cloak thrown over
you and flowers crowning your hair . . .

"Praxinoa, my child, will you please
roast nuts for our breakfast? One
of the gods is being good to us: 15

"today we are going at last
into Mytilene,[8] our favorite
city, with Sappho, loveliest

---

[7] *Chian:* of Chios, an island south of Lesbos thought to be Homer's birthplace. [Editors' note.]

[8] *Mytilene:* the chief city of Lesbos. [Editors' note.]

"of its women; she will walk
among us like a mother with   20
all her daughters around her

"when she comes home from exile . . ."

But you forget everything

Death is an evil;
we have the gods'
word for it; they too
would die if death
were a good thing   5

Gongyla; I ask only
that you wear the cream
white dress when you come

Desire darts about your
loveliness, drawn down in
circling flight at sight of it   5

and I am glad, although
once I too quarrelled
with Aphrodite
              to whom   10
I pray that you will
come soon

Death will finish
you: afterwards no
one will remember

or want you: you
had no share in   5
the Pierian roses[9]

You will flitter
invisible among
the indistinct dead
in Hell's palace   10
darting fitfully

Let me tell you
this: someone in
some future time
will think of us

Questions for Discussion and Writing

1. It could be said that Sappho's poetry emphasizes the sensual and the physical characteristics of her subjects. If this is true, what is the effect of these emphases on the reader? What is gained—and what is sacrificed—by Sappho's strategic choices?

2. Several centuries after Sappho's lifetime, the ancient writer Antipater of Sidon wrote the following words for her burial place: "That which thou coverest, Aeolian[10] soil, is Sappho, one that sang for a mortal Muse among Muses immortal, one that was reared by Cypris[11] and Eros[12] too, one that helped Persuasion[13] weave the everlasting garland of the Pierian Maids, a delight unto Greece, a glory unto thee." After reading the fragments, how would you

[9] *Pierian roses:* Pieria was a place in Macedonia sacred to the Muses (the daughters of Memory), who were the deities presiding over the arts. "Pierian roses" are "roses sacred to the Muses," that is, works of art such as poetry, music, and so on. [Editors' note.]

[10] *Aeolian:* of Aeolis (or Aeolia), an ancient country in northwest Asia Minor. [Editors' note.]

[11] *Cypris:* another name for Aphrodite, whose sacred place of origin was thought to be the Mediterranean island of Cyprus. [Editors' note.]

[12] *Eros:* desire, attraction, love. Eros, the god, was thought to be the son of Aphrodite; he is still with us today, in his Roman form, as Cupid. [Editors' note.]

[13] *Persuasion:* Peitho, the goddess of persuasion and belief. [Editors' note.]

interpret Antipater's comment that Sappho "helped Persuasion weave the everlasting garland of the Pierian Maids"? In what sense can we think of Sappho's poems as persuasion? How does this way of considering poetry fit or conflict with the way you typically think about poems?

3. How much do you feel that you are part of Sappho's audience? In what ways does her poetry seem to speak to you? How convincing do you find it? In what ways might it seem entirely ancient, strange, irrelevant, unmoving, or dead? What is your attitude toward Sappho and her world? Consider your response carefully and explain why you feel as you do.

4. Imagine that a Mr. Gore G. Haas, superintendent of schools in your home district, sends you—along with other alumni of your high school, parents, and other concerned citizens—a survey letter soliciting your opinion on the advisability of including Sappho's poems in a new "classics-oriented" program aimed at deepening the historical and cultural awareness of high school students. The proposed program would become a part of the general requirements for graduation. There has been, as Haas hints in his letter, some controversy over Sappho, but he does not elaborate and leaves you to speculate about the exact nature of the debate. Do you think that Sappho's poems ought to be included or excluded from the program? Write a letter to Mr. Haas in which you set forth and defend your opinion in this matter.

GORGIAS OF LEONTINI

(c. 483–376 B.C.)

Although little is known about him today, Gorgias was one of the most influential and controversial figures of the early "Golden Age" of Greek culture. As an ambassador from his native Leontini (a Greek city in Sicily), Gorgias arrived in Athens in 427. Already thoroughly steeped in the art of speaking, Gorgias enthralled—and terrified—the Athenians with his eloquence. It was not long before he acquired great wealth and fame as a professional orator and teacher of the art of rhetoric. Among his pupils and protégés were the historian Thucydides, the statesman Pericles, and the orators Antiphon and Isocrates.

In a famous philosophical treatise known as On the Nonexistent—which, appropriately, no longer exists—Gorgias argued the following rather startling theses:

Nothing exists.

If anything exists, the human mind cannot perceive it.

If anything exists and if the human mind perceives it, it cannot be expressed or explained in human language.

This skepticism about the possibility of knowing and/or communicating truth was characteristic of the ancient Sophists, with whom Gorgias has been traditionally identified. The Sophists were frequently accused of being irresponsible—indifferent to truth, unconcerned with justice, preoccupied only with persuasiveness and style, and perpetually "on the make."

The Sophistic view of things, however, possessed considerable philosophical integrity, an integrity that is often overlooked by its detractors, both then and now. As empiricists, they shunned the pursuit of absolute truth and chose rather to base their approach to life and argumentation on probability and direct experience of the world. Of Gorgias, the ancient historian Philostratus tells us (in Lives of the Sophists) that he delivered ceremonial speeches (at public festivals) on political matters of the highest importance, and that in times of dissension he became a "counselor of concord" to the Greeks.

The following selection, "Encomium of Helen," is one of Gorgias' few surviving works. Ostensibly, it is an encomium (a speech of praise) defending Helen of Troy against the charge of adultery. In its original context, it was probably meant to be a kind of literary entertainment, a tour de force in which Gorgias showcases his great skill by arguing this most difficult of cases.

The background of Gorgias' encomium is Homer's Iliad, as well as the folklore and legends surrounding the story of Helen and the Trojan war, which took place (if it happened at all) several centuries before Gorgias' time, in the shadowy prehistory of Greek civilization. Also part of the background is the fact that Helen, in the Greek imagination of Gorgias' time, had become a standard mythic example of the "bad woman": that is, the astonishingly beautiful adulteress; the woman "shaped by heaven" (as Homer says) who betrayed her kingly husband Menelaus by running away with a sexy young prince; the woman who let passion overwhelm her and thereby set in motion a chain of events that ended in catastrophic tragedy. But, so the legends went, Helen was also fated: She herself was the daughter of the god Zeus, who, in an amorous mood, had assumed the form of a swan to rape her mother, Leda; furthermore, her passion for the Trojan prince was caused by the love goddess Aphrodite. In Book III of the Iliad, Helen complains to Aphrodite, "Immortal madness, why do you have this craving to seduce me?" Gorgias plays with this double image of the fabled Helen as he argues her defense.

Ultimately, Gorgias' "Encomium of Helen" does more than present an unusual interpretation of a literary character for the fifth-century B.C. Greek mind; it also offers to the modern reader ways of considering some persistent questions—questions that can never have a final answer but that must be answered somehow and are still important today.

ENCOMIUM OF HELEN

What is becoming to a city is manpower, to a body beauty, to a soul   1
wisdom, to an action virtue, to a speech truth, and the opposites of these
are unbecoming. Man and woman and speech and deed and city and object
should be honored with praise if praiseworthy and incur blame if unworthy,
for it is an equal error and mistake to blame the praisable and to praise the
blamable. It is the duty of one and the same man both to speak the needful
rightly and to refute the unrightfully spoken. Thus it is right to refute
those who rebuke Helen, a woman about whom the testimony of inspired
poets has become univocal and unanimous as had the ill omen of her name,
which has become a reminder of misfortunes. For my part, by introducing
some reasoning into my speech, I wish to free the accused of blame and,
having reproved her detractors as prevaricators and proved the truth, to
free her from their ignorance.

Now it is not unclear, not even to a few, that in nature and in blood the   2
woman who is the subject of this speech is preeminent among preeminent
men and women. For it is clear that her mother was Leda, and her father
was in fact a god, Zeus, but allegedly a mortal, Tyndareus, of whom the

former was shown to be her father because he was and the latter was disproved because he was said to be, and the one was the most powerful of men and the other the lord of all.

Born from such stock, she had godlike beauty, which taking and not 3 mistaking, she kept. In many did she work much desire for her love, and her one body was the cause of bringing together many bodies of men thinking great thoughts for great goals, of whom some had greatness of wealth, some the glory of ancient nobility, some the vigor of personal agility, some command of acquired knowledge. And all came because of a passion which loved to conquer and a love of honor which was unconquered. Who it was and why and how he sailed away, taking Helen as his love, I shall not say. To tell the knowing what they know shows it is right but brings no delight. Having now gone beyond the time once set for my speech, I shall go on to the beginning of my future speech, and I shall set forth the causes through which it was likely that Helen's voyage to Troy should take place.

For either by will of Fate and decision of the gods and vote of Necessity[1] 4 did she do what she did, or by force reduced or by words seduced or by love possessed. Now if through the first, it is right for the responsible one to be held responsible; for god's predetermination cannot be hindered by human premeditation. For it is the nature of things, not for the strong to be hindered by the weak, but for the weaker to be ruled and drawn by the stronger, and for the stronger to lead and the weaker to follow. God is a stronger force than man in might and in wit and in other ways. If then one must place blame on Fate and on a god, one must free Helen from disgrace.

But if she was raped by violence and illegally assaulted and unjustly 5 insulted, it is clear that the raper, as the insulter, did the wronging, and the raped, as the insulted, did the suffering. It is right then for the barbarian who undertook a barbaric undertaking in word and law and deed to meet with blame in word, exclusion in law, and punishment in deed. And surely it is proper for a woman raped and robbed of her country and deprived of her friends to be pitied rather than pilloried. He did the dread deeds; she suffered them. It is just therefore to pity her but to hate him.

But if it was speech which persuaded her and deceived her heart, not 6 even to this is it difficult to make an answer and to banish blame as follows. Speech is a powerful lord, which by means of the finest and most invisible body effects the divinest works: it can stop fear and banish grief and create joy and nurture pity. I shall show how this is the case, since it is necessary to offer proof to the opinion of my hearers: I both deem and define all

---

[1] *Fate . . . Necessity:* The words are capitalized here because they are the names of gods. [Editors' note.]

poetry as speech with meter. Fearful shuddering and tearful pity and grievous longing come upon its hearers, and at the actions and physical sufferings of others in good fortunes and in evil fortunes, through the agency of words, the soul is wont to experience a suffering of its own. But come, I shall turn from one argument to another. Sacred incantations sung with words are bearers of pleasure and banishers of pain, for, merging with opinion in the soul, the power of the incantation is wont to beguile it and persuade it and alter it by witchcraft. There have been discovered two arts of witchcraft and magic: one consists of errors of soul and the other of deceptions of opinion. All who have and do persuade people of things do so by molding a false argument. For if all men on all subjects had both memory of things past and awareness of things present and foreknowledge of the future, speech would not be similarly similar, since as things are now it is not easy for them to recall the past nor to consider the present nor to predict the future. So that on most subjects most men take opinion as counselor to their soul, but since opinion is slippery and insecure it casts those employing it into slippery and insecure successes. What cause then prevents the conclusion that Helen similarly, against her will, might have come under the influence of speech, just as if ravished by the force of the mighty? For it was possible to see how the force of persuasion prevails; persuasion has the form of necessity, but it does not have the same power. For speech constrained the soul, persuading it which it persuaded, both to believe the things said and to approve the things done. The persuader, like a constrainer, does the wrong and the persuaded, like the constrained, in speech is wrongly charged. To understand that persuasion, when added to speech, is wont also to impress the soul as it wishes, one must study: first, the words of astronomers who, substituting opinion for opinion, taking away one but creating another, make what is incredible and unclear seem true to the eyes of opinion; then, second, logically necessary debates in which a single speech, written with art but not spoken with truth, bends a great crowd and persuades; and third, the verbal disputes of philosophers in which the swiftness of thought is also shown making the belief in an opinion subject to easy change. The effect of speech upon the condition of the soul is comparable to the power of drugs over the nature of bodies. For just as different drugs dispel different secretions from the body, and some bring an end to disease and others to life, so also in the case of speeches, some distress, others delight, some cause fear, others make the hearers bold, and some drug and bewitch the soul with a kind of evil persuasion.

It has been explained that if she was persuaded by speech she did not do wrong but was unfortunate. I shall discuss the fourth cause in a fourth passage. For if it was love which did all these things, there will be no difficulty in escaping the charge of the sin which is alleged to have taken place. For the things we see do not have the nature which we wish them to have, but the nature which each actually has. Through sight the soul receives an impression even in its inner features. When belligerents in war buckle on their warlike acouterments of bronze and steel, some designed for defense, others for offense, if the sight sees this, immediately it is alarmed and it alarms the soul, so that often men flee, panic-stricken, from future danger as though it were present. For strong as is the habit of obedience to the law, it is ejected by fear resulting from sight, which coming to a man causes him to be indifferent both to what is judged honorable because of the law and to the advantage to be derived from victory. It has happened that people, after having seen frightening sights, have also lost presence of mind for the present moment; in this way fear extinguishes and excludes thought. And many have fallen victim to useless labor and dread diseases and hardly curable madnesses. In this way the sight engraves upon the mind images of things which have been seen. And many frightening impressions linger, and what lingers is exactly analogous to what is spoken. Moreover, whenever pictures perfectly create a single figure and form from many colors and figures, they delight the sight, while the creation of statues and the production of works of art furnish a pleasant sight to the eyes. Thus it is natural for the sight to grieve for some things and to long for others, and much love and desire for many objects and figures is engraved in many men. If, therefore, the eye of Helen, pleased by the figure of Alexander,[2] presented to her soul eager desire and contest of love, what wonder? If, being a god, love has the divine power of the gods, how could a lesser being reject and refuse it? But if it is a disease of human origin and a fault of the soul, it should not be blamed as a sin, but regarded as an affliction. For she came, as she did come, caught in the net of Fate, not by the plans of the mind, and by the constraints of love, not by the devices of art.

How then can one regard blame of Helen as just, since she is utterly acquitted of all charge, whether she did what she did through falling in love or persuaded by speech or ravished by force or constrained by divine constraint? 8

I have by means of speech removed disgrace from a woman; I have observed the procedure which I set up at the beginning of the speech; I have tried to end the injustice of blame and the ignorance of opinion; I wished to write a speech which would be a praise of Helen and a diversion to myself. 9

Questions for Discussion and Writing

1. Analyze the overall arrangement of the "Encomium of Helen." What, in effect, is Gorgias' basic structural strategy? How would you characterize the argument's *cumulative development*?

---

[2] *Alexander:* Helen's Trojan lover; also known as Paris. [Editors' note.]

2. For the reasoning in this argument to be persuasive, Gorgias' conclusions must be based on a number of given assumptions, beliefs, and values that his listeners are already willing to accept—ideas about what is "fair," for example, or about the nature of "love" or of "justice," to name only a few. What assumptions (stated or unstated) do you think Gorgias is depending on? How can they be recognized? Is there a central assumption? Consider what these assumptions tell us about Gorgias' audience. How many of these assumptions are still present in today's discourse on such subjects?

3. Considering Gorgias' famous three theses from *On the Nonexistent* (summarized in the introductory headnote), what does Gorgias mean when he says "All who . . . persuade people of things do so by molding a false argument"? When he says that love is a god, how much do you think he believes his own statement? How much should Gorgias be trusted? How could we decide?

4. Imagine that you are visited by an ancient Athenian gentleman who claims to be a direct descendant of Menelaus. Not surprisingly, he takes considerable offense at Gorgias' "Encomium of Helen," and he begs you to write a reply that he can use to defend the honor of his family. Your visitor's persistence inspires you to grant his request. As you craft the argument, consider the values of this special audience.

LYSIAS

(c. 459–c. 380 b.c.)

As an orator, professional speech writer, and teacher of rhetoric, Lysias occupies an important place in the history of Greek political discourse. Although his reputation has been permanently stained by Plato's unflattering portrayal in the Phaedrus, Lysias was a sincere patriot and staunch democrat who stood up for good government, even in the face of harsh persecution. A resident of Athens in his early youth, Lysias came of age in the Athenian colony of Thurii, where he honed his argumentative skills and worked for democracy. After he was banished from that city in 412 b.c., he returned to Athens. As a resident alien, he was forbidden to enter politics, so he manufactured arms with his brother and taught rhetoric on the side. He joined Socrates' circle of disciples and mingled with the intellectual elite of the city.

In the year 404 b.c., Lysias' fortunes changed. Identified as an undesirable by the Thirty, a group of antidemocratic oligarchs, he fled Athens and spent a year in exile. His brother Polemarchus was not so lucky; he was murdered by the Thirty for his democratic tendencies and his wealth. After aiding in the fall of the Thirty and returning to Athens, Lysias won, then once again lost, the rights of a citizen. For the rest of his life, he was unable to speak in court, and though he delivered the occasional ceremonial oration he made a living by writing legal orations for others. Indeed, Lysias was prolific—his courtroom speeches alone numbered over two hundred. Although only a small fraction of his work is extant, the surviving speeches are a rich source of vital information about Greek society.

The following selection, "On the Murder of Eratosthenes: Defence" was written by Lysias for the cuckolded Euphiletus. The purpose of the speech was to justify the killing of the rakish oligarch Eratosthenes, who was carrying on a clandestine affair with Euphiletus' wife. Although the speech was delivered by Euphiletus, Lysias' interest in the case was more than professional; as a member of the Thirty, Eratosthenes was at least partly responsible for the murder of Lysias' brother, Polemarchus.

ON THE MURDER OF ERATOSTHENES

Defence

I should be only too pleased, sirs, to have you so disposed towards me in judging this case as you would be to yourselves, if you found yourselves in my plight. For I am sure that, if you had the same feelings about others as about yourselves, not one of you but would be indignant at what has been done; you would all regard the penalties appointed for those who resort to such practices as too mild. And these feelings would be found, not only amongst you, but in the whole of Greece: for in the case of this crime alone, under both democracy and oligarchy, the same requital is accorded to the weakest against the strongest, so that the lowest gets the same treatment as the highest.[1] Thus you see, sirs, how all men abominate this outrage. Well, I conceive that, in regard to the severity of the penalty, you are all of the same mind, and that not one of you is so easygoing as to think it right that men who are guilty of such acts should obtain pardon, or to presume that slight penalties suffice for their deserts. But I take it, sirs, that what I have to show is that Eratosthenes had an intrigue with my wife, and not only corrupted her but inflicted disgrace upon my children and an outrage on myself by entering my house; that this was the one and only enmity between him and me; that I have not acted thus for the sake of money, so as to raise myself from poverty to wealth; and that all I seek to gain is the requital accorded by our laws. I shall therefore set forth to you the whole of my story from the beginning; I shall omit nothing, but will tell the truth. For I consider that my own sole deliverance rests on my telling you, if I am able, the whole of what has occurred.

When I, Athenians, decided to marry, and brought a wife into my house, for some time I was disposed neither to vex her nor to leave her too free to do just as she pleased; I kept a watch on her as far as possible, with such observation of her as was reasonable. But when a child was born to me, thenceforward I began to trust her, and placed all my affairs in her hands, presuming that we were now in perfect intimacy. It is true that in the early days, Athenians, she was the most excellent of wives; she was a clever, frugal housekeeper, and kept everything in the nicest order. But as soon as I lost my mother, her death became the cause of all my troubles. For it was in attending her funeral that my wife was seen by this man, who in time corrupted her. He looked out for the servant-girl who went to market, and so paid addresses to her mistress by which he wrought her ruin. Now

1

2

---

[1] The general statement in these last words shows that the full sense of the preceding is: "the same requital is accorded to the weakest against the strongest as to the strongest against the weakest." [Translator's note.]

in the first place I must tell you, sirs (for I am obliged to give you these particulars), my dwelling is on two floors, the upper being equal in space to the lower, with the women's quarters above and the men's below. When the child was born to us, its mother suckled it; and in order that, each time that it had to be washed, she might avoid the risk of descending by the stairs, I used to live above, and the women below. By this time it had become such an habitual thing that my wife would often leave me and go down to sleep with the child, so as to be able to give it the breast and stop its crying. Things went on in this way for a long time, and I never suspected, but was simpleminded enough to suppose that my own was the chastest wife in the city. Time went on, sirs; I came home unexpectedly from the country, and after dinner the child started crying in a peevish way, as the servant-girl was annoying it on purpose to make it so behave; for the man was in the house,—I learnt it all later. So I bade my wife go and give the child her breast, to stop its howling. At first she refused, as though delighted to see me home again after so long; but when I began to be angry and bade her go,—"Yes, so that you," she said, "may have a try here at the little maid. Once before, too, when you were drunk, you pulled her about." At that I laughed, while she got up, went out of the room, and closed the door, feigning to make fun, and she turned the key in the lock. I, without giving a thought to the matter, or having any suspicion, went to sleep in all content after my return from the country. Towards daytime she came and opened the door. I asked why the doors made a noise in the night; she told me that the child's lamp had gone out, and she had lit it again at our neighbour's. I was silent and believed it was so. But it struck me, sirs, that she had powdered her face,[2] though her brother had died not thirty days before; even so, however, I made no remark on the fact, but left the house in silence. After this, sirs, an interval occurred in which I was left quite unaware of my own injuries; I was then accosted by a certain old female, who was secretly sent by a woman with whom that man was having an intrigue, as I heard later. This woman was angry with him and felt herself wronged, because he no longer visited her so regularly, and she kept a close watch on him until she discovered what was the cause. So the old creature accosted me where she was on the look-out, near my house, and said,—"Euphiletus, do not think it is from any meddlesomeness that I have approached you; for the man who is working both your and your wife's dishonour happens to be our enemy. If, therefore, you take the servant-girl who goes to market and waits on you, and torture her, you will learn all. It is," she said, "Eratosthenes of Oë who is doing this; he has debauched not only your wife, but many others besides; he makes an art of it." With these words, sirs, she took herself off; I was at once

---

[2] Athenian women used white lead to give an artificial delicacy to their complexion; cf. Aristoph. *Ecclesiazusae* 878, 929. [Translator's note.]

perturbed; all that had happened came into my mind, and I was filled with suspicion,—reflecting first how I was shut up in my chamber, and then remembering how on that night the inner and outer doors made a noise, which had never occurred before, and how it struck me that my wife had put on powder. All these things came into my mind, and I was filled with suspicion. Returning home, I bade the servant-girl follow me to the market, and taking her to the house of an intimate friend, I told her I was fully informed of what was going on in my house: "So it is open to you," I said, "to choose as you please between two things,—either to be whipped and thrown into a mill, never to have any rest from miseries of that sort, or else to speak out the whole truth and, instead of suffering any harm, obtain my pardon for your transgressions. Tell no lies, but speak the whole truth." The girl at first denied it, and bade me do what I pleased, for she knew nothing; but when I mentioned Eratosthenes to her, and said that he was the man who visited my wife, she was dismayed, supposing that I had exact knowledge of everything. At once she threw herself down at my knees, and having got my pledge that she should suffer no harm, she accused him, first, of approaching her after the funeral, and then told how at last she became his messenger; how my wife in time was persuaded, and by what means she procured his entrances, and how at the Thesmophoria,[3] while I was in the country, she went off to the temple with his mother. And the girl gave an exact account of everything else that had occurred. When her tale was all told, I said,—"Well now, see that nobody in the world gets knowledge of this; otherwise, nothing in your arrangement with me will hold good. And I require that you show me their guilt in the very act; I want no words, but manifestation of the fact, if it really is so." She agreed to do this. Then came an interval of four or five days . . .[4] as I shall bring strong evidence to show. But first I wish to relate what took place on the last day. I had an intimate friend named Sostratus. After sunset I met him as he came from the country. As I knew that, arriving at that hour, he would find none of his circle at home, I invited him to dine with me; we came to my house, mounted to the upper room, and had dinner. When he had made a good meal, he left me and departed; then I went to bed. Eratosthenes, sirs, entered, and the maid-servant roused me at once, and told me that he was in the house. Bidding her look after the door, I descended and went out in silence; I called on one friend and another, and found some of them at home, while others were out of town. I took with me as many as I could among those who were there, and so came along. Then we got torches from the nearest shop, and went in; the door was open, as the girl had it in readiness. We pushed open the door of the

---

[3] A festival in honour of Demeter, celebrated by Athenian matrons in October. [Translator's note.]

[4] Some words are missing here in the text. [Translator's note.]

bedroom, and the first of us to enter were in time to see him lying down by my wife; those who followed saw him standing naked on the bed. I gave him a blow, sirs, which knocked him down, and pulling round his two hands behind his back, and tying them, I asked him why he had the insolence to enter my house. He admitted his guilt; then he besought and implored me not to kill him, but to exact a sum of money. To this I replied,—"It is not I who am going to kill you, but our city's law, which you have transgressed and regarded as of less account than your pleasures, choosing rather to commit this foul offence against my wife and my children than to obey the laws like a decent person."

Thus it was, sirs, that this man incurred the fate that the laws ordain for 3 those who do such things;[5] he had not been dragged in there from the street, nor had he taken refuge at my hearth,[6] as these people say. For how could it be so, when it was in the bedroom that he was struck and fell down then and there, and I pinioned his arms, and so many persons were in the house that he could not escape them, as he had neither steel nor wood nor anything else with which he might have beaten off those who had entered? But, sirs, I think you know as well as I that those whose acts are against justice do not acknowledge that their enemies speak the truth, but lie themselves and use other such devices to foment anger in their hearers against those whose acts are just. So, first read the law.

LAW

He did not dispute it, sirs: he acknowledged his guilt, and besought and 4 implored that he might not be killed, and was ready to pay compensation in money. But I would not agree to his estimate, as I held that our city's law should have higher authority; and I obtained that satisfaction which you deemed most just when you imposed it on those who adopt such courses. Now, let my witnesses come forward in support of these statements.

WITNESSES

Read out also, please, that law from the pillar in the Areopagus. 5

LAW

You hear, sirs, how the Court of the Areopagus itself, to which has been 6 assigned, in our own as in our fathers' time, the trial of suits for murder,

---

[5] Athenian law provided that a husband could kill his wife's seducer if the killing was unpremeditated. [Editors' note.]

[6] The hearth in a Greek house retained its primitive sanctity as a centre of the family religion, and it would be sacrilege to kill anyone there. [Translator's note.]

has expressly stated that whoever takes this vengeance on an adulterer caught in the act with his spouse shall not be convicted of murder. And so strongly was the lawgiver convinced of the justice of this in the case of wedded wives, that he even applied the same penalty in the case of mistresses, who are of less account. Now surely it is clear that, if he had had any heavier punishment than this for the case of married women, he would have imposed it. But in fact, as he was unable to devise a severer one for wives, he ordained that it should be the same for that of mistresses also. Please read this law besides.

LAW

You hear, sirs, how it directs that, if anyone forcibly debauches a free adult or child, he shall be liable to double[7] damages; while if he so debauches a woman, in any of the cases where it is permitted to kill him, he is subject to the same rule. Thus the lawgiver, sirs, considered that those who use force deserve a less penalty than those who use persuasion; for the latter he condemned to death, whereas for the former he doubled the damages, considering that those who achieve their ends by force are hated by the persons forced; while those who used persuasion corrupted thereby their victims' souls, thus making the wives of others more closely attached to themselves than to their husbands, and got the whole house into their hands, and caused uncertainty as to whose the children really were, the husbands' or the adulterers'. In view of all this the author of the law made death their penalty. Wherefore I, sirs, not only stand acquitted of wrongdoing by the laws, but am also directed by them to take this satisfaction: it is for you to decide whether they are to be valid or of no account. For to my thinking every city makes its laws in order that on any matter which perplexes us we may resort to them and inquire what we have to do. And so it is they who, in cases like the present, exhort the wronged parties to obtain this kind of satisfaction. I call upon you to support their opinion: otherwise, you will be giving adulterers such licence that you will encourage thieves as well to call themselves adulterers; since they will feel assured that, if they plead this reason in their defence, and allege that they enter other men's houses for this purpose, nobody will touch them. For everyone will know that the laws on adultery are to be dismissed, and that it is your vote that one has to fear, because this has supreme authority over all the city's affairs.

Do not consider, sirs, what they say: they accuse me of ordering the maid-servant on that day to go and fetch the young man. Now I, sirs, could have held myself justified in using any possible means to catch the corrupter of my wife. For if I had bidden the girl fetch him, when words

7

8

---

[7] i.e., double the amount laid down for violating a slave. [Translator's note.]

alone had been spoken and no act had been committed, I should have been in the wrong: but if, when once he had compassed all his ends, and had frequently entered my house, I had then used any possible means to catch him, I should have considered myself quite in order. And observe how on this point also they are lying: you will perceive it easily in this way. As I told you, sirs, before, Sostratus was a friend of mine, on intimate terms with me; he met me as he came from the country about sunset, and had dinner with me, and when he had made a good meal he left me and departed. Now in the first place, sirs, you must bear this in mind: if on that night I had designs on Eratosthenes, which was more to my advantage,— to go and take my dinner elsewhere, or to bring in my guest to dinner with me? For in the latter case that man would have been less likely to venture on entering my house. And in the second place, do you suppose that I should have let my dinner-guest go and leave me there alone and unsupported, and not rather have bidden him stay, in order that he might stand by me in taking vengeance upon the adulterer? Then again, sirs, do you not think that I should have sent word to my intimate acquaintances in the daytime, and bidden them assemble at the house of one of my friends living nearest to me, rather than have waited till the moment of making my discovery to run round in the night, without knowing whom I should find at home, and who were away? Thus I called on Harmodius, and one other, who were not in town—of this I was not aware—and others, I found, were not in; but those whom I could I took along with me. Yet if I had foreknown this, do you not think that I should have called up servants and passed the word to my friends, in order that I might have gone in myself with all possible safety,—for how could I tell whether he too had some weapon?—and so I might have had as many witnesses as possible with me when I took my vengeance? But as in fact I knew nothing of what was to befall on that night, I took with me those whom I could. Now let my witnesses come forward in support of all this.

WITNESSES

You have heard the witnesses, sirs; and consider this affair thus in your 9
own minds, asking yourselves whether any enmity has ever arisen before this between me and Eratosthenes. I say you will discover none. For he had neither subjected me to slanderous impeachment, nor attempted to expel me from the city, nor brought any private suit against me, nor was he privy to any wrongdoing which I was so afraid of being divulged that I was intent on his destruction, nor, should I accomplish this, had I any hope of getting money from anywhere: for there are people who plot each other's death for such purposes. So far, indeed, from either abuse or a drunken brawl or any other quarrel having occurred between us, I had never even seen the man before that night. For what object, then, should I run so grave a risk, unless I had received from him the greatest of injuries? Why,

again, did I choose to summon witnesses for my wicked act, when it was open to me, if I was thus criminally intent on his destruction, to have none of them privy to it?

I therefore, sirs, do not regard this requital as having been exacted in my own private interest, but in that of the whole city. For those who behave in that way, when they see the sort of prizes offered for such transgressions, will be less inclined to trespass against their neighbours, if they see that you also take the same view. Otherwise it were better far to erase our established laws, and ordain others which will inflict the penalties on men who keep watch on their own wives, and will allow full immunity to those who would debauch them. This would be a far juster way than to let the citizens be entrapped by the laws; these may bid a man, on catching an adulterer, to deal with him in whatever way he pleases, but the trials are found to be more dangerous to the wronged parties than to those who, in defiance of the laws, dishonour the wives of others. For I am now risking the loss of life, property and all else that I have, because I obeyed the city's laws.

Questions for Discussion and Writing

1. In describing Lysias' craft, W. R. M. Lamb declares, "The arrangement of subject matter is orderly and lucid: we have usually a preface, a narrative, an argued proof, and a conclusion, and we are led by easy steps from one section to another." Is this an accurate description of the speech you have just read? Describe the way that Lysias unfolds his argument in time.

2. The headnote mentions that Lysias' speeches tell us much of interest about Athenian life. Precisely what does this speech tell us? More specifically, what do we learn about attitudes toward gender, male-female relations, marital responsibility, and mistresses? How do these attitudes compare with the beliefs of today?

3. Considering the Athenian attitudes that seem to be reflected in Lysias' speech (see question 2), do you feel that he has assembled an effective argument? Should he win the case?

4. Imagine that you are a Greek writer hired by Eratosthenes' relatives to compose a speech prosecuting Euphiletus. As you compose this speech, think carefully about how you will counter the kinds of arguments presented by Lysias.

PLATO

(c. 427–347 b.c.)

No matter whose list you consult, Plato ranks with the most important philosophers the world has known. Even if you have never read a word he wrote, chances are excellent that you have encountered, in various contexts, the concepts of "Platonic love," "philosopher king," or "ideal forms." In fact, a working knowledge of the writings of Plato and his pupil Aristotle provides a philosophical framework for understanding a surprisingly large portion of Western thought. The ubiquity of their influence moved the nineteenth-century poet and literary critic Samuel Taylor Coleridge to claim, "Every man is either a Platonist or an Aristotelian."

The son of distinguished Athenians, Plato became the most famous pupil of the philosopher Socrates. In lively discussions with his teacher and fellow students, Plato began to formulate his ideas about language, argument, politics, law, ethics, love, justice, and other timeless human subjects. Because Socrates wrote no philosophy himself, we have no way of determining precisely how great his influence was on Plato. Today most scholars believe that although Socrates had a major role in shaping Plato's philosophical positions, the student was no mere recorder of his teacher's lectures. Like most great thinkers, Plato absorbed the wisdom of his predecessors but also moved beyond it to fresh new territory.

Although his original intention was to pursue politics, Plato soon became disillusioned with the volatile government of Athens. When his beloved teacher was tried and executed on charges of introducing strange gods and corrupting the youth, Plato left the city for a number of years. Eventually he made his way back to Athens, where he began a school known as the Academy. Aside from a distracting entanglement with politics in the city of Syracuse, Plato dedicated himself to the task of training statesmen. That the Academy functioned as a school until A.D. 529 is a great tribute to its founder's enduring influence.

A great believer in the power of the spoken word, Plato wrote dialogues to record and disseminate his philosophy. Through this form of discourse, he attempted to combine the depth of careful reflection with the immediacy of personal encounter. Although the dialogues consist of realistic-sounding exchanges among people whom Plato actually knew, his intention was not to record history or to transcribe actual conversations, but to marshal poetic license in the service of a philosophical education. The Socrates who appears in Plato's dialogues is thus not necessarily the historical Socrates at whose knee Plato sat as a young man.

The following selection has been taken from the Phaedrus, one of Plato's later works. The dialogue begins when Socrates encounters the youthful Phaedrus on the streets of Athens. Phaedrus has just come from the orator Lysias, whose eloquence *charms him. In fact, he is hiding one of his idol's compositions under his cloak. After a bit of friendly joking, Phaedrus agrees to read the speech to Socrates. As our selection begins, they quit the bustle of Athens for a cool spot under a plane tree in the countryside. Here the philosopher listens carefully to Lysias' "feast of eloquence," in which the famous Greek orator paradoxically praises lust, disparages romantic love, and claims that it is better to yield sexual favors to a nonlover than to a lover. From this opening gambit, the dialogue proceeds to a discussion of the art of rhetoric and the nature of love. As you will see, Socrates offers two intriguing speeches of his own.*

In the last half of the dialogue, which is not included here, Socrates marshals carefully structured discourse to persuade the youthful and impressionable Phaedrus that a "true art of rhetoric" must necessarily be philosophical. True rhetoric, unlike the brand of discourse practiced by Lysias and taught by Sophists such as Gorgias, is not simply a collection of formulae and mechanical techniques for creating crowd-pleasing effects. True rhetoricians cannot be satisfied with appealing to popular opinion, nor can they forsake the search for true knowledge. For Socrates, an art of rhetoric worthy of the name must do more than produce technically impressive style and persuasiveness; it must also foster the ability to lead one's fellow citizens to understand the truth about such things as justice and help them choose a way of life that is genuinely good.

In short, a true art of rhetoric, Socrates argues, is like a true art of medicine. Its function is not merely to entertain, impress, or manipulate, or make the practitioner wealthy, but to improve people's lives. To accomplish this goal, according to Socrates, a rhetorician must have three kinds of knowledge: (1) You must know the truth of the subject matter about which you wish to speak; (2) you must know the "soul" or mind set of your listener; and (3) you must know the kind of speaking most appropriate for each soul and each situation. As the dialogue concludes, Phaedrus promises to act on the new lessons he has learned by encouraging his beloved Lysias to engage in philosophical, rather than merely manipulative, rhetoric.

As you read this selection and consider these weighty lessons for yourself, please keep in mind a point mentioned earlier about historical accuracy: Socrates, Phaedrus, and Lysias were real persons, but it is doubtful that the speeches and conversations in this dialogue took place in the way they are recorded. The Lysias who composed "On the Murder of Eratosthenes: Defence" may have had a hand in composing a speech something like the one recorded by Plato in the Phaedrus, but no definitive claims can be made for the accuracy or legitimacy of the speech that Plato puts in Phaedrus' youthful hands.

FROM PHAEDRUS

SOCRATES   Let's leave the road here and go along the Ilissus. Then   1
we can sit in peace wherever you like.

PHAEDRUS   It's a good thing I've come without shoes. You, of   2
course, never wear them. Our easiest course will be to go wading, and
pleasant too, especially at this time of year and day.

SOCRATES   Lead on. And keep an eye out for a place to sit.   3

PHAEDRUS   Do you see that tall plane tree?   4

SOCRATES   Yes?   5

PHAEDRUS   There's shade there and a bit of a breeze and grass to   6
sit on or, if we like, even to lie in.

SOCRATES   Lead on, please.   7

PHAEDRUS   Tell me, Socrates, isn't it from somewhere around   8
here, from the Ilissus, that Boreas is said to have carried off Oreithyia?[1]

SOCRATES   So it's said.   9

PHAEDRUS   Was it really from this very spot? To be sure, the   10
waters are lovely and pure and clear, just right for young girls to play
beside.

SOCRATES   No, the actual place is downstream, a couple of hundred   11
yards or so, where we cross over to the Agra precinct. There is, I think,
an altar to Boreas there.

PHAEDRUS   I'd never noticed it. But tell me, Socrates, do you   12
really believe in the truth of this tale?

SOCRATES   If I followed the learned in disbelieving it, I should   13
be more in fashion than I am; for I would rationalize and say that while
the maiden was at play with Pharmaceia, she was pushed by the North
Wind over the neighboring cliff and so it finally came about that the tale
was told that she had been ravished away by Boreas. But as for me,
Phaedrus, though I allow that such explanations are generally pleasant
enough, yet they must proceed from too clever and laborious a person, and
one not altogether to be envied if only for the reason that after this
rationalization he has to go on to straighten out the appearance of
Hippocentaurs, and then Chimaeras: there floods in a great horde of such
creatures as Gorgons and Pegasuses and masses of other impossible,
portentous beings. If one doubts the existence of these and proceeds with
his simple-minded erudition to reduce each one to verisimilitude, he'll need
quite a bit of leisure. That is what I entirely lack, to make such speculations.
And the reason, my friend, is this: I am not yet in a position to follow the
Delphian inscription and come to know myself;[2] while I still lack this
knowledge, it seems ridiculous to investigate irrelevant matters. So that is

---

[1] *Boreas is said to have carried off Oreithyia:* Phaedrus refers to a traditional myth. Boreas is
the god of the North Wind; Oreithyia was a human maiden. [Editors' note.]

[2] *the Delphian inscription:* At the shrine of the famous oracle at Delphi there was an inscription
that said KNOW THYSELF. [Editors' note.]

the reason I leave such subjects alone and adopt the common view about them; and, as I said just now, I conduct my researches not into them, but into myself. Am I perhaps a creature more involved, more puffed with passion than Typhon?[3] Or am I a gentler, more straightforward animal, to whom the gods have given a modest nature? But look, friend, while we talk on, isn't this the tree to which you were leading us?

PHAEDRUS   The very one.   14

SOCRATES   And a fine retreat it is. Here is the lofty, spreading   15
plane tree and the agnus castus,[4] high clustering with delightful shade.
Now that it is in full bloom, the whole place will be wonderfully fragrant;
and the stream that flows beneath the plane is delightfully cool to the feet.
To judge from the figurines and images, this must be a spot sacred to
Achelous and the Nymphs.[5] And please note how welcome and sweet the
fresh air is, resounding with the summer chirping of the cicada chorus.
But the finest thing of all is the grass, thick enough on the gentle slope to
rest one's head most comfortably. It turns out, dear Phaedrus, that you're
the best of guides for a stranger.

PHAEDRUS   You, strange friend, are the most extraordinary man   16
I know. Just as you say, you really do give the effect of a stranger and no
native. That's because you never leave the city. Why, you never even leave
the walls, let alone crossing the frontier.

SOCRATES   Forgive me. My appetite is for learning. Trees and   17
countryside have no desire to teach me anything; it's only the men in the
city that do. You, however, seem to have found the remedy to draw me
out. Just as men can lead hungry beasts by shaking a bait of fruit or leaves
in front of them, so you brandish before me words in books and could lead
me on a tour of all Attica[6] and anywhere else you pleased. So now that I've
got here, I intend for the present to lie down; but do you take the most
comfortable position for reading, open your book, and begin.

PHAEDRUS   Then listen.   18

---

[3] *more puffed with passion than Typhon:* When Hera, the queen of the gods, was angry with her husband Zeus, she gave birth in revenge to a cruel monster-son, Typhon, to be a plague to humankind. [Editors' note.]

[4] *agnus castus:* an ornamental shrub with blue and white flowers and fruit; sometimes used as a stimulant or carminative (antiflatulent). [Editors' note.]

[5] *figurines and images:* small votive figures and relief sculptures. In the fifth and fourth centuries B.C., such figures and reliefs around Athens typically showed dancing nymphs led by the god Hermes while the god Pan and the river-spirit Achelous looked on. Hermes was the messenger of the gods and sometimes a trickster also (as a baby, he stole some cows from the god Apollo). Called the "guide of souls," he was a patron-deity for travellers, heralds, and orators as well. [Editors' note.]

[6] *a tour of all Attica:* Attica is the region of Greece surrounding Athens. [Editors' note.]

The Speech of Lysias[7]

What my circumstances are, you know; and you have heard how I believe   19
they should be settled to our best advantage. I claim that I should not fail
to obtain what I ask merely because I am not a lover of yours. As soon
as their passion abates, lovers always feel that their favors have been
wasted, but non-lovers never have reason for regrets. It is not under
constraint, but as free agents, taking careful thought for what is within
their power to control, that they regulate favors in proportion to their
means.

Again, lovers reckon losses incurred in their affairs because of their   20
love, and also the favors they have bestowed, and even add the trouble
they have taken; then they make up their minds that they have long since
given ample satisfaction to the beloved. But non-lovers cannot adduce
neglect of their property because of their passion, or reckon in any past
exertions, or blame the beloved for their quarrels with relatives. The
result of this is that, since so many evils have been removed, nothing
remains but to perform with eagerness such actions as they believe will
gratify.

Again, if it is right for lovers to be highly valued because they profess   21
to have particular affection for those they love, and are ready, both in
word and deed, to give pleasure to the beloved at the cost of being detested
by everyone else, it is easy to recognize (if they speak the truth) that when
later on they fall in love with someone else, they will value the new love
more highly than the old; consequently it is obvious that they will do evil
to the former beloved if it so please the new one.

Yet how is it seemly to entrust a matter of such importance to a man   22
suffering the kind of affliction that no one of any experience would even
try to drive away? It is a fact that lovers themselves acknowledge that they
are not sound, but sick; they know that they are incapable of good
judgment, but cannot control themselves. How, then, when they come to
their senses, can they approve of the intentions they formed when they
were in an abnormal condition?

Moreover, if you were to choose the best of your lovers, your choice   23
would be limited to only a few; but if from all the non-lovers you choose
the one most suited to you, you will have a wide field. The result of this,
then, is that there is a far greater expectation of hitting on a man worthy
of your affections in the vast crowd of non-lovers.

---

[7] It is doubtful that this speech was actually written by Lysias; what Plato offers here is
really a portrait—or parody, or caricature—of sophistical rhetoric. For comparison, examine
Lysias' *On the Murder of Eratosthenes: Defence* or Gorgias' *Encomium of Helen*. [Editors'
note.]

Now if you respect established custom and are apprehensive that people 24
may hear about you and reproach you, it is entirely likely that the lover,
thinking that everyone else will find him as enviable as he finds himself,
will become excited by possession and will flatter his vanity by proving
to the world at large that his efforts have not been in vain; but the non-
lover, in full self-possession, will choose what is really best in preference
to a bit of glory in the eyes of the public.

Again, a lover must necessarily be seen and heard accompanying his 25
beloved and making this his chief business, so that, when they are observed
talking with one another, other people will suppose that they have either
already satisfied their desires or will soon do so. The non-lover, on the
other hand, no one will dream of inculpating for this association, realizing
as people do that a man must talk with someone, for friendship's sake or
some other pleasant reason.

Moreover, you may be afraid that it is difficult for friendship to last 26
and that, though a quarrel under other circumstances would be an equal
disaster to both, if it occurs when you have sacrificed what you value most
highly, it is to you alone that great damage accrues. If you have such
fears, it is only natural that you should be more afraid of lovers. For
many are the things that offend them and they interpret everything as
being done for their hurt. This is the reason why they discourage any
association of the beloved with other men, fearing that the wealthy may
surpass them in material assets, that the cultured may prove superior in
intelligence. They are always on guard against the influence of anyone
who possesses any other advantage, too, and so they will persuade you to
incur the dislike of all such men and leave you without a friend in the
world. And if you try to look after your own interests and use better
judgment than your lover, you will only quarrel with him. But non-
lovers who have gained what they wanted through their own merits will
not be jealous of your associations; rather, they would dislike those who
did not wish to be with you, believing that you are slighted by such
people, but derive benefit by associating with others. The result, then, is
that you may have much more expectation of friendship than of enmity
arising from such an affair.

Moreover, many lovers conceive a desire for the body before they come 27
to know the character or have become familiar with personal traits so that
they have no way of telling whether they will still desire to be friends
when they shall be quit of their passion. But non-lovers, who have become
friends before the affair took place, will naturally not allow its course to
diminish their friendship: the past will, rather, remain as a reminder that
there are more favors to come.

Moreover, it is for your own improvement to be persuaded by me 28
rather than by a lover. For lovers praise your deeds and words far beyond
your best advantage, partly in fear that they may offend you if they do

not, partly because their judgment is impaired by their desires. Such, in fact, are the manifestations of love: when circumstances go badly, it makes a man count as a dreadful affliction the sort of thing that would not give trouble to anyone else; but when they go well, it compels him to greet with extravagant praise what no one else would find pleasant at all. So, you see, lovers should inspire far more pity than envy in the beloved. If, however, you yield to me, my relations with you will be, not with a view toward present pleasure, but toward future benefits. I shall not be subdued by love, but remain master of myself, not conceiving a violent antipathy because of petty faults, but being moved only slowly into a mild anger when great shortcomings are revealed. I shall forgive involuntary slips and voluntary ones I shall endeavor to prevent. And these are proofs that our friendship will last a long time. If, however, your present belief is that a firm friendship cannot come about unless one is already in love, you would also have to subscribe to the notion that we put no great value on our sons and our fathers and our mothers, that we cannot acquire loyal friends—for it is not to passion that we owe these [relationships], but to considerations of a different order.

Again, if we should show favor to those who press us most eagerly, 29 then in other matters also we ought to confer benefits upon the neediest, not the best; for the former will be quit of the greatest evils and so return us the greatest gratitude. In that case, even to our private banquets we ought not to invite our friends, but beggars instead and those who need a square meal. For it is they who will be fond of us and attend us and flock to our doors; it is they who will be most delighted and grateful and will call down blessings upon us. But actually the proper course is not to gratify the most importunate, but rather those who are most capable of returning the favor; not mere lovers, but the deserving; not those who will enjoy your youth and beauty, but those who, when you are older, will let you share their wealth; not those who, when they have gained their intent, will boast to the world of their success, but those who would modestly keep it a complete secret; not those who will be enthusiastic for a moment or two, but those whose friendship will continue uninterrupted through your whole life; not those who, when desire shall fail, will seek a pretext for a quarrel, but those who, when your beauty is gone, will exhibit their real goodness.

Remember, then, what I have said and reflect that while lovers' friends 30 admonish them because of the evil inherent in their practices, no friend or relation has ever blamed a non-lover for badly managing his affairs because of a disinterested attachment.

Perhaps you may ask me if I am advising you to grant favors to all 31 non-lovers. Well, I don't think even a lover would urge you to comply with the requests of all lovers. Impartial favors are not received with equal gratitude; nor, since you wish to keep it a secret, would that be equally possible. No harm must come from it, and benefits must accrue to both.

As for me, I think I've said enough. But if you believe anything has been neglected and want to hear more, you have only to question me. 32

Well, Socrates, how does the speech seem to you? Isn't it marvelously eloquent, especially in its use of language? 33

SOCRATES Wonderfully, my friend, to the point of quite overcoming me. This was due to you, Phaedrus; I was watching you and observed how you were enjoying the speech as you read it. And because I know that you understand such things better than I, I followed your guidance and entered into your ecstasy, my holy companion. 34

PHAEDRUS So! You want to make fun of it? 35

SOCRATES Do you really think I'm joking? Don't I seem serious? 36

PHAEDRUS Please don't joke, Socrates. Now tell me truly, as friend to friend, do you believe that any other Greek could have spoken more impressively or more copiously on the same subject? 37

SOCRATES How's that? Are you and I to praise the speech on the grounds of the author's relevance? Or rather only on this score: that the language was clear and precise, turned out in accurately balanced periods? But if we are to praise it for saying what it ought, I can do only for your sake; my insignificance failed to grasp it. I listened to it merely as a piece of rhetoric, and in this I don't believe even Lysias himself would regard it as adequate. To me, in fact, Phaedrus—if you don't disagree—it seemed that the author was saying the same thing two or three times, as though he weren't capable of saying a great deal on a single topic—or perhaps he wasn't especially interested in the matter. I thought it quite a virtuoso performance, to show himself capable of saying the same thing in two different ways, and both of them excellently. 38

PHAEDRUS Now, Socrates, that's ridiculous. Why, that is the outstanding quality of the speech: of all the points of the subject worthy to be enumerated he has neglected not one! I conclude that, in comparison with Lysias's speech, no one could treat the topic more exhaustively or more worthily. 39

SOCRATES Here I must cease to agree with you. You must know that ancient history has produced sages, both men and woman, who have written and spoken on the same topic. They will rise up and confute me if, through deference to you, I agree. 40

PHAEDRUS Now who may they be? And where have you heard anything better than this? 41

SOCRATES At the moment I can't tell you. But I'm quite sure I've heard it somewhere—from the fair Sappho, perhaps, or the wise Anacreon or one of the prose writers. Do you know why I suppose so? My dear boy, there is something welling up inside me which makes me feel that I could 42 speak in different terms, and not inferior ones, on these same lines. I am quite aware that it is not from myself that such ideas come, for I know my own ignorance. They can only come, I suppose, from some other source, flowing in through my ears, filling me like a pitcher; though again, because of my stupidity I can't remember how and from whom I've heard them. . . .

[Phaedrus challenges Socrates' claim, and now Socrates must deliver a speech of his own. Socrates notes that he will be obliged to use some of the same ideas that Lysias has used, covers his head because "If I catch your eye, I may be ashamed and falter," calls on the Muses to help him, and begins:]

SOCRATES' FIRST SPEECH

Once upon a time there was a boy, or a youth rather, of great beauty who had a large number of lovers. And one of them was a certain cunning fellow who had persuaded the boy that he did not love him, though he really loved him all the time. On one occasion of his courtship he tried to convince the lad of this precise point: that it is better to give one's favors to a non-lover than to a lover. And this is what he said: 43

"There is only one way, my child, to begin deliberations auspiciously; one must first understand what the deliberations are about or the whole matter will fail of its purpose. Most people are unaware that they do not know the true nature of the things they discuss; but since they assume that they do know, no basic agreement is reached before they begin their discussion. So, as the inquiry proceeds, the result is what one might expect: they can neither remain consistent nor agree with one another. But as for you and me, let us see to it that we do not have that trouble which we censure in others. Since the question before us is whether one should consort with a non-lover rather than a lover, let us agree on a definition of love, its nature and its power; then we can keep it before our eyes and refer to it as we examine the question of whether it brings advantage or harm. 44

"Everyone knows quite well that love is a desire of some sort; and further, we also know that even non-lovers desire what is beautiful. Then by what token shall we distinguish the lover and the non-lover? Again, we must observe that in each of us there are two ruling and guiding principles which we follow wherever they may lead: one of them is an innate desire for pleasure, the other, an acquired opinion which strives for the best. And sometimes these forces within us are at harmony and sometimes at variance; now one gains the mastery, now the other. When opinion leads through reason to what is best and dominates the other, the name given to this dominance is self-control; but when desire irrationally drags us toward pleasures and gains the mastery within us, this mastery is called wantonness. This wantonness has many names, for it has many 45 branches and many aspects. And whichever of these forms gains supremacy gives its name to the man who possesses it, a name neither honorable nor creditable. If desire for food masters the judgment of what is best and also the other desires, then this is called gluttony and the man who possesses it will have a corresponding name. Again, if desire for drinking seizes supreme power, we know what appellation the man who follows that path will have. And it is no less plain what appropriate names of the same sort will be given in each case when any desire akin to these achieves dominion.

"The reason for this preamble must be fairly obvious; yet what is stated 46 outright will be clearer than what is not. So I say that the irrational desire which overcomes the opinion that prompts to right conduct and pursues the enjoyment of beauty, acquiring fresh strength from other desires akin to it for an assault on carnal beauty—that very strength provides its name, it is the power called love."[8]

Well, dear Phaedrus, do you think, as I do, that I am inspired? 47

PHAEDRUS   Certainly, Socrates, you are dominated by an unusual 48 eloquence.

SOCRATES   Then listen to me in silence; for this place gives the 49 impression of being truly divine, so much so that if, as the speech proceeds, I often seem to be in a frenzy, don't be surprised. Already my words are almost dithyrambic. . . .[9]

Well then, dear friend, we have stated and defined the topic for our 50 present deliberations. And let us keep our eyes firmly fastened on this while we proceed with the question of what advantage or harm will be likely to come from the lover and non-lover respectively to a lad who consorts with them. Now the one is mastered by desire and a slave to pleasure, so that it follows that he will try to get the greatest possible pleasure from his beloved. When a man is ill, everything that doesn't thwart him is pleasant, whereas whatever is stronger than he or on equal terms is objectionable. So the lover will not willingly endure to have his beloved stronger or an equal but will continually strive to make him weaker or inferior. The ignorant man is inferior to the wise man, the coward to the brave, the poor speaker to the eloquent, the slow witted to the quick. All these and more defects of intelligence in the beloved, whether acquired or innate, will necessarily please the lover; and if they are lacking he must try to produce them or be deprived of his immediate pleasure. He is, of course, bound to be jealous and does great harm by trying to keep his favorite from many other advantageous associations which would tend to make a man of him, and especially from the one that would most increase his wisdom (thereby doing him the greatest harm of all). This is divine philosophy, from which the lover must necessarily

---

[8] A fanciful etymology: "love" from "strength," *eros* from *rhomê*. [Translators' note.]

[9] *almost dithyrambic:* Dithyrambs were a type of lyric song. [Editors' note.]

and strictly bar his beloved, for he fears that he would then be despised; and he will contrive, besides, to make the boy totally ignorant and totally dependent on himself and his standards of conduct, securing the greatest pleasure for himself, but the greatest harm for the boy. So much, then, for the intellect: a man in love is an utterly unprofitable guardian or associate.

As for the condition and care of the body, let us next observe how the 51 man who is forced to pursue pleasure instead of goodness will attend to this and what will be the result of his care in the boy he has come to possess. You will note that the object of his pursuit will be no stalwart, but a weakling, not accustomed to sun and fresh air but to the half-lights of delicate shadow; the boy will know nothing of manly toil and the sweat of ardor, but will indulge in soft, effeminate living, adorned with an artificial complexion since he has none of his own. The rest of his practices will be like these and obviously need no further enumeration here. To sum up briefly and pass on: the boy will have the sort of body that, in war or any other crisis, will bring help and comfort to his enemies, but to his friends and even his lovers, not a little alarm.

Since this is quite plain, let us abandon the topic and proceed to list 52 the advantages and disadvantages that the association or guardianship of a lover will bring in the matter of the boy's possessions. Here, too, it is clear to everyone, and especially to the lover, that his fondest wish must be to see the beloved stripped of his dearest and kindest and most sacred belongings: father, mother, kinsmen, friends—the lover will welcome seeing him lose them all, for he looks upon them as trying to prevent or to censure this sweetest of associations. And that's not all: if the boy actually has money or property, the lover will realize that he's not so easy to capture, or, once captured, to manage; so he will most certainly begrudge the beloved any possessions and rejoice when they are lost. And furthermore, a lover will try to keep the boy unmarried, childless, and without a home for as long as may be, desiring to savor as long as possible his own delights.

Now there are, of course, other evils in life; but in most of them, the 53 gods have mingled some temporary ability to please. The flatterer, for instance, is a hideous creature that does great harm; yet nature has seasoned him with a dash of cultivated charm. The courtesan you may revile as pernicious—and so on with the rest of such creatures and occupations; yet in everyday life they may be quite agreeable. But the lover, in addition to the harm he does, must be the most disagreeable of all persons for the boy to spend his days with. There's an old proverb, "birds of a feather," meaning, I suppose, that equality of years is conducive to similar pleasures and so begets friendship. Even so, such an association is apt to pall. Furthermore, compulsion in anything is disagreeable to everyone; and beside the inequality in age, there is precisely this compulsion in the relationship of lover and lad. For the older man lives with the younger and never leaves him, if he can help it, by day or by night, driven on, as he is, by the goading of his own compulsion which constantly gives him pleasure in seeing, hearing, touching the beloved, in experiencing him in every sensuous way; and it is these compulsive pleasures that accompany his adhesive enslavement to the boy. Yet what consolation, what pleasure can he give to the beloved to prevent him from reaching the extremity of disgust in this same period of continuous association, over the course of which the lad not only gazes at a face which time has stripped of its freshness, but has experience of the other concomitants of age as well, which, disagreeable as these are to hear about, are far more unpleasant to deal with day in, day out, in grim reality? What of the constant suspicious vigilance against everybody, the unseasonable, exaggerated praise the boy has to hear, the reproaches which, when the man is sober, are unendurable, but when he's drunk and pours out his emotions with no sense of propriety or restraint are not only unbearable but disgusting as well?

Now while he's in love he is merely harmful and disagreeable; but 54 when love ceases, from then on he's disloyal as well to the boy whom, with many promises and vows and prayers, he had only by great effort constrained to endure a relationship even then hard to accept; yet he did accept it because of the expectation of benefits to come. But now it's time to pay! Another set of rulers and controllers have ousted the old ones in him: sense and sanity have taken the place of madness and love. He's become another person, but the boy doesn't know it and keeps on asking for a return of former favors, reminding the man of what was said and done, just as though he were talking to the same person. And the man is ashamed to say that he's changed nor does he have a mind to redeem the vows and promises made during the regime of his old folly, now that he's come to his senses and sobered up. He's afraid that, if he does the same things again, he'll become the same man that he once was. So he runs away: the former lover must now become a defaulter. The shoe's on the other foot; the roles are changed and he flies. The boy is forced to follow with indignant cries to heaven, still not realizing the fundamental truth; he should not in the first place have yielded to a lover, to a man necessarily out of his mind; a non-lover, a man perfectly in his senses, is what it should have been. The wrong choice means surrendering oneself to a man who is disloyal, bad tempered, jealous, offensive, harmful to one's income, harmful to one's physical being, most harmful of all to the development of one's soul; and there neither is nor ever can be anything of more real importance in heaven or earth than the soul.

This, my boy, you must bear in mind and realize that the lover's 55 fondness is not accompanied by good will; it is rather a hunger that demands food to satisfy it:

"As wolf loves lamb, so lovers love their lads."

There, Phaedrus. That's it! Don't expect to hear more from me. My speech 56
is done. . . .

*[Phaedrus is impressed but wonders why Socrates stopped halfway, without going
on to enumerate the advantages of the nonlover, and then suggests they stay in
the shade a while and discuss the two speeches. Suddenly Socrates announces that
he will now make another speech:]*

SOCRATES   My friend, when I was about to cross the river, there 57
came to me the divine familiar sign which always holds me back from
something I'm about to do. I thought I heard a voice which forbade me to
go away until I had made atonement for an impiety to heaven. Now I am
something of a diviner, though not a very good one, but enough for my
own needs—as you might say of a bad writer, "his work is good enough
for *him.*" So now I can clearly understand my sin. The fact is, my friend,
that the soul is a kind of diviner; quite early in the course of my speech I
felt a sort of disturbance—I was "put out of countenance" as Ibycus[10] has
it, lest "through some sin against the gods I win renown from men." And
now I have come to realize the sin.

PHAEDRUS   What do you mean?   58

SOCRATES   Phaedrus, it was a dreadful, dreadful speech, both the 59
one you brought and the one you forced me to deliver.

PHAEDRUS   How, please?   60

SOCRATES   It was fatuous, and also concealed something impious. 61
What could be more dreadful than that?

PHAEDRUS   Nothing, if you're right about it.   62

SOCRATES   Well, don't you believe Love is a god, the son of 63
Aphrodite?[11]

PHAEDRUS   So it's said, at any rate.   64

SOCRATES   But not by Lysias, and not by that speech of yours 65
which was spoken by you through my bewitched mouth. If Love is, as he
certainly is, a god, or something divine, he cannot be anything evil. But
the two speeches just now spoke of him as evil. This, then, is their sin
against Love. And besides, their fatuousness was really charming: they put
on airs as if they amounted to something, while not uttering a syllable of
sense or truth—as though, if you please, they could win applause from a
couple of little manikins by deceiving them. And so, friend, I must purify
myself. For those who have sinned by lying about gods or heroes there is
an ancient rite of purification, unknown to Homer, but familiar to
Stesichorus.[12] When he was struck blind for speaking evil of Helen, he

---

[10] *Ibycus:* a lyric poet. [Editors' note.]

[11] *Love is a god, the son of Aphrodite:* Aphrodite was the goddess of love, and Eros (Love)
was her son. Eros is known to us today in his Roman form as Cupid. [Editors' note.]

[12] *Stesichorus:* a lyric poet. [Editors' note.]

was not, like Homer, ignorant of the reason.[13] Like a true artist, he recognized the cause and immediately wrote the lines:

> It is not true, that tale!
> You never embarked in the well-decked ships,
> Nor came to the towers of Troy.

And when he had completed this so-called Recantation, he recovered his sight at once. Now I shall be wiser than these worthies in just this particular: before I undergo any ill effects from my defamation of Love, I shall attempt to atone to him with my Recantation—this time with bared head, not, as before, veiled in shame.

PHAEDRUS   Nothing you could say, Socrates, would please me   66
more.

SOCRATES   That proves, dear Phaedrus, that you recognize the   67
utter shamelessness of the two speeches, both mine and the one read from
the book. Wouldn't anyone who was himself of a gentle, noble nature, who
loved or had loved a nature like his own, when he heard us speaking of
the petty causes of the jealousies and the bitter animosities engendered and
the injuries done the beloved—hearing all this, would he not imagine that
our ideas of love were taken from some haunt of sailors who had never
known a generous, decent love? Wouldn't he completely refuse to accept
our defamation of Love?

PHAEDRUS   Very probably, Socrates.   68

SOCRATES   Then in shame before this good man and in fear of   69
Love himself, I desire to rinse away the brackish taste, as it were, of what
I have said with fresh and drinkable discourse. . . . Where is that boy I
was addressing? This, too, he must hear and not slip off to yield to his non-
lover before he listens to what I have to say.

PHAEDRUS   He's here beside you, very close, always present when   70
you want him.

SOCRATES' SECOND SPEECH

Now you must understand, fair youth, that the last speech was that of   71
Phaedrus, son of Pythocles, from Myrrinous; but the one I am about to
deliver is by Stesichorus, son of Euphemus, from Himera. It should
proceed as follows:

> It is not true, that tale which declares that if taking a lover is in view,   72
> one should rather yield to a non-lover on the ground that a lover is out

---

[13] *Helen . . . like Homer:* Socrates refers to Helen of Troy; Homer was blind. Homer, of course, told the story of Helen of Troy's adultery and "elopement" with her illicit lover, which Homer claimed was caused by a spell cast over her by Aphrodite. In Socrates' opinion, then, Homer had lied about a goddess by making her the cause of mischief and evil. [Editors' note.]

of his senses, while a non-lover is perfectly sane. If it were true that madness is invariably an evil, then the statement would be correct; but in fact, the greatest benefits come to us through madness when it is bestowed on us as a gift of the gods. For example, the prophetess at Delphi and the priestesses at Dodona have conferred many splendid benefits on Greece for both private citizens and whole states through their madness; while in their right minds they have done little or nothing.[14] And if we were to mention the Sibyl[15] and all the others who through their inspired prophecies have foretold many future events to many people and so guided them aright, it would be a tedious recital of what everyone knows.

This too is worth mentioning: our ancestors who invented our vocabulary thought there was no shame or reproach in madness; otherwise they would not have connected the noblest of arts, which foretells the future, with this very word *mania*, and named it accordingly. It was because they regarded madness under divine guidance as a splendid thing that they gave it this name. But nowadays people have inserted a T, a tasteless modern addition, and changed *manic* to *mantic*. The proof of this is the name our forefathers gave to the art of the uninspired and sane who inquire into the future by observing bird-flights and other such indications: on the ground that this skill, proceeding from purely human reasoning, produced merely understanding and information, they called it *oionïstic*,[16] which our modern contemporaries call *oiónistic*, lengthening the o to make it sound impressive. Our ancestors, then, testify to the fact that in proportion as prophecy is superior in value and perfection to augury (*oiónistic*), both in name and in fact, so also is madness nobler than sanity: the first proceeds from a god, the other from mere man. 73

Moreover, when great plagues and troubles are visited on certain families by reason of an ancient guilt, madness has appeared among them and spoken in true prophetic terms and found release by recourse to prayers and worship of heaven. In consequence rites of purification have become established to protect such sufferers for the present and the future alike; thus, for him who is insane and possessed in the correct way, an escape by madness from his troubles has been secured. 74

---

[14] *Delphi . . . Dodona:* At each of these places was an ancient shrine in which a priestess delivered prophecies, messages from the gods, in answer to questions put to them. The priestess would be in a state of trance, to all appearances insane; the answers given typically took bizarre and riddlelike form (sometimes in verse) and required interpretation. [Editors' note.]

[15] *the Sibyl:* another prophetess. [Editors' note.]

[16] Playfully derived from *oio-* (thinking), *nous* (understanding), and *hist-* (inquiry). . . . [Translators' note.] *Oionistic* refers to an indirect process of acquiring knowledge through reasoning and the interpretation of evidence; *mantic* or *manic* arts depend on a direct process of acquiring knowledge by inspired intuition and divine revelation. [Editors' note.]

A third kind of possession or madness comes from the Muses. It takes   75
hold upon a gentle virginal soul, awakens and inspires it to song and
poetry and so, glorifying the innumerable deeds of our forefathers,
educates posterity. He who without the Muses' madness in his soul comes
knocking at the door of poetry, thinking that art alone will make him fit
to be called a poet, will find that he is found wanting and that the verse
he writes in his sober senses is beaten hollow by the poetry of madmen.

Such, and even more, is the tale of the achievements of madness that   76
comes from the gods. Let us, therefore, not be alarmed on this score; let
us not fear any argument that seeks to frighten us into preferring the
rational friend to one whose senses are disturbed. Let it demonstrate also,
if it is to win us over, that love is not sent from heaven for the benefit of
lover and beloved alike. We, on the contrary, must prove the opposite,
that such a madness is indeed bestowed by the gods for our greatest
happiness. Our proof will fail to convince the merely clever, but it will
be acceptable to the truly wise.

First, we must discover the truth about the nature of the soul, both the   77
divine and the human, and examine its experiences and activities. And
the beginning of our proof is this:

Every soul is immortal, for that which moves itself is immortal; but   78
that which, though it moves something at one time, may yet have its
motion transmitted to it by another at another time, when it ceases from
movement, ceases from life. Only that which moves itself, since its motion
does not derive from any source outside itself, never ceases to move.
Moreover this is the source and beginning for all other things which are
in motion. Now a first principle cannot be derived. For everything that
is derived must come from a first principle, but the principle itself cannot
be derived from anything at all; for if a principle should be derived from
something else, it would lose its nature *quâ* beginning in the process of
derivation. And since it does not come into being, it must also be
imperishable; for if a first principle were to perish, it could never come
into being from anything else or anything else from it, since it is true
that we must have a first principle to bring about the coming into being
of everything [else]. So that which by itself moves itself is a beginning
of movement. It is capable of neither destruction nor derivation; otherwise
the whole universe would collapse into uniformity and come to a halt and
could never thereafter find a source from which it might derive the motion
of its parts.

Since that which is moved by itself has been shown to be immortal, we   79
shall not be disgraced if we declare that this self-motion is the essence,
the very definition of the soul. For every body that is moved from without
is soulless; and every body that derives its motion from within itself has
a soul, since that is indeed the soul's nature. But if this is so, that what
really moves itself is not the body and is nothing else but the soul, then
the soul must necessarily be uncreated and immortal.

As for the soul's immortality, enough has been said. But about its form, 80
the following must be stated: To tell what it really is would be a theme
for a divine and a very long discourse; what it resembles, however, may
be expressed more briefly and in human language. Let us say that it is
like the composite union of powers in a team of winged horses and their
charioteer. Now all the gods' horses and charioteers are good and of good
descent, but those of other beings are mixed. In the case of the human
soul, first of all, it is a pair of horses that the charioteer dominates; one
of them is noble and handsome and of good breeding, while the other is
the very opposite, so that our charioteer necessarily has a difficult and
troublesome task.

I must try to tell how it is that a living being is called both mortal and 81
immortal. Soul, taking it collectively, has charge of all that is soulless. It
traverses the entire heaven, appearing sometimes in one form, sometimes
in another. When it is perfect and fully winged, it soars on high and is
responsible for all order in the universe; but if it loses its wings, it is
carried down until it can fasten on something solid. It settles there, taking
on an earthly body which seems to be self-moving because of the power
of soul within. This composite structure of body and soul joined together
is called a living being and is further designated as mortal. Immortal it
is not on any reasonable supposition: in fact, it is our imagination, not
our vision, not our adequate comprehension, that presents us with the
notion of a god as an immortal living being equipped both with soul and
with body, and with these, moreover, joined together for all time. Let
this, however, and our words concerning it, be as the god pleases. We
must now consider the reason for the soul's loss of wings. It is somewhat
as follows:

The natural function of a wing is to raise what is heavy and soar with 82
it to where the race of gods dwells. More than any other part of the body
the soul partakes of the divine nature which is beautiful, wise, good, and
all such qualities. Nothing, certainly, contributes more than these to the
nourishment and development of the soul's wing; while by their opposites,
ugliness and evil, it is wasted away and destroyed.

Now the great leader in heaven, Zeus, comes first, driving a winged 83
chariot, imposing order upon all things and caring for them; and the host
of gods and spirits follows him, marshaled in eleven sections, for Hestia
alone remains in the House of the Gods.[17] But for the others, all that are

---

[17] *Hestia:* the goddess of the home and hearth, protector spirit of domestic concord and
hospitality. An eternal virgin and unmarried maiden (she refused to marry either Apollo or
Poseidon, who courted her, and she had no interest in Aphrodite's arts of love), Hestia was
given a special place of honor, by Zeus, in the household of the gods on Mount Olympus.
In Rome, Hestia was worshipped as Vesta and her priestesses were the Vestal Virgins.
Though a homebody, Hestia/Vesta was one of the twelve ruling gods. [Editors' note.]

counted among the Twelve Ruling Gods proceed in due order according to rank, each at the head of his own division.

Many and wonderful to see are the orbits within the heavens and the blessed gods constantly turn to contemplate these as each busies himself with his special duties. There follows whoever will and can, for envy has no place in the company of heaven. But when they proceed to the divine banquet, they mount the steep ascent to the top of the vault of heaven; and here the advance is easy for the gods' chariots, well balanced and guided as they are, but the others have difficulty: the horse of evil nature weighs down their chariots, pulling heavily toward the earth any charioteer who has not trained him well. And here the extremity of toil and struggle awaits the soul. 84

Now when those souls that are called immortal come to the summit, they proceed without and take their stand upon the back of heaven, where its revolution carries them in full circle as they gaze upon what is without. 85

Of that region beyond no one of our earthly poets has ever sung, nor will any ever sing worthily. Its description follows, for I must dare to speak the truth, especially since the nature of truth is my theme. It is there that Reality lives, without shape or color, intangible, visible only to reason, the soul's pilot; and all true knowledge is knowledge of her. Now a god's faculty of understanding is sustained by experiencing direct and pure knowledge, as is that part of every soul that is concerned to receive what is akin to this experience. Consequently, when the soul has at long last beheld Reality, it rejoices, finding sustenance in its direct contemplation of the truth and in the immediate experience of it until, in the revolution of its orbit, it is brought round again to the point of departure. And in the course of the revolution it beholds absolute justice and temperance and knowledge, not such knowledge as is subject to process, and varies with its various objects to which we ascribe reality; no, it is Real Knowledge whose object is the truly existent. And when the soul has similarly seen and feasted upon all the other true realities, it comes back again within the heavens and returns home. And when it has arrived, the charioteer brings the horses to the manger and feeds them ambrosia and gives them nectar to drink. 86

This, then, is the god's life; but of the other souls, that which best follows and most closely resembles a god and has raised its charioteer's head up into the outer region is carried around with the gods in their revolution—yet it is troubled by the horses and only beholds Reality with much difficulty. Another sometimes rises, sometimes sinks; because the horses are unruly it beholds some part of Reality, but fails to see others. And other souls follow after, all desirous to gain the upper region, but unable to reach it; their circuit is far below where they jostle and trample on one another, each trying to outstrip his neighbor. So there is confusion and rivalry and the sweat of desperate competition in which many are lamed and many have their wings broken through the incompetence of 87 their charioteers. And, for all their struggle, not one of them is able to gain a glimpse of Reality; and so they go away and feed on the food of illusion. The reason for this great eagerness to behold the plain of truth is that the pasturage proper to the best part lies in that meadow: the wings on which the soul is to be borne aloft must find their nourishment there.

This is the Decree of Destiny: whatever soul has followed in the train   88 of a god and has caught some sight of any truth, it shall be free from harm until the next revolution; and, if it can continually do this, it shall remain forever free from harm. But when a soul is unable to keep up with the train and fails to catch sight of Reality and through some mischance is filled with forgetfulness and weakness and grows heavy and in its heaviness molts its wings and falls to earth, then it is the Law that such a soul shall not be planted in any beast in its first birth. The one which has seen the most Reality shall at birth enter into a future seeker for wisdom or beauty, a follower of the Muses or a lover; the second soul into a law-abiding monarch or warlike ruler; the third into a statesman or a man of business or a merchant; the fourth into some hard-working athlete or physician; the fifth into a prophet's life or a priest of the mysteries; to the sixth a poet's life or some other devoted to imitation will be proper; the seventh shall be a craftsman or a farmer; the eighth a sophist or a demagogue; the ninth a tyrant.

Now in all these transformations whoever lives a just life shall obtain   89 a better lot; and conversely with an evil-doer. For the soul does not return to the place of its origin for 10,000 years, since in no less time can it regain its wings. The sole exception is the soul of a man whose pursuit of wisdom has had no ulterior motive, whose search for love has involved the pursuit of wisdom. Such a soul, if it choose this life three times in succession, will become winged in the third period of 1000 years and so depart in the 3000th year. But when the others have finished their first life, they receive judgment. After it some go beneath the earth to places of chastisement and are punished while others are carried aloft by Justice to some part of the heavens where they live in a manner commensurate with their life while they were men. And after a thousand years both of these groups come to draw lots and choose their second life, each soul as it wishes. At that point a human soul may enter into the life of a beast; and conversely a beast who was once human may become a man again, for a soul which has never seen the truth cannot pass into this human form of ours. For to be a man, one must understand the content of a general term, leaving the field of manifold sense-perceptions, and entering that in which the object of knowledge is unique and grasped only by reasoning. This process is a remembering of what our soul once saw as it made its journey with a god, looking down upon what we now assert to be real and gazing upwards at what is Reality itself. This is clearly the reason why it is right for only the philosopher's mind to have wings; for he remains always, so far as he can, through memory in the field of precisely those entities in whose presence, as though he were a god, he is himself divine. And if a man makes a right use of such entities as memoranda,[18] always being perfectly initiated into perfect mysteries, he alone becomes truly perfected. He separates himself from the busy interests of men and approaches the divine. He is rebuked by the vulgar as insane, for they cannot know that he is possessed by divinity.

This, then, is the summation and completion of our discourse on the fourth sort of madness: when a man sees beauty in this world and has a remembrance of true beauty, he begins to grow wings. While they are sprouting, he is eager to fly, but he cannot. He gazes upward as though he were a bird and cares nothing for what is here below, so that he is accused of being mad. I have shown that this, of all forms of divine possession, is the best and has the highest origin, both for him that has it and for him who shares in it; and that the man who partakes of this madness and loves beauty is called a lover. For, as I said, every human soul by reason of its nature has had a view of Reality, otherwise it could not have entered this human form of ours. But to derive a clear memory of those real truths from these earthly perceptions is not easy for every soul—not for such as have had only a brief view in their former existence, or for such as suffered misfortune, when they fell into this world, to form evil connections and turned to unrighteousness, forgetting the holy vision they once had. Few indeed remain who can still remember much; yet when they see here some resemblance to those former sights, they are stricken with amazement and are no longer able to control themselves. Yet they do not recognize the reason for their emotion, for their perceptions are quite dim.

Now with justice, temperance, and all the other values of the soul, their copies have here no attribute of luminousness: only a few of us, with the greatest difficulty, working through our lusterless organs of sense, can approach the images and behold in them the kind of nature they resemble. But beauty! We were once able to behold it shining clear at the same time when we followed in the happy troop, some of us with Zeus, others with another god; and we saw this blessed vision and were initiated into that mystery which it is right to call the most blessed of all. This we celebrated, perfect as we then were and without experience of any of the evils which awaited us later. Whole and unblemished also, steadfast and blissful were the spectacles we gazed at in the pure light of final revelation, pure initiates as we were, not disfigured by this so-called body that we carry about with us, imprisoned in it like oysters in a shell.

Let this tribute, then, be paid to memory, which has caused us to enlarge upon it now, yearning for what we once possessed. But as for beauty, as I said, it shone brightly among those former sights and, even

90

91

92

---

[18] *memoranda:* aids to recollection, memory. [Editors' note.]

though we have descended here on earth, we can still recapture it, gleaming most clearly as it does, through the clearest of our senses. For sight is the keenest of our physical perceptions, though through it wisdom cannot be perceived. For marvelous would be the love excited by wisdom, if wisdom were capable of presenting to vision such a clear image of itself as is presented by beauty—and all other objects of love would be marvelously loved too, if they could do this. But as it is, only to beauty has it been allotted to be most manifest in this world, and the loveliest of all.

Now a man whose initiation is long past or has been corrupted here 93 cannot pass quickly from this world to the other, to beauty itself, when he beholds its namesake in the flesh. He feels no reverence for the sight, but surrenders to pleasure. Like a beast he proceeds to lust and procreation; he takes wantonness as his companion and is not fearful or ashamed to practice unnatural pleasure. But when a man recently initiated, who has looked upon many of the great realities, sees a god-like countenance or physical form the beauty of which is a faithful imitation of true beauty, a shudder runs through him and something of the old awe steals over him. Beholding it, he reverences it as he would a god; and if he were not afraid of being accounted stark mad, he would offer sacrifice to the beloved as to a holy image of divinity. As he gazes there comes over him a reaction from the shudder, an unusual fever and perspiration. Once he has received the emanation of beauty through his eyes, he grows warm, and through the perspiration that ensues, he irrigates the sprouting of his wing. When he is quite warm, the outer layers of the seedling unfurl—parts which by reason of their close-drawn rigidity had for a long time prevented anything from blossoming. As nourishment streams upon it the stump of the wing begins to swell and grow from the root upward as a support for the entire structure of the soul, fully developing the wing which every soul possessed in the past.

During this process the soul is completely in a state of ferment and 94 palpitation: just as there is irritation and pain in the gums felt at the time of cutting teeth, so the soul of one beginning to sprout wings feels ferment and painful irritation. Now sometimes while it gazes at the youth's beauty and admits a flood of particles streaming therefrom (that is why this process is called a "flood of passion"), the soul is irrigated and warmed and rejoices at the abatement of pain. But at other times, when it is alone and grown dry, the mouths of the passages through which the wing is beginning to grow also become dry; they close up and shut off the wing's sprouting. And the sprouts within, enclosed with the flood of passion, throb like a pulse in fever, each pricking at its proper outlet so that the whole soul, wounded time and time again in every part, is goaded into anguish; yet again it retains the memory of beauty and so rejoices. And because of these two confused sensations the soul is troubled and perplexed by its extraordinary condition and becomes distraught: in its madness it can neither sleep by night nor keep still by day. Desire forces it to hurry to wherever it thinks it can catch sight of the possessor of this beauty. And when it does see him and is bathed in the flood of passion, the passages that were sealed are opened; then the soul has respite from stings and anguish and again for the moment enjoys this sweetest of all pleasures. So it will not, if it can help it, abandon its joy; it esteems this beauty above everything else. Mother, brother, friends, they are all forgotten; property is neglected, and the soul cares nothing; conventions and proprieties in which it formerly took pride are all despised. It is ready to be a slave, to rest anywhere it may be allowed, to remain as close to the beloved as may be. For not only does the soul revere the possessor of beauty, it has found in him the only healer of terrible sufferings.

Now this condition, fair youth to whom I speak, men call love; but 95 when you hear what the gods call it, you will probably laugh because you are so young. Some of the Homeridae, I believe, recite two verses on love taken from the Homeric Apocrypha;[19] the second of them is rather bold and not quite metrical. They go as follows:

Though mortal men call Eros winged Love,
Gods call him Pteros for he fathers wings.[20]

You may believe this or not as you like; but the condition of lovers and the reason for it are just as I have stated.

Now if the man whom love has captured was among the followers of 96 Zeus, he is able to bear a heavier burden of the Winged One,[21] but when those who are servants of Ares[22] and used to follow in his train are caught by Love and believe that they have been injured by the beloved, they become muderous and are ready to sacrifice both themselves and the loved one. And so it is with regard to each god that a man may once have followed: this is the divinity he honors and imitates as he is best able so long as he remains uncorrupted and continues living through his first incarnation upon earth; and in this way he conducts himself toward the beloved and all his other associates. So each selects his love according to character; and as though the youth were the very god whom he once followed, the lover fashions and adorns him like an image to be the object of his worship and his veneration. So the followers of Zeus desire that the soul of their beloved should resemble that god; they look for one who loves wisdom and has a commanding nature. And when they have found him and fallen in love, they do everything in their power to produce this

[19] *Homeridae:* reciters of Homer's poetry. *Homeric Apocrypha:* verses attributed to Homer, but not a part of his principal works. [Editors' note.]

[20] The word play seems to involve *Eros* (love), *pteron* (wing), and *p[a]ter* (father). [Translators' note.]

[21] *the Winged One:* Eros. [Editors' note.]

[22] *Ares:* the god of war. [Editors' note.]

resemblance. If they are novices in this pursuit, they try to learn all they can from whatever source, though they must set forth upon this quest alone. In their search, however, they find it not at all difficult to recognize the person whose nature is their god's, for, by reason of their long and concentrated vision of the god in the past, they need draw on their own resources and nothing else. When they come upon such a person, the memory of the god they followed is aroused; enraptured, they pattern their way and manner of life upon his—in so far as a man can partake of a god's ways. And they consider the beloved the cause of all this and love him still more: the drafts of inspiration which they draw from Zeus they pour like Bacchants[23] into the boy's soul, making him so far as they can exactly like their god.

Again, those who followed Hera[24] look for a kingly nature; and when 97 they have found him they behave in a manner toward him in all their actions. And similarly the followers of Apollo and the other gods proceed to seek a youth whose nature corresponds to their god: when they have won him, they pattern themselves upon the god and by persuasion and discipline they lead the beloved to the way and conduct appropriate to each god so far as they can. They exhibit no jealousy or pettiness toward the loved one; rather, every act is aimed at bringing the beloved to be as much as possible like themselves, that is, like the god they honor.

The zeal, therefore, of true lovers to initiate their beloved is beautiful 98 and brings happiness from the inspired lover to his loved one if they accomplish what they desire in the manner I am describing. But the youth must first be caught; and caught he is in the following way:

At the beginning of this story of ours we divided every soul into three 99 parts, two of which had the form of horses, the third that of a charioteer. Let us retain this. As we said, one of the horses is good, the other not. But we did not define the goodness of the one or the badness of the other, which we must now do. The horse that holds the nobler position is upright and clean-limbed; it carries its head high, its nose is aquiline, its color wine, its eyes dark; it is a lover of honor only when that may be joined with temperance and decency: in other words a follower of true renown; it needs no whip, but is driven by word of command alone. The other horse, however, is huge, but crooked, a great jumble of a creature, with a short thick neck, a flat nose, dark color, grey bloodshot eyes, the mate of insolence and knavery, shaggy-eared and deaf, hardly heeding whip or spur.

Now when the charioteer beholds the love-inspiring sight and his whole 100 soul is warmed by the vision and becomes filled with the tickling and prickling of desire, the obedient horse, then as always constrained by

---

[23] *like Bacchants:* like followers of Bacchus, the god of wine. [Editors' note.]

[24] *Hera:* wife and sister of Zeus, queen of the gods. [Editors' note.]

decorum, controls itself and does not leap onto the beloved. The other, however, no longer pays any attention to the driver's spur or whip, but leaps wildly forward, causing all possible trouble to its mate and to the driver, trying to force them to approach the beloved and propose the pleasures of love. At first, they pull back, indignant at being forced to a dreadful, lawless thing; but at last, since there is no end to the evil insistence, they are dragged forward, yielding and agreeing to do its bidding. And they come to the beloved and behold his radiant face.

At this sight the charioteer's memory is borne back to the form of real 101 beauty: again he beholds it seated beside Temperance on a throne of holiness. He sees this and is afraid and falls backward in awe and reverence, necessarily pulling the reins so violently that both horses are brought down to their haunches, the one willingly, without opposition, but the wanton one very much against its will.

When they have withdrawn, the good horse in shame and horror 102 drenches all the soul with sweat; but the other, as soon as it has recovered from the pain of the bit and the fall and has barely regained its wind, bitterly reviles its mate and the charioteer for their cowardice and weakness in deserting and forsaking their agreement. And against their will it tries to force another approach and hardly will yield to their pleas for postponement. And when the time appointed comes, the others pretend to have forgotten, but the bad horse reminds them; struggling and neighing and dragging them on, again it forces them to approach the beloved to make the same proposal. And when they are near at hand, it lowers its head, elevates its tail, takes the bit in its teeth, and pulls shamelessly. But the charioteer has the same feeling as before, only it is more pronounced: like a racer recoiling from the starting-rope, he jerks back the bit even more violently than before from the teeth of the wanton horse, bespatters its malicious tongue and jaws with blood, forces its legs and haunches to the ground and causes it much pain. So when the bad horse has gone through the same experience again and again, it finally has enough of wantonness. Now it has been humbled and follows the driver's instructions; when it catches sight of the beautiful, it is like to die of fear. So from this time on the soul of the lover may follow the beloved with reverence and awe.

Now the beloved is served with every attention, as though he were the 103 peer of the gods, by the lover who is making no pretence but loves in all sincerity; and since the beloved is naturally kind to one who serves him, in spite of the fact that in the past he may have rejected his friend, prejudiced by schoolmates or others who claimed that it was a disgrace to deal with a lover, yet as time goes on youth and destiny bring him to welcome the lover into his society. For it is a law of fate that no evil man may be a friend to another who is bad and no good man may fail to be a friend to another who is good.

And now that he has welcomed his lover and takes pleasure in his 104 company and conversation, the lover's good will, discovered by this intimacy, astonishes the beloved who perceives that not all other men together, friends and relatives, can contribute even a little of affection in comparison with his inspired friend. So when this intimacy continues and the lover comes near and touches the beloved in the gymnasia and elsewhere, then the fountain of that stream, which Zeus, when he was in love with Ganymede,[25] called the "flood of passion," pours abundantly upon the lover; some of it flows into him and some, when he is filled, passes away without. Just as wind or echo rebounds from smooth, hard surfaces and returns whence it came, so the stream of beauty flows back again into the beautiful beloved through his eyes, the natural inlet to the soul. There it comes and excites the soul, watering the outlets of the wings and quickening them to sprout; so in his turn the soul of the loved one is filled with love.

He loves, but does not know whom or what; he does not understand, he cannot tell what has happened to him. Like one who has caught a disease of the eyes from another, he can give no reason for it; as in a mirror, in his lover he beholds himself and does not know it. When he is with him, he too ceases from pain; when he is away, he too yearns and is yearned for, possessing the image of love, requited love, though he calls it friendship, not love, and believes it to be so. He desires, like the lover, though less passionately than he, to see, to touch, to kiss, to lie down together. And indeed it is likely that this soon comes to pass. 105

So when they lie down together the lover's wanton horse has something to say to the charioteer, demanding a little enjoyment in return for all his sufferings. But the bad horse of the beloved has nothing to say; teeming with passion and confusion he embraces and kisses the lover in grateful acknowledgement of his many kindnesses. When they lie together he is minded, for his part, not to refuse any favor the lover might ask; yet his yoke-fellow joins with the charioteer, and with modesty and reason, in opposing any of this. 106

If, then, the better part of the intelligence wins the victory and guides them to an orderly and philosophic way of life, their life on earth will be happy and harmonious since they have attained discipline and self-control: they have subdued the source of evil in the soul and set free the source of goodness. At the end of life they will have full-grown wings and cast off the burdens of the flesh: they will stand victorious in the first bout of a truly Olympian victory.[26] Nor can human discipline or divine madness confer any greater blessing on man than this. 107

---

[25] *Ganymede:* a human boy whom Zeus fell in love with and spirited away (in some versions of the story) to Olympus. [Editors' note.]

[26] *Olympian victory:* a godlike victory. [Editors' note.]

If, however, they turn to a way of life less noble and without philosophy, 108 yet ordained by a love of honor, then perhaps when they are drinking or otherwise careless, their two wanton beasts may catch the soul off guard and bring them together to that act and choice which most people regard as blissful. Once joined they will continue the act, though rarely, for it is not approved by the whole intelligence. So these two are friends, though less so than the others, both during their love affair and when it is past, believing that they have exchanged the most binding pledges which it would be wrong ever to break and so to become enemies. In the end, as they leave the body, they are still not fully winged, though wings have begun to sprout. So that it is no small prize for their love-madness that they win: for it is the law that those who have once begun the journey to heaven shall never pass down into the dark path beneath the earth. Their life henceforward shall be a journey of radiant happiness together, and when they grow their wings, these shall be alike, because of their love.

These benefits, so great and so divine, the friendship of a lover will 109 confer upon you, my boy. He who is no lover can offer merely a relationship tempered with worldly self-discipline, dispensing niggardly and transitory gifts. It will beget in the soul it seeks to befriend only that illiberality which most people admiringly call "virtue." It will cause you to float for 9000 years around the earth and beneath it—a fool!

Thus, dear Love, I have made and paid my recantation as well and as 110 fairly as I could; the poetical figures I was forced to use, for Phaedrus would have them. Please forgive my former speech; grant this one your favor. Be kind and merciful to me. Do not take away this knowledge of love that you have given. Do not blind me in anger. Grant me to be even more esteemed than I am now by the beautiful. If in our former speech Phaedrus or I said anything harsh against you, blame Lysias, the begetter of that discourse. Make him cease from such speeches and turn him to philosophy, just as his brother Polemarchus has been turned; so that his lover here may no longer waver as he does now, but may wholeheartedly live for love, together with philosophy.

PHAEDRUS I join in your prayer, Socrates, and pray that this may 111 come to pass if it is best for us. . . .

[Socrates and Phaedrus then turn to a long discussion of the art of rhetoric.]

Questions for Discussion and Writing

1. How does Socrates' character compare with that of Phaedrus or of Lysias (as we know him from this speech)? What attitudes might Plato want his reader to take toward each of these characters? On the basis of what values? What evidence and reasoning lead you to your judgment?

2. Analyze the *structure* of each of the three speeches presented in this selection. In what ways do Socrates' speeches differ from Lysias' speech? What effects do these differences produce? What might be the effect of rearranging the parts of Lysias' speech? What if the sections of Socrates' speeches were reordered? Why might Lysias avoid extended discussion of the definition of love he is using and concentrate instead on love's disadvantages?

3. Socrates' theory of rhetoric assumes that there *is* a truth apart from human opinion, an absolute reality that can be discovered, understood, and communicated in language. These assumptions are what Sophists such as Gorgias questioned and what their present-day descendents continue to doubt. What is your opinion of Socrates' theory? Furthermore, what do you think of Socrates' rhetorical practice? Is he able to base his persuasion of Phaedrus on truth? Do you ever find him appealing to Phaedrus' preexisting beliefs, values, feelings, and opinions? Does he live up to the ideals he sets forth?

4. What place can women have in Socrates' myths of love, or in Lysias'? Would you expect a woman to be cast in the role of "lover" or "beloved"? Why? What about the myth of love—or one of the myths of love—presented to us now through television, music, films, advertisements, novels, and the like? Would you call it Socratic (or Platonic) or Lysianic? Is it a myth of love or nonlove? Or something else? How should the current myth be judged, and on what basis? After carefully collecting and analyzing your evidence, write an essay that addresses one or more of these concerns.

RENÉ DESCARTES

(1596–1650)

As we read earlier, Gorgias, Lysias, and Plato developed their arguments primarily through social interaction. Sappho's poetry represented her feelings for her intimates. In the discourse of René Descartes, however, we find a rather different sort of writing.

As a boy, Descartes studied with the Jesuits—a religious order affiliated with the Catholic church—in the French city of La Flèche. He was drawn to mathematics, a specialty of the school. In 1612, he left La Flèche to study at the University of Poitiers. He received a law degree in 1616 but never practiced.

In 1617, Descartes began a decade or so of military service and European travel. He applied his mathematical ability to military engineering. In 1619, while wintering in the German city of Neuburg on the Danube River, the young French soldier experienced an epiphany that eventually produced his revolutionary philosophical system. His practice of universal methodic doubt in philosophical inquiry led him to believe that all ideas must be subjected to rigorous intellectual scrutiny, that a theory or hypothesis must be considered false until all doubt concerning its veracity can be removed. Furthermore, he developed his notion that "the mysteries of Nature and the laws of Mathematics could be unlocked by the same key." In 1629, Descartes settled in Holland, where he published his most important works of philosophy: Discourse on the Method (1637), Meditations on First Philosophy (1641), and Philosophic Principles (1644). On a visit to Sweden to tutor Queen Christina, he caught a severe chill and died within two weeks.

Like Plato, Descartes must be counted among the most influential figures of the Western philosophical tradition. Modern science and philosophy alike claim this innovative thinker as a patron saint. Reading his work, one is immediately struck by Descartes's ability to question the beliefs his society had taken for granted for hundreds of years. He has long been admired for his effort to isolate himself from the discourse of others in order to develop new first principles based on his own thought process and his own empirical experience of the world. Descartes's acute skepticism, his unwillingness to accept on faith those premises that his predecessors and contemporaries in philosophy all too willingly endorsed, and his tenacious application of trenchant reason are the striking characteristics of his work that became in turn the guiding principles of the great philosophical movement that succeeded him, the "Enlightenment." Voltaire, whose work follows Descartes's in this reader, represents the crowning intellectual achievement of this new age.

The first reading, which serves as a prelude to the selections from Discourse on the Method, is the beginning section of Meditations on First Philosophy. It is extracted from a longer series of arguments, most of which consider specific philosophical *and scientific problems. Many of these problems, in fact, are presented in the selections from* Discourse on the Method. *These passages from the* Discourse *and the* Meditations *contain some of Descartes's most well-known philosophical speculations, including* cogito ergo sum—*"I am thinking, therefore I exist." Yet despite the fame of this and other quotations, Descartes's arguments are subtle and require careful attention. As you read, consider applying "universal methodic doubt" to Descartes's own arguments. Is he able to meet his own standards of philosophic rigor?*

FROM MEDITATIONS ON FIRST PHILOSOPHY

In Which Are Demonstrated the Existence of God and the Distinction Between the Human Soul and the Body

FIRST MEDITATION

WHAT CAN BE CALLED INTO DOUBT

Some years ago I was struck by the large number of falsehoods that I had   1
accepted as true in my childhood, and by the highly doubtful nature of the
whole edifice that I had subsequently based on them. I realized that it was
necessary, once in the course of my life, to demolish everything completely
and start again right from the foundations if I wanted to establish anything
at all in the sciences that was stable and likely to last. But the task looked
an enormous one, and I began to wait until I should reach a mature enough
age to ensure that no subsequent time of life would be more suitable for
tackling such inquiries. This led me to put the project off for so long that
I would now be to blame if by pondering over it any further I wasted the
time still left for carrying it out. So today I have expressly rid my mind
of all worries and arranged for myself a clear stretch of free time. I am
here quite alone, and at last I will devote myself sincerely and without
reservation to the general demolition of my opinions.

But to accomplish this, it will not be necessary for me to show that all   2
my opinions are false, which is something I could perhaps never manage.
Reason now leads me to think that I should hold back my assent from
opinions which are not completely certain and indubitable just as carefully
as I do from those which are patently false. So, for the purpose of rejecting
all my opinions, it will be enough if I find in each of them at least some
reason for doubt. And to do this I will not need to run through them all
individually, which would be an endless task. Once the foundations of a
building are undermined, anything built on them collapses of its own

accord; so I will go straight for the basic principles on which all my former beliefs rested.

Whatever I have up till now accepted as most true I have acquired either 3 from the senses or through the senses. But from time to time I have found that the senses deceive, and it is prudent never to trust completely those who have deceived us even once.

Yet although the senses occasionally deceive us with respect to objects 4 which are very small or in the distance, there are many other beliefs about which doubt is quite impossible, even though they are derived from the senses—for example, that I am here, sitting by the fire, wearing a winter dressing-gown, holding this piece of paper in my hands, and so on. Again, how could it be denied that these hands or this whole body are mine? Unless perhaps I were to liken myself to madmen, whose brains are so damaged by the persistent vapours of melancholia that they firmly maintain they are kings when they are paupers, or say they are dressed in purple when they are naked, or that their heads are made of earthenware, or that they are pumpkins, or made of glass. But such people are insane, and I would be thought equally mad if I took anything from them as a model for myself.

A brilliant piece of reasoning! As if I were not a man who sleeps at 5 night, and regularly has all the same experiences[1] while asleep as madmen do when awake—indeed sometimes even more improbable ones. How often, asleep at night, am I convinced of just such familiar events—that I am here in my dressing-gown, sitting by the fire—when in fact I am lying undressed in bed! Yet at the moment my eyes are certainly wide awake when I look at this piece of paper; I shake my head and it is not asleep; as I stretch out and feel my hand I do so deliberately, and I know what I am doing. All this would not happen with such distinctness to someone asleep. Indeed! As if I did not remember other occasions when I have been tricked by exactly similar thoughts while asleep! As I think about this more carefully, I see plainly that there are never any sure signs by means of which being awake can be distinguished from being asleep. The result is that I begin to feel dazed, and this very feeling only reinforces the notion that I may be asleep.

Suppose then that I am dreaming, and that these particulars—that my 6 eyes are open, that I am moving my head and stretching out my hands— are not true. Perhaps, indeed, I do not even have such hands or such a body at all. Nonetheless, it must surely be admitted that the visions which come in sleep are like paintings, which must have been fashioned in the likeness of things that are real, and hence that at least these general kinds of things—eyes, head, hands and the body as a whole—are things which are not imaginary but are real and exist. For even when painters try to create sirens and satyrs with the most extraordinary bodies, they cannot give

---

[1] '. . . and in my dreams regularly represent to myself the same things' (French version) [Translators' note.]

them natures which are new in all respects; they simply jumble up the limbs of different animals. Or if perhaps they manage to think up something so new that nothing remotely similar has ever been seen before—something which is therefore completely fictitious and unreal—at least the colours used in the composition must be real. By similar reasoning, although these general kinds of things—eyes, head, hands and so on—could be imaginary, it must at least be admitted that certain other even simpler and more universal things are real. These are as it were the real colours from which we form all the images of things, whether true or false, that occur in our thought.

This class appears to include corporeal nature in general, and its extension; the shape of extended things; the quantity, or size and number of these things; the place in which they may exist, the time through which they may endure,[2] and so on.

So a reasonable conclusion from this might be that physics, astronomy, medicine, and all other disciplines which depend on the study of composite things, are doubtful; while arithmetic, geometry and other subjects of this kind, which deal only with the simplest and most general things, regardless of whether they really exist in nature or not, contain something certain and indubitable. For whether I am awake or asleep, two and three added together are five, and a square has no more than four sides. It seems impossible that such transparent truths should incur any suspicion of being false.

And yet firmly rooted in my mind is the long-standing belief that there is an omnipotent God who made me the kind of creature that I am. How do I know that he has not brought it about that there is no earth, no sky, no extended thing, no shape, no size, no place, while at the same time ensuring that all these things appear to me to exist just as they do now? Moreover, since I sometimes consider that others go astray in cases where they think they have the most perfect knowledge, may I not similarly go wrong every time I add two and three or count the sides of a square, or in some even simpler matter, if that is imaginable? But perhaps God would not have wished me to be deceived in this way, since he is said to be supremely good. But if it were inconsistent with his goodness to have created me such that I am deceived all the time, it would seem equally foreign to his goodness to allow me to be deceived even occasionally; yet this last assertion cannot be made.[3]

Perhaps there may be some who would prefer to deny the existence of so powerful a God rather than believe that everything else is uncertain. Let us not argue with them, but grant them that everything said about God is a fiction. According to their supposition, then, I have arrived at my present

---

[2] '. . . the place where they are, the time which measures their duration' (French version). [Translators' noted.]

[3] '. . . yet I cannot doubt that he does allow this' (French version). [Translators' note.]

state by fate or chance or a continuous chain of events, or by some other means; yet since deception and error seem to be imperfections, the less powerful they make my original cause, the more likely it is that I am so imperfect as to be deceived all the time. I have no answer to these arguments, but am finally compelled to admit that there is not one of my former beliefs about which a doubt may not properly be raised; and this is not a flippant or ill-considered conclusion, but is based on powerful and well thought-out reasons. So in future I must withhold my assent from these former beliefs just as carefully as I would from obvious falsehoods, if I want to discover any certainty.[4]

But it is not enough merely to have noticed this; I must make an effort 11 to remember it. My habitual opinions keep coming back, and, despite my wishes, they capture my belief, which is as it were bound over to them as a result of long occupation and the law of custom. I shall never get out of the habit of confidently assenting to these opinions, so long as I suppose them to be what in fact they are, namely highly probable opinions—opinions which, despite the fact that they are in a sense doubtful, as has just been shown, it is still much more reasonable to believe than to deny. In view of this, I think it will be a good plan to turn my will in completely the opposite direction and deceive myself, by pretending for a time that these former opinions are utterly false and imaginary. I shall do this until the weight of preconceived opinion is counter-balanced and the distorting influence of habit no longer prevents my judgement from perceiving things correctly. In the meantime, I know that no danger or error will result from my plan, and that I cannot possibly go too far in my distrustful attitude. This is because the task now in hand does not involve action but merely the acquisition of knowledge.

I will suppose therefore that not God, who is supremely good and the 12 source of truth, but rather some malicious demon of the utmost power and cunning has employed all his energies in order to deceive me. I shall think that the sky, the air, the earth, colours, shapes, sounds and all external things are merely the delusions of dreams which he has devised to ensnare my judgement. I shall consider myself as not having hands or eyes, or flesh, or blood or senses, but as falsely believing that I have all these things. I shall stubbornly and firmly persist in this meditation; and, even if it is not in my power to know any truth, I shall at least do what is in my power,[5] that is, resolutely guard against assenting to any falsehoods, so that the deceiver, however powerful and cunning he may be, will be unable to impose on me in the slightest degree. But this is an arduous undertaking, and a kind of laziness brings me back to normal life. I am like a prisoner

---

[4] '. . . in the sciences' (added in French version). [Translators' note.]

[5] '. . . nevertheless it is in my power to suspend my judgement' (French version). [Translators' note.]

who is enjoying an imaginary freedom while asleep; as he begins to suspect that he is asleep, he dreads being woken up, and goes along with the pleasant illusion as long as he can. In the same way, I happily slide back into my old opinions and dread being shaken out of them, for fear that my peaceful sleep may be followed by hard labour when I wake, and that I shall have to toil not in the light, but amid the inextricable darkness of the problems I have now raised.

from DISCOURSE ON THE METHOD

Of Rightly Conducting One's Reason and Seeking the Truth in the Sciences

Part One

Good sense is the best distributed thing in the world: for everyone thinks himself so well endowed with it that even those who are the hardest to please in everything else do not usually desire more of it than they possess. In this it is unlikely that everyone is mistaken. It indicates rather that the power of judging well and of distinguishing the true from the false—which is what we properly call "good sense" or "reason"—is naturally equal in all men, and consequently that the diversity of our opinions does not arise because some of us are more reasonable than others but solely because we direct our thoughts along different paths and do not attend to the same things. For it is not enough to have a good mind; the main thing is to apply it well. The greatest souls are capable of the greatest vices as well as the greatest virtues; and those who proceed but very slowly can make much greater progress, if they always follow the right path, than those who hurry and stray from it.

For my part, I have never presumed my mind to be in any way more perfect than that of the ordinary man; indeed, I have often wished to have as quick a wit, or as sharp and distinct an imagination, or as ample or prompt a memory as some others. And apart from these, I know of no other qualities which serve to perfect the mind; for, as regards reason or sense, since it is the only thing that makes us men and distinguishes us from the beasts, I am inclined to believe that it exists whole and complete in each of us. Here I follow the common opinion of the philosophers, who say there are differences of degree only between the *accidents*, and not between the *forms* (or natures) of *individuals* of the same *species*.

But I say without hesitation that I consider myself very fortunate to have ³ happened upon certain paths in my youth which led me to considerations and maxims from which I formed a method whereby, it seems to me, I can increase my knowledge gradually and raise it little by little to the highest point allowed by the mediocrity of my mind and the short duration of my life. Now I always try to lean towards diffidence rather than presumption in the judgements I make about myself; and when I cast a philosophical eye upon the various activities and undertakings of mankind, there are almost none which I do not consider vain and useless. Nevertheless I have already reaped such fruits from this method that I cannot but feel extremely satisfied with the progress I think I have already made in the search for truth, and I cannot but entertain such hopes for the future as to venture the opinion that if any purely human occupation has solid worth and importance, it is the one I have chosen.

Yet I may be wrong: perhaps what I take for gold and diamonds is ⁴ nothing but a bit of copper and glass. I know how much we are liable to err in matters that concern us, and also how much the judgements of our friends should be distrusted when they are in our favour. I shall be glad, nevertheless, to reveal in this discourse what paths I have followed, and to represent my life in it as if in a picture, so that everyone may judge it for himself; and thus, learning from public response the opinions held of it, I shall add a new means of self-instruction to those I am accustomed to using.

My present aim, then, is not to teach the method which everyone must ⁵ follow in order to direct his reason correctly, but only to reveal how I have tried to direct my own. One who presumes to give precepts must think himself more skilful than those to whom he gives them; and if he makes the slightest mistake, he may be blamed. But I am presenting this work only as a history or, if you prefer, a fable in which, among certain examples worthy of imitation, you will perhaps also find many others that it would be right not to follow; and so I hope it will be useful for some without being harmful to any, and that everyone will be grateful to me for my frankness.

From my childhood I enjoyed the benefits of a literary education; and ⁶ because I was persuaded that by this means one could acquire a clear and certain knowledge of all that is useful in life, I was extremely eager to learn. But as soon as I had completed the course of study at the end of which one is normally admitted to the ranks of the learned, I completely changed my opinion. For I found myself beset by so many doubts and errors that I came to think I had gained nothing from my attempts to become educated but increasing recognition of my ignorance. And yet I was at one of the most famous schools in Europe, where I thought there must be learned men if they existed anywhere on earth. There I had learned everything that the others were learning; moreover, not content with the subjects they taught us, I had gone through all the books that fell into my hands concerning the subjects that are considered most abstruse and unusual.

At the same time, I knew how the others judged me, and I saw that they did not regard me as inferior to my fellow students, even though several among them were already destined to take the place of our teachers. And finally, the age in which we live seemed to me to be as flourishing, and as rich in good minds, as any before it. This made me feel free to judge all others by reference to myself and think there was no knowledge in the world such as I had previously been led to hope for.

I did not, however, cease to value the exercises done in the Schools. I knew that the languages learned there are necessary for understanding the works of the ancients; that the charm of fables awakens the mind, while the memorable deeds told in histories uplift it and help to shape one's judgement if they are read with discretion; that reading good books is like having a conversation with the most distinguished men of past ages— indeed, a rehearsed conversation in which these authors reveal to us only the best of their thoughts; that oratory has incomparable powers and beauties; that poetry has quite ravishing delicacy and sweetness; that mathematics contains some very subtle devices which serve as much to satisfy the curious as to further all the arts and lessen man's labours; that writings on morals contain many very useful teachings and exhortations to virtue; that theology instructs us how to reach heaven; that philosophy gives us the means of speaking plausibly about any subject and of winning the admiration of the less learned; that jurisprudence, medicine, and other sciences bring honours and riches to those who cultivate them; and, finally, that it is good to have examined all these subjects, even those full of superstition and falsehood, in order to know their true value and guard against being deceived by them.

But I thought I had already given enough time to languages and likewise to reading the works of the ancients, both their histories and their fables. For conversing with those of past centuries is much the same as travelling. It is good to know something of the customs of various peoples, so that we may judge our own more soundly and not think that everything contrary to our own ways is ridiculous and irrational, as those who have seen nothing of the world ordinarily do. But one who spends too much time travelling eventually becomes a stranger in his own country; and one who is too curious about the practices of past ages usually remains quite ignorant about those of the present. Moreover, fables make us imagine many events as possible when they are not. And even the most accurate histories, while not altering or exaggerating the importance of matters to make them more worthy of being read, at any rate almost always omit the baser and less notable events; as a result, the other events appear in a false light, and those who regulate their conduct by examples drawn from these works are liable to fall into the excesses of the knights-errant in our tales of chivalry, and conceive plans beyond their powers.

I valued oratory highly and loved poetry; but I thought both were gifts of the mind rather than fruits of study. Those with the strongest reasoning and the most skill at ordering their thoughts so as to make them clear and intelligible are always the most persuasive, even if they speak only low Breton and have never learned rhetoric. And those with the most pleasing conceits and the ability to express them with the most embellishment and sweetness would still be the best poets, even if they knew nothing of the theory of poetry.

Above all I delighted in mathematics, because of the certainty and self-evidence of its reasonings. But I did not yet notice its real use; and since I thought it was of service only in the mechanical arts, I was surprised that nothing more exalted had been built upon such firm and solid foundations. On the other hand, I compared the moral writings of the ancient pagans to very proud and magnificent palaces built only on sand and mud. They extol the virtues, and make them appear more estimable than anything else in the world; but they do not adequately explain how to recognize a virtue, and often what they call by this fine name is nothing but a case of callousness, or vanity, or desperation, or parricide.   10

I revered our theology, and aspired as much as anyone else to reach heaven. But having learned as an established fact that the way to heaven is open no less to the most ignorant than to the most learned, and that the revealed truths which guide us there are beyond our understanding, I would not have dared submit them to my weak reasonings; and I thought that to undertake an examination of them and succeed, I would need to have some extraordinary aid from heaven and to be more than a mere man.   11

Regarding philosophy, I shall say only this: seeing that it has been cultivated for many centuries by the most excellent minds and yet there is still no point in it which is not disputed and hence doubtful, I was not so presumptuous as to hope to achieve any more in it than others had done. And, considering how many diverse opinions learned men may maintain on a single question—even though it is impossible for more than one to be true—I held as well-nigh false everything that was merely probable.   12

As for the other sciences, in so far as they borrow their principles from philosophy I decided that nothing solid could have been built upon such shaky foundations. Neither the honour nor the riches they offered was enough to induce me to learn them. For my circumstances did not, thank God, oblige me to augment my fortune by making science my profession; and although I did not profess to scorn glory, like a Cynic, yet I thought very little of the glory which I could hope to acquire only through false pretences. Finally, as for the false sciences, I thought that I already knew their worth well enough not to be liable to be deceived by the promises of an alchemist or the predictions of an astrologer, the tricks of a magician or the frauds and boasts of those who profess to know more than they do.   13

That is why, as soon as I was old enough to emerge from the control of my teachers, I entirely abandoned my literary studies. Resolving to seek no knowledge other than that which could be found in myself or else in the great book of the world, I spent the rest of my youth travelling, visiting courts and armies, mixing with people of diverse temperaments and ranks,   14 gathering various experiences, testing myself in the situations which fortune offered me, and at all times reflecting upon whatever came my way so as to derive some profit from it. For it seemed to me that much more truth could be found in the reasonings which a man makes concerning matters that concern him than in those which some scholar makes in his study about speculative matters. For the consequences of the former will soon punish the man if he judges wrongly, whereas the latter have no practical consequences and no importance for the scholar except that perhaps the further they are from common sense the more pride he will take in them, since he will have had to use so much more skill and ingenuity in trying to render them plausible. And it was always my most earnest desire to learn to distinguish the true from the false in order to see clearly into my own actions and proceed with confidence in this life.

It is true that, so long as I merely considered the customs of other men, 15 I found hardly any reason for confidence, for I observed in them almost as much diversity as I had found previously among the opinions of philosophers. In fact the greatest benefit I derived from these observations was that they showed me many things which, although seeming very extravagant and ridiculous to us, are nevertheless commonly accepted and approved in other great nations; and so I learned not to believe too firmly anything of which I had been persuaded only by example and custom. Thus I gradually freed myself from many errors which may obscure our natural light and make us less capable of heeding reason. But after I had spent some years pursuing these studies in the book of the world and trying to gain some experience, I resolved one day to undertake studies within myself too and to use all the powers of my mind in choosing the paths I should follow. In this I have had much more success, I think, than I would have had if I had never left my country or my books.

PART TWO

At that time I was in Germany, where I had been called by the wars that 16 are not yet ended there. While I was returning to the army from the coronation of the Emperor, the onset of winter detained me in quarters where, finding no conversation to divert me and fortunately having no cares or passions to trouble me, I stayed all day shut up alone in a stove-heated room, where I was completely free to converse with myself about my own thoughts.[1] Among the first that occurred to me was the thought that there is not usually so much perfection in works composed of several parts and

---

[1] In 1619 Descartes attended the coronation of Ferdinand II in Frankfurt, which took place from 20 July to 9 September. The mentioned army was that of the Catholic Duke Maximilian of Bavaria. It is thought that Descartes was detained in a village near Ulm. His day of solitary reflection in a stove-heated room was, according to Baillet, 10 November 1619. [Translators' note.]

produced by various different craftsmen as in the works of one man. Thus we see that buildings undertaken and completed by a single architect are usually more attractive and better planned than those which several have tried to patch up by adapting old walls built for different purposes. Again, ancient cities which have gradually grown from mere villages into large towns are usually ill-proportioned, compared with those orderly towns which planners lay out as they fancy on level ground. Looking at the buildings of the former individually, you will often find as much art in them, if not more, than in those of the latter; but in view of their arrangement—a tall one here, a small one there—and the way they make the streets crooked and irregular, you would say it is chance, rather than the will of men using reason, that placed them so. And when you consider that there have always been certain officials whose job is to see that private buildings embellish public places, you will understand how difficult it is to make something perfect by working only on what others have produced. Again, I thought, peoples who have grown gradually from a half-savage to a civilized state, and have made their laws only in so far as they were forced to by the inconvenience of crimes and quarrels, could not be so well governed as those who from the beginning of their society have observed the basic laws laid down by some wise law-giver. Similarly, it is quite certain that the constitution of the true religion, whose articles have been made by God alone, must be incomparably better ordered than all the others. And to speak of human affairs, I believe that if Sparta was at one time very flourishing, this was not because each of its laws in particular was good (seeing that some were very strange and even contrary to good morals), but because they were devised by a single man and hence all tended to the same end.[2] And so I came to think that the sciences contained in books, at least those involving merely probable arguments and having no demonstrative basis, being built up and developed little by little from the opinions of many different persons, do not get so close to the truth as do the simple reasonings which a man of good sense, using his natural powers, can carry out in dealing with whatever objects he may come across. So, too, I reflected that we were all children before being men and had to be governed for some time by our appetites and our teachers, which were often opposed to each other and neither of which, perhaps, always gave us the best advice; hence I thought it virtually impossible that our judgements should be as unclouded and firm as they would have been if we had had the full use of our reason from the moment of our birth, and if we had always been guided by it alone.

Admittedly, we never see people pulling down all the houses of a city 17 for the sole purpose of rebuilding them in a different style to make the streets more attractive; but we do see many individuals having their houses

---

[2] By tradition the constitution of Sparta was attributed to Lycurgus. [Translators' note.]

pulled down in order to rebuild them, some even being forced to do so when the houses are in danger of falling down and their foundations are insecure. This example convinced me that it would be unreasonable for an individual to plan to reform a state by changing it from the foundations up and overturning it in order to set it up again; or again for him to plan to reform the body of the sciences or the established order of teaching them in the schools. But regarding the opinions which I had hitherto given credence, I thought that I could not do better than undertake to get rid of them, all at one go, in order to replace them afterwards with better ones, or with the same ones once I had squared them with the standards of reason. I firmly believed that in this way I would succeed in conducting my life much better than if I built only upon old foundations and relied only upon principles that I had accepted in my youth without ever examining whether they were true. For although I noted various difficulties in this undertaking, they were not insurmountable. Nor could they be compared with those encountered in the reform of even minor matters affecting public institutions. These large bodies are too difficult to raise up once overthrown, or even to hold up once they begin to totter, and their fall cannot but be a hard one. Moreover, any imperfections they may possess—and their very diversity suffices to ensure that many do possess them—have doubtless been much smoothed over by custom; and custom has even prevented or imperceptibly corrected many imperfections that prudence could not so well provide against. Finally, it is almost always easier to put up with their imperfections than to change them, just as it is much better to follow the main roads that wind through mountains, which have gradually become smooth and convenient through frequent use, than to try to take a more direct route by clambering over rocks and descending to the foot of precipices.

That is why I cannot by any means approve of those meddlesome and 18 restless characters who, called neither by birth nor by fortune to the management of public affairs, are yet forever thinking up some new reform. And if I thought this book contained the slightest ground for suspecting me of such folly, I would be very reluctant to permit its publication. My plan has never gone beyond trying to reform my own thoughts and construct them upon a foundation which is all my own. If I am sufficiently pleased with my work to present you with this sample of it, this does not mean that I would advise anyone to imitate it. Those on whom God has bestowed more of his favours will perhaps have higher aims; but I fear that even my aim may be too bold for many people. The simple resolution to abandon all the opinions one has hitherto accepted is not an example that everyone ought to follow. The world is largely composed of two types of minds for whom it is quite unsuitable. First, there are those who, believing themselves cleverer than they are, cannot avoid precipitate judgements and never have the patience to direct all their thoughts in an orderly manner; consequently, if they once took the liberty of doubting the principles they accepted and of straying from the common path, they could never stick to the track that must be taken as a short-cut, and they would remain lost all their lives. Secondly, there are those who have enough reason or modesty to recognize that they are less capable of distinguishing the true from the false than certain others by whom they can be taught; such people should be content to follow the opinions of these others rather than seek better opinions themselves.

For myself, I would undoubtedly have been counted among the latter if   19 I had had only one teacher or if I had never known the differences that have always existed among the opinions of the most learned. But in my college days I discovered that nothing can be imagined which is too strange or incredible to have been said by some philosopher; and since then I have recognized through my travels that those with views quite contrary to ours are not on that account barbarians or savages, but that many of them make use of reason as much or more than we do. I thought, too, how the same man, with the same mind, if brought up from infancy among the French or Germans, develops otherwise than he would if he had always lived among the Chinese or cannibals; and how, even in our fashions of dress, the very thing that pleased us ten years ago, and will perhaps please us again ten years hence, now strikes us as extravagant and ridiculous. Thus it is custom and example that persuade us, rather than any certain knowledge. And yet a majority vote is worthless as a proof of truths that are at all difficult to discover; for a single man is much more likely to hit upon them than a group of people. I was, then, unable to choose anyone whose opinions struck me as preferable to those of all others, and I found myself as it were forced to become my own guide.

But, like a man who walks alone in the dark, I resolved to proceed so   20 slowly, and to use such circumspection in all things, that even if I made but little progress I should at least be sure not to fall. Nor would I begin rejecting completely any of the opinions which may have slipped into my mind without having been introduced there by reason, until I had first spent enough time in planning the work I was undertaking and in seeking the true method of attaining the knowledge of everything within my mental capabilities.

When I was younger, my philosophical studies had included some logic,   21 and my mathematical studies some geometrical analysis and algebra. These three arts or sciences, it seemed, ought to contribute something to my plan. But on further examination I observed with regard to logic that syllogisms and most of its other techniques are of less use for learning things than for explaining to others the things one already knows or even, as in the art of Lully, for speaking without judgement about matters of which one is ignorant.[3] And although logic does contain many excellent and true precepts,

---

[3] Raymond Lully (1232–1315) was a Catalan theologian whose *Ars Magna* purported to provide a universal method of discovery. [Translators' note.]

these are mixed up with so many others which are harmful or superfluous that it is almost as difficult to distinguish them as it is to carve a Diana or a Minerva from an unhewn block of marble. As to the analysis of the ancients and the algebra of the moderns, they cover only highly abstract matters, which seem to have no use. Moreover the former is so closely tied to the examination of figures that it cannot exercise the intellect without greatly tiring the imagination; and the latter is so confined to certain rules and symbols that the end result is a confused and obscure art which encumbers the mind, rather than a science which cultivates it. For this reason I thought I had to seek some other method comprising the advantages of these three subjects but free from their defects. Now a multiplicity of laws often provides an excuse for vices, so that a state is much better governed when it has only a few laws which are strictly observed; in the same way, I thought, in place of the large number of rules that make up logic, I would find the following four to be sufficient, provided that I made a strong and unswerving resolution never to fail to observe them.

The first was never to accept anything as true if I did not have evident 22 knowledge of its truth: that is, carefully to avoid precipitate conclusions and preconceptions, and to include nothing more in my judgements than what presented itself to my mind so clearly and so distinctly that I had no occasion to call it into doubt.

The second, to divide each of the difficulties I examined into as many 23 parts as possible and as may be required in order to resolve them better.

The third, to direct my thoughts in an orderly manner, by beginning 24 with the simplest and most easily known objects in order to ascend little by little, step by step, to knowledge of the most complex, and by supposing some order even among objects that have no natural order of precedence.

And the last, throughout to make enumerations so complete, and reviews 25 so comprehensive, that I could be sure of leaving nothing out.

Those long chains composed of very simple and easy reasonings, which 26 geometers customarily use to arrive at their most difficult demonstrations, had given me occasion to suppose that all the things which come within the scope of human knowledge are interconnected in the same way. And I thought that, provided we refrain from accepting anything as true which is not, and always keep to the order required for deducing one thing from another, there can be nothing too remote to be reached in the end or too well hidden to be discovered. I had no great difficulty in deciding which things to begin with, for I knew already that it must be with the simplest and most easily known. Reflecting, too, that of all those who have hitherto sought after truth in the sciences, mathematicians alone have been able to find any demonstrations—that is to say, certain and evident reasonings—I had no doubt that I should begin with the very things that they studied. From this, however, the only advantage I hoped to gain was to accustom my mind to nourish itself on truths and not to be satisfied with bad reasoning. Nor did I have any intention of trying to learn all the special sciences commonly called "mathematics."[4] For I saw that, despite the diversity of their objects, they agree in considering nothing but the various relations or proportions that hold between these objects. And so I thought it best to examine only such proportions in general, supposing them to hold only between such items as would help me to know them more easily. At the same time I would not restrict them to these items, so that I could apply them the better afterwards to whatever others they might fit. Next I observed that in order to know these proportions I would need sometimes to consider them separately and sometimes merely to keep them in mind or understand many together. And I thought that in order the better to consider them separately I should suppose them to hold between lines, because I did not find anything simpler, nor anything that I could represent more distinctly to my imagination and senses. But in order to keep them in mind or understand several together, I thought it necessary to designate them by the briefest possible symbols. In this way I would take over all that is best in geometrical analysis and in algebra, using the one to correct all the defects of the other.

In fact, I venture to say that by strictly observing the few rules I had 27 chosen, I became very adept at unravelling all the questions which come within the scope of these two sciences. So much so, in fact, that in the two or three months I spent in examining them—beginning with the simplest and most general and using each truth I found as a rule for finding further truths—not only did I solve many problems which I had previously thought very difficult, but also it seemed to me towards the end that even in those cases where I was still in the dark I could determine by what means and to what extent it was possible to find a solution. This claim will not appear too arrogant if you consider that since there is only one truth concerning any matter, whoever discovers this truth knows as much about it as can be known. For example, if a child who has been taught arithmetic does a sum following the rules, he can be sure of having found everything the human mind can discover regarding the sum he was considering. In short, the method which instructs us to follow the correct order, and to enumerate exactly all the relevant factors, contains everything that gives certainty to the rules of arithmetic.

But what pleased me most about this method was that by following it I 28 was sure in every case to use my reason, if not perfectly, at least as well as was in my power. Moreover, as I practised the method I felt my mind gradually become accustomed to conceiving its objects more clearly and distinctly; and since I did not restrict the method to any particular subject-matter, I hoped to apply it as usefully to the problems of the other sciences as I had to those of algebra. Not that I would have dared to try at the outset

---

[4] These are subjects with a theoretical basis in mathematics, such as astronomy, music and optics. [Translators' note.]

to examine every problem that might arise, for that would itself have been contrary to the order which the method prescribes. But observing that the principles of these sciences must all be derived from philosophy, in which I had not yet discovered any certain ones, I thought that first of all I had to try to establish some certain principles in philosophy. And since this is the most important task of all, and the one in which precipitate conclusions and preconceptions are most to be feared, I thought that I ought not try to accomplish it until I had reached a more mature age than twenty-three, as I then was, and until I had first spent a long time in preparing myself for it. I had to uproot from my mind all the wrong opinions I had previously accepted, amass a variety of experiences to serve as the subject-matter of my reasonings, and practise constantly my self-prescribed method in order to strengthen myself more and more in its use.

Part Three

Now, before starting to rebuild your house, it is not enough simply to pull   29
it down, to make provision for materials and architects (or else train yourself in architecture), and to have carefully drawn up the plans; you must also provide yourself with some other place where you can live comfortably while building is in progress. Likewise, lest I should remain indecisive in my actions while reason obliged me to be so in my judgements, and in order to live as happily as I could during this time, I formed for myself a provisional moral code consisting of just three or four maxims, which I should like to tell you about.

The first was to obey the laws and customs of my country, holding   30
constantly to the religion in which by God's grace I had been instructed from my childhood, and governing myself in all other matters according to the most moderate and least extreme opinions—the opinions commonly accepted in practice by the most sensible of those with whom I should have to live. For I had begun at this time to count my own opinions as worthless, because I wished to submit them all to examination, and so I was sure I could do no better than follow those of the most sensible men. And although there may be men as sensible among the Persians or Chinese as among ourselves, I thought it would be most useful for me to be guided by those with whom I should have to live. I thought too that in order to discover what opinions they really held I had to attend to what they did rather than what they said. For with our declining standards of behaviour, few people are willing to say everything that they believe; and besides, many people do not know what they believe, since believing something and knowing that one believes it are different acts of thinking, and the one often occurs without the other. Where many opinions were equally well accepted, I chose only the most moderate, both because these are always the easiest to act upon and probably the best (excess being usually bad), and also so that if I made a mistake, I should depart less from the right path than I would

if I chose one extreme when I ought to have pursued the other. In particular, I counted as excessive all promises by which we give up some of our freedom. It was not that I disapproved of laws which remedy the inconstancy of weak minds by allowing us to make vows or contracts that oblige perseverance in some worthy project (or even, for the security of commerce, in some indifferent one). But I saw nothing in the world which remained always in the same state, and for my part I was determined to make my judgements more and more perfect, rather than worse. For these reasons I thought I would be sinning against good sense if I were to take my previous approval of something as obliging me to regard it as good later on, when it had perhaps ceased to be good or I no longer regarded it as such.

My second maxim was to be as firm and decisive in my actions as I 31 could, and to follow even the most doubtful opinions, once I had adopted them, with no less constancy than if they had been quite certain. In this respect I would be imitating a traveller who, upon finding himself lost in a forest, should not wander about turning this way and that, and still less stay in one place, but should keep walking as straight as he can in one direction, never changing it for slight reasons even if mere chance made him choose it in the first place; for in this way, even if he does not go exactly where he wishes, he will at least end up in a place where he is likely to be better off than in the middle of a forest. Similarly, since in everyday life we must often act without delay, it is a most certain truth that when it is not in our power to discern the truest opinions, we must follow the most probable. Even when no opinions appear more probable than any others, we must still adopt some; and having done so we must then regard them not as doubtful, from a practical point of view, but as most true and certain, on the grounds that the reason which made us adopt them is itself true and certain. By following this maxim I could free myself from all the regrets and remorse which usually trouble the consciences of those weak and faltering spirits who allow themselves to set out on some supposedly good course of action which later, in their inconstancy, they judge to be bad.

My third maxim was to try always to master myself rather than fortune, 32 and change my desires rather than the order of the world. In general I would become accustomed to believing that nothing lies entirely within our power except our thoughts, so that after doing our best in dealing with things external to us, whatever we fail to achieve is absolutely impossible so far as we are concerned. This alone, I thought, would be sufficient to prevent me from desiring in future something I could not get, and so to make me content. For our will naturally tends to desire only what our intellect represents to it as somehow possible; and so it is certain that if we consider all external goods as equally beyond our power, we shall not regret the absence of goods which seem to be our birthright when we are deprived of them through no fault of our own, any more than we regret not possessing the kingdom of China or of Mexico. Making a virtue of necessity, as they say, we shall not desire to be healthy when ill or free when imprisoned, any more than we now desire to have bodies of a material as indestructible as diamond or wings to fly like the birds. But I admit that it takes long practice and repeated meditation to become accustomed to seeing everything in this light. In this, I believe, lay the secret of those philosophers who in earlier times were able to escape from the dominion of fortune and, despite suffering and poverty, rival their gods in happiness. Through constant reflection upon the limits prescribed for them by nature, they became perfectly convinced that nothing was in their power but their thoughts, and this alone was sufficient to prevent them from being attracted to other things. Their mastery over their thoughts was so absolute that they had reason to count themselves richer, more powerful, freer and happier than other men who, because they lack this philosophy, never achieve such mastery over all their desires, however favoured by nature and fortune they may be.

Finally, to conclude this moral code, I decided to review the various 33 occupations which men have in this life, in order to try to choose the best. Without wishing to say anything about the occupations of others, I thought I could do no better than to continue with the very one I was engaged in, and devote my whole life to cultivating my reason and advancing as far as I could in the knowledge of the truth, following the method I had prescribed for myself. Since beginning to use this method I had felt such great satisfaction that I thought one could not have any sweeter or purer enjoyment in this life. Every day I discovered by its means truths which, it seemed to me, were quite important and were generally unknown by other men; and the satisfaction they gave me so filled my mind that nothing else mattered to me. Besides, the sole basis of the foregoing three maxims was the plan I had to continue my self-instruction. For since God has given each of us a light to distinguish truth from falsehood, I should not have thought myself obliged to rest content with the opinions of others for a single moment if I had not intended in due course to examine them using my own judgement; and I could not have avoided having scruples about following these opinions, if I had not hoped to take every opportunity to discover better ones, in case there were any. Lastly, I could not have limited my desires, or been happy, had I not been following a path by which I thought I was sure to acquire all the knowledge of which I was capable, and in this way all the true goods within my reach. For since our will tends to pursue or avoid only what our intellect represents to it as good or bad, we need only to judge well in order to act well, and to judge as well as we can in order to do our best—that is to say, in order to acquire all the virtues and in general all the other goods we can acquire. And when we are certain of this, we cannot fail to be happy.

Once I had established these maxims and set them on one side together 34 with the truths of faith, which have always been foremost among my beliefs, I judged that I could freely undertake to rid myself of all the rest of my opinions. As I expected to be able to achieve this more readily by talking with other men than by staying shut up in the stove-heated room where I had had all these thoughts, I set out on my travels again before the end of winter. Throughout the following nine years I did nothing but roam about in the world, trying to be a spectator rather than an actor in all the comedies that are played out there. Reflecting especially upon the points in every subject which might make it suspect and give occasion for us to make mistakes, I kept uprooting from my mind any errors that might previously have slipped into it. In doing this I was not copying the sceptics, who doubt only for the sake of doubting and pretend to be always undecided; on the contrary, my whole aim was to reach certainty—to cast aside the loose earth and sand so as to come upon rock or clay. In this I think I was quite successful. For I tried to expose the falsity or uncertainty of the propositions I was examining by clear and certain arguments, not by weak conjectures; and I never encountered any proposition so doubtful that I could not draw from it some quite certain conclusion—if only the conclusion that it contained nothing certain. And, just as in pulling down an old house we usually keep the remnants for use in building a new one, so in destroying all those opinions of mine that I judged ill-founded I made various observations and acquired many experiences which I have since used in establishing more certain opinions. Moreover, I continued practising the method I had prescribed for myself. Besides taking care in general to conduct all my thoughts according to its rules, I set aside some hours now and again to apply it more particularly to mathematical problems. I also applied it to certain other problems which I could put into something like mathematical form by detaching them from all the principles of the other sciences, which I did not find sufficiently secure (as you will see I have done in many problems discussed later in this book).[5] Thus, while appearing to live like those concerned only to lead an agreeable and blameless life, who take care to keep their pleasures free from vices, and who engage in every honest pastime in order to enjoy their leisure without boredom, I never stopped pursuing my project, and I made perhaps more progress in the knowledge of the truth than I would have if I had done nothing but read books or mix with men of learning.

Those nine years passed by, however, without my taking any side 35 regarding the questions which are commonly debated among the learned, or beginning to search for the foundations of any philosophy more certain than the commonly accepted one. The example of many fine intellects who had previously had this project, but had not, I thought, met with success, made me imagine the difficulties to be so great that I would not have dared to embark upon it so soon if I had not noticed that some people were spreading the rumour that I had already completed it. I cannot say what

---

[5] Here Descartes is referring to the scientific problems which he deals with in the essays published with the *Discourse on the Method*. [Translators' note.]

basis they had for this opinion. If I contributed anything to it by my conversation, it must have been because I confessed my ignorance more ingenuously than is customary for those with a little learning, and perhaps also because I displayed the reasons I had for doubting many things which others regard as certain, rather than because I boasted of some learning. But as I was honest enough not to wish to be taken for what I was not, I thought I had to try by every means to become worthy of the reputation that was given me. Exactly eight years ago this desire made me resolve to move away from any place where I might have acquaintances and retire to this country, where the long duration of the war has led to the establishment of such order that the armies maintained here seem to serve only to make the enjoyment of the fruits of peace all the more secure.[6] Living here, amidst this great mass of busy people who are more concerned with their own affairs than curious about those of others, I have been able to lead a life as solitary and withdrawn as if I were in the most remote desert, while lacking none of the comforts found in the most populous cities.

Part Four

I do not know whether I should tell you of the first meditations that I had there, for they are perhaps too metaphysical and uncommon for everyone's taste. And yet, to make it possible to judge whether the foundations I have chosen are firm enough, I am in a way obliged to speak of them. For a long time I had observed, as noted above, that in practical life it is sometimes necessary to act on opinions as if they were indubitable, even when one knows that they are quite uncertain. But since I now wished to devote myself solely to the search for truth, I thought it necessary to do the very opposite and reject as if absolutely false everything in which I could imagine the least doubt, in order to see if I was left believing anything that was entirely indubitable. Thus, because our senses sometimes deceive us, I decided to suppose that nothing was such as they led us to imagine. And since there are men who make mistakes in reasoning, committing logical fallacies concerning the simplest questions in geometry, and because I judged that I was as prone to error as anyone else, I rejected as unsound all the arguments I had previously taken as demonstrative proofs. Lastly, considering that the very thoughts we have while awake may also occur while we sleep without any of them being at that time true, I resolved to pretend that all the things that had ever entered my mind were no more true than the illusions of my dreams. But immediately I noticed that while I was endeavouring in this way to think that everything was false, it was necessary that I, who was thinking this, was something. And observing that

36

---

[6] Descartes settled in Holland in 1629. The war was that conducted by the United Provinces against Spain from 1572 to 1648. [Translators' note.]

this truth *"I am thinking, therefore I exist"*[7] was so firm and sure that all the most extravagant suppositions of the sceptics were incapable of shaking it, I decided that I could accept it without scruple as the first principle of the philosophy I was seeking.

Next I examined attentively what I was. I saw that while I could pretend that I had no body and that there was no world and no place for me to be in, I could not for all that pretend that I did not exist. I saw on the contrary that from the mere fact that I thought of doubting the truth of other things, it followed quite evidently and certainly that I existed; whereas if I had merely ceased thinking, even if everything else I had ever imagined had been true, I should have had no reason to believe that I existed. From this I knew I was a substance whose whole essence or nature is solely to think, and which does not require any place, or depend on any material thing, in order to exist. Accordingly this "I"—that is, the soul by which I am what I am—is entirely distinct from the body, and indeed is easier to know than the body, and would not fail to be whatever it is, even if the body did not exist.

After this I considered in general what is required of a proposition in order for it to be true and certain; for since I had just found one that I knew to be such, I thought that I ought also to know what this certainty consists in. I observed that there is nothing at all in the proposition *"I am thinking, therefore I exist"* to assure me that I am speaking the truth, except that I see very clearly that in order to think it is necessary to exist. So I decided that I could take it as a general rule that the things we conceive very clearly and very distinctly are all true; only there is some difficulty in recognizing which are the things that we distinctly conceive.

Next, reflecting upon the fact that I was doubting and that consequently my being was not wholly perfect (for I saw clearly that it is a greater perfection to know than to doubt), I decided to inquire into the source of my ability to think of something more perfect than I was; and I recognized very clearly that this had to come from some nature that was in fact more perfect. Regarding the thoughts I had of many other things outside me, like the heavens, the earth, light, heat and numerous others, I had no such difficulty in knowing where they came from. For I observed nothing in them that seemed to make them superior to me; and so I could believe that, if they were true, they depended on my nature in so far as it had any perfection, and if they were not true, I got them from nothing—in other words, they were in me because I had some defect. But the same could not hold for the idea of a being more perfect than my own. For it was manifestly impossible to get this from nothing; and I could not have got it from myself since it is no less contradictory that the more perfect should result from the

[7] This is the famous *cogito ergo sum*, familiar in popular quotation as "I think, therefore I am." [Editors' note.]

less perfect, and depend on it, than that something should proceed from nothing. So there remained only the possibility that the idea had been put into me by a nature truly more perfect than I was and even possessing in itself all the perfections of which I could have any idea, that is—to explain myself in one word—by God. To this I added that since I knew of some perfections that I did not possess, I was not the only being which existed (here, by your leave, I shall freely use some scholastic terminology), but there had of necessity to be some other, more perfect being on which I depended and from which I had acquired all that I possessed. For if I had existed alone and independently of every other being, so that I had got from myself what little of the perfect being I participated in, then for the same reason I could have got from myself everything else I knew I lacked, and thus been myself infinite, eternal, immutable, omniscient, omnipotent; in short, I could have had all the perfections which I could observe to be in God. For, according to the arguments I have just advanced, in order to know the nature of God, as far as my own nature was capable of knowing it, I had only to consider, for each thing of which I found in myself some idea, whether or not it was a perfection to possess it; and I was sure that none of those which indicated any imperfection was in God, but that all the others were. Thus I saw that doubt, inconstancy, sadness and the like could not be in God, since I myself would have been very glad to be free from them. Besides this, I had ideas of many corporeal things capable of being perceived by the senses; for even if I were to suppose that I was dreaming and that whatever I saw or imagined was false, yet I could not deny that the ideas were truly in my mind. But since I had already recognized very clearly from my own case that the intellectual nature is distinct from the corporeal, and as I observed that all composition is evidence of dependence and that dependence is manifestly a defect, I concluded that it could not be a perfection in God to be composed of these two natures, and consequently that he was not composed of them. But if there were any bodies in the world, or any intelligences or other natures that were not wholly perfect, their being must depend on God's power in such a manner that they could not subsist for a single moment without him.

After that, wishing to seek other truths, I considered the object studied by geometers. I conceived of this as a continuous body, or a space indefinitely extended in length, breadth and height or depth, and divisible into different parts which may have various shapes and sizes, and may be moved or transposed in every way: for all this is assumed by geometers in their object of study. I went through some of their simpler demonstrations and noted that the great certainty which everyone ascribes to them is founded solely on their being conceived as evident (in accordance with the rule stated above). I noted also that there was nothing at all in these demonstrations which assured me of the existence of their object. For example, I saw clearly that the three angles of any given triangle must equal two right angles; yet

40

for all that, I saw nothing which assured me that there existed any triangle in the world. Whereas when I looked again at the idea I had of a perfect being, I found that this included existence in the same way as—or even more evidently than—the idea of a triangle includes the equality of its three angles to two right angles, or the idea of a sphere includes the equidistance of all the points on the surface from the centre. Thus I concluded that it is at least as certain as any geometrical proof that God, who is this perfect being, is or exists.

But many are convinced that there is some difficulty in knowing God, 41 and even in knowing what their soul is. The reason for this is that they never raise their minds above things which can be perceived by the senses: they are so used to thinking of things only by imagining them (a way of thinking specially suited to material things) that whatever is unimaginable seems to them unintelligible. This is sufficiently obvious from the fact that even the scholastic philosophers take it as a maxim that there is nothing in the intellect which has not previously been in the senses; and yet it is certain that the ideas of God and of the soul have never been in the senses. It seems to me that trying to use one's imagination in order to understand these ideas is like trying to use one's eyes in order to hear sounds or smell odours— though there is this difference, that the sense of sight gives us no less assurance of the reality of its objects than do the senses of smell and hearing, while neither our imagination nor our senses could ever assure us of anything without the intervention of our intellect.

Finally, if there are still people who are not sufficiently convinced of the 42 existence of God and of their soul by the arguments I have proposed, I would have them know that everything else of which they may think themselves more sure—such as their having a body, there being stars and an earth, and the like—is less certain. For although we have a moral certainty about these things, so that it seems we cannot doubt them without being extravagant, nevertheless when it is a question of metaphysical certainty, we cannot reasonably deny that there are adequate grounds for not being entirely sure about them. We need only observe that in sleep we may imagine in the same way that we have a different body and see different stars and a different earth, without there being any of these things. For how do we know that the thoughts which come to us in dreams are any more false than the others, seeing that they are often no less lively and distinct? However much the best minds study this question, I do not believe they will be able to give any reason sufficient to remove this doubt unless they presuppose the existence of God. For in the first place, what I took just now as a rule, namely that everything we conceive very clearly and very distinctly is true, is assured only for the reasons that God is or exists, that he is a perfect being, and that everything in us comes from him. It follows that our ideas or notions, being real things and coming from God, cannot be anything but true, in every respect in which they are clear and distinct. Thus, if we frequently have ideas containing some falsity, this can happen only because there is something confused and obscure in them, for in that respect they participate in nothingness, that is, they are in us in this confused state only because we are not wholly perfect. And it is evident that it is no less contradictory that falsity or imperfection as such should proceed from God than that truth or perfection should proceed from nothingness. But if we did not know that everything real and true within us comes from a perfect and infinite being then, however clear and distinct our ideas were, we would have no reason to be sure that they had the perfection of being true.

But once the knowledge of God and the soul has made us certain of this 43 rule, it is easy to recognize that the things we imagine in dreams should in no way make us doubt the truth of the thoughts we have when awake. For if one happened even in sleep to have some very distinct idea (if, say, a geometer devised some new proof), one's being asleep would not prevent the idea from being true. And as to the most common error of our dreams, which consists in their representing various objects to us in the same way as our external senses do, it does not matter that this gives us occasion to doubt the truth of such ideas, for often they can also mislead us without our being asleep—as when those with jaundice see everything coloured yellow, or when stars or other very distant bodies appear to us much smaller than they are. For after all, whether we are awake or asleep, we ought never to let ourselves be convinced except by the evidence of our reason. It will be observed that I say "our reason," not "our imagination" or "our senses." Even though we see the sun very clearly, we must not judge on that account that it is only as large as we see it; and we can distinctly imagine a lion's head on a goat's body without having to conclude from this that a chimera exists in the world. For reason does not insist that what we thus see or imagine is true. But it does insist that all our ideas or notions must have some foundation of truth; for otherwise it would not be possible that God, who is all-perfect and all-truthful, should have placed them in us. And our reasonings are never so evident or complete in sleep as in waking life, although sometimes our imaginings in sleep are as lively and distinct as in waking life, or more so. Hence reason also demands that, since our thoughts cannot all be true because we are not wholly perfect, what truth they do possess must inevitably be found in the thoughts we have when awake, rather than in our dreams.

PART SIX

It is now three years since I reached the end of the treatise that contains all 44 these things. I was beginning to revise it in order to put it in the hands of a publisher, when I learned that some persons to whom I defer and who have hardly less authority over my actions than my own reason has over my thoughts, had disapproved of a physical theory published a little while before by someone else.[8] I will not say that I accepted this theory, but only that before their condemnation I had noticed nothing in it that I could imagine to be prejudicial either to religion or to the state, and hence nothing that would have prevented me from publishing it myself, if reason had convinced me of it. This made me fear that there might be some mistake in one of my own theories, in spite of the great care I had always taken never to adopt any new opinion for which I had no certain demonstration, and never to write anything that might work to anyone's disadvantage. That was enough to make me change my previous decision to publish my views. For although I had had very strong reasons for this decision, my inclination, which has always made me dislike the business of writing books, prompted me to find excuses enough for deciding otherwise. The reasons, on one side and the other, are such that not only do I have some interest in stating them here, but also the public may be interested to know what they are.

I have never made much of the products of my own mind; and so long as the only fruits I gathered from the method I use were my own satisfaction regarding certain difficulties in the speculative sciences, or else my attempts to govern my own conduct by the principles I learned from it, I did not think I was obliged to write anything about it. For as regards conduct, everyone is so full of his own wisdom that we might find as many reformers as heads if permission to institute change in these matters were granted to anyone other than those whom God has set up as sovereigns over his people or those on whom he has bestowed sufficient grace and zeal to be prophets. As regards my speculations, although they pleased me very much, I realized that other people had their own which perhaps pleased them more. But as soon as I had acquired some general notions in physics and had noticed, as I began to test them in various particular problems, where they could lead and how much they differ from the principles used up to now, I believed that I could not keep them secret without sinning gravely against the law which obliges us to do all in our power to secure the general welfare of mankind. For they opened my eyes to the possibility of gaining knowledge which would be very useful in life, and of discovering a practical philosophy which might replace the speculative philosophy taught in the schools. Through this philosophy we could know the power and action of fire, water, air, the stars, the heavens and all the other bodies in our environment, as distinctly as we know the various crafts of our artisans; and we could use this knowledge—as the artisans use theirs—for all the purposes for which it is appropriate, and thus make ourselves, as it were, the lords and masters of nature. This is desirable not only for the invention of innumerable devices which would facilitate our enjoyment of the fruits of the earth and all the goods we find there, but also, and most importantly, for the

[8] Galileo, whose *Dialogue Concerning the Two Chief World Systems* was published in 1632 and condemned by the Congregation of the Holy Office in 1633. [Translators' note.]

maintenance of health, which is undoubtedly the chief good and the foundation of all the other goods in this life. For even the mind depends so much on the temperament and disposition of the bodily organs that if it is possible to find some means of making men in general wiser and more skilful than they have been up till now, I believe we must look for it in medicine. It is true that medicine as currently practised does not contain much of any significant use; but without intending to disparage it, I am sure there is no one, even among its practitioners, who would not admit that all we know in medicine is almost nothing in comparison with what remains to be known, and that we might free ourselves from innumerable diseases, both of the body and of the mind, and perhaps even from the infirmity of old age, if we had sufficient knowledge of their causes and of the remedies that nature has provided. Intending as I did to devote my life to the pursuit of such indispensable knowledge, I discovered a path which would, I thought, inevitably lead us to it, unless prevented by the brevity of life or the lack of observations.[9] And I judged that the best remedy against these two obstacles was to communicate faithfully to the public what little I had discovered, and to urge the best minds to try and make further progress by helping with the necessary observations, each according to his inclination and ability, and by communicating to the public everything they learn. Thus, by building upon the work of our predecessors and combining the lives and labours of many, we might make much greater progress working together than anyone could make on his own.

I also noticed, regarding observations, that the further we advance in our knowledge, the more necessary they become. At the beginning, rather than seeking those which are more unusual and highly contrived, it is better to resort only to those which, presenting themselves spontaneously to our senses, cannot be unknown to us if we reflect even a little. The reason for this is that the more unusual observations are apt to mislead us when we do not yet know the causes of the more common ones, and the factors on which they depend are almost always so special and so minute that it is very difficult to discern them. But the order I have adopted in this regard is the following. First I tried to discover in general the principles or first causes of everything that exists or can exist in the world. To this end I considered nothing but God alone, who created the world; and I derived these principles only from certain seeds of truth which are naturally in our souls. Next I examined the first and most ordinary effects deducible from these causes. In this way, it seems to me, I discovered the heavens, the stars, and an earth; and, on the earth, water, air, fire, minerals, and other such things which, being the most common of all and the simplest, are consequently

---

[9] Fr. *expériences*, a term which Descartes often uses when talking of scientific observations, and which sometimes comes close to meaning "experiments" in the modern sense (its root being derived from Lat. *experiri*, "to test"). [Translators' note.]

the easiest to know. Then, when I sought to descend to more particular things, I encountered such a variety that I did not think the human mind could possibly distinguish the forms or species of bodies that are on the earth from an infinity of others that might be there if it had been God's will to put them there; nor could it relate them to our purposes except by progressing to the causes by way of the effects and making use of many special observations. And now, reviewing in my mind all the objects that have ever been present to my senses, I venture to say that I have never noticed anything in them which I could not explain quite easily by the principles I had discovered. But I must also admit that the power of nature is so ample and so vast, and these principles so simple and so general, that I notice hardly any particular effect of which I do not know at once that it can be deduced from the principles in many different ways—and my greatest difficulty is usually to discover in which of these ways it depends on them. I know no other means to discover this than by seeking further observations whose outcomes vary according to which of these ways provides the correct explanation. Moreover, I have now reached a point where I think I can see quite clearly what line we should follow in making most of the observations which serve this purpose; but I see also that they are of such a kind and so numerous that neither my dexterity nor my income (were it even a thousand times greater than it is) could suffice for all of them. And so the advances I make in the knowledge of nature will depend henceforth on the opportunities I get to make more or fewer of these observations. I resolved to make this known in the treatise I had written, and to show clearly how the public could benefit from such knowledge. This would oblige all who desire the general well-being of mankind—that is, all who are really virtuous, not virtuous only in appearance or merely in repute— both to communicate to me the observations they have already made and to assist me in seeking those which remain to be made.

Since then, however, other considerations have made me change my 47 mind. I have come to think that I must continue writing down anything I consider at all important, when I discover its truth, and that I should take as much care over these writings as I would if I intended to have them published. For this will give me all the more reason to examine them closely, as undoubtedly we always look more carefully at something we think is to be seen by others than at something we do only for ourselves; and often what seemed true to me when I first conceived it has looked false when I tried to put it on paper. This plan will also ensure both that I lose no opportunity to benefit the public if I can, and that if my writings have any value, those who get them after my death can make the most appropriate use of them. But I was determined not to agree to their publication during my lifetime, so that neither the opposition and controversy they might arouse, nor the reputation they might gain for me, would make me lose any of the time I planned to devote to my self-instruction. Every man is indeed bound to do what he can to procure the good of others, and a man who is of no use to anyone else is strictly worthless. Nevertheless it is also true that our concern ought to extend beyond the present, and that it is good to neglect matters which may profit the living when we aim to do other things which will benefit posterity even more. In any case I am willing to acknowledge that the little I have learned so far is almost nothing in comparison with that which I do not know but which I hope to be able to learn. Those who gradually discover the truth in the sciences are like people who become rich and find they have less trouble making large profits than they had in making much smaller ones when they were poorer. Or they may be compared with military commanders, whose forces tend to grow in proportion to their victories, but who need more skill to maintain their position after losing a battle than they do to take towns and provinces after winning one. For attempting to overcome all the difficulties and errors that prevent our arriving at knowledge of the truth is indeed a matter of fighting battles: we lose a battle whenever we accept some false opinion concerning an important question of general significance, and we need much more skill afterwards to regain our former position than we do to make good progress when we already have principles which are well-founded. For my part, if I have hitherto discovered a number of truths in the sciences (and I trust that the contents of this volume warrant the judgement that I have discovered some), I may say that they are merely the results and consequences of some five or six fundamental difficulties which I surmounted and which I count as so many battles where I had fortune on my side. I even venture to say that I think I need to win only two or three further such battles in order to achieve my aims completely, and that my age is not so far advanced that I may not in the normal course of nature still have the time to do this. But the more hopeful I am of being able to use my remaining years effectively, the more I think I am obliged to plan my time carefully; and many occasions for wasting time would undoubtedly arise if I published the fundamental principles of my physics. For although these principles are almost all so evident that they need only to be understood to be believed, and although I think I can demonstrate all of them, yet since it is impossible that they should accord with all the diverse opinions of other men, I foresee that I should often be distracted by the controversies they would arouse.

It may be claimed that such controversies would be useful. Not only 48 would they make me aware of my mistakes, but also they would enable others to have a better understanding of anything worthwhile that I may have discovered; and, just as many people are able to see more than one person can on his own, so these others might begin to make use of my discoveries and help me with theirs. But although I recognize that I am extremely prone to error, and I almost never trust the first thoughts that come to me, at the same time my acquaintance with the objections that may be raised prevents me from expecting any benefit from them. For I have already had frequent experience of the judgements both of those I held to be my friends and of some I thought indifferent towards me, and even of certain others whose malice and envy would, I knew, make them eager enough to reveal what affection would hide from my friends. But it has rarely happened that an objection has been raised which I had not wholly foreseen, except when it was quite wide of the mark. Thus I have almost never encountered a critic of my views who did not seem to be either less rigorous or less impartial than myself. Nor have I ever observed that any previously unknown truth has been discovered by means of the disputations practised in the schools. For so long as each side strives for victory, more effort is put into establishing plausibility than in weighing reasons for and against; and those who have long been good advocates do not necessarily go on to make better judges.

As for the benefit that others might gain from the communication of my 49 thoughts, this could not be so very great. For I have not yet taken them sufficiently far: I need to add many things to them before applying them in practice. And I think I can say without vanity that if anyone is capable of making these additions it must be myself rather than someone else—not that there may not be many minds in the world incomparably better than mine, but because no one can conceive something so well, and make it his own, when he learns it from someone else as when he discovers it himself. This is especially true in the case under consideration. I have often explained some of my opinions to highly intelligent persons who seemed to understand them quite distinctly when I told them about them; but, when they repeated them, I observed that they almost always changed them in such a way that I could no longer acknowledge them as my own. For this reason I should like to beg future generations never to believe that I am the source of an opinion they hear unless I have published it myself. I do not wonder at the absurdities attributed to all the ancient philosophers whose writings we do not possess; nor do I conclude from these attributions that their thoughts were highly unreasonable. As they were some of the best minds of their time, I conclude rather that their thoughts have been misreported. We see too that it has almost never happened that any of their followers has surpassed them; and I am sure that Aristotle's most enthusiastic contemporary followers would count themselves fortunate if they had as much knowledge of nature as he had, even on the condition that they should never know any more. They are like ivy, which never seeks to climb higher than the trees which support it, and often even grows downward after reaching the tree tops. For it seems to me that they too take downward steps, or become somehow less knowledgeable than if they refrained from study, when, not content with knowing everything which is intelligibly explained in their author's writings, they wish in addition to find there the solution to many problems about which he says nothing and about which perhaps he never thought. But this manner of philosophizing is very convenient for those with only mediocre minds, for the obscurity of the distinctions and principles they use makes it possible for them to speak about everything as confidently as if they knew it, and to defend all they say against the most subtle and clever thinkers without anyone having the means to convince them that they are wrong. In this they seem to resemble a blind man who, in order to fight without disadvantage against someone who can see, lures him into the depths of a very dark cellar. These philosophers, I may say, have an interest in my refraining from publishing the principles of the philosophy I use. For my principles are so very simple and evident that in publishing them I should, as it were, be opening windows and admitting daylight into that cellar where they have gone down to fight. But even the best minds have no reason to wish to know my principles. For if they want to be able to speak about everything and acquire the reputation of being learned, they will achieve this more readily by resting content with plausibility, which can be found without difficulty in all kinds of subjects, than by seeking the truth; for the truth comes to light only gradually in certain subjects, and it obliges us frankly to confess our ignorance where other subjects are concerned. But if they prefer the knowledge of some few truths to the vanity of appearing ignorant of nothing (and undoubtedly the former is preferable), and if they wish to follow a plan similar to mine, then in that case I need tell them nothing more than I have already said in this discourse. For if they are capable of making further progress than I have made, they will be all the more capable of discovering for themselves everything I think I have discovered. Inasmuch as I have examined everything in an orderly manner, it is certain that what still remains for me to discover is in itself more difficult and more hidden than anything I have thus far been able to discover; and they would have much less pleasure in learning it from me than in learning it for themselves. Besides, by investigating easy matters first and then moving on gradually to more difficult ones, they will acquire habits more useful to them than all my instructions could be. For my part, I am convinced that if from my youth I had been taught all the truths I have since sought to demonstrate, and so had learned them without any difficulty, I should perhaps never have known any others; or at least I should never have acquired the habit and facility, which I think I have, for always finding new truths whenever I apply myself in searching for them. In short, if there was ever a task which could not be completed so well by someone other than the person who began it, it is the one on which I am working.

True, as regards observations which may help in this work, one man 50 could not possibly make them all. But he could not effectively use hands other than his own, except by employing artisans, or other persons whom he could pay and who would be led by the hope of gain (a most effective motive) to do precisely what he ordered them to do. For voluntary helpers, who might offer their assistance from curiosity or a desire to learn, usually promise more than they achieve and make fine proposals which never come to anything. In addition, they would inevitably wish to be rewarded by having certain difficulties explained to them, or at any rate by compliments and useless conversation, which could not but waste a lot of his time. And as for the observations that others have already made, even if they were willing to communicate them to him (something which those who call them "secrets" would never do), they are for the most part bound up with so many details or superfluous ingredients that it would be very hard for him to make out the truth in them. Besides, he would find almost all of these observations to be so badly explained or indeed so mistaken—because those who made them were eager to have them appear to conform with their principles—that it would simply not be worthwhile for him to spend the time required to pick out those which he might find useful. So if there were someone in the world whom we knew for sure to be capable of making discoveries of the greatest possible importance and public utility, and whom other men accordingly were eager to help in every way to achieve his ends, I do not see how they could do anything for him except to contribute towards the expenses of the observations that he would need and, further, prevent unwelcome visitors from wasting his free time. But I am not so presumptuous that I wish to promise anything extraordinary, nor do I entertain thoughts so vain as the supposition that the public ought to take a great interest in my projects. Apart from that, I am not so mean-spirited that I would willingly accept from anyone a favour that I might be thought not to deserve.

All these considerations taken together caused me to decide, three years ago, that I did not wish to publish the treatise I had ready then, and make me resolve not to publish any other work during my lifetime which was so general in scope or by which the foundations of my physics might be understood. Since then, however, two further reasons have compelled me to include here some essays on particular topics and to give to the public some account of my actions and plans. The first is that, if I failed to do so, then many who knew of my earlier intention to publish certain writings might suppose that my reasons for not doing so were more discreditable to me than they are. I am not excessively fond of glory—indeed if I may say so, I dislike it—in so far as I regard it as opposed to that tranquillity which I value above everything else. At the same time I have never tried to conceal my actions as if they were crimes, or taken many precautions to remain unknown. For if I had done this I thought I would do myself an injustice, and moreover that would have given me a certain sort of disquiet, which again would have been opposed to the perfect peace of mind I am seeking. And since my indifference as to whether I was well-known or not made it unavoidable that I should gain some sort of reputation, I thought I ought to do my best at least to avoid getting a bad one. The other reason compelling me to write this is that every day I am becoming more and more aware of the delay which my project of self-instruction is suffering because of the need for innumerable observations which I cannot possibly make without the help of others. Although I do not flatter myself with any expectation that the public will share my interests, yet at the same time I am unwilling to be so unfaithful to myself as to give those who come after me cause to reproach me one day on the grounds that I could have left them many far better things if I had not been so remiss in making them understand how they could contribute to my projects.

I thought it convenient for me to choose certain subjects which, without   52
being highly controversial and without obliging me to reveal more of my principles than I wished, would nevertheless show quite clearly what I can, and what I cannot, achieve in the sciences. I cannot tell if I have succeeded in this, and I do not wish to anticipate anyone's judgements about my writings by speaking about them myself. But I shall be very glad if they are examined. In order to provide more opportunity for this, I beg all who have any objections to take the trouble to send them to my publisher, and when he informs me about them I shall attempt to append my reply at the same time, so that readers can see both sides together, and decide the truth all the more easily. I do not promise to make very long replies, but only to acknowledge my errors very frankly if I recognize them; and where I cannot see them I shall simply say what I consider is required for defending what I have written, without introducing any new material, so as to avoid getting endlessly caught up in one topic after another.

Should anyone be shocked at first by some of the statements I make at   53
the beginning of the *Optics* and the *Meteorology* because I call them "suppositions" and do not seem to care about proving them, let him have the patience to read the whole book attentively, and I trust that he will be satisfied. For I take my reasonings to be so closely interconnected that just as the last are proved by the first, which are their causes, so the first are proved by the last, which are their effects. It must not be supposed that I am here committing the fallacy which logicians call "arguing in a circle." For as experience renders most of these effects quite certain, the causes from which I deduce them serve not so much to prove them as to explain them; indeed, quite to the contrary, it is the causes which are proved by the effects. And I have called them "suppositions" simply to make it known that I think I can deduce them from the primary truths I have expounded above; but I have deliberately avoided carrying out these deductions in order to prevent certain ingenious persons from taking the opportunity to construct, on what they believe to be my principles, some extravagant philosophy for which I shall be blamed. These persons imagine that they can learn in a single day what it has taken someone else twenty years to think out, as soon as he has told them only two or three words about it; whereas the more penetrating and acute they are, the more prone to error they are and less capable of truth. As to the opinions that are wholly mine, I do not apologize for their novelty. If the reasons for them are properly considered, I am sure they will be found to be so simple and so much in agreement with common sense as to appear less extraordinary and strange

than any other views that people may hold on the same subjects. I do not boast of being the first to discover any of them, but I do claim to have accepted them not because they have, or have not, been expressed by others, but solely because reason has convinced me of them.

If artisans are not immediately able to put into operation the invention 54
explained in the *Optics,* I do not think it can on that account be said to be defective.[10] For much skill and practice are needed for making and adjusting the machines I have described, and although my description does not omit any details, I should be no less astonished if they succeeded at the first attempt than if someone could learn to play the lute excellently in a single day simply by being given a good fingering chart. And if I am writing in French, my native language, rather than Latin, the language of my teachers, it is because I expect that those who use only their natural reason in all its purity will be better judges of my opinions than those who give credence only to the writings of the ancients. As to those who combine good sense with application—the only judges I wish to have—I am sure they will not be so partial to Latin that they will refuse to listen to my arguments because I expound them in the vernacular.

For the rest, I do not wish to speak here in detail about the further 55
progress I hope to make in the sciences, or to commit myself in the eyes of the public by making any promise that I am not sure of fulfilling. I will say only that I have resolved to devote the rest of my life to nothing other than trying to acquire some knowledge of nature from which we may derive rules in medicine which are more reliable than those we have had up till now. Moreover, my inclination makes me so strongly opposed to all other projects, and especially to those which can be useful to some persons only by harming others, that if circumstances forced me to engage in any such pursuit, I do not think I would be capable of succeeding in it. Of this I make here a public declaration, fully recognizing that it cannot serve to make me eminent in the world; but then I have no desire to be such. And I shall always hold myself more obliged to those by whose favour I enjoy uninterrupted leisure than to any who might offer me the most honourable positions in the world.

Questions for Discussion and Writing

1. Students are sometimes told *not* to write in the first person. In light of this proscription, what do you think of Descartes's use of the word "I"? Can you think of any rhetorical reason why he uses the first person as he does?

---

[10] Here Descartes refers to the method of cutting lenses described in Discourse 10 of the *Optics.* [Translators' note.]

2. What values and premises does Descartes seem to accept at face value? Do you agree with him? In what ways are or are you not a member of his intended audience?

3. All in all, do you find Descartes's argument democratic or undemocratic? What sort of person is able to pursue knowledge the way he does? For Descartes, is education a fundamentally democratic or aristocratic pursuit?

4. While pondering the nature of God and knowledge and truth, Descartes writes a good deal about the process of writing itself. How would you characterize his ideas about writing? Do they seem to form a consistent view of the subject? How might the concept of audience fit into his view of prose? What, for Descartes, is the relationship between knowledge and writing? Write an essay in which you present and evaluate Descartes's approach to the composition process.

ANDREW MARVELL
(1621–1678)

LADY MARY WORTLEY MONTAGU
(1689–1762)

The son of a Yorkshire minister, Andrew Marvell received the education of a gentleman at Cambridge. Unfortunately, he lived most of his life in an England rocked by civil war and revolution, ideological strife, and religious conflict. Although he worked for the antiroyalist Puritan government of Oliver Cromwell and served as secretary to fellow poet John Milton, he was never the ardent follower of the cause that his superior was. After the Restoration of the English monarchy, Marvell's rhetorical efforts helped save Milton from prison and execution.

Ever a pragmatist, Marvell demonstrated a practical interest in argumentation that is forever captured in his most famous poem, "To His Coy Mistress." Obviously, all was not gloomy political struggle in seventeenth-century England. Marvell was not considered a strong public speaker, but clearly he had an interest in speeches of a sort. Today he is considered by many to be the best "minor" poet of the English language.

Lady Mary Wortley Montagu was the product of a very different England. Her era was marked more by political and social continuity and by gradual, evolutionary change. Like Marvell, however, she lived in a world dominated by men. An intelligent, well-educated, independent-minded woman with a marvelous eye for detail, Lady Montagu struggled against the chauvinistic attitudes that pervaded her culture. As a rebellious teenager who questioned the traditional role of women, she secretly taught herself Latin, a language then considered the exclusive property of men. Unlike most aristocratic young ladies, she married for love and traveled extensively throughout Europe and Turkey with her ambassador husband. She was a pioneer in the campaign to bring the smallpox inoculation to England.

After her marriage deteriorated, Lady Montagu lived abroad until the very end of her life. In her own time, she was considered a formidable poet. Although it was not meant entirely as a compliment, the fact that Alexander Pope called her "Sappho" signified that her verse was not treated lightly. Today, though, we remember Lady Montagu chiefly for her courageous stand against narrow thinking, her independent mind, and her wonderful letters.

Because eighteenth-century women were not afforded the same opportunities as men, Lady Montagu's poetry, travel narratives, and epistles demonstrate the ethos of a marginalized figure. Although she moved in the highest social circles, attended more than one coronation, and counted as friends and close acquaintances some of *the most important literary and political figures of the century (such as the essayists Addison and Steele, the playwrights Congreve and Gay, and the poet Pope), she wrote essentially as an outsider in her own society.*

It must have been difficult for Lady Montagu to watch as other less talented individuals achieved—solely because of gender—the kind of recognition and power that she deserved. Even so, she wrote vividly of her society and maintained a lively sense of humor throughout her work.

The following poems, the first from Andrew Marvell and the second from Lady Montagu, illustrate provocative rhetorical similarities and differences. Marvell, the seventeenth-century man, writes from the perspective of the lover; Montagu, the eighteenth-century woman, adopts the voice of the beloved.

TO HIS COY MISTRESS

ANDREW MARVELL

Had we but world enough, and time,
This coyness, lady, were no crime.
We would sit down, and think which way
To walk, and pass our long love's day.
Thou by the Indian Ganges' side[1]   5
Shouldst rubies[2] find; I by the tide
Of Humber[3] would complain. I would
Love you ten years before the flood,
And you should, if you please, refuse
Till the conversion of the Jews.[4]   10
My vegetable[5] love should grow
Vaster than empires and more slow;
An hundred years should go to praise
Thine eyes, and on thy forehead gaze;
Two hundred to adore each breast,   15
But thirty thousand to the rest;
An age at least to every part,
And the last age should show your heart.

---

[1] *Ganges:* the holy river of India. [Editors' note.]

[2] *rubies:* thought to preserve virginity. [Editors' note.]

[3] *Humber:* a river in England. [Editors' note.]

[4] *the conversion of the Jews:* i.e., to Christianity. According to Christian tradition, this unlikely event was to occur at the end of history. [Editors' note.]

[5] *vegetable:* unconscious, achieved through unconscious effort. [Editors' note.]

For, lady, you deserve this state,
Nor would I love at lower rate.   20
 But at my back I always hear
Time's wingéd chariot hurrying near;
And yonder all before us lie
Deserts of vast eternity.
Thy beauty shall no more be found;   25
Nor, in the marble vault, shall sound
My echoing song; then worms shall try
That long-preserved virginity,
And your quaint honor turn to dust,
And into ashes all my lust: 30
The grave's a fine and private place,
But none, I think, do there embrace.
 Now therefore, while the youthful hue
Sits on thy skin like morning glow,
And while thy willing soul transpires   35
At every pore with instant fires,
Now let us sport us while we may,
And now, like amorous birds of prey,
Rather at once our time devour
Than languish in his slow-chapped power.   40
Let us roll our strength and all
Our sweetness up into one ball,
And tear our pleasures with rough strife
Through the iron gates of life:
Thus, though we cannot make our sun   45
Stand still, yet we will make him run.

THE LOVER: A BALLAD

LADY MARY WORTLEY MONTAGU

At length, by so much importunity pressed,
Take, C—,[1] at once, the inside of my breast;
This stupid[2] indifference so often you blame
Is not owing to nature, to fear, or to shame;

---

[1] *C—*: possibly a reference to Richard Chandler, a friend of the poet. [Editors' note.]

[2] *stupid:* torpid, dulled in feeling or sensation. [Editors' note.]

I am not as cold as a Virgin in lead,   5
Nor is Sunday's sermon so strong in my head;
I know but too well how time flies along,
That we live but few years and yet fewer are young.

But I hate to be cheated, and never will buy
Long years of repentance for moments of joy.   10
Oh was there a man (but where shall I find
Good sense and good nature so equally joined?)
Would value his pleasure, contribute to mine,
Not meanly would boast, nor would lewdly design,
Not over severe, yet not stupidly vain,   15
For I would have the power though not give the pain;

No pedant yet learnéd, not rakehelly gay
Or laughing because he has nothing to say,
To all my whole sex obliging and free,
Yet never be fond of any but me;   20
In public preserve the decorum that's just,
And show in his eyes he is true to his trust,
Then rarely approach, and respectfully bow,
Yet not fulsomely pert, nor yet foppishly low.

But when the hours of public are past   25
And we meet with champagne and a chicken at last,
May every fond pleasure that hour endear,
Be banished afar both discretion and fear,
Forgetting or scorning the airs of the crowd
He may cease to be formal, I to be proud,   30
Till lost in the joy we confess that we live,
And he may be rude, and yet I may forgive.

And that my delight may be solidly fixed,
Let the friend and the lover be handsomely mixed,
In whose tender bosom my soul might confide,   35
Whose kindness can soothe me, whose counsel could guide.
From such a dear lover as here I describe
No danger should fright me, no millions should bribe;
But till this astonishing creature I know,
As I long have lived chaste, I will keep myself so.   40

I never will share with the wanton coquette,
Or be caught by a vain affectation of wit.
The toasters and songsters may try all their art
But never shall enter the pass of my heart.

I loathe the lewd rake, the dressed fopling despise;   45
Before such pursuers the nice[3] virgin flies;
And as Ovid[4] has sweetly in parables told
We harden like trees, and like rivers are cold.

Questions for Discussion and Writing

1. In "To His Coy Mistress," Marvell's persona combines the rhetorical strategies of the libertine playboy with the decorous language of courtly love. How does he effect this unlikely hybrid? Is he, in your eyes, successful?

2. Discuss the *logical* structure of Marvell's persona's "speech." How does he move from premises to conclusions? What is the speech's overall structure? On the whole, how *logical* do you find the argument?

3. How does Lady Montagu's speaker seem to *answer* Marvell's? As you respond to this question, consider both the form and the content of the "speeches." If Marvell had lived to read Lady Montagu's poem, how do you suppose he might have responded?

4. How has the territory in the battle of the sexes changed and how has it remained the same since the writing of these poems? How might more contemporary versions of these arguments go? Write an essay in which you compare contemporary attitudes about gender, seduction, romance, and role playing with those of Marvell's and Montagu's times.

---

[3] *nice:* fastidious. [Editors' note.]

[4] *Ovid:* Roman poet, author of *Metamorphoses,* a collection of mythical tales in which the characters undergo various kinds of transformations, becoming trees, rocks, animals, and the like. [Editors' note.]

VOLTAIRE

(1694–1778)

François Marie Arouet de Voltaire is an outstanding representative of the intellectual movement commonly known as the "Enlightenment" or the "Age of Reason." Born into a bourgeois Parisian family, Voltaire received a strong classical education at the hand of the Jesuits. At school he was characterized as "a talented boy, but a notable scamp." This roguish behavior, so brilliantly expressed in keen wit and biting satire, earned him generous portions of honor and notoriety throughout his life.

Forsaking his father's advice, Voltaire rejected a career in the law and began writing for the stage. After an aborted duel and a brief stint in the Bastille, Voltaire sought exile in England for several years. Experiencing the comparative freedoms of English society made him bitterly aware of the social injustices that stifled his native land. His controversial Philosophical Letters, or Letters Concerning the English Nation (1734), courageously addressed these problems. Throughout his life, in fact, he worked for social justice, tolerance, and freedom. Whether composing philosophical prose or acting directly to aid specific victims of political oppression, Voltaire defended the liberties he believed should distinguish a civilized and rational society. He also wrote influential historical treatises, studied science with a passion, and served at the royal courts of Paris and Potsdam.

Because of legal difficulties, Voltaire eventually settled into exile in Switzerland. Here, besides pursuing an active social life and carrying on his indefatigable quest for social justice, he continued to write prolifically. Among the writings of this period is his most enduring literary work, Candide (1759), a portion of which is presented here. At the very end of his life, Voltaire was hailed as a hero in his native Paris.

Candide concerns the life and adventures of a "candid" young man of sound judgment and simple mind who is brought up in the Westphalian castle of "My Lord the Baron of Thunder-ten-tronckh." There he is tutored by the utterly optimistic Doctor Pangloss (from the Greek: "all tongue"), who blithely asserts that "there is no effect without a cause and that, in this best of all possible worlds, My Lord the Baron's castle [is] the finest of castles, and My Lady the best of all possible Baronesses." (Pangloss's philosophy is partially a parody of the work of Gottfried Wilhelm Leibniz, a German philosophical optimist and mathematician who preceded Voltaire.) But when Candide is discovered amorously cavorting with the beautiful young daughter of the Baron, Lady Cunegonde, he is expelled from this aristocratic life of leisurely reflection and forced to fend for himself.

An inquisitive and philosophical chap, the ever-innocent Candide roams the world in search of truth and the meaning of life, braving capture by barbaric Bulgarians; shipwreck; the Lisbon earthquake; torture at the hands of the Spanish Inquisition;

and a host of other trials and tribulations. The episode that follows takes place in South America. Candide—having left his Lady Cunegonde and her faithful friend "the old woman" in the hands of the lecherous governor of Buenos Aires, stabbed Cunegonde's brother in an argument in Paraguay, and escaped being devoured by the primitive Oreillons—along with his faithful servant Cacambo finds himself quite by accident in a country of vast material wealth.

FROM CANDIDE; OR, OPTIMISM

17

CANDIDE AND HIS VALET ARRIVE IN THE COUNTRY OF EL DORADO. WHAT THEY SAW THERE.

When they reached the frontiers of the Oreillons, "You see," said Cacambo to Candide, "this hemisphere is no better than the other; take my advice, and let us return to Europe by the shortest way possible." "But how can we return?" said Candide; "and whither shall we go? If I go to my own country, the Bulgarians and the Abares are laying that waste with fire and sword; if I return to Portugal, I shall be burned; if we remain in this country, we are every moment in danger of being spitted. But how can I bring myself to quit that part of the world where Miss Cunegonde dwells?" 1

"Let us turn toward Cayenne," said Cacambo; "there we shall meet with some Frenchmen who ramble all over the world; they may assist us, and God will perhaps have pity on us." 2

It was not so easy to get to Cayenne. They knew pretty nearly whereabouts it lay; but the mountains, rivers, precipices, robbers, savages, were dreadful obstacles in the way. Their horses died with fatigue; their provisions were at an end; they subsisted a whole month upon wild fruit, and finally they came to a little river bordered with cocoa-trees which sustained their lives and their hopes. 3

Cacambo, who was always giving as good advice as the old woman herself, said to Candide: "We can do no more, we have traveled enough on foot; I see an empty canoe near the river-side; let us fill it with cocoanuts, get into it, and go down with the stream; a river always leads to some inhabited place. If we do not meet with agreeable things, we shall at least meet with something new." "Agreed," replied Candide; "let us recommend ourselves to Providence." 4

They drifted a few leagues down the river, between banks which were in some places covered with flowers, in others barren; in some parts smooth and level, and in others steep and rugged. The stream constantly widened; at length it disappeared under a vault of frightful rocks, whose summits seemed to reach the clouds. The two travelers had the courage to commit 5 themselves to the current under this vault; the river, contracting in this part, hurried them along with a dreadful noise and rapidity. At the end of four-and-twenty hours, they saw daylight again; but their canoe was dashed to pieces against the rocks. They were obliged to creep along from rock to rock for the space of a league, till at last a spacious plain presented itself to their sight, bounded by inaccessible mountains. The country appeared cultivated equally for pleasure and to produce the necessaries of life; the useful was everywhere agreeable here: the roads were covered, or rather adorned, with carriages formed of glittering materials, in which were men and women of a surprising beauty, drawn with great rapidity by red sheep of a very large size, which surpassed in swiftness the finest coursers of Andalusia, Tetuan, or Mequinez.

"Here is a country, however," said Candide, "which is preferable to 6 Westphalia." He and Cacambo landed near the first village they saw, at the entrance of which they perceived some children covered with tattered garments of gold brocade, playing at quoits. Our two inhabitants of the other hemisphere amused themselves by looking at them; their quoits were large, round pieces, yellow, red, and green, which had a singular lustre. Our travelers picked up some of them, and they proved to be gold, emeralds, rubies, the least of which would have been the greatest ornament to the throne of the great Mogul. "Without doubt," said Cacambo, "these children are the king's sons that are playing at quoits." As he was uttering these words, the schoolmaster of the village appeared, who came to call them to school. "There," said Candide, "is the preceptor of the royal family."

The little ragamuffins immediately quitted their diversion, leaving the 7 quoits on the ground with all their other playthings. Candide gathers them up, runs to the schoolmaster, and presents them to him, humbly giving him to understand by signs that their royal highnesses had forgotten their gold and precious stones. The schoolmaster, with a smile, flung them upon the ground, examined Candide with much surprise, and went on his way.

The travelers did not fail to gather up the gold, the rubies, and the 8 emeralds. "Where are we?" cried Candide. "The king's children in this country must have an excellent education, since they are taught to show such a contempt for gold and precious stones." Cacambo was as much surprised as his master. They then drew near the first house in the village, which was built after the manner of an European palace. There was a crowd of people about the door, and a still greater number in the house; the sound of the most delightful instruments of music was heard, and the most agreeable smell came from the kitchen. Cacambo went up to the door, and heard those within talking in the Peruvian language, which was his mother-tongue; for every one knows that Cacambo was born in a village of Tucuman in which no other language was spoken. "I will be your interpreter here," said he to Candide, "let us go in; this is an eating-house."

Immediately two waiters and two servant-girls, dressed in cloth of gold 9 and their hair braided with ribbons, accost the strangers and invite them to sit down to the ordinary. Their dinner consisted of four dishes of different soups, each garnished with two young paroquets, a large dish of boiled meat that weighed two hundred pounds, two roasted monkeys of a delicious flavor, three hundred humming-birds in one dish, and six hundred of another species in another; some excellent ragouts, some delicate tarts, and the whole served up in dishes of a sort of rock-crystal. Several sorts of liquors, extracted from the sugar-cane, were handed about by the waiters and the servant-girls.

Most of the company were dealers and wagoners, all extremely polite; 10 they asked Cacambo a few questions with the utmost discretion and circumspection, and replied to his in a most obliging and satisfactory manner.

When the repast was ended, both Candide and Cacambo thought they 11 should pay very handsomely for their entertainment by laying upon the table two of those large gold pieces which they had picked off the ground; but the landlord and landlady burst into a fit of laughing, and held their sides for some time. When the fit was over, "Gentlemen," said the landlord, "we plainly perceive you are strangers, and such we are not accustomed to see; pardon us, therefore, for laughing when you offered us the common pebbles of our highways for payment of your reckoning. You doubtless have none of the coin of this country; but there is no necessity of having any money at all to dine in this house. All the inns, which are established for the convenience of those who carry on the trade of this nation, are maintained by the government. You have found but very indifferent entertainment here, because this is only a poor village; but everywhere else you will meet with a reception worthy of persons of your merit." Cacambo explained the whole of this speech of the landlord to Candide, who listened to it with the same astonishment and admiration with which his friend communicated it. "What sort of a country is this," said the one to the other, "that is unknown to all the world, and in which Nature has everywhere an appearance so different from that she has in ours? This is probably the country in which everything is right, for there must certainly be some such place; and, for all that Master Pangloss could say, I often perceived that things went very ill in Westphalia."

18

What They Saw in the Country of El Dorado.

Cacambo expressed all his curiosity to his landlord; the latter answered him 12 thus: "I am very ignorant, and I get along very well with it; however, we have in this neighborhood an old man, retired from court, who is the most learned man in the kingdom and the most communicative." He then led Cacambo to the old man; Candide was now only a secondary character, and attended his valet. They entered a very plain house, for the door was nothing but silver, and the ceiling of the apartments only of gold, but wrought in so elegant a taste as to vie with the richest ceilings; the antechamber, indeed, was incrusted only with rubies and emeralds; but the order in which everything was disposed made amends for this extreme simplicity.

The old man received the strangers on his sofa, which was stuffed with 13 humming-birds' feathers, and ordered his servants to present them with liquors in diamond vases, after which he satisfied their curiosity in the following terms:

"I am now one hundred and seventy-two years old; and I learned from 14 my late father, who was equerry to the king, the amazing revolutions of Peru, to which he had been an eyewitness. This kingdom in which we are is the ancient patrimony of the Incas, who very imprudently quitted it to conquer another part of the world, and were at length conquered and destroyed themselves by the Spaniards.

"Those princes of their family who remained in their native country 15 acted more wisely. They ordained, with the consent of the whole nation, that none of the inhabitants of our little kingdom should ever quit it; and to this wise ordinance we owe the preservation of our innocence and our happiness. The Spaniards had some confused notion of this country, to which they gave the name of El Dorado; and an Englishman named Sir Walter Raleigh actually came very near it about a hundred years ago; but the inaccessible rocks and precipices with which our country is surrounded on all sides has hitherto secured us from the rapacious fury of the people of Europe, who have an unaccountable craving for the pebbles and dirt of our land, for the sake of which they would murder us all to the very last man."

The conversation lasted some time, and turned chiefly on their form of 16 government, their manners and customs, their women, their public diversions, and the arts. At length, Candide, who had always had a taste for metaphysics, asked through Cacambo whether the people of that country had any religion.

The old man reddened a little at this question. "Can you doubt it?" said 17 he; "do you take us for wretches lost to all sense of gratitude?" Cacambo asked, in a respectful manner, what was the established religion of El Dorado. The old man blushed again. "Can there be two religions, then?" said he; "ours, I apprehend, is the religion of the whole world; we worship God from night till morning." "Do you worship but one God?" said Cacambo, who still acted as the interpreter of Candide's doubts. "Certainly," said the old man; "there are not two, nor three, nor four gods. I must confess the people of your world ask very extraordinary questions." However, Candide could not refrain from making many more inquiries of the old man; he wanted to know in what manner they prayed to God in El Dorado.

"We do not pray to Him at all," said the reverend sage; "we have nothing to ask of Him, He has given us all we want, and we return thanks to Him incessantly." Candide had a curiosity to see some of their priests, and desired Cacambo to ask the old man where they were; the good old man smiled. "My friends, we are all of us priests; the king, and all the heads of families, sing solemn hymns of thanksgiving every morning, accompanied by five or six thousand musicians." "What! have you no monks among you, to dispute, to govern, to intrigue, and to burn people who are not of the same opinion with themselves?" "Do you take us for fools?" said the old man; "here we are all of one opinion, and know not what you mean by your monks." At all these replies Candide was in raptures, and he said to himself: "This is all very different from Westphalia and the baron's castle. Ah, if our friend Pangloss had seen El Dorado, he would no longer have maintained that the castle of Thunder-ten-tronckh was the finest in the world; and it is certain that every one should travel."

This long conversation being ended, the old man ordered six sheep to 18 be harnessed and put to the coach, and sent twelve of his servants to escort the travelers to court. "Excuse me," said he, "for not waiting on you in person; my age deprives me of that honor; the king will receive you in such a manner that you will have no reason to complain; and doubtless you will make a proper allowance for the customs of the country if there should be some that should not altogether please you."

Candide and Cacambo took their seats in the coach, the six sheep flew, 19 and in less than four hours they arrived at the king's palace, which was situated at the farther end of the capital. The portal was two hundred and twenty feet high and one hundred wide; but it is impossible for words to express the material of which it was built. It could readily be perceived that it had a prodigious superiority over the pebbles and sand, which we call gold and precious stones.

Twenty beautiful young virgins of the body-guard received Candide and 20 Cacambo on their alighting from the coach, conducted them to the bath, and clad them in robes woven of the down of humming-birds; after which they were introduced by the great officers of the crown of both sexes to the king's apartment, between two files of musicians, each a thousand in number, according to the custom of the country. When they drew near to the throne-room, Cacambo asked one of the great officers in what manner they were to pay their obeisance to His Majesty: whether it was the custom to fall upon their knees, or to prostrate themselves upon the ground; whether they were to put their hands upon their heads or upon their buttocks; whether they were to lick the dust of the floor,—in short, what was the ceremony usual on such occasions. "The custom," said the great officer, "is to embrace the king, and kiss him on each cheek." Candide and Cacambo accordingly threw their arms around His Majesty's neck, who received them in the most gracious manner imaginable, and very politely asked them to sup with him.

While supper was preparing, orders were given to show them the city, the public structures that reared their lofty heads to the clouds; the market-places decorated with a thousand columns; fountains of spring-water, fountains of rosewater, and of liquors drawn from the sugar-cane, incessantly flowing in the great squares, which were paved with a kind of precious stones that emitted an odor like that of cloves and cinnamon. Candide asked to see the high court of justice, the parliament; he was answered that there were none, and that law-suits were unknown. He inquired if they had any prisons; they replied, none. But what gave him at once the greatest surprise and pleasure was the palace of sciences, where he saw a gallery two thousand feet long, filled with various instruments of mathematics and natural philosophy. 21

After having spent the whole afternoon in seeing only about the thousandth part of the city, they were brought back to the king's palace. Candide sat down at the table with His Majesty, his valet Cacambo, and several ladies. Never was entertainment more elegant, nor could any one possibly show more wit at supper than His Majesty displayed. Cacambo explained all the king's *bonmots* to Candide, and, although they were translated, they still appeared to be *bonmots*. Of all the things that surprised Candide, this was not the least. 22

They spent a whole month in this hospitable place. But Candide was continually saying to Cacambo: "I own, my friend, once more, that the castle where I was born cannot compare with the place where we now are; but still Miss Cunegonde is not here, and you yourself have doubtless some mistress in Europe. If we remain here, we shall be only as others are; whereas, if we return to our own world with only a dozen of the El Dorado sheep, loaded with the pebbles of this country, we shall be richer than all the kings in Europe; we shall no longer need to stand in awe of the Inquisitors, and we may easily recover Miss Cunegonde." 23

This speech met with Cacambo's approval: a fondness for roving, for making a figure in your own country, for boasting of what you had seen in your travels, is so common a trait that the two happy ones resolved to be so no longer, and they demanded permission of the king to quit the country. 24

"You are about to do a stupid action," said the king. "I am sensible that my kingdom is an inconsiderable spot; but when people are tolerably at their ease in any place, it is advisable to remain there. Most assuredly, I have no right to detain any strangers against their own wills; this is an act of tyranny to which our manners and our laws are equally repugnant; all men are by nature free; you have therefore an undoubted liberty to depart whenever you please, but you will have many and great difficulties to encounter in passing the frontiers. It is impossible to ascend that rapid river, which runs under high and vaulted rocks, and by which you were conveyed hither by a kind of miracle. The mountains which enclose my 25 kingdom on all sides are ten thousand feet high, and as perpendicular as walls; they are above ten leagues in width, and the descent from them is one continued precipice. However, since you are determined to leave us, I will immediately give orders to the superintendent of machines to cause one to be made that will transport you comfortably. When they have conducted you to the back of the mountains, no one can attend you farther; for my subjects have made a vow never to quit the kingdom, and they are too prudent to break it. Ask of me whatever else you please." "All we shall ask of Your Majesty," said Cacambo, "is only a few sheep laden with provisions, pebbles, and the clay of your country." The king laughed. "I cannot imagine," said he, "what pleasure you Europeans find in our yellow clay; but take away as much of it as you will, and much good may it do you."

He immediately gave orders to his engineers to make a machine to hoist   26
these two extraordinary men out of the kingdom. Three thousand good mathematicians went to work and finished it in about fifteen days; and it did not cost more than twenty millions sterling of the money of the country. Candide and Cacambo were placed in this machine, and they took with them two large red sheep, bridled and saddled, to ride upon when they had crossed the mountains; twenty others as pack animals for carrying provisions; thirty laden with presents of whatever was most curious in the country; and fifty with gold, diamonds, and other precious stones. The king, at parting with our two adventurers, embraced them with affection.

It was a curious sight to behold the manner of their setting off, and the   27
ingenious method by which they and their sheep were hoisted to the top of the mountains. The mathematicians and engineers took leave of them as soon as they had conveyed them to a place of safety, and Candide was wholly occupied with the thoughts of presenting his sheep to Miss Cunegonde. "We have," said he, "sufficient to pay the Governor of Buenos Ayres for Miss Cunegonde, if she is redeemable. Let us make the best of our way to Cayenne, where we will take shipping, and then we may at leisure think of what kingdom we shall purchase with our riches."

Questions for Discussion and Writing

1. Verbal irony can be defined as a discrepancy between what is literally *said* and what is actually *meant*. How does Voltaire employ verbal irony in this episode from *Candide*? What is the purpose of this irony?

2. Unlike many storytellers that you may have read, Voltaire's narrator chooses to provide very little explicit commentary as he relates the adventures of Candide and his friends. What is the effect of this authorial decision on the reader? Without such explicit commentary to guide us, how do we come to understand Voltaire's intention?

3. At the conclusion of *Candide*, our hero, having traveled the world and experienced the follies and vices of people everywhere, and having lost all of his riches, tells his friends "that we must cultivate our garden." In terms of the specific lessons of the El Dorado section of the narrative, what might that dictum mean? Does the notion of cultivating one's own garden seem a proper ethic in today's society?

4. The fact that *Candide* was condemned and banned by various groups for years and years after Voltaire's death demonstrates that both irony and fictive narrative can help authors to make strong arguments about social issues. Identify a current social issue that concerns you and write a brief fictive narrative that addresses your concern. You might wish to invoke irony to help make your argument.

THOMAS PAINE

(1737–1809)

lthough he is remembered as the writer who inspired the American colonists to declare their independence in 1776, Thomas Paine was born and raised in England, and he spent a surprisingly small percentage of his years in America. The son of a poor corsetmaker, he received minimal formal schooling and was apprenticed to his father's trade at age thirteen. He ran away from home three years later and worked at a wide variety of jobs— including staymaker, excise officer, and sailor. As he could afford, he purchased books and studied to compensate for his weak formal education. Like Voltaire, Paine was an Enlightenment thinker who put great stock in reason and who sought out and addressed social inequities. He had a keen eye for injustice, and he was distressed by the destructive effects of England's class system, its enclosure movement (a policy of redefining property rights that systematically deprived a large portion of that country's small farmers of their arable land), and its corrupt, unrepresentative government. His first important pamphlet, The Case of the Officers of Excise (1772), was written to help improve the lot of his fellow laborers.

In 1774, financial difficulties drove Paine out of England. With a letter of introduction from Benjamin Franklin, he found work in America in the printing business. As the editor of the Pennsylvania Magazine, Paine published articles about social and political issues such as slavery. Soon, however, the struggle for independence from England became the all-important issue for journalists and publishers. At first, Paine favored reconciliation with England, but after the Battle of Lexington and Concord in 1775, he became convinced that the time had come to sever the tie.

Like many Americans, Paine had tired of the out-of-touch Hanoverian monarchs who had ruled England for most of the century and was frustrated by the archaic, unwieldy, largely unwritten English Constitution. He was painfully aware that the British bicameral parliamentary system, with its aristocratic House of Lords and its corruptly elected House of Commons, poorly represented the English population, not to mention the American colonists. He knew that although the colonists did have some influential English friends such as Edmund Burke, other political figures such as Lord North carried more weight and swayed the English government to adopt a harsh line against the colonies.

Acting decisively on his belief, Paine published Common Sense in January of 1776. He was by no means the first person to call for American independence, but his impassioned pamphlet had great influence and ignited passionate debate among the colonists. It sold out in a matter of days, and before long it was produced and *sold from Boston to Charleston. From America,* Common Sense *rapidly made its way to Britain and the Continent. By spring, several less successful pamphlets— including James Chalmers's stolid* Plain Truth—*were published in opposition to Paine's argument. Because of the importance of* Common Sense *to America's fight for independence, Paine is considered one of the most influential pamphleteers of all time.*

Paine left the fledgling new nation in 1787 to return to his native England. Two years later, he traveled to France to further the cause of revolution there. Paine's bold arguments continued to send shock waves through Europe and America. His controversial apology for the French Revolution, The Rights of Man *(1791–1792), was condemned in England, and his radical religious treatise,* The Age of Reason *(1794–1796), earned him the hatred of many who must have admired his earlier work. At the end of his life he returned to America, where he was received not as a hero but as a radical freethinker out of step with the morals of his age. He died, as he was born, in poverty. Twenty years later, his bones were stolen and taken to England, where they disappeared.*

COMMON SENSE

INTRODUCTION

Perhaps the sentiments contained in the following pages, are not *yet* 1 sufficiently fashionable to procure them general Favor; a long Habit of not thinking a Thing *wrong*, gives it a superficial appearance of being *right*, and raises at first a formidable outcry in defence of Custom. But the Tumult soon subsides. Time makes more Converts than Reason.

As a long and violent abuse of power is generally the means of calling 2 the right of it in question, (and in matters too which might never have been thought of, had not the sufferers been aggravated into the inquiry,) and as the King of England hath undertaken in his *own right*, to support the Parliament in what he calls *Theirs*, and as the good People of this Country are grievously oppressed by the Combination, they have an undoubted privilege to enquire into the Pretensions of both, and equally to reject the Usurpation of *either*.

In the following Sheets, the Author hath studiously avoided every thing 3 which is personal among ourselves. Compliments as well as censure to individuals make no part thereof. The wise and the worthy need not the triumph of a Pamphlet; and those whose sentiments are injudicious or unfriendly will cease of themselves, unless too much pains is bestowed upon their conversions.

The cause of America is in a great measure the cause of all mankind. 4

Many circumstances have, and will arise, which are not local, but universal, and through which the principles of all lovers of mankind are affected, and in the event of which their affections are interested. The laying a country desolate with fire and sword, declaring war against the natural rights of all mankind, and extirpating the defenders thereof from the face of the earth, is the concern of every man to whom nature hath given the power of feeling; of which class, regardless of party censure, is

The Author

POSTSCRIPT TO PREFACE IN THE THIRD EDITION

P.S. The Publication of this new Edition hath been delayed, with a view   5
of taking notice (had it been necessary) of any attempt to refute the Doctrine of Independence: As no answer hath yet appeared, it is now presumed that none will, the time needful for getting such a Performance ready for the Public being considerably past.

Who the Author of this Production is, is wholly unnecessary to the   6
Public, as the Object for Attention is the *Doctrine itself,* not the *Man.* Yet is may not be unnecessary to say, That he is unconnected with any party, and under no sort of Influence, public or private, but the influence of reason and principle.

PHILADELPHIA, FEBRUARY 14, 1776

COMMON SENSE

ON THE ORIGIN AND DESIGN OF GOVERNMENT IN GENERAL, WITH
CONCISE REMARKS ON THE ENGLISH CONSTITUTION

Some writers have so confounded society with government, as to leave little   7
or no distinction between them; whereas they are not only different, but have different origins. Society is produced by our wants, and government by our wickedness; the former promotes our happiness *positively* by uniting our affections, the latter *negatively* by restraining our vices. The one encourages intercourse, the other creates distinctions. The first is a patron, the last a punisher.

Society in every state is a blessing, but Government, even in its best   8
state, is but a necessary evil; in its worst state an intolerable one: for when we suffer, or are exposed to the same miseries *by a Government,* which we might expect in a country *without Government,* our calamity is heightened by reflecting that we furnish the means by which we suffer. Government,

like dress, is the badge of lost innocence; the palaces of kings are built upon the ruins of the bowers of paradise. For were the impulses of conscience clear, uniform and irresistibly obeyed, man would need no other lawgiver; but that not being the case, he finds it necessary to surrender up a part of his property to furnish means for the protection of the rest; and this he is induced to do by the same prudence which in every other case advises him, out of two evils to choose the least. Wherefore, security being the true design and end of government, it unanswerably follows that whatever form thereof appears most likely to ensure it to us, with the least expence and greatest benefit, is preferable to all others.

In order to gain a clear and just idea of the design and end of government,   9 let us suppose a small number of persons settled in some sequestered part of the earth, unconnected with the rest; they will then represent the first peopling of any country, or of the world. In this state of natural liberty, society will be their first thought. A thousand motives will excite them thereto; the strength of one man is so unequal to his wants, and his mind so unfitted for perpetual solitude, that he is soon obliged to seek assistance and relief of another, who in his turn requires the same. Four or five united would be able to raise a tolerable dwelling in the midst of a wilderness, but one man might labour out the common period of life without accomplishing any thing; when he had felled his timber he could not remove it, nor erect it after it was removed; hunger in the mean time would urge him to quit his work, and every different want would call him a different way. Disease, nay even misfortune, would be death; for though neither might be mortal, yet either would disable him from living, and reduce him to a state in which he might rather be said to perish than to die.

Thus necessity, like a gravitating power, would soon form our newly   10 arrived emigrants into society, the reciprocal blessings of which would supercede, and render the obligations of law and government unnecessary while they remained perfectly just to each other; but as nothing but Heaven is impregnable to vice, it will unavoidably happen that in proportion as they surmount the first difficulties of emigration, which bound them together in a common cause, they will begin to relax in their duty and attachment to each other: and this remissness will point out the necessity of establishing some form of government to supply the defect of moral virtue.

Some convenient tree will afford them a State House, under the branches   11 of which the whole Colony may assemble to deliberate on public matters. It is more than probable that their first laws will have the title only of Regulations and be enforced by no other penalty than public disesteem. In this first parliament every man by natural right will have a seat.

But as the Colony encreases, the public concerns will encrease likewise,   12 and the distance at which the members may be separated, will render it too inconvenient for all of them to meet on every occasion as at first, when their number was small, their habitations near, and the public concerns few and trifling. This will point out the convenience of their consenting to leave the legislative part to be managed by a select number chosen from the whole body, who are supposed to have the same concerns at stake which those have who appointed them, and who will act in the same manner as the whole body would act were they present. If the colony continue encreasing, it will become necessary to augment the number of representatives, and that the interest of every part of the colony may be attended to, it will be found best to divide the whole into convenient parts, each part sending its proper number: and that the *elected* might never form to themselves an interest separate from the *electors*, prudence will point out the propriety of having elections often: because as the *elected* might by that means return and mix again with the general body of the *electors* in a few months, their fidelity to the public will be secured by the prudent reflection of not making a rod for themselves. And as this frequent interchange will establish a common interest with every part of the community, they will mutually and naturally support each other, and on this, (not on the unmeaning name of king,) depends the *strength of government, and the happiness of the governed*.

Here then is the origin and rise of government; namely, a mode rendered necessary by the inability of moral virtue to govern the world; here too is the design and end of government, viz. Freedom and security. And however our eyes may be dazzled with show, or our ears deceived by sound; however prejudice may warp our wills, or interest darken our understanding, the simple voice of nature and reason will say, 'tis right. 13

I draw my idea of the form of government from a principle in nature which no art can overturn, viz. that the more simple any thing is, the less liable it is to be disordered, and the easier repaired when disordered; and with this maxim in view I offer a few remarks on the so much boasted constitution of England. That it was noble for the dark and slavish times in which it was erected, is granted. When the world was overrun with tyranny the least remove therefrom was a glorious rescue. But that it is imperfect, subject to convulsions, and incapable of producing what it seems to promise, is easily demonstrated. 14

Absolute governments, (tho' the disgrace of human nature) have this advantage with them, they are simple; if the people suffer, they know the head from which their suffering springs; know likewise the remedy; and are not bewildered by a variety of causes and cures. But the constitution of England is so exceedingly complex, that the nation may suffer for years together without being able to discover in which part the fault lies; some will say in one and some in another, and every political physician will advise a different medicine. 15

I know it is difficult to get over local or long standing prejudices, yet if we will suffer ourselves to examine the component parts of the English constitution, we shall find them to be the base remains of two ancient tyrannies, compounded with some new Republican materials. 16

First.—The remains of Monarchical tyranny in the person of the King.   17

Secondly.—The remains of Aristocratical tyranny in the persons of the   18
Peers.[1]

Thirdly.—The new Republican materials, in the persons of the Commons,[2]   19
on whose virtue depends the freedom of England.

The two first, by being hereditary, are independant of the People;   20
wherefore in a *constitutional sense* they contribute nothing towards the
freedom of the State.

To say that the constitution of England is an *union* of three powers,   21
reciprocally *checking* each other, is farcical; either the words have no
meaning, or they are flat contradictions.

To say that the Commons is a check upon the King, presupposes two   22
things.

First.—That the King is not to be trusted without being looked after; or   23
in other words, that a thirst for absolute power is the natural disease of
monarchy.

Secondly.—That the Commons, by being appointed for that purpose, are   24
either wiser or more worthy of confidence than the Crown.

But as the same constitution which gives the Commons a power to check   25
the King by withholding the supplies, gives afterwards the King a power
to check the Commons, by empowering him to reject their other bills; it
again supposes that the King is wiser than those whom it has already
supposed to be wiser than him. A mere absurdity!

There is something exceedingly ridiculous in the composition of Mon-   26
archy; it first excludes a man from the means of information, yet empowers
him to act in cases where the highest judgment is required. The state of a
king shuts him from the World, yet the business of a king requires him
to know it thoroughly; wherefore the different parts, by unnaturally opposing
and destroying each other, prove the whole character to be absurd and
useless.

Some writers have explained the English constitution thus: the King, say   27
they, is one, the people another; the Peers are a house in behalf of the
King, the commons in behalf of the people; but this hath all the distinctions
of a house divided against itself; and though the expressions be pleasantly
arranged, yet when examined they appear idle and ambiguous; and it will
always happen, that the nicest construction that words are capable of, when
applied to the description of something which either cannot exist, or is too
incomprehensible to be within the compass of description, will be words of
sound only, and though they may amuse the ear, they cannot inform the
mind: for this explanation includes a previous question, viz. *how came the
king by a power which the people are afraid to trust, and always obliged to*

---

[1] *Peers*: the British aristocracy comprising the House of Lords. [Editors' note.]

[2] *Commons*: the House of Commons. [Editors' note.]

check? Such a power could not be the gift of a wise people, neither can any power, *which needs checking*, be from God; yet the provision which the constitution makes supposes such a power to exist.

But the provision is unequal to the task; the means either cannot or will not accomplish the end, and the whole affair is a *Felo de se:*[3] for as the greater weight will always carry up the less, and as all the wheels of a machine are put in motion by one, it only remains to know which power in the constitution has the most weight, for that will govern: and tho' the others, or a part of them, may clog, or, as the phrase is, check the rapidity of its motion, yet so long as they cannot stop it, their endeavours will be ineffectual: The first moving power will at last have its way, and what it wants in speed is supplied by time.

That the crown is this overbearing part in the English constitution needs not be mentioned, and that it derives its whole consequence merely from being the giver of places and pensions is self-evident; wherefore, though we have been wise enough to shut and lock a door against absolute Monarchy, we at the same time have been foolish enough to put the Crown in possession of the key.

The prejudice of Englishmen, in favour of their own government, by King, Lords and Commons, arises as much or more from national pride than reason. Individuals are undoubtedly safer in England than in some other countries: but the will of the king is as much the law of the land in Britain as in France, with this difference, that instead of proceeding directly from his mouth, it is handed to the people under the formidable shape of an act of parliament. For the fate of Charles the First hath only made kings more subtle—not more just.

Wherefore, laying aside all national pride and prejudice in favour of modes and forms, the plain truth is that *it is wholly owing to the constitution of the people, and not to the constitution of the government* that the crown is not as oppressive in England as in Turkey.

An inquiry into the *constitutional errors* in the English form of government, is at this time highly necessary; for as we are never in a proper condition of doing justice to others, while we continue under the influence of some leading partiality, so neither are we capable of doing it to ourselves while we remain fettered by any obstinate prejudice. And as a man who is attached to a prostitute is unfitted to choose or judge of a wife, so any prepossession in favour of a rotten constitution of government will disable us from discerning a good one.

OF MONARCHY AND HEREDITARY SUCCESSION

Mankind being originally equals in the order of creation, the equality could only be destroyed by some subsequent circumstance: the distinctions of rich

[3] *Felo de se*: suicide. [Editors' note.]

and poor may in a great measure be accounted for, and that without having recourse to the harsh ill-sounding names of oppression and avarice. Oppression is often the *consequence*, but seldom or never the *means* of riches; and tho' avarice will preserve a man from being necessitously poor, it generally makes him too timorous to be wealthy.

But there is another and greater distinction for which no truly natural   34 or religious reason can be assigned, and that is the distinction of men into KINGS and SUBJECTS. Male and female are the distinctions of nature, good and bad the distinctions of Heaven; but how a race of men came into the world so exalted above the rest, and distinguished like some new species, is worth inquiring into, and whether they are the means of happiness or of misery to mankind.

In the early ages of the world, according to the scripture chronology   35 there were no kings; the consequence of which was, there were no wars; it is the pride of kings which throws mankind into confusion. Holland, without a king hath enjoyed more peace for this last century than any of the monarchical governments in Europe. Antiquity favours the same remark; for the quiet and rural lives of the first Patriarchs have a happy something in them, which vanishes when we come to the history of Jewish royalty.

Government by kings was first introduced into the world by the Heathens,   36 from whom the children of Israel copied the custom. It was the most prosperous invention the Devil ever set on foot for the promotion of idolatry. The Heathens paid divine honours to their deceased kings, and the Christian World hath improved on the plan by doing the same to their living ones. How impious is the title of sacred Majesty applied to a worm, who in the midst of his splendor is crumbling into dust!

As the exalting one man so greatly above the rest cannot be justified on   37 the equal rights of nature, so neither can it be defended on the authority of scripture; for the will of the Almighty as declared by Gideon, and the prophet Samuel, expressly disapproves of government by Kings. All anti-monarchical parts of scripture, have been very smoothly glossed over in monarchical governments, but they undoubtedly merit the attention of countries which have their governments yet to form. *Render unto Cesar the things which are Cesar's*, is the scripture doctrine of courts, yet it is no support of monarchical government, for the Jews at that time were without a king, and in a state of vassalage to the Romans.

Near three thousand years passed away, from the Mosaic account of the   38 creation, till the Jews under a national delusion requested a king. Till then their form of government (except in extraordinary cases where the Almighty interposed) was a kind of Republic, administered by a judge and the elders of the tribes. Kings they had none, and it was held sinful to acknowledge any being under that title but the Lord of Hosts. And when a man seriously reflects on the idolatrous homage which is paid to the persons of kings, he need not wonder that the Almighty, ever jealous of his honour, should disapprove a form of government which so impiously invades the prerogative of Heaven.

Monarchy is ranked in scripture as one of the sins of the Jews, for which a curse in reserve is denounced against them. The history of that transaction is worth attending to. 39

The children of Israel being oppressed by the Midianites, Gideon marched against them with a small army, and victory thro' the divine interposition decided in his favour. The Jews, elate with success, and attributing it to the generalship of Gideon, proposed making him a king, saying, *Rule thou over us, thou and thy son, and thy son's son.* Here was temptation in its fullest extent; not a kingdom only, but an hereditary one; but Gideon in the piety of his soul replied, *I will not rule over you, neither shall my son rule over you.* THE LORD SHALL RULE OVER YOU. Words need not be more explicit; Gideon doth not decline the honour, but denieth their right to give it; neither doth he compliment them with invented declarations of his thanks, but in the positive stile of a prophet charges them with disaffection to their proper Sovereign, the King of Heaven. 40

About one hundred and thirty years after this, they fell again into the same error. The hankering which the Jews had for the idolatrous customs of the Heathens, is something exceedingly unaccountable; but so it was, that laying hold of the misconduct of Samuel's two sons, who were intrusted with some secular concerns, they came in an abrupt and clamorous manner to Samuel, saying, *Behold thou art old, and thy sons walk not in thy ways, now make us a king to judge us like all the other nations.* And here we cannot but observe that their motives were bad, viz. that they might be *like* unto other nations, i.e., the Heathens, whereas their true glory lay in being as much *unlike* them as possible. *But the thing displeased Samuel when they said, give us a King to judge us; and Samuel prayed unto the Lord, and the Lord said unto Samuel, hearken unto the voice of the people in all that they say unto thee, for they have not rejected thee, but they have rejected me,* THAT I SHOULD NOT REIGN OVER THEM. *According to all the works which they have done since the day that I brought them up out of Egypt even unto this day, wherewith they have forsaken me, and served other Gods: so do they also unto thee. Now therefore hearken unto their voice, howbeit, protest solemnly unto them and show them the manner of the King that shall reign over them,* i. e. not of any particular King, but the general manner of the Kings of the earth whom Israel was so eagerly copying after. And notwithstanding the great distance of time and difference of manners, the character is still in fashion. *And Samuel told all the words of the Lord unto the people, that asked of him a King. And he said, This shall be the manner of the King that shall reign over you. He will take your sons and appoint them for himself for his chariots and to be his horsemen, and some shall run before his chariots* (this description agrees with the present mode of impressing men) *and he will appoint him captains over thousands and captains over fifties, will set them to ear his ground and to* 41 *reap his harvest, and to make his instruments of war, and instruments of his chariots. And he will take your daughters to be confectionaries, and to be cooks, and to be bakers* (this describes the expense and luxury as well as the oppression of Kings) *and he will take your fields and your vineyards, and your olive yards, even the best of them, and give them to his servants. And he will take the tenth of your seed, and of your vineyards, and give them to his officers and to his servants* (by which we see that bribery, corruption, and favouritism, are the standing vices of Kings) *and he will take the tenth of your men servants, and your maid servants, and your goodliest young men, and your asses, and put them to his work: and he will take the tenth of your sheep, and ye shall be his servants, and ye shall cry out in that day because of your king which ye shall have chosen,* AND THE LORD WILL NOT HEAR YOU IN THAT DAY. This accounts for the continuation of Monarchy; neither do the characters of the few good kings which have lived since, either sanctify the title, or blot out the sinfulness of the origin; the high encomium given of David takes no notice of him *officially as a King,* but only as a *Man* after God's own heart. *Nevertheless the people refused to obey the voice of Samuel, and they said, Nay but we will have a king over us, that we may be like all the nations, and that our king may judge us, and go out before us and fight our battles.* Samuel continued to reason with them but to no purpose; he set before them their ingratitude, but all would not avail; and seeing them fully bent on their folly, he cried out, *I will call unto the Lord, and he shall send thunder and rain* (which was then a punishment, being in the time of wheat harvest) *that ye may perceive and see that your wickedness is great which ye have done in the sight of the Lord,* IN ASKING YOU A KING. *So Samuel called unto the Lord, and the Lord sent thunder and rain that day, and all the people greatly feared the Lord and Samuel. And all the people said unto Samuel, Pray for thy servants unto the Lord thy God that we die not, for* WE HAVE ADDED UNTO OUR SINS THIS EVIL, TO ASK A KING. These portions of scripture are direct and positive. They admit of no equivocal construction. That the Almighty hath here entered his protest against monarchical government is true, or the scripture is false. And a man hath good reason to believe that there is as much of kingcraft as priestcraft in withholding the scripture from the public in popish countries. For monarchy in every instance is the popery of government.

To the evil of monarchy we have added that of hereditary succession; and as the first is a degradation and lessening of ourselves, so the second, claimed as a matter of right, is an insult and imposition on posterity. For all men being originally equals, no one by birth could have a right to set up his own family in perpetual preference to all others for ever, and tho' himself might deserve some decent degree of honours of his cotemporaries, yet his descendants might be far too unworthy to inherit them. One of the strongest natural proofs of the folly of hereditary right in Kings, is that nature disapproves it, otherwise she would not so frequently turn it into ridicule, by giving mankind an *Ass for a Lion.* 42

Secondly, as no man at first could possess any other public honors than   43
were bestowed upon him, so the givers of those honors could have no power
to give away the right of posterity, and though they might say "We choose
you for our head," they could not without manifest injustice to their children
say "that your children and your children's children shall reign over ours
forever." Because such an unwise, unjust, unnatural compact might (perhaps)
in the next succession put them under the government of a rogue or a fool.
Most wise men in their private sentiments have ever treated hereditary
right with contempt; yet it is one of those evils which when once established
is not easily removed; many submit from fear, others from superstition,
and the more powerful part shares with the king the plunder of the rest.

This is supposing the present race of kings in the world to have had an   44
honorable origin: whereas it is more than probable, that, could we take off
the dark covering of antiquity and trace them to their first rise, we should
find the first of them nothing better than the principal ruffian of some
restless gang, whose savage manners or pre-eminence in subtilty obtained
him the title of chief among plunderers: and who by increasing in power
and extending his depredations, overawed the quiet and defenceless to
purchase their safety by frequent contributions. Yet his electors could have
no idea of giving hereditary right to his descendants, because such a
perpetual exclusion of themselves was incompatible with the free and
unrestrained principles they professed to live by. Wherefore, hereditary
succession in the early ages of monarchy could not take place as a matter of
claim, but as something casual or complemental; but as few or no records
were extant in those days, and traditionary history stuff'd with fables, it
was very easy, after the lapse of a few generations, to trump up some
superstitious tale conveniently timed, Mahomet-like, to cram hereditary
right down the throats of the vulgar. Perhaps the disorders which threatened,
or seemed to threaten, on the decease of a leader and the choice of a new
one (for elections among ruffians could not be very orderly) induced many
at first to favour hereditary pretensions; by which means it happened, as it
hath happened since, that what at first was submitted to as a convenience
was afterwards claimed as a right.

England since the conquest hath known some few good monarchs, but   45
groaned beneath a much larger number of bad ones: yet no man in his
senses can say that their claim under William the Conqueror is a very
honourable one. A French bastard landing with an armed Banditti and
establishing himself king of England against the consent of the natives, is
in plain terms a very paltry rascally original. It certainly hath no divinity
in it. However it is needless to spend much time in exposing the folly of
hereditary right; if there are any so weak as to believe it, let them pro-
miscuously worship the Ass and the Lion, and welcome. I shall neither
copy their humility, nor disturb their devotion.

Yet I should be glad to ask how they suppose kings came at first? The   46
46   question admits but of three answers, viz. either by lot, by election, or by

usurpation. If the first king was taken by lot, it establishes a precedent for the next, which excludes hereditary succession. Saul was by lot, yet the succession was not hereditary, neither does it appear from that transaction that there was any intention it ever should. If the first king of any country was by election, that likewise establishes a precedent for the next; for to say, that the right of all future generations is taken away, by the act of the first electors, in their choice not only of a king but of a family of kings for ever, hath no parallel in or out of scripture but the doctrine of original sin, which supposes the free will of all men lost in Adam; and from such comparison, and it will admit of no other, hereditary succession can derive no glory. For as in Adam all sinned, and as in the first electors all men obeyed; as in the one all mankind were subjected to Satan, and in the other to sovereignty; as our innocence was lost in the first, and our authority in the last; and as both disable us from re-assuming some former state and privilege, it unanswerably follows that original sin and hereditary succession are parallels. Dishonourable rank! inglorious connection! yet the most subtle sophist cannot produce a juster simile.

As to usurpation, no man will be so hardy as to defend it; and that 47 William the Conqueror was an usurper is a fact not to be contradicted. The plain truth is, that the antiquity of English monarchy will not bear looking into.

But it is not so much the absurdity as the evil of hereditary succession 48 which concerns mankind. Did it ensure a race of good and wise men it would have the seal of divine authority, but as it opens a door to the *foolish*, the *wicked*, and the *improper*, it hath in it the nature of oppression. Men who look upon themselves born to reign, and others to obey, soon grow insolent. Selected from the rest of mankind, their minds are early poisoned by importance; and the world they act in differs so materially from the world at large, that they have but little opportunity of knowing its true interests, and when they succeed to the government are frequently the most ignorant and unfit of any throughout the dominions.

Another evil which attends hereditary succession is, that the throne is 49 subject to be possessed by a minor at any age; all which time the regency acting under the cover of a king have every opportunity and inducement to betray their trust. The same national misfortune happens when a king worn out with age and infirmity enters the last stage of human weakness. In both these cases the public becomes a prey to every miscreant who can tamper successfully with the follies either of age or infancy.

The most plausible plea which hath ever been offered in favor of 50 hereditary succession is, that it preserves a nation from civil wars; and were this true, it would be weighty; whereas it is the most bare-faced falsity ever imposed upon mankind. The whole history of England disowns the fact. Thirty kings and two minors have reigned in that distracted kingdom since the conquest, in which time there has been (including the revolution) no less than eight civil wars and nineteen Rebellions. Wherefore instead of making for peace, it makes against it, and destroys the very foundation it seems to stand upon.

The contest for monarchy and succession, between the houses of York 51 and Lancaster, laid England in a scene of blood for many years. Twelve pitched battles besides skirmishes and sieges were fought between Henry and Edward. Twice was Henry prisoner to Edward, who in his turn was prisoner to Henry. And so uncertain is the fate of war and the temper of a nation, when nothing but personal matters are the ground of a quarrel, that Henry was taken in triumph from a prison to a palace, and Edward obliged to fly from a palace to a foreign land; yet, as sudden transitions of temper are seldom lasting, Henry in his turn was driven from the throne, and Edward re-called to succeed him. The parliament always following the strongest side.

This contest began in the reign of Henry the Sixth, and was not entirely 52 extinguished till Henry the Seventh, in whom the families were united. Including a period of 67 years, viz. from 1422 to 1489.

In short, monarchy and succession have laid (not this or that kingdom 53 only) but the world in blood and ashes. 'Tis a form of government which the word of God bears testimony against, and blood will attend it.

If we enquire into the business of a King, we shall find that in some 54 countries they may have none; and after sauntering away their lives without pleasure to themselves or advantage to the nation, withdraw from the scene, and leave their successors to tread the same idle round. In absolute monarchies the whole weight of business civil and military lies on the King; the children of Israel in their request for a king urged this plea, "that he may judge us, and go out before us and fight our battles." But in countries where he is neither a Judge nor a General, as in England, a man would be puzzled to know what *is* his business.

The nearer any government approaches to a Republic, the less business 55 there is for a King. It is somewhat difficult to find a proper name for the government of England. Sir William Meredith calls it a Republic; but in its present state it is unworthy of the name, because the corrupt influence of the Crown, by having all the places in its disposal, hath so effectually swallowed up the power, and eaten out the virtue of the House of Commons (the Republican part in the constitution) that the government of England is nearly as monarchical as that of France or Spain. Men fall out with names without understanding them. For 'tis the Republican and not the Monarchical part of the constitution of England which Englishmen glory in, viz. the liberty of choosing an House of Commons from out of their own body—and it is easy to see that when Republican virtues fails, slavery ensues. Why is the constitution of England sickly, but because monarchy hath poisoned the Republic; the Crown hath engrossed the Commons.

In England a King hath little more to do than to make war and give 56 away places; which, in plain terms, is to empoverish the nation and set it together by the ears. A pretty business indeed for a man to be allowed eight hundred thousand sterling a year for, and worshipped into the bargain! Of more worth is one honest man to society, and in the sight of God, than all the crowned ruffians that ever lived.

THOUGHTS ON THE PRESENT STATE OF AMERICAN AFFAIRS

In the following pages I offer nothing more than simple facts, plain 57 arguments, and common sense: and have no other preliminaries to settle with the reader, than that he will divest himself of prejudice and prepossession, and suffer his reason and his feelings to determine for themselves: that he will put on, or rather that he will not put off, the true character of a man, and generously enlarge his views beyond the present day.

Volumes have been written on the subject of the struggle between England 58 and America. Men of all ranks have embarked in the controversy, from different motives, and with various designs; but all have been ineffectual, and the period of debate is closed. Arms as the last resource decide the contest; the appeal was the choice of the King, and the Continent has accepted the challenge.

It hath been reported of the late Mr. Pelham (who tho' an able minister 59 was not without his faults) that on his being attacked in the House of Commons on the score that his measures were only of a temporary kind, replied, *"they will last my time."* Should a thought so fatal and unmanly possess the Colonies in the present contest, the names of ancestors will be remembered by future generations with detestation.

The Sun never shined on a cause of greater worth. 'Tis not the affair of 60 a City, a County, a Province, or a Kingdom; but of a Continent—of at least one eighth part of the habitable Globe. 'Tis not the concern of a day, a year, or an age; posterity are virtually involved in the contest, and will be more or less affected even to the end of time, by the proceedings now. Now is the seed-time of Continental union, faith and honour. The least fracture now will be like a name engraved with the point of a pin on the tender rind of a young oak; the wound would enlarge with the tree, and posterity read it in full grown characters.

By referring the matter from argument to arms, a new æra for politics 61 is struck—a new method of thinking hath arisen. All plans, proposals, &c. prior to the nineteenth of April, *i.e.* to the commencement of hostilities,[4] are like the almanacks of the last year; which tho' proper then, are superceded and useless now. Whatever was advanced by the advocates on either side of the question then, terminated in one and the same point, viz. a union with Great Britain; the only difference between the parties was the method of effecting it; the one proposing force, the other friendship; but it hath so

---

[4] *hostilities:* the Battle of Lexington and Concord in 1775. [Editors' note.]

far happened that the first hath failed, and the second hath withdrawn her influence.

As much hath been said of the advantages of reconciliation, which, like 62 an agreeable dream, hath passed away and left us as we were, it is but right that we should examine the contrary side of the argument, and enquire into some of the many material injuries which these Colonies sustain, and always will sustain, by being connected with and dependant on Great-Britain. To examine that connection and dependance, on the principles of nature and common sense, to see what we have to trust to, if separated, and what we are to expect, if dependant.

I have heard it asserted by some, that as America has flourished under 63 her former connection with Great-Britain, the same connection is necessary towards her future happiness, and will always have the same effect. Nothing can be more fallacious than this kind of argument. We may as well assert that because a child has thrived upon milk, that it is never to have meat, or that the first twenty years of our lives is to become a precedent for the next twenty. But even this is admitting more than is true; for I answer roundly, that America would have flourished as much, and probably much more, had no European power taken any notice of her. The commerce by which she hath enriched herself are the necessaries of life, and will always have a market while eating is the custom of Europe.

But she has protected us, say some. That she hath engrossed us is true, 64 and defended the Continent at our expense as well as her own, is admitted; and she would have defended Turkey from the same motive, *viz.* for the sake of trade and dominion.

Alas! we have been long led away by ancient prejudices and made large 65 sacrifices to superstition. We have boasted the protection of Great Britain, without considering, that her motive was *interest* not *attachment*; and that she did not protect us from *our enemies* on *our account*; but from *her enemies* on *her own account*, from those who had no quarrel with us on any *other account*, and who will always be our enemies on the *same account*. Let Britain waive her pretensions to the Continent, or the Continent throw off the dependance, and we should be at peace with France and Spain, were they at war with Britain. The miseries of Hanover last war ought to warn us against connections.

It hath lately been asserted in parliament, that the Colonies have no 66 relation to each other but through the Parent Country, *i.e.* that Pennsylvania and the Jerseys, and so on for the rest, are sister Colonies by the way of England; this is certainly a very roundabout way of proving relationship, but it is the nearest and only true way of proving enmity (or enemyship, if I may so call it.) France and Spain never were, nor perhaps ever will be, our enemies as *Americans*, but as our being the *subjects of Great Britain*.

But Britain is the parent country, say some. Then the more shame upon 67 her conduct. Even brutes do not devour their young, nor savages make war upon their families; Wherefore, the assertion, if true, turns to her reproach; but it happens not to be true, or only partly so, and the phrase *parent* or *mother country* hath been jesuitically adopted by the King and his parasites, with a low papistical design of gaining an unfair bias on the credulous weakness of our minds. Europe, and not England, is the parent country of America. This new World hath been the asylum for the persecuted lovers of civil and religious liberty from *every part* of Europe. Hither have they fled, not from the tender embraces of the mother, but from the cruelty of the monster; and it is so far true of England, that the same tyranny which drove the first emigrants from home, pursues their descendants still.

In this extensive quarter of the globe, we forget the narrow limits of   68
three hundred and sixty miles (the extent of England) and carry our friendship on a larger scale; we claim brotherhood with every European Christian, and triumph in the generosity of the sentiment.

It is pleasant to observe by what regular gradations we surmount the   69
force of local prejudices, as we enlarge our acquaintance with the World. A man born in any town in England divided into parishes, will naturally associate most with his fellow parishioners (because their interests in many cases will be common) and distinguish him by the name of *neighbour;* if he meet him but a few miles from home, he drops the narrow idea of a street, and salutes him by the name of *townsman;* if he travel out of the county and meet him in any other, he forgets the minor divisions of street and town, and calls him *countryman, i.e. countyman:* but if in their foreign excursions they should associate in France, or any other part of *Europe,* their local remembrance would be enlarged into that of *Englishmen.* And by a just parity of reasoning, all Europeans meeting in America; or any other quarter of the globe, are *countrymen;* for England, Holland, Germany, or Sweden, when compared with the whole, stand in the same places on the larger scale, which the divisions of street, town, and county do on the smaller ones; Distinctions too limited for Continental minds. Not one third of the inhabitants, even of this province, [Pennsylvania], are of English descent. Wherefore, I reprobate the phrase of Parent or Mother Country applied to England only, as being false, selfish, narrow and ungenerous.

But, admitting that we were all of English descent, what does it amount   70
to? Nothing. Britain, being now an open enemy, extinguishes every other name and title: and to say that reconciliation is our duty, is truly farcical. The first king of England, of the present line (William the Conqueror) was a Frenchman, and half the peers of England are descendants from the same country; wherefore, by the same method of reasoning, England ought to be governed by France.

Much hath been said of the united strength of Britain and the Colonies,   71
that in conjunction they might bid defiance to the world: But this is mere presumption; the fate of war is uncertain, neither do the expressions mean any thing; for this continent would never suffer itself to be drained of inhabitants, to support the British arms in either Asia, Africa, or Europe.

Besides, what have we to do with setting the world at defiance? Our plan 72
is commerce, and that, well attended to, will secure us the peace and
friendship of all Europe; because it is the interest of all Europe to have
America a free port. Her trade will always be a protection, and her bar-
renness of gold and silver secure her from invaders.

I challenge the warmest advocate for reconciliation to show a single 73
advantage that this continent can reap by being connected with Great Britain.
I repeat the challenge; not a single advantage is derived. Our corn will
fetch its price in any market in Europe, and our imported goods must be
paid for buy them where we will.

But the injuries and disadvantages which we sustain by that connection, 74
are without number; and our duty to mankind at large, as well as to
ourselves, instruct us to renounce the alliance: because, any submission to,
or dependance on, Great Britain, tends directly to involve this Continent
in European wars and quarrels, and set us at variance with nations who
would otherwise seek our friendship, and against whom we have neither
anger nor complaint. As Europe is our market for trade, we ought to form
no partial connection with any part of it. It is the true interest of America
to steer clear of European contentions, which she never can do, while, by
her dependance on Britain, she is made the make-weight in the scale of
British politics.

Europe is too thickly planted with Kingdoms to be long at peace, and 75
whenever a war breaks out between England and any foreign power, the
trade of America goes to ruin, *because of her connection with Britain.* The
next war may not turn out like the last, and should it not, the advocates
for reconciliation now will be wishing for separation then, because neutrality
in that case would be a safer convoy than a man of war. Every thing that
is right or reasonable pleads or separation. The blood of the slain, the
weeping voice of nature cries, 'TIS TIME TO PART. Even the distance at
which the Almighty hath placed England and America is a strong and
natural proof that the authority of the one over the other, was never the
design of Heaven. The time likewise at which the Continent was discovered,
adds weight to the argument, and the manner in which it was peopled,
encreases the force of it. The Reformation was preceded by the discovery
of America: As if the Almighty graciously meant to open a sanctuary to the
persecuted in future years, when home should afford neither friendship nor
safety.

The authority of Great Britain over this continent, is a form of government, 76
which sooner or later must have an end: And a serious mind can draw no
true pleasure by looking forward, under the painful and positive conviction
that what he calls "the present constitution" is merely temporary. As parents,
we can have no joy, knowing that this government is not sufficiently lasting
to ensure any thing which we may bequeath to posterity: And by a plain
method of argument, as we are running the next generation into debt, we
ought to do the work of it, otherwise we use them meanly and pitifully. In

order to discover the line of our duty rightly, we should take our children in our hand, and fix our station a few years farther into life; that eminence will present a prospect which a few present fears and prejudices conceal from our sight.

Though I would carefully avoid giving unnecessary offence, yet I am   77
inclined to believe, that all those who espouse the doctrine of reconciliation, may be included within the following descriptions.

Interested men, who are not to be trusted, weak men who *cannot* see,   78
prejudiced men who will not see, and a certain set of moderate men who think better of the European world than it deserves; and this last class, by an ill-judged deliberation, will be the cause of more calamities to this Continent than all the other three.

It is the good fortune of many to live distant from the scene of present   79
sorrow; the evil is not sufficiently brought to their doors to make them feel the precariousness with which all American property is possessed. But let our imaginations transport us a few moments to Boston; that seat of wretchedness will teach us wisdom, and instruct us for ever to renounce a power in whom we can have no trust. The inhabitants of that unfortunate city who but a few months ago were in ease and affluence, have now no other alternative than to stay and starve, or turn out to beg. Endangered by the fire of their friends if they continue within the city, and plundered by the soldiery if they leave it, in their present situation they are prisoners without the hope of redemption, and in a general attack for their relief they would be exposed to the fury of both armies.

Men of passive tempers look somewhat lightly over the offences of Great   80
Britain, and, still hoping for the best, are apt to call out, *Come, come, we shall be friends again for all this*. But examine the passions and feelings of mankind: bring the doctrine of reconciliation to the touchstone of nature, and then tell me whether you can hereafter love, honour, and faithfully serve the power that hath carried fire and sword into your land? If you cannot do all these, then are you only deceiving yourselves, and by your delay bringing ruin upon posterity. Your future connection with Britain, whom you can neither love nor honour, will be forced and unnatural, and being formed only on the plan of present convenience, will in a little time fall into a relapse more wretched than the first. But if you say, you can still pass the violations over, then I ask, hath your house been burnt? Hath your property been destroyed before your face? Are your wife and children destitute of a bed to lie on, or bread to live on? Have you lost a parent or a child by their hands, and yourself the ruined and wretched survivor? If you have not, then are you not a judge of those who have. But if you have, and can still shake hands with the murderers, then are you unworthy the name of husband, father, friend, or lover, and whatever may be your rank or title in life, you have the heart of a coward, and the spirit of a sycophant.

This is not inflaming or exaggerating matters, but trying them by those   81
feelings and affections which nature justifies, and without which we should

be incapable of discharging the social duties of life, or enjoying the felicities of it. I mean not to exhibit horror for the purpose of provoking revenge, but to awaken us from fatal and unmanly slumbers, that we may pursue determinately some fixed object. 'Tis not in the power of Britain or of Europe to conquer America, if she doth not conquer herself by delay and timidity. The present winter is worth an age if rightly employed, but if lost or neglected the whole Continent will partake of the misfortune; and there is no punishment which that man doth not deserve, be he who, or what, or where he will, that may be the means of sacrificing a season so precious and useful.

'Tis repugnant to reason, to the universal order of things, to all examples 82 from former ages, to suppose that this Continent can long remain subject to any external power. The most sanguine in Britain doth not think so. The utmost stretch of human wisdom cannot, at this time, compass a plan, short of separation, which can promise the continent even a year's security. Reconciliation is *now* a fallacious dream. Nature hath deserted the connection, and art cannot supply her place. For, as Milton wisely expresses, "never can true reconcilement grow where wounds of deadly hate have pierced so deep."

Every quiet method for peace hath been ineffectual. Our prayers have 83 been rejected with disdain; and hath tended to convince us that nothing flatters vanity or confirms obstinacy in Kings more than repeated petition- ing—and nothing hath contributed more than that very measure to make the Kings of Europe absolute. Witness Denmark and Sweden. Wherefore, since nothing but blows will do, for God's sake let us come to a final separation, and not leave the next generation to be cutting throats under the violated unmeaning names of parent and child.

To say they will never attempt it again is idle and visionary; we thought 84 so at the repeal of the stamp act, yet a year or two undeceived us; as well may we suppose that nations which have been once defeated will never renew the quarrel.

As to government matters, 'tis not in the power of Britain to do this 85 continent justice: the business of it will soon be too weighty and intricate to be managed with any tolerable degree of convenience, by a power so distant from us, and so very ignorant of us; for if they cannot conquer us, they cannot govern us. To be always running three or four thousand miles with a tale or a petition, waiting four or five months for an answer, which, when obtained, requires five or six more to explain it in, will in a few years be looked upon as folly and childishness. There was a time when it was proper, and there is a proper time for it to cease.

Small islands not capable of protecting themselves are the proper objects 86 for government to take under their care; but there is something absurd, in supposing a Continent to be perpetually governed by an island. In no instance hath nature made the satellite larger than its primary planet; and as England and America, with respect to each other, reverse the common order of nature, it is evident that they belong to different systems. England to Europe: America to itself.

I am not induced by motives of pride, party, or resentment to espouse the doctrine of separation and independence; I am clearly, positively, and conscientiously persuaded that it is the true interest of this Continent to be so; that every thing short of *that* is mere patchwork, that it can afford no lasting felicity,—that it is leaving the sword to our children, and shrinking back at a time when a little more, a little further, would have rendered this Continent the glory of the earth. 87

As Britain hath not manifested the least inclination towards a compromise, we may be assured that no terms can be obtained worthy the acceptance of the Continent, or any ways equal to the expence of blood and treasure we have been already put to. 88

The object contended for, ought always to bear some just proportion to the expense. The removal of North, or the whole detestable junto, is a matter unworthy the millions we have expended. A temporary stoppage of trade was an inconvenience, which would have sufficiently ballanced the repeal of all the acts complained of, had such repeals been obtained; but if the whole Continent must take up arms, if every man must be a soldier, 'tis scarcely worth our while to fight against a contemptible ministry only. Dearly, dearly do we pay for the repeal of the acts, if that is all we fight for; for, in a just estimation 'tis as great a folly to pay a Bunker-hill price for law as for land. As I have always considered the independancy of this continent, as an event which sooner or later must arrive, so from the late rapid progress of the Continent to maturity, the event cannot be far off. Wherefore, on the breaking out of hostilities, it was not worth the while to have disputed a matter which time would have finally redressed, unless we meant to be in earnest: otherwise it is like wasting an estate on a suit at law, to regulate the trespasses of a tenant whose lease is just expiring. No man was a warmer wisher for a reconciliation than myself, before the fatal nineteenth of April, 1775, but the moment the event of that day was made known, I rejected the hardened, sullen-tempered Pharaoh of England for ever; and disdain the wretch, that with the pretended title of FATHER OF HIS PEOPLE can unfeelingly hear of their slaughter, and composedly sleep with their blood upon his soul. 89

But admitting that matters were now made up, what would be the event? I answer, the ruin of the Continent. And that for several reasons. 90

First. The power of governing still remaining in the hands of the King, he will have a negative over the whole legislation of this Continent. And as he hath shown himself such an inveterate enemy to liberty, and discovered such a thirst for arbitrary power, is he, or is he not, a proper person to say to these colonies, *You shall make no laws but what I please!?* And is there any inhabitant of America so ignorant as not to know, that according to what is called the *present constitution*, this Continent can make no laws but what the king gives leave to; and is there any man so unwise as not to see, 91 that (considering what has happened) he will suffer no law to be made here but such as suits *his* purpose? We may be as effectually enslaved by the want of laws in America, as by submitting to laws made for us in England. After matters are made up (as it is called) can there be any doubt, but the whole power of the crown will be exerted to keep this continent as low and humble as possible? Instead of going forward we shall go backward, or be perpetually quarrelling, or ridiculously petitioning. We are already greater than the King wishes us to be, and will he not hereafter endeavor to make us less? To bring the matter to one point, Is the power who is jealous of our prosperity, a proper power to govern us? Whoever says *No*, to this question, is an Independant for independency means no more than this, whether we shall make our own laws, or, whether the King, the greatest enemy this continent hath, or can have, shall tell us *there shall be no laws but such as I like.*

But the King, you will say, has a negative in England; the people there 92 can make no laws without his consent. In point of right and good order, it is something very ridiculous that a youth of twenty-one (which hath often happened) shall say to several millions of people older and wiser than himself, "I forbid this or that act of yours to be law." But in this place I decline this sort of reply, though I will never cease to expose the absurdity of it, and only answer that England being the King's residence, and America not so, makes quite another case. The King's negative here is ten times more dangerous and fatal than it can be in England; for there he will scarcely refuse his consent to a bill for putting England into as strong a state of defense as possible, and in America he would never suffer such a bill to be passed.

America is only a secondary object in the system of British politics. 93 England consults the good of this country no further than it answers her own purpose. Wherefore, her own interest leads her to suppress the growth of ours in every case which doth not promote her advantage, or in the least interferes with it. A pretty state we should soon be in under such a second hand government, considering what has happened! Men do not change from enemies to friends by the alteration of a name: And in order to show that reconciliation now is a dangerous doctrine, I affirm, *that it would be policy in the King at this time to repeal the acts, for the sake of reinstating himself in the government of the provinces;* In order that HE MAY ACCOMPLISH BY CRAFT AND SUBTLETY, IN THE LONG RUN, WHAT HE CANNOT DO BY FORCE AND VIOLENCE IN THE SHORT ONE. Reconciliation and ruin are nearly related.

Secondly. That as even the best terms which we can expect to obtain can 94 amount to no more than a temporary expedient, or a kind of government by guardianship, which can last no longer than till the Colonies come of age, so the general face and state of things in the interim will be unsettled and unpromising. Emigrants of property will not choose to come to a country whose form of government hangs but by a thread, and who is every day tottering on the brink of commotion and disturbance; and numbers of the present inhabitants would lay hold of the interval to dispose of their effects, and quit the Continent.

But the most powerful of all arguments is, that nothing but independance, 95 *i. e.* a Continental form of government, can keep the peace of the Continent and preserve it inviolate from civil wars. I dread the event of a reconciliation with Britain now, as it is more than probable that it will be followed by a revolt some where or other, the consequences of which may be far more fatal than all the malice of Britain.

Thousands are already ruined by British barbarity; (thousands more will 96 probably suffer the same fate.) Those men have other feelings than us who have nothing suffered. All they now possess is liberty; what they before enjoyed is sacrificed to its service, and having nothing more to lose they disdain submission. Besides, the general temper of the Colonies, towards a British government will be like that of a youth who is nearly out of his time; they will care very little about her: And a government which cannot preserve the peace is no government at all, and in that case we pay our money for nothing; and pray what is it that Britain can do, whose power will be wholly on paper, should a civil tumult break out the very day after reconciliation? I have heard some men say, many of whom I believe spoke without thinking, that they dreaded an independance, fearing that it would produce civil wars: It is but seldom that our first thoughts are truly correct, and that is the case here; for there is ten times more to dread from a patched up connection than from independance. I make the sufferer's case my own, and I protest, that were I driven from house and home, my property destroyed, and my circumstances ruined, that as a man, sensible of injuries, I could never relish the doctrine of reconciliation, or consider myself bound thereby.

The Colonies have manifested such a spirit of good order and obedience 97 to Continental government, as is sufficient to make every reasonable person easy and happy on that head. No man can assign the least pretence for his fears, on any other grounds, than such as are truly childish and ridiculous, viz., that one colony will be striving for superiority over another.

Where there are no distinctions there can be no superiority; perfect 98 equality affords no temptation. The Republics of Europe are all (and we may say always) in peace. Holland and Switzerland are without wars, foreign or domestic: Monarchical governments, it is true, are never long at rest: the crown itself is a temptation to enterprising ruffians at home; and that degree of pride and insolence ever attendant on regal authority, swells into a rupture with foreign powers in instances where a republican government, by being formed on more natural principles, would negociate the mistake.

If there is any true cause of fear respecting independance, it is because 99 no plan is yet laid down. Men do not see their way out. Wherefore, as an opening into that business I offer the following hints; at the same time modestly affirming, that I have no other opinion of them myself, than that they may be the means of giving rise to something better. Could the straggling thoughts of individuals be collected, they would frequently form materials for wise and able men to improve into useful matter.

Let the assemblies be annual, with a president only. The representation 100 more equal, their business wholly domestic, and subject to the authority of a Continental Congress.

Let each Colony be divided into six, eight, or ten, convenient districts, 101 each district to send a proper number of Delegates to Congress, so that each Colony send at least thirty. The whole number in Congress will be at least 390. Each congress to sit and to choose a President by the following method. When the Delegates are met, let a Colony be taken from the whole thirteen Colonies by lot, after which let the Congress choose (by ballot) a president from out of the Delegates of that Province. In the next Congress, let a colony be taken by lot from twelve only, omitting that Colony from which the president was taken in the former Congress, and so proceeding on till the whole thirteen shall have had their proper rotation. And in order that nothing may pass into a law but what is satisfactorily just, not less than three fifths of the Congress to be called a majority. He that will promote discord, under a government so equally formed as this, would have joined Lucifer in his revolt.

But as there is a peculiar delicacy from whom, or in what manner, this 102 business must first arise, and as it seems most agreeable and consistent that it should come from some intermediate body between the governed and the governors, that is, between the Congress and the People, let a Continental Conference be held in the following manner, and for the following purpose,

A Committee of twenty six members of congress, *viz.* Two for each 103 Colony. Two Members from each House of Assembly, or Provincial Convention; and five Representatives of the people at large, to be chosen in the capital city or town of each Province, for, and in behalf of the whole Province, by as many qualified voters as shall think proper to attend from all parts of the Province for that purpose; or, if more convenient, the Representatives may be chosen in two or three of the most populous parts thereof. In this conference, thus assembled, will be united the two grand principles of business, *knowledge* or *power*. The Members of Congress, Assemblies, or Conventions, by having had experience in national concerns, will be able and useful counsellors, and the whole, being impowered by the people, will have a truly legal authority.

The conferring members being met, let their business be to frame a 104 Continental Charter, or Charter of the United Colonies; (answering to what is called the Magna Charta of England) fixing the number and manner of choosing Members of Congress, Members of Assembly, with their date of sitting; and drawing the line of business and jurisdiction between them: Always remembering, that our strength is Continental, not Provincial. Securing freedom and property to all men, and above all things, the free exercise of religion, according to the dictates of conscience; with such other matter as it is necessary for a charter to contain. Immediately after which, the said conference to dissolve, and the bodies which shall be chosen conformable to the said charter, to be the Legislators and Governors of this Continent for the time being: Whose peace and happiness, may GOD preserve. AMEN.

Should any body of men be hereafter delegated for this or some similar 105 purpose, I offer them the following extracts from that wise observer on Governments, Dragonetti. "The science," says he, "of the Politician consists in fixing the true point of happiness and freedom. Those men would deserve the gratitude of ages, who should discover a mode of government that contained the greatest sum of individual happiness, with the least national expense." (Dragonetti on "Virtues and Reward.")

But where, say some, is the King of America? I'll tell you, friend, he 106 reigns above, and doth not make havoc of mankind like the Royal Brute of Great Britain. Yet that we may not appear to be defective even in earthly honours, let a day be solemnly set apart for proclaiming the Charter; let it be brought forth placed on the Divine Law, the Word of God; let a crown be placed thereon, by which the world may know, that so far as we approve of monarchy, that in America the law is king. For as in absolute governments the King is law, so in free countries the law ought to be king; and there ought to be no other. But lest any ill use should afterwards arise, let the Crown at the conclusion of the ceremony be demolished, and scattered among the people whose right it is.

A government of our own is our natural right: and when a man seriously 107 reflects on the precariousness of human affairs, he will become convinced, that it is infinitely wiser and safer, to form a constitution of our own in a cool deliberate manner, while we have it in our power, than to trust such as interesting event to time and chance. If we omit it now, some Massanello[5] may hereafter arise, who, laying hold of popular disquietudes, may collect together the desperate and the discontented, and by assuming to themselves the powers of government, finally sweep away the liberties of the Continent like a deluge. Should the government of America return again into the hands of Britain, the tottering situation of things will be a temptation for some desperate adventurer to try his fortune; and in such a case, what relief can Britain give? Ere she could hear the news, the fatal business might be done; and ourselves suffering like the wretched Britons under the oppression of the Conqueror. Ye that oppose independance now, ye know not what ye do: ye are opening a door to eternal tyranny, by keeping vacant the seat of

[5] Thomas Anello, otherwise Massanello, a fisherman of Naples, who after spiriting up his countrymen in the public market place, against the oppression of the Spaniards, to whom the place was then subject, prompted them to revolt, and in the space of a day became King. [Author's note.]

government. There are thousands and tens of thousands, who would think it glorious to expel from the Continent, that barbarous and hellish power, which hath stirred up the Indians and the Negroes to destroy us; the cruelty hath a double guilt, it is dealing brutally by us, and treacherously by them.

To talk of friendship with those in whom our reason forbids us to have 108 faith, and our affections wounded thro' a thousand pores instruct us to detest, is madness and folly. Every day wears out the little remains of kindred between us and them; and can there be any reason to hope, that as the relationship expires, the affection will encrease, or that we shall agree better when we have ten times more and greater concerns to quarrel over than ever?

Ye that tell us of harmony and reconciliation, can ye restore to us the 109 time that is past? Can ye give to prostitution its former innocence? neither can ye reconcile Britain and America. The last cord now is broken, the people of England are presenting addresses against us. There are injuries which nature cannot forgive; she would cease to be nature if she did. As well can the lover forgive the ravisher of his mistress, as the Continent forgive the murders of Britain. The Almighty hath implanted in us these unextinguishable feelings for good and wise purposes. They are the Guardians of his Image in our hearts. They distinguish us from the herd of common animals. The social compact would dissolve, and justice be extirpated from the earth, or have only a casual existence were we callous to the touches of affection. The robber and the murderer would often escape unpunished, did not the injuries which our tempers sustain, provoke us into justice.

O! ye that love mankind! Ye that dare oppose not only the tyranny but 110 the tyrant, stand forth! Every spot of the old world is overrun with oppression. Freedom hath been hunted round the Globe. Asia and Africa have long expelled her. Europe regards her like a stranger, and England hath given her warning to depart. O! receive the fugitive, and prepare in time an asylum for mankind.

Of the Present Ability of America: With Some Miscellaneous Reflections

I have never met with a man, either in England or America, who hath not 111 confessed his opinion, that a separation between the countries would take place one time or other: And there is no instance in which we have shown less judgment, than in endeavoring to describe, what we call, the ripeness or fitness of the Continent for independance.

As all men allow the measure, and vary only in their opinion of the 112 time, let us, in order to remove mistakes, take a general survey of things, and endeavor if possible to find out the *very* time. But I need not go far, the inquiry ceases at once, for the *time hath found us*. The general concurrence, the glorious union of all things, proves the fact.

'Tis not in numbers but in unity that our great strength lies: yet our 113 present numbers are sufficient to repel the force of all the world. The Continent hath at this time the largest body of armed and disciplined men of any power under Heaven: and is just arrived at that pitch of strength, in which no single colony is able to support itself, and the whole, when united, is able to do any thing. Our land force is more than sufficient, and as to Naval affairs, we cannot be insensible that Britain would never suffer an American man of war to be built, while the Continent remained in her hands. Wherefore, we should be no forwarder an hundred years hence in that branch than we are now; but the truth is, we should be less so, because the timber of the Country is every day diminishing, and that which will remain at last, will be far off or difficult to procure.

Were the Continent crowded with inhabitants, her sufferings under the 114 present circumstances would be intolerable. The more seaport-towns we had, the more should we have both to defend and to lose. Our present numbers are so happily proportioned to our wants, that no man need be idle. The diminution of trade affords an army, and the necessities of an army create a new trade.

Debts we have none: and whatever we may contract on this account will 115 serve as a glorious memento of our virtue. Can we but leave posterity with a settled form of government, an independant constitution of its own, the purchase at any price will be cheap. But to expend millions for the sake of getting a few vile acts repealed, and routing the present ministry only, is unworthy the charge, and is using posterity with the utmost cruelty; because it is leaving them the great work to do, and a debt upon their backs from which they derive no advantage. Such a thought's unworthy a man of honour, and is the true characteristic of a narrow heart and a pidling politician.

The debt we may contract doth not deserve our regard if the work be 116 but accomplished. No nation ought to be without a debt. A national debt is a national bond; and when it bears no interest, is in no case a grievance. Britain is oppressed with a debt of upwards of one hundred and forty millions sterling, for which she pays upwards of four millions interest. And as a compensation for her debt, she has a large navy; America is without a debt, and without a navy; yet for the twentieth part of the English national debt, could have a navy as large again. The navy of England is not worth at this time more than three millions and a half sterling.

The first and second editions of this pamphlet were published without 117 the following calculations, which are now given as a proof that the above estimation of the navy is a just one. See Entic's "Naval History," Intro., p. 56.

The charge of building a ship of each rate, and furnishing her with 118 masts, yards, sails, and rigging, together with a proportion of eight months boatswain's and carpenter's seastores, as calculated by Mr. Burchett, Secretary to the navy.

For a ship of 100 guns,	• •	35,553 *l.*[6]
90	• •	29,886
80	• •	23,638
70	• •	17,785
60	• •	14,197
50	• •	10,606
40	• •	7,558
30	• •	5,846
20	• •	3,710

And hence it is easy to sum up the value, or cost, rather, of the whole 119 British navy, which, in the year 1757, when it was at its greatest glory, consisted of the following ships and guns.

Ships.	Guns.	Cost of one.	Cost of all.
6 •	100 •	55,553*l.* •	213,318 *l.*
12 •	90 •	29,886 •	358,632
12 •	80 •	23,638 •	283,656
43 •	70 •	17,785 •	764,755
35 •	60 •	14,197 •	496,895
40 •	50 •	10,605 •	424,240
45 •	40 •	7,558 •	340,110
58 •	20 •	3,710 •	215,180
85 Sloops, bombs, and fireships, one with another, at }		2,000 •	170,000
		Cost,	3,266,786 *l.*
		Remains for guns,	233,214
		Total,	3,500,000 *l.*

No country on the globe is so happily situated, or so internally capable 120 of raising a fleet as America. Tar, timber, iron, and cordage are her natural produce. We need go abroad for nothing. Whereas the Dutch, who make large profits by hiring out their ships of war to the Spaniards and Portugese, are obliged to import most of the materials they use. We ought to view the building a fleet as an article of commerce, it being the natural manufactory of this country. 'Tis the best money we can lay out. A navy when finished is worth more than it cost: And is that nice point in national policy, in which commerce and protection are united. Let us build; if we want them not, we can sell; and by that means replace our paper currency with ready gold and silver.

---

[6] *l.*: pound, Britain's basic monetary unit. [Editors' note.]

In point of manning a fleet, people in general run into great errors; it is 121 not necessary that one fourth part should be sailors. The Terrible privateer, captain Death, stood the hottest engagement of any ship last war, yet had not twenty sailors on board, though her complement of men was upwards of two hundred. A few able and social sailors will soon instruct a sufficient number of active landsmen in the common work of a ship. Wherefore we never can be more capable of beginning on maritime matters than now, while our timber is standing, our fisheries blocked up, and our sailors and shipwrights out of employ. Men of war, of seventy and eighty guns, were built forty years ago in New England, and why not the same now? Ship building is America's greatest pride, and in which she will, in time, excel the whole world. The great empires of the east are mostly inland, and consequently excluded from the possibility of rivalling her. Africa is in a state of barbarism; and no power in Europe, hath either such an extent of coast, or such an internal supply of materials. Where nature hath given the one, she hath withheld the other; to America only hath she been liberal to both. The vast empire of Russia is almost shut out from the sea; wherefore her boundless forests, her tar, iron, and cordage are only articles of commerce.

In point of safety, ought we to be without a fleet? We are not the little 122 people now, which we were sixty years ago; at that time we might have trusted our property in the streets, or fields rather, and slept securely without locks or bolts to our doors and windows. The case is now altered, and our methods of defence ought to improve with our encrease of property. A common pirate, twelve months ago, might have come up the Delaware, and laid the city of Philadelphia under contribution for what sum he pleased; and the same might have happened to other places. Nay, any daring fellow, in the brig of fourteen or sixteen guns, might have robbed the whole Continent, and carried off half a million of money. These are circumstances which demand our attention, and point out the necessity of naval protection.

Some perhaps will say, that after we have made it up with Britain, she 123 will protect us. Can they be so unwise as to mean, that she will keep a navy in our Harbours for that purpose? Common sense will tell us, that the power which hath endeavoured to subdue us, is of all others, the most improper to defend us. Conquest may be effected under the pretence of friendship; and ourselves, after a long and brave resistance, be at last cheated into slavery. And if her ships are not to be admitted into our harbours, I would ask, how is she to protect us? A navy three or four thousand miles off can be of little use, and on sudden emergencies, none at all. Wherefore if we must hereafter protect ourselves, why not do it for ourselves? Why do it for another?

The English list of ships of war, is long and formidable, but not a tenth 124 part of them are at any one time fit for service, numbers of them are not in being; yet their names are pompously continued in the list, if only a plank be left of the ship: and not a fifth part of such as are fit for service, can be spared on any one station at one time. The East and West Indies, Mediterranean, Africa, and other parts, over which Britain extends her claim, make large demands upon her navy. From a mixture of prejudice and inattention, we have contracted a false notion respecting the navy of England, and have talked as if we should have the whole of it to encounter at once, and, for that reason, supposed that we must have one as large; which not being instantly practicable, has been made use of by a set of disguised Tories to discourage our beginning thereon. Nothing can be further from truth than this; for if America had only a twentieth part of the naval force of Britain, she would be by far an over-match for her; because, as we neither have, nor claim any foreign dominion, our whole force would be employed on our own coast, where we should, in the long run, have two to one the advantage of those who had three or four thousand miles to sail over, before they could attack us, and the same distance to return in order to refit and recruit. And although Britain, by her fleet, hath a check over our trade to Europe, we have as large a one over her trade to the West Indies, which, by laying in the neighborhood of the Continent, lies entirely as its mercy.

Some method might be fallen on to keep up a naval force in time of 125 peace, if we should not judge it necessary to support a constant navy. If premiums were to be given to Merchants to build and employ in their service, ships mounted with twenty, thirty, forty, or fifty guns, (the premiums to be in proportion to the loss of bulk to the merchant,) fifty or sixty of those ships, with a few guardships on constant duty, would keep up a sufficient navy, and that without burdening ourselves with the evil so loudly complained of in England, of suffering their fleet in time of peace to lie rotting in the docks. To unite the sinews of commerce and defence is sound policy; for when our strength and our riches play into each other's hand, we need fear no external enemy.

In almost every article of defence we abound. Hemp flourishes even to 126 rankness, so that we need not want cordage. Our iron is superior to that of other countries. Our small arms equal to any in the world. Cannon we can cast at pleasure. Saltpetre and gunpowder we are every day producing. Our knowledge is hourly improving. Resolution is our inherent character, and courage hath never yet forsaken us. Wherefore, what is it that we want? Why is it that we hesitate? From Britain we can expect nothing but ruin. If she is once admitted to the government of America again, this Continent will not be worth living in. Jealousies will be always arising; insurrections will be constantly happening; and who will go forth to quell them? Who will venture his life to reduce his own countrymen to a foreign obedience? The difference between Pennsylvania and Connecticut, respecting some unlocated lands, shows the insignificance of a British government, and fully proves that nothing but Continental authority can regulate Continental matters.

Another reason why the present time is preferable to all others, is, that 127 the fewer our numbers are, the most land there is yet unoccupied, which, instead of being lavished by the king on his worthless dependants, may be hereafter applied, not only to the discharge of the present debt, but to the constant support of government. No nation under Heaven hath such an advantage as this.

The infant state of the Colonies, as it is called, so far from being against, 128 is an argument in favour of independance. We are sufficiently numerous, and were we more so we might be less united. 'Tis a matter worthy of observation, that the more a country is peopled, the smaller their armies are. In military numbers, the ancients far exceeded the moderns: and the reason is evident, for trade being the consequence of population, men became too much absorbed thereby to attend to any thing else. Commerce diminishes the spirit both of patriotism and military defence. And history sufficiently informs us, that the bravest achievements were always accomplished in the non-age of a nation. With the increase of commerce England hath lost its spirit. The city of London, notwithstanding its numbers, submits to continued insults with the patience of a coward. The more men have to lose, the less willing are they to venture. The rich are in general slaves to fear, and submit to courtly power with the trembling duplicity of a spaniel.

Youth is the seed-time of good habits as well in nations as in individuals. 129 It might be difficult, if not impossible, to form the Continent into one Government half a century hence. The vast variety of interests, occasioned by an increase of trade and population, would create confusion. Colony would be against Colony. Each being able would scorn each other's assistance: and while the proud and foolish gloried in their little distinctions, the wise would lament that the union had not been formed before. Wherefore the present time is the true time for establishing it. The intimacy which is contracted in infancy, and the friendship which is formed in misfortune, are of all others the most lasting and unalterable. Our present union is marked with both these characters: we are young, and we have been distressed; but our concord hath withstood our troubles, and fixes a memorable Æra for posterity to glory in.

The present time, likewise, is that peculiar time which never happens to 130 a nation but once, viz. the time of forming itself into a government. Most nations have let slip the opportunity, and by that means have been compelled to receive laws from their conquerors, instead of making laws for themselves. First, they had a king, and then a form of government; whereas the articles or charter of government should be formed first, and men delegated to execute them afterwards: but from the errors of other nations let us learn wisdom, and lay hold of the present opportunity—*to begin government at the right end*.

When William the Conqueror subdued England, he gave them law at 131 the point of the sword; and, until we consent that the seat of government in America be legally and authoritatively occupied, we shall be in danger of having it filled by some fortunate ruffian, who may treat us in the same manner, and then, where will be our freedom? where our property?

As to religion, I hold it to be the indispensable duty of government to 132 protect all conscientious professors thereof, and I know of no other business which government hath to do therewith. Let a man throw aside that narrowness of soul, that selfishness of principle, which the niggards of all professions are so unwilling to part with, and he will be at once delivered of his fears on that head. Suspicion is the companion of mean souls, and the bane of all good society. For myself, I fully and conscientiously believe, that it is the will of the Almighty that there should be a diversity of religious opinions among us. It affords a larger field for our Christian kindness: were we all of one way of thinking, our religious dispositions would want matter for probation; and on this liberal principle I look on the various denominations among us, to be like children of the same family, differing only in what is called their Christian names.

In page [170] I threw out a few thoughts on the propriety of a Continental 133 Charter (for I only presume to offer hints, not plans) and in this place, I take the liberty of re-mentioning the subject, by observing, that a charter is to be understood as a bond of solemn obligation, which the whole enters into, to support the right of every separate part, whether of religion, pro- fessional freedom, or property. A firm bargain and a right reckoning make long friends.

I have heretofore likewise mentioned the necessity of a large and equal 134 representation; and there is no political matter which more deserves our attention. A small number of electors, or a small number of representatives, are equally dangerous. But if the number of the representatives be not only small, but unequal, the danger is encreased. As an instance of this, I mention the following; when the petition of the associators was before the House of Assembly of Pennsylvania, twenty-eight members only were present; all the Bucks county members, being eight, voted against it, and had seven of the Chester members done the same, this whole province had been governed by two counties only; and this danger it is always exposed to. The unwarrantable stretch likewise, which that house made in their last sitting, to gain an undue authority over the Delegates of that Province, ought to warn the people at large, how they trust power out of their own hands. A set of instructions for their Delegates were put together, which in point of sense and business would have dishonoured a school-boy, and after being approved by a few, a very few, without doors, were carried into the house, and there passed *in behalf of the whole Colony;* whereas, did the whole colony know with what ill will that house had entered on some necessary public measures, they would not hesitate a moment to think them unworthy of such a trust.

Immediate necessity makes many things convenient, which if continued 135 would grow into oppressions. Expedience and right are different things. When the calamities of America required a consultation, there was no method so ready, or at that time so proper, as to appoint persons from the several houses of Assembly for that purpose; and the wisdom with which they have proceeded hath preserved this Continent from ruin. But as it is more than probable that we shall never be without a CONGRESS, every well wisher to good order must own that the mode for choosing members of that body, deserves consideration. And I put it as a question to those who make a study of mankind, whether representation and election is not too great a power for one and the same body of men to possess? When we are planning for posterity, we ought to remember that virtue is not hereditary.

It is from our enemies that we often gain excellent maxims, and are 136 frequently surprised into reason by their mistakes. Mr. Cornwall (one of the Lords of the Treasury) treated the petition of the New York Assembly with contempt, because *that* house, he said, consisted but of twenty-six members, which trifling number, he argued, could not with decency be put for the whole. We thank him for his involuntary honesty.[7]

To conclude, however strange it may appear to some, or however un- 137 willing they may be to think so, matters not, but many strong and striking reasons may be given to show, that nothing can settle our affairs so expeditiously as an open and determined declaration for independance. Some of which are,

First—It is the custom of Nations, when any two are at war, for some 138 other powers, not engaged in the quarrel, to step in as mediators, and bring about the preliminaries of a peace: But while America calls herself the subject of Great Britain, no power, however well disposed she may be, can offer her mediation. Wherefore, in our present state we may quarrel on for ever.

Secondly—It is unreasonable to suppose, that France or Spain will give 139 us any kind of assistance, if we mean only to make use of that assistance for the purpose of repairing the breach, and strengthening the connection between Britain and America; because, those powers would be sufferers by the consequences.

Thirdly—While we profess ourselves the subjects of Britain, we must, 140 in the eyes of foreign nations, be considered as Rebels. The precedent is somewhat dangerous to their peace, for men to be in arms under the name of subjects: we, on the spot, can solve the paradox; but to unite resistance and subjection, requires an idea much too refined for common understanding.

Fourthly—Were a manifesto to be published, and despatched to foreign 141 Courts, setting forth the miseries we have endured, and the peaceful methods which we have ineffectually used for redress; declaring at the same time, that not being able any longer to live happily or safely under the cruel disposition of the British Court, we had been driven to the necessity of

---

[7] Those who would fully understand of what great consequence a large and equal representation is to a state, should read Burgh's *Political Disquisitions*. [Author's note.]

breaking off all connections with her; at the same time, assuring all such Courts of our peaceable disposition towards them, and of our desire of entering into trade with them: such a memorial would produce more good effects to this Continent, than if a ship were freighted with petitions to Britain.

Under our present denomination of British subjects, we can neither be received nor heard abroad: the custom of all Courts is against us, and will be so, until by an independance we take rank with other nations. 142

These proceedings may at first seem strange and difficult, but like all other steps which we have already passed over, will in a little time become familiar and agreeable: and until an independance is declared, the Continent will feel itself like a man who continues putting off some unpleasant business from day to day, yet knows it must be done, hates to set about it, wishes it over, and is continually haunted with the thoughts of its necessity. 143

Questions for Discussion and Writing

1. What are the ramifications of Paine's title, *Common Sense*? What claims is Paine making about revolution, the rights of the governed, and human nature? How broad is his application of these claims? Do you support his arguments?

2. Discuss the overall structure of *Common Sense*. How does Paine move from point to point, unfolding his argument through time? Where does his thesis come? How do Paine's opening premises form the foundation of his entire piece?

3. The terms *nature* and *natural* appear over and over again in this treatise. What do you suppose they mean? Is Paine's use of them consistent? Is it similar to ours? How might nature relate to common sense?

4. Imagine yourself an American Tory, a colonist loyal to the king of England. Appealing to the same audience that read *Common Sense*, write a refutation of Paine's argument that supports the case for remaining loyal to the ruling monarch. How might you coopt Paine's use of such concepts as common sense, nature, and reason? How might you use the Bible to *your* advantage?

ALEXANDER HAMILTON

(1755–1804)

JAMES MADISON

(1751–1836)

$\mathbf{A}$lthough we consider July 4, 1776, a proper date for marking the birth of our nation, it was—as we all know— simply the day when a collection of disgruntled colonists decided that they had had enough of British rule. The Declaration of Independence, as wonderful a piece of rhetoric as it is, neither established nor even outlined a workable form of government for the thirteen independently minded, diverse colonies that originally united to fight for freedom.

The first official guidelines for the government of the fledgling republic—drafted during the Revolution itself—were known as the Articles of Confederation. Still in the process of freeing themselves from the clutches of an authoritarian government and an autocratic king, the framers of the Articles felt obligated not to establish an American version of British rule. To break the spiritual tie to the British system, they emphasized freedom and autonomy, redistributing most governmental power to the individual states.

Before long, though, the loosely constructed Articles of Confederation were deemed ineffective. One political writer even declared the state of affairs under the Articles "the last stage of national humiliation." To address this crisis, a national convention was called in Philadelphia in 1787. At this meeting, discussion and debate—some of which you will read in this selection—led to the formulation of a new blueprint for American government that emphasized a stronger federal government with greater centralized power. This document, approved by the convention on September 17, 1787, and ratified by the individual states in the following year, is the same Constitution that continues to direct our political system at the close of the twentieth century.

As with the debate over the Declaration of Independence, the controversy surrounding ratification of the Constitution was fierce. To many Americans— including highly respected figures such as Patrick Henry—the Revolutionary War had been fought precisely for the purpose of ending the rule of an authoritarian centralized government, and too much American blood had been spilled in defense of freedom to endorse quickly another strong national political system. Those supporting the Constitution had the advantage, yet the "Antifederalists" were numerous and eloquent, and ratification was by no means guaranteed. Orators and pamphleteers churned out mountains of argument on both sides of the issue. Although much of this rhetoric has now been relegated to specialized anthologies and relatively obscure library collections, a few texts have earned reputations as major works. In particular, the collection of pro-Constitution arguments known as The Federalist forms the pinnacle of eighteenth-century American political theory.

The Federalist is a series of letters published anonymously in New York City newspapers under the pseudonym "Publius." New York was seen as a vital state in the ratification campaign, and its governor, George Clinton, supported the Antifederalist cause. Alexander Hamilton, an energetic Federalist who served as a delegate at the national convention in 1787, believed that ratification would have a better chance if he could publish a sustained argument in favor of the new Constitution. With his two coauthors James Madison, a Virginia delegate to the convention in Philadelphia whose work there eventually earned him the title of "Father of the Constitution," and John Jay (1745–1829), a New York lawyer and statesman who wrote his own state's constitution, Hamilton published the eighty-five letters that comprise The Federalist between October 1787 and August 1788. At that time Jay was the best known of the three, but Hamilton and Madison did most of the writing. At its state convention, New York ratified the Constitution by a narrow margin.

Although The Federalist is a work of considerable originality and foresight, it did not spring from thin air. Hamilton, Madison, and Jay worked from a rich tradition of political writing. Ancient Greek and Roman politics, the British political system (see the headnote for Thomas Paine), and the experience of the American Revolution all provided background for these letters. In addition, The Spirit of Law, the influential treatise by the great eighteenth-century French political scientist Charles de Secondat, Baron de Montesquieu, informs the work of these three Federalists.

Hamilton, Madison, and Jay all set aside "Publius" for greater political fame. Before Aaron Burr fatally wounded him in a duel, Hamilton served as the influential Secretary of the Treasury to President George Washington. Madison served eight years as a congressman, eight years as Secretary of State, and eight years as President. Jay became chief justice of the Supreme Court.

In the readings that follow, you will find excerpts from the debates of the national convention of 1787 and The Federalist. Bear in mind, however, that these readings have been chosen from a large body of discourse. Although we can only feature a few of the arguments by Hamilton and Madison, each spoke and wrote at length in the great constitutional debate.

from DEBATES ON THE ADOPTION OF THE FEDERAL CONSTITUTION

MONDAY, JUNE 18, 1787

Met pursuant to adjournment. Present, eleven states.   1

    MR. HAMILTON.   To deliver my sentiments on so important a subject,   2
when the first characters of the Union have gone before me, inspires me
with the greatest diffidence, especially when my own ideas are so materially
dissimilar to the plans now before the committee. My situation is disagreeable;
but it would be criminal not to come forward on a question of such
magnitude. I have well considered the subject, and am convinced that no
amendment of the Confederation can answer the purpose of a good
government, so long as the state sovereignties do, in any shape, exist; and
I have great doubts whether a national government on the Virginia plan
can be made effectual. What is federal? An association of several independent
states into one. How or in what manner this association is formed, is not
so clearly distinguishable. We find the diet of Germany[1] has, in some
instances, the power of legislation on individuals. We find the United States
of America have it in an extensive degree in the case of piracies.

    Let us now review the powers with which we are invested. We are   3
appointed for the sole and express purpose of revising the Confederation,
and to alter or amend it, so as to render it effectual for the purposes of a
good government. Those who suppose it to be federal, lay great stress on
the terms *sole* and *express,* as if these words intended a confinement to a
federal government; when the manifest import is no more than that the
institution of a good government must be the *sole* and *express* object of your
deliberations. Nor can we suppose an annihilation of our powers by forming
a national government, as many of the states have made, in their constitutions,
no provision for any alteration; and thus much I can say for the state I have
the honor to represent, that, when our credentials were under consideration
in the Senate, some members were for inserting a restriction in the powers,
to prevent an encroachment on the constitution: it was answered by others,
and thereupon the resolve carried on the credentials, that it might abridge
the constitutional powers of the state, and that possibly, in the formation of
a new union, it would be found necessary. This appears reasonable, and
therefore leaves us at liberty to form such a national government as we
think best adapted for the good of the whole. I have therefore no difficulty
as to the extent of our powers, nor do I feel myself restrained in the exercise
of my judgment under them. We can only propose and recommend;—the
power of ratifying or rejecting is still in the states. But on this great question
I am still greatly embarrassed. . . .

---

[1] *diet of Germany:* German parliament. [Editors' note.]

I confess I am at a loss. I foresee the difficulty, on a consolidated plan,   4
of drawing a representation from so extensive a continent to one place.
What can be the inducements for gentlemen to come six hundred miles to
a national legislature! The expense would at least amount to a hundred
thousand pounds. This, however, can be no conclusive objection, if it
eventuates in an extinction of state governments. The burden of the latter
would be saved, and the expense, then, would not be great. State distinctions
would be found unnecessary; and yet, I confess, to carry government to the
extremities, the state governments, reduced to corporations, and with very
limited powers, might be necessary, and the expense of the national
government become less burdensome.

Yet, I confess, I see great difficulty of drawing forth a good representation.   5
What, for example, will be the inducements for gentlemen of fortune and
abilities to leave their houses and business to attend annually and long? It
cannot be the wages; for these, I presume, must be small. Will not the
power, therefore, be thrown into the hands of the demagogue, or middling
politician—who, for the sake of a small stipend, and the hopes of advancement, will offer himself as a candidate, and the real men of weight
and influence, by remaining at home, add strength to the state governments?
I am at a loss to know what must be done. I despair that a republican form
of government can remove the difficulties. Whatever may be my opinion,
I would hold it, however, unwise to change that form of government. I
believe the British government forms the best model the world ever
produced; and such has been its progress in the minds of the many, that
the truth gradually gains ground. This government has for its object *public
strength* and *individual security*. It is said with us to be unattainable. If it
was once formed, it would maintain itself. All communities divide themselves
into the few and the many. The first are the rich and well born, the other
the mass of the people. The voice of the people has been said to be the
voice of God; and, however generally this maxim has been quoted and
believed, it is not true in fact. The people are turbulent and changing; they
seldom judge or determine right. Give, therefore, to the first class a distinct,
permanent share in the government. They will check the unsteadiness of
the second; and, as they cannot receive any advantage by a change, they
therefore will ever maintain good government. Can a democratic assembly,
who annually revolve in the mass of the people, be supposed steadily to
pursue the public good? Nothing but a permanent body can check the
imprudence of democracy. Their turbulent and uncontrollable disposition
requires checks. The Senate of New York, although chosen for four years,
we have found to be inefficient. Will, on the Virginia plan, a continuance
of seven years do it? It is admitted that you cannot have a good executive
upon a democratic plan. See the excellency of the British executive. He is
placed above temptation—he can have no distinct interests from the public
welfare. Nothing short of such an executive can be efficient. The weak side
of a republican government is the danger of foreign influence. This is

unavoidable, unless it is so constructed as to bring forward its first characters in its support. I am therefore for a general government, yet would wish to go the full length of republican principles.

Let one body of the legislature be constituted during good behavior or life.   6

Let one executive be appointed, who dares execute his powers. It may be asked, Is this a republican system? It is strictly so, as long as they remain elective.   7

And let me observe, that an executive is less dangerous to the liberties of the people when in office during life, than for seven years.   8

It may be said this constitutes an elective monarchy. Pray what is a monarchy? May not the governors of the respective states be considered in that light? But by making the executive subject to impeachment, the term *monarchy* cannot apply. These elective monarchs have produced tumults in Rome, and are equally dangerous to peace in Poland; but this cannot apply to the mode in which I propose the election. Let electors be appointed in each of the states to elect the legislature, [*Here Mr. H. produced his plan. . . .*] to consist of two branches; and I would give them the unlimited power of passing *all laws* without exception. The Assembly to be elected for three years, by the people, in districts; the Senate to be elected by electors to be chosen for that purpose by the people, and to remain in office during life. The executive to have the power of negativing all laws; to make war or peace, with the advice of the Senate; to make treaties with their advice, but to have the sole direction of all military operations; and to send ambassadors, and appoint all military officers, and to pardon all offenders, treason excepted, unless by advice of the Senate. On his death or removal, the president of the Senate to officiate, with the same powers, until another is elected. Supreme judicial officers to be appointed by the executive and the Senate. The legislature to appoint courts in each state, so as to make the state governments unnecessary to it.   9

All state laws to be absolutely void which contravene the general laws. An officer to be appointed in each state to have a negative on all state laws. All the militia, and the appointment of officers, to be under the national government.   10

I confess that this plan, and that from Virginia, are very remote from the idea of the people. Perhaps the Jersey plan is nearest their expectation. But the people are gradually ripening in their opinions of government— they begin to be tired of an excess of democracy—and what even is the Virginia plan, but *pork still, with a little change of the sauce?*   11

Then adjourned to to-morrow.   12

FROM THE FEDERALIST

NUMBER 9

BY MR. HAMILTON

The utility of the Union, as a Safeguard against Domestic Faction and Insurrection.

A firm union will be of the utmost moment to the peace and liberty of the states, as a barrier against domestic faction and insurrection. 1

It is impossible to read the history of the petty republics of Greece and Italy, without feeling sensations of horror and disgust at the distractions with which they were continually agitated, and at the rapid succession of revolutions, by which they were kept perpetually vibrating between the extremes of tyranny and anarchy. If they exhibit occasional calms, these only serve as short-lived contrasts to the furious storms that are to succeed. If now and then intervals of felicity open themselves to view, we behold them with a mixture of regret, arising from the reflection, that the pleasing scenes before us are soon to be overwhelmed by the tempestuous waves of sedition and party rage. If momentary rays of glory break forth from the gloom, while they dazzle us with a transient and fleeting brilliancy, they at the same time admonish us to lament that the vices of government should pervert the direction, and tarnish the lustre of those bright talents and exalted endowments, for which the favoured soils that produced them have been so justly celebrated. 2

From the disorders that disfigure the annals of those republics, the advocates of despotism have drawn arguments, not only against the forms of republican government, but against the very principles of civil liberty. They have decried all free government, as inconsistent with the order of society, and have indulged themselves in malicious exultation over its friends and partizans. Happily for mankind, stupendous fabrics reared on the basis of liberty, which have flourished for ages, have in a few glorious instances refuted their gloomy sophisms. And, I trust, America will be the broad and solid foundation of other edifices not less magnificent, which will be equally permanent monuments of their error. 3

But it is not to be denied, that the portraits they have sketched of republican government, were too just copies of the originals from which they were taken. If it had been found impracticable to have devised models of a more perfect structure, the enlightened friends of liberty would have been obliged to abandon the cause of that species of government as indefensible. The science of politics, however, like most other sciences, has received great improvement. The efficacy of various principles is now well understood, which were either not known at all, or imperfectly known to the ancients. The regular distribution of power into distinct departments— the introduction of legislative balances and checks—the institution of courts 4 composed of judges, holding their offices during good behaviour—the representation of the people in the legislature, by deputies of their own election—these are either wholly new discoveries, or have made their principal progress towards perfection in modern times. They are means, and powerful means, by which the excellencies of republican government may be retained, and its imperfections lessened or avoided. To this catalogue of circumstances that tend to the amelioration of popular systems of civil government, I shall venture, however novel it may appear to some, to add one more, on a principle which has been made the foundation of an objection to the new constitution; I mean the ENLARGEMENT of the ORBIT within which such systems are to revolve, either in respect to the dimensions of a single state, or to the consolidation of several smaller states into one great confederacy. The latter is that which immediately concerns the object under consideration. It will, however, be of use to examine the principle in its application to a single state, which shall be attended to in another place.

The utility of a confederacy, as well to suppress faction and to guard the internal tranquillity of states, as to increase their external force and security, is in reality not a new idea. It has been practised upon in different countries and ages, and has received the sanction of the most approved writers on the subjects of politics. The opponents of the PLAN proposed, have, with great assiduity, cited and circulated the observations of Montesquieu on the necessity of a contracted territory for a republican government. But they seem not to have been apprised of the sentiments of that great man expressed in another part of his work, nor to have adverted to the consequences of the principle to which they subscribe with such ready acquiescence.   5

When Montesquieu recommends a small extent for republics, the standards he had in view were of dimensions, far short of the limits of almost every one of these states. Neither Virginia, Massachusetts, Pennsylvania, New-York, North-Carolina, nor Georgia, can by any means be compared with the models from which he reasoned, and to which the terms of his description apply. If we therefore receive his ideas on this point, as the criterion of truth, we shall be driven to the alternative, either of taking refuge at once in the arms of monarchy, or of splitting ourselves into an infinity of little, jealous, clashing, tumultuous commonwealths, the wretched nurseries of unceasing discord, and the miserable objects of universal pity or contempt. Some of the writers who have come forward on the other side of the question, seem to have been aware of the dilemma; and have even been bold enough to hint at the division of the larger states, as a desirable thing. Such an infatuated policy—such a desperate expedient—might, by the multiplication of petty offices, answer the views of men who possess not qualifications to extend their influence beyond the narrow circles of personal intrigue; but it could never promote the greatness or happiness of the people of America.   6

Referring the examination of the principle itself to another place, as has been already mentioned, it will be sufficient to remark here, that in the   7 sense of the author who has been most emphatically quoted upon the occasion, it would only dictate a reduction of the SIZE of the more considerable MEMBERS of the union; but would not militate against their being all comprehended in one confederate government. And this is the true question, in the discussion of which we are at present interested.

So far are the suggestions of Montesquieu from standing in opposition 8 to a general union of the states, that he explicitly treats of a CONFEDERATE REPUBLIC as the expedient for extending the sphere of popular government, and reconciling the advantages of monarchy with those of republicanism.

"It is very probable, says he,[1] that mankind would have been obliged, 9 at length, to live constantly under the government of a SINGLE PERSON, had they not contrived a kind of constitution, that has all the internal advantages of a republican, together with the external force of a monarchial government. I mean a CONFEDERATE REPUBLIC.

"This form of government is a convention, by which several smaller 10 *states* agree to become members of a larger *one*, which they intend to form. It is a kind of assemblage of societies, that constitute a new one, capable of increasing by means of new associations, till they arrive to such a degree of power as to be able to provide for the security of the united body.

"A republic of this kind, able to withstand an external force, may support 11 itself without any internal corruption. The form of this society prevents all manner of inconveniences.

"If a single member should attempt to usurp the supreme authority, he 12 could not be supposed to have an equal authority and credit in all the confederate states. Were he to have too great influence over one, this would alarm the rest. Were he to subdue a part, that which would still remain free might oppose him with forces, independent of those which he had usurped, and overpower him before he could be settled in his usurpation.

"Should a popular insurrection happen in one of the confederate states, 13 the others are able to quell it. Should abuses creep into one part, they are reformed by those that remain sound. The state may be destroyed on one side, and not on the other; the confederacy may be dissolved, and the confederates preserve their sovereignty.

"As this government is composed of small republics, it enjoys the internal 14 happiness of each, and with respect to its external situation, it is possessed, by means of the association, of all the advantages of large monarchies."

I have thought it proper to quote at length these interesting passages, 15 because they contain a luminous abridgment of the principal arguments in favour of the union, and must effectually remove the false impressions which a misapplication of the other parts of the work was calculated to produce. They have, at the same time, an intimate connexion with the more

---

[1] Spirit of Laws, Vol. I. Book IX. Chap. I. [Author's note.]

immediate design of this paper; which is to illustrate the tendency of the union to repress domestic faction and insurrection.

A distinction, more subtle than accurate, has been raised between a *confederacy* and a *consolidation* of the states. The essential characteristic of the first, is said to be the restriction of its authority to the members in their collective capacities, without reaching to the individuals of whom they are composed. It is contended that the national council ought to have no concern with any object of internal administration. An exact equality of suffrage between the members, has also been insisted upon as a leading feature of a confederate government. These positions are, in the main, arbitrary; they are supported neither by principle nor precedent. It has indeed happened, that governments of this kind have generally operated in the manner which the distinction taken notice of supposes to be inherent in their nature; but there have been in most of them extensive exceptions to the practice, which serve to prove, as far as example will go, that there is no absolute rule on the subject. And it will be clearly shown, in the course of this investigation, that, as far as the principle contended for has prevailed, it has been the cause of incurable disorder and imbecility in the government. 16

The definition of a *confederate republic* seems simply to be, "an assemblage of societies," or an association of two or more states into one state. The extent, modifications, and objects of the federal authority, are mere matters of discretion. So long as the separate organization of the members be not abolished—so long as it exists by a constitutional necessity for local purposes, though it should be in perfect subordination to the general authority of the union—it would still be, in fact and in theory, an association of states, or a confederacy. The proposed constitution, so far from implying an abolition of the state governments, makes them constituent parts of the national sovereignty, by allowing them a direct representation in the senate, and leaves in their possession certain exclusive and very important portions of the sovereign power. This fully corresponds, in every rational import of the terms, with the idea of a federal government. 17

In the Lycian confederacy,[2] which consisted of twenty-three CITIES or republics, the largest were entitled to *three* votes in the COMMON COUNCIL, those of the middle class to *two*, and the smallest to *one*. The COMMON COUNCIL had the appointment of all the judges and magistrates of the respective CITIES. This was certainly the most delicate species of interference in their internal administration; for if there be any thing that seems exclusively appropriated to the local jurisdictions, it is the appointment of their own officers. Yet Montesquieu, speaking of this association, says, "Were I to give a model of an excellent confederate republic, it would be that of Lycia." Thus we perceive, that the distinctions insisted upon, were 18

---

[2] *Lycian confederacy:* Lycia was an ancient country in southwestern Asia Minor. The Lycians were known for their ability to form confederacies and alliances. [Editors' note.]

not within the contemplation of this enlightened writer; and we shall be led to conclude that they are the novel refinements of an erroneous theory.

PUBLIUS

NUMBER 10

BY MR. MADISON

The same Subject continued.

Among the numerous advantages promised by a well constructed union, none deserves to be more accurately developed, than its tendency to break and control the violence of faction. The friend of popular governments, never finds himself so much alarmed for their character and fate, as when he contemplates their propensity to this dangerous vice. He will not fail, therefore, to set a due value on any plan which, without violating the principles to which he is attached, provides a proper cure for it. The instability, injustice, and confusion introduced into the public councils, have, in truth, been the mortal diseases under which popular governments have every where perished; as they continue to be the favourite and fruitful topics from which the adversaries to liberty derive their most specious declamations. The valuable improvements made by the American constitutions on the popular models, both ancient and modern, cannot certainly be too much admired; but it would be an unwarrantable partiality, to contend that they have as effectually obviated the danger on this side, as was wished and expected. Complaints are every where heard from our most considerate and virtuous citizens, equally the friends of public and private faith, and of public and personal liberty, that our governments are too unstable; that the public good is disregarded in the conflicts of rival parties; and that measures are too often decided, not according to the rules of justice, and the rights of the minor party, but by the superior force of an interested and overbearing majority. However anxiously we may wish that these complaints had no foundation, the evidence of known facts will not permit us to deny that they are in some degree true. It will be found, indeed, on a candid review of our situation, that some of the distresses under which we labour, have been erroneously charged on the operation of our governments; but it will be found, at the same time, that other causes will not alone account for many of our heaviest misfortunes; and, particularly, for that prevailing and increasing distrust of public engagements, and alarm for private rights, which are echoed from one end of the continent to the other. These must be chiefly, if not wholly, effects of the unsteadiness and injustice, with which a factious spirit has tainted our public administration.

By a faction, I understand a number of citizens, whether amounting to a majority or minority of the whole, who are united and actuated by some common impulse of passion, or of interest, adverse to the rights of other citizens, or to the permanent and aggregate interests of the community.

There are two methods of curing the mischiefs of faction: The one, by removing its causes; the other, by controlling its effects. 3

There are again two methods of removing the causes of faction: The one, by destroying the liberty which is essential to its existence; the other, by giving to every citizen the same opinions, the same passions, and the same interests. 4

It could never be more truly said, than of the first remedy, that it is worse than the disease. Liberty is to faction, what air is to fire, an aliment, without which it instantly expires. But it could not be a less folly to abolish liberty, which is essential to political life, because it nourishes faction, than it would be to wish the annihilation of air, which is essential to animal life, because it imparts to fire its destructive agency. 5

The second expedient is as impracticable, as the first would be unwise. As long as the reason of man continues fallible, and he is at liberty to exercise it, different opinions will be formed. As long as the connexion subsists between his reason and his self-love, his opinions and his passions will have a reciprocal influence on each other; and the former will be objects to which the latter will attach themselves. The diversity in the faculties of men, from which the rights of property originate, is not less an insuperable obstacle to an uniformity of interests. The protection of these faculties, is the first object of government. From the protection of different and unequal faculties of acquiring property, the possession of different degrees and kinds of property immediately results: and from the influence of these on the sentiments and views of the respective proprietors, ensues a division of the society into different interests and parties. 6

The latent causes of faction are thus sown in the nature of man; and we see them every where brought into different degrees of activity, according to the different circumstances of civil society. A zeal for different opinions concerning religion, concerning government, and many other points, as well of speculation as of practice; an attachment to different leaders, ambitiously contending for pre-eminence and power; or to persons of other descriptions, whose fortunes have been interesting to the human passions, have, in turn, divided mankind into parties, inflamed them with mutual animosity, and rendered them much more disposed to vex and oppress each other, than to co-operate for their common good. So strong is this propensity of mankind, to fall into mutual animosities, that where no substantial occasion presents itself, the most frivolous and fanciful distinctions have been sufficient to kindle their unfriendly passions, and excite their most violent conflicts. But the most common and durable source of factions, has been the various and unequal distribution of property.—Those who hold, and those who are without property, have ever formed distinct interests in society. Those who are creditors, and those who are debtors, fall under a like discrimination. A landed interest, a manufacturing interest, a mercantile 7 interest, a monied interest, with many lesser interests, grow up of necessity in civilized nations, and divide them into different classes, actuated by different sentiments and views. The regulation of these various and interfering interests, forms the principal task of modern legislation, and involves the spirit of party and faction in the necessary and ordinary operations of government.

No man is allowed to be a judge in his own cause; because his interest would certainly bias his judgment, and, not improbably, corrupt his integrity. With equal, nay, with greater reason, a body of men, are unfit to be both judges and parties, at the same time; yet, what are many of the most important acts of legislation, but so many judicial determinations, not indeed concerning the rights of single persons, but concerning the rights of large bodies of citizens? and what are the different classes of legislators, but advocates and parties to the causes which they determine? Is a law proposed concerning private debts? It is a question to which the creditors are parties on one side, and the debtors on the other. Justice ought to hold the balance between them. Yet the parties are, and must be, themselves the judges; and the most numerous party, or, in other words, the most powerful faction, must be expected to prevail. Shall domestic manufactures be encouraged, and in what degree, by restrictions on foreign manufactures? are questions which would be differently decided by the landed and the manufacturing classes; and probably by neither with a sole regard to justice and the public good. The apportionment of taxes, on the various descriptions of property, is an act which seems to require the most exact impartiality; yet there is, perhaps, no legislative act in which greater opportunity and temptation are given to a predominant party, to trample on the rules of justice. Every shilling with which they over-burden the inferior number, is a shilling saved to their own pockets. 8

It is in vain to say, that enlightened statesmen will be able to adjust these clashing interests, and render them all subservient to the public good. Enlightened statesmen will not always be at the helm: nor, in many cases, can such an adjustment be made at all, without taking into view indirect and remote considerations, which will rarely prevail over the immediate interest which one party may find in disregarding the rights of another, or the good of the whole. 9

The inference to which we are brought is, that the *causes* of faction cannot be removed; and that relief is only to be sought in the means of controlling its *effects*. 10

If a faction consists of less than a majority, relief is supplied by the republican principle, which enables the majority to defeat its sinister views, by regular vote. It may clog the administration, it may convulse the society; but it will be unable to execute and mask its violence under the forms of the constitution. When a majority is included in a faction, the form of popular government, on the other hand, enables it to sacrifice to its ruling passion or interest, both the public good, and the rights of other citizens. 11

To secure the public good and private rights against the danger of such a faction, and at the same time to preserve the spirit and the form of popular government, is then the great object to which our inquiries are directed. Let me add, that it is the great desideratum, by which alone this form of government can be rescued from the opprobrium under which it has so long laboured, and be recommended to the esteem and adoption of mankind.

By what means is this object attainable? Evidently by one of two only. 12 Either the existence of the same passion or interest in a majority, at the same time, must be prevented; or the majority, having such co-existent passion or interest, must be rendered, by their number and local situation, unable to concert and carry into effect schemes of oppression. If the impulse and the opportunity be suffered to coincide, we well know, that neither moral nor religious motives can be relied on as an adequate control. They are not found to be such on the injustice and violence of individuals, and lose their efficacy in proportion to the number combined together; that is, in proportion as their efficacy becomes needful.

From this view of the subject, it may be concluded that a pure democracy, 13 by which I mean a society consisting of a small number of citizens, who assemble and administer the government in person, can admit of no cure for the mischiefs of faction. A common passion or interest will, in almost every case, be felt by a majority of the whole; a communication and concert, results from the form of government itself; and there is nothing to check the inducements to sacrifice the weaker party, or an obnoxious individual. Hence it is, that such democracies have ever been spectacles of turbulence and contention; have ever been found incompatible with personal security, or the rights of property; and have in general, been as short in their lives, as they have been violent in their deaths. Theoretic politicians, who have patronised this species of government, have erroneously supposed, that by reducing mankind to a perfect equality in their political rights, they would, at the same time, be perfectly equalised and assimilated in their possessions, their opinions, and their passions.

A republic, by which I mean a government in which the scheme of 14 representation takes place, opens a different prospect, and promises the cure for which we are seeking. Let us examine the points in which it varies from pure democracy, and we shall comprehend both the nature of the cure, and the efficacy which it must derive from the union.

The two great points of difference, between a democracy and a republic, 15 are, first, the delegation of the government, in the latter, to a small number of citizens elected by the rest; secondly, the greater number of citizens, and greater sphere of country, over which the latter may be extended.

The effect of the first difference is, on the one hand, to refine and enlarge 16 the public views, by passing them through the medium of a chosen body of citizens, whose wisdom may best discern the true interest of their country, and whose patriotism and love of justice, will be least likely to sacrifice it to temporary or partial considerations. Under such a regulation, it may well happen, that the public voice, pronounced by the representatives of the people, will be more constant to the public good, than if pronounced by the people themselves, convened for the purpose. On the other hand, the effect may be inverted. Men of factious tempers, of local prejudices, or of sinister designs, may by intrigue, by corruption, or by other means, first obtain the suffrages, and then betray the interest of the people. The question resulting is, whether small or extensive republics are most favourable to the election of proper guardians of the public weal; and it is clearly decided in favour of the latter by two obvious considerations.

In the first place, it is to be remarked, that however small the republic   17
may be, the representatives must be raised to a certain number, in order to guard against the cabals of a few; and that, however large it may be, they must be limited to a certain number, in order to guard against the confusion of a multitude. Hence the number of representatives in the two cases not being in proportion to that of the constituents, and being proportionably greatest in the small republic, it follows, that if the proportion of fit characters be not less in the large than in the small republic, the former will present a greater option, and consequently a greater probability of a fit choice.

In the next place, as each representative will be chosen by a greater   18
number of citizens in the large than in the small republic, it will be more difficult for unworthy candidates to practise with success the vicious arts, by which elections are too often carried; and the suffrages of the people being more free, will be more likely to center in men who possess the most attractive merit, and the most diffusive and established characters.

It must be confessed, that in this, as in most other cases, there is a mean,   19
on both sides of which inconveniences will be found to lie. By enlarging too much the number of electors, you render the representative too little acquainted with all their local circumstances and lesser interests; as by reducing it too much, you render him unduly attached to these, and too little fit to comprehend and pursue great and national objects. The federal constitution forms, in this respect, a happy combination; the great and aggregate interest being referred to the national—the local and particular, to the state legislatures.

The other point of difference is, the greater number of citizens, and   20
extent of territory, which may be brought within the compass of republican, than of democratic government; and it is this circumstance principally which renders factious combinations less to be dreaded in the former, than in the latter. The smaller the society, the fewer probably will be the distinct parties and interests composing it; the fewer the distinct parties and interests, the more frequently will a majority be found of the same party; and the smaller the number of individuals composing a majority, and the smaller the compass within which they are placed, the more easily will they concert and execute their plans of oppression. Extend the sphere, and you take in a greater variety of parties and interest; you make it less probable that a

majority of the whole will have a common motive to invade the rights of other citizens; or if such a common motive exists, it will be more difficult for all who feel it to discover their own strength, and to act in unison with each other. Besides other impediments, it may be remarked, that where there is a consciousness of unjust or dishonourable purpose, communication is always checked by distrust, in proportion to the number whose concurrence is necessary.

Hence it clearly appears, that the same advantage, which a republic has   21
over a democracy, in controlling the effects of faction, is enjoyed by a large over a small republic—is enjoyed by the union over the states composing it. Does this advantage consist in the substitution of representatives, whose enlightened views and virtuous sentiments render them superior to local prejudices, and to schemes of injustice? It will not be denied, that the representation of the union will be most likely to possess these requisite endowments. Does it consist in the greater security afforded by a greater variety of parties, against the event of any one party being able to outnumber and oppress the rest? In an equal degree does the increased variety of parties, comprised within the union, increase this security. Does it, in fine, consist in the greater obstacles opposed to the concert and accomplishment of the secret wishes of an unjust and interested majority? Here, again, the extent of the union gives it the most palpable advantage.

The influence of factious leaders may kindle a flame within their particular   22
states, but will be unable to spread a general conflagration through the other states: A religious sect may degenerate into a political faction in a part of the confederacy; but the variety of sects dispersed over the entire face of it, must secure the national councils against any danger from the source: A rage for paper money, for an abolition of debts, for an equal division of property, or for any other improper or wicked project, will be less apt to pervade the whole body of the union, than a particular member of it; in the same proportion as such a malady is more likely to taint a particular county or district, than an entire state.

In the extent and proper structure of the union, therefore, we behold a   23
republican remedy for the diseases most incident to a republican government. And according to the degree of pleasure and pride we feel in being republicans, ought to be our zeal in cherishing the spirit, and supporting the character of federalists.

PUBLIUS

Questions for Discussion and Writing

1. In the first selection, Hamilton claims—among other things—that "all communities divide themselves into the few and the many" (paragraph 5) and that people will grow tired of "an excess of democracy" (paragraph 11). What do you think of

these claims.? How do they correspond with your conception of contemporary American government?

2. Does "Publius" seem to have a split personality? Compare the argumentative strategies employed by Hamilton and Madison. Consider elements such as structure, use of examples, and style. Do you notice any important similarities or differences in their rhetoric?

3. In Paine's *Common Sense,* the terms *nature* and *natural* appeared again and again. In the discourse of Madison and Hamilton, the adjective *enlightened* is pervasive. What do you make of this term? How does it specifically help to shape this argument about political reform? How might it be used to appeal to the values of this particular audience?

4. However brilliant, Hamilton and Madison were typical statesmen of their era, and their method of political argument is representative of the late eighteenth century. How do their rhetorical strategies compare to the rhetoric practiced by contemporary politicians you have seen on television and read in the press? Find an article or transcript of a speech written by a politician in the last few years and compare it to a passage from Madison or Hamilton. What distinctive similarities or differences do you discover? Write an essay that argues for the significance of one or two key similarities or differences.

WILLIAM WORDSWORTH

(1770–1850)

William Wordsworth was a native of England's Lake District, an enchanted land of pristine, windswept lakes and rugged mountains located near the Scottish border. The beauty and sublimity of his homeland affected him profoundly; throughout his life, Wordsworth drew great inspiration from the wonders of the natural world.

Along with his three brothers and his sister Dorothy (to whom he was particularly close), the young Wordsworth grew up relatively isolated from the other residents of Cockermouth, his hometown. This isolation may have been at least partly responsible for his introspective, contemplative frame of mind. After completing a fine grammar school education in the Lake District, he entered Cambridge. His years there were fairly uneventful, and he graduated without a firm sense of direction. Like his countryman Thomas Paine, he traveled to the Continent to observe the French Revolution, and he returned to England imbued with the revolutionary spirit. His inheritance temporarily deprived him by his dead father's superior, Wordsworth attempted to raise a little money publishing poetry. Like many intellectuals of his age, he became increasingly disillusioned with the course of the French Revolution when promises of freedom and democratic reform brought only tyranny and terror. As many literary historians have noted, Wordsworth grew increasingly conservative throughout his adult life.

In 1795, after setting up house with his sister in Dorsetshire, Wordsworth met the budding poet Samuel Taylor Coleridge, with whom he established one of the most famous friendships in the history of English literature. William and Dorothy moved their residence to further William's creative collaboration with his new friend. Two years before the turn of the century, they produced the Lyrical Ballads, an innovative collection that changed the course of British poetry. After traveling on the Continent with Coleridge, William and Dorothy settled permanently in the Lake District. There he married a childhood friend, raised a family, and lived what was in many respects a rather ordinary rural life.

The steady growth of Wordsworth's literary reputation, though, was extraordinary. Year after year his fame as a poet grew, and many of the most distinguished figures in Europe made their way to the Lake District to pay him homage. In 1843, he became poet laureate of his country. Although his literary power declined in his later years, he remained a senior statesman of British letters until his death.

Today Wordsworth is considered one of the greatest of the Romantic poets who dominated the English literary scene from the close of the eighteenth century through the first half of the nineteenth. Born in the last years of the "Enlightenment," Romantics such as Wordsworth and Coleridge worshipped less ardently at the shrine of reason than did their predecessors, as they reacted against what seemed to them the deadening influences of industrialism, mass society, abstract logic, and a scientific world view that reduced the universe to a soulless machine. Instead, they turned to the shrine of nature, which they felt to be saturated with divinity. Accordingly, they placed great stress on intuitive understanding, imagination, inspiration, the complexity of human feeling, and the primacy of the individual person. Perhaps more than any other poet of his era, Wordsworth epitomizes the Romantic sensibility.

The poem reprinted here was originally published as part of the Lyrical Ballads. It was composed in 1798, after the poet had paid his second visit to the picturesque ruin of Tintern Abbey. He had this to say of his composing process:

> No poem of mine was composed under circumstances more pleasant for me to remember than this. I began it upon leaving Tintern, after crossing the Wye, and concluded it just as I was entering Bristol in the evening, after a ramble of four or five days, with my sister. Not a line of it was altered, and not any part of it written down till I reached Bristol.

LINES

Composed a Few Miles Above Tintern Abbey, on Revisiting the Banks of the Wye During a Tour, July 13, 1798

Five years have past; five summers, with the length
Of five long winters! and again I hear
These waters, rolling from their mountain-springs
With a soft inland murmur.—Once again
Do I behold these steep and lofty cliffs,   5
That on a wild secluded scene impress
Thoughts of more deep seclusion; and connect
The landscape with the quiet of the sky.
The day is come when I again repose
Here, under this dark sycamore, and view   10
These plots of cottage-ground, these orchard-tufts,
Which at this season, with their unripe fruits,
Are clad in one green hue, and lose themselves
'Mid groves and copses. Once again I see
These hedge-rows, hardly hedge-rows, little lines   15
Of sportive wood run wild: these pastoral farms,
Green to the very door; and wreaths of smoke
Sent up, in silence, from among the trees!

With some uncertain notice, as might seem
Of vagrant dwellers in the houseless woods.   20
Or of some Hermit's cave, where by his fire
The Hermit sits alone.

                  These beauteous forms,
Through a long absence, have not been to me
As is a landscape to a blind man's eye: 25
But oft, in lonely rooms, and 'mid the din
Of towns and cities, I have owed to them,
In hours of weariness, sensations sweet,
Felt in the blood, and felt along the heart;
And passing even into my purer mind,   30
With tranquil restoration:—feelings too
Of unremembered pleasure: such, perhaps,
As have no slight or trivial influence
On that best portion of a good man's life,
His little, nameless, unremembered, acts   35
Of kindness and of love. Nor less, I trust,
To them I may have owed another gift,
Of aspect more sublime; that blessed mood,
In which the burthen of the mystery,
In which the heavy and the weary weight   40
Of all this unintelligible world,
Is lightened:—that serene and blessed mood,
In which the affections gently lead us on,—
Until, the breath of this corporeal frame
And even the motion of our human blood   45
Almost suspended, we are laid asleep
In body, and become a living soul:
While with an eye made quiet by the power
Of harmony, and the deep power of joy,
We see into the life of things.   50
                      If this
Be but a vain belief, yet, oh! how oft—
In darkness and amid the many shapes
Of joyless daylight; when the fretful stir
Unprofitable, and the fever of the world,   55
Have hung upon the beatings of my heart—
How oft, in spirit, have I turned to thee,
O sylvan Wye! thou wanderer thro' the woods,
How often has my spirit turned to thee!
  And now, with gleams of half-extinguished thought,   60
With many recognitions dim and faint,
And somewhat of a sad perplexity,

The picture of the mind revives again:
While here I stand, not only with the sense
Of present pleasure, but with pleasing thoughts   65
That in this moment there is life and food
For future years. And so I dare to hope,
Though changed, no doubt, from what I was when first
I came among these hills; when like a roe
I bounded o'er the mountains, by the sides   70
Of the deep rivers, and the lonely streams,
Wherever nature led: more like a man
Flying from something that he dreads than one
Who sought the thing he loved. For nature then
(The coarser pleasures[1] of my boyish days,   75
And their glad animal movements all gone by)
To me was all in all.—I cannot paint
What then I was. The sounding cataract
Haunted me like a passion: the tall rock,
The mountain, and the deep and gloomy wood,   80
Their colours and their forms, were then to me
An appetite; a feeling and a love,
That had no need of a remoter charm,
By thought supplied, nor any interest
Unborrowed from the eye.—That time is past,   85
And all its aching joys are now no more,
And all its dizzy raptures. Not for this
Faint[2] I, nor mourn nor murmur; other gifts
Have followed; for such loss, I would believe,
Abundant recompense. For I have learned   90
To look on nature, not as in the hour
Of thoughtless youth; but hearing oftentimes
The still, sad music of humanity,
Nor harsh nor grating, though of ample power
To chasten and subdue. And I have felt   95
A presence that disturbs me with the joy
Of elevated thoughts; a sense sublime
Of something far more deeply interfused,
Whose dwelling is the light of setting suns,
And the round ocean and the living air,   100
And the blue sky, and in the mind of man:
A motion and a spirit, that impels
All thinking things, all objects of all thought,

---

[1] *coarser pleasures:* physical pleasures. [Editors' note.]

[2] *Faint:* become discouraged. [Editors' note.]

And rolls through all things. Therefore am I still
A lover of the meadows and the woods,   105
And mountains; and of all that we behold
From this green earth; of all the mighty world
Of eye, and ear,—both what they half create,
And what perceive; well pleased to recognise
In nature and the language of the sense   110
The anchor of my purest thoughts, the nurse,
The guide, the guardian of my heart, and soul
Of all my moral being.
                   Nor perchance,
If I were not thus taught, should I the more   115
Suffer my genial spirits[3] to decay:
For thou art with me here upon the banks
Of this fair river; thou my dearest Friend,
My dear, dear Friend; and in thy voice I catch
The language of my former heart, and read   120
My former pleasures in the shooting lights
Of thy wild eyes. Oh! yet a little while
May I behold in thee what I was once,
My dear, dear Sister! and this prayer I make,
Knowing that Nature never did betray   125
The heart that loved her; 'tis her privilege,
Through all the years of this our life, to lead
From joy to joy: for she can so inform
The mind that is within us, so impress
With quietness and beauty, and so feed   130
With lofty thoughts, that neither evil tongues,
Rash judgments, nor the sneers of selfish men,
Nor greetings where no kindness is, nor all
The dreary intercourse of daily life,
Shall e'er prevail against us, or disturb   135
Our cheerful faith, that all which we behold
Is full of blessings. Therefore let the moon
Shine on thee in thy solitary walk;
And let the misty mountain-winds be free
To blow against thee: and, in after years,   140
When these wild ecstasies shall be matured
Into a sober pleasure; when thy mind
Shall be a mansion for all lovely forms,
Thy memory be as a dwelling-place

---

[3] *genial spirits:* This phrase has a variety of possible meanings, including cheerfulness, enlivening feelings, vital energies, and creative powers (genius). [Editors' note.]

For all sweet sounds and harmonies; oh! then,   145
If solitude, or fear, or pain, or grief,
Should be thy portion, with what healing thoughts
Of tender joy wilt thou remember me,
And these my exhortations! Nor, perchance—
If I should be where I no more can hear   150
Thy voice, nor catch from thy wild eyes these gleams
Of past existence—wilt thou then forget
That on the banks of this delightful stream
We stood together; and that I, so long
A worshipper of Nature, hither came   155
Unwearied in that service: rather say
With warmer love—oh! with far deeper zeal
Of holier love. Nor wilt thou then forget
That after many wanderings, many years
Of absence, these steep woods and lofty cliffs,   160
And this green pastoral landscape, were to me
More dear, both for themselves and for thy sake!

Questions for Discussion and Writing

1. Describe the ethos of the "I," the persona who speaks within the context of this poem. To whom does he speak? What are the rhetorical ramifications of this speaking situation for the implied reader?

2. How would you describe the change from youth to middle age portrayed by the persona of the poem? How is the concept of nature employed by the persona to illustrate or illuminate this change?

3. Although "Tintern Abbey" is not explicitly argumentative, its structure has been carefully fashioned to move the reader from easily accepted—perhaps mundane— premises about nature and emotion to more profound conclusions. Like an essayist, Wordsworth carefully introduces his key terms and concepts over the course of the entire text. As you may have done with selected prose arguments in this reader, outline the structural development of Wordsworth's poem as it unfolds in time. Look for crucial transitions in which the poet moves the discourse in a new or unexpected direction. How do these new or unexpected directions become the foundation for later developments in the poem?

4. What is the rhetorical intention of this poem? How might the *specific* personal experiences described by the persona be marshaled by the implied author in order to convey a more *general* message, argument, or effect to the implied reader of the poem? Based on your reading of this poem, what are the strengths and weaknesses of texts that attempt to use deeply personal reflections to establish more general points about the human condition? Write an essay that addresses one or more of these questions.

ALEXIS DE TOCQUEVILLE

(1805–1859)

After the French Revolution brought down the reigning royalty (and encouraged progressive-minded British intellectuals of the time such as Paine and Wordsworth to sing the praises of the French political reform), no James Madison or Alexander Hamilton arose to establish a successful blueprint for a representative democracy. The new order that ensued in the wake of the French Revolution was established not by the republican principle of a written constitution, but by the charismatic and autocratic rule of Napoleon. In short, the road toward true democratic reform in France was a long one, and although the French system of government moved toward greater representativeness, it moved extremely slowly.

Thus, the France in which Alexis Charles Henri Clerel de Tocqueville came of age was characterized more by elitist than by democratic ideas. Born into an aristocratic Parisian family, Tocqueville received all the benefits and privileges common to his high station in life. In 1831, he left his position as a magistrate and journeyed to America. The official purpose of the trip was to study the American prison system, but his real interest was in learning more about American democracy. Despite the fact that his family had been ravaged by the French Revolution, Tocqueville wanted to see for himself the strengths and weaknesses of popular government. During his nine-month tour, he and a friend scoured the United States, collecting information about this alien land. The spirit of Jacksonian democracy was in the air, and Tocqueville absorbed it like a sponge.

After the obligatory prison report was out of the way, Tocqueville went to work on a more ambitious project, a two-volume work entitled Democracy in America. Volume 1, published in 1835, was an analysis of contemporary American government. Volume 2, a more general study of the American character, was published in 1840.

Tocqueville held several political positions and published again in the field of political science, but Democracy in America remains his primary claim to fame. As a foreign observer unfamiliar with American ways of thinking, Tocqueville was able to isolate and identify key traits that his subjects simply took for granted. Like Paine urging American colonialists to fight for independence, Tocqueville employed his initial perspective as an outsider to generate fresh insights into the American condition. The book was instantly recognized as a classic and was translated widely; the English edition of the first volume was published even before Tocqueville had completed the second volume.

Today Democracy in America remains required reading for most political science majors in this country, and Tocqueville is cited in scholarly studies of history, *sociology, politics, literature, media, and popular culture. The selection that follows, "In What Spirit the Americans Cultivate the Arts," comprises a chapter from the second volume.*

IN WHAT SPIRIT THE AMERICANS CULTIVATE THE ARTS

It would be to waste the time of my readers and my own if I strove to demonstrate how the general mediocrity of fortunes, the absence of superfluous wealth, the universal desire for comfort, and the constant efforts by which everyone attempts to procure it make the taste for the useful predominate over the love of the beautiful in the heart of man. Democratic nations, among whom all these things exist, will therefore cultivate the arts that serve to render life easy in preference to those whose object is to adorn it. They will habitually prefer the useful to the beautiful, and they will require that the beautiful should be useful. 1

But I propose to go further, and, after having pointed out this first feature, to sketch several others. 2

It commonly happens that in the ages of privilege the practice of almost all the arts becomes a privilege, and that every profession is a separate sphere of action, into which it is not allowable for everyone to enter. Even when productive industry is free, the fixed character that belongs to aristocratic nations gradually segregates all the persons who practice the same art till they form a distinct class, always composed of the same families, whose members are all known to each other and among whom a public opinion of their own and a species of corporate pride soon spring up. In a class or guild of this kind each artisan has not only his fortune to make, but his reputation to preserve. He is not exclusively swayed by his own interest or even by that of his customer, but by that of the body to which he belongs; and the interest of that body is that each artisan should produce the best possible workmanship. In aristocratic ages the object of the arts is therefore to manufacture as well as possible, not with the greatest speed or at the lowest cost. 3

When, on the contrary, every profession is open to all, when a multitude of persons are constantly embracing and abandoning it, and when its several members are strangers, indifferent to and because of their numbers hardly seen by each other, the social tie is destroyed, and each workman, standing alone, endeavors simply to gain the most money at the least cost. The will of the customer is then his only limit. But at the same time a corresponding change takes place in the customer also. In countries in which riches as well as power are concentrated and retained in the hands of a few, the use of 4 the greater part of this world's goods belongs to a small number of individuals, who are always the same. Necessity, public opinion, or moderate desires exclude all others from the enjoyment of them. As this aristocratic class remains fixed at the pinnacle of greatness on which it stands, without diminution or increase, it is always acted upon by the same wants and affected by them in the same manner. The men of whom it is composed naturally derive from their superior and hereditary position a taste for what is extremely well made and lasting. This affects the general way of thinking of the nation in relation to the arts. It often occurs among such a people that even the peasant will rather go without the objects he covets than procure them in a state of imperfection. In aristocracies, then, the handicraftsmen work for only a limited number of fastidious customers; the profit they hope to make depends principally on the perfection of their workmanship.

Such is no longer the case when, all privileges being abolished, ranks 5
are intermingled and men are forever rising or sinking in the social scale. Among a democratic people a number of citizens always exists whose patrimony is divided and decreasing. They have contracted, under more prosperous circumstances, certain wants, which remain after the means of satisfying such wants are gone; and they are anxiously looking out for some surreptitious method of providing for them. On the other hand, there is always in democracies a large number of men whose fortune is on the increase, but whose desires grow much faster than their fortunes, and who gloat upon the gifts of wealth in anticipation, long before they have means to obtain them. Such men are eager to find some short cut to these gratifications, already almost within their reach. From the combination of these two causes the result is that in democracies there is always a multitude of persons whose wants are above their means and who are very willing to take up with imperfect satisfaction rather than abandon the object of their desires altogether.

The artisan readily understands these passions, for he himself partakes 6
in them. In an aristocracy he would seek to sell his workmanship at a high price to the few; he now conceives that the more expeditious way of getting rich is to sell them at a low price to all. But there are only two ways of lowering the price of commodities. The first is to discover some better, shorter, and more ingenious method of producing them; the second is to manufacture a larger quantity of goods, nearly similar, but of less value. Among a democratic population all the intellectual faculties of the workman are directed to these two objects: he strives to invent methods that may enable him not only to work better, but more quickly and more cheaply; or if he cannot succeed in that, to diminish the intrinsic quality of the thing he makes, without rendering it wholly unfit for the use for which it is intended. When none but the wealthy had watches, they were almost all very good ones; few are now made that are worth much, but everybody has one in his pocket. Thus the democratic principle not only tends to direct

the human mind to the useful arts, but it induces the artisan to produce with great rapidity many imperfect commodities, and the consumer to content himself with these commodities.

Not that in democracies the arts are incapable, in case of need, of producing wonders. This may occasionally be so if customers appear who are ready to pay for time and trouble. In this rivalry of every kind of industry, in the midst of this immense competition and these countless experiments, some excellent workmen are formed who reach the utmost limits of their craft. But they rarely have an opportunity of showing what they can do; they are scrupulously sparing of their powers; they remain in a state of accomplished mediocrity, which judges itself, and though well able to shoot beyond the mark before it, aims only at what it hits. In aristocracies, on the contrary, workmen always do all they can; and when they stop, it is because they have reached the limit of their art. 7

When I arrive in a country where I find some of the finest productions of the arts, I learn from this fact nothing of the social condition or of the political constitution of the country. But if I perceive that the productions of the arts are generally of an inferior quality, very abundant, and very cheap, I am convinced that among the people where this occurs privilege is on the decline and that ranks are beginning to intermingle and will soon become one. 8

The handicraftsmen of democratic ages not only endeavor to bring their useful productions within the reach of the whole community, but strive to give to all their commodities attractive qualities that they do not in reality possess. In the confusion of all ranks everyone hopes to appear what he is not, and makes great exertions to succeed in this object. This sentiment, indeed, which is only too natural to the heart of man, does not originate in the democratic principle; but that principle applies it to material objects. The hypocrisy of virtue is of every age, but the hypocrisy of luxury belongs more particularly to the ages of democracy. 9

To satisfy these new cravings of human vanity the arts have recourse to every species of imposture; and these devices sometimes go so far as to defeat their own purpose. Imitation diamonds are now made which may be easily mistaken for real ones; as soon as the art of fabricating false diamonds becomes so perfect that they cannot be distinguished from real ones, it is probable that both will be abandoned and become mere pebbles again. 10

This leads me to speak of those arts which are called, by way of distinction, the fine arts. I do not believe that it is a necessary effect of a democratic social condition and of democratic institutions to diminish the number of those who cultivate the fine arts, but these causes exert a powerful influence on the manner in which these arts are cultivated. Many of those who had already contracted a taste for the fine arts are impoverished; on the other hand, many of those who are not yet rich begin to conceive that taste, at least by imitation; the number of consumers increases, but opulent and fastidious consumers become more scarce. Something analogous to what I 11 have already pointed out in the useful arts then takes place in the fine arts; the productions of artists are more numerous, but the merit of each production is diminished. No longer able to soar to what is great, they cultivate what is pretty and elegant, and appearance is more attended to than reality.

In aristocracies a few great pictures are produced; in democratic countries   12 a vast number of insignificant ones. In the former statues are raised of bronze; in the latter, they are modeled in plaster.

When I arrived for the first time at New York, by that part of the   13 Atlantic Ocean which is called the East River, I was surprised to perceive along the shore, at some distance from the city, a number of little palaces of white marble, several of which were of classic architecture. When I went the next day to inspect more closely one which had particularly attracted my notice, I found that its walls were of whitewashed brick, and its columns of painted wood. All the edifices that I had admired the night before were of the same kind.

The social condition and the institutions of democracy impart, moreover,   14 certain peculiar tendencies to all the imitative arts, which it is easy to point out. They frequently withdraw them from the delineation of the soul to fix them exclusively on that of the body, and they substitute the representation of motion and sensation for that of sentiment and thought; in a word, they put the real in the place of the ideal.

I doubt whether Raphael studied the minute intricacies of the mechanism   15 of the human body as thoroughly as the draftsmen of our own time. He did not attach the same importance as they do to rigorous accuracy on this point because he aspired to surpass nature. He sought to make of man something which should be superior to man and to embellish beauty itself. David and his pupils, on the contrary, were as good anatomists as they were painters. They wonderfully depicted the models that they had before their eyes, but they rarely imagined anything beyond them; they followed nature with fidelity, while Raphael sought for something better than nature. They have left us an exact portraiture of man, but he discloses in his works a glimpse of the Divinity.

This remark as to the manner of treating a subject is no less applicable   16 to its choice. The painters of the Renaissance generally sought far above themselves, and away from their own time, for mighty subjects, which left to their imagination an unbounded range. Our painters often employ their talents in the exact imitation of the details of private life, which they have always before their eyes; and they are forever copying trivial objects, the originals of which are only too abundant in nature.

Questions for Discussion and Writing

1. What does Tocqueville seem to mean when he asserts, in paragraph 9: "The hypocrisy of virtue is of every age, but the hypocrisy of luxury belongs more particularly to the ages of democracy"?

2. Tocqueville begins this chapter by talking generally about the relationship of the arts to political systems, moves to a specific discussion of the practical and fine arts of America, jumps to a specific comparison of the European painters Raphael and David, and then closes with a brief discussion of Renaissance art. Why does he employ such an odd succession of subjects to convey to his reader the "spirit" in which "the Americans cultivate the arts"? Why might not Tocqueville return to his central subject at the end of the chapter?

3. How does Tocqueville use the ethos of an "outsider" to enhance his argument? Examine specific passages in which his ethos is particularly noticeable.

4. In your estimation, is Tocqueville's claim that Americans, as citizens of a democratic nation, "cultivate the arts that serve to render life easy in preference to those whose object is to adorn it" (paragraph 1) still true at the close of the twentieth century? Do we, as Tocqueville claimed in the 1830s, "habitually prefer the useful to the beautiful," and do we "require that the beautiful should be useful" (paragraph 1)? How do artifacts from our media rhetoric and mass culture support or undermine Tocqueville's original argument? Write an essay that addresses one or more of these questions.

KARL MARX

(1818–1883)

FREDERICK ENGELS

(1820–1895)

Karl Marx was the most influential— and most controversial—economist of all time. He was a saint to some and a devil to others, but every economist who has followed him has had no choice but to grapple with his monumental contribution to the field. In twentieth-century revolutions across the globe from Cuba to China, Marx's ideas have inspired the disenchanted to topple time-honored regimes and experiment with alternative forms of government. What is it that is so special about this man, his ideas, and his rhetorical practice?

In fact, Marx's life lacked most of the revolutionary excitement of his ideological legacy. He was born of Jewish parents in the city of Trier in the Prussian Rhineland. His father converted to Christianity while Karl was a child, and he was baptized a Protestant. Marx came of age as the Holy Alliance—a conservative faction of European countries that included Russia, Prussia, and Austria—was attempting to wipe out the memory of the French Revolution, and he came to resent this reactionary backlash.

As a student at the universities of Bonn and Berlin, Marx studied history and philosophy. He was strongly influenced by the work of the great German philosopher Georg Wilhelm Friedrich Hegel. Hegel's dialectical method, a process in which a "thesis" generates its own "antithesis" to produce a new "synthesis," shaped Marx's world view. For socialist-leaning Marx, though, who admired the democratic ideals of the French Revolution, Hegel's conservative philosophy needed to be applied to the world of material and social reality. After receiving his doctorate at the University of Jena, Marx began work as an editor in Cologne and married the daughter of a high government official. When Marx's paper was suppressed because it ran counter to the interests of the government, he and his wife sought refuge in Paris. It was there that he met many of the important socialists of the age, including Frederick Engels.

Engels, the eldest child of a wealthy German textile manufacturer, grew up with a keen awareness of the problems of class structure in Europe. When he moved to Manchester, England in 1842 to work at one of his father's factories, he had already rubbed elbows with French socialists and developed a left-of-center outlook on the world. Outraged over the plight of poor laborers, he was soon to publish a work entitled The Condition of the Working Class in England. It is no surprise, then, that he and Marx would have much to talk about, and they soon established a friendship that would last until Marx's death.

In 1848, while Marx was living in exile in Brussels, he and Engels collaborated on The Manifesto of the Communist Party, *their concise statement of the history of economics and the role of the worker in the future of civilization. Although the first draft of the* Manifesto *was written by Engels, Marx is given more credit for its final form and content. Hegel's philosophical dialectic became Marx's "dialectical materialism," an economic theory in which the shortcomings of capitalism and the class struggle it inevitably perpetuates lead first to the dictatorship of the proletariat and ultimately to a democratic form of communism.*

In 1849, Marx and his family settled in permanent exile in London. Although they lived in grinding poverty for the rest of his life, Marx, with the financial support and encouragement of his friend Engels, conducted extensive economic research and wrote prolifically. Unlike Engels', Marx's leadership role in the actual organization of labor was minimal, but he continued to support their cause, and his published work demonstrated his deep-seated belief. His greatest contribution to economic theory, Das Kapital, *filled three volumes, but only the first was published in his lifetime. Engels himself oversaw the publication of the second two. After Marx's death, in fact, Engels continued to promote Marxism and organize labor. Although he was not the thinker his friend was, he nonetheless must be remembered as a socialist crusader who made his own important contributions to nineteenth-century social thought.*

As one reads Marx—and Engels, for that matter—it is important to realize that the original theories of the man and many of the actions taken in his name long after his death cannot necessarily be equated. There is no reason to believe that Marx (who loved democracy, treasured the nineteenth-century liberal-humanitarian tradition, and hated autocratic monarchy and slavery), would have supported most of the all-too-familiar crimes committed by "Marxist" dictators around the world. In fact, Engels reported that his friend actually once declared, "I am not a Marxist."

As you read the Communist Manifesto, *consider what made it such a powerful document in its time and try to determine the grounds on which its persuasion depends.*

MANIFESTO OF THE COMMUNIST PARTY

A spectre is haunting Europe—the spectre of Communism. All the Powers   1
of old Europe have entered into a holy alliance to exorcise this spectre:
Pope and Czar, Metternich[1] and Guizot,[2] French Radicals and German
police-spies.

Where is the party in opposition that has not been decried as Communistic   2
by its opponents in power? Where the Opposition that has not hurled back
the branding reproach of Communism, against the more advanced opposition
parties, as well as against its reactionary adversaries?

Two things result from this fact.   3

I.   Communism is already acknowledged by all European Powers to be
      itself a Power.
II.   It is high time that Communists should openly, in the face of the
      whole world, publish their views, their aims, their tendencies, and
      meet this nursery tale of the Spectre of Communism with a Manifesto
      of the party itself.

To this end, Communists of various nationalities have assembled in   4
London, and sketched the following Manifesto, to be published in the
English, French, German, Italian, Flemish and Danish languages.

I

BOURGEOISIE AND PROLETARIANS[3]

The history of all hitherto existing society[4] is the history of class struggles.   5

Freeman and slave, patrician and plebeian, lord and serf, guild-master[5]   6
and journeyman, in a word, oppressor and oppressed, stood in constant

---

The footnotes by Engels are highly Marxist in perspective and therefore must be read as
part of the overall argument. [Editors' note.]

[1] *Metternich*: Prince Klemens Wenzel Nepomuk Lothar von Metternich (1773–1859), a
conservative Austrian statesman who amassed great power in nineteenth-century Europe.
He was an important player in the Holy Alliance. [Editors' note.]

[2] *Guizot:* François Pierre Guillaume Guizot (1787–1874), a French historian and statesman.
[Editors' note.]

[3] By bourgeoisie is meant the class of modern Capitalists, owners of the means of social
production and employers of wage-labour. By proletariat, the class of modern wage-labourers
who, having no means of production of their own, are reduced to selling their labour-power
in order to live. [Note by Engels to the English edition of 1888.]

[4] That is, all *written* history. In 1824, the pre-history of society, the social organisation
existing previous to recorded history, was all but unknown. Since then, Haxthausen

opposition to one another, carried on an uninterrupted, now hidden, now open fight, a fight that each time ended, either in a revolutionary re-constitution of society at large, or in the common ruin of the contending classes.

In the earlier epochs of history, we find almost everywhere a complicated arrangement of society into various orders, a manifold gradation of social rank. In ancient Rome we have patricians, knights, plebeians, slaves; in the Middle Ages, feudal lords, vassals, guild-masters, journeymen, ap-prentices, serfs; in almost all of these classes, again, subordinate gradations. 7

The modern bourgeois society that has sprouted from the ruins of feudal society has not done away with class antagonisms. It has but established new classes, new conditions of oppression, new forms of struggle in place of the old ones. 8

Our epoch, the epoch of the bourgeoisie, possesses, however, this distinctive feature: it has simplified the class antagonisms. Society as a whole is more and more splitting up into two great hostile camps, into two great classes directly facing each other: Bourgeoisie and Proletariat. 9

From the serfs of the Middle Ages sprang the chartered burghers of the earliest towns. From these burgesses the first elements of the bourgeoisie were developed. 10

The discovery of America, the rounding of the Cape, opened up fresh ground for the rising bourgeoisie. The East-Indian and Chinese markets, the colonisation of America, trade with the colonies, the increase in the means of exchange and in commodities generally, gave to commerce, to navigation, to industry, an impulse never before known, and thereby, to the revolutionary element in the tottering feudal society, a rapid development. 11

The feudal system of industry, under which industrial production was monopolised by closed guilds, now no longer sufficed for the growing wants of the new markets. The manufacturing system took its place. The guild-masters were pushed on one side by the manufacturing middle class; division of labour between the different corporate guilds vanished in the face of division of labour in each single workshop. 12

---

discovered common ownership of land in Russia, Maurer proved it to be the social foundation from which all Teutonic races started in history, and by and by village communities were found to be, or to have been the primitive form of society everywhere from India to Ireland. The inner organisation of this primitive Communistic society was laid bare, in its typical form, by Morgan's crowning discovery of the true nature of the *gens* and its relation to the *tribe*. With the dissolution of these primaeval communities society begins to be differentiated into separate and finally antagonistic classes. I have attempted to retrace this process of dissolution in: "Der Ursprung der Familie, des Privateigenthums und des Staats" [*The Origin of the Family, Private Property and the State*—Ed.], 2nd edition, Stuttgart 1886. [Note by Engels to the English edition of 1888].

[5] Guild-master, that is, a full member of a guild, a master within, not a head of a guild. [Note by Engels to the English edition of 1888.]

Meantime the markets kept ever growing, the demand ever rising. Even 13 manufacture no longer sufficed. Thereupon, steam and machinery revolutionised industrial production. The place of manufacture was taken by the giant, Modern Industry, the place of the industrial middle class, by industrial millionaires, the leaders of whole industrial armies, the modern bourgeois.

Modern industry has established the world-market, for which the 14 discovery of America paved the way. This market has given an immense development to commerce, to navigation, to communication by land. This development has, in its turn, reacted on the extension of industry; and in proportion as industry, commerce, navigation, railways extended, in the same proportion the bourgeoisie developed, increased its capital, and pushed into the background every class handed down from the Middle Ages.

We see, therefore, how the modern bourgeoisie is itself the product of 15 a long course of development, of a series of revolutions in the modes of production and of exchange.

Each step in the development of the bourgeoisie was accompanied by a 16 corresponding political advance of that class. An oppressed class under the sway of the feudal nobility, an armed and self-governing association in the mediaeval commune[6]; here independent urban republic (as in Italy and Germany), there taxable "third estate" of the monarchy (as in France), afterwards, in the period of manufacture proper, serving either the semi-feudal or the absolute monarchy as a counterpoise against the nobility, and, in fact, corner-stone of the great monarchies in general, the bourgeoisie has at last, since the establishment of Modern Industry and of the world-market, conquered for itself, in the modern representative State, exclusive political sway. The executive of the modern State is but a committee for managing the common affairs of the whole bourgeoisie.

The bourgeoisie, historically, has played a most revolutionary part. 17

The bourgeoisie, wherever it has got the upper hand, has put an end to 18 all feudal, patriarchal, idyllic relations. It has pitilessly torn asunder the motley feudal ties that bound man to his "natural superiors," and has left remaining no other nexus between man and man than naked self-interest, than callous "cash payment." It has drowned the most heavenly ecstasies of religious fervour, or chivalrous enthusiasm, of philistine sentimentalism, in the icy water of egotistical calculation. It has resolved personal worth

---

[6] "Commune" was the name taken, in France, by the nascent towns even before they had conquered from their feudal lords and masters local self-government and political rights as the "Third Estate". Generally speaking, for the economical development of the bourgeoisie, England is here taken as the typical country; for its political development, France. [Note by Engels to the English edition of 1888.]

This was the name given their urban communities by the townsmen of Italy and France, after they had purchased or wrestled their initial rights of self-government from their feudal lords. [Note by Engels to the German edition of 1890.]

into exchange value, and in place of the numberless indefeasible chartered freedoms, has set up that single, unconscionable freedom—Free Trade. In one word, for exploitation, veiled by religious and political illusions, it has substituted naked, shameless, direct, brutal exploitation.

The bourgeoisie has stripped of its halo every occupation hitherto honoured 19 and looked up to with reverent awe. It has converted the physician, the lawyer, the priest, the poet, the man of science, into its paid wage-labourers.

The bourgeoisie has torn away from the family its sentimental veil, and 20 has reduced the family relation to a mere money relation.

The bourgeoisie has disclosed how it came to pass that the brutal display 21 of vigour in the Middle Ages, which Reactionists[7] so much admire, found its fitting complement in the most slothful indolence. It has been the first to show what man's activity can bring about. It has accomplished wonders far surpassing Egyptian pyramids, Roman aqueducts, and Gothic cathedrals; it has conducted expeditions that put in the shade all former Exoduses of nations and crusades.

The bourgeoisie cannot exist without constantly revolutionising the 22 instruments of production, and thereby the relations of production, and with them the whole relations of society. Conservation of the old modes of production in unaltered form, was, on the contrary, the first condition of existence for all earlier industrial classes. Constant revolutionising of production, uninterrupted disturbance of all social conditions, everlasting uncertainty and agitation distinguish the bourgeois epoch from all earlier ones. All fixed, fast-frozen relations, with their train of ancient and venerable prejudices and opinions, are swept away, all new-formed ones become antiquated before they can ossify. All that is solid melts into air, all that is holy is profaned, and man is at last compelled to face with sober senses, his real conditions of life, and his relations with his kind.

The need of a constantly expanding market for its products chases the 23 bourgeoisie over the whole surface of the globe. It must nestle everywhere, settle everywhere, establish connexions everywhere.

The bourgeoisie has through its exploitation of the world-market given 24 a cosmopolitan character to production and consumption in every country. To the great chagrin of Reactionists, it has drawn from under the feet of industry the national ground on which it stood. All old-established national industries have been destroyed or are daily being destroyed. They are dislodged by new industries, whose introduction becomes a life and death question for all civilised nations, by industries that no longer work up indigenous raw material, but raw material drawn from the remotest zones; industries whose products are consumed, not only at home, but in every quarter of the globe. In place of the old wants, satisfied by the productions

---

[7] *Reactionists:* nineteenth-century conservatives who wished Europe to return to the aristocratic attitudes of the era preceding the French Revolution. [Editors' note.]

of the country, we find new wants, requiring for their satisfaction the products of distant lands and climes. In place of the old local and national seclusion and self-sufficiency, we have intercourse in every direction, universal inter-dependence of nations. And as in material, so also in intellectual production. The intellectual creations of individual nations become common property. National one-sidedness and narrow-mindedness become more and more impossible, and from the numerous national and local literatures, there arises a world literature.

The bourgeoisie, by the rapid improvement of all instruments of production, by the immensely facilitated means of communication, draws all, even the most barbarian, nations into civilisation. The cheap prices of its commodities are the heavy artillery with which it batters down all Chinese walls, with which it forces the barbarians' intensely obstinate hatred of foreigners to capitulate. It compels all nations, on pain of extinction, to adopt the bourgeois mode of production; it compels them to introduce what it calls civilisation into their midst, *i.e.*, to become bourgeois themselves. In one word, it creates a world after its own image. 25

The bourgeoisie has subjected the country to the rule of the towns. It has created enormous cities, has greatly increased the urban population as compared with the rural, and has thus rescued a considerable part of the population from the idiocy of rural life. Just as it has made the country dependent on the towns, so it has made barbarian and semi-barbarian countries dependent on the civilised ones, nations of peasants on nations of bourgeois, the East on the West. 26

The bourgeoisie keeps more and more doing away with the scattered state of the population, of the means of production, and of property. It has agglomerated population, centralised means of production, and has concentrated property in a few hands. The necessary consequence of this was political centralisation. Independent, or but loosely connected provinces, with separate interests, laws, governments and systems of taxation, became lumped together into one nation, with one government, one code of laws, one national class-interest, one frontier and one customs-tariff. 27

The bourgeoisie, during its rule of scarce one hundred years, has created more massive and more colossal productive forces than have all preceding generations together. Subjection of Nature's forces to man, machinery, application of chemistry to industry and agriculture, steam-navigation, railways, electric telegraphs, clearing of whole continents for cultivation, canalisation of rivers, whole populations conjured out of the ground—what earlier century had even a presentiment that such productive forces slumbered in the lap of social labour? 28

We see then: the means of production and of exchange, on whose foundation the bourgeoisie built itself up, were generated in feudal society. At a certain stage in the development of these means of production and of exchange, the conditions under which feudal society produced and exchanged, the feudal organisation of agriculture and manufacturing industry, in one 29 word, the feudal relations of property became no longer compatible with the already developed productive forces; they became so many fetters. They had to be burst asunder; they were burst asunder.

Into their place stepped free competition, accompanied by a social and political constitution adapted to it, and by the economical and political sway of the bourgeois class. ₃₀

A similar movement is going on before our own eyes. Modern bourgeois society with its relations of production, of exchange and of property, a society that has conjured up such gigantic means of production and of exchange, is like the sorcerer, who is no longer able to control the powers of the nether world whom he has called up by his spells. For many a decade past the history of industry and commerce is but the history of the revolt of modern productive forces against modern conditions of production, against the property relations that are the conditions for the existence of the bourgeoisie and of its rule. It is enough to mention the commercial crises that by their periodical return put on trial, each time more threateningly, the existence of the entire bourgeois society. In these crises a great part not only of the existing products, but also of the previously created productive forces, are periodically destroyed. In these crises there breaks out an epidemic that, in all earlier epochs, would have seemed an absurdity—the epidemic of over-production. Society suddenly finds itself put back into a state of momentary barbarism; it appears as if a famine, a universal war of devastation had cut off the supply of every means of subsistence; industry and commerce seem to be destroyed; and why? Because there is too much civilisation, too much means of subsistence, too much industry, too much commerce. The productive forces at the disposal of society no longer tend to further the development of the conditions of bourgeois property; on the contrary, they have become too powerful for these conditions, by which they are fettered, and so soon as they overcome these fetters, they bring disorder into the whole of bourgeois society, endanger the existence of bourgeois property. The conditions of bourgeois society are too narrow to comprise the wealth created by them. And how does the bourgeoisie get over these crises? On the one hand by enforced destruction of a mass of productive forces; on the other, by the conquest of new markets, and by the more thorough exploitation of the old ones. That is to say, by paving the way for more extensive and more destructive crises, and by diminishing the means whereby crises are prevented.

The weapons with which the bourgeoisie felled feudalism to the ground are now turned against the bourgeoisie itself. ₃₂

But not only has the bourgeoisie forged the weapons that bring death to itself; it has also called into existence the men who are to wield those weapons—the modern working class—the proletarians. ₃₃

In proportion as the bourgeoisie, *i.e.*, capital, is developed, in the same proportion is the proletariat, the modern working class, developed—a class of labourers, who live only so long as they find work, and who find work ₃₄

only so long as their labour increases capital. These labourers, who must sell themselves piecemeal, are a commodity, like every other article of commerce, and are consequently exposed to all the vicissitudes of competition, to all the fluctuations of the market.

Owing to the extensive use of machinery and to division of labour, the 35 work of the proletarians has lost all individual character, and, consequently, all charm for the workman. He becomes an appendage of the machine, and it is only the most simple, most monotonous, and most easily acquired knack, that is required of him. Hence, the cost of production of a workman is restricted, almost entirely, to the means of subsistence that he requires for his maintenance, and for the propagation of his race. But the price of a commodity, and therefore also of labor, is equal to its cost of production. In proportion, therefore, as the repulsiveness of the work increases, the wage decreases. Nay more, in proportion as the use of machinery and division of labour increases, in the same proportion the burden of toil also increases, whether by prolongation of the working hours, by increase of the work exacted in a given time or by increased speed of the machinery, etc.

Modern industry has converted the little workshop of the patriarchal 36 master into the great factory of the industrial capitalist. Masses of labourers, crowded into the factory, are organised like soldiers. As privates of the industrial army they are placed under the command of a perfect hierarchy of officers and sergeants. Not only are they slaves of the bourgeois class, and of the bourgeois State; they are daily and hourly enslaved by the machine, by the overlooker, and, above all, by the individual bourgeois manufacturer himself. The more openly this despotism proclaims gain to be its end and aim, the more petty, the more hateful and the more embittering it is.

The less the skill and exertion of strength implied in manual labour, in 37 other words, the more modern industry becomes developed, the more is the labour of men superseded by that of women. Differences of age and sex have no longer any distinctive social validity for the working class. All are instruments of labour, more or less expensive to use, according to their age and sex.

No sooner is the exploitation of the labourer by the manufacturer, so 38 far, at an end, and he receives his wages in cash, than he is set upon by the other portions of the bourgeoisie, the landlord, the shopkeeper, the pawnbroker, etc.

The lower strata of the middle class—the small tradespeople, shopkeepers, 39 and retired tradesmen generally, the handicraftsmen and peasants—all these sink gradually into the proletariat, partly because their diminutive capital does not suffice for the scale on which Modern Industry is carried on, and is swamped in the competition with the large capitalists, partly because their specialised skill is rendered worthless by new methods of production. Thus the proletariat is recruited from all classes of the population.

The proletariat goes through various stages of development. With its 40
birth begins its struggle with the bourgeoisie. At first the contest is carried
on by individual labourers, then by the workpeople of a factory, then by
the operatives of one trade, in one locality, against the individual bourgeois
who directly exploits them. They direct their attacks not against the bourgeois
conditions of production, but against the instruments of production themselves; they destroy imported wares that compete with their labour, they
smash to pieces machinery, they set factories ablaze, they seek to restore by
force the vanished status of the workman of the Middle Ages.

At this stage the labourers still form an incoherent mass scattered over 41
the whole country, and broken up by their mutual competition. If anywhere
they unite to form more compact bodies, this is not yet the consequence of
their own active union, but of the union of the bourgeoisie, which class,
in order to attain its own political ends, is compelled to set the whole
proletariat in motion, and is moreover yet, for a time, able to do so. At
this stage, therefore, the proletarians do not fight their enemies, but the
enemies of their enemies, the remnants of absolute monarchy, the landowners,
the non-industrial bourgeois, the petty bourgeoisie. Thus the whole historical
movement is concentrated in the hands of the bourgeoisie; every victory so
obtained is a victory for the bourgeoisie.

But with the development of industry the proletariat not only increases 42
in number; it becomes concentrated in greater masses, its strength grows,
and it feels that strength more. The various interests and conditions of life
within the ranks of the proletariat are more and more equalised, in
proportion as machinery obliterates all distinctions of labour, and nearly
everywhere reduces wages to the same low level. The growing competition
among the bourgeois, and the resulting commercial crises, make the wages
of the workers ever more fluctuating. The unceasing improvement of
machinery, ever more rapidly developing, makes their livelihood more and
more precarious; the collisions between individual workmen and individual
bourgeois take more and more the character of collisions between two
classes. Thereupon the workers begin to form combinations (Trades' Unions)
against the bourgeois; they club together in order to keep up the rate of
wages; they found permanent associations in order to make provision
beforehand for these occasional revolts. Here and there the contest breaks
out into riots.

Now and then the workers are victorious, but only for a time. The real 43
fruit of their battles lies, not in the immediate result, but in the ever-
expanding union of the workers. This union is helped on by the improved
means of communication that are created by modern industry and that place
the workers of different localities in contact with one another. It was just
this contact that was needed to centralise the numerous local struggles, all
of the same character, into one national struggle between classes. But every
class struggle is a political struggle. And that union, to attain which the
burghers of the Middle Ages, with their miserable highways, required

centuries, the modern proletarians, thanks to railways, achieve in a few years.

This organisation of the proletarians into a class, and consequently into 44 a political party, is continually being upset again by the competition between the workers themselves. But it ever rises up again, stronger, firmer, mightier. It compels legislative recognition of particular interests of the workers, by taking advantage of the divisions among the bourgeoisie itself. Thus the ten-hours' bill in England was carried.

Altogether collisions between the classes of the old society further, in 45 many ways, the course of development of the proletariat. The bourgeoisie finds itself involved in a constant battle. At first with the aristocracy; later on, with those portions of the bourgeoisie itself, whose interests have become antagonistic to the progress of industry; at all times, with the bourgeoisie of foreign countries. In all these battles it sees itself compelled to appeal to the proletariat, to ask for its help, and thus, to drag it into the political arena. The bourgeoisie itself, therefore, supplies the proletariat with its own elements of political and general education, in other words, it furnishes the proletariat with weapons for fighting the bourgeoisie.

Further, as we have already seen, entire sections of the ruling classes 46 are, by the advance of industry, precipitated into the proletariat, or are at least threatened in their conditions of existence. These also supply the proletariat with fresh elements of enlightenment and progress.

Finally, in times when the class struggle nears the decisive hour, the 47 process of dissolution going on within the ruling class, in fact within the whole range of old society, assumes such a violent, glaring character, that a small section of the ruling class cuts itself adrift, and joins the revolutionary class, the class that holds the future in its hands. Just as, therefore, at an earlier period, a section of the nobility went over to the bourgeoisie, so now a portion of the bourgeoisie goes over to the proletariat, and in particular, a portion of the bourgeois ideologists, who have raised themselves to the level of comprehending theoretically the historical movement as a whole.

Of all the classes that stand face to face with the bourgeoisie today, the 48 proletariat alone is a really revolutionary class. The other classes decay and finally disappear in the face of Modern Industry; the proletariat is its special and essential product.

The lower middle class, the small manufacturer, the shopkeeper, the 49 artisan, the peasant, all these fight against the bourgeoisie, to save from extinction their existence as fractions of the middle class. They are therefore not revolutionary, but conservative. Nay more, they are reactionary, for they try to roll back the wheel of history. If by chance they are revolutionary, they are so only in view of their impending transfer into the proletariat, they thus defend not their present, but their future interests, they desert their own standpoint to place themselves at that of the proletariat.

The "dangerous class," the social scum, that passively rotting mass thrown   50
off by the lowest layers of old society, may, here and there, be swept into
the movement by a proletarian revolution, its conditions of life, however,
prepare it far more for the part of a bribed tool of reactionary intrigue.

In the conditions of the proletariat, those of old society at large are   51
already virtually swamped. The proletarian is without property; his relation
to his wife and children has no longer anything in common with the
bourgeois family-relations; modern industrial labour, modern subjection to
capital, the same in England as in France, in America as in Germany, has
stripped him of every trace of national character. Law, morality, religion,
are to him so many bourgeois prejudices, behind which lurk in ambush
just as many bourgeois interests.

All the preceding classes that got the upper hand, sought to fortify their   52
already acquired status by subjecting society at large to their conditions of
appropriation. The proletarians cannot become masters of the productive
forces of society, except by abolishing their own previous mode of
appropriation, and thereby also every other previous mode of appropriation.
They have nothing of their own to secure and to fortify; their mission is to
destroy all previous securities for, and insurances of, individual property.

All previous historical movements were movements of minorities, or in   53
the interests of minorities. The proletarian movement is the self-conscious,
independent movement of the immense majority, in the interests of the
immense majority. The proletariat, the lowest stratum of our present society,
cannot stir, cannot raise itself up, without the whole superincumbent strata
of official society being sprung into the air.

Though not in substance, yet in form, the struggle of the proletariat   54
with the bourgeoisie is at first a national struggle. The proletariat of each
country must, of course, first of all settle matters with its own bourgeoisie.

In depicting the most general phases of the development of the proletariat,   55
we traced the more or less veiled civil war, raging within existing society,
up to the point where that war breaks out into open revolution, and where
the violent overthrow of the bourgeoisie lays the foundation for the sway
of the proletariat.

Hitherto, every form of society has been based, as we have already seen,   56
on the antagonism of oppressing and oppressed classes. But in order to
oppress a class, certain conditions must be assured to it under which it can,
at least, continue its slavish existence. The serf, in the period of serfdom,
raised himself to membership in the commune, just as the petty bourgeois,
under the yoke of feudal absolutism, managed to develop into a bourgeois.
The modern labourer, on the contrary, instead of rising with the progress
of industry, sinks deeper and deeper below the conditions of existence of
his own class. He becomes a pauper, and pauperism develops more rapidly
than population and wealth. And here it becomes evident, that the bourgeoisie
is unfit any longer to be the ruling class in society, and to impose its

conditions of existence upon society as an over-riding law. It is unfit to rule because it is incompetent to assure an existence to its slave within his slavery, because it cannot help letting him sink into such a state, that it has to feed him, instead of being fed by him. Society can no longer live under this bourgeoisie, in other words, its existence is no longer compatible with society.

The essential condition for the existence, and for the sway of the bourgeois 57 class, is the formation and augmentation of capital; the condition for capital is wage-labour. Wage-labour rests exclusively on competition between the labourers. The advance of industry, whose involuntary promoter is the bourgeoisie, replaces the isolation of the labourers, due to competition, by their revolutionary combination, due to association. The development of Modern Industry, therefore, cuts from under its feet the very foundation on which the bourgeoisie produces and appropriates products. What the bourgeoisie, therefore, produces, above all, is its own grave-diggers. Its fall and the victory of the proletariat are equally inevitable.

II

PROLETARIANS AND COMMUNISTS

In what relation do the Communists stand to the proletarians as a whole? 58

The Communists do not form a separate party opposed to other working- 59 class parties.

They have no interests separate and apart from those of the proletariat as 60 a whole.

They do not set up any sectarian principles of their own, by which to 61 shape and mould the proletarian movement.

The Communists are distinguished from the other working-class parties 62 by this only: 1. In the national struggles of the proletarians of the different countries, they point out and bring to the front the common interests of the entire proletariat, independently of all nationality. 2. In the various stages of development which the struggle of the working class against the bourgeoisie has to pass through, they always and everywhere represent the interests of the movement as a whole.

The Communists, therefore, are on the one hand, practically, the most 63 advanced and resolute section of the working-class parties of every country, that section which pushes forward all others; on the other hand, theoretically, they have over the great mass of the proletariat the advantage of clearly understanding the line of march, the conditions, and the ultimate general results of the proletarian movement.

The immediate aim of the Communists is the same as that of all the other 64 proletarian parties: formation of the proletariat into a class, overthrow of the bourgeois supremacy, conquest of political power by the proletariat.

The theoretical conclusions of the Communists are in no way based on 65 ideas or principles that have been invented, or discovered, by this or that would-be universal reformer.

They merely express, in general terms, actual relations springing from 66 an existing class struggle, from a historical movement going on under our very eyes. The abolition of existing property relations is not at all a distinctive feature of Communism.

All property relations in the past have continually been subject to historical 67 change consequent upon the change in historical conditions.

The French Revolution, for example, abolished feudal property in favour 68 of bourgeois property.

The distinguishing feature of Communism is not the abolition of property 69 generally, but the abolition of bourgeois property. But modern bourgeois private property is the final and most complete expression of the system of producing and appropriating products, that is based on class antagonisms, on the exploitation of the many by the few.

In this sense, the theory of the Communists may be summed up in the 70 single sentence: Abolition of private property.

We Communists have been reproached with the desire of abolishing the 71 right of personally acquiring property as the fruit of a man's own labour, which property is alleged to be the groundwork of all personal freedom, activity and independence.

Hard-won, self-acquired, self-earned property! Do you mean the property 72 of the petty artisan and of the small peasant, a form of property that preceded the bourgeois form? There is no need to abolish that; the development of industry has to a great extent already destroyed it, and is still destroying it daily.

Or do you mean modern bourgeois private property? 73

But does wage-labour create any property for the labourer? Not a bit. It 74 creates capital, *i.e.*, that kind of property which exploits wage-labour, and which cannot increase except upon condition of begetting a new supply of wage-labour for fresh exploitation. Property, in its present form, is based on the antagonism of capital and wage-labour. Let us examine both sides of this antagonism.

To be a capitalist, is to have not only a purely personal, but a social 75 *status* in production. Capital is a collective product, and only by the united action of many members, nay, in the last resort, only by the united action of all members of society, can it be set in motion.

Capital is, therefore, not a personal, it is a social power. 76

When, therefore, capital is converted into common property, into the 77 property of all members of society, personal property is not thereby transformed into social property. It is only the social character of the property that is changed. It loses its class-character.

Let us now take wage-labour. 78

The average price of wage-labour is the minimum wage, *i.e.*, that 79 quantum of the means of subsistence, which is absolutely requisite to keep the labourer in bare existence as a labourer. What, therefore, the wage-labourer appropriates by means of his labour, merely suffices to prolong and reproduce a bare existence. We by no means intend to abolish this personal appropriation of the products of labour, an appropriation that is made for the maintenance and reproduction of human life, and that leaves no surplus wherewith to command the labour of others. All that we want to do away with, is the miserable character of this appropriation, under which the labourer lives merely to increase capital, and is allowed to live only in so far as the interest of the ruling class requires it.

In bourgeois society, living labour is but a means to increase accumulated labour. In Communist society, accumulated labour is but a means to widen, to enrich, to promote the existence of the labourer. 80

In bourgeois society, therefore, the past dominates the present; in Communist society, the present dominates the past. In bourgeois society capital is independent and has individuality, while the living person is dependent and has no individuality. 81

And the abolition of this state of things is called by the bourgeois, abolition of individuality and freedom! And rightly so. The abolition of bourgeois individuality, bourgeois independence, and bourgeois freedom is undoubtedly aimed at. 82

By freedom is meant, under the present bourgeois conditions of production, free trade, free selling and buying. 83

But if selling and buying disappears, free selling and buying disappears also. This talk about free selling and buying, and all the other "brave words" of our bourgeoisie about freedom in general, have a meaning, if any, only in contrast with restricted selling and buying, with the fettered traders of the Middle Ages, but have no meaning when opposed to the Communistic abolition of buying and selling, of the bourgeois conditions of production, and of the bourgeoisie itself. 84

You are horrified at our intending to do away with private property. But in your existing society, private property is already done away with for nine-tenths of the population; its existence for the few is solely due to its non-existence in the hands of those nine-tenths. You reproach us, therefore, with intending to do away with a form of property, the necessary condition for whose existence is the non-existence of any property for the immense majority of society. 85

In one word, you reproach us with intending to do away with your property. Precisely so; that is just what we intend. 86

From the moment when labour can no longer be converted into capital, money, or rent, into a social power capable of being monopolised, *i.e.*, from the moment when individual property can no longer be transformed into bourgeois property, into capital, from that moment, you say, individuality vanishes. 87

You must, therefore, confess that by "individual" you mean no other 88 person than the bourgeois, than the middle-class owner of property. This person must, indeed, be swept out of the way, and made impossible.

Communism deprives no man of the power to appropriate the products   89
of society; all that it does is to deprive him of the power to subjugate the labour of others by means of such appropriation.

It has been objected that upon the abolition of private property all work   90
will cease, and universal laziness will overtake us.

According to this, bourgeois society ought long ago to have gone to the   91
dogs through sheer idleness; for those of its members who work, acquire nothing, and those who acquire anything, do not work. The whole of this objection is but another expression of the tautology: that there can no longer be any wage-labour when there is no longer any capital.

All objections urged against the Communistic mode of producing and   92
appropriating material products, have, in the same way, been urged against the Communistic modes of producing and appropriating intellectual prod-ucts. Just as, to the bourgeois, the disappearance of class property is the disappearance of production itself, so the disappearance of class culture is to him identical with the disappearance of all culture.

That culture, the loss of which he laments, is, for the enormous majority,   93
a mere training to act as a machine.

But don't wrangle with us so long as you apply, to our intended abolition   94
of bourgeois property, the standard of your bourgeois notions of freedom, culture, law, &c. Your very ideas are but the outgrowth of the conditions of your bourgeois production and bourgeois property, just as your juris-prudence is but the will of your class made into a law for all, a will, whose essential character and direction are determined by the economical conditions of existence of your class.

The selfish misconception that induces you to transform into eternal laws   95
of nature and of reason, the social forms springing from your present mode of production and form of property—historical relations that rise and disappear in the progress of production—this misconception you share with every ruling class that has preceded you. What you see clearly in the case of ancient property, what you admit in the case of feudal property, you are of course forbidden to admit in the case of your own bourgeois form of property.

Abolition of the family! Even the most radical flare up at this infamous   96
proposal of the Communists.

On what foundation is the present family, the bourgeois family, based?   97
On capital, on private gain. In its completely developed form this family exists only among the bourgeoisie. But this state of things finds its complement in the practical absence of the family among the proletarians, and in public prostitution.

The bourgeois family will vanish as a matter of course when its complement   98
vanishes, and both will vanish with the vanishing of capital.

Do you charge us with wanting to stop the exploitation of children by 99 their parents? To this crime we plead guilty.

But, you will say, we destroy the most hallowed of relations, when we 100 replace home education by social.

And your education! Is not that also social, and determined by the social 101 conditions under which you educate, by the intervention, direct or indirect, of society, by means of schools, &c.? The Communists have not invented the intervention of society in education; they do but seek to alter the character of that intervention, and to rescue education from the influence of the ruling class.

The bourgeois clap-trap about the family and education, about the 102 hallowed co-relation of parent and child, becomes all the more disgusting, the more, by the action of Modern Industry, all family ties among the proletarians are torn asunder, and their children transformed into simple articles of commerce and instruments of labour.

But you Communists would introduce community of women, screams 103 the whole bourgeoisie in chorus.

The bourgeois sees in his wife a mere instrument of production. He 104 hears that the instruments of production are to be exploited in common, and, naturally, can come to no other conclusion than that the lot of being common to all will likewise fall to the women.

He has not even a suspicion that the real point aimed at is to do away 105 with the status of women as mere instruments of production.

For the rest, nothing is more ridiculous than the virtuous indignation of 106 our bourgeois at the community of women which, they pretend, is to be openly and officially established by the Communists. The Communists have no need to introduce community of women; it has existed almost from time immemorial.

Our bourgeois, not content with having the wives and daughters of their 107 proletarians at their disposal, not to speak of common prostitutes, take the greatest pleasure in seducing each other's wives.

Bourgeois marriage is in reality a system of wives in common and thus, 108 at the most, what the Communists might possibly be reproached with, is that they desire to introduce, in substitution for a hypocritically concealed, an openly legalised community of women. For the rest, it is self-evident that the abolition of the present system of production must bring with it the abolition of the community of women springing from that system, *i.e.*, of prostitution both public and private.

The Communists are further reproached with desiring to abolish countries 109 and nationality.

The working men have no country. We cannot take from them what 110 they have not got. Since the proletariat must first of all acquire political supremacy, must rise to be the leading class of the nation, must constitute itself *the* nation, it is, so far, itself national, though not in the bourgeois sense of the word.

National differences and antagonisms between peoples are daily more and 111
more vanishing, owing to the development of the bourgeoisie, to freedom
of commerce, to the world-market, to uniformity in the mode of production
and in the conditions of life corresponding thereto.

The supremacy of the proletariat will cause them to vanish still faster. 112
United action, of the leading civilised countries at least, is one of the first
conditions for the emancipation of the proletariat.

In proportion as the exploitation of one individual by another is put an 113
end to, the exploitation of one nation by another will also be put an end to.
In proportion as the antagonism between classes within the nation vanishes,
the hostility of one nation to another will come to an end.

The charges against Communism made from a religious, a philosophical, 114
and, generally, from an ideological standpoint, are not deserving of serious
examination.

Does it require deep intuition to comprehend that man's ideas, views and 115
conceptions, in one word, man's consciousness, changes with every change
in the conditions of his material existence, in his social relations and in his
social life?

What else does the history of ideas prove, than that intellectual production 116
changes its character in proportion as material production is changed? The
ruling ideas of each age have ever been the ideas of its ruling class.

When people speak of ideas that revolutionise society, they do but express 117
the fact, that within the old society, the elements of a new one have been
created, and that the dissolution of the old ideas keeps even pace with the
dissolution of the old conditions of existence.

When the ancient world was in its last throes, the ancient religions were 118
overcome by Christianity. When Christian ideas succumbed in the 18th
century to rationalist ideas, feudal society fought its death battle with the
then revolutionary bourgeoisie. The ideas of religious liberty and freedom
of conscience merely gave expression to the sway of free competition within
the domain of knowledge.

"Undoubtedly," it will be said, "religious, moral, philosophical and 119
juridical ideas have been modified in the course of historical development.
But religion, morality, philosophy, political science, and law, constantly
survived this change."

"There are, besides, eternal truths, such as Freedom, Justice, etc., that 120
are common to all states of society. But Communism abolishes eternal
truths, it abolishes all religion, and all morality, instead of constituting
them on a new basis; it therefore acts in contradiction to all past historical
experience."

What does this accusation reduce itself to? The history of all past society 121
has consisted in the development of class antagonisms, antagonisms that
assumed different forms at different epochs.

But whatever form they may have taken, one fact is common to all past 122
ages, *viz.*, the exploitation of one part of society by the other. No wonder,

then, that the social consciousness of past ages, despite all the multiplicity and variety it displays, moves within certain common forms, or general ideas, which cannot completely vanish except with the total disappearance of class antagonisms.

The Communist revolution is the most radical rupture with traditional 123 property relations; no wonder that its development involves the most radical rupture with traditional ideas.

But let us have done with the bourgeois objections to Communism. 124

We have seen above, that the first step in the revolution by the working 125 class, is to raise the proletariat to the position of ruling class, to win the battle of democracy.

The proletariat will use its political supremacy to wrest, by degrees, all 126 capital from the bourgeoisie, to centralise all instruments of production in the hands of the State, *i.e.*, of the proletariat organised as the ruling class; and to increase the total of productive forces as rapidly as possible.

Of course, in the beginning, this cannot be effected except by means of 127 despotic inroads on the rights of property, and on the conditions of bourgeois production; by means of measures, therefore, which appear economically insufficient and untenable, but which, in the course of the movement, outstrip themselves, necessitate further inroads upon the old social order, and are unavoidable as a means of entirely revolutionising the mode of production.

These measures will of course be different in different countries. 128

Nevertheless in the most advanced countries, the following will be pretty 129 generally applicable.

1. Abolition of property in land and application of all rents of land to public purposes.
2. A heavy progressive or graduated income tax.
3. Abolition of all right of inheritance.
4. Confiscation of the property of all emigrants and rebels.
5. Centralisation of credit in the hands of the State, by means of a national bank with State capital and an exclusive monopoly.
6. Centralisation of the means of communication and transport in the hands of the State.
7. Extension of factories and instruments of production owned by the State; the bringing into cultivation of waste-lands, and the improvement of the soil generally in accordance with a common plan.
8. Equal liability of all to labour. Establishment of industrial armies, especially for agriculture.
9. Combination of agriculture with manufacturing industries; gradual abolition of the distinction between town and country, by a more equable distribution of the population over the country.

10. Free education for all children in public schools. Abolition of children's factory labour in its present form. Combination of education with industrial production, &c., &c.

When, in the course of development, class distinctions have disappeared, 130 and all production has been concentrated in the hands of a vast association of the whole nation, the public power will lose its political character. Political power, properly so called, is merely the organised power of one class for oppressing another. If the proletariat during its contest with the bourgeoisie is compelled, by the force of circumstances, to organise itself as a class, if, by means of a revolution, it makes itself the ruling class, and, as such, sweeps away by force the old conditions of production, then it will, along with these conditions, have swept away the conditions for the existence of class antagonisms and of classes generally, and will thereby have abolished its own supremacy as a class.

In place of the old bourgeois society, with its classes and class antagonisms, 131 we shall have an association, in which the free development of each is the condition for the free development of all.

III
SOCIALIST AND COMMUNIST LITERATURE

I. REACTIONARY SOCIALISM

A. FEUDAL SOCIALISM

Owing to their historical position, it became the vocation of the aristocracies 132 of France and England to write pamphlets against modern bourgeois society. In the French revolution of July 1830, and in the English reform agitation, these aristocracies again succumbed to the hateful upstart. Thenceforth, a serious political contest was altogether out of question. A literary battle alone remained possible. But even in the domain of literature the old cries of the restoration period[8] had become impossible.

In order to arouse sympathy, the aristocracy were obliged to lose sight, 133 apparently, of their own interests, and to formulate their indictment against the bourgeoisie in the interest of the exploited working class alone. Thus the aristocracy took their revenge by singing lampoons on their new master, and whispering in his ears sinister prophecies of coming catastrophe.

In this way arose Feudal Socialism: half lamentation, half lampoon; half 134

---

[8] Not the English Restoration 1660 to 1689, but the French Restoration 1814 to 1830. [Note by Engels to the English edition of 1888.]

echo of the past, half menace of the future; at times, by its bitter, witty and incisive criticism, striking the bourgeoisie to the very heart's core; but always ludicrous in its effect, through total incapacity to comprehend the march of modern history.

The aristocracy, in order to rally the people to them, waved the proletarian 135 alms-bag in front for a banner. But the people, so often as it joined them, saw on their hindquarters the old feudal coats of arms, and deserted with loud and irreverent laughter.

One section of the French Legitimists and "Young England" exhibited 136 this spectacle.

In pointing out that their mode of exploitation was different to that of 137 the bourgeoisie, the feudalists forget that they exploited under circumstances and conditions that were quite different, and that are now antiquated. In showing that, under their rule, the modern proletariat never existed, they forget that the modern bourgeoisie is the necessary offspring of their own form of society.

For the rest, so little do they conceal the reactionary character of their 138 criticism that their chief accusation against the bourgeoisie amounts to this, that under the bourgeois *régime* a class is being developed, which is destined to cut up root and branch the old order of society.

What they upbraid the bourgeoisie with is not so much that it creates a 139 proletariat, as that it creates a *revolutionary* proletariat.

In political practice, therefore, they join in all coercive measures against 140 the working class; and in ordinary life, despite their high-falutin phrases, they stoop to pick up the golden apples dropped from the tree of industry, and to barter truth, love, and honour for traffic in wool, beetroot-sugar, and potato spirits.[9]

As the parson has ever gone hand in hand with the landlord, so has 141 Clerical Socialism with Feudal Socialism.

Nothing is easier than to give Christian asceticism a Socialist tinge. Has 142 not Christianity declaimed against private property, against marriage, against the State? Has it not preached in the place of these, charity and poverty, celibacy and mortification of the flesh, monastic life and Mother Church? Christian Socialism is but the holy water with which the priest consecrates the heartburnings of the aristocrat.

---

[9] This applies chiefly to Germany where the landed aristocracy and squirearchy have large portions of their estates cultivated for their own account by stewards, and are, moreover, extensive beetroot-sugar manufacturers and distillers of potato spirits. The wealthier British aristocracy are, as yet, rather above that; but they, too, know how to make up for declining rents by lending their names to floaters of more or less shady joint-stock companies. [Note by Engels to the English edition of 1888.]

B. PETTY-BOURGEOIS SOCIALISM

The feudal aristocracy was not the only class that was ruined by the 143
bourgeoisie, not the only class whose conditions of existence pined and
perished in the atmosphere of modern bourgeois society. The mediaeval
burgesses and the small peasant proprietors were the precursors of the
modern bourgeoisie. In those countries which are but little developed,
industrially and commercially, these two classes still vegetate side by side
with the rising bourgeoisie.

In countries where modern civilisation has become fully developed, a 144
new class of petty bourgeois has been formed, fluctuating between proletariat
and bourgeoisie and ever renewing itself as a supplementary part of
bourgeois society. The individual members of this class, however, are being
constantly hurled down into the proletariat by the action of competition,
and, as modern industry develops, they even see the moment approaching
when they will completely disappear as an independent section of modern
society, to be replaced, in manufactures, agriculture and commerce, by
overlookers, bailiffs and shopmen.

In countries like France, where the peasants constitute far more than half 145
of the population, it was natural that writers who sided with the proletariat
against the bourgeoisie, should use, in their criticism of the bourgeois
régime, the standard of the peasant and petty bourgeois, and from the
standpoint of these intermediate classes should take up the cudgels for the
working class. Thus arose petty-bourgeois Socialism. Sismondi was the head
of this school, not only in France but also in England.

This school of Socialism dissected with great acuteness the contradictions 146
in the conditions of modern production. It laid bare the hypocritical
apologies of economists. It proved, incontrovertibly, the disastrous effects
of machinery and division of labour; the concentration of capital and land
in a few hands; overproduction and crises; it pointed out the inevitable ruin
of the petty bourgeois and peasant, the misery of the proletariat, the anarchy
in production, the crying inequalities in the distribution of wealth, the
industrial war of extermination between nations, the dissolution of old moral
bonds, of the old family relations, of the old nationalities.

In its positive aims, however, this form of Socialism aspires either to 147
restoring the old means of production and of exchange, and with them the
old property relations, and the old society, or to cramping the modern
means of production and of exchange, within the framework of the old
property relations that have been, and were bound to be, exploded by those
means. In either case, it is both reactionary and Utopian.

Its last words are: corporate guilds for manufacture, patriarchal relations 148
in agriculture.

Ultimately, when stubborn historical facts had dispersed all intoxicating 149
effects of self-deception, this form of Socialism ended in a miserable fit of
the blues.

C. GERMAN, OR "TRUE," SOCIALISM

The Socialist and Communist literature of France, a literature that originated 150 under the pressure of a bourgeoisie in power, and that was the expression of the struggle against this power, was introduced into Germany at a time when the bourgeoisie, in that country, has just begun its contest with feudal absolutism.

German philosophers, would-be philosophers, and *beaux esprits*, eagerly 151 seized on this literature, only forgetting, that when these writings immigrated from France into Germany, French social conditions had not immigrated along with them. In contact with German social conditions, this French literature lost all its immediate practical significnce, and assumed a purely literary aspect. Thus, to the German philosophers of the eighteenth century, the demands of the first French Revolution were nothing more than the demands of "Practical Reason" in general, and the utterance of the will of the revolutionary French bourgeoisie signified in their eyes the laws of pure Will, of Will as it was bound to be, of true human Will generally.

The work of the German *literati* consisted solely in bringing the new 152 French ideas into harmony with their ancient philosophical conscience, or rather, in annexing the French ideas without deserting their own philosophic point of view.

This annexation took place in the same way in which a foreign language 153 is appropriated, namely, by translation.

It is well known how the monks wrote silly lives of Catholic Saints *over* 154 the manuscripts on which the classical works of ancient heathendom had been written. The German *literati* reversed this process with the profane French literature. They wrote their philosophical nonsense beneath the French original. For instance, beneath the French criticism of the economic functions of money, they wrote "Alienation of Humanity," and beneath the French criticism of the bourgeois State they wrote "Dethronement of the Category of the General," and so forth.

The introduction of these philosophical phrases at the back of the French 155 historical criticisms they dubbed "Philosophy of Action," "True Socialism," "German Science of Socialism," "Philosophical Foundation of Socialism," and so on.

The French Socialist and Communist literature was thus completely 156 emasculated. And, since it ceased in the hands of the German to express the struggle of one class with the other, he felt conscious of having overcome "French one-sidedness" and of representing, not true requirements, but the requirements of Truth; not the interests of the proletariat, but the interests of Human Nature, of Man in general, who belongs to no class, has no reality, who exists only in the misty realm of philosophical fantasy.

This German Socialism, which took its schoolboy task so seriously and 157 solemnly, and extolled its poor stock-in-trade in such mountebank fashion, meanwhile gradually lost its pedantic innocence.

The fight of the German, and, especially, of the Prussian bourgeoisie, 158 against feudal aristocracy and absolute monarchy, in other words, the liberal movement, became more earnest.

By this, the long wished-for opportunity was offered to "True" Socialism 159 of confronting the political movement with the Socialist demands, of hurling the traditional anathemas against liberalism, against representative government, against bourgeois competition, bourgeois freedom of the press, bourgeois legislation, bourgeois liberty and equality, and of preaching to the masses that they had nothing to gain, and everything to lose, by this bourgeois movement. German Socialism forgot, in the nick of time, that the French criticism, whose silly echo it was, presupposed the existence of modern bourgeois society, with its corresponding economic conditions of existence, and the political constitution adapted thereto, the very things whose attainment was the object of the pending struggle in Germany.

To the absolute governments, with their following of parsons, professors, 160 country squires and officials, it served as a welcome scarecrow against the threatening bourgeoisie.

It was a sweet finish after the bitter pills of floggings and bullets with 161 which these same governments, just at that time, dosed the German working-class risings.

While this "true" Socialism thus served the governments as a weapon 162 for fighting the German bourgeoisie, it, at the same time, directly represented a reactionary interest, the interest of the German Philistines. In Germany the *petty-bourgeois* class, a relic of the sixteenth century, and since then constantly cropping up again under various forms, is the real social basis of the existing state of things.

To preserve this class is to preserve the existing state of things in 163 Germany. The industrial and political supremacy of the bourgeoisie threatens it with certain destruction; on the one hand, from the concentration of capital; on the other, from the rise of a revolutionary proletariat. "True" Socialism appeared to kill these two birds with one stone. It spread like an epidemic.

The robe of speculative cobwebs, embroidered with flowers of rhetoric, 164 steeped in the dew of sickly sentiment, this transcendental robe in which the German Socialists wrapped their sorry "eternal truths," all skin and bone, served to wonderfully increase the sale of their goods amongst such a public.

And on its part, German Socialism recognised, more and more, its own 165 calling as the bombastic representative of the petty-bourgeois Philistine.

It proclaimed the German nation to be the model nation, and the German 166 petty Philistine to be the typical man. To every villainous meanness of this model man it gave a hidden, higher, Socialistic interpretation, the exact contrary of its real character. It went to the extreme length of directly opposing the "brutally destructive" tendency of Communism, and of proclaiming its supreme and impartial contempt of all class struggles. With very few exceptions, all the so-called Socialist and Communist publications that now (1847) circulate in Germany belong to the domain of this foul and enervating literature.[10]

2. CONSERVATIVE, OR BOURGEOIS, SOCIALISM

A part of the bourgeoisie is desirous of redressing social grievances, in order to secure the continued existence of bourgeois society. 167

To this section belong economists, philanthropists, humanitarians, improvers of the condition of the working class, organisers of charity, members of societies for the prevention of cruelty to animals, temperance fanatics, hole-and-corner reformers of every imaginable kind. This form of Socialism has, moreover, been worked out into complete systems. 168

We may cite Proudhon's *Philosophie de la Misère* as an example of this form. 169

The Socialistic bourgeois want all the advantages of modern social conditions without the struggles and dangers necessarily resulting therefrom. They desire the existing state of society minus its revolutionary and disintegrating elements. They wish for a bourgeoisie without a proletariat. The bourgeoisie naturally conceives the world in which it is supreme to be the best; and bourgeois Socialism develops this comfortable conception into various more or less complete systems. In requiring the proletariat to carry out such a system, and thereby to march straightway into the social New Jerusalem, it but requires in reality, that the proletariat should remain within the bounds of existing society, but should cast away all its hateful ideas concerning the bourgeoisie. 170

A second and more practical, but less systematic, form of this Socialism sought to depreciate every revolutionary movement in the eyes of the working class, by showing that no mere political reform, but only a change in the material conditions of existence, in economical relations, could be of any advantage to them. By changes in the material conditions of existence, this form of Socialism, however, by no means understands abolition of the bourgeois relations of production, an abolition that can be effected only by a revolution, but administrative reforms, based on the continued existence of these relations; reforms, therefore, that in no respect affect the relations between capital and labour, but, at the best, lessen the cost, and simplify the administrative work, of bourgeois government. 171

Bourgeois Socialism attains adequate expression, when, and only when, it becomes a mere figure of speech. 172

---

[10] The revolutionary storm of 1848 swept away this whole shabby tendency and cured its protagonists of the desire to dabble further in Socialism. The chief representative and classical type of this tendency is Herr Karl Grün. [Note by Engels to the German edition of 1890.]

Free trade: for the benefit of the working class. Protective duties: for 173
the benefit of the working class. Prison Reform: for the benefit of the
working class. This is the last word and the only seriously meant word of
bourgeois Socialism.

It is summed up in the phrase: the bourgeois is a bourgeois—for the 174
benefit of the working class.

3. CRITICAL-UTOPIAN SOCIALISM AND COMMUNISM

We do not here refer to that literature which, in every great modern 175
revolution, has always given voice to the demands of the proletariat, such
as the writings of Babeuf and others.

The first direct attempts of the proletariat to attain its own ends, made 176
in times of universal excitement, when feudal society was being overthrown,
these attempts necessarily failed, owing to the then undeveloped state of the
proletariat, as well as to the absence of the economic conditions for its
emancipation, conditions that had yet to be produced, and could be produced
by the impending bourgeois epoch alone. The revolutionary literature that
accompanied these first movements of the proletariat had necessarily a
reactionary character. It inculcated universal asceticism and social levelling
in its crudest form.

The Socialist and Communist systems properly so called, those of Saint- 177
Simon, Fourier, Owen and others, spring into existence in the early
undeveloped period, described above, of the struggle between proletariat
and bourgeoisie (see Section I. Bourgeoisie and Proletariat).

The founders of these systems see, indeed, the class antagonisms, as well 178
as the action of the decomposing elements, in the prevailing form of society.
But the proletariat, as yet in its infancy, offers to them the spectacle of a
class without any historical initiative or any independent political movement.

Since the development of class antagonism keeps even pace with the 179
development of industry, the economic situation, as they find it, does not
as yet offer to them the material conditions for the emancipation of the
proletariat. They therefore search after a new social science, after new social
laws, that are to create these conditions.

Historical action is to yield to their personal inventive action, historically 180
created conditions of emancipation to fantastic ones, and the gradual,
spontaneous class-organisation of the proletariat to an organisation of society
specially contrived by these inventors. Future history resolves itself, in their
eyes, into the propaganda and the practical carrying out of their social plans.

In the formation of their plans they are conscious of caring chiefly for 181
the interests of the working class, as being the most suffering class. Only
from the point of view of being the most suffering class does the proletariat
exist for them.

The undeveloped state of the class struggle, as well as their own 182
surroundings, causes Socialists of this kind to consider themselves far

superior to all class antagonisms. They want to improve the condition of every member of society, even that of the most favoured. Hence, they habitually appeal to society at large, without distinction of class; nay, by preference, to the ruling class. For how can people, when once they understand their system, fail to see in it the best possible plan of the best possible state of society?

Hence, they reject all political, and especially all revolutionary, action; they wish to attain their ends by peaceful means, and endeavour, by small experiments, necessarily doomed to failure, and by the force of example, to pave the way for the new social Gospel. 183

Such fantastic pictures of future society, painted at a time when the proletariat is still in a very undeveloped state and has but a fantastic conception of its own position, correspond with the first instinctive yearnings of that class for a general reconstruction of society. 184

But these Socialist and Communist publications contain also a critical element. They attack every principle of existing society. Hence they are full of the most valuable materials for the enlightenment of the working class. The practical measures proposed in them—such as the abolition of the distinction between town and country, of the family, of the carrying on of industries for the account of private individuals, and of the wage system, the proclamation of social harmony, the conversion of the functions of the State into a mere superintendence of production, all these proposals point solely to the disappearance of class antagonisms which were, at that time, only just cropping up, and which, in these publications, are recognised in their earliest, indistinct and undefined forms only. These proposals, therefore, are of a purely Utopian character. 185

The significance of Critical-Utopian Socialism and Communism bears an inverse relation to historical development. In proportion as the modern class struggle develops and takes definite shape, this fantastic standing apart from the contest, these fantastic attacks on it, lose all practical value and all theoretical justification. Therefore, although the originators of these systems were, in many respects, revolutionary, their disciples have, in every case, formed mere reactionary sects. They hold fast by the original views of their masters, in opposition to the progressive historical development of the proletariat. They, therefore, endeavour, and that consistently, to deaden the class struggle and to reconcile the class antagonisms. They still dream of experimental realisation of their social Utopias, of founding isolated *"phalanstères,"* of establishing "Home Colonies," of setting up a "Little Icaria"[11]—duodecimo editions of the New Jerusalem—and to realise all 186

---

[11] *Phalanstères* were Socialist colonies on the plan of Charles Fourier; *Icaria* was the name given by Cabet to his Utopia and, later on, to his American Communist colony. [Note by Engels to the English edition of 1888.]

"Home colonies" were what Owen called his Communist model societies. *Phalanstères* these castles in the air, they are compelled to appeal to the feelings and purses of the bourgeois. By degrees they sink into the category of the reactionary conservative Socialists depicted above, differing from these only by more systematic pedantry, and by their fanatical and superstitious belief in the miraculous effects of their social science.

They, therefore, violently oppose all political action on the part of the 187 working class; such action, according to them, can only result from blind unbelief in the new Gospel.

The Owenites in England, and the Fourierists in France, respectively, 188 oppose the Chartists and the *Réformistes*.

IV
POSITION OF THE COMMUNISTS IN RELATION TO THE VARIOUS EXISTING OPPOSITION PARTIES

Section II has made clear the relations of the Communists to the existing 189 working-class parties, such as the Chartists in England and the Agrarian Reformers in America.

The Communists fight for the attainment of the immediate aims, for the 190 enforcement of the momentary interests of the working class; but in the movement of the present, they also represent and take care of the future of that movement. In France the Communists ally themselves with the Social-Democrats,[12] against the conservative and radical bourgeoisie, reserving, however, the right to take up a critical position in regard to phrases and illusions traditionally handed down from the great Revolution.

In Switzerland they support the Radicals, without losing sight of the fact 191 that this party consists of antagonistic elements, partly of Democratic Socialists, in the French sense, partly of radical bourgeois.

In Poland they support the party that insists on an agrarian revolution 192 as the prime condition for national emancipation, that party which fomented the insurrection of Cracow in 1846.

---

was the name of the public palaces planned by Fourier. *Icaria* was the name given to the Utopian land of fancy, whose Communist institutions Cabet portrayed. [Note by Engels to the German edition of 1890.]

[12] The party then represented in Parliament by Ledru-Rollin, in literature by Louis Blanc, in the daily press by the *Réforme*. The name of Social-Democracy signified, with these its inventors, a section of the Democratic or Republican party more or less tinged with Socialism. [Note by Engels to the English edition of 1888.]

The party in France which at that time called itself Socialist-Democratic was represented in political life by Ledru-Rollin and in literature by Louis Blanc; thus it differed immeasurably from present-day German Social-Democracy. [Note by Engels to the German edition of 1890.]

In Germany they fight with the bourgeoisie whenever it acts in a 193 revolutionary way, against the absolute monarchy, the feudal squirearchy, and the petty bourgeoisie.

But they never cease, for a single instant, to instil into the working class 194 the clearest possible recognition of the hostile antagonism between bourgeoisie and proletariat, in order that the German workers may straightway use, as so many weapons against the bourgeoisie, the social and political conditions that the bourgeoisie must necessarily introduce along with its supremacy, and in order that, after the fall of the reactionary classes in Germany, the fight against the bourgeoisie itself may immediately begin.

The Communists turn their attention chiefly to Germany, because that 195 country is on the eve of a bourgeois revolution that is bound to be carried out under more advanced conditions of European civilisation, and with a much more developed proletariat, than that of England was in the seventeenth, and of France in the eighteenth century, and because the bourgeois revolution in Germany will be but the prelude to an immediately following proletarian revolution.

In short, the Communists everywhere support every revolutionary 196 movement against the existing social and political order of things.

In all these movements they bring to the front, as the leading question 197 in each, the property question, no matter what its degree of development at the time.

Finally, they labour everywhere for the union and agreement of the 198 democratic parties of all countries.

The Communists disdain to conceal their views and aims. They openly 199 declare that their ends can be attained only by the forcible overthrow of all existing social conditions. Let the ruling classes tremble at a Communistic revolution. The proletarians have nothing to lose but their chains. They have a world to win.

WORKING MEN OF ALL COUNTRIES, UNITE! 200

Written by Marx and Engels in December 1847–January 1848

Originally published in German in London in February 1848

Printed according to the 1888 English edition

Tr. Samuel Moore
Ed. Frederick Engels

Questions for Discussion and Writing

1. How would you characterize Marx's[13] use of ethos? Does he act the part of a prophet, a priest, a political scientist, or merely a crank? Does his ethos appear to change over the course of the treatise, or does it remain relatively constant?

[13] We have referred to the author of the *Manifesto of the Communist Party* as "Marx" simply to avoid clumsy phrasing, not to deny Engels' role in the writing of the text. [Editors' note.]

2. Structurally speaking, Marx's treatise may appear strange to you. He begins with a sweeping economic history of Western civilization. From there, he moves to a rather specific discussion of nineteenth-century European social movements before summing up the general argument. What is the relationship between his economic history and the discussion that follows? Do you find his analysis of history persuasive?

3. Marx's argument seems to present the audience with black and white, either/or alternatives. What are the inherent strengths and weaknesses of theory and practice built on such strong distinctions? How well, in your opinion, do Marx's either/ or alternatives describe today's society?

4. Imagine that you represent labor or management at a congressional investigation of wages for factory workers. Marshaling the *Manifesto of the Communist Party* or its arguments, prepare written testimony that supports or attacks a significant pay raise. Be sure to consider the special needs of your audience.

WALT WHITMAN

(1819–1892)

Walt Whitman, considered by many the father of modern American poetry, was born into a simple farm family family and grew up rather uneventfully on Long Island and in Brooklyn. His parents received little formal education, and young Walt himself, the second of nine children, left school around the age of thirteen to be trained as a printer. He worked in printing in New York City for a while, then spent a few years teaching school on Long Island. During these years he supplemented his meager education by reading widely. He began to write poetry, but it was of the most conventional sort.

In the 1840s, Whitman moved back to New York City and began working as a journalist. He worked for a variety of papers and submitted stories to The Democratic Review, the best literary magazine of the day, but he took his most important job in 1848 with the Brooklyn Eagle, which he edited for two years. After his strong antislavery stance cost him his job, Whitman visited New Orleans for a few months before returning to New York City to resume his career in journalism. He also worked with his father as a carpenter and dabbled in real estate.

What was most significant about this period of Whitman's life, though, was the highly innovative poetry he began to write. In 1855, he published (at his own expense) the first edition of Leaves of Grass, a 150-page poem in twelve sections, in which Whitman announced himself as America's true bard and self-appointed prophet of independence, frank sexuality, working-class democracy, and American destiny. This poetry was intensely admired by some (including the influential philosopher Ralph Waldo Emerson), but most of Whitman's contemporaries found it confusing, shocking, even obscene. Although his unusual and controversial book was not a popular success, Whitman believed in his work and for the rest of his life published and republished it, constantly revising and expanding the original text and incorporating into it all his poetic output. Eventually, Leaves of Grass earned Whitman a growing number of imitators and established his place among the first rank of American writers.

Whitman was a literary man, but he often preferred the company of uneducated workingmen and was known for his compassion for those in need. During the Civil War, he moved to the nation's capital to nurse wounded soldiers, supporting himself by working as a clerk in a military office. His experiences are recorded in two sections of Leaves of Grass called "Drum-Taps" and "Memories of President Lincoln," and in Specimen Days, a collection of prose pieces published in 1882. After the war was over, Whitman settled in Washington, where he worked in the government. In 1873, however, he suffered a crippling stroke and was forced to leave his job and live with his brother in Camden, New Jersey. He remained in Camden

*for the rest of his life, eventually earning enough money from his poetry to buy a
small house. There the elderly Whitman played the part of a snowy-bearded sage,
receiving visits from literary friends, admirers, and disciples—some of whom regarded
him as a savior figure. Whitman died in 1892, having just completed his final
edition of* Leaves of Grass.

*In 1871, during his Washington period, Whitman published "Passage to India,"
the poem reprinted here. In it he celebrates the technological feats of modern
civilization and at the same time gestures toward the ultimate vistas of America's
destiny—the completion of Columbus' passage to India. Late in life, Whitman would
call this his most important poem. Indeed, it embodied what he felt his nation should
believe was the truest version of the American dream.*

PASSAGE TO INDIA

I

Singing my days,
Singing the great achievements of the present,
Singing the strong light works of engineers,
Our modern wonders, (the antique ponderous Seven outvied,)
In the Old World the east the Suez canal,   5
The New by its mighty railroad spann'd,
The seas inlaid with eloquent gentle wires;
Yet first to sound, and ever sound, the cry with thee O soul,
The Past! the Past! the Past!

The Past—the dark unfathom'd retrospect!   10
The teeming gulf—the sleepers and the shadows!
The past—the infinite greatness of the past!
For what is the present after all but a growth out of the past?
(As a projectile form'd, impell'd, passing a certain line, still keeps
    on,
So the present, utterly form'd, impell'd by the past.)   15

2

Passage O soul to India!
Eclaircise the myths Asiatic, the primitive fables.

Not you alone proud truths of the world,
Nor you alone ye facts of modern science,
But myths and fables of eld, Asia's, Africa's fables,   20

The far-darting beams of the spirit, the unloos'd dreams,
The deep diving bibles and legends,
The daring plots of the poets, the elder religions;
O you temples fairer than lilies pour'd over by the rising sun!
O you fables spurning the known, eluding the hold of the known,   25
    mounting to heaven!
You lofty and dazzling towers, pinnacled, red as roses, burnish'd
    with gold!
Towers of fables immortal fashion'd from mortal dreams!
You too I welcome and fully the same as the rest!
You too with joy I sing.

Passage to India!   30
Lo, soul, seest thou not God's purpose from the first?
The earth to be spann'd, connected by network,
The races, neighbors, to marry and be given in marriage,
The oceans to be cross'd, the distant brought near,
The lands to be welded together.   35

A worship new I sing,
You captains, voyagers, explorers, yours,
You engineers, you architects, machinists, yours,
You, not for trade or transportation only,
But in God's name, and for thy sake O soul.   40

3

Passage to India!
Lo soul for thee of tableaus twain,
I see in one the Suez canal initiated, open'd,
I see the procession of steamships, the Empress Eugenie's leading
    the van,
I mark from on deck the strange landscape, the pure sky, the level   45
    sand in the distance,
I pass swiftly the picturesque groups, the workmen gather'd,
The gigantic dredging machines.

In one again, different, (yet thine, all thine, O soul, the same,)
I see over my own continent the Pacific railroad surmounting every
    barrier,
I see continual trains of cars winding along the Platte carrying   50
    freight and passengers,
I hear the locomotives rushing and roaring, and the shrill steam-
    whistle,

I hear the echoes reverberate through the grandest scenery in the
 world,
I cross the Laramie plains, I note the rocks in grotesque shapes,
 the buttes,
I see the plentiful larkspur and wild onions, the barren, colorless,
 sage-deserts,
I see in glimpses afar or towering immediately above me the great 55
 mountains, I see the Wind river and the Wahsatch mountains,
I see the Monument mountain and the Eagle's Nest, I pass the
 Promontory, I ascend the Nevadas,
I scan the noble Elk mountain and wind around its base,
I see the Humboldt range, I thread the valley and cross the river,
I see the clear waters of lake Tahoe, I see forests of majestic pines,
Or crossing the great desert, the alkaline plains, I behold enchanting 60
 mirages of waters and meadows,
Marking through these and after all, in duplicate slender lines,
Bridging the three or four thousand miles of land travel,
Tying the Eastern to the Western sea,
The road between Europe and Asia.

(A Genoese[1] thy dream! thy dream!   65
Centuries after thou art laid in thy grave,
The shore thou foundest verifies thy dream.)

4

Passage to India!
Struggles of many a captain, tales of many a sailor dead,
Over my mood stealing and spreading they come,   70
Like clouds and cloudlets in the unreach'd sky.

Along all history, down the slopes,
As a rivulet running, sinking now, and now again to the surface
 rising,
A ceaseless thought, a varied train—lo, soul, to thee, thy sight,
 they rise,
The plans, the voyages again, the expeditions;   75
Again Vasco de Gama[2] sails forth,
Again the knowledge gain'd, the mariner's compass,

---

[1] *Genoese:* Christopher Columbus (1451?–1506), a native of Genoa. [Editors' note.]

[2] *Vasco de Gama:* a Portuguese explorer (1469?–1524) who in 1498 reached India by sailing
around the Cape of Good Hope in southern Africa. [Editors' note.]

Lands found and nations born, thou born America,
For purpose vast, man's long probation fill'd,
Thou rondure of the world at last accomplish'd.   80

5

O vast Rondure, swimming in space,
Cover'd all over with visible power and beauty,
Alternate light and day and the teeming spiritual darkness,
Unspeakable high processions of sun and moon and countless
          stars above,
Below, the manifold grass and waters, animals, mountains, trees,   85
With inscrutable purpose, some hidden prophetic intention,
Now first it seems my thought begins to span thee.

Down from the gardens of Asia descending radiating,
Adam and Eve appear, then their myriad progeny after them,
Wandering, yearning, curious, with restless explorations,   90
With questionings, baffled, formless, feverish, with never-happy
          hearts,
With that sad incessant refrain, *Wherefore unsatisfied soul?* and
          Whither O mocking life?

Ah who shall soothe these feverish children?
Who justify these restless explorations?
Who speak the secret of impassive earth?   95
Who bind it to us? what is this separate Nature so unnatural?
What is this earth to our affections? (unloving earth, without a
          throb to answer ours,
Cold earth, the place of graves.)

Yet soul be sure the first intent remains, and shall be carried out,
Perhaps even now the time has arrived.   100
After the seas are all cross'd, (as they seem already cross'd,)
After the great captains and engineers have accomplish'd their
          work,
After the noble inventors, after the scientists, the chemist, the
          geologist, ethnologist,
Finally shall come the poet worthy that name,
The true son of God shall come singing his songs.   105

Then not your deeds only O voyagers, O scientists and inventors,
          shall be justified,
All these hearts as of fretted children shall be sooth'd,

All affection shall be fully responded to, the secret shall be told,
All these separations and gaps shall be taken up and hook'd and
    link'd together,
The whole earth, this cold, impassive, voiceless earth, shall be 110
    completely justified,
Trinitas divine shall be gloriously accomplish'd and compacted by
    the true son of God, the poet,
(He shall indeed pass the straits and conquer the mountains,
He shall double the cape of Good Hope to some purpose,)
Nature and Man shall be disjoin'd and diffused no more,
The true son of God shall absolutely fuse them.   115

6

Year at whose wide-flung door I sing!
Year of the purpose accomplish'd!
Year of the marriage of continents, climates and oceans!
(No mere doge of Venice now wedding the Adriatic,)
I see O year in you the vast terraqueous globe given and giving 120
    all,
Europe to Asia, Africa join'd, and they to the New World,
The lands, geographies, dancing before you, holding a festival
    garland,
As brides and bridegrooms hand in hand.

Passage to India!
Cooling airs from Caucasus far, soothing cradle of man,   125
The river Euphrates flowing, the past lit up again.

Lo soul, the retrospect brought forward,
The old, most populous, wealthiest of earth's lands,
The streams of the Indus and the Ganges and their many affluents,
(I my shores of America walking to-day behold, resuming all,)   130
The tale of Alexander on his warlike marches suddenly dying,
On one side China and on the other side Persia and Arabia,
To the south the great seas and the bay of Bengal,
The flowing literatures, tremendous epics, religions, castes,
Old occult Brahma interminably far back, the tender and junior 135
    Buddha,
Central and southern empires and all their belongings, possessors,
The wars of Tamerlane, the reign of Aurungzebe,
The traders, rulers, explorers, Moslems, Venetians, Byzantium,
    the Arabs, Portuguese,
The first travelers famous yet, Marco Polo, Batouta the Moor,

245

Doubts to be solv'd, the map incognita, blanks to be fill'd,   140
The foot of man unstay'd, the hands never at rest,
Thyself O soul that will not brook a challenge.

The mediæval navigators rise before me,
The world of 1492, with its awaken'd enterprise,
Something swelling in humanity now like the sap of the earth in 145
    spring,
The sunset splendor of chivalry declining.

And who art thou sad shade?
Gigantic, visionary, thyself a visionary,
With majestic limbs and pious beaming eyes,
Spreading around with every look of thine a golden world,   150
Enhuing it with gorgeous hues.

As the chief histrion,[3]
Down to the footlights walks in some great scena,
Dominating the rest I see the Admiral himself,
(History's type of courage, action, faith,)   155
Behold him sail from Palos[4] leading his little fleet,
His voyage behold, his return, his great fame,
His misfortunes, calumniators, behold him a prisoner, chain'd,
Behold his dejection, poverty, death.

(Curious in time I stand, noting the efforts of heroes,   160
Is the deferment long? bitter the slander, poverty, death?
Lies the seed unreck'd for centuries in the ground? lo, to God's
    due occasion,
Uprising in the night, it sprouts, blooms,
And fills the earth with use and beauty.)

7

Passage indeed O soul to primal thought,   165
Not lands and seas alone, thy own clear freshness,
The young maturity of brood and bloom,
To realms of budding bibles.

---

[3] *histrion:* actor. [Editors' note.]

[4] *Palos:* Spanish seaport from which Columbus launched his first voyage to the New World.
[Editors' note.]

O soul, repressless, I with thee and thou with me,
Thy circumnavigation of the world begin,   170
Of man, the voyage of his mind's return,
To reason's early paradise,
Back, back to wisdom's birth, to innocent intuitions,
Again with fair creation.

8

O we can wait no longer,   175
We too take ship O soul,
Joyous we too launch out on trackless seas,
Fearless for unknown shores on waves of ecstasy to sail,
Amid the wafting winds, (thou pressing me to thee, I thee to me,
     O soul,)
Caroling free, singing our song of God,   180
Chanting our chant of pleasant exploration.

With laugh and many a kiss,
(Let others deprecate, let others weep for sin, remorse, humiliation,)
O soul thou pleasest me, I thee.

Ah more than any priest O soul we too believe in God,   185
But with the mystery of God we dare not dally.

O soul thou pleasest me, I thee,
Sailing these seas or on the hills, or waking in the night,
Thoughts, silent thoughts, of Time and Space and Death, like
     waters flowing,
Bear me indeed as through the regions infinite,   190
Whose air I breathe, whose ripples hear, lave me all over,
Bathe me O God in thee, mounting to thee,
I and my soul to range in range of thee.

O Thou transcendent,
Nameless, the fibre and the breath,   195
Light of the light, shedding forth universes, thou centre of them,
Thou mightier centre of the true, the good, the loving,
Thou moral, spiritual fountain—affection's source—thou reservoir,
(O pensive soul of me—O thirst unsatisfied—waitest not there?
Waitest not haply for us somewhere there the Comrade perfect?)   200
Thou pulse—thou motive of the stars, suns, systems,
That, circling, move in order, safe, harmonious,
Athwart the shapeless vastnesses of space,

247

How should I think, how breathe a single breath, how speak, if,
   out of myself,
I could not launch, to those, superior universes?   205

Swiftly I shrivel at the thought of God,
At Nature and its wonders, Time and Space and Death,
But that I, turning, call to thee O soul, thou actual Me,
And lo, thou gently masterest the orbs,
Thou matest Time, smilest content at Death,   210
And fillest, swellest full the vastnesses of Space.

Greater than stars or suns,
Bounding O soul thou journeyest forth;
What love than thine and ours could wider amplify?
What aspirations, wishes, outvie thine and ours O soul?   215
What dreams of the ideal? what plans of purity, perfection, strength?
What cheerful willingness for others' sake to give up all?
For others' sake to suffer all?

Reckoning ahead O soul, when thou, the time achiev'd,
The seas all cross'd, weather'd the capes, the voyage done,   220
Surrounded, copest, frontest God, yieldest, the aim attain'd,
As fill'd with friendship, love complete, the Elder Brother found,
The Younger melts in fondness in his arms.

9

Passage to more than India!
Are thy wings plumed indeed for such far flights?   225
O soul, voyagest thou indeed on voyages like those?
Disportest thou on waters such as those?
Soundest below the Sanscrit and the Vedas?[5]
Then have thy bent unleash'd.

Passage to you, your shores, ye aged fierce enigmas!   230
Passage to you, to mastership of you, ye strangling problems!
You, strew'd with the wrecks of skeletons, that, living, never
   reach'd you.

Passage to more than India!
O secret of the earth and sky!
Of you O waters of the sea! O winding creeks and rivers!   235

---

[5] *Vedas:* sacred texts of the Hindu religion. [Editors' note.]

Of you O woods and fields! of you strong mountains of my land!
Of you O prairies! of you gray rocks!
O morning red! O Clouds! O rain and snows!
O day and night, passage to you!

O sun and moon and all you stars! Sirius and Jupiter!   240
Passage to you!

Passage, immediate passage! the blood burns in my veins!
Away O soul! hoist instantly the anchor!
Cut the hawsers—haul out—shake out every sail!
Have we not stood here like trees in the ground long enough?   245
Have we not grovel'd here long enough, eating and drinking like
   mere brutes?
Have we not darken'd and dazed ourselves with books long enough?

Sail forth—steer for the deep waters only,
Reckless O soul, exploring, I with thee, and thou with me,
For we are bound where mariner has not yet dared to go,   250
And we will risk the ship, ourselves and all.

O my brave soul!
O farther farther sail!
O daring joy, but safe! are they not all the seas of God?
O farther, farther, farther sail!   255

Questions for Discussion and Writing

1. When Whitman says "O soul," what is he gesturing toward? How are the primary
    elements of this poem—"O soul" and "passage to India"—linked?

2. How might the main "argument" or "effect" of this poem be translated into late
    twentieth-century terms? Have the primary issues Whitman grapples with changed
    or have they remained essentially the same?

3. Describe the structure of "Passage to India." Is it linear? Cyclical? Repetitive?
    Tight? Loose? Discursive? Deductive? Anecdotal? How does the structure of this
    poem compare to others you have read? Overall, do you find Whitman's structural
    choices successful?

4. While describing the great procession of nature, Whitman alludes to an "inscrutable
    purpose" and "some hidden prophetic intention" (l. 86). How do this "inscrutable
    purpose" and this "hidden prophetic intention" relate to Whitman's vision of
    America? Do you find his argument compelling? Write an essay in which you
    explicate and critique Whitman's vision.

SUSAN B. ANTHONY

(1820–1906)

EMMELINE PANKHURST

(1858–1928)

I magine rising to speak at a public meeting only to be greeted by jeers, rotten eggs and vegetables, and crude attacks from the press. Or even worse, imagine that your effort to get your message across will lead to your immediate arrest and incarceration. Only a hunger strike will secure you a temporary release from jail, and most likely you will be back behind bars again soon. Do these scenarios remind you of the plight of an activist in a faraway totalitarian government? In fact, such cruel treatment was inflicted for years on American and English women who simply desired the right to vote. Although today it may be hard for us to believe that so basic a right was ever denied half the adult population of these two ostensibly freedom-loving nations, not until after World War I did the women's vote become a national standard in either country. Although many women—and men—worked courageously for women's suffrage between 1840 and 1928, two women in particular, Susan B. Anthony and Emmeline Pankhurst, are remembered for their tireless efforts and eloquent rhetoric in aid of the cause.

Susan B. Anthony, the daughter of independent-minded Quakers, was born in Adams, Massachusetts, and raised in upstate New York, where she learned to respect egalitarianism, self-reliance, and social action. Working as a schoolteacher, Anthony became involved in the temperance movement, and her first public speech was sponsored by the Daughters of Temperance.

In 1850, Anthony befriended Elizabeth Cady Stanton, with whom she remained close for fifty years. Stanton, together with women such as Lucretia Mott, was already working for the rights of women. During this time, Anthony herself was becoming more and more aware of the problems women faced in this country. In 1852, when she rose to speak at a temperance rally, she was told that "the sisters were not invited here to speak, but to listen and to learn." Disgusted by this sexist attitude, she organized the Women's State Temperance Society of New York.

Ultimately, though, the antislavery cause was a much more important influence than the temperance movement on Anthony's feminist convictions, for it led much more directly to the issues of equality and suffrage. An enthusiastic abolitionist, she worked as a paid organizer for the American Anti-Slavery Society from 1856 until the outbreak of the Civil War. After the war, she was one of the first to call for federal voting rights for African Americans, which they eventually won through passage of the Fifteenth Amendment.

Meanwhile, Anthony's work with women's suffrage gained momentum. From 1868 to 1870, Anthony and Stanton published The Revolution, a feminist New York weekly paper. They also organized the National Woman Suffrage Association, which sought to amend the Constitution to allow for the female vote. This organization held annual meetings for fifty years and pleaded with every Congress for justice until women's suffrage was mandated.

For the rest of her life, Anthony worked singlemindedly for the women's vote. She traveled the lecture circuit heavily until 1897; she organized the International Council of Women and the International Woman Suffrage Alliance; and she helped compile a definitive multiple-volume work entitled The History of Woman Suffrage. Sadly, it was not until 1920, fourteen years after her death, that women gained the right to vote.

In 1872, to test the applicability of the Fourteenth and Fifteenth Amendments, Anthony voted in the U.S. Presidential election in Rochester, New York. She was arrested and ordered to stand trial. In the spring of 1873, to help influence public opinion, she traveled through upstate New York, speaking on behalf of women's suffrage. The text reprinted here is a version of the basic speech she delivered about forty times before the trial. Despite her strong arguments, she was convicted and ordered to pay a $100 fine. Not surprisingly, she never paid it.

England's Emmeline Pankhurst was exposed to progressive ideas when, as a student in a Parisian boarding school, she became friends with the daughter of the French radical Henri Rochefort. In 1879, she married Richard Marsden Pankhurst, a lawyer with a professional interest in women's issues. They had five children, and when her husband died in 1898 she was left with the financial responsibility of the family.

As Pankhurst became more involved in women's issues, her life began to heat up. In 1903, she founded the Women's Social and Political Union; in 1905, her daughter and another woman were arrested and thrown in prison for speaking up at a political meeting. Fighting fire with fire, Pankhurst and her colleagues adopted militaristic strategies to push for suffrage. Members of her group interrupted public meetings, chained themselves to public places, and vandalized property. Arrest was all in a day's work.

Eventually, the increasing militancy of the suffragists led to government charges of conspiracy. Pankhurst was sent to prison for nine months and was released only after she embarked on a hunger strike. This sort of activity continued until the outbreak of World War I, when the campaign was halted. In 1918, the Representation Act of the People gave a limited number of women the right to vote. Pankhurst lived abroad from 1919 until 1925. On her return, she sought to enter politics, but her health failed. She died one month before Britain adopted full equality in voting. "Militant Suffragists" is the text of a speech delivered in Hartford, Connecticut, November 13, 1913.

ON WOMEN'S RIGHT TO SUFFRAGE

SUSAN B. ANTHONY

Friends and fellow-citizens: I stand before you tonight under indictment   1
for the alleged crime of having voted at the last Presidential election,
without having a lawful right to vote. It shall be my work this evening to
prove to you that in thus voting, I not only committed no crime, but,
instead, simply exercised my citizen's rights, guaranteed to me and all
United States citizens by the National Constitution, beyond the power of
any State to deny.

The preamble of the Federal Constitution says: 2

"We, the people of the United States, in order to form a more perfect   3
union, establish justice, insure domestic tranquillity, provide for the common
defense, promote the general welfare, and secure the blessings of liberty to
ourselves and our posterity, do ordain and establish this Constitution for
the United States of America."

It was we, the people; not we, the white male citizens; nor yet we, the   4
male citizens; but we, the whole people, who formed the Union. And we
formed it, not to give the blessings of liberty, but to secure them; not to
the half of ourselves and the half of our posterity, but to the whole people—
women as well as men. And it is a downright mockery to talk to women
of their enjoyment of the blessings of liberty while they are denied the use
of the only means of securing them provided by this democratic-republican
government—the ballot.

For any State to make sex a qualification that must ever result in the   5
disfranchisement of one entire half of the people is to pass a bill of attainder,
or an *ex post facto* law, and is therefore a violation of the supreme law of
the land. By it the blessings of liberty are forever withheld from women
and their female posterity. To them this government has no just powers
derived from the consent of the governed. To them this government is not
a democracy. It is not a republic. It is an odious aristocracy; a hateful
oligarchy of sex; the most hateful aristocracy ever established on the face of
the globe; an oligarchy of wealth, where the rich govern the poor. An
oligarchy of learning, where the educated govern the ignorant, or even an
oligarchy of race, where the Saxon rules the African, might be endured;
but this oligarchy of sex, which makes father, brothers, husband, sons, the
oligarchs over the mother and sisters, the wife and daughters of every
household—which ordains all men sovereigns, all women subjects, carries
dissension, discord and rebellion into every home of the nation.

Webster,[1] Worcester[2] and Bouvier[3] all define a citizen to be a person in   6
the United States, entitled to vote and hold office.

---

[1] *Webster:* Noah Webster (1758–1843), an American lexicographer. [Editors' note.]

The only question left to be settled now is: Are women persons? And I 7
hardly believe any of our opponents will have the hardihood to say they are
not. Being persons, then, women are citizens; and no State has a right to
make any law, or to enforce any old law, that shall abridge their privileges
or immunities. Hence, every discrimination against women in the constitutions and laws of the several States is today null and void, precisely as is
every one against Negroes.

MILITANT SUFFRAGISTS
EMMELINE PANKHURST

I do not come here as an advocate, because whatever position the suffrage 1
movement may occupy in the United States of America, in England it has
passed beyond the realm of advocacy and it has entered into the sphere of
practical politics. It has become the subject of revolution and civil war, and
so to-night I am not here to advocate woman suffrage. American suffragists
can do that very well for themselves. I am here as a soldier who has
temporarily left the field of battle in order to explain—it seems strange it
should have to be explained—what civil war is like when civil war is waged
by women. I am not only here as a soldier temporarily absent from the
field of battle; I am here—and that, I think, is the strangest part of my
coming—I am here as a person who, according to the law courts of my
country, it has been decided, is of no value to the community at all; and I
am adjudged because of my life to be a dangerous person, under sentence
of penal servitude in a convict prison. So you see there is some special
interest in hearing so unusual a person address you. I dare say, in the minds
of many of you—you will perhaps forgive me this personal touch—that I
do not look either very like a soldier or very like a convict, and yet I am
both.

It would take too long to trace the course of militant methods as adopted 2
by women, because it is about eight years since the word militant was first
used to describe what we were doing; it is about eight years since the first
militant action was taken by women. It was not militant at all, except that
it provoked militancy on the part of those who were opposed to it. When
women asked questions in political meetings and failed to get answers, they

---

[2] *Worcester:* Joseph Emerson Worcester (1784–1865), an American lexicographer. [Editors' note.]

[3] *Bouvier:* John Bouvier (1787–1851), a Franco-American judge and legal scholar. [Editors' note.]

were not doing anything militant. To ask questions at political meetings is an acknowledged right of all people who attend public meetings; certainly in my country, men have always done it, and I hope they do it in America, because it seems to me that if you allow people to enter your legislatures without asking them any questions as to what they are going to do when they get there you are not exercising your citizen rights and your citizen duties as you ought. At any rate in Great Britain it is a custom, a time-honored one, to ask questions of candidates for Parliament and ask questions of members of the government. No man was ever put out of a public meeting for asking a question until Votes for Women came onto the political horizon. The first people who were put out of a political meeting for asking questions, were women; they were brutally ill-used; they found themselves in jail before twenty-four hours had expired. But instead of the newspapers, which are largely inspired by the politicians, putting militancy and the reproach of militancy, if reproach there is, on the people who had assaulted the women, they actually said it was the women who were militant and very much to blame.

It was not the speakers on the platform who would not answer them, who were to blame, or the ushers at the meeting; it was the poor women who had had their bruises and their knocks and scratches, and who were put into prison for doing precisely nothing but holding a protest meeting in the street after it was all over. However, we were called militant for doing that, and we were quite willing to accept the name, because militancy for us is time-honored; you have the church militant and in the sense of spiritual militancy we were very militant indeed. We were determined to press this question of the enfranchisement of the women to the point where we were no longer to be ignored by the politicians as had been the case for about fifty years, during which time women had patiently used every means open to them to win their political enfranchisement.

Experience will show you that if you really want to get anything done, it is not so much a matter of whether you alienate sympathy; sympathy is a very unsatisfactory thing if it is not practical sympathy. It does not matter to the practical suffragist whether she alienates sympathy that was never of any use to her. What she wants is to get something practical done, and whether it is done out of sympathy or whether it is done out of fear, or whether it is done because you want to be comfortable again and not be worried in this way, doesn't particularly matter so long as you get it. We had enough of sympathy for fifty years; it never brought us anything; and we would rather have an angry man going to the government and saying, my business is interfered with and I won't submit to its being interfered with any longer because you won't give women the vote, than to have a gentleman come onto our platforms year in and year out and talk about his ardent sympathy with woman suffrage.

"Put them in prison," they said; "that will stop it." But it didn't stop it.   5
They put women in prison for long terms of imprisonment, for making a
nuisance of themselves—that was the expression when they took petitions
in their hands to the door of the House of Commons; and they thought
that by sending them to prison, giving them a day's imprisonment, would
cause them to all settle down again and there would be no further trouble.
But it didn't happen so at all: instead of the women giving it up, more
women did it, and more and more and more women did it until there were
three hundred women at a time, who had not broken a single law, only
"made a nuisance of themselves" as the politicians say.

The whole argument with the anti-suffragists, or even the critical suffragist   6
man, is this: that you can govern human beings without their consent. They
have said to us, "Government rests upon force; the women haven't force,
so they must submit." Well, we are showing them that government does
not rest upon force at all; it rests upon consent. As long as women consent
to be unjustly governed, they can be; but directly women say: "We withhold
our consent, we will not be governed any longer so long as that government
is unjust," not by the forces of civil war can you govern the very weakest
woman. You can kill that woman, but she escapes you then; you cannot
govern her. And that is, I think, a most valuable demonstration we have
been making to the world.

Now, I want to say to you who think women cannot succeed, we have   7
brought the government of England to this position, that it has to face this
alternative; either women are to be killed or women are to have the vote.
I ask American men in this meeting, what would you say if in your State
you were faced with that alternative, that you must either kill them or give
them their citizenship,—women, many of whom you respect, women whom
you know have lived useful lives, women whom you know, even if you do
not know them personally, are animated with the highest motives, women
who are in pursuit of liberty and the power to do useful public service?
Well, there is only one answer to that alternative; there is only one way out
of it, unless you are prepared to put back civilization two or three
generations; you must give those women the vote. Now that is the outcome
of our civil war.

You won your freedom in America when you had the Revolution, by   8
bloodshed, by sacrificing human life. You won the Civil War by the sacrifice
of human life when you decided to emancipate the negro. You have left it
to the women in your land, the men of all civilized countries have left it
to women, to work out their own salvation. That is the way in which we
women of England are doing. Human life for us is sacred, but we say if
any life is to be sacrificed it shall be ours; we won't do it ourselves, but we
will put the enemy in the position where they will have to choose between
giving us freedom or giving us death.

Questions for Discussion and Writing

1. What is the essence of Anthony's argument? Could you restate Anthony's entire argument as a single sentence?

2. Apparently, Anthony's early speeches about temperance and slavery relied heavily on vivid language and overt appeals to pathos. Would you describe Anthony's rhetoric in "On Women's Right to Suffrage" as oriented primarily toward ethos, logos, or pathos? Considering Anthony's status as a nineteenth-century woman, is this primary orientation significant?

3. Compare Anthony's rhetoric with Pankhurst's. Do they employ similar types of appeals? Has the forty-year period between the speeches changed the rhetoric of the women's suffrage movement? If so, how?

4. How might you apply arguments made by Anthony and Pankhurst to contemporary discussions of gender or racial issues? In an essay of your own design, experiment with such applications.

T. H. HUXLEY

(1825–1895)

Although Thomas Henry Huxley's primary expertise was in biology, he was a "Renaissance man" whose interests and contributions to society were diverse. And he was, as his biography demonstrates, one who could make the most of a difficult situation.

Huxley was born in Ealing, England, the son of a schoolmaster. There were eight children in the family, and formal education was a scarce enough commodity that Thomas received only two years of it. Despite this handicap, he read widely in an effort to educate himself. Later, he received a scholarship to attend the Charing Cross Hospital Medical School, where he distinguished himself. While still a student there, he published his first scientific paper, a study of hair.

Unfortunately, the scholarship ran out before Huxley could graduate. He promptly joined the Royal Navy and became the assistant surgeon aboard the H.M.S. Rattlesnake. Taking advantage of every opportunity and improvising whenever necessary, Huxley set up a lab on the ship and studied marine biology from voyage to voyage. He published many important papers during this time and was elected to the Royal Society, England's prestigious scientific organization, in 1851.

A few years later, when he was forced out of the navy on a technicality, Huxley took a job as a lecturer at the London School of Mines. Although the school went through many changes over the years, he taught there until 1885. Huxley continued to publish important papers and to sharpen his biological theories through exchanges with great scientists of the day such as Herbert Spencer and Charles Darwin. He and Darwin became good friends.

In 1859, Darwin published the most important—and controversial—work of nineteenth-century science, On the Origin of Species. In the era before Darwin, most biologists believed Lamarck's idea that species evolved through use and disuse of various elements of their anatomy and that traits acquired by an organism while it lived could be inherited by its descendants. Thus, according to this theory, the giraffe's neck was long because centuries of giraffes kept stretching for the leaves of tall trees. The Lamarckian approach to biological change fit the then-current conception of natural reason: Effort is rewarded as the world evolves predictably, as though the invisible hand of the deity were at work.

Darwin's essential thesis, that life on earth evolved not because of some carefully designed plan but because of a series of random accidents, shook Western society's assumptions about God, fate, and reason to the core. "Natural selection" meant that the survival of an individual organism or an entire species was a chance occurrence based on somewhat arbitrarily inherited traits that just happened to be useful or useless in the brutal war of nature. Within this theory biological fitness emerged more as a matter of coincidence than plan.

A further implication of evolutionary theory was this: If God's decisions have little to do with biology, His role in the formation of societies also falls into question. If our culture has evolved in the same manner as individual species, then perhaps our social structures are more the product of random occurrence than omnipotent design. Evolution forced nineteenth-century thinkers to raise serious questions about the integrity and certainty of our values, ethics, and beliefs. If success in this world is simply a matter of chance, then how can we possibly talk about good and bad people? If our fate is predetermined by some random throw of the evolutionary dice, then what good is it to discuss free will, social justice, or divine providence? At the very least, the rules of the discourse had to change because a new set of premises had come into effect. Nietzsche's rejection of traditional values can be seen as one result of this major intellectual upheaval.

Realizing the merit of Darwin's theory, Huxley jumped to defend it, and became one of Darwin's most enthusiastic and energetic supporters. Huxley participated in many important debates, including a particularly famous exchange with Bishop Samuel Wilberforce. His own work moved into the areas of evolution, paleontology, and biological classification, and his book-length study, Man's Place in Nature (1863), popularized the theory that man evolved from animals.

Yet other challenges lay ahead for this versatile man. In the 1870s, Huxley involved himself in administrative work and served on many committees. He was a member of the first London school board and was an instrumental figure in the revolutionary school reform that characterized the late nineteenth century. Never one to avoid an opportunity to face his opposition, he continued to debate in public.

In later years, Huxley focused his efforts primarily on philosophy, theology, and ethics. As a natural scientist, he felt confident only about what he could actually observe in the natural world. Further, he believed that one must subordinate beliefs to evidence and reason. He grew to distrust the teachings of orthodox religions, and although he admired some aspects of Christianity, he rejected its formal rules. His own uncertainty concerning the existence of a superior being led him to agnosticism ("not knowing"), a term he himself coined. It is no surprise, thus, that he was disliked by the orthodox clergy of the day, but he got along well with their more liberal colleagues.

Although Huxley had no firm religious belief, he was capable of demonstrating much concern for his fellow human being and for society as a whole. He despised slavery and supported the North during the American Civil War. He fought racism, arguing that the doctrine of inborn racial superiority was scientifically indefensible. He was a friend of workers, and he promoted education for women.

Huxley's genius was passed along to his children and grandchildren. Several of his descendents were important scientists, and one grandson, Aldous Huxley, was the world-famous author of the prophetic novel Brave New World.

The essay that follows, "Evolution and Ethics," presents a combination of several important topics pondered by Huxley over his lifetime. It was delivered at Oxford in 1894, the year before his death.

FROM EVOLUTION AND ETHICS

Prolegomena

I

It may be safely assumed that, two thousand years ago, before Cæsar set foot in southern Britain, the whole country-side visible from the windows of the room in which I write, was in what is called "the state of nature." Except, it may be, by raising a few sepulchral mounds, such as those which still, here and there, break the flowing contours of the downs, man's hands had made no mark upon it; and the thin veil of vegetation which overspread the broad-backed heights and the shelving sides of the coombs was unaffected by his industry. The native grasses and weeds, the scattered patches of gorse, contended with one another for the possession of the scanty surface soil; they fought against the droughts of summer, the frosts of winter, and the furious gales which swept, with unbroken force, now from the Atlantic, and now from the North Sea, at all times of the year; they filled up, as they best might, the gaps made in their ranks by all sorts of underground and overground animal ravagers. One year with another, an average population, the floating balance of the unceasing struggle for existence among the indigenous plants, maintained itself. It is as little to be doubted, that an essentially similar state of nature prevailed, in this region, for many thousand years before the coming of Cæsar; and there is no assignable reason for denying that it might continue to exist through an equally prolonged futurity, except for the intervention of man. 1

Reckoned by our customary standards of duration, the native vegetation, like the "everlasting hills" which it clothes, seems a type of permanence. The little Amarella Gentians, which abound in some places to-day, are the descendants of those that were trodden underfoot by the prehistoric savages who have left their flint tools about, here and there; and they followed ancestors which, in the climate of the glacial epoch, probably flourished better than they do now. Compared with the long past of this humble plant, all the history of civilized men is but an episode. 2

Yet nothing is more certain than that, measured by the liberal scale of time-keeping of the universe, this present state of nature, however it may seem to have gone and to go on for ever, is but a fleeting phase of her infinite variety; merely the last of the series of changes which the earth's surface has undergone in the course of the millions of years of its existence. Turn back a square foot of the thin turf, and the solid foundation of the land, exposed in cliffs of chalk five hundred feet high on the adjacent shore, yields full assurance of a time when the sea covered the site of the "everlasting hills"; and when the vegetation of what land lay nearest, was as different from the present Flora of the Sussex downs, as that of Central Africa now 3

259

is.[1] No less certain is it that, between the time during which the chalk was formed and that at which the original turf came into existence, thousands of centuries elapsed, in the course of which, the state of nature of the ages during which the chalk was deposited, passed into that which now is, by changes so slow that, in the coming and going of the generations of men, had such witnessed them, the contemporary conditions would have seemed to be unchanging and unchangeable.

But it is also certain that, before the deposition of the chalk, a vastly   4
longer period had elapsed, throughout which it is easy to follow the traces of the same process of ceaseless modification and of the internecine struggle for existence of living things; and that even when we can get no further back, it is not because there is any reason to think we have reached the beginning, but because the trail of the most ancient life remains hidden, or has become obliterated.

Thus that state of nature of the world of plants which we began by   5
considering, is far from possessing the attribute of permanence. Rather its very essence is impermanence. It may have lasted twenty or thirty thousand years, it may last for twenty or thirty thousand years more, without obvious change; but, as surely as it has followed upon a very different state, so it will be followed by an equally different condition. That which endures is not one or another association of living forms, but the process of which the cosmos is the product, and of which these are among the transitory expressions. And in the living world, one of the most characteristic features of this cosmic process is the struggle for existence, the competition of each with all, the result of which is the selection, that is to say, the survival of those forms which, on the whole, are best adapted to the conditions which at any period obtain; and which are, therefore, in that respect, and only in that respect, the fittest.[2] The acme reached by the cosmic process in the vegetation of the downs is seen in the turf, with its weeds and gorse. Under the conditions, they have come out of the struggle victorious; and, by surviving, have proved that they are the fittest to survive.

That the state of nature, at any time, is a temporary phase of a process   6
of incessant change, which has been going on for innumerable ages, appears to me to be a proposition as well established as any in modern history. Paleontology assures us, in addition, that the ancient philosophers who,

---

[1] See "On a piece of Chalk" in the preceding volume of these Essays (vol. viii. p. 1). [Author's note.] The *Collected Essays* to which Huxley refers is a nine-volume set of his works. [Editors' note.]

[2] That every theory of evolution must be consistent not merely with progressive development, but with indefinite persistence in the same condition and with retrogressive modification, is a point which I have insisted upon repeatedly from the year 1862 till now. See *Collected Essays*, vol. ii. pp. 461–89; vol. iii. p. 33; vol. viii. p. 304. In the address on "Geological Contemporaneity and Persistent Types" (1862), the paleontological proofs of this proposition were, I believe, first set forth. [Author's note.]

with less reason, held the same doctrine, erred in supposing that the phases formed a cycle, exactly repeating the past, exactly foreshadowing the future, in their rotations. On the contrary, it furnishes us with conclusive reasons for thinking that, if every link in the ancestry of these humble indigenous plants had been preserved and were accessible to us, the whole would present a converging series of forms of gradually diminishing complexity, until, at some period in the history of the earth, far more remote than any of which organic remains have yet been discovered, they would merge in those low groups among which the boundaries between animal and vegetable life become effaced.[3]

The word "evolution," now generally applied to the cosmic process, has   7
had a singular history, and is used in various senses.[4] Taken in its popular signification it means progressive development, that is, gradual change from a condition of relative uniformity to one of relative complexity; but its connotation has been widened to include the phenomena of retrogressive metamorphosis, that is, of progress from a condition of relative complexity to one of relative uniformity.

As a natural process, of the same character as the development of a tree   8
from its seed, or of a fowl from its egg, evolution excludes creation and all other kinds of supernatural intervention. As the expression of a fixed order, every stage of which is the effect of causes operating according to definite rules, the conception of evolution no less excludes that of chance. It is very desirable to remember that evolution is not an explanation of the cosmic process, but merely a generalized statement of the method and results of that process. And, further, that, if there is proof that the cosmic process was set going by any agent, then that agent will be the creator of it and of all its products, although supernatural intervention may remain strictly excluded from its further course.

So far as that limited revelation of the nature of things, which we call   9
scientific knowledge, has yet gone, it tends, with constantly increasing emphasis, to the belief that, not merely the world of plants, but that of animals; nor merely living things, but the whole fabric of the earth; not merely our planet, but the whole solar system; not merely our star and its satellites, but the millions of similar bodies which bear witness to the order which pervades boundless space, and has endured through boundless time; are all working out their predestined courses of evolution.

With none of these have I anything to do, at present, except with that   10
exhibited by the forms of life which tenant the earth. All plants and animals exhibit the tendency to vary, the causes of which have yet to be ascertained; it is the tendency of the conditions of life, at any given time, while favouring

---

[3] "On the Border Territory between the Animal and the Vegetable Kingdoms," Essays, vol. viii. p. 162. [Author's note.]

[4] See "Evolution in Biology," Essays, vol. ii. p. 187. [Author's note.]

the existence of the variations best adapted to them, to oppose that of the rest and thus to exercise selection; and all living things tend to multiply without limit, while the means of support are limited; the obvious cause of which is the production of offspring more numerous than their progenitors, but with equal expectation of life in the actuarial sense. Without the first tendency there could be no evolution. Without the second, there would be no good reason why one variation should disappear and another take its place; that is to say there would be no selection. Without the third, the struggle for existence, the agent of the selective process in the state of nature, would vanish.[5]

Granting the existence of these tendencies, all the known facts of the   11
history of plants and of animals may be brought into rational correlation. And this is more than can be said for any other hypothesis that I know of. Such hypotheses, for example, as that of the existence of a primitive, orderless chaos; of a passive and sluggish eternal matter moulded, with but partial success, by archetypal ideas; of a brand-new world-stuff suddenly created and swiftly shaped by a supernatural power; receive no encouragement, but the contrary, from our present knowledge. That our earth may once have formed part of a nebulous cosmic magma is certainly possible, indeed seems highly probable; but there is no reason to doubt that order reigned there, as completely as amidst what we regard as the most finished works of nature or of man.[6] The faith which is born of knowledge, finds its object in an eternal order, bringing forth ceaseless change, through endless time, in endless space; the manifestations of the cosmic energy alternating between phases of potentiality and phases of explication. It may be that, as Kant suggests,[7] every cosmic magma predestined to evolve into a new world, has been the no less predestined end of a vanished predecessor.

2

Three or four years have elapsed since the state of nature, to which I have   12
referred, was brought to an end, so far as a small patch of the soil is concerned, by the intervention of man. The patch was cut off from the rest by a wall; within the area thus protected, the native vegetation was, as far as possible, extirpated; while a colony of strange plants was imported and set down in its place. In short, it was made into a garden. At the present time, this artificially treated area presents an aspect extraordinarily different from that of so much of the land as remains in the state of nature, outside the wall. Trees, shrubs, and herbs, many of them appertaining to the state

---

[5] *Collected Essays*, vol. ii. *passim*. [Author's note.]

[6] *Ibid.*, vol. iv. p. 138; vol. v. pp. 71–73. [Author's note.]

[7] *Ibid.*, vol. viii. p. 321. [Author's note.]

of nature of remote parts of the globe, abound and flourish. Moreover, considerable quantities of vegetables, fruits, and flowers are produced, of kinds which neither now exist, nor have ever existed, except under conditions such as obtain in the garden; and which, therefore, are as much works of the art of man as the frames and glass-houses in which some of them are raised. That the "state of Art," thus created in the state of nature by man, is sustained by and dependent on him, would at once become apparent, if the watchful supervision of the gardener were withdrawn, and the antagonistic influences of the general cosmic process were no longer sedulously warded off, or counteracted. The walls and gates would decay; quadrupedal and bipedal intruders would devour and tread down the useful and beautiful plants; birds, insects, blight, and mildew would work their will; the seeds of the native plants, carried by winds or other agencies, would immigrate, and in virtue of their long-earned special adaptation to the local conditions, these despised native weeds would soon choke their choice exotic rivals. A century or two hence, little beyond the foundations of the wall and of the houses and frames would be left, in evidence of the victory of the cosmic powers at work in the state of nature, over the temporary obstacles to their supremacy, set up by the art of the horticulturist.

It will be admitted that the garden is as much a work of art,[8] or artifice,   13 as anything that can be mentioned. The energy localised in certain human bodies, directed by similarly localised intellects, has produced a collocation of other material bodies which could not be brought about in the state of nature. The same proposition is true of all the works of man's hands, from a flint implement to a cathedral or a chronometer; and it is because it is true, that we call these things artificial, term them works of art, or artifice, by way of distinguishing them from the products of the cosmic process, working outside man, which we call natural, or works of nature. The distinction thus drawn between the works of nature and those of man, is universally recognized; and it is, as I conceive, both useful and justifiable.

3

No doubt, it may be properly urged that the operation of human energy   14 and intelligence, which has brought into existence and maintains the garden, by what I have called "the horticultural process," is, strictly speaking, part and parcel of the cosmic process. And no one could more readily agree to that proposition than I. In fact, I do not know that any one has taken more pains than I have, during the last thirty years, to insist upon the doctrine, so much reviled in the early part of that period, that man, physical,

---

[8] The sense of the term "Art" is becoming narrowed; "work of Art" to most people means a picture, a statue, or a piece of *bijouterie;* by way of compensation "artist" has included in its wide embrace cooks and ballet girls, no less than painters and sculptors. [Author's note.]

intellectual, and moral, is as much a part of nature, as purely a product of the cosmic process, as the humblest weed.[9]

But if, following up this admission, it is urged that, such being the case, the cosmic process cannot be in antagonism with that horticultural process which is part of itself—I can only reply, that if the conclusion that the two are antagonistic is logically absurd, I am sorry for logic, because, as we have seen, the fact is so. The garden is in the same position as every other work of man's art; it is a result of the cosmic process working through and by human energy and intelligence; and, as is the case with every other artificial thing set up in the state of nature, the influences of the latter are constantly tending to break it down and destroy it. No doubt, the Forth bridge and an ironclad in the offing, are, in ultimate resort, products of the cosmic process; as much so as the river which flows under the one, or the seawater on which the other floats. Nevertheless, every breeze strains the bridge a little, every tide does something to weaken its foundations; every change of temperature alters the adjustment of its parts, produces friction and consequent wear and tear. From time to time, the bridge must be repaired, just as the ironclad must go into dock; simply because nature is always tending to reclaim that which her child, man, has borrowed from her and has arranged in combinations which are not those favoured by the general cosmic process.

Thus, it is not only true that the cosmic energy, working through man upon a portion of the plant world, opposes the same energy as it works through the state of nature, but a similar antagonism is everywhere manifest between the artificial and the natural. Even in the state of nature itself, what is the struggle for existence but the antagonism of the results of the cosmic process in the region of life, one to another?[10]

4

Not only is the state of nature hostile to the state of art of the garden; but the principle of the horticultural process, by which the latter is created and maintained, is antithetic to that of the cosmic process. The characteristic feature of the latter is the intense and unceasing competition of the struggle for existence. The characteristic of the former is the elimination of that struggle, by the removal of the conditions which give rise to it. The tendency of the cosmic process is to bring about the adjustment of the forms of plant life to the current conditions; the tendency of the horticultural

---

[9] See "Man's Place in Nature," *Collected Essays*, vol. vii., and "On the Struggle for Existence in Human Society" (1888). . . . [Author's note.]

[10] Or to put the case still more simply. When a man lays hold of the two ends of a piece of string and pulls them, with intent to break it, the right arm is certainly exerted in antagonism to the left arm; yet both arms derive their energy from the same original source. [Author's note.]

process is the adjustment of the conditions to the needs of the forms of plant life which the gardener desires to raise.

The cosmic process uses unrestricted multiplication as the means whereby hundreds compete for the place and nourishment adequate for one; it employs frost and drought to cut off the weak and unfortunate; to survive, there is need not only of strength, but of flexibility and of good fortune. 18

The gardener, on the other hand, restricts multiplication; provides that each plant shall have sufficient space and nourishment; protects from frost and drought; and, in every other way, attempts to modify the conditions, in such a manner as to bring about the survival of those forms which most nearly approach the standard of the useful, or the beautiful, which he has in his mind. 19

If the fruits and the tubers, the foliage and the flowers thus obtained, reach, or sufficiently approach, that ideal, there is no reason why the *status quo* attained should not be indefinitely prolonged. So long as the state of nature remains approximately the same, so long will the energy and intelligence which created the garden suffice to maintain it. However, the limits within which this mastery of man over nature can be maintained are narrow. If the conditions of the cretaceous epoch returned, I fear the most skilful of gardeners would have to give up the cultivation of apples and gooseberries; while, if those of the glacial period once again obtained, open asparagus beds would be superfluous, and the training of fruit trees against the most favourable of south walls, a waste of time and trouble. 20

But it is extremely important to note that, the state of nature remaining the same, if the produce does not satisfy the gardener, it may be made to approach his ideal more closely. Although the struggle for existence may be at end, the possibility of progress remains. In discussions on these topics, it is often strangely forgotten that the essential conditions of the modification, or evolution, of living things are variation and hereditary transmission. Selection is the means by which certain variations are favoured and their progeny preserved. But the struggle for existence is only one of the means by which selection may be effected. The endless varieties of cultivated flowers, fruits, roots, tubers, and bulbs are not products of selection by means of the struggle for existence, but of direct selection, in view of an ideal of utility or beauty. Amidst a multitude of plants, occupying the same station and subjected to the same conditions, in the garden, varieties arise. The varieties tending in a given direction are preserved, and the rest are destroyed. And the same process takes place among the varieties until, for example, the wild kale becomes a cabbage, or the wild *Viola tricolor* a prize pansy. 21

5

The process of colonisation presents analogies to the formation of a garden which are highly instructive. Suppose a shipload of English colonists sent 22

265

to form a settlement, in such a country as Tasmania was in the middle of the last century. On landing, they find themselves in the midst of a state of nature, widely different from that left behind them in everything but the most general physical conditions. The common plants, the common birds and quadrupeds, are as totally distinct as the men from anything to be seen on the side of the globe from which they come. The colonists proceed to put an end to this state of things over as large an area as they desire to occupy. They clear away the native vegetation, extirpate or drive out the animal population, so far as may be necessary, and take measures to defend themselves from the re-immigration of either. In their place, they introduce English grain and fruit trees; English dogs, sheep, cattle, horses; and English men; in fact they set up a new Flora and Fauna and a new variety of mankind, within the old state of nature. Their farms and pastures represent a garden on a great scale, and themselves the gardeners who have to keep it up, in watchful antagonism to the old *régime*. Considered as a whole, the colony is a composite unit introduced into the old state of nature; and, thenceforward, a competitor in the struggle for existence, to conquer or be vanquished.

Under the conditions supposed, there is no doubt of the result, if the 23 work of the colonists be carried out energetically and with intelligent combination of all their forces. On the other hand, if they are slothful, stupid, and careless; or if they waste their energies in contests with one another, the chances are that the old state of nature will have the best of it. The native savage will destroy the immigrant civilized man; of the English animals and plants some will be extirpated by their indigenous rivals, others will pass into the feral state and themselves become components of the state of nature. In a few decades, all other traces of the settlement will have vanished.

6

Let us now imagine that some administrative authority, as far superior in 24 power and intelligence to men, as men are to their cattle, is set over the colony, charged to deal with its human elements in such a manner as to assure the victory of the settlement over the antagonistic influences of the state of nature in which it is set down. He would proceed in the same fashion as that in which the gardener dealt with his garden. In the first place, he would, as far as possible, put a stop to the influence of external competition by thoroughly extirpating and excluding the native rivals, whether men, beasts, or plants. And our administrator would select his human agents, with a view to his ideal of a successful colony, just as the gardener selects his plants with a view to his ideal of useful or beautiful products.

In the second place, in order that no struggle for the means of existence 25 between these human agents should weaken the efficiency of the corporate whole in the battle with the state of nature, he would make arrangements by which each would be provided with those means; and would be relieved from the fear of being deprived of them by his stronger or more cunning fellows. Laws, sanctioned by the combined force of the colony, would restrain the self-assertion of each man within the limits required for the maintenance of peace. In other words, the cosmic struggle for existence, as between man and man, would be rigorously suppressed; and selection, by its means, would be as completely excluded as it is from the garden.

At the same time, the obstacles to the full development of the capacities 26 of the colonists by other conditions of the state of nature than those already mentioned, would be removed by the creation of artificial conditions of existence of a more favourable character. Protection against extremes of heat and cold would be afforded by houses and clothing; drainage and irrigation works would antagonise the effects of excessive rain and excessive drought; roads, bridges, canals, carriages, and ships would overcome the natural obstacles to locomotion and transport; mechanical engines would supplement the natural strength of men and of their draught animals; hygienic precautions would check, or remove, the natural causes of disease. With every step of this progress in civilization, the colonists would become more and more independent of the state of nature; more and more, their lives would be conditioned by a state of art. In order to attain his ends, the administrator would have to avail himself of the courage, industry, and co-operative intelligence of the settlers; and it is plain that the interest of the community would be best served by increasing the proportion of persons who possess such qualities, and diminishing that of persons devoid of them. In other words, by selection directed towards an ideal.

Thus the administrator might look to the establishment of an earthly 27 paradise, a true garden of Eden, in which all things should work together towards the well-being of the gardeners: within which the cosmic process, the coarse struggle for existence of the state of nature, should be abolished; in which that state should be replaced by a state of art; where every plant and every lower animal should be adapted to human wants, and would perish if human supervision and protection were withdrawn; where men themselves should have been selected, with a view to their efficiency as organs for the performance of the functions of a perfected society. And this ideal polity would have been brought about, not by gradually adjusting the men to the conditions around them, but by creating artificial conditions for them; not by allowing the free play of the struggle for existence, but by excluding that struggle; and by substituting selection directed towards the administrator's ideal for the selection it exercises.

7

But the Eden would have its serpent, and a very subtle beast too. Man 28 shares with the rest of the living world the mighty instinct of reproduction and its consequence, the tendency to multiply with great rapidity. The better the measures of the administrator achieved their object, the more completely the destructive agencies of the state of nature were defeated, the less would that multiplication be checked.

On the other hand, within the colony, the enforcement of peace, which 29 deprives every man of the power to take away the means of existence from another, simply because he is the stronger, would have put an end to the struggle for existence between the colonists, and the competition for the commodities of existence, which would alone remain, is no check upon population.

Thus, as soon as the colonists began to multiply, the administrator would 30 have to face the tendency to the reintroduction of the cosmic struggle into his artificial fabric, in consequence of the competition, not merely for the commodities, but for the means of existence. When the colony reached the limit of possible expansion, the surplus population must be disposed of somehow; or the fierce struggle for existence must recommence and destroy that peace, which is the fundamental condition of the maintenance of the state of art against the state of nature.

Supposing the administrator to be guided by purely scientific considera- 31 tions, he would, like the gardener, meet this most serious difficulty by systematic extirpation, or exclusion, of the superfluous. The hopelessly diseased, the infirm aged, the weak or deformed in body or in mind, the excess of infants born, would be put away, as the gardener pulls up defective and superfluous plants, or the breeder destroys undesirable cattle. Only the strong and the healthy, carefully matched, with a view to the progeny best adapted to the purposes of the administrator, would be permitted to perpetuate their kind.

8

Of the more thoroughgoing of the multitudinous attempts to apply the 32 principles of cosmic evolution, or what are supposed to be such, to social and political problems, which have appeared of late years, a considerable proportion appear to me to be based upon the notion that human society is competent to furnish, from its own resources, an administrator of the kind I have imagined. The pigeons, in short, are to be their own Sir John Sebright.[11] A despotic government, whether individual or collective, is to be endowed with the preternatural intelligence, and with what, I am afraid, many will consider the preternatural ruthlessness, required for the purpose

---

[11] Not that the conception of such a society is necessarily based upon the idea of evolution. The Platonic state testifies to the contrary. [Author's note.] *Sir John Sebright:* a British politician and agriculturalist (1767–1846), an authority on the breeding of domestic animals. [Editors' note.]

of carrying out the principle of improvement by selection, which the somewhat drastic thoroughness upon which the success of the method depends. Experience certainly does not justify us in limiting the ruthlessness of individual "saviours of society"; and, on the well-known grounds of the aphorism which denies both body and soul to corporations, it seems probable (indeed the belief is not without support in history) that a collective despotism, a mob got to believe in its own divine right by demagogic missionaries, would be capable of more thorough work in this direction than any single tyrant, puffed up with the same illusion, has ever achieved. But intelligence is another affair. The fact that "saviours of society" take to that trade is evidence enough that they have none to spare. And such as they possess is generally sold to the capitalists of physical force on whose resources they depend. However, I doubt whether even the keenest judge of character, if he had before him a hundred boys and girls under fourteen, could pick out, with the least chance of success, those who should be kept, as certain to be serviceable members of the polity, and those who should be chloroformed, as equally sure to be stupid, idle, or vicious. The "points" of a good or of a bad citizen are really far harder to discern than those of a puppy or a short-horn calf; many do not show themselves before the practical difficulties of life stimulate manhood to full exertion. And by that time the mischief is done. The evil stock, if it be one, has had time to multiply, and selection is nullified.

9

I have other reasons for fearing that this logical ideal of evolutionary regimentation—this pigeon-fancier's polity—is unattainable. In the absence of any such a severely scientific administrator as we have been dreaming of, human society is kept together by bonds of such a singular character, that the attempt to perfect society after his fashion would run serious risk of loosening them.   33

Social organization is not peculiar to men. Other societies, such as those constituted by bees and ants, have also arisen out of the advantage of co-operation in the struggle for existence; and their resemblances to, and their differences from, human society are alike instructive. The society formed by the hive bee fulfils the ideal of the communistic aphorism "to each according to his needs, from each according to his capacity." Within it, the struggle for existence is strictly limited. Queen, drones, and workers have each their allotted sufficiency of food; each performs the function assigned to it in the economy of the hive, and all contribute to the success of the whole co-operative society in its competition with rival collectors of nectar and pollen and with other enemies, in the state of nature without. In the same sense as the garden, or the colony, is a work of human art, the bee polity is a work of apiarian art, brought about by the cosmic process, working through the organization of the hymenopterous type.   34

Now this society is the direct product of an organic necessity, impelling   35
every member of it to a course of action which tends to the good of the
whole. Each bee has its duty and none has any rights. Whether bees are
susceptible of feeling and capable of thought is a question which cannot be
dogmatically answered. As a pious opinion, I am disposed to deny them
more than the merest rudiments of consciousness.[12] But it is curious to
reflect that a thoughtful drone (workers and queens would have no leisure
for speculation) with a turn for ethical philosophy, must needs profess
himself an intuitive moralist of the purest water. He would point out, with
perfect justice, that the devotion of the workers to a life of ceaseless toil for
a mere subsistence wage, cannot be accounted for either by enlightened
selfishness, or by any other sort of utilitarian motives; since these bees begin
to work, without experience or reflection, as they emerge from the cell in
which they are hatched. Plainly, an eternal and immutable principle, innate
in each bee, can alone account for the phenomena. On the other hand, the
biologist, who traces out all the extant stages of gradation between solitary
and hive bees, as clearly sees in the latter, simply the perfection of an
automatic mechanism, hammered out by the blows of the struggle for
existence upon the progeny of the former, during long ages of constant
variation.

10

I see no reason to doubt that, at its origin, human society was as much a   36
product of organic necessity as that of the bees.[13] The human family, to
begin with, rested upon exactly the same conditions as those which gave
rise to similar associations among animals lower in the scale. Further, it is
easy to see that every increase in the duration of the family ties, with the
resulting co-operation of a larger and larger number of descendants for
protection and defence, would give the families in which such modification
took place a distinct advantage over the others. And, as in the hive, the
progressive limitation of the struggle for existence between the members of
the family would involve increasing efficiency as regards outside competition.

But there is this vast and fundamental difference between bee society and   37
human society. In the former, the members of the society are each organically
predestined to the performance of one particular class of functions only. If
they were endowed with desires, each could desire to perform none but
those offices for which its organization specially fits it; and which, in view
of the good of the whole, it is proper it should do. So long as a new queen

---

[12] *Collected Essays*, vol. i., "Animal Automatism"; vol. v., "Prologue," pp. 45 *et seq.*
[Author's note.]

[13] *Collected Essays*, vol. v., Prologue, pp. 50–54. [Author's note.]

does not make her appearance, rivalries and competition are absent from the bee polity.

Among mankind, on the contrary, there is no such predestination to a sharply defined place in the social organism. However much men may differ in the quality of their intellects, the intensity of their passions, and the delicacy of their sensations, it cannot be said that one is fitted by his organization to be an agricultural labourer and nothing else, and another to be a landowner and nothing else. Moreover, with all their enormous differences in natural endowment, men agree in one thing, and that is their innate desire to enjoy the pleasures and to escape the pains of life; and, in short, to do nothing but that which it pleases them to do, without the least reference to the welfare of the society into which they are born. That is their inheritance (the reality at the bottom of the doctrine of original sin) from the long series of ancestors, human and semi-human and brutal, in whom the strength of this innate tendency to self-assertion was the condition of victory in the struggle for existence. That is the reason of the *aviditas vitæ*—the insatiable hunger for enjoyment—of all mankind, which is one of the essential conditions of success in the war with the state of nature outside; and yet the sure agent of the destruction of society if allowed free play within. 38

The check upon this free play of self-assertion, or natural liberty, which is the necessary condition for the origin of human society, is the product of organic necessities of a different kind from those upon which the constitution of the hive depends. One of these is the mutual affection of parent and offspring, intensified by the long infancy of the human species. But the most important is the tendency, so strongly developed in man, to reproduce in himself actions and feelings similar to, or correlated with, those of other men. Man is the most consummate of all mimics in the animal world; none but himself can draw or model; none comes near him in the scope, variety, and exactness of vocal imitation; none is such a master of gesture; while he seems to be impelled thus to imitate for the pure pleasure of it. And there is no such another emotional chameleon. By a purely reflex operation of the mind, we take the hue of passion of those who are about us, or, it may be, the complementary colour. It is not by any conscious "putting one's self in the place" of a joyful or a suffering person that the state of mind we call sympathy usually arises;[14] indeed, it is often contrary to one's sense of right, and in spite of one's will, that 39

---

[14] Adam Smith makes the pithy observation that the man who sympathises with a woman in childbed, cannot be said to put himself in her place. ("The Theory of the Moral Sentiments," Part vii. sec. iii. chap. i.) Perhaps there is more humour than force in the example; and, in spite of this and other observations of the same tenor, I think that the one defect of the remarkable work in which is occurs is that it lays too much stress on conscious substitution, too little on purely reflex sympathy. [Author's note.]

"fellow-feeling makes us wondrous kind," or the reverse. However complete may be the indifference to public opinion, in a cool, intellectual view, of the traditional sage, it has not yet been my fortune to meet with any actual sage who took its hostile manifestations with entire equanimity. Indeed, I doubt if the philosopher lives, or ever has lived, who could know himself to be heartily despised by a street boy without some irritation. And, though one cannot justify Haman for wishing to hang Mordecai on such a very high gibbet, yet, really, the consciousness of the Vizier of Ahasuerus, as he went in and out of the gate, that this obscure Jew had no respect for him, must have been very annoying.[15]

It is needful only to look around us, to see that the greatest restrainer of   40
the anti-social tendencies of men is fear, not of the law, but of the opinion of their fellows. The conventions of honour bind men who break legal, moral, and religious bonds; and, while people endure the extremity of physical pain rather than part with life, shame drives the weakest to suicide.

Every forward step of social progress brings men into closer relations   41
with their fellows, and increases the importance of the pleasures and pains derived from sympathy. We judge the acts of others by our own sympathies, and we judge our own acts by the sympathies of others, every day and all day long, from childhood upwards, until associations, as indissoluble as those of language, are formed between certain acts and the feelings of approbation or disapprobation. It becomes impossible to imagine some acts without disapprobation, or others without approbation of the actor, whether he be one's self, or any one else. We come to think in the acquired dialect of morals. An artificial personality, the "man within," as Adam Smith[16] calls conscience, is built up beside the natural personality. He is the watchman of society, charged to restrain the anti-social tendencies of the natural man within the limits required by social welfare.

I I

I have termed this evolution of the feelings out of which the primitive   42
bonds of human society are so largely forged, into the organized and

---

[15] Esther v. 9–13. ". . . but when Haman saw Mordecai in the king's gate, that he stood not up, nor moved for him, he was full of indignation against Mordecai. . . . And Haman told them of the glory of his riches . . . and all the things wherein the king had promoted him. . . . Yet all this availeth me nothing, so long as I see Mordecai the Jew sitting at the king's gate." What a shrewd exposure of human weakness it is! [Author's note.] Haman was a vizier (a government official) in the service of King Ahasuerus (or Xerxes) of Persia. Haman's plot to execute the Jews was exposed by Esther, Ahasuerus' Jewish wife. Mordecai was Esther's cousin. [Editors' note.]

[16] "Theory of the Moral Sentiments," Part iii. chap. 3, *On the influence and authority of conscience*. [Author's note.] Adam Smith (1723–1790) was a Scottish economist, moral philosopher, and rhetorician. [Editors' note.]

personified sympathy we call conscience, the ethical process.[17] So far as it tends to make any human society more efficient in the struggle for existence with the state of nature, or with other societies, it works in harmonious contrast with the cosmic process. But it is none the less true that, since law and morals are restraints upon the struggle for existence between men in society, the ethical process is in opposition to the principle of the cosmic process, and tends to the suppression of the qualities best fitted for success in that struggle.[18]

It is further to be observed that, just as the self-assertion, necessary to   43
the maintenance of society against the state of nature, will destroy that society if it is allowed free operation within; so the self-restraint, the essence of the ethical process, which is no less an essential condition of the existence of every polity, may, by excess, become ruinous to it.

Moralists of all ages and of all faiths, attending only to the relations of   44
men towards one another in an ideal society, have agreed upon the "golden rule," "Do as you would be done by." In other words, let sympathy be your guide; put yourself in the place of the man towards whom your action is directed; and do to him what you would like to have done to yourself under the circumstances. However much one may admire the generosity of such a rule of conduct; however confident one may be that average men may be thoroughly depended upon not to carry it out to its full logical consequences; it is nevertheless desirable to recognise the fact that these consequences are incompatible with the existence of a civil state, under any circumstances of this world which have obtained, or, so far as one can see, are, likely to come to pass.

For I imagine there can be no doubt that the great desire of every   45
wrongdoer is to escape from the painful consequences of his actions. If I put myself in the place of the man who has robbed me, I find that I am possessed by an exceeding desire not to be fined or imprisoned; if in that of the man who has smitten me on one cheek, I contemplate with satisfaction the absence of any worse result than the turning of the other cheek for like treatment. Strictly observed, the "golden rule" involves the negation of law by the refusal to put it in motion against law-breakers; and, as regards the

---

[17] Worked out, in its essential features, chiefly by Hartley and Adam Smith, long before the modern doctrine of evolution was thought of. [Author's note.] David Hartley (1705–1757) was an English physician and philosopher. [Editors' note.] It seems the fashion nowadays to ignore Hartley; though, a century and a half ago, he not only laid the foundations but built up much of the superstructure of a true theory of the Evolution of the intellectual and moral faculties. He speaks of what I have termed the ethical process as "our Progress from Self-interest to Self-annihilation." *Observations on Man* (1749), vol. ii, p. 281. [Author's note.]

[18] See the essay "On the Struggle for Existence in Human Society" below; and *Collected Essays*, vol. i, p. 276, for Kant's recognition of these facts. [Author's note.]

external relations of a polity, it is the refusal to continue the struggle for existence. It can be obeyed, even partially, only under the protection of a society which repudiates it. Without such shelter, the followers of the "golden rule" may indulge in hopes of heaven, but they must reckon with the certainty that other people will be masters of the earth.

What would become of the garden if the gardener treated all the weeds 46 and slugs and birds and trespassers as he would like to be treated, if he were in their place?

12

Under the preceding heads, I have endeavoured to represent in broad, but 47 I hope faithful, outlines the essential features of the state of nature and of that cosmic process of which it is the outcome, so far as was needful for my argument; I have contrasted with the state of nature the state of art, produced by human intelligence and energy, as it is exemplified by a garden; and I have shown that the state of art, here and elsewhere, can be maintained only by the constant counteraction of the hostile influences of the state of nature. Further, I have pointed out that the "horticultural process," which thus sets itself against the "cosmic process" is opposed to the latter in principle, in so far as it tends to arrest the struggle for existence, by restraining the multiplication which is one of the chief causes of that struggle, and by creating artificial conditions of life, better adapted to the cultivated plants than are the conditions of the state of nature. And I have dwelt upon the fact that, though the progressive modification, which is the consequence of the struggle for existence in the state of nature, is at an end, such modification may still be effected by that selection, in view of an ideal of usefulness, or of pleasantness, to man, of which the state of nature knows nothing.

I have proceeded to show that a colony, set down in a country in the 48 state of nature, presents close analogies with a garden; and I have indicated the course of action which an administrator, able and willing to carry out horticultural principles, would adopt, in order to secure the success of such a newly formed polity, supposing it to be capable of indefinite expansion. In the contrary case, I have shown that difficulties must arise; that the unlimited increase of the population over a limited area must, sooner or later, reintroduce into the colony that struggle for the means of existence between the colonists, which it was the primary object of the administrator to exclude, insomuch as it is fatal to the mutual peace which is the prime condition of the union of men in society.

I have briefly described the nature of the only radical cure, known to 49 me, for the disease which would thus threaten the existence of the colony; and, however regretfully, I have been obliged to admit that this rigorously scientific method of applying the principles of evolution to human society hardly comes within the region of practical politics; not for want of will on the part of a great many people; but because, for one reason, there is no hope that mere human beings will ever possess enough intelligence to select the fittest. And I have adduced other grounds for arriving at the same conclusion.

I have pointed out that human society took its rise in the organic necessities 50 expressed by imitation and by the sympathetic emotions; and that, in the struggle for existence with the state of nature and with other societies, as part of it, those in which men were thus led to close co-operation had a great advantage.[19] But, since each man retained more or less of the faculties common to all the rest, and especially a full share of the desire for unlimited self-gratification, the struggle for existence within society could only be gradually eliminated. So long as any of it remained, society continued to be an imperfect instrument of the struggle for existence and, consequently, was improvable by the selective influence of that struggle. Other things being alike, the tribe of savages in which order was best maintained; in which there was most security within the tribe and the most loyal mutual support outside it, would be the survivors.

I have termed this gradual strengthening of the social bond, which, 51 though it arrest the struggle for existence inside society, up to a certain point improves the chances of society, as a corporate whole, in the cosmic struggle—the ethical process. I have endeavoured to show that, when the ethical process has advanced so far as to secure every member of the society in the possession of the means of existence, the struggle for existence, as between man and man, within that society is, *ipso facto*, at an end. And, as it is undeniable that the most highly civilized societies have substantially reached this position, it follows that, so far as they are concerned, the struggle for existence can play no important part within them.[20] In other words, the kind of evolution which is brought about in the state of nature cannot take place.

I have further shown cause for the belief that direct selection, after the 52 fashion of the horticulturist and the breeder, neither has played, nor can play, any important part in the evolution of society; apart from other reasons, because I do not see how such selection could be practised without a serious weakening, it may be the destruction, of the bonds which hold society together. It strikes me that men who are accustomed to contemplate the active or passive extirpation of the weak, the unfortunate, and the superfluous; who justify that conduct on the ground that it has the sanction

---

[19] *Collected Essays*, vol. v., Prologue, p. 52. [Author's note.]

[20] Whether the struggle for existence with the state of nature and with other societies, so far as they stand in the relation of the state of nature with it, exerts a selective influence upon modern society, and in what direction, are questions not easy to answer. The problem of the effect of military and industrial warfare upon those who wage it is very complicated. [Author's note.]

of the cosmic process, and is the only way of ensuring the progress of the race; who, if they are consistent, must rank medicine among the black arts and count the physician a mischievous preserver of the unfit; on whose matrimonial undertakings the principles of the stud have the chief influence; whose whole lives, therefore, are an education in the noble art of suppressing natural affection and sympathy, are not likely to have any large stock of these commodities left. But, without them, there is no conscience, nor any restraint on the conduct of men, except the calculation of self-interest, the balancing of certain present gratifications against doubtful future pains; and experience tells us how much that is worth. Every day, we see firm believers in the hell of the theologians commit acts by which, as they believe when cool, they risk eternal punishment; while they hold back from those which are opposed to the sympathies of their associates.

13

That progressive modification of civilization which passes by the name of 53 the "evolution of society," is, in fact, a process of an essentially different character, both from that which brings about the evolution of species, in the state of nature, and from that which gives rise to the evolution of varieties, in the state of art.

There can be no doubt that vast changes have taken place in English 54 civilizaiton since the reign of the Tudors.[21] But I am not aware of a particle of evidence in favour of the conclusion that this evolutionary process has been accompanied by any modification of the physical, or the mental, characters of the men who have been the subjects of it. I have not met with any grounds for suspecting that the average Englishmen of to-day are sensibly different from those that Shakespeare knew and drew. We look into his magic mirror of the Elizabethan age, and behold, nowise darkly, the presentment of ourselves.

During these three centuries, from the reign of Elizabeth to that of 55 Victoria,[22] the struggle for existence between man and man has been so largely restrained among the great mass of the population (except for one or two short intervals of civil war), that it can have had little, or no, selective operation. As to anything comparable to direct selection, it has been practised on so small a scale that it may also be neglected. The criminal law, in so far as by putting to death or by subjecting to long periods of imprisonment, those who infringe its provisions, prevents the propagation of hereditary criminal tendencies; and the poor-law, in so far as it separates

---

[21] *Tudors:* the ruling family of England from 1485 to 1603. Queen Elizabeth I was the last Tudor to hold the throne. The Elizabethan age (the latter half of the sixteenth century) was named for her. [Editors' note.]

[22] *Victoria:* Queen Victoria (1819–1901), ruler of Britain from 1837 to 1901. The Victorian age was named for her. [Editors' note.]

married couples, whose destitution arises from hereditary defects of character, are doubtless selective agents operating in favour of the non-criminal and the more effective members of society. But the proportion of the population which they influence is very small; and, generally, the hereditary criminal and the hereditary pauper have propagated their kind before the law affects them. In a large proportion of cases, crime and pauperism have nothing to do with heredity; but are the consequence, partly, of circumstances and, partly, of the possession of qualities, which, under different conditions of life, might have excited esteem and even admiration. It was a shrewd man of the world who, in discussing sewage problems, remarked that dirt is riches in the wrong place; and that sound aphorism has moral applications. The benevolence and open-handed generosity which adorn a rich man, may make a pauper of a poor one; the energy and courage to which the successful soldier owes his rise, the cool and daring subtlety to which the great financier owes his fortune, may very easily, under unfavourable conditions, lead their possessors to the gallows, or to the hulks. Moreover, it is fairly probable that the children of a "failure" will receive from their other parent just that little modification of character which makes all the difference. I sometimes wonder whether people, who talk so freely about extirpating the unfit, ever dispassionately consider their own history. Surely, one must be very "fit," indeed, not to know of an occasion, or perhaps two, in one's life, when it would have been only too easy to qualify for a place among the "unfit."

In my belief the innate qualities, physical, intellectual, and moral, of 56
our nation have remained substantially the same for the last four or five centuries. If the struggle for existence has affected us to any serious extent (and I doubt it) it has been, indirectly, through our military and industrial wars with other nations.

14

What is often called the struggle for existence in society (I plead guilty to 57
having used the term too loosely myself), is a contest, not for the means of existence, but for the means of enjoyment. Those who occupy the first places in this practical competitive examination are the rich and the influential; those who fail, more or less, occupy the lower places, down to the squalid obscurity of the pauper and the criminal. Upon the most liberal estimate, I suppose the former group will not amount to two per cent. of the population. I doubt if the latter exceeds another two per cent.; but let it be supposed, for the sake of argument, that it is as great as five per cent.[23]

As it is only in the latter group that any thing comparable to the struggle 58
for existence in the state of nature can take place; as it is only among this twentieth of the whole people that numerous men, women, and children

---

[23] Those who read the last Essay in this volume ["Social Diseases and Worse Remedies," vol. ix of *Collected Essays*] will not accuse me of wishing to attenuate the evil of the existence of this group, whether great or small. [Author's note.]

die of rapid or slow starvation, or of the diseases incidental to permanently bad conditions of life; and as there is nothing to prevent their multiplication before they are killed off, while, in spite of greater infant mortality, they increase faster than the rich; it seems clear that the struggle for existence in this class can have no appreciable selective influence upon the other 95 per cent. of the population.

What sort of a sheep breeder would he be who should content himself 59 with picking out the worst fifty out of a thousand, leaving them on a barren common till the weakest starved, and then letting the survivors go back to mix with the rest? And the parallel is too favourable; since in a large number of cases, the actual poor and the convicted criminals are neither the weakest nor the worst.

In the struggle for the means of enjoyment, the qualities which ensure 60 success are energy, industry, intellectual capacity, tenacity of purpose, and, at least, as much sympathy as is necessary to make a man understand the feelings of his fellows. Were there none of those artificial arrangements by which fools and knaves are kept at the top of society instead of sinking to their natural place at the bottom,[24] the struggle for the means of enjoyment would ensure a constant circulation of the human units of the social compound, from the bottom to the top and from the top to the bottom. The survivors of the contest, those who continued to form the great bulk of the polity, would not be those "fittest" who got to the very top, but the great body of the moderately "fit," whose numbers and superior propagative power, enable them always to swamp the exceptionally endowed minority.

I think it must be obvious to every one, that, whether we consider the 61 internal or the external interests of society, it is desirable they should be in the hands of those who are endowed with the largest share of energy, of industry, of intellectual capacity, of tenacity of purpose, while they are not devoid of sympathetic humanity; and, in so far as the struggle for the means of enjoyment tends to place such men in possession of wealth and influence, it is a process which tends to the good of society. But the process, as we have seen, has no real resemblance to that which adapts living beings to current conditions in the state of nature; nor any to the artificial selection of the horticulturist.

15

To return, once more, to the parallel of horticulture. In the modern world, 62 the gardening of men by themselves is practically restricted to the performance, not of selection, but of that other function of the gardener, the creation of conditions more favourable than those of the state of nature; to the end of facilitating the free expansion of the innate faculties of the citizen,

[24] I have elsewhere lamented the absence from society of a machinery for facilitating the descent of incapacity. "Administrative Nihilism." *Collected Essays*, vol. i. p. 54. [Author's note.]

so far as it is consistent with the general good. And the business of the moral and political philosopher appears to me to be the ascertainment, by the same method of observation, experiment, and ratiocination, as is practised in other kinds of scientific work, of the course of conduct which will best conduce to that end.

But, supposing this course of conduct to be scientifically determined and 63 carefully followed out, it cannot put an end to the struggle for existence in the state of nature; and it will not so much as tend, in any way, to the adaptation of man to that state. Even should the whole human race be absorbed in one vast polity, within which "absolute political justice" reigns, the struggle for existence with the state of nature outside it, and the tendency to the return to the struggle within, in consequence of over-multiplication, will remain; and, unless men's inheritance from the ancestors who fought a good fight in the state of nature, their dose of original sin, is rooted out by some method at present unrevealed, at any rate to disbelievers in supernaturalism, every child born into the world will still bring with him the instinct of unlimited self-assertion. He will have to learn the lesson of self-restraint and renunciation. But the practice of self-restraint and renunciation is not happiness, though it may be something much better.

That man, as a "political animal," is susceptible of a vast amount of 64 improvement, by education, by instruction, and by the application of his intelligence to the adaptation of the conditions of life to his higher needs, I entertain not the slightest doubt. But so long as he remains liable to error, intellectual or moral; so long as he is compelled to be perpetually on guard against the cosmic forces, whose ends are not his ends, without and within himself; so long as he is haunted by inexpugnable memories and hopeless aspirations; so long as the recognition of his intellectual limitations forces him to acknowledge his incapacity to penetrate the mystery of existence; the prospect of attaining untroubled happiness, or of a state which can, even remotely, deserve the title of perfection, appears to me to be as misleading an illusion as ever was dangled before the eyes of poor humanity. And there have been many of them.

That which lies before the human race is a constant struggle to maintain 65 and improve, in opposition to the State of Nature, the State of Art of an organized polity; in which, and by which, man may develop a worthy civilization, capable of maintaining and constantly improving itself, until the evolution of our globe shall have entered so far upon its downward course that the cosmic process resumes its sway; and, once more, the State of Nature prevails over the surface of our planet.

Questions for Discussion and Writing

1. Compare Huxley's introduction to his conclusion. In your estimation, does the latter seem to "answer" the questions or problems raised by the former? Do these

two sections of the piece seem to complement each other, or do you sense disjunction?

2. Retrace Huxley's steps as he gradually approaches the topics of ethics and evolution. Where do the terms *evolution* and *ethical* first actually appear? Why might Huxley prepare the way for these terms so cautiously? What, finally, is the relationship between them?

3. For the purposes of his argument, how does Huxley link the terms *art, men,* and *nature*? How might his opposition confront these terms?

4. How should one go about making ethical decisions of the sort that Huxley confronts in this essay? Do you believe that science has any role in such decision making? What characteristics, ultimately, do you believe are essential for great leadership? Write an essay that addresses one or more of these questions.

ANDREW CARNEGIE

(1835–1919)

We are all familiar with the traditional American success story. The leading character, often an immigrant, makes the best of initiative, ingenuity, self-reliance, hard work, and bold dreams in the struggle to rise from the bottom to the top of society. Once he—"he," since the story reflects the values of a historically male-dominated society—has reached the pinnacle of success, he charitably stoops down to help others make their way up. This assistance, of course, is offered on the philanthropist's own terms.

Andrew Carnegie fits the tradition perfectly. He was born in Dunfermline, Scotland, where his father worked as a handloom weaver. The family was very poor, and their prospects in Scotland remained bleak. In 1848, they scraped together enough money for passage and immigrated to Pennsylvania in search of greater opportunity. Beginning at $1.20 per week, young Andrew worked at a variety of jobs as he read his way through the private library of a local philanthropist. In 1853, he began working for the Pennsylvania Railroad for a whopping $35 per month. There, he distinguished himself with such innovations as the Pullman sleeping car.

In 1865, Carnegie left the railroad to pursue his interest in oil and to manage his new enterprise, the Keystone Bridge Company. An extremely able salesman who took advantage of his prior railroad contacts and considerable personal charm, Carnegie successfully promoted iron railroad bridges as the much-needed replacement for the older wooden variety. By 1873, he had imported Britain's industry-leading technology and was focusing most of his attention on steel production. Carnegie was an adroit competitor and a strong judge of talent. He surrounded himself with the most capable workers available and practiced democratic management. All the company's stock was held by Carnegie and his working associates. In relatively little time, he built a steel empire that flourished despite labor disputes and industrial slumps. There is no doubt that his contribution to the industry made it possible for the United States to eclipse Britain in steel production during this period.

In 1901, after selling his steel interests to the U.S. Steel Corporation for $250,000,000, Carnegie retired from business so that he could concentrate on the final element of the traditional American success story: helping others help themselves. He erected libraries in America and Great Britain, established pension plans for former employees and college professors, and set up a trust to assist Scottish universities. Furthermore, he founded the Carnegie Institute of Technology at Pittsburgh and the Carnegie Institution at Washington, D.C., and he contributed generously to Booker T. Washington's Tuskegee Institute. Before he died, he had given away $350,000,000.

But Carnegie's version of the American dream had a unique twist. Not only did this rags-to-riches industrialist reach the very top of the social ladder, but he chose to write eloquently about the nature of wealth and the duties of the wealthy. In The Gospel of Wealth, published in 1889, Carnegie sang the praises of both wealth acquisition and distribution, but his conditions for "philanthropy" were very specific. In the following excerpt, he sets forth in precise terms his beliefs about wealth, poverty, and assistance for the less fortunate.

As one evaluates Carnegie's argument in The Gospel of Wealth, it is important to consider social context. When the work was published, there existed no income tax and few government-sponsored services such as welfare. Charity was a matter for churches and individuals. Unions had limited power, and most laborers worked at the mercy of management. There was no minimum wage, and no laws regulating child labor. It was a time when a great premium was placed on individual ability as the means to better one's situation. America was the land of opportunity, but each person was solely responsible for his or her success or failure.

FROM THE GOSPEL OF WEALTH

THE PROBLEM OF THE ADMINISTRATION OF WEALTH

The problem of our age is the proper administration of wealth, that the ties of brotherhood may still bind together the rich and poor in harmonious relationship. The conditions of human life have not only been changed, but revolutionized, within the past few hundred years. In former days there was little difference between the dwelling, dress, food, and environment of the chief and those of his retainers. The Indians are to-day where civilized man then was. When visiting the Sioux, I was led to the wigwam of the chief. It was like the others in external appearance, and even within the difference was trifling between it and those of the poorest of his braves. The contrast between the palace of the millionaire and the cottage of the laborer with us to-day measures the change which has come with civilization. This change, however, is not to be deplored, but welcomed as highly beneficial. It is well, nay, essential, for the progress of the race that the houses of some should be homes for all that is highest and best in literature and the arts, and for all the refinements of civilization, rather than that none should be so. Much better this great irregularity than universal squalor. Without wealth there can be no Mæcenas.[1] The "good old times" were not

1

---

[1] *Mæcenas:* Gaius Maecenas, a Roman statesman (d. 8 B.C.) who was a friend and patron of the poets Horace and Virgil. Today the name is used to refer to any patron, especially a patron of literature and the arts. [Editors' note.]

good old times. Neither master nor servant was as well situated then as to-day. A relapse to old conditions would be disastrous to both—not the least so to him who serves—and would sweep away civilization with it. But whether the change be for good or ill, it is upon us, beyond our power to alter, and, therefore, to be accepted and made the best of. It is a waste of time to criticize the inevitable.

It is easy to see how the change has come. One illustration will serve for almost every phase of the cause. In the manufacture of products we have the whole story. It applies to all combinations of human industry, as stimulated and enlarged by the inventions of this scientific age. Formerly, articles were manufactured at the domestic hearth, or in small shops which formed part of the household. The master and his apprentices worked side by side, the latter living with the master, and therefore subject to the same conditions. When these apprentices rose to be masters, there was little or no change in their mode of life, and they, in turn, educated succeeding apprentices in the same routine. There was, substantially, social equality, and even political equality, for those engaged in industrial pursuits had then little or no voice in the State. 2

The inevitable result of such a mode of manufacture was crude articles at high prices. To-day the world obtains commodities of excellent quality at prices which even the preceding generation would have deemed incredible. In the commercial world similar causes have produced similar results, and the race is benefited thereby. The poor enjoy what the rich could not before afford. What were the luxuries have become the necessaries of life. The laborer has now more comforts than the farmer had a few generations ago. The farmer has more luxuries than the landlord had, and is more richly clad and better housed. The landlord has books and pictures rarer and appointments more artistic than the king could then obtain. 3

The price we pay for this salutary change is, no doubt, great. We assemble thousands of operatives in the factory, and in the mine, of whom the employer can know little or nothing, and to whom he is little better than a myth. All intercourse between them is at an end. Rigid castes are formed, and, as usual, mutual ignorance breeds mutual distrust. Each caste is without sympathy with the other, and ready to credit anything disparaging in regard to it. Under the law of competition, the employer of thousands is forced into the strictest economies, among which the rates paid to labor figure prominently, and often there is friction between the employer and the employed, between capital and labor, between rich and poor. Human society loses homogeneity. 4

The price which society pays for the law of competition, like the price it pays for cheap comforts and luxuries, is also great; but the advantages of this law are also greater still than its cost—for it is to this law that we owe our wonderful material development, which brings improved conditions in its train. But, whether the law be benign or not, we must say of it, as we say of the change in the conditions of men to which we have referred: It is 5 here; we cannot evade it; no substitutes for it have been found; and while the law may be sometimes hard for the individual, it is best for the race, because it insures the survival of the fittest in every department. We accept and welcome, therefore, as conditions to which we must accommodate ourselves, great inequality of environment; the concentration of business, industrial and commercial, in the hands of a few; and the law of competition between these, as being not only beneficial, but essential to the future progress of the race. Having accepted these, it follows that there must be great scope for the exercise of special ability in the merchant and in the manufacturer who has to conduct affairs upon a great scale. That this talent for organization and management is rare among men is proved by the fact that it invariably secures enormous rewards for its possessor, no matter where or under what laws or conditions. The experienced in affairs always rate the MAN whose services can be obtained as a partner as not only the first consideration, but such as render the question of his capital scarcely worth considering: for able men soon create capital; in the hands of those without the special talent required, capital soon takes wings. Such men become interested in firms or corporations using millions; and, estimating only simple interest to be made upon the capital invested, it is inevitable that their income must exceed their expenditure and that they must, therefore, accumulate wealth. Nor is there any middle ground which such men can occupy, because the great manufacturing or commercial concern which does not earn at least interest upon its capital soon becomes bankrupt. It must either go forward or fall behind; to stand still is impossible. It is a condition essential to its successful operation that it should be thus far profitable, and even that, in addition to interest on capital, it should make profit. It is a law, as certain as any of the other named, that men possessed of this peculiar talent for affairs, under the free play of economic forces must, of necessity, soon be in receipt of more revenue than can be judiciously expended upon themselves; and this law is as beneficial for the race as the others.

Objections to the foundations upon which society is based are not in order, because the condition of the race is better with these than it has been with any other which has been tried. Of the effect of any new substitutes proposed we cannot be sure. The Socialist or Anarchist who seeks to overturn present conditions is to be regarded as attacking the foundation upon which civilization itself rests, for civilization took its start from the day when the capable, industrious workman said to his incompetent and lazy fellow, "If thou dost not sow, thou shalt not reap," and thus ended primitive Communism by separating the drones from the bees. One who studies this subject will soon be brought face to face with the conclusion that upon the sacredness of property civilization itself depends—the right of the laborer to his hundred dollars in the savings-bank, and equally the legal right of the millionaire to his millions. Every man must be allowed "to sit under his own vine and fig-tree, with none to make afraid," if

6

human society is to advance, or even to remain so far advanced as it is. To those who propose to substitute Communism for this intense Individualism, the answer therefore is: The race has tried that. All progress from that barbarous day to the present time has resulted from its displacement. Not evil, but good, has come to the race from the accumulation of wealth by those who have had the ability and energy to produce it. But even if we admit for a moment that it might be better for the race to discard its present foundation, Individualism,—that it is a nobler ideal that man should labor, not for himself alone, but in and for a brotherhood of his fellows, and share with them all in common, realizing Swedenborg's idea of heaven, where, as he says, the angels derive their happiness, not from laboring for self, but for each other,—even admit all this, and a sufficient answer is, This is not evolution, but revolution. It necessitates the changing of human nature itself—a work of eons, even if it were good to change it, which we cannot know.

It is not practicable in our day or in our age. Even if desirable theo-   7
retically, it belongs to another and long-succeeding sociological stratum. Our duty is with what is practicable now—with the next step possible in our day and generation. It is criminal to waste our energies in endeavoring to uproot, when all we can profitably accomplish is to bend the universal tree of humanity a little in the direction most favorable to the production of good fruit under existing circumstances. We might as well urge the destruction of the highest existing type of man because he failed to reach our ideal as to favor the destruction of Individualism, Private Property, the Law of Accumulation of Wealth, and the Law of Competition; for these are the highest result of human experience, the soil in which society, so far, has produced the best fruit. Unequally or unjustly, perhaps, as these laws sometimes operate, and imperfect as they appear to the Idealist, they are, nevertheless, like the highest type of man, the best and most valuable of all that humanity has yet accomplished.

We start, then, with a condition of affairs under which the best interests   8
of the race are promoted, but which inevitably gives wealth to the few. Thus far, accepting conditions as they exist, the situation can be surveyed and pronounced good. The question then arises,—and if the foregoing be correct, it is the only question with which we have to deal,—What is the proper mode of administering wealth after the laws upon which civilization is founded have thrown it into the hands of the few? And it is of this great question that I believe I offer the true solution. It will be understood that fortunes are here spoken of, not moderate sums saved by many years of effort, the returns from which are required for the comfortable maintenance and education of families. This is not wealth, but only competence, which it should be the aim of all to acquire, and which it is for the best interests of society should be acquired.

There are but three modes in which surplus wealth can be disposed of.   9
It can be left to the families of the decedents; or it can be bequeathed for

public purposes; or, finally, it can be administered by its possessors during their lives. Under the first and second modes most of the wealth of the world that has reached the few has hitherto been applied. Let us in turn consider each of these modes. The first is the most injudicious. In monarchical countries, the estates and the greatest portion of the wealth are left to the first son, that the vanity of the parent may be gratified by the thought that his name and title are to descend unimpaired to succeeding generations. The condition of this class in Europe to-day teaches the failure of such hopes or ambitions. The successors have become impoverished through their follies, or from the fall in the value of land. Even in Great Britain the strict law of entail has been found inadequate to maintain an hereditary class. Its soil is rapidly passing into the hands of the stranger. Under republican institutions the division of property among the children is much fairer; but the question which forces itself upon thoughtful men in all lands is, Why should men leave great fortunes to their children? If this is done from affection, is it not misguided affection? Observation teaches that, generally speaking, it is not well for the children that they should be so burdened. Neither is it well for the State. Beyond providing for the wife and daughters moderate sources of income, and very moderate allowances indeed, if any, for the sons, men may well hesitate; for it is no longer questionable that great sums bequeathed often work more for the injury than for the good of the recipients. Wise men will soon conclude that, for the best interests of the members of their families, and of the State, such bequests are an improper use of their means.

It is not suggested that men who have failed to educate their sons to earn   10
a livelihood shall cast them adrift in poverty. If any man has seen fit to rear his sons with a view to their living idle lives, or, what is highly commendable, has instilled in them the sentiment that they are in a position to labor for public ends without reference to pecuniary considerations, then, of course, the duty of the parent is to see that such are provided for in moderation. There are instances of millionaires' sons unspoiled by wealth, who, being rich, still perform great services to the community. Such are the very salt of the earth, as valuable as, unfortunately, they are rare. It is not the exception, however, but the rule, that men must regard; and, looking at the usual result of enormous sums conferred upon legatees, the thoughtful man must shortly say, "I would as soon leave to my son a curse as the almighty dollar," and admit to himself that it is not the welfare of the children, but family pride, which inspires these legacies.

As to the second mode, that of leaving wealth at death for public uses,   11
it may be said that this is only a means for the disposal of wealth, provided a man is content to wait until he is dead before he becomes of much good in the world. Knowledge of the results of legacies bequeathed is not calculated to inspire the brightest hopes of much posthumous good being accomplished by them. The cases are not few in which the real object sought by the testator is not attained, nor are they few in which his real wishes are

thwarted. In many cases the bequests are so used as to become only monuments of his folly. It is well to remember that it requires the exercise of not less ability than that which acquires it, to use wealth so as to be really beneficial to the community. Besides this, it may fairly be said that no man is to be extolled for doing what he cannot help doing, nor is he to be thanked by the community to which he only leaves wealth at death. Men who leave vast sums in this way may fairly be thought men who would not have left it at all had they been able to take it with them. The memories of such cannot be held in grateful remembrance, for there is no grace in their gifts. It is not to be wondered at that such bequests seem so generally to lack the blessing.

The growing disposition to tax more and more heavily large estates left 12 at death is a cheering indication of the growth of a salutary change in public opinion. The State of Pennsylvania now takes—subject to some exceptions— one tenth of the property left by its citizens. The budget presented in the British Parliament the other day proposes to increase the death duties; and, most significant of all, the new tax is to be a graduated one. Of all forms of taxation this seems the wisest. Men who continue hoarding great sums all their lives, the proper use of which for public ends would work good to the community from which it chiefly came, should be made to feel that the community, in the form of the State, cannot thus be deprived of its proper share. By taxing estates heavily at death the State marks its condemnation of the selfish millionaire's unworthy life.

It is desirable that nations should go much further in this direction. 13 Indeed, it is difficult to set bounds to the share of a rich man's estate which should go at his death to the public through the agency of the State, and by all means such taxes should be graduated, beginning at nothing upon moderate sums to dependants, and increasing rapidly as the amounts swell, until of the millionaire's hoard, as of Shylock's, at least

> The other half
> Comes to the privy coffer of the State.

This policy would work powerfully to induce the rich man to attend to the administration of wealth during his life, which is the end that society should always have in view, as being by far the most fruitful for the people. Nor need it be feared that this policy would sap the root of enterprise and render men less anxious to accumulate, for, to the class whose ambition it is to leave great fortunes and be talked about after their death, it will attract even more attention, and, indeed, be a somewhat nobler ambition, to have enormous sums paid over to the State from their fortunes.

There remains, then, only one mode of using great fortunes; but in this 14 we have the true antidote for the temporary unequal distribution of wealth, the reconciliation of the rich and the poor—a reign of harmony, another ideal, differing, indeed, from that of the Communist in requiring only the further evolution of existing conditions, not the total overthrow of our civilization. It is founded upon the present most intense Individualism, and the race is prepared to put it in practice by degrees whenever it pleases. Under its sway we shall have an ideal State, in which the surplus wealth of the few will become, in the best sense, the property of the many, because administered for the common good; and this wealth, passing through the hands of the few, can be made a much more potent force for the elevation of our race than if distributed in small sums to the people themselves. Even the poorest can be made to see this, and to agree that great sums gathered by some of their fellow-citizens and spent for public purposes, from which the masses reap the principal benefit, are more valuable to them than if scattered among themselves in trifling amounts through the course of many years.

If we consider the results which flow from the Cooper Institute,[2] for in-   15
stance, to the best portion of the race in New York not possessed of means, and compare these with those which would have ensued for the good of the masses from an equal sum distributed by Mr. Cooper in his lifetime in the form of wages, which is the highest form of distribution, being for work done and not for charity, we can form some estimate of the possibilities for the improvement of the race which lie embedded in the present law of the accumulation of wealth. Much of this sum, if distributed in small quantities among the people, would have been wasted in the indulgence of appetite, some of it in excess, and it may be doubted whether even the part put to the best use, that of adding to the comforts of the home, would have yielded results for the race, as a race, at all comparable to those which are flowing and are to flow from the Cooper Institute from generation to generation. Let the advocate of violent or radical change ponder well this thought.

We might even go so far as to take another instance—that of Mr. Til-   16
den's[3] bequest of five millions of dollars for a free library in the city of New York; but in referring to this one cannot help saying involuntarily: How much better if Mr. Tilden had devoted the last years of his own life to the proper administration of this immense sum; in which case neither legal contest nor any other cause of delay could have interfered with his aims. But let us assume that Mr. Tilden's millions finally become the means of giving to this city a noble public library, where the treasures of the world contained in books will be open to all forever, without money and without

---

[2] *Cooper Institute:* an institution of higher learning in New York City founded by Peter Cooper (1791–1883), an industrialist, inventor, and philanthropist. Traditionally Cooper Institute (or Cooper Union) has charged no tuition. [Editors' note.]

[3] *Mr. Tilden:* Samuel Jones Tilden (1814–1886), a politician who served as governor of New York and nearly became president of the United States. Tilden left most of his estate to New York for the building of a free public library. [Editors' note.]

price. Considering the good of that part of the race which congregates in and around Manhattan Island, would its permanent benefit have been better promoted had these millions been allowed to circulate in small sums through the hands of the masses? Even the most strenuous advocate of Communism must entertain a doubt upon this subject. Most of those who think will probably entertain no doubt whatever.

Poor and restricted are our opportunities in this life, narrow our horizon, our best work most imperfect; but rich men should be thankful for one inestimable boon. They have it in their power during their lives to busy themselves in organizing benefactions from which the masses of their fellows will derive lasting advantage, and thus dignify their own lives. The highest life is probably to be reached, not by such imitation of the life of Christ as Count Tolstoi[4] gives us, but, while animated by Christ's spirit, by recognizing the changed conditions of this age, and adopting modes of expressing this spirit suitable to the changed conditions under which we live, still laboring for the good of our fellows, which was the essence of his life and teaching, but laboring in a different manner. 17

This, then, is held to be the duty of the man of wealth: To set an example of modest, unostentatious living, shunning display or extravagance; to provide moderately for the legitimate wants of those dependent upon him; and, after doing so, to consider all surplus revenues which come to him simply as trust funds, which he is called upon to administer, and strictly bound as a matter of duty to administer in the manner which, in his judgment, is best calculated to produce the most beneficial results for the community— the man of wealth thus becoming the mere trustee and agent for his poorer brethren, bring to their service his superior wisdom, experience, and ability to administer, doing for them better than they would or could do for themselves. 18

We are met here with the difficulty of determining what are moderate sums to leave to members of the family; what is modest, unostentatious living; what is the test of extravagance. There must be different standards for different conditions. The answer is that it is as impossible to name exact amounts or actions as it is to define good manners, good taste, or the rules of propriety; but, nevertheless, these are verities, well known, although indefinable. Public sentiment is quick to know and to feel what offends these. So in the case of wealth. The rule in regard to good taste in the dress of men or women applies here. Whatever makes one conspicuous offends the canon. If any family be chiefly known for display, for extravagance in 19

---

[4] *Count Tolstoi:* Leo Nikolayevich Tolstoi (1828–1910), a Russian aristocrat, novelist, and religious thinker. After a spiritual crisis relatively late in life, Tolstoi came to believe that life is most fully realized through Christian charity, hard work, poverty, and nonviolence. [Editors' note.]

home, table, or equipage, for enormous sums ostentatiously spent in any form upon itself—if these be its chief distinctions, we have no difficulty in estimating its nature or culture. So likewise in regard to the use or abuse of its surplus wealth, or to generous, free-handed coöperation in good public uses, or to unabated efforts to accumulate and hoard to the last, or whether they administer or bequeath. The verdict rests with the best and most enlightened public sentiment. The community will surely judge, and its judgments will not often be wrong.

The best uses to which surplus wealth can be put have already been 20 indicated. Those who would administer wisely must, indeed, be wise; for one of the serious obstacles to the improvement of our race is indiscriminate charity. It were better for mankind that the millions of the rich were thrown into the sea than so spent as to encourage the slothful, the drunken, the unworthy. Of every thousand dollars spent in so-called charity to-day, it is probable that nine hundred and fifty dollars is unwisely spent—so spent, indeed, as to produce the very evils which it hopes to mitigate or cure. A well-known writer of philosophic books admitted the other day that he had given a quarter of a dollar to a man who approached him as he was coming to visit the house of his friend. He knew nothing of the habits of this beggar, knew not the use that would be made of this money, although he had every reason to suspect that it would be spent improperly. This man professed to be a disciple of Herbert Spencer;[5] yet the quarter-dollar given that night will probably work more injury than all the money will do good which its thoughtless donor will ever be able to give in true charity. He only gratified his own feelings, saved himself from annoyance—and this was probably one of the most selfish and very worst actions of his life, for in all respects he is most worthy.

In bestowing charity, the main consideration should be to help those who 21 will help themselves; to provide part of the means by which those who desire to improve may do so; to give those who desire to rise the aids by which they may rise; to assist, but rarely or never to do all. Neither the individual nor the race is improved by almsgiving. Those worthy of assistance, except in rare cases, seldom require assistance. The really valuable men of the race never do, except in case of accident or sudden change. Every one has, of course, cases of individuals brought to his own knowledge where temporary assistance can do genuine good, and these he will not overlook. But the amount which can be wisely given by the individual for individuals is necessarily limited by his lack of knowledge of the circumstances connected with each. He is the only true reformer who is as careful and as anxious not to aid the unworthy as he is to aid the worthy, and, perhaps, even more so, for in almsgiving more injury is probably done by rewarding vice than by relieving virtue.

------

[5] *Herbert Spencer:* an English philosopher (1820–1903). [Editors' note.]

The rich man is thus almost restricted to following the examples of Peter   22
Cooper, Enoch Pratt[6] of Baltimore, Mr. Pratt[7] of Brooklyn, Senator Stanford,[8] and others, who know that the best means of benefiting the community is to place within its reach the ladders upon which the aspiring can
rise—free libraries, parks, and means of recreation, by which men are
helped in body and mind; works of art, certain to give pleasure and improve
the public taste; and public institutions of various kinds, which will improve
the general condition of the people; in this manner returning their surplus
wealth to the mass of their fellows in the forms best calculated to do them
lasting good.

Thus is the problem of rich and poor to be solved. The laws of   23
accumulation will be left free, the laws of distribution free. Individualism
will continue, but the millionaire will be but a trustee for the poor, intrusted
for a season with a great part of the increased wealth of the community,
but administering it for the community far better than it could or would
have done for itself. The best minds will thus have reached a stage in the
development of the race in which it is clearly seen that there is no mode of
disposing of surplus wealth creditable to thoughtful and earnest men into
whose hands it flows, save by using it year by year for the general good.
This day already dawns. Men may die without incurring the pity of their
fellows, still sharers in great business enterprises from which their capital
cannot be or has not been withdrawn, and which is left chiefly at death for
public uses; yet the day is not far distant when the man who dies leaving behind him millions of available wealth, which was free for him to administer
during life, will pass away "unwept, unhonored, and unsung," no matter
to what uses he leaves the dross which he cannot take with him. Of such
as these the public verdict will then be: "The man who dies thus rich dies
disgraced."

Such, in my opinion, is the true gospel concerning wealth, obedience to   24
which is destined some day to solve the problem of the rich and the poor,
and to bring "Peace on earth, among men good will."

Questions for Discussion and Writing

1. What does the word *gospel* literally mean? Why has Carnegie chosen this term
    for the title of his essay? What are the rhetorical consequences—both positive and

---

[6] *Enoch Pratt:* a financier and philanthropist (1808–1896) who founded Baltimore's Enoch
Pratt Free Library in 1882. [Editors' note.]

[7] *Mr. Pratt:* Charles Pratt (1854–1921), an industrialist who founded Brooklyn's Pratt
Institute in 1887 and established the Pratt Institute Free Library. [Editors' note.]

[8] *Senator Stanford:* Leland Stanford (1824–1893), a railroad developer, politician, and
philanthropist. He served California as both governor and a senator. [Editor's note.]

negative—of this choice? In what other ways might Carnegie develop a pseudo-religious argument?

2. Do you believe, as Carnegie states in his opening paragraph, that "in former days there was little difference between the dwelling, dress, food, and environment of the chief and those of his retainers"? Would his audience have believed this claim? How important is it to his overall argument?

3. Throughout the essay, Carnegie continually refers to economic activity that benefits the "race." What do you make of these claims? Why are they repeated? To which race is he referring?

4. How would you evaluate the American success story that Carnegie typifies? Is it a socially productive or destructive tale? Has the plot evolved since Carnegie's days, or has it remained essentially the same? What figures today—real or fictional—have replaced the Carnegies of yesterday? Write an argument about the character and ultimate value of the American success story.

WILLIAM JAMES

(1842–1910)

lthough William James and Thomas Huxley formulated different answers to several of the most important religious, philosophical, and scientific questions of their day, including the challenge of Darwinism, both men possessed the kind of broad knowledge of the liberal arts and sciences that is largely missing in today's academy. Both James and Huxley moved gracefully from field to field, breaking intellectual ground and laying theoretical foundations on which other more specialized scholars would later build. If today we have surpassed many of their conclusions, we have, for the most part, lost their versatility.

James, the eldest of five children, was born in New York City. The wealth amassed by his grandfather made James's youth comfortable, if rootless: His father, in pursuit of his intellectual and spiritual interests, moved the family across the Atlantic and around Europe. Because of this nomadic childhood, James's formal education was spotty. He was extremely well read, however, and well versed in European languages.

At eighteen, James spent a year studying painting before entering Harvard as a science student. In 1865, he enrolled in the Harvard Medical School, only to interrupt his studies with a nine-month stint with a research team in the Amazon. He also spent some time studying in Germany before taking his medical degree in 1869.

James's postgraduation years were extremely painful. A combination of ill health and melancholy left James in a state of acute withdrawal. For three years, he lived as an invalid in his father's house and did almost nothing but read. What finally saved him from suicidal depression was a belief in free will. Fighting the spiritual fatalism and skepticism that dominated the intellectual community at the time, James came to the conclusions that life is not necessarily predetermined at the outset, that Darwin's theory of random selection does not preclude the possibility of free will and providential design, and that a person can affect the course of his or her existence. If we are not automatons, James concluded, then our beliefs about the future can shape our destinies for the better. In short, James's newfound confidence in free will and his defiance toward the reigning belief in determinism yanked him from his paralyzing despair and became the cornerstone for all his work.

Having fully regained his spirits, James was launched on a remarkable career path. In 1872, he joined the faculty of Harvard as a physiology instructor. Before long, he moved himself into the discipline of psychology and by 1876 had established the first American laboratory of psychology. He married in 1878 and began writing a book on psychology. In 1880, he was appointed assistant professor of philosophy.

Ten years later, he published Principles of Psychology, *which set forth a functional, biological approach to consciousness yet left a place for free will. Although his publisher found this work "a loathsome, distended, tumefied, bloated, dropsical mass," it became an industry standard. Though much of James's psychology is now obsolete, the book remains in print to this day. In the 1893–94 school year, he taught what was most probably the first American course in abnormal psychology.*

If, ultimately, James moved away from the laboratory and set his sights on more spiritual topics such as the nature of God, free will, and the purpose of life, his pursuit of the philosophical was never conducted at the expense of science or scientific thinking. Ingeniously, he incorporated Darwin's theory of natural selection into his philosophical position on free will. His theory of Pragmatism, which grew out of the pioneering work of his friend Charles Sanders Peirce, was based on the idea that our beliefs should be grounded in practical experience and our perception of the natural world rather than abstract philosophizing. It has been suggested that James's approach altered twentieth-century philosophy with the same impact that Einstein's theories had on physics.

Brilliant, cosmopolitan, witty, and passionately committed to his beliefs, James became an extremely popular lecturer and spoke on campuses across America and in Britain. "The Will to Believe," reproduced here, was originally delivered to the Philosophical Clubs of Yale and Brown universities and was published in a volume of the same name in 1897. James was generous to his students and, in the spirit of fair play and pluralism, was fond of championing underdogs and popular social causes. In fact, he was even known to work to secure the rights of those with whom he vehemently disagreed.

James's depth and breadth of thought humbles us. Few in his own time or since have been able to match his abilities. Ironically, one individual whose reputation ranks as high as the noble Pragmatist is none other than his younger brother Henry, the great American novelist.

THE WILL TO BELIEVE

In the recently published Life by Leslie Stephen of his brother, Fitz-James, there is an account of a school to which the latter went when he was a boy. The teacher, a certain Mr. Guest, used to converse with his pupils in this wise: "Gurney, what is the difference between justification and sanctification?—Stephen, prove the omnipotence of God!" etc. In the midst of our Harvard freethinking and indifference we are prone to imagine that here at your good old orthodox College conversation continues to be somewhat upon this order; and to show you that we at Harvard have not lost all interest in these vital subjects, I have brought with me to-night something like a sermon on justification by faith to read to you,—I mean an essay in justification *of* faith, a defence of our right to adopt a believing attitude in religious matters, in spite of the fact that our merely logical intellect may not have been coerced. "The Will to Believe," accordingly, is the title of my paper.

I have long defended to my own students the lawfulness of voluntarily   2 adopted faith; but as soon as they have got well imbued with the logical spirit, they have as a rule refused to admit my contention to be lawful philosophically, even though in point of fact they were personally all the time chock-full of some faith or other themselves. I am all the while, however, so profoundly convinced that my own position is correct, that your invitation has seemed to me a good occasion to make my statements more clear. Perhaps your minds will be more open than those with which I have hitherto had to deal. I will be as little technical as I can, though I must begin by setting up some technical distinctions that will help us in the end.

I

Let us give the name of *hypothesis* to anything that may be proposed to our   3 belief; and just as the electricians speak of live and dead wires, let us speak of any hypothesis as either *live* or *dead*. A live hypothesis is one which appeals as a real possibility to him to whom it is proposed. If I ask you to believe in the Mahdi,[1] the notion makes no electric connection with your nature,—it refuses to scintillate with any credibility at all. As an hypothesis it is completely dead. To an Arab, however (even if he be not one of the Mahdi's followers), the hypothesis is among the mind's possibilities: it is alive. This shows that deadness and liveness in an hypothesis are not intrinsic properties, but relations to the individual thinker. They are measured by his willingness to act. The maximum of liveness in an hypothesis means willingness to act irrevocably. Practically, that means belief; but there is some believing tendency wherever there is willingness to act at all.

Next, let us call the decision between two hypotheses an *option*. Options   4 may be of several kinds. They may be—1, *living* or *dead*; 2, *forced* or *avoidable*; 3, *momentous* or *trivial*; and for our purposes we may call an option a *genuine* option when it is of the forced, living, and momentous kind.

1. A living option is one in which both hypotheses are live ones. If I   5 say to you: "Be a theosophist or be a Mohammedan," it is probably a dead option, because for you neither hypothesis is likely to be alive. But if I say: "Be an agnostic or be a Christian," it is otherwise: trained as you are, each hypothesis makes some appeal, however small, to your belief.

2. Next, if I say to you: "Choose between going out with your umbrella   6

---

[1] *Mahdi:* the Muslim messiah. [Editors' note.]

or without it," I do not offer you a genuine option, for it is not forced. You can easily avoid it by not going out at all. Similarly, if I say, "Either love me or hate me," "Either call my theory true or call it false," your option is avoidable. You may remain indifferent to me, neither loving nor hating, and you may decline to offer any judgment as to my theory. But if I say, "Either accept this truth or go without it," I put on you a forced option, for there is no standing place outside of the alternative. Every dilemma based on a complete logical disjunction, with no possibility of not choosing, is an option of this forced kind.

3. Finally, if I were Dr. Nansen[2] and proposed to you to join my North Pole expedition, your option would be momentous; for this would probably be your only similar opportunity, and your choice now would either exclude you from the North Pole sort of immortality altogether or put at least the chance of it into your hands. He who refuses to embrace a unique opportunity loses the prize as surely as if he tried and failed. *Per contra*, the option is trivial when the opportunity is not unique, when the stake is insignificant, or when the decision is reversible if it later prove unwise. Such trivial options abound in the scientific life. A chemist finds an hypothesis live enough to spend a year in its verification: he believes in it to that extent. But if his experiments prove inconclusive either way, he is quit for his loss of time, no vital harm being done.

It will facilitate our discussion if we keep all these distinctions well in mind.

2

The next matter to consider is the actual psychology of human opinion. When we look at certain facts, it seems as if our passional and volitional nature lay at the root of all our convictions. When we look at others, it seems as if they could do nothing when the intellect had once said its say. Let us take the latter facts up first.

Does it not seem preposterous on the very face of it to talk of our opinions being modifiable at will? Can our will either help or hinder our intellect in its perceptions of truth? Can we, by just willing it, believe that Abraham Lincoln's existence is a myth, and that the portraits of him in McClure's Magazine are all of some one else? Can we, by any effort of our will, or by any strength of wish that it were true, believe ourselves well and about when we are roaring with rheumatism in bed, or feel certain that the sum of the two one-dollar bills in our pocket must be a hundred dollars? We can *say* any of these things, but we are absolutely impotent to believe them;

---

[2] *Dr. Nansen:* Fridtjof Nansen (1861–1930), a Norwegian Arctic explorer and statesman. [Editors' note.]

and of just such things is the whole fabric of the truths that we do believe in made up,—matters of fact, immediate or remote, as Hume[3] said, and relations between ideas, which are either there or not there for us if we see them so, and which if not there cannot be put there by any action of our own.

In Pascal's[4] Thoughts there is a celebrated passage known in literature as Pascal's wager. In it he tries to force us into Christianity by reasoning as if our concern with truth resembled our concern with the stakes in a game of chance. Translated freely his words are these: You must either believe or not believe that God is—which will you do? Your human reason cannot say. A game is going on between you and the nature of things which at the day of judgment will bring out either heads or tails. Weigh what your gains and your losses would be if you should stake all you have on heads, or God's existence: if you win in such case, you gain eternal beatitude; if you lose, you lose nothing at all. If there were an infinity of chances, and only one for God in this wager, still you ought to stake your all on God; for though you surely risk a finite loss by this procedure, any finite loss is reasonable, even a certain one is reasonable, if there is but the possibility of infinite gain. Go, then, and take holy water, and have masses said; belief will come and stupefy your scruples,—*Cela vous fera croire et vous abêtira.*[5] Why should you not? At bottom, what have you to lose? 11

You probably feel that when religious faith expresses itself thus, in the language of the gaming-table, it is put to its last trumps. Surely Pascal's own personal belief in masses and holy water had far other springs; and this celebrated page of his is but an argument for others, a last desperate snatch at a weapon against the hardness of the unbelieving heart. We feel that a faith in masses and holy water adopted wilfully after such a mechanical calculation would lack the inner soul of faith's reality; and if we were ourselves in the place of the Deity, we should probably take particular pleasure in cutting off believers of this pattern from their infinite reward. It is evident that unless there be some pre-existing tendency to believe in masses and holy water, the option offered to the will by Pascal is not a living option. Certainly no Turk ever took to masses and holy water on its account; and even to us Protestants these means of salvation seem such foregone impossibilities that Pascal's logic, invoked for them specifically, leaves us unmoved. As well might the Mahdi write to us, saying, "I am the Expected One whom God has created in his effulgence. You shall be 12

---

[3] *Hume:* David Hume (1711–1776), a British philosopher and skeptic. [Editors' note.]

[4] *Pascal:* Blaise Pascal (1623–1662), a French philosopher and mathematician. [Editors' note.]

[5] *"Cela vous . . . abêtira":* "This will make you believe and you will be stupefied." [Editors' note.]

infinitely happy if you confess me; otherwise you shall be cut off from the light of the sun. Weigh, then, your infinite gain if I am genuine against your finite sacrifice if I am not!" His logic would be that of Pascal; but he would vainly use it on us, for the hypothesis he offers us is dead. No tendency to act on it exists in us to any degree.

The talk of believing by our volition seems, then, from one point of view, simply silly. From another point of view it is worse than silly, it is vile. When one turns to the magnificent edifice of the physical sciences, and sees how it was reared; what thousands of disinterested moral lives of men lie buried in its mere foundations; what patience and postponement, what choking down of preference, what submission to the icy laws of outer fact are wrought into its very stones and mortar; how absolutely impersonal it stands in its vast augustness,—then how besotted and contemptible seems every little sentimentalist who comes blowing his voluntary smoke-wreaths, and pretending to decide things from out of his private dream! Can we wonder if those bred in the rugged and manly school of science should feel like spewing such subjectivism out of their mouths? The whole system of loyalties which grow up in the schools of science go dead against its toleration; so that it is only natural that those who have caught the scientific fever should pass over to the opposite extreme, and write sometimes as if the incorruptibly truthful intellect ought positively to prefer bitterness and unacceptableness to the heart in its cup.

> It fortifies my soul to know
> That, though I perish, Truth is so—

sings Clough,[6] while Huxley exclaims: "My only consolation lies in the reflection that, however bad our posterity may become, so far as they hold by the plain rule of not pretending to believe what they have no reason to believe, because it may be to their advantage so to pretend [the word "pretend" is surely here redundant], they will not have reached the lowest depth of immorality." And that delicious *enfant terrible* Clifford[7] writes: "Belief is desecrated when given to unproved and unquestioned statements for the solace and private pleasure of the believer. . . . Whoso would deserve well of his fellows in this matter will guard the purity of his belief with a very fanaticism of jealous care, lest at any time it should rest on an unworthy object, and catch a stain which can never be wiped away. . . . If [a] belief has been accepted on insufficient evidence [even though the belief be true, as Clifford on the same page explains] the pleasure is a stolen one. . . . It is sinful because it is stolen in defiance of our duty to mankind. That duty is to guard ourselves from such beliefs as from a pestilence which

---

[6] *Clough:* Arthur Clough (1819–1861), an English poet. [Editors' note.]

[7] *Clifford:* William Kingdon Clifford (1845–1899), an English mathematician and philosopher. [Editors' note.]

may shortly master our own body and then spread to the rest of the town. . . . It is wrong always, everywhere, and for every one, to believe anything upon insufficient evidence."

3

All this strikes one as healthy, even when expressed, as by Clifford, with   14
somewhat too much of robustious pathos in the voice. Free-will and simple wishing do seem, in the matter of our credences, to be only fifth wheels to the coach. Yet if any one should thereupon assume that intellectual insight is what remains after wish and will and sentimental preference have taken wing, or that pure reason is what then settles our opinions, he would fly quite as directly in the teeth of the facts.

It is only our already dead hypotheses that our willing nature is unable   15
to bring to life again. But what has made them dead for us is for the most part a previous action of our willing nature of an antagonistic kind. When I say "willing nature," I do not mean only such deliberate volitions as may have set up habits of belief that we cannot now escape from,—I mean all such factors of belief as fear and hope, prejudice and passion, imitation and partisanship, the circumpressure of our caste and set. As a matter of fact we find ourselves believing, we hardly know how or why. Mr. Balfour[8] gives the name of "authority" to all those influences, born of the intellectual climate, that make hypotheses possible or impossible for us, alive or dead. Here in this room, we all of us believe in molecules and the conservation of energy, in democracy and necessary progress, in Protestant Christianity and the duty of fighting for "the doctrine of the immortal Monroe," all for no reasons worthy of the name. We see into these matters with no more inner clearness, and probably with much less, than any disbeliever in them might possess. His unconventionality would probably have some grounds to show for its conclusions; but for us, not insight, but the *prestige* of the opinions, is what makes the spark shoot from them and light up our sleeping magazines of faith. Our reason is quite satisfied, in nine hundred and ninety-nine cases out of every thousand of us, if it can find a few arguments that will do to recite in case our credulity is criticised by some one else. Our faith is faith in some one else's faith, and in the greatest matters this is most the case. Our belief in truth itself, for instance, that there is a truth, and that our minds and it are made for each other,—what is it but a passionate affirmation of desire, in which our social system backs us up? We want to have a truth; we want to believe that our experiments and studies and discussions must put us in a continually better and better position

---

[8] *Mr. Balfour:* Arthur James Balfour (1848–1930), first Earl of Balfour, a British statesman and writer. In 1879 James reviewed Balfour's *A Defence of Philosophic Doubt.* [Editors' note.]

towards it; and on this line we agree to fight out our thinking lives. But if a pyrrhonistic sceptic asks us *how we know* all this, can our logic find a reply? No! certainly it cannot. It is just one volition against another,—we willing to go in for life upon a trust or assumption which he, for his part, does not care to make.[9]

As a rule we disbelieve all facts and theories for which we have no use.   16
Clifford's cosmic emotions find no use for Christian feelings. Huxley belabors the bishops because there is no use for sacerdotalism in his scheme of life. Newman,[10] on the contrary, goes over to Romanism, and finds all sorts of reasons good for staying there, because a priestly system is for him an organic need and delight. Why do so few "scientists" even look at the evidence for telepathy, so called? Because they think, as a leading biologist, now dead, once said to me, that even if such a thing were true, scientists ought to band together to keep it suppressed and concealed. It would undo the uniformity of Nature and all sorts of other things without which scientists cannot carry on their pursuits. But if this very man had been shown something which as a scientist he might *do* with telepathy, he might not only have examined the evidence, but even have found it good enough. This very law which the logicians would impose upon us—if I may give the name of logicians to those who would rule out our willing nature here— is based on nothing but their own natural wish to exclude all elements for which they, in their professional quality of logicians, can find no use.

Evidently, then, our non-intellectual nature does influence our convic-   17
tions. There are passional tendencies and volitions which run before and others which come after belief, and it is only the latter that are too late for the fair; and they are not too late when the previous passional work has been already in their own direction. Pascal's argument, instead of being powerless, then seems a regular clincher, and is the last stroke needed to make our faith in masses and holy water complete. The state of things is evidently far from simple; and pure insight and logic, whatever they might do ideally, are not the only things that really do produce our creeds.

4

Our next duty, having recognized this mixed-up state of affairs, is to ask   18
whether it be simply reprehensible and pathological, or whether, on the contrary, we must treat it as a normal element in making up our minds. The thesis I defend is, briefly stated, this: *Our passional nature not only lawfully may, but must, decide an option between propositions, whenever it is a*

---

[9] Compare the admirable page 310 in S. H. Hodgson's "Time and Space," London, 1865. [Author's note.]

[10] *Newman:* John Henry Newman (1801–1890), a British theologian who converted from Protestantism to Roman Catholicism and became a cardinal. [Editors' note.]

genuine option that cannot by its nature be decided on intellectual grounds; for to say, under such circumstances, "Do not decide, but leave the question open," is itself a passional decision,—just like deciding yes or no,—and is attended with the same risk of losing the truth. The thesis thus abstractly expressed will, I trust, soon become quite clear. But I must first indulge in a bit more of preliminary work.

5

It will be observed that for the purposes of this discussion we are on "dogmatic" ground,—ground, I mean, which leaves systematic philosophical scepticism altogether out of account. The postulate that there is truth, and that it is the destiny of our minds to attain it, we are deliberately resolving to make, though the sceptic will not make it. We part company with him, therefore, absolutely, at this point. But the faith that truth exists, and that our minds can find it, may be held in two ways. We may talk of the *empiricist* way and of the *absolutist* way of believing in truth. The absolutists in this matter say that we not only can attain to knowing truth, but we can *know when* we have attained to knowing it; while the empiricists think that although we may attain it, we cannot infallibly know when. To *know* is one thing, and to know for certain *that* we know is another. One may hold to the first being possible without the second; hence the empiricists and the absolutists, although neither of them is a sceptic in the usual philosophic sense of the term, show very different degrees of dogmatism in their lives. 19

If we look at the history of opinions, we see that the empiricist tendency has largely prevailed in science, while in philosophy the absolutist tendency has had everything its own way. The characteristic sort of happiness, indeed, which philosophies yield has mainly consisted in the conviction felt by each successive school or system that by it bottom-certitude had been attained. "Other philosophies are collections of opinions, mostly false; *my* philosophy gives standing-ground forever,"—who does not recognize in this the key-note of every system worthy of the name? A system, to be a system at all, must come as a *closed* system, reversible in this or that detail, perchance, but in its essential features never! 20

Scholastic orthodoxy, to which one must always go when one wishes to find perfectly clear statement, has beautifully elaborated this absolutist conviction in a doctrine which it calls that of "objective evidence." If, for example, I am unable to doubt that I now exist before you, that two is less than three, or that if all men are mortal then I am mortal too, it is because these things illumine my intellect irresistibly. The final ground of this objective evidence possessed by certain propositions is the *adæquatio intellectûs nostri cum rê.*[11] The certitude it brings involves an *aptitudinem ad extor-* 21

---

[11] *adaequatio intellectûs . . . rê:* congruence of our intellect with the thing. [Editors' note.]

301

quendum certum assensum[12] on the part of the truth envisaged, and on the side of the subject a *quietem in cognitione*,[13] when once the object is mentally received, that leaves no possibility of doubt behind; and in the whole transaction nothing operates but the *entitas ipsa*[14] of the object of the *entitas ipsa* of the mind. We slouchy modern thinkers dislike to talk in Latin,—indeed, we dislike to talk in set terms at all; but at bottom our own state of mind is very much like this whenever we uncritically abandon ourselves: You believe in objective evidence, and I do. Of some things we feel that we are certain: we know, and we know that we do know. There is something that gives a click inside of us, a bell that strikes twelve, when the hands of our mental clock have swept the dial and meet over the meridian hour. The greatest empiricists among us are only empiricists on reflection: when left to their instincts, they dogmatize like infallible popes. When the Cliffords tell us how sinful it is to be Christians on such "insufficient evidence," insufficiency is really the last thing they have in mind. For them the evidence is absolutely sufficient, only it makes the other way. They believe so completely in an anti-christian order of the universe that there is no living option: Christianity is a dead hypothesis from the start.

6

But now, since we are all such absolutists by instinct, what in our quality   22 of students of philosophy ought we to do about the fact? Shall we espouse and indorse it? Or shall we treat it as a weakness of our nature from which we must free ourselves, if we can?

    I sincerely believe that the latter course is the only one we can follow as   23 reflective men. Objective evidence and certitude are doubtless very fine ideals to play with, but where on this moonlit and dream-visited planet are they found? I am, therefore, myself a complete empiricist so far as my theory of human knowledge goes. I live, to be sure, by the practical faith that we must go on experiencing and thinking over our experience, for only thus can our opinions grow more true; but to hold any one of them— I absolutely do not care which—as if it never could be reinterpretable or corrigible, I believe to be a tremendously mistaken attitude, and I think that the whole history of philosophy will bear me out. There is but one indefectibly certain truth, and that is the truth that pyrrhonistic scepticism itself leaves standing,—the truth that the present phenomenon of conscious-

---

[12] *aptitudinem ad . . . assensum:* aptitude to force certain agreement. [Editors' note.]

[13] *quietem in cognitione:* peace in recognition. [Editors' note.]

[14] *entitas ipsa:* existence itself. [Editors' note.]

ness exists. That, however, is the bare starting-point of knowledge, the mere admission of a stuff to be philosophized about. The various philosophies are but so many attempts at expressing what this stuff really is. And if we repair to our libraries what disagreement do we discover! Where is a certainly true answer found? Apart from abstract propositions of comparison (such as two and two are the same as four), propositions which tell us nothing by themselves about concrete reality, we find no proposition ever regarded by any one as evidently certain that has not either been called a falsehood, or at least had its truth sincerely questioned by some one else. The transcending of the axioms of geometry, not in play but in earnest, by certain of our contemporaries (as Zöllner[15] and Charles H. Hinton[16]), and the rejection of the whole Aristotelian logic by the Hegelians,[17] are striking instances in point.

No concrete test of what is really true has ever been agreed upon. Some make the criterion external to the moment of perception, putting it either in revelation, the *consensus gentium*,[18] the instincts of the heart, or the systematized experience of the race. Others make the perceptive moment its own test,—Descartes, for instance, with his clear and distinct ideas guaranteed by the veracity of God; Reid[19] with his "common-sense"; and Kant[20] with his forms of synthetic judgment *a priori*. The inconceivability of the opposite; the capacity to be verified by sense; the possession of complete organic unity or self-relation, realized when a thing is its own other,—are standards which, in turn, have been used. The much lauded objective evidence is never triumphantly there; it is a mere aspiration or *Grenzbegriff*,[21] marking the infinitely remote ideal of our thinking life. To claim that certain truths now possess it, is simply to say that when you think them true and they *are* true, then their evidence is objective, otherwise it is not. But practically one's conviction that the evidence one goes by is of the real objective brand, is only one more subjective opinion added to the lot. For what a contradictory array of opinions have objective evidence and absolute certitude been claimed! The world is rational through and through,—its existence is an ultimate brute fact; there is a personal God,— a personal God is inconceivable; there is an extra-mental physical world

24

---

[15] *Zöllner:* Johann Carl Friedrich Zöllner (1834–1882), a German physicist. [Editors' note.]

[16] *Charles H. Hinton:* Charles Howard Hinton (1853–1907), an English mathematician and writer. [Editors' note.]

[17] *Hegelians:* followers of Georg Wilhelm Friedrich Hegel (1770–1831), a German philosopher. For more on Hegel, see pages 210–211. [Editors' note.]

[18] *consensus gentium:* universal agreement or common consent. [Editors' note.]

[19] *Reid:* Thomas Reid (1710–1796), a Scottish philosopher. [Editors' note.]

[20] *Kant:* Immanuel Kant (1724–1804), a German philosopher. [Editors' note.]

[21] *Grenzbegriff:* limiting concept. [Editors' note.]

immediately known,—the mind can only know its own ideas; a moral imperative exists,—obligation is only the resultant of desires; a permanent spiritual principle is in every one,—there are only shifting states of mind; there is an endless chain of causes,—there is an absolute first cause; an eternal necessity,—a freedom; a purpose,—no purpose; a primal One,—a primal Many; a universal continuity,—an essential discontinuity in things; an infinity,—no infinity. There is this,—there is that; there is indeed nothing which some one has not thought absolutely true, while his neighbor deemed it absolutely false; and not an absolutist among them seems ever to have considered that the trouble may all the time be essential, and that the intellect, even with truth directly in its grasp, may have no infallible signal for knowing whether it be truth or no. When, indeed, one remembers that the most striking practical application to life of the doctrine of objective certitude has been the conscientious labors of the Holy Office of the Inquisition, one feels less tempted than ever to lend the doctrine a respectful ear.

But please observe, now, that when as empiricists we give up the doctrine 25 of objective certitude, we do not thereby give up the quest or hope of truth itself. We still pin our faith on its existence, and still believe that we gain an ever better position towards it by systematically continuing to roll up experiences and think. Our great difference from the scholastic lies in the way we face. The strength of his system lies in the principles, the origin, the *terminus a quo*[22] of his thought; for us the strength is in the outcome, the upshot, the *terminus ad quem*.[23] Not where it comes from but what it leads to is to decide. It matters not to an empiricist from what quarter an hypothesis may come to him: he may have acquired it by fair means or by foul; passion may have whispered or accident suggested it; but if the total drift of thinking continues to confirm it, that is what he means by its being true.

7

One more point, small but important, and our preliminaries are done. 26 There are two ways of looking at our duty in the matter of opinion,—ways entirely different, and yet ways about whose difference the theory of knowledge seems hitherto to have shown very little concern. *We must know the truth;* and *we must avoid error,*—these are our first and great commandments as would-be knowers; but they are not two ways of stating an identical commandment, they are two separable laws. Although it may indeed happen that when we believe the truth *A*, we escape as an incidental consequence

---

[22] *terminus a quo:* beginning point. [Editors' note.]

[23] *terminus ad quem:* ending point. [Editor's note.]

from believing the falsehood B, it hardly ever happens that by merely disbelieving B we necessarily believe A. We may in escaping B fall into believing other falsehoods, C or D, just as bad as B; or we may escape B by not believing anything at all, not even A.

Believe truth! Shun error!—these, we see, are two materially different   27
laws; and by choosing between them we may end by coloring differently our whole intellectual life. We may regard the chase for truth as paramount, and the avoidance of error as secondary; or we may, on the other hand, treat the avoidance of error as more imperative, and let truth take its chance. Clifford, in the instructive passage which I have quoted, exhorts us to the latter course. Believe nothing, he tells us, keep your mind in suspense forever, rather than by closing it on insufficient evidence incur the awful risk of believing lies. You, on the other hand, may think that the risk of being in error is a very small matter when compared with the blessings of real knowledge, and be ready to be duped many times in your investigation rather than postpone indefinitely the chance of guessing true. I myself find it impossible to go with Clifford. We must remember that these feelings of our duty about either truth or error are in any case only expressions of our passional life. Biologically considered, our minds are as ready to grind out falsehood as veracity, and he who says, "Better go without belief forever than believe a lie!" merely shows his own preponderant private horror of becoming a dupe. He may be critical of many of his desires and fears, but this fear he slavishly obeys. He cannot imagine any one questioning its binding force. For my own part, I have also a horror of being duped; but I can believe that worse things than being duped may happen to a man in this world: so Clifford's exhortation has to my ears a thoroughly fantastic sound. It is like a general informing his soldiers that it is better to keep out of battle forever than to risk a single wound. Not so are victories either over enemies or over nature gained. Our errors are surely not such awfully solemn things. In a world where we are so certain to incur them in spite of all our caution, a certain lightness of heart seems healthier than this excessive nervousness on their behalf. At any rate, it seems the fittest thing for the empiricist philosopher.

8

And now, after all this introduction, let us go straight at our question. I   28
have said, and now repeat it, that not only as a matter of fact do we find our passional nature influencing us in our opinions, but that there are some options between opinions in which this influence must be regarded both as an inevitable and as a lawful determinant of our choice.

I fear here that some of you my hearers will begin to scent danger, and   29
lend an inhospitable ear. Two first steps of passion you have indeed had to

admit as necessary,—we must think so as to avoid dupery, and we must think so as to gain truth; but the surest path to those ideal consummations, you will probably consider, is from now onwards to take no further passional step.

Well, of course, I agree as far as the facts will allow. Wherever the option between losing truth and gaining it is not momentous, we can throw the chance of *gaining truth* away, and at any rate save ourselves from any chance of *believing falsehood*, by not making up our minds at all till objective evidence has come. In scientific questions, this is almost always the case; and even in human affairs in general, the need of acting is seldom so urgent that a false belief to act on is better than no belief at all. Law courts, indeed, have to decide on the best evidence attainable for the moment, because a judge's duty is to make law as well as to ascertain it, and (as a learned judge once said to me) few cases are worth spending much time over: the great thing is to have them decided on *any* acceptable principle, and got out of the way. But in our dealings with objective nature we obviously are recorders, not makers, of the truth; and decisions for the mere sake of deciding promptly and getting on to the next business would be wholly out of place. Throughout the breadth of physical nature facts are what they are quite independently of us, and seldom is there any such hurry about them that the risks of being duped by believing a premature theory need be faced. The questions here are always trivial options, the hypotheses are hardly living (at any rate not living for us spectators), the choice between believing truth or falsehood is seldom forced. The attitude of sceptical balance is therefore the absolutely wise one if we would escape mistakes. What difference, indeed, does it make to most of us whether we have or have not a theory of the Röntgen rays, whether we believe or not in mind-stuff, or have a conviction about the causality of conscious states? It makes no difference. Such options are not forced on us. On every account it is better not to make them, but still keep weighing reasons *pro et contra*[24] with an indifferent hand.

I speak, of course, here of the purely judging mind. For purposes of discovery such indifference is to be less highly recommended, and science would be far less advanced than she is if the passionate desires of individuals to get their own faiths confirmed had been kept out of the game. See for example the sagacity which Spencer and Weismann now display. On the other hand, if you want an absolute duffer in an investigation, you must, after all, take the man who has no interest whatever in its results: he is the warranted incapable, the positive fool. The most useful investigator, because the most sensitive observer, is always he whose eager interest in one side of the question is balanced by an equally keen nervousness lest he become

30

31

---

[24] *pro et contra:* pro and con, for and against. [Editors' note.]

deceived.[25] Science has organized this nervousness into a regular *technique,* her so-called method of verification; and she has fallen so deeply in love with the method that one may even say she has ceased to care for truth by itself at all. It is only truth as technically verified that interests her. The truth of truths might come in merely affirmative form, and she would decline to touch it. Such truth as that, she might repeat with Clifford, would be stolen in defiance of her duty to mankind. Human passions, however, are stronger than technical rules. "Le cœur a ses raisons," as Pascal says, "que la raison ne connaît pas";[26] and however indifferent to all but the bare rules of the game the umpire, the abstract intellect, may be, the concrete players who furnish him the materials to judge of are usually, each one of them, in love with some pet "live hypothesis" of his own. Let us agree, however, that wherever there is no forced option, the dispassionately judicial intellect with no pet hypothesis, saving us, as it does, from dupery at any rate, ought to be our ideal.

The question next arises: Are there not somewhere forced options in our speculative questions, and can we (as men who may be interested at least as much in positively gaining truth as in merely escaping dupery) always wait with impunity till the coercive evidence shall have arrived? It seems *a priori* improbable that the truth should be so nicely adjusted to our needs and powers as that. In the great boarding-house of nature, the cakes and the butter and the syrup seldom come out so even and leave the plates so clean. Indeed, we should view them with suspicion if they did.

9

Moral questions immediately present themselves as questions whose solution cannot wait for sensible proof. A moral question is a question not of what sensibly exists, but of what is good, or would be good if it did exist. Science can tell us what exists; but to compare the *worths,* both of what exists and of what does not exist, we must consult not science, but what Pascal calls our heart. Science herself consults her heart when she lays it down that the infinite ascertainment of fact and correction of false belief are the supreme goods for man. Challenge the statement, and science can only repeat it oracularly, or else prove it by showing that such ascertainment and correction bring man all sorts of other goods which man's heart in turn declares. The question of having moral beliefs at all or not having them is decided by our will. Are our moral preferences true or false, or are they only odd biological phenomena, making things good or bad for *us,* but in themselves

---

[25] Compare Wilfrid Ward's Essay, "The Wish to Believe," in his *Witnesses to the Unseen,* Macmillan & Co., 1893. [Author's note.]

[26] *Le cœur . . . pas:* The heart has its reasons that reason does not understand. [Editors' note.]

indifferent? How can your pure intellect decide? If your heart does not *want* a world of moral reality, your head will assuredly never make you believe in one. Mephistophelian scepticism, indeed, will satisfy the head's play-instincts much better than any rigorous idealism can. Some men (even at the student age) are so naturally cool-hearted that the moralistic hypothesis never has for them any pungent life, and in their supercilious presence the hot young moralist always feels strangely ill at ease. The appearance of knowingness is on their side, of *naïveté* and gullibility on his. Yet, in the inarticulate heart of him, he clings to it that he is not a dupe, and that there is a realm in which (as Emerson[27] says) all their wit and intellectual superiority is no better than the cunning of a fox. Moral scepticism can no more be refuted or proved by logic than intellectual scepticism can. When we stick to it that there *is* truth (be it of either kind), we do so with our whole nature, and resolve to stand or fall by the results. The sceptic with his whole nature adopts the doubting attitude; but which of us is the wiser, Omniscience only knows.

Turn now from these wide questions of good to a certain class of questions of fact, questions concerning personal relations, states of mind between one man and another. *Do you like me or not?*—for example. Whether you do or not depends, in countless instances, on whether I meet you half-way, am willing to assume that you must like me, and show you trust and expectation. The previous faith on my part in your liking's existence is in such cases what makes your liking come. But if I stand aloof, and refuse to budge an inch until I have objective evidence, until you shall have done something apt, as the absolutists say, *ad extorquendum assensum meum*,[28] ten to one your liking never comes. How many women's hearts are vanquished by the mere sanguine insistence of some man that they *must* love him! he will not consent to the hypothesis that they cannot. The desire for a certain kind of truth here brings about that special truth's existence; and so it is in innumerable cases of other sorts. Who gains promotions, boons, appointments, but the man in whose life they are seen to play the part of live hypotheses, who discounts them, sacrifices other things for their sake before they have come, and takes risks for them in advance? His faith acts on the powers above him as a claim, and creates its own verification.

A social organism of any sort whatever, large or small, is what it is because each member proceeds to his own duty with a trust that the other members will simultaneously do theirs. Wherever a desired result is achieved by the co-operation of many independent persons, its existence as a fact is a pure consequence of the precursive faith in one another of those immediately

34

35

---

[27] *Emerson:* Ralph Waldo Emerson (1803–1882), an American writer and philosopher. [Editors' note.]

[28] *ad extorquendum . . . meum:* to wrench out my agreement. [Editors' note.]

THE WILL TO BELIEVE

concerned. A government, an army, a commercial system, a ship, a college, an athletic team, all exist on this condition, without which not only is nothing achieved, but nothing is even attempted. A whole train of passengers (individually brave enough) will be looted by a few highwaymen, simply because the latter can count on one another, while each passenger fears that if he makes a movement of resistance, he will be shot before any one else backs him up. If we believed that the whole car-full would rise at once with us, we should each severally rise, and train-robbing would never even be attempted. There are, then, cases where a fact cannot come at all unless a preliminary faith exists in its coming. *And where faith in a fact can help create the fact,* that would be an insane logic which should say that faith running ahead of scientific evidence is the "lowest kind of immorality" into which a thinking being can fall. Yet such is the logic by which our scientific absolutists pretend to regulate our lives!

10

In truths dependent on our personal action, then, faith based on desire is   36 certainly a lawful and possibly an indispensable thing.

But now, it will be said, these are all childish human cases, and have   37 nothing to do with great cosmical matters, like the question of religious faith. Let us then pass on to that. Religions differ so much in their accidents that in discussing the religious question we must make it very generic and broad. What then do we now mean by the religious hypothesis? Science says things are; morality says some things are better than other things; and religion says essentially two things.

First, she says that the best things are the more eternal things, the over-   38 lapping things, the things in the universe that throw the last stone, so to speak, and say the final word. "Perfection is eternal,"—this phrase of Charles Secrétan[29] seems a good way of putting this first affirmation of religion, an affirmation which obviously cannot yet be verified scientifically at all.

The second affirmation of religion is that we are better off even now if   39 we believe her first affirmation to be true.

Now, let us consider what the logical elements of this situation are *in*   40 *case the religious hypothesis in both its branches be really true.* (Of course, we must admit that possibility at the outset. If we are to discuss the question at all, it must involve a living option. If for any of you religion be a hypothesis that cannot, by any living possibility be true, then you need go no farther. I speak to the "saving remnant" alone.) So proceeding, we see, first, that religion offers itself as a *momentous* option. We are supposed to gain, even now, by our belief, and to lose by our nonbelief, a certain vital

---

[29] *Charles Secrétan:* a Swiss philosopher and moralist (1815–1895). [Editors' note.]

good. Secondly, religion is a *forced* option, so far as that good goes. We cannot escape the issue by remaining sceptical and waiting for more light, because, although we do avoid error in that way *if religion be untrue,* we lose the good, *if it be true,* just as certainly as if we positively chose to disbelieve. It is as if a man should hesitate indefinitely to ask a certain woman to marry him because he was not perfectly sure that she would prove an angel after he brought her home. Would he not cut himself off from that particular angel-possibility as decisively as if he went and married some one else? Scepticism, then, is not avoidance of option; it is option of a certain particular kind of risk. *Better risk loss of truth than chance of error,*—that is your faith-vetoer's exact position. He is actively playing his stake as much as the believer is; he is backing the field against the religious hypothesis, just as the believer is backing the religious hypothesis against the field. To preach scepticism to us as a duty until "sufficient evidence" for religion be found, is tantamount therefore to telling us, when in presence of the religious hypothesis, that to yield to our fear of its being error is wiser and better than to yield to our hope that it may be true. It is not intellect against all passions, then; it is only intellect with one passion laying down its law. And by what, forsooth, is the supreme wisdom of this passion warranted? Dupery for dupery, what proof is there that dupery through hope is so much worse than dupery through fear? I, for one, can see no proof; and I simply refuse obedience to the scientist's command to imitate his kind of option, in a case where my own stake is important enough to give me the right to choose my own form of risk. If religion be true and the evidence for it be still insufficient, I do not wish, by putting your extinguisher upon my nature (which feels to me as if it had after all some business in this matter), to forfeit my sole chance in life of getting upon the winning side,—that chance depending, of course, on my willingness to run the risk of acting as if my passional need of taking the world religiously might be prophetic and right.

All this is on the supposition that it really may be prophetic and right, 41 and that, even to us who are discussing the matter, religion is a live hypothesis which may be true. Now, to most of us religion comes in a still further way that makes a veto on our active faith even more illogical. The more perfect and more eternal aspect of the universe is represented in our religions as having personal form. The universe is no longer a mere *It* to us, but a *Thou,* if we are religious; and any relation that may be possible from person to person might be possible here. For instance, although in one sense we are passive portions of the universe, in another we show a curious autonomy, as if we were small active centres on our own account. We feel, too, as if the appeal of religion to us were made to our own active good-will, as if evidence might be forever withheld from us unless we met the hypothesis half-way. To take a trivial illustration; just as a man who in a company of gentlemen made no advances, asked a warrant for every concession, and believed no one's word without proof, would cut himself off by such churlishness from all the social rewards that a more trusting spirit would earn,—so here, one who should shut himself up in snarling logicality and try to make the gods extort his recognition willy-nilly, or not get it at all, might cut himself off forever from his only opportunity of making the gods' acquaintance. This feeling, forced on us we know not whence, that by obstinately believing that there are gods (although not to do so would be so easy both for our logic and our life) we are doing the universe the deepest service we can, seems part of the living essence of the religious hypothesis. If the hypothesis *were* true in all its parts, including this one, then pure intellectualism, with its veto on our making willing advances, would be an absurdity; and some participation of our sympathetic nature would be logically required. I, therefore, for one, cannot see my way to accepting the agnostic rules for truth-seeking, or wilfully agree to keep my willing nature out of the game. I cannot do so for this plain reason, that *a rule of thinking which would absolutely prevent me from acknowledging certain kinds of truth if those kinds of truth were really there, woud be an irrational rule.* That for me is the long and short of the formal logic of the situation, no matter what the kinds of truth might materially be.

I confess I do not see how this logic can be escaped. But sad experience makes me fear that some of you may still shrink from radically saying with me, *in abstracto*,[30] that we have the right to believe at our own risk any hypothesis that is live enough to tempt our will. I suspect, however, that if this is so, it is because you have got away from the abstract logical point of view altogether, and are thinking (perhaps without realizing it) of some particular religious hypothesis which for you is dead. The freedom to "believe what we will" you apply to the case of some patent superstition; and the faith you think of is the faith defined by the schoolboy when he said, "Faith is when you believe something that you know ain't true." I can only repeat that this is misapprehension. *In concreto*,[31] the freedom to believe can only cover living options which the intellect of the individual cannot by itself resolve; and living options never seem absurdities to him who has them to consider. When I look at the religious question as it really puts itself to concrete men, and when I think of all the possibilities which both practically and theoretically it involves, then this command that we shall put a stopper on our heart, instincts, and courage, and *wait*—acting of course meanwhile more or less as if religion were *not* true[32]—till doomsday,

42

---

[30] *in abstracto:* in the abstract. [Editors' note.]

[31] *in concreto:* in concrete terms. [Editors' note.]

[32] Since belief is measured by action, he who forbids us to believe religion to be true, necessarily also forbids us to act as we should if we did believe it to be true. The whole defence of religious faith hinges upon action. If the action required or inspired by the

or till such time as our intellect and senses working together may have raked in evidence enough,—this command, I say, seems to me the queerest idol ever manufactured in the philosophic cave. Were we scholastic absolutists, there might be more excuse. If we had an infallible intellect with its objective certitudes, we might feel ourselves disloyal to such a perfect organ of knowledge in not trusting to it exclusively, in not waiting for its releasing word. But if we are empiricists, if we believe that no bell in us tolls to let us know for certain when truth is in our grasp, then it seems a piece of idle fantasticality to preach so solemnly our duty of waiting for the bell. Indeed we *may* wait if we will,—I hope you do not think that I am denying that,—but if we do so, we do so at our peril as much as if we believed. In either case we *act*, taking our life in our hands. No one of us ought to issue vetoes to the other, nor should we bandy words of abuse. We ought, on the contrary, delicately and profoundly to respect one another's mental freedom: then only shall we bring about the intellectual republic; then only shall we have that spirit of inner tolerance without which all our outer tolerance is soulless, and which is empiricism's glory; then only shall we live and let live, in speculative as well as in practical things.

I began by a reference to Fitz James Stephen; let me end by a quotation from him. "What do you think of yourself? What do you think of the world? . . . These are questions with which all must deal as it seems good to them. They are riddles of the Sphinx, and in some way or other we must deal with them. . . . In all important transactions of life we have to take a leap in the dark. . . . If we decide to leave the riddles unanswered, that is a choice; if we waver in our answer, that, too, is a choice: but whatever choice we make, we make it at our peril. If a man chooses to turn his back altogether on God and the future, no one can prevent him; no one can show beyond reasonable doubt that he is mistaken. If a man thinks otherwise and acts as he thinks, I do not see that any one can prove that *he* is mistaken. Each must act as he thinks best; and if he is wrong, so much the worse for him. We stand on a mountain pass in the midst of whirling snow and blinding mist, through which we get glimpses now and then of paths which may be deceptive. If we stand still we shall be frozen to death. If we take the wrong road we shall be dashed to pieces. We do not certainly know whether there is any right one. What must we do? 'Be strong and of a good courage.' Act for the best, hope for the best, and take what comes. . . . If death ends all, we cannot meet death better."[33]

---

religious hypothesis is in no way different from that dictated by the naturalistic hypothesis, then religious faith is a pure superfluity, better pruned away, and controversy about its legitimacy is a piece of idle trifling, unworthy of serious minds. I myself believe, of course, that the religious hypothesis gives to the world an expression which specifically determines our reactions, and makes them in a large part unlike what they might be on a purely naturalistic scheme of belief. [Author's note.]

[33] Liberty, Equality, Fraternity, p. 353, 2d edition. London, 1874. [Author's note.]

Questions for Discussion and Writing

1. How does James characterize his relationship with his own students at Harvard? How might this characterization help establish his ethos and cement his bond with this audience? Much later in the essay, how might this bond enhance his argument about belief in a supreme being?

2. Keeping in mind the oral nature of this piece, analyze James's transitions. Identify transitional passages in which James both *summarizes* the previous arguments and *projects* the audience ahead into his next point.

3. How does James seek to argue *logically* about the inherently *emotional* subjects of will, belief, and God? Is James able to handle this ostensible contradiction?

4. In an essay of your own design, adapt James's discussion of belief to argue for or against one of the following: (a) prayer in public schools; (b) state funding of private religious schools; (c) strict separation of church and state; or (d) religious leaders running for high office.

FRIEDRICH NIETZSCHE

(1844–1900)

L ike Karl Marx, Friedrich Nietzsche has slipped into the category of great thinkers with serious image problems. Perhaps the super bad boy of the Western philosophical tradition, Nietzsche continues to draw fire from many quarters. His famous exclamation, "God is dead" (from The Gay Science, a section of which is featured here) has become one of the most well-known and controversial battle cries of the modern age. Before you judge the value of his arguments for yourself, let us take a brief look at the man who has raised such a ruckus.

Nietzsche was born in the Prussian province of Saxony. His family was Lutheran, and church and state were of great importance to them. In fact, young Friedrich was named for the reigning king of Prussia. Although it would be simpleminded to attempt to explain away the revolutionary attitudes of the adult in terms of the rebelliousness of the adolescent, it is prudent to take into account the intellectual and spiritual context of any writer. There is little doubt that Nietzsche's early experiences with and reaction against religious and political autocracy profoundly influenced his mature work.

Nietzsche studied Latin and Greek authors at the universities of Bonn and Leipzig. One of his intellectual idols during his student days was the German philosopher Arthur Schopenhauer. In 1869, before he had completed his doctorate, he became a professor of classical philology and rhetoric at the University of Basel, in Switzerland. During the Franco-Prussian War, Nietzsche worked as a medical orderly for his native country. After the war, he returned to Basel a sick man. Nietzsche had contracted syphilis, a much more dangerous disease before the age of modern antibiotics. Eventually, the malady destroyed him.

The next great influence in Nietzsche's life was Richard Wagner, with whom he had a close friendship for a number of years. In fact, Nietzsche's first book-length study, The Birth of Tragedy out of the Spirit of Music (1872), contained much praise for the great German composer of operas. As Wagner became more and more traditional in his thought and Nietzsche continued to reach for bold new ideas, however, their friendship dissolved. In fact, Nietzsche despised Parsifal, one of Wagner's most famous operas.

In 1879, Nietzsche's declining health forced him to resign his position at Basel. For the next ten years, he isolated himself from society and, with the asceticism that characterized most of his adult life, focused strictly on writing. It was during this period that Nietzsche produced his most important works. In 1882, he published The Gay Science (or The Joyful Wisdom). Thus Spake Zarathustra (1885), considered one of the great classics of world literature, was written during this time, *as well as* Beyond Good and Evil *(1886) and* The Genealogy of Morals *(1887). Despite the fact that his health declined while he was producing his major work, it is not realistic to attribute his revolutionary ideas to feebleness of mind. Nietzsche's output went unnoticed until 1888, when it was first studied seriously at the university level. By 1898, he was world famous. Sadly, though, Nietzsche himself was utterly unaware of his great success. In 1889, as the result of his syphilitic infection, he suffered a serious breakdown and never recovered his sanity.*

Since Nietzsche's ideas first surfaced, he had been misquoted and misunderstood. His sister unscrupulously edited his work for publication, and the Nazis unfairly marshaled bits and pieces of Nietzsche in support of their cause. And, of course, he had his legitimate detractors. H. Thirring, an Austrian physicist, declared that Nietzsche was "a not ungifted poet but no thinker at all." On the other hand, he was admired by major literary figures such as Thomas Mann, Hermann Hesse, Rainer Maria Rilke, André Gide, George Bernard Shaw, André Malraux, and Jean-Paul Sartre, and by such philosophers as Martin Heidegger. Sigmund Freud had great praise for Nietzsche, claiming that his self-knowledge was unparalleled. High words, indeed, from the father of modern psychology.

To attempt to summarize the essence of Nietzschean philosophy would be extremely difficult. It can be said, though, that he placed great emphasis on the natural drive for power that he believed dominated the human psyche, and he argued that much of this power came when one liberated oneself from the burdensome traditions imposed by one's culture. Nietzsche was a thoroughgoing skeptic and nonconformist who brilliantly challenged the values of conventional belief systems. His ideal "overman" or "superman" rejected the beliefs of the herd to forge a personal value system that met his own needs. Like philosophers as conservative and as mainstream as Plato, Nietzsche placed a high premium on self-mastery. His idols were not warriors or dictators but creative geniuses such as the great Italian painter Leonardo da Vinci and the eighteenth-century German poet and dramatist Johann Wolfgang von Goethe.

FROM THE GAY SCIENCE

108

New struggles. After Buddha was dead, his shadow was still shown for 1 centuries in a cave—a tremendous, gruesome shadow. God is dead; but given the way of men, there may still be caves for thousands of years in which his shadow will be shown. —And we—we still have to vanquish his shadow, too.

109

Let us beware. Let us beware of thinking that the world is a living being. 2 Where should it expand? On what should it feed? How could it grow and multiply? We have some notion of the nature of the organic; and we should not reinterpret the exceedingly derivative, late, rare, accidental, that we perceive only on the crust of the earth and make of it something essential, universal, and eternal, which is what those people do who call the universe an organism. This nauseates me. Let us even beware of believing that the universe is a machine: it is certainly not constructed for one purpose, and calling it a "machine" does it far too much honor.

Let us beware of positing generally and everywhere anything as elegant as the cyclical movements of our neighboring stars; even a glance into the Milky Way raises doubts whether there are not far coarser and more contradictory movements there, as well as stars with eternally linear paths, etc. The astral order in which we live is an exception; this order and the relative duration that depends on it have again made possible an exception of exceptions: the formation of the organic. The total character of the world, however, is in all eternity chaos—in the sense not of a lack of necessity but of a lack of order, arrangement, form, beauty, wisdom, and whatever other names there are for our aesthetic anthropomorphisms. Judged from the point of view of our reason, unsuccessful attempts are by all odds the rule, the exceptions are not the secret aim, and the whole musical box repeats eternally its tune which may never be called a melody—and ultimately even the phrase "unsuccessful attempt" is too anthropomorphic and reproachful. But how could we reproach or praise the universe? Let us beware of attributing to it heartlessness and unreason or their opposites: it is neither perfect nor beautiful, nor noble, nor does it wish to become any of these things; it does not by any means strive to imitate man. None of our aesthetic and moral judgments apply to it. Nor does it have any instinct for self-preservation or any other instinct; and it does not observe any laws either. Let us beware of saying that there are laws in nature. There are only necessities: there is nobody who commands, nobody who obeys, nobody who trespasses. Once you know that there are no purposes, you also know that there is no accident; for it is only beside a world of purposes that the word "accident" has meaning. Let us beware of saying that death is opposed to life. The living is merely a type of what is dead, and a very rare type.

Let us beware of thinking that the world eternally creates new things. There are no eternally enduring substances: matter is as much of an error as the God of the Eleatics.[1] But when shall we ever be done with our caution and care? When will all these shadows of God cease to darken our minds? When will we complete our de-deification of nature? When may we begin to *"naturalize"* humanity in terms of a pure, newly discovered, newly redeemed nature?[2]

---

[1] A group of early Greek philosophers who lived in Southern Italy. The most famous among them, Parmenides, was born about 510 B.C. [Translator's note.]

[2] "Naturalize" is here used in the sense of naturalism, as opposed to supernaturalism. Man is to be reintegrated into nature. [Translator's note.]

110

Origin of knowledge.   Over immense periods of time the intellect produced   5
nothing but errors. A few of these proved to be useful and helped to
preserve the species: those who hit upon or inherited these had better luck
in their struggle for themselves and their progeny. Such erroneous articles
of faith, which were continually inherited, until they became almost part
of the basic endowment of the species, include the following: that there are
enduring things; that there are equal things; that there are things, substances,
bodies; that a thing is what it appears to be; that our will is free; that what
is good for me is also good in itself. It was only very late that such
propositions were denied and doubted; it was only very late that truth
emerged—as the weakest form of knowledge. It seemed that one was unable
to live with it: our organism was prepared for the opposite; all its higher
functions, sense perception and every kind of sensation worked with those
basic errors which had been incorporated since time immemorial. Indeed,
even in the realm of knowledge these propositions became the norms
according to which "true" and "untrue" were determined—down to the
most remote regions of logic.

Thus the *strength* of knowledge does not depend on its degree of truth   6
but on its age, on the degree to which it has been incorporated, on its
character as a condition of life. Where life and knowledge seemed to be at
odds there was never any real fight, but denial and doubt were simply
considered madness. Those exceptional thinkers, like the Eleatics, who
nevertheless posited and clung to the opposites of the natural errors, believed
that it was possible to *live* in accordance with these opposites: they invented
the sage as the man who was unchangeable and impersonal, the man of the
universality of intuition who was One and All at the same time, with a
special capacity for his inverted knowledge: they had the faith that their
knowledge was also the principle of *life.* But in order to claim all of this,
they had to *deceive* themselves about their own state: they had to attribute
to themselves, fictitiously, impersonality and changeless duration; they had
to misapprehend the nature of the knower; they had to deny the role of the
impulses in knowledge; and quite generally they had to conceive of reason
as a completely free and spontaneous activity. They shut their eyes to the
fact that they, too, had arrived at their propositions through opposition to
common sense, or owing to a desire for tranquillity, for sole possession, or
for dominion. The subtler development of honesty and skepticism eventually
made these people, too, impossible; their ways of living and judging were
seen to be also dependent upon the primeval impulses and basic errors of
all sentient existence.

This subtler honesty and skepticism came into being wherever two   7
contradictory sentences appeared to be *applicable* to life because *both* were
compatible with the basic errors, and it was therefore possible to argue
about the higher or lower degree of *utility* for life; also wherever new

propositions, though not useful for life, were also evidently not harmful to life: in such cases there was room for the expression of an intellectual play impulse, and honesty and skepticism were innocent and happy like all play. Gradually, the human brain became full of such judgments and convictions, and a ferment, struggle, and lust for power developed in this tangle. Not only utility and delight but every kind of impulse took sides in this fight about "truths." The intellectual fight became an occupation, an attraction, a profession, a duty, something dignified—and eventually knowledge and the striving for the true found their place as a need among other needs. Henceforth not only faith and conviction but also scrutiny, denial, mistrust, and contradiction became a *power*; all "evil" instincts were subordinated to knowledge, employed in her service, and acquired the splendor of what is permitted, honored, and useful—and eventually even the eye and innocence of the *good*.

Thus knowledge became a piece of life itself, and hence a continually   8
growing power—until eventually knowledge collided with those primeval basic errors: two lives, two powers, both in the same human being. A thinker is now that being in whom the impulse for truth and those life-preserving errors clash for their first fight, after the impulse for truth has proved to be also a life-preserving power. Compared to the significance of this fight, everything else is a matter of indifference: the ultimate question about the conditions of life has been posed here, and we confront the first attempt to answer this question by experiment. To what extent can truth endure incorporation? That is the question; that is the experiment.

I I I

Origin of the logical.   How did logic come into existence in man's head?   9
Certainly out of illogic, whose realm originally must have been immense. Innumerable beings who made inferences in a way different from ours perished; for all that, their ways might have been truer. Those, for example, who did not know how to find often enough what is "equal" as regards both nourishment and hostile animals—those, in other words, who subsumed things too slowly and cautiously—were favored with a lesser probability of survival than those who guessed immediately upon encountering similar instances that they must be equal. The dominant tendency, however, to treat as equal what is merely similar—an illogical tendency, for nothing is really equal—is what first created any basis for logic.

In order that the concept of substance could originate—which is indis-   10
pensable for logic although in the strictest sense nothing real corresponds to it—it was likewise necessary that for a long time one did not see nor perceive the changes in things. The beings that did not see so precisely had an advantage over those that saw everything "in flux." At bottom, every high degree of caution in making inferences and every skeptical tendency constitute a great danger for life. No living beings would have survived if

the opposite tendency—to affirm rather than suspend judgment, to err and *make up* things rather than wait, to assent rather than negate, to pass judgment rather than be just—had not been bred to the point where it became extraordinarily strong.

The course of logical ideas and inferences in our brain today corresponds   11
to a process and a struggle among impulses that are, taken singly, very illogical and unjust. We generally experience only the result of this struggle because this primeval mechanism now runs its course so quickly and is so well concealed.

112

Cause and effect. "Explanation" is what we call it, but it is "description"   12
that distinguishes us from older stages of knowledge and science. Our descriptions are better—we do not explain any more than our predecessors. We have uncovered a manifold one-after-another where the naive man and inquirer of older cultures saw only two separate things. "Cause" and "effect" is what one says; but we have merely perfected the image of becoming without reaching beyond the image or behind it. In every case the series of "causes" confronts us much more completely, and we infer: first, this and that has to precede in order that this or that may then follow—but this does not involve any *comprehension*. In every chemical process, for example, quality appears as a "miracle," as ever; also, every locomotion; nobody has "explained" a push. But how could we possibly explain anything? We operate only with things that do not exist: lines, planes, bodies, atoms, divisible time spans, divisible spaces. How should explanations be at all possible when we first turn everything into an *image*, our image!

It will do to consider science as an attempt to humanize things as faithfully   13
as possible; as we describe things and their one-after-another, we learn how to describe ourselves more and more precisely. Cause and effect: such a duality probably never exists; in truth we are confronted by a continuum out of which we isolate a couple of pieces, just as we perceive motion only as isolated points and then infer it without ever actually seeing it. The suddenness with which many effects stand out misleads us; actually, it is sudden only for us. In this moment of suddenness there is an infinite number of processes that elude us. An intellect that could see cause and effect as a continuum and a flux and not, as we do, in terms of an arbitrary division and dismemberment, would repudiate the concept of cause and effect and deny all conditionality.

113

On the doctrine of poisons. So many things have to come together for   14
scientific thinking to originate; and all these necessary strengths had to be invented, practiced, and cultivated separately. As long as they were still

separate, however, they frequently had an altogether different effect than they do now that they are integrated into scientific thinking and hold each other in check. Their effect was that of poisons; for example, that of the impulse to doubt, to negate, to wait, to collect, to dissolve. Many hecatombs[3] of human beings were sacrificed before these impulses learned to comprehend their coexistence and to feel that they were all functions of one organizing force within one human being. And even now the time seems remote when artistic energies and the practical wisdom of life will join with scientific thinking to form a higher organic system in relation to which scholars, physicians, artists, and legislators—as we know them at present—would have to look like paltry relics of ancient times.

114

How far the moral sphere extends.   As soon as we see a new image, we   15 immediately construct it with the aid of all our previous experiences, *depending on the degree* of our honesty and justice. All experiences are moral experiences, even in the realm of sense perception.

115

The four errors.   Man has been educated by his errors. First, he always   16 saw himself only incompletely; second, he endowed himself with fictitious attributes; third, he placed himself in a false order of rank in relation to animals and nature; fourth, he invented ever new tables of goods and always accepted them for a time as eternal and unconditional: as a result of this, now one and now another human impulse and state held first place and was ennobled because it was esteemed so highly. If we removed the effects of these four errors, we should also remove humanity, humaneness, and "human dignity."

116

Herd instinct.   Wherever we encounter a morality, we also encounter   17 valuations and an order of rank of human impulses and actions. These valuations and orders of rank are always expressions of the needs of a community and herd: whatever benefits it most—and second most, and third most—that is also considered the first standard for the value of all individuals. Morality trains the individual to be a function of the herd and to ascribe value to himself only as a function. The conditions for the preservation of different communities were very different; hence there were very different moralities. Considering essential changes in the forms of

---

[3] *hecatombs:* Greek and Roman sacrifice of 100 victims, usually cattle. [Editors' note.]

future herds and communities, states and societies, we can prophesy that there will yet be very divergent moralities. Morality is herd instinct in the individual.

117

Herd remorse.   During the longest and most remote periods of the human past, the sting of conscience was not at all what it is now. Today one feels responsible only for one's will and actions, and one finds one's pride in oneself. All our teachers of law start from this sense of self and pleasure in the individual, as if this had always been the fount of law. But during the longest period of the human past nothing was more terrible than to feel that one stood by oneself. To be alone, to experience things by oneself, neither to obey nor to rule, to be an individual—that was not a pleasure but a punishment; one was sentenced "to individuality." Freedom of thought was considered discomfort itself. While we experience law and submission as compulsion and loss, it was egoism that was formerly experienced as something painful and as real misery. To be a self and to esteem oneself according to one's own weight and measure—that offended taste in those days. An inclination to do this would have been considered madness; for being alone was associated with every misery and fear. In those days, "free will" was very closely associated with a bad conscience; and the more unfree one's actions were and the more the herd instinct rather than any personal sense found expression in an action, the more moral one felt. Whatever harmed the herd, whether the individual had wanted it or not wanted it, prompted the sting of conscience in the individual—and in his neighbor, too, and even in the whole herd. —There is no point on which we have learned to think and feel more differently. [18]

118

Benevolence.   Is it virtuous when a cell transforms itself into a function of a stronger cell? It has no alternative. And is it evil when the stronger cell assimilates the weaker? It also has no alternative; it follows necessity, for it strives for superabundant substitutes and wants to regenerate itself. Hence we should make a distinction in benevolence between the impulse to appropriate and the impulse to submit, and ask whether it is the stronger or the weaker that feels benevolent. Joy and desire appear together in the stronger that wants to transform something into a function; joy and the wish to be desired appear together in the weaker that wants to become a function. [19]

Pity is essentially of the former type: an agreeable impulse of the instinct for appropriation at the sight of what is weaker. But it should be kept in mind that "strong" and "weak" are relative concepts. [20]

119

No altruism! In many people I find an overwhelmingly forceful and 21
pleasurable desire to be a function: they have a very refined sense for all
those places where precisely *they* could "function" and push in those
directions. Examples include those women who transform themselves into
some function of a man that happens to be underdeveloped in him, and
thus become his purse or his politics or his sociability. Such beings preserve
themselves best when they find a fitting place in another organism; if they
fail to do this, they become grumpy, irritated, and devour themselves.

120

Health of the soul. The popular medical formulation of morality that goes 22
back to Ariston of Chios,⁴ "virtue is the health of the soul," would have to
be changed to become useful, at least to read: "*your* virtue is the health of
your soul." For there is no health as such, and all attempts to define a thing
that way have been wretched failures. Even the determination of what is
healthy for your *body* depends on your goal, your horizon, your energies,
your impulses, your errors, and above all on the ideals and phantasms of
your soul. Thus there are innumerable healths of the body; and the more
we allow the unique and incomparable to raise its head again, and the more
we abjure the dogma of the "equality of men," the more must the concept
of a *normal* health, along with a normal diet and the normal course of an
illness, be abandoned by medical men. Only then would the time have
come to reflect on the health and illness of the *soul*, and to find the peculiar
virtue of each man in the health of his soul. In one person, of course, this
health could look like its opposite in another person.

Finally, the great question would still remain whether we can really 23
dispense with illness—even for the sake of our virtue—and whether our
thirst for knowledge and self-knowledge in particular does not require the
sick soul as much as the healthy, and whether, in brief, the will to health
alone, is not a prejudice, cowardice, and perhaps a bit of very subtle
barbarism and backwardness.

121

Life no argument. We have arranged for ourselves a world in which we 24
can live—by positing bodies, lines, planes, causes and effects, motion and
rest, form and content; without these articles of faith nobody now could
endure life. But that does not prove them. Life is no argument. The
conditions of life might include error.

---

⁴ A pupil of Zeno, the founder of Stoicism. Ariston founded an independent branch of this
school and had great influence in Athens around 250 B.C. . . . [Translators' note.]

122

Moral skepticism in Christianity.   Christianity, too, has made a great   25
contribution to the enlightenment, and taught moral skepticism very
trenchantly and effectively, accusing and embittering men, yet with untiring
patience and subtlety; it destroyed the faith in his "virtues" in every single
individual; it led to the disappearance from the face of the earth of all those
paragons of virtue of whom there was no dearth in antiquity—those popular
personalities who, imbued with faith in their own perfection, went about
with the dignity of a great matador.

When we today, trained in this Christian school of skepticism, read the   26
moral treatises of the ancients—for example, Seneca and Epictetus—we
have a diverting sense of superiority and feel full of secret insights and
over-sights: we feel as embarrassed as if a child were talking before an old
man, or an over-enthusiastic young beauty before La Rochefoucauld[5]: we
know better what virtue is.

In the end, however, we have applied this same skepticism also to all   27
religious states and processes, such as sin, repentance, grace, sanctification,
and we have allowed the worm to dig so deep that now we have the same
sense of subtle superiority and insight when we read any Christian book:
we also know religious feelings better! And it is high time to know them
well and to describe them well, for the pious people of the old faith are
dying out, too. Let us save their image and their type at least for knowledge.

123

Knowledge as more than a mere means.   *Without* this new passion—I mean   28
the passion to know—science would still be promoted; after all, science has
grown and matured without it until now. The good faith in science, the
prejudice in its favor that dominates the modern state (and formerly
dominated even the church) is actually based on the fact that this unconditional
urge and passion has manifested itself so rarely and that science is considered
not a passion but a mere condition or an "ethos." Often mere *amour-plaisir*[6]
of knowledge (curiosity) is felt to be quite sufficient, or *amour-vanité,*[7]
being accustomed to it with the ulterior motive of honors and sustenance;
for many people it is actually quite enough that they have too much leisure
and do not know what to do with it except to read, collect, arrange, observe,
and recount—their "scientific impulse" is their boredom.

---

[5] François de La Rochefoucauld (1613–80) whose *Maxims* are among the treasures of French
literature. . . . [Translator's note.]

[6] Love based on pleasure. [Translator's note.]

[7] Love based on vanity. [Translator's note.]

Pope Leo X once sang the praises of science (in his brief to Beroaldo): 29 he called it the most beautiful ornament and the greatest pride of our life and a noble occupation in times of happiness as well as unhappiness; and finally he said: "without it all human endeavors would lack any firm foothold—and even with it things are changeable and insecure enough." But this tolerably skeptical pope keeps silent, like all other ecclesiastical eulogists of science, about his ultimate judgment. From his words one might infer, although this is strange enough for such a friend of the arts, that he places science above art; but in the end it is nothing but good manners when he does not speak at this point of what he places high above all of the sciences, too: "revealed truth" and the "eternal salvation of the soul." Compared to that, what are ornaments, pride, entertainment, and the security of life to him? "Science is something second-class, not anything ultimate, unconditional, not an object of passion"—this judgment Leo retained in his soul: the truly Christian judgment about science.

In antiquity the dignity and recognition of science were diminished by 30 the fact that even her most zealous disciples placed the striving for *virtue* first, and one felt that knowledge had received the highest praise when one celebrated it as the best means to virtue. It is something new in history that knowledge wants to be more than a mere means.

124

In the horizon of the infinite.　We have left the land and have embarked. 31 We have burned our bridges behind us—indeed, we have gone farther and destroyed the land behind us. Now, little ship, look out! Beside you is the ocean: to be sure, it does not always roar, and at times it lies spread out like silk and gold and reveries of graciousness. But hours will come when you will realize that it is infinite and that there is nothing more awesome than infinity. Oh, the poor bird that felt free and now strikes the walls of this cage! Woe, when you feel homesick for the land as if it had offered more *freedom*—and there is no longer any "land."

125

The madman.　Have you not heard of that madman who lit a lantern in 32 the bright morning hours, ran to the market place, and cried incessantly: "I seek God! I seek God!" —As many of those who did not believe in God were standing around just then, he provoked much laughter. Has he got lost? asked one. Did he lose his way like a child? asked another. Or is he hiding? Is he afraid of us? Has he gone on a voyage? emigrated? —Thus they yelled and laughed.

The madman jumped into their midst and pierced them with his eyes. 33 "Whither is God?" he cried; "I will tell you. *We have killed him*—you and I. All of us are his murderers. But how did we do this? How could we drink up the sea? Who gave us the sponge to wipe away the entire horizon? What were we doing when we unchained this earth from its sun? Whither is it moving now? Whither are we moving? Away from all suns? Are we not plunging continually? Backward, sideward, forward, in all directions? Is there still any up or down? Are we not straying as through an infinite nothing? Do we not feel the breath of empty space? Has it not become colder? Is not night continually closing in on us? Do we not need to light lanterns in the morning? Do we hear nothing as yet of the noise of the gravediggers who are burying God? Do we smell nothing as yet of the divine decomposition? Gods, too, decompose. God is dead. God remains dead. And we have killed him.

"How shall we comfort ourselves, the murderers of all murderers? What 34 was holiest and mightiest of all that the world has yet owned has bled to death under our knives: who will wipe this blood off us? What water is there for us to clean ourselves? What festivals of atonement, what sacred games shall we have to invent? Is not the greatness of this deed too great for us? Must we ourselves not become gods simply to appear worthy of it? There has never been a greater deed; and whoever is born after us—for the sake of this deed he will belong to a higher history than all history hitherto."

Here the madman fell silent and looked again at his listeners; and they, 35 too, were silent and stared at him in astonishment. At last he threw his lantern on the ground, and it broke into pieces and went out. "I have come too early," he said then; "my time is not yet. This tremendous event is still on its way, still wandering; it has not yet reached the ears of men. Lightning and thunder require time; the light of the stars requires time; deeds, though done, still require time to be seen and heard. This deed is still more distant from them than the most distant stars—*and yet they have done it themselves.*"

It has been related further that on the same day the madman forced his 36 way into several churches and there struck up his *requiem aeternam deo.*[8] Led out and called to account, he is said always to have replied nothing but: "What after all are these churches now if they are not the tombs and sepulchers of God?"

Questions for Discussion and Writing

1. How does Nietzsche prepare the reader for startling claims such as "God is dead" and "The character of the world . . . is in all eternity chaos"? What kind of proof and support does he offer for such claims? What serves to make his claims persuasive?

---

[8] *requiem aeternam deo:* eternal funeral dirge for God. [Editors' note.]

2. Nietzsche's prose in texts such as *The Gay Science* has been described as aphoristic. What does this description mean? Overall, do you find such discourse structurally coherent? How are transitions handled? Is the argument sufficiently unified such that one can form a consistent counterargument to oppose it?

3. For what kind of an audience do you suppose this text is fashioned? To what values and beliefs would they ascribe? Is Nietzsche's intention to reinforce or to assault his audience's belief system? Said another way, does Nietzsche seem to be preaching to the converted, or is he actually out to change someone's mind? How would a critical reader make such a distinction?

4. You are the principal at a Christian high school, and recently your librarian has come under attack from some parents of students for stocking the shelves of the philosophy section with a brand-new edition of the complete works of Friedrich Nietzsche. You've received mixed reviews of Nietzsche from your faculty. The board of directors of the school has asked you to state your position on the matter in writing. Considering the fact that your statement may become a matter of public record, what would you write?

SIGMUND FREUD

(1856–1939)

J ust as Marx's proclamations about capitalism and communism forever altered
the study of economics, so have Freud's
writings about the subconscious, the structure of personality, and the importance of
childhood experience to the adult psyche determined the agenda for twentieth-century
psychology. Even those with little or no interest in the field of psychology may call
attention to a friend's "ego trip," "Freudian slip," or "Oedipus complex." Whether
you admire or detest Freudian theory, you cannot help but grapple with his writings
if you wish to join in the modern dialogue about the human mind.

Freud was born to Jewish parents in Freiberg, Moravia (now Czechoslovakia).
When he was four, his family moved to Vienna, where he lived until the final year
of his life. The young Freud had wide-ranging interests. He admired Darwin's work,
and it has been argued that this interest in evolution influenced Freud's developmental
approach to both the human psyche and civilization as a whole. He dabbled in
social studies, philosophy, and chemistry before focusing on human physiology and
medicine at the University of Vienna, where he became deeply involved in research.
It was here that Freud was exposed to the organic view of human consciousness.
Rather than approaching character in traditional moral or religious terms, Freud's
professors at the University of Vienna studied how physiological phenomena shaped
human personality and behavior. By learning to emphasize the role of physiology in
forming the psyche, Freud came to embrace a degree of psychic determinism that
was to characterize all his work.

After graduating in 1881, Freud married and began practicing neurology, but
his desire to conduct research remained strong. In 1885, he joined Josef Breuer in
an investigation of hysteria. Together, they experimented with a developmental
approach to therapy, helping patients analyze their pasts to understand the deep-
seated origins of their disorders. That this approach seems virtually intuitive to us
testifies to the momentous nature of Breuer and Freud's discovery. Although Breuer
used hypnotism to plumb the patient's subconscious and uncover revealing memories,
Freud's technique of free association gained more popularity. Breuer and Freud
published their findings in Studies in Hysteria (1895). With their advancements,
the theory, the treatment, and the movement of psychoanalysis were born.

What were the fundamental principles of psychoanalysis? Aside from the
developmental approach and the psychic determinism mentioned, Freud's new
approach stressed the following points:

1. The personality has a three-part structure that includes the "ego" (self), the
    "super ego" (conscience), and the "id" (the subconscious).

2. *The subconscious has a tremendous impact on our thoughts and actions, and thus we must try to understand its contents.*

3. *Infant sexuality helps shape our adult psyches. Human sexuality progresses from an infantile fascination with the oral, to the anal, and finally to the adult interest in the genital.*

4. *Instinctual desires play a key role in our lives and require satisfaction, either in direct and indirect ("sublimated") ways, or in distorted ("neurotic") ways.*

5. *Mental conflict and struggle are not confined to the realm of abnormal psychology but are a part of normal mental development. (Again, Darwin's influence is evident.)*

6. *Most people resist, repress, or sublimate their deep-seated feelings. The analyst's job is to help the patient release these feelings so that healing can occur.*

The publication of The Interpretation of Dreams *(1900), perhaps Freud's most important work, further established his reputation. He was appointed professor extraordinarius of neurology at the University of Vienna in 1902. A world-famous figure by 1908, he was instrumental in organizing the First International Congress of Psychoanalysis. Freud rapidly developed a flock of devoted followers; many such as Carl Jung later severed their ties with their mentor and began major psychological movements of their own. Freud's work was rapidly translated into many languages. (The Hogarth Press, operated by Virginia and Leonard Woolf, published most of his English translations.) He won the Goethe Prize in 1930 and was made a member of the Royal Society in 1936. Always a controversial figure, Freud never became a full professor at the University of Vienna despite his great fame. He and his wife had six children; Anna, the youngest, became a famous psychoanalyst in her own right. When the Nazis invaded Austria in 1938, Freud fled to London, where he spent his final year.*

The scope of Freud's publications is daunting. Totem and Taboo *(1913) traces the sources of social mores.* Leonardo da Vinci *(1916) attempts to psychoanalyze the great artist from evidence present in his painting.* The Ego and the Id *(1923) outlines the theory of personality structure. In* The Future of an Illusion *(1927) and* Civilization and Its Discontents *(1930, excerpted below), Freud applies psychoanalytic principles and psychic determinism to suggest causes for larger social problems. Just as an individual's consciousness inevitably evolves from the infantile stage through adulthood, he argues, so does a civilization's mind set grow from a primitive form to an adult configuration. Productive until the end of his life, Freud tackles large religious questions in* Moses and Monotheism *(1939).*

Like the economic debates that surround Marx and Marxism, the controversy over Freud and psychoanalysis has long outlived the man himself. Today many reject Freud's ideas about the importance of infant sexuality and the development of sex drive. His low estimation of women's intelligence and abilities is infuriating. Freud did not benefit from careful research methods that today we take for granted, and he did not support many of his theories with the kind of empirical proof we have come to expect from social scientists. Still, our debt to Freud is immeasurable, especially in America, where psychoanalysis continues to dominate our therapeutic practice. And no wonder, since the American dream is tied inescapably to the notion of limitless self-improvement.

We present here the concluding paragraphs from the third chapter of Freud's Civilization and Its Discontents. *Freud begins Chapter 3 by asserting that though dramatic scientific advancements have improved the "material" quality of life immensely, unhappiness still plagues our civilization. The gains achieved by revolutionary inventions such as the telephone, the train, and the airplane seem to create as many problems as they solve. Technologically, we have reached a "Godlike character," yet psychologically we labor to find happiness.*

In order to explore this problem further, Freud analyzes the essential elements of our civilization. Most obviously, civilization serves the utilitarian purpose of protecting us from the dangers and hardships present in our natural environment. In addition to utility, civilization encourages beauty, cleanliness, order, and intellectual activity. It is at this point in the discussion that our excerpt begins.

In the remaining chapters of Civilization and Its Discontents, *Freud refines the basic argument expressed in Chapter 3 and demonstrates its relevance in terms of the basic ego states. As mentioned, Freud's analogy between the individual psyche and the mental health of the entire civilization is key to his overall social arguments.*

FROM CIVILIZATION AND ITS DISCONTENTS

If we assume quite generally that the motive force of all human activities is a striving towards the two confluent goals of utility and a yield of pleasure, we must suppose that this is also true of the manifestations of civilization which we have been discussing here, although this is easily visible only in scientific and aesthetic activities. But it cannot be doubted that the other activities, too, correspond to strong needs in men—perhaps to needs which are only developed in a minority. Nor must we allow ourselves to be misled by judgements of value concerning any particular religion, or philosophic system, or ideal. Whether we think to find in them the highest achievements of the human spirit, or whether we deplore them as aberrations, we cannot but recognize that where they are present, and, in especial, where they are dominant, a high level of civilization is implied.

The last, but certainly not the least important, of the characteristic features of civilization remains to be assessed: the manner in which the relationships of men to one another, their social relationships, are regulated—relationships which affect a person as a neighbour, as a source of help, as another person's sexual object, as a member of a family and of a State. Here it is especially difficult to keep clear of particular ideal demands and to see what is civilized in general. Perhaps we may begin by explaining that the element of civilization enters on the scene with the first attempt to regulate these social relationships. If the attempt were not made, the relationships would be subject to the arbitrary will of the individual: that is to say, the physically stronger man would decide them in the sense of his own interests and instinctual impulses. Nothing would be changed in this if this stronger man should in his turn meet someone even stronger than he. Human life in common is only made possible when a majority comes together which is stronger than any separate individual and which remains united against all separate individuals. The power of this community is then set up as 'right' in opposition to the power of the individual, which is condemned as 'brute force'. This replacement of the power of the individual by the power of a community constitutes the decisive step of civilization. The essence of it lies in the fact that the members of the community restrict themselves in their possibilities of satisfaction, whereas the individual knew no such restrictions. The first requisite of civilization, therefore, is that of justice—that is, the assurance that a law once made will not be broken in favour of an individual. This implies nothing as to the ethical value of such a law. The further course of cultural development seems to tend towards making the law no longer an expression of the will of a small community—a caste or a stratum of the population or a racial group—which, in its turn, behaves like a violent individual towards other, and perhaps more numerous, collections of people. The final outcome should be a rule of law to which all—except those who are not capable of entering a community—have contributed by a sacrifice of their instincts, and which leaves no one—again with the same exception—at the mercy of brute force.

The liberty of the individual is no gift of civilization. It was greatest before there was any civilization, though then, it is true, it had for the most part no value, since the individual was scarcely in a position to defend it. The development of civilization imposes restrictions on it, and justice demands that no one shall escape those restrictions. What makes itself felt in a human community as a desire for freedom may be their revolt against some existing injustice, and so may prove favourable to a further development of civilization; it may remain compatible with civilization. But it may also spring from the remains of their original personality, which is still untamed by civilization and may thus become the basis in them of hostility to civilization. The urge for freedom, therefore, is directed against particular forms and demands of civilization or against civilization altogether. It does not seem as though any influence could induce a man to change his nature into a termite's. No doubt he will always defend his claim to individual liberty against the will of the group. A good part of the struggles of mankind centre round the single task of finding an expedient accommodation—one, that is, that will bring happiness—between this claim of the individual and the cultural claims of the group; and one of the problems that touches the fate of humanity is whether such an accommodation can be reached by means of some particular form of civilization or whether this conflict is irreconcilable.

By allowing common feeling to be our guide in deciding what features of human life are to be regarded as civilized, we have obtained a clear impression of the general picture of civilization; but it is true that so far we have discovered nothing that is not universally known. At the same time we have been careful not to fall in with the prejudice that civilization is syn-onymous with perfecting, that it is the road to perfection pre-ordained for men. But now a point of view presents itself which may lead in a different direction. The development of civilization appears to us as a peculiar process which mankind undergoes, and in which several things strike us as familiar. We may characterize this process with reference to the changes which it brings about in the familiar instinctual dispositions of human beings, to satisfy which is, after all, the economic task of our lives. A few of these instincts are used up in such a manner that something appears in their place which, in an individual, we describe as a character-trait. The most remarkable example of such a process is found in the anal erotism of young human beings. Their original interest in the excretory function, its organs and products, is changed in the course of their growth into a group of traits which are familiar to us as parsimony, a sense of order and cleanliness— qualities which, though valuable and welcome in themselves, may be intensified till they become markedly dominant and produce what is called the anal character. How this happens we do not know, but there is no doubt about the correctness of the finding.[1] Now we have seen that order and cleanliness are important requirements of civilization, although their vital necessity is not very apparent, any more than their suitability as sources of enjoyment. At this point we cannot fail to be struck by the similarity between the process of civilization and the libidinal development of the individual. Other instincts [besides anal erotism] are induced to displace the conditions for their satisfaction, to lead them into other paths. In most cases this process coincides with that of the *sublimation* (of instinctual aims) with which we are familiar, but in some it can be differentiated from it. Sublimation of instinct is an especially conspicuous feature of cultural development; it is what makes it possible for higher psychical activities, scientific, artistic or ideological, to play such an important part in civilized life. If one were to yield to a first impression, one would say that sublimation is a vicissitude which has been forced upon the instincts entirely by civilization. But it would be wiser to reflect upon this a little longer. In

4

---

[1] Cf. my 'Character and Anal Erotism' (1908b), and numerous further contributions, by Ernest Jones [1918] and others. [Author's note.] The 1918 Ernest Jones publication is 'Anal-Erotic Character Traits.' [Editors' note.]

the third place,[2] finally, and this seems the most important of all, it is impossible to overlook the extent to which civilization is built up upon a renunciation of instinct, how much it presupposes precisely the non-satisfaction (by suppression, repression or some other means?) of powerful instincts. This 'cultural frustration' dominates the large field of social relationships between human beings. As we already know, it is the cause of the hostility against which all civilizations have to struggle. It will also make severe demands on our scientific work, and we shall have much to explain here. It is not easy to understand how it can become possible to deprive an instinct of satisfaction. Nor is doing so without danger. If the loss is not compensated for economically, one can be certain that serious disorders will ensue. . . .

Questions for Discussion and Writing

1. Note that Freud's rhetorical situation includes not only his intended audience, but also those people and ideas he *opposes*. Who, in your opinion, is Freud's principal opposition? Describe both Freud's audience and his adversaries, and explain how his argument is tailored to confront and defuse the contentions of his chief opponents.

2. How is Freud's audience meant to react to his claim that our "Godlike character" has failed to bring us complete happiness? How might a reader who is *not* part of Freud's intended audience respond to it? How, for example, would a Christian or other religious believer respond? Or a person who sees technology purely as a matter of beneficial "progress"? Consider what counterarguments such audiences might present, and how persuasive they might be for the kind of audience that Freud addresses.

3. What, in Freud's hands, becomes of common terms such as *justice, utility, beauty, liberty, will, individual,* and *community*? Do you agree with the way he uses them in his argument? How might a different writer—in a different setting—use these same terms—or terms like them—in support of a very different argument?

4. On what problem, principally, does Freud pin the "discontents" of our civilization? Why, with all our technological advances, are we so unhappy? What component or components of the human condition might be missing from his account? Using Freud's argument as a springboard, write an argument defending or opposing the proposition that our civilization is itself the cause of our unhappiness. Write for those who (1) have read this chapter of Freud and (2) are inclined to be skeptical of the basic claim you wish to make.

---

[2] Freud had already mentioned two other factors playing a part in the 'process' of civilization: character-formation and sublimation. [Translator's note.]

W. E. B. DUBOIS

(1868–1963)

Today, when we consider the civil rights movement, the name Dr. Martin Luther King, Jr., quickly comes to mind. Other figures such as Jesse Jackson, Ralph Abernathy, and Rosa Parks are also usually mentioned. One name, though, that is not normally included among these stars is William Edward Burghardt DuBois. The irony behind this omission is startling: DuBois's contributions to the African-American community are unparalleled. Why is it that we have chosen to "forget" this leader?

DuBois was born in Great Barrington, Massachusetts, just a few years after the conclusion of the Civil War. Of mixed African-American and European ancestry, he grew up in a predominantly white culture that inflicted little prejudice on him. Although his African-American heritage determined his self-concept, he readily absorbed the traditional Puritan values prevalent in the Northeast. As a young person, he served as a correspondent for the New York Globe, an African-American paper. With this assignment began his lifelong commitment to civil rights issues.

DuBois attended Fisk University in Nashville, Tennessee, a school established specifically for African-American students. He was an excellent student and edited the college paper in his senior year. Having grown up in the Northeast, he was utterly shocked by the racism and segregation that choked the South. Thus, his experience as an undergraduate was instrumental in shaping his approach to racial issues.

After graduating from Fisk in 1888, DuBois went to Harvard to pursue doctoral studies. It was there that he became friends with William James, whom he considered one of the great influences on his life. DuBois studied in Germany and taught at Wilberforce University in Ohio before receiving his Ph.D. in 1895. His dissertation, The Suppression of the African Slave-Trade in the United States of America, was published in 1896 as the first volume of the Harvard Historical Series. After spending a year in Philadelphia studying the urban African American and working as an assistant instructor at the University of Pennsylvania, he produced The Philadelphia Negro (1899), a ground-breaking study that emphasized cultural and historical, rather than genetic, explanations of racial differences and problems.

For the first decade of the new century, DuBois served as a professor of economics and sociology at Atlanta University. During this time, he became convinced that the way for African Americans to better their lot was not through vocational education but through political action and advanced education. He believed that his people should be assertive about their rights and that they should adopt a less passive, less compromising approach to advancement. Today the civil rights movement takes this position for granted, but in DuBois's time the leadership of African-

American society, epitomized by men such as Booker T. Washington of the Tuskegee Institute, rejected the more active approach. In The Souls of Black Folk (1903), his most famous work, DuBois eloquently described the plight of his fellow African Americans and outlined his disagreement with Washington. In 1905, DuBois launched the Niagara Movement, which took a more militant stance on social advancement for African Americans. In 1910, the group became the National Association for the Advancement of Colored People (NAACP), which is still an active force in American politics today. For twenty-four years, DuBois edited Crisis, the official organ of the association, and consistently called attention to institutionalized racism in the United States. His writing had a profound impact on African-American intellectuals, who looked to DuBois for spiritual leadership. Crisis, in fact, may have been at least partially responsible for the flowering of the Harlem Renaissance in the 1920s.

Around the time of the founding of the NAACP, DuBois was drawn to socialism, and he began to sound more and more like a Marxist. He visited the USSR with great enthusiasm in 1924. As he grew progressively more and more attached to the left, DuBois gradually lost the support of the African-American community. In "The White World," reprinted here from Dusk of Dawn: An Essay Toward an Autobiography of Race Concept (1940), DuBois's disgust with America's capitalist system and his optimism about Marxism moved him to present some arguments about race, economics, and war that shocked his original audience and still may shock the modern reader.

Along with his Marxist tendencies, DuBois became increasingly concerned with the plight of Africa itself, and he participated in many discussions about colonialism and self-rule. In 1945, he met Kwame Nkrumah, the great African nationalist. Late in his life, DuBois was invited by Nkrumah, then leader of Ghana, to move to Africa and help with scholarship there. In 1961, DuBois joined the Communist party and moved to Ghana and became a citizen of that country. He died there the year of King's March on Washington.

DuBois's radicalism, his somewhat naive attitude about the Marxist world, and his rather difficult personality damaged his reputation deeply, and they continue to mar his memory. We must remember, though, that his great positive influence should not be buried under the less popular aspects of his life and work. Through the twenty-one books he wrote, the fifteen he edited, and the 100 or more major articles he published, DuBois contributed immeasurably to African-American scholarship. When he left the NAACP in 1934, they wrote that he "created what never existed before, a Negro intelligentsia, and many who have never read a word of his writings are his spiritual disciples and descendants." These words remain true to this day. By standing up boldly for his race when others chose to adopt a more cautious posture, DuBois led the way for those who came of age in less racist, more tolerant eras.

As we read "The White World," it is important for us to understand that DuBois's hard-line position toward American society comes not from an idiosyncratic malcontent, but from someone who saw the system fail to serve his people. Clearly, the promise of the Emancipation Proclamation and the Reconstruction period had died at the hands of a stubborn racist spirit. The African Americans of DuBois's

*era were by and large poor, uneducated, and unskilled, and many were
disenfranchised. Across the South, "Jim Crow" laws officially sanctioned oppressive
segregation. Even in the North, where superficial equality existed, African Americans
were systematically discriminated against. As W. E. B. DuBois expresses his
arguments about racial theory and racism, it is important to read his frustration
and anger within the context that produced them. It was a radical message that
DuBois sought to deliver, because it was, and—more than we would like to
admit—still is, a radical problem.*

THE WHITE WORLD

The majority of men resent and always have resented the idea of equality
with most of their fellow men. This has had physical, economic, and
cultural reasons: the physical fear of attack; the economic strife to avert
starvation and secure protection and shelter; but more especially I presume
the cultural and spiritual desire to be one's self without interference from
others; to enjoy that anarchy of the spirit which is inevitably the goal of all
consciousness. It is only in highly civilized times and places that the
conception arises of an individual freedom and development, and even that
was conceived of as the right of a privileged minority, and was based on
the degradation, the exclusion, the slavery of most others. The history of
tribes and clans, of social classes and all nations, and of race antipathies in
our own world, is an exemplification of this fight against equality and
inability even to picture its possibility.

The result is that men are conditioned and their actions forced not simply
by their physical environment, powerful as mountains and rain, heat and
cold, forest and desert always have been and will be. When we modify the
effects of this environment by what we call the social environment, we have
conceived a great and important truth. But even this needs further revision.
A man lives today not only in his physical environment and in the social
environment of ideas and customs, laws and ideals; but that total environment
is subjected to a new socio-physical environment of other groups, whose
social environment he shares but in part.

A man in the European sixteenth century was born not simply in the
valley of the Thames or Seine, but in a certain social class and the environment of that class made and limited his world. He was then, consciously or not, not fully a man; he was an artisan and until he complied
with the limitations of that class he was continually knocking his hands,
head and heart against an environment, composed of other classes, which
limited what he could and could not do and what he must do; and this
greater group environment was not a matter of mere ideas and thought; it

was embodied in muscles and armed men, in scowling faces, in the majesty of judge and police and in human law which became divine.

Much as I knew of this class structure of the world, I should never have 4 realized it vividly and fully if I had not been born into its modern counterpart, racial segregation; first into a world composed of people with colored skins who remembered slavery and endured discrimination; and who had to a degree their own habits, customs, and ideals; but in addition to this I lived in an environment which I came to call the white world. I was not an American; I was not a man; I was by long education and continual compulsion and daily reminder, a colored man in a white world; and that white world often existed primarily, so far as I was concerned, to see with sleepless vigilance that I was kept within bounds. All this made me limited in physical movement and provincial in thought and dream. I could not stir, I could not act, I could not live, without taking into careful daily account the reaction of my white environing world. How I traveled and where, what work I did, what income I received, where I ate, where I slept, with whom I talked, where I sought recreation, where I studied, what I wrote and what I could get published—all this depended and depended primarily upon an overwhelming mass of my fellow citizens in the United States, from whose society I was largely excluded.

Of course, there was no real wall between us. I knew from the days of 5 my childhood and in the elementary school, on through my walks in the Harvard yard and my lectures in Germany, that in all things in general, white people were just the same as I: their physical possibilities, their mental processes were no different from mine; even the difference in skin color was vastly overemphasized and intrinsically trivial. And yet this fact of racial distinction based on color was the greatest thing in my life and absolutely determined it, because this surrounding group, in alliance and agreement with the white European world, was settled and determined upon the fact that I was and must be a thing apart.

It was impossible to gainsay this. It was impossible for any time and to 6 any distance to withdraw myself and look down upon these absurd assumptions with philosophical calm and humorous self-control. If, as happened to a friend of mine, a lady in a Pullman car ordered me to bring her a glass of water, mistaking me for a porter, the incident in its essence was a joke to be chuckled over; but in its hard, cruel significance and its unending inescapable sign of slavery, it was something to drive a man mad.

For long years it seemed to me that this imprisonment of a human group 7 with chains in hands of an environing group, was a singularly unusual characteristic of the Negro in the United States in the nineteenth century. But since then it has been easy for me to realize that the majority of mankind has struggled through this inner spiritual slavery and that while a dream which we have easily and jauntily called democracy envisages a day when the environing group looses the chains and compulsion, and is willing and even eager to grant families, nations, subraces, and races equality of opportunity among larger groups, that even this grand equality has not come; and until it does, individual equality and the free soul is impossible. All our present frustration in trying to realize individual equality through communism, fascism, and democracy arises from our continual unwillingness to break the intellectual bonds of group and racial exclusiveness.

Thus it is easy to see that scientific definition of race is impossible; it is easy to prove that physical characteristics are not so inherited as to make it possible to divide the world into races; that ability is the monopoly of no known aristocracy; that the possibilities of human development cannot be circumscribed by color, nationality, or any conceivable definition of race; all this has nothing to do with the plain fact that throughout the world today organized groups of men by monopoly of economic and physical power, legal enactment and intellectual training are limiting with determination and unflagging zeal the development of other groups; and that the concentration particularly of economic power today puts the majority of mankind into a slavery to the rest.

There has been an understandable determination in the United States among both Negro and white thinkers to minimize and deny the realities of racial difference. The race problem has been rationalized in every way. It has been called the natural result of slavery; the effect of poverty and ignorance; the situation consequent upon lack of effort and thought on the part of Americans and of other races. But all this reasoning has its logical pitfalls: granted that poverty causes color prejudice, color prejudice certainly is a cause of poverty. Ignorance leads to exploitation and mistreatment, but the black child is more often forced into ignorance and kept there than the white child. Thus it is impossible for the clear-headed student of human action in the United States and in the world, to avoid facing the fact of a white world which is today dominating human culture and working for the continued subordination of the colored races.

It may be objected here that so general a statement is not fair; that there are many white folk who feel the unfairness and crime of color and race prejudice and have toiled and sacrificed to counteract it. This brings up the whole question of social guilt. When, for instance, one says that the action of England toward the darker races has been a course of hypocrisy, force and greed covering four hundred years it does not mean to include in that guilt many persons of the type of William Wilberforce[1] and Granville Sharpe.[2] On the other hand because British history has not involved the guilt of all Britons we cannot jump to the opposite and equally fallacious conclusion that there has been no guilt; that the development of the British Empire is a sort of cosmic process with no individual human being at fault.

---

[1] *William Wilberforce:* an English politician (1759–1833) who worked for the abolition of the slave trade. [Editors' note.]

[2] *Granville Sharpe:* an abolitionist who worked with Wilberforce. [Editors' note.]

In the history of England, France, America, Germany and Italy, we have villains who have selfishly and criminally desired and accomplished what made for the suffering and degradation of mankind. We have had others who desired the uplift and worked for the uplift of all men. And we have had a middle class of people who sometimes ignorantly and sometimes consciously shifted the balance now here, and now there; and when, in the end, this balance of public opinion, this effective social action, has made for the degradation of mankind or in so far as it has done this, that part of England which has allowed this or made it possible is blood-guilty of the result. So in America, not the philosophy of Jefferson nor the crusade of Garrison[3] nor the reason of Sumner[4] was able to counterbalance the race superiority doctrines of Calhoun,[5] the imperialism of Jefferson Davis,[6] nor the race hate of Ben Tillman.[7] As a result white America has crucified, enslaved, and oppressed the Negro group and holds them still, especially in the South, in a legalized position of inferior caste.

With the best will the factual outline of a life misses the essence of its spirit. Thus in my life the chief fact has been race—not so much scientific race, as that deep conviction of myriads of men that congenital differences among the main masses of human beings absolutely condition the individual destiny of every member of a group. Into the spiritual provincialism of this belief I have been born and this fact has guided, embittered, illuminated and enshrouded my life. Yet, how shall I explain and clarify its meaning for a soul? Description fails—I have tried that. Yet, lest I omit the most important thing in the life of an American Negro today and the only thing that adequately explains his success, failures and foibles, let me attempt its exposition by personifying my white and colored environment. 11

When, for example, the obsession of his race consciousness leaves him, my white friend, Roger Van Dieman (who, I hasten to add, is an abstraction and integration and never existed), is quite companionable; otherwise he is impossible. He has a way of putting an excessive amount of pity in his look and of stating as a general and incontrovertible fact that it is "horrible" to be an Exception. By this he means me. He is more than certain that I prove the rule. He is not a bright person, but of that famous average, 12

---

[3] *Garrison:* William Lloyd Garrison (1805–1879), an American abolitionist. [Editors' note.]

[4] *Sumner:* Charles Sumner (1840–1910), an American abolitionist. [Editors' note.]

[5] *Calhoun:* John Caldwell Calhoun (1782–1850), an American statesman who served as vice president from 1825 to 1832. Later, as a senator from South Carolina, he argued the Southern position in famous pre–Civil War senatorial debates. [Editors' note.]

[6] *Jefferson Davis:* an American statesman (1808–1889) who served as the only president of the Confederacy. [Editors' note.]

[7] *Ben Tillman:* Benjamin Ryan Tillman (1847–1918), an American legislator and white supremacist. [Editors' note.]

standardized and astonished at anything that even seems original. His thesis is simple: the world is composed of Race superimposed on Race; classes superimposed on classes; beneath the whole thing is "Our Family" in capitals, and under that is God. God seems to be a cousin, or at least a blood relative, of the Van Diemans.

"Of course," he says, "you know Negroes are inferior."   13

I admit nothing of the sort, I maintain. In fact, having known with   14
some considerable intimacy both male and female, the people of the British Isles, of Scandinavia, of Russia, of Germany, north and south, of the three ends of France and the two ends of Italy; specimens from the Balkans and black and white Spain; the three great races of Asia and the melange of Africa, without mentioning America, I sit here and maintain that black folk are much superior to white.

"You are either joking or mad," he says.   15

Both and neither. This race talk is, of course, a joke, and frequently it   16
has driven me insane and probably will permanently in the future; and yet, seriously and soberly, we black folk are the salvation of mankind.

He regards me with puzzled astonishment and says confidentially: 17

"Do you know that sometimes I am half afraid that you really believe   18
this? At other times I see clearly the inferiority complex."

The former after lunch, I reply, and the latter before.   19

"Very well," he says, "let's lunch."   20

Where? I ask quizzically, we being at the time in the Roaring Forties.   21

"Why—oh, well—their refusal to serve you lunch at least does not prove   22
your superiority."

Nor yet theirs, I answer; but never mind, come with me to Second   23
Avenue, where Labor lives and food is bad.

We start again with the salad.   24

"Now, superiority consists of what?" he argues.   25

Life is, I remark, (1) Beauty and health of body. (2) Mental clearness   26
and creative genius. (3) Spiritual goodness and receptivity. (4) Social adaptability and constructiveness.

"Not bad," he answers. "Not bad at all. Now I contend that the white   27
race conspicuously excels in beauty, genius, and construction, and is well abreast even in goodness."

And I maintain that the black race excels in beauty, goodness, and   28
adaptability, and is well abreast in genius.

"Sheer nonsense and pure balderdash. Compare the Venus of Milo[8] and   29
the Apollo Belvedere[9] with a Harlem or Beale Street[10] couple."

---

[8] *Venus of Milo:* a Greek marble statue of the goddess Venus, now housed at the Louvre Museum in Paris. [Editors' note.]

[9] *Apollo Belvedere:* a Roman marble statue. [Editors' note.]

[10] *Beale Street:* a street in Memphis, Tennessee, known during the early 1900s for its

I retort: in short, compare humanity at its worst with the Ideal, and   30
humanity suffers. But black folk in most attributes of physical beauty, in
line and height and curve, have the same norms as whites and differ only
in small details of color, hair and curve of countenance. Now can there be
any question but that as colors, bronze, mahogany, coffee and gold are far
lovelier than pink, gray, and marble? Hair is a matter of taste. Some will
have it drab and stringy and others in a gray, woven, unmoving mass.
Most of us like it somewhere between, in tiny tendrils, smoking curls and
sweeping curves. I have loved all these varieties in my day. I prefer the
crinkly kind, almost wavy, in black, brown, and glistening gold. In faces,
I hate straight features; needles and razors may be sharp—but beautiful,
never.

"All that is personal opinion. I prefer the colors of heaven and day: 31
sunlight hair and sky-blue eyes; straight noses and thin lips, and that
incomparable air of haughty aloofness and aristocracy."

And I, on the contrary, am the child of twilight and night, and choose   32
intricately curly hair, black eyes, full and luscious features; and that air of
humility and wonder which streams from moonlight. Add to this voices
that caress instead of rasp, glances that appeal rather than repel, and a
sinuous litheness of movement to replace Anglo-Saxon stalking—there you
have my ideal. Of course, you can bury any human body in dirt and misery
and make it horrible. I have seen the East End of London.

"Beauty seems to be simply opinion, if you put it that way."   33

To be sure. But whose opinion?   34

"Bother beauty. Here we shall never agree. But, after all, I doubt if it   35
makes much difference. The real point is Brains: clear thinking, pure
reason, mathematical precision and creative genius. Now, without blague,[11]
stand and acknowledge that here the white race is supreme."

Quite the contrary. I know no attribute in which the white race has more   36
conspicuously failed. This is white and European civilization; and as a
system of culture it is idiotic, addle-brained, unreasoning, topsy-turvy,
without precision; and its genius chiefly runs to marvelous contrivances for
enslaving the many, and enriching the few, and murdering both. I see
absolutely no proof that the average ability of the white man's brain to
think clearly is any greater than that of the yellow man or of the black
man. If we take even that doubtful but widely heralded test, the frequency
of individual creative genius (when a real racial test should be the frequency
of ordinary common sense)—if we take the Genius as the savior of mankind,

---

legitimate and illegitimate businesses and its bawdy entertainment, and the inspiration for
W. C. Handy's jazz tune "Beale Street Blues."

[11] *blague*: pretentious, boastful, inaccurate talk. [Editors' note.]

it is only possible for the white race to prove its own incontestable superiority by appointing both judge and jury and summoning its own witnesses.

I freely admit that, according to white writers, white teachers, white   37
historians, and white molders of public opinion, nothing ever happened in the world of any importance that could not or should not be labeled "white." How silly. I place black iron-welding and village democracy, and yellow printing and state building, side by side with white representative government and the steam engine, and unhesitatingly give the palm to the first. I hand the first vast conception of the solar system to the Africanized Egyptians, the creation of Art to the Chinese, the highest conception of Religion to the Asiatic Semites, and then let Europe rave over the Factory system.

"But is not well-being more widely diffused among white folk than   38
among yellow and black, and general intelligence more common?"

True, and why? Ask the geography of Europe, the African Slave Trade   39
and the industrial technique of the nineteenth-century white man. Turn the thing around, and let a single tradition of culture suddenly have thrust into its hands the power to bleed the world of its brawn and wealth, and the willingness to do this, and you will have exactly what we have today, under another name and color.

"Precisely. Then, at least, the white race is more advanced and no more   40
blameworthy than others because, as I insist, its native intelligence is greater. It is germ plasm, seed, that I am talking about. Do you believe in heredity?"

Not blindly; but I should be mildly surprised to see a dog born of a cat.   41

"Exactly; or a genius born of a fool."   42

No, no; on the contrary, I rather expect fools of geniuses and geniuses   43
of fools. And while I stoutly maintain that cattiness and dogginess are as far apart as the East from the West, on the other hand, I just as strongly believe that the human ass and the superman have much in common and can often, if not always, spawn each other.

"Is it possible that you have never heard of the Jukes,[12] or of the plain   44
results of hereditary degeneration and the possibilities of careful breeding?"

It is not possible; they have been served up to me ad infinitum. But they   45
are nothing. I know greater wonders: Lincoln from Nancy Hanks,[13] Dumas[14]

---

[12] *Jukes:* the fictitious name of an actual white family that was the subject of a nineteenth-century sociological study of inherited feeblemindedness. Modern sociologists and geneticists have rejected the results of the study. [Editors' note.]

[13] *Nancy Hanks:* Abraham Lincoln's mother (1783–1818). Her ancestry was obscure; most likely, she was illegitimate. [Editors' note.]

[14] *Dumas:* Alexandre Dumas (1802–1870), the French author of *The Count of Monte Cristo* and *The Three Musketeers*. His grandmother, Marie Dumas, was of African ancestry.

from a black beast of burden, Kant[15] from a saddler, and Jesus Christ from a manger.

"All of which, instead of disproving, is exact and definite proof of the persistence of good blood."   46

Precisely, and of the catholicity of its tastes; the method of proof is this: 47
when anything good occurs, it is proof of good blood; when anything bad occurs, it is proof of bad blood. Very well. Now good and bad, native endowment and native deficiency, do not follow racial lines. There is good stock in all races and the outcropping of bad individuals, too; and there has been absolutely no proof that the white race has any larger share of the gifted strains of human heritage than the black race or the yellow race. To be sure, good seed proves itself in the flower and the fruit, but the failure of seed to sprout is no proof that it is not good. It may be proof simply of the absence of manure—or its excessive presence.

Granted, that when time began, there was hidden in a Seed that tiny   48
speck that spelled the world's salvation, do you think today it would manifest itself crudely and baldly in a dash of skin color and a crinkle of hair? Is the subtle mystery of life and consciousness and of ability portrayed in any such slapdash and obvious marks of difference?

"Go out upon the street; choose ten white men and ten colored men.   49
Which can carry on and preserve American civilization?"

The whites.   50

"Well, then."   51

You evidently consider that a compliment. Let it pass. Go out upon the   52
street and choose ten men and ten women. Which could best run a Ford car? The men, of course; but hold. Fly out into the sky and look down upon ten children of Podunk and ten children of Chicago. Which would know most about elevated railroads, baseball, zoology, and movies?

"The point is visible, but beyond that, outside of mere experience and   53
education, and harking back to native gift and intelligence, on your honor, which has most, white folk or black folk?"

There you have me deep in the shadows, beyond the benign guidance of   54
words. Just what is gift and intelligence, especially of the native sort? And when we compare the gift of one human soul with that of another, are we not seeking to measure incommensurable things; trying to lump things like sunlight and music and love? And if a certain shadowy Over-soul can really compare the incomparable with some transcendental yardstick, may we not here emerge into a super-equality of man? At least this I can quite believe.

"But it is a pious belief, not more."   55

Not more; but a pious belief outweighs an impious unbelief.   56

Admitting that the problem of native human endowment is obscure,   57
there is no corresponding obscurity in spiritual values. Goodness and

---

[15] *Kant:* Immanuel Kant (1724–1804), a German philosopher. [Editors' note.]

unselfishness; simplicity and honor; tolerance, susceptibility to beauty in form, color, and music; courage to look truth in the face; courage to live and suffer in patience and humility, in forgiveness and in hope; eagerness to turn, not simply the other cheek, but the face and the bowed back; capacity to love. In all these mighty things, the greatest things in the world, where do black folk and white folk stand?

Why, man of mine, you would not have the courage to live one hour as   58
a black man in America, or as a Negro in the whole wide world. Ah, yes, I know what you whisper to such accusation. You say dryly that if we had good sense, we would not live either; and that the fact that we do submit to life as it is and yet laugh and dance and dream, is but another proof that we are idiots.

This is the truly marvelous way in which you prove your superiority by   59
admitting that our love of life can only be intelligently explained on the hypothesis of inferiority. What finer tribute is possible to our courage?

What great works of Art have we made? Very few. The Pyramids,   60
Luxor,[16] the Bronzes of Benin,[17] the Spears of the Bongo,[18] "When Malinda Sings"[19] and the Sorrow Song she is always singing. Oh, yes, and the love of her dancing.

But art is not simply works of art; it is the spirit that knows Beauty, that   61
has music in its soul and the color of sunsets in its headkerchiefs; that can dance on a flaming world and make the world dance, too. Such is the soul of the Negro.

Why, do you know the two finest things in the industry of the West,   62
finer than factory, shop or ship? One is the black laborer's Saturday off. Neither the whip of the driver, nor the starvation wage, nor the disgust of the Yankee, nor the call of the cotton crop, has yet convinced the common black variety of plantation laborer that one day in the week is enough for rest and play. He wants two days. And, from California to Texas, from Florida to Trinidad, he takes two days while the planter screams and curses. They have beaten the English slavey, the French and German peasants, and the North Italian contadini[20] into twelve-hour, six-day slaves. They crushed the Chinese and Indian coolie into a twenty-four-hour beast of burden; they have even made the American, free, white and twenty-one, believe that daily toil is one of the Ten Commandments. But not the Negro.

---

[16] *Luxor:* an Egyptian city across the Nile from the ruins of Thebes. [Editors' note.]

[17] *Bronzes of Benin:* ancient works of art cast in bronze by artists in the kingdom of Benin, an area of modern-day Nigeria. [Editors' note.]

[18] *Spears of the Bongo:* weapons crafted by the Bongo, a Sudanese people once noted for their metal work. [Editors' note.]

[19] *"When Malinda Sings":* a poem by African-American poet Paul Laurence Dunbar. [Editors' note.]

[20] *contadini:* peasants. [Editors' note.]

From Monday to Friday the field hand is a slave; then for forty-eight golden hours he is free, and through these same forty-eight hours he may yet free the dumb, driven cattle of the world.

Then the second thing, laughter. This race has the greatest of the gifts 63 of God, laughter. It dances and sings; it is humble; it longs to learn; it loves men; it loves women. It is frankly, baldly, deliciously human in an artificial and hypocritical land. If you will hear men laugh, go to Guinea, "Black Bottom," "Niggertown," Harlem. If you want to feel humor too exquisite and subtle for translation, sit invisibly among a gang of Negro workers. The white world has its gibes and cruel caricatures; it has its loud guffaws; but to the black world alone belongs the delicious chuckle.

"But the State; the modern industrial State. Wealth of work, wealth of 64 commerce, factory and mine, skyscrapers; New York, Chicago, Johannesburg, London and Buenos Aires!"

This is the best expression of the civilization in which the white race 65 finds itself today. This is what the white world means by culture.

"Does it not excel the black and yellow race here?" 66

It does. But the excellence here raises no envy; only regrets. If this vast 67 Frankenstein monster really served its makers; if it were their minister and not their master, god and king; if their machines gave us rest and leisure, instead of the drab uniformity of uninteresting drudgery; if their factories gave us gracious community of thought and feeling; beauty enshrined, free and joyous; if their work veiled them with tender sympathy at human distress and wide tolerance and understanding—then, all hail, White Imperial Industry! But it does not. It is a Beast! Its creators even do not understand it, cannot curb or guide it. They themselves are but hideous, groping higher Hands, doing their bit to oil the raging devastating machinery which kills men to make cloth, prostitutes women to rear buildings and eats little children.

Is this superiority? It is madness. We are the supermen who sit idly by 68 and laugh and look at civilization. We, who frankly want the bodies of our mates and conjure no blush to our bronze cheeks when we own it. We, who exalt the Lynched above the Lyncher, and the Worker above the Owner, and the Crucified above Imperial Rome.

"But why have you black and yellow men done nothing better or even 69 as good in the history of the world?"

We have, often. 70

"I never heard of it." 71

Lions have no historians. 72

"It is idiotic even to discuss it. Look around and see the pageantry of 73 the world. It belongs to white men; it is the expression of white power; it is the product of white brains. Who can have the effrontery to stand for a moment and compare with this white triumph, yellow and brown anarchy and black savagery?"

You are obsessed by the swiftness of the gliding of the sled at the bottom 74 of the hill. You say: what tremendous power must have caused its speed, and how wonderful is Speed. You think of the rider as the originator and inventor of that vast power. You admire his poise and *sangfroid*,[21] his utter self-absorption. You say: surely here is the son of God and he shall reign forever and forever.

You are wrong, quite wrong. Away back on the level stretches of the 75 mountain tops in the forests, amid drifts and driftwood, this sled was slowly and painfully pushed on its little hesitating start. It took power, but the power of sweating, courageous men, not of demigods. As the sled slowly started and gained momentum, it was the Law of Being that gave it speed, and the grace of God that steered its lone, scared passengers. Those passengers, white, black, red and yellow, deserve credit for their balance and pluck. But many times it was sheer luck that made the road not land the white man in the gutter, as it had others so many times before, and as it may him yet. He has gone farther than others because of others whose very falling made hard ways iced and smooth for him to traverse. His triumph is a triumph not of himself alone, but of humankind, from the pusher in the primeval forests to the last flier through the winds of the twentieth century.

And so to leave our parable and come to reality. Great as has been the 76 human advance in the last one thousand years, it is, so far as native human ability, so far as intellectual gift and moral courage are concerned, nothing as compared with any one of ten and more millenniums before, far back in the forests of tropical Africa and in hot India, where brown and black humanity first fought climate and disease and bugs and beasts; where man dared simply to live and propagate himself. There was the hardest and greatest struggle in all the human world. If in sheer exhaustion or in desperate self-defense during this last moment of civilization he has rested, half inert and blinded with the sweat of his efforts, it is only the silly onlooker who sees but the passing moment of time, who can think of him as subhuman and inferior.

All this is Truth, but unknown, unapprehended Truth. Indeed, the 77 greatest and most immediate danger of white culture, perhaps least sensed, is its fear of the Truth, its childish belief in the efficacy of lies as a method of human uplift. The lie is defensible; it has been used widely and often profitably among humankind. But it may be doubted if ever before in the world so many intelligent people believed in it so deeply. We deliberately and continuously deceive not simply others, but ourselves as to the truth about them, us, and the world. We have raised Propaganda to a capital "P" and elaborated an art, almost a science, of how one may make the world believe what is not true, provided the untruth is a widely wished-for thing like the probable extermination of Negroes, the failure of Japanese Imperialism,

---

[21] *sangfroid:* cold-bloodedness, cool, composure. [Editors' note.]

the incapacity of India for self-rule, collapse of the Russian Revolution. When in other days the world lied, it was a world that expected lies and consciously defended them; when the world lies today it is to a world that pretends to love truth.

"In other words, according to you, white folk are about the meanest and 78 lowest on earth."

They are human, even as you and I. 79

"Why don't you leave them, then? Get out, go to Africa or to the North 80 Pole; shake the dust of their hospitality from off your feet?"

There are abundant reasons. First, they have annexed the earth and hold 81 it by transient but real power. Thus, by running away, I shall not only not escape them, but succeed in hiding myself in out of the way places where they can work their deviltry on me without photograph, telegraph, or mail service. But even more important than this: I am as bad as they are. In fact, I am related to them and they have much that belongs to me—this land, for instance, for which my fathers starved and fought; I share their sins; in fine, I am related to them.

"By blood?" 82

By Blood. 83

"Then you are railing at yourself. You are not black; you are no Negro." 84

And you? Yellow blood and black has deluged Europe in days past even 85 more than America yesterday. You are not white, as the measurements of your head will show.

"What then becomes of all your argument, if there are no races and we 86 are all so horribly mixed as you maliciously charge?"

Oh, my friend, can you not see that I am laughing at you? Do you 87 suppose this world of men is simply a great layer cake with superimposed slices of inferior and superior races, interlaid with mud?

No, no. Human beings are infinite in variety, and when they are 88 agglutinated in groups, great and small, the groups differ as though they, too, had integrating souls. But they have not. The soul is still individual if it is free. Race is a cultural, sometimes an historical fact. And all that I really have been trying to say is that a certain group that I know and to which I belong, as contrasted with the group you know and to which you belong, and in which you fanatically and glorifyingly believe, bears in its bosom just now the spiritual hope of this land because of the persons who compose it and not by divine command.

"But what is this group; and how do you differentiate it; and how can 89 you call it 'black' when you admit it is not black?"

I recognize it quite easily and with full legal sanction; the black man is 90 a person who must ride "Jim Crow"[22] in Georgia.

---

[22] *Jim Crow:* a slang term for discrimination against African-Americans, often in the form of laws enforcing segregation. [Editors' note.]

My mythical friend Van Dieman is not my only white companion. I have 91 others—many others; one and one especially I want to bring to your attention not because of his attitude toward me but rather because of his attitude toward himself. He represents the way in which my environing white group distorts and frustrates itself even as it strives toward Justice and all because of me. In other words, because of the Negro problem. The average reasonable, conscientious, and fairly intelligent white American faces continuing paradox.

This other friend of mine is free, white, and twenty-one. Which is to 92 say—he is as free as the law and his income, his family and friends, and his formal and informal education allow. He is "white" so far as the records show and as tradition tells; he is not simply twenty-one—he is fifty-one. He is respectable, that is, he belongs to the Episcopal Church, the Union League and Harvard Clubs, and the Republican Party. He is educated, in the sense that he can read if he will, he can write in case his stenographer is absent and he has the privilege of listening to Metropolitan Opera on Tuesdays. He is a Son of the American Revolution, a reserve officer and a member of the American Legion. He reads the *Times* and the *Evening Post* (Saturday); he subscribes for the *Atlantic* and last year he read two books. He also began "Man the Unknown." He owns a home in Westchester assessed at fifty thousand; he drives a Buick. He associates quite often with a wife and a child of fifteen and more often with his fellow employees of the wholesale house which pays him ten thousand a year.

Frankly, my friend faces a dilemma. It is this: his pastor, the Reverend 93 J. Simpson Stodges, D.D., preaches to him Sundays (except July, August and September) a doctrine that sounds like this (I say "sounds" because Dr. Stodges has explanations which mitigate the extremities of his ex cathedra statements): The Doctor asserts in sermons that Peace on Earth is the message of Christ, the Divine leader of men; that this means Good Will to all human beings; that it means Freedom, Toleration of the mistakes, sins and shortcomings of not only your friends but of your enemies. That the Golden Rule of Christianity is to treat others as you want to be treated and that finally you should be willing to sacrifice your comfort, your convenience, your wealth and even your life for mankind; in other words, that Poverty is better than riches and that the meek shall inherit the earth.

Stated thus plainly, this is to my friend's mind pretty stiff doctrine for 94 an ordinary human being in A.D. 1940; and while he believes it in a sense (having been reared in a Godly and Presbyterian household and by a father who spared no rods and spoiled no children), yet, as he puts it to Dr. Stodges in his own parlor, Could a man live up to all that today?

Now, Dr. Stodges out of the pulpit is a most companionable fellow; 95 excellent family, good manners, Oxford accent and Brooks Brothers to-order clothes. He plays keen golf, smokes a rare weed and knows a Bronx cocktail from a Manhattan. Well, the Doctor explained things rather satisfactorily. This Christian business of Peace, Good Will, the Golden

Rule, Liberty and Poverty, was, of course, the Ideal. But, bless your soul, man, we can't all always attain the heights, much less live in their rarefied atmosphere. Aim at 'em—that's the point, and in fact, at least live a Gentleman with the "G" capitalized.

Now my friend is exceedingly anxious to be a gentleman. His father, to 96 be sure, sneered at gentlemen and his grandfather for certain obscure reasons both hated them and denied their existence. His great-great-great-grand-father, whose existence the Media Research Bureau had discovered, was, however, high-bred enough to shoulder a pitchfork against England. But at college, at his club, and with his daily companions it appeared altogether desirable to be genteel—to have manners, an "air," and a tailor. As there was no one to preach gentility in plain words, my friend has gathered this rather vague definition: a Gentleman relies on the Police and Law for protection and self-assertion; he is sustained by a fine sense of Justice for himself and his Family, past and present; he is always courteous in public with "ladies first" and precedence to "gray hairs"; and even in private, he minds his manners and dignity and resists his neighbor's wife; he is charitable, giving to the needy and deserving, to the poor and proud, to inexplicable artists and to the Church. He certainly does not believe in the WPA or other alphabetical ways of encouraging laziness and waste and increasing his taxes. And finally, without ostentation, he is exclusive; picking his associates with care and fine discrimination and appearing socially only where the Best People appear. All this calls for money and a good deal of it. He does not want to be vulgarly and ostentatiously rich. As millionaires go, he is relatively poor, which is poverty as he understands it.

Now my friend knows that this conception lets one in for a certain 97 snobbishness and tendency toward "climbing." And yet it does furnish atmosphere, comfort and a reasonable rule of life for a modern man of position. It is not, of course, the Christianity of the Gospels, nor the career of the Knight Errant; but it is a good, honest, middle path suited to good, honest, middle-aged men.

If the matter halted here, my friend might be vaguely disappointed, but 98 fairly well satisfied. After all, in the workaday life we can't expect moral heroes in quantity. But the trouble is, my friend saw the edges of the Great War (from a swivel chair in America) and he belongs to the American Legion. Also he reads the papers and converses in club lobbies. From this he has assimilated a new and alarming code of action. As Americans we've got to be "prepared" for "defense." Well enough to think of a world of peace, but we haven't got it. Not only that, but the world is not preparing for peace. Everywhere and all over it is not only preparing for war—it is fighting. What is the sense of man, even though he be big, strong, well, sitting down empty-handed while around him are grouped a dozen men armed to the teeth with every device that brains and money can furnish? No, no, this will never do. We've got to have an army and a big army for a big country. We need a militia and a universal draft; we need several big seventy-five million dollar battle-ships with cruisers, airplane carriers and submersibles. We must play expensively at war with elaborate maneuvers. Defense, Preparedness—that's the word.

America must be prepared for all eventualities. England wants her trade, 99 France wants her gold, Germany wants her markets, Russia wants her laborers remade into Bolsheviks. Italy wants her raw material; and above all—Japan! Japan is about to conquer the world for the yellow race and then she'll be ready to swallow America. We must, therefore, be prepared to defend ourselves.

In order to defend America and make an efficient, desirable country, we 100 must have authority and discipline. This may not sound like the Good Will of the Christian but at bottom, it is. There is no use pretending any longer that all men are equal. We know perfectly well that Negroes, Chinamen, Mexicans and a lot of others who are presuming to exercise authority in this country are not our equals. Human beings should be considered as facts and not as possibilities and most of them have no possibilities. Unless, therefore, we have Efficiency—Ability at the top and submission and thrift at the bottom—we are going to come a cropper. Critics may sneer at this and call it caste or fascism, but a country and a world governed by gentlemen for gentlemen is after all the only one worth living in.

There may come some argument as to who should belong to this ruling 101 caste of the Efficient. My friend does not want to be snobbish nor assume too much. Ability will rise. On the whole it would seem that well-bred persons of English descent and New England nurture are the kernel and hope of the land. There will, of course, be modifications in the membership of this group. Without doubt remnants of the Southern slave-holding aristocracy and some of the Mid-Western agrarian stock belong. But we have got to have the best at the top and we know pretty well who the best are.

This hierarchy we should defend vigorously. For this, deliberate prop- 102 aganda is necessary and permissible; propaganda assists the truth and hurries it on; it may at times exaggerate and distort but all this is for a defensible end and newspapers, radio channels, and news distribution agencies should be owned and used for this end. Here comes the necessity of smoking out radicals. Radicals are insidious intellectuals, themselves usually unsuccessful misfits, envious of success and misled by cranks. They not only advocate impossible panaceas but they undermine the safety of the state. If honest and able, they are even more dangerous. They should be sternly dealt with.

Having thus established a country worth saving, patriotism comes next; 103 and patriotism means standing by your country, thick and thin. It means not simply being an American but feeling proud of America and publicly asserting the fact from time to time. Also, it means seeing to it that other people are patriotic; looking about carefully when the "Star-Spangled Banner" is played to see who is sitting down and why; keeping a watchful eye on the flag. Americans traveling abroad, or at any rate white Americans, should, like the English, have such a panoply thrown about them that street urchins will be afraid to make faces and throw stones.

Finally, my friend learned that a nation must not only be powerful; that power must expand; more territory; more commerce; widened influence and that sort of thing. America must no longer be provincial. It must sit among the great powers of the earth, consulted for all world movements. In fact, it is not too much to think of this marvelous country as a sort of super-power, umpire of humanity, tremendous, irresistible. 104

Now all these things intrigue my friend. On his trip to Europe last summer he was made to feel more strongly his Americanism, partly in protest against the outrageous misunderstanding and apparent jealousy of America which he met, and partly from the complacency which swelled his breast when he noted what a great country America was in the eyes of Europe and how everybody was hanging on her lightest whisper. Would she please call a peace conference? Would she please restore the gold standard? Would she kindly sell her raw materials cheap? Would she please lend a helping hand in China and Africa? Would she forbear from completely swallowing South America? And so forth and so on. 105

But there was one difficulty about this code of Americanism which my friend learned; and that was that it led directly and inevitably to another code to which, theoretically, he was definitely opposed, but which, logically, he could not see his way to resist. It was not stated as clearly as any of the other codes; it certainly did not echo in Sunday sermons, although he sometimes suspected it lurked there. It did not enter into his definition of "gentleman" and seemed in fact opposed to it. And yet, somehow, all the gentlemen that he knew were strongly for it. It did seem bound up with his Americanism and yet there again, he resented the logical imputation. 106

The statement of this fourth code of action was found in unfinished assumption rather than plain words; in unfinished sentences, in novels, in editorials written for country papers by city scriveners; in organizations like the Ku Klux Klan which he thought was extremely silly; or the Security League, which was very respectable. This code rested upon the fact that he was a White Man. Now until my friend had reached the age of thirty he had not known that he was a white man, or at least he had not realized it. Certainly, so far as his skin was concerned, he knew that he was not black, brown, or very yellow. But it never occurred to him that there was any divine significance in that rather negative fact. But lately he had come to realize that his whiteness was fraught with tremendous responsibilities, age-old and infinite in future possibilities. It would seem that colored folks were a threat to the world. They were going to overthrow white folk by sheer weight of numbers, destroy their homes and marry their daughters. 107

It was this last point that particularly got upon his nerves. He had, as I've said, a girl of fifteen, rather pretty and fragile; and he and his wife were planning already certain advantageous family and economic alliances 108 for the young miss. Much of their social life was already being guided to this end. Now, imagine a world where she would have to repel the advances of Japanese or Negroes!

He had noticed with some disturbed feeling that Negroes in particular 109 were not nearly as agreeable and happy as they used to be. He had not for years been able to get a cheap, good colored cook and the last black yard man asked quite exorbitant wages. He now had white help. They were expensive but in fashion. He had had only last year to join in a neighborhood association to keep a Negro from buying a lot right in the next block!

Now all this led him to understand, if not to sympathize with, a code 110 which began with War. Not only preparedness nor simply defense, but war against the darker races, carried out now and without too nice discrimination as to who were dark: war against the Riff,[23] the Turk, Chinese, Japanese, Indians, Negroes, Mulattoes, Italians and South Americans. Recently this fact, which he knew perfectly well himself, has been confirmed by that great authority, Charles Lindbergh, who flew into wealth and omniscience through one trip to Paris. War and all that goes to implement war: We must hate our enemies. That sounds heathenish; but there can be no effective war, no determination to fight evil to the death, without full-bellied Hate! We need to lay emphasis upon "white": acting like a "White" man, doing things "white"; "white" angels, etc.; efforts to boost novels which paint white heroes, black devils and brown scoundrels with yellow souls; efforts to use the theater and the movies for the same reason; emphasis upon the race element in crime.

In this matter, too, there cannot unfortunately be too nice an honesty. 111 Self-preservation is a First Law; the crimes and shortcomings of white people, while unfortunate, are incidental; news of them must be ignored or suppressed; crimes of colored people are characteristic and must be advertised as stern warnings. He had noted with surprise and satisfaction that the only place in the movies where Negroes were in special evidence was in jails. That was the only way to make that true which ought to be true and which was true but hidden. War, righteous Hate and then Suspicion. It was very easy to be deceived by other races; to think of the Negro as good-natured; of the Chinaman as simply "queer"; of the Japanese as "imitative." No. Look for low subtle methods and death-dealing ideals. Meet them by full-blooded contempt for other races. Teach this to children so that it will become instinctive. Then they won't get into trouble by playing artlessly with colored children or even with colored dolls unless, of course, they are attired as servants.

Next, Exploitation. No use wincing at the word. No sense in letting 112 Roosevelt and the "New Deal" mislead you. The poor must be poor so that the Rich may be Rich. That's clear and true. It merely means using the

---

[23] *Riff:* a native people of northern Morocco. [Editors' note.]

world for the good of the world and those who own it; bringing out its wealth and abundance; making the lazy and shiftless and ignorant work for their soul's good and for the profit of their betters, who alone are capable of using Wealth to promote Culture.

And finally, Empire: the white race as ruler of all the world and the world working for it, and the world's wealth piled up for the white man's 113 use. This may seem harsh and selfish and yet, of course, it was perfectly natural. Naturally white men would and must rule and any question of their ruling should be met and settled promptly. My friend had not thought that there was any question of this, and there was not before the first World War. There we made the wretched mistake of letting the colored folk dip in, and it turned their weak heads. They almost thought they won the war. He remembered his own disgust at seeing American Negroes actually tricked up as officers—shoulder-straps, Sam Browne belts, and all. He could not conceive of a world where white people did not rule colored people, and certainly if the matter actually came to a trial of force, would he not naturally have to stand for War, Hate, Suspicion and Exploitation in order to put over the Empire of the Whites?

The trouble was, however, that when my friend tabulated all of the codes 114 which he at once and apparently simultaneously was to put in action, he found a most astonishing result, and here it is:

CHRISTIAN	GENTLEMAN	AMERICAN	WHITE MAN
Peace	Justice	Defense	War
Good Will	Manners	Caste	Hate
Golden Rule	Exclusiveness	Propaganda	Suspicion
Liberty	Police	Patriotism	Exploitation
Poverty	Wealth	Power	Empire

Looking them over, he doesn't know what on earth to do. It is not only 115 dilemma, it is almost quadri-lemma. Perhaps he might put a line between "Christian Gentleman" on the one hand and the "American White Man" on the other, and so arrange a very tremendous and puzzling dilemma.

My friend comes and sits down with me and asks me frankly what to do 116 about it. And I? Why, I appeal to you, Gentle Reader. What should he do about it?

My friend's fault is that he is logical. His reasoning is a clean, simple 117 process like two plus two equal four. This is the cause of his present unrest. Other folk are deliciously impervious to reason. They are pacifists with the help of the police and backed by careful preparation for war. They are filled with Good Will for all men, provided these men are in their places and certain of them kept there by severe discountenance. In that case courtesy smooths human relations. They certainly aim to treat others as they want to be treated themselves, so far as this is consistent with their own necessarily exclusive position. This position must be maintained by propaganda inculcating a perfectly defensible contempt for inferiors and suspicion of strangers and radicals. They believe in liberty under a firm police system backed by patriotism and an organization of work which will yield profit to capital. And, of course, they believe in poverty so long as they have sufficient wealth. This they are certain is the way to make America the greatest country on earth for white supremacy.

This makes my friend tear his pale hair. "How can they do it?" he yells. 118 "It ain't reasonable." I explained patiently: possibly they are playing acrostics. See how they might arrange their meanings?

Peace			
	Manners		
		Propaganda	
			Exploitation
Good Will			
	Exclusiveness		
		Patriotism	
			Empire

			Hate
		Propaganda	
	Police		
Poverty			
			War
		Caste	
	Exclusiveness		
Liberty			

"Fact is," I add, "I've heard them singing in St. Thomas's: 119

> The Prince of *Peace* goes forth to *War*
> A *Kingly Crown* to ga-a-ain!
> His *blood-red banner* floats afar.
> Who follows *in his Name!*"

"Your quotation is not exact," responds my literal friend. 120

"Perhaps not, but it comes to the same thing: they combine Peace, War, 121 Empire, Bolshevism and Jesus Christ in one happy family."

My friend waves all this aside. "Outside of spoofing and horse-play," he 122 insists, "it's all both reasonable and impossible. Take each column alone and it is to me absolutely convincing. I believe in it. Think of a world with Peace, Good Will, Freedom, the Golden Rule and Poverty! My God, what a Paradise, despite death and accident, cold and heat—what? That fellow Gandhi is the only human leader today with the right idea. It's magnificent. It's tremendous."

"Plain living and high thinking," I suggest.   123

"Of course," he responds, "only—well, one wants some Beauty—travel, 124 gowns, palaces, diamonds, and Grand Opera—"

I intervene, "But don't forget the preceding lines: 'never to blend our 125 pleasure or our pride, with sorrow of the meanest thing that feels.' "

"But—well, that brings me down out of the clouds," he complains. 126 "This can't be a world of saints. We have got to have wealth and servants. Servants must be cheap and willing and the mean ought not to be so sensitive. Perhaps they are not. But why not have a world of gentlemen— well-policed, everybody in his place; all the rich, courteous and generous and all the poor appreciative; propaganda for the right, love of country and prosperous business; White World leading the Colored as far as the darkies can go. Certainly despite all your democracy, blood will tell. Now that seems to be *practical*. They've got something like that in England. Or at least, they think they have.

"But if I put this thing to the club, as man to man, no sooner have I 127 mentioned England than they're in arms. England, dammit, has a bigger navy and merchant marine than we, with which she monopolizes the world-carrying trade; she patronizes and despises us, and then pats us on the back when her chestnuts are red-hot; she rules a bigger empire. And France won't pay us and has a big black army; and Russia is stirring up Revolution with a big Red army; and Germany! Good Lord! Hitler is anti-Christ. I tell you what, we got to watch out. America is the greatest nation on earth and the world is jealous of her. We got to be prepared if it takes a billion a year for powder and guns. We've got to be disciplined; a stern, severe code for the lazy and criminal; training for boy scouts and militia. We must put patriotism before everything—make 'em salute the flag, stop radical treason, keep out the dirty foreigners, disfranchise niggers and make America a Power!

"Well, I like America. Darn it! I *love* it. My father died for it, although 128 not in war—and I am reasonably willing to. There's no doubt about it, lambs have got no business prowling about lions and—oh, Hell! Honest to God, what do you think Asia and Africa would do to us, if they got a chance?"

"Skin us alive," I answer cheerfully, loving the "us."   129

"Well, then! Skin them and skin 'em first and keep 'em skinned. I'm a 130 He-White-Man, get me?

"Then, look at these other columns. Suppose they are not logical, correct, 131 compelling. We cannot run this world without the police and courts of Justice. We must not be discourteous even to the pushing, careless, impudent American fellow-citizen, but something is due our own self-respect. Can we get on without being exclusive? I don't mean downright snobbishness, but be careful, nice, 'aristocratic' in the best meaning of the term. Finally, we of the upper class must have money. We must have it, no matter how we get it, or civilization is lost.

"Well, now, if we cannot do without these things, then, they must 132 become our rule of life. But no sooner have you settled it this way than there comes that business of being an American. Can we give that up? Can we go in for Humanity and the Internation? Lord knows I'd like to but somehow, I can't see it. Suppose America disarmed like Denmark, gave up poison gas, big battleships and dinky little officers in khaki? Suppose we continue to neglect discipline for the mob and stop teaching thick and thin patriotism? I admit it isn't exactly honest business; America isn't so wonderful as nations go, but must we not make Americans believe it wonderful? Can we emphasize the fact that Lincoln told smutty stories and Washington held slaves and Jefferson begat bastards, and Webster drank more than was good for him? Suppose we did not become powerful as well as big? What is going to happen to us? Well, there you are. We've got to be Americans even if we give up being Christians and Gentlemen."

Or again, and here my friend gets a bit embarrassed and red in the face: 133 "You see," he says to me confidentially, "I've got a little daughter, young yet, but a nice little thing. Probably she is going to be pretty, certainly is going to have some money from her aunt as well as a bit from me. She is being educated, and I may say rather expensively educated, in a private school. She may go in for art or some high class profession, or she may not; but certainly, I hope she will marry and marry well. There will be children and grandchildren and great-grandchildren and so on ad infinitum. Now, I tell you frankly, I want them all white. Even if she were a son, while the case wouldn't be so bad, still I don't want to think of colored folk sharing my blood. Can you for a moment conceive a world where brown men and dagoes[24] were giving orders to white men and women? It would spell the end of civilization. Of course, there may be a few exceptions, but the mass of the colored world can't think, they can't rule, they can't direct, and we mustn't let them try. And to keep them from trying we've got to pound them back into their places every time they show their heads above the ramparts!"

Then my friend stopped. He turned red and grew apologetic. "Of 134 course," he stammered, "I don't exactly mean you—you are an Exception, at least in some respects—"

"In some respects?" I rejoin helplessly. But my friend stiffened. Suddenly 135 he ceased speaking and stared at the headlines in the evening paper. The world had gone to war again to defend Democracy!

---

[24] *dagoes:* a derogatory name for people of Mediterranean, usually Spanish or Italian, ancestry. [Editors' note.]

The democracy which the white world seeks to defend does not exist. It has 136
been splendidly conceived and discussed, but not realized. If it ever is to
grow strong enough for self-defense and for embracing the world and
developing human culture to its highest, it must include not simply the
lower classes among the whites now excluded from voice in the control of
industry; but in addition to that it must include the colored peoples of Asia
and Africa, now hopelessly imprisoned by poverty and ignorance. Unless
these latter are included and in so far as they are not, democracy is a
mockery and contains within itself the seeds of its own destruction.

Hitler is the late crude but logical exponent of white world race philosophy 137
since the Conference of Berlin[25] in 1884. Europe had followed the high,
ethical dream of a young Jew but twisted that ethic beyond recognition to
any end that Europe wanted. If that end was murder, the "Son of God
went forth to war!" If that end was slavery, God thundered, "Cursed be
Canaan," and Paul echoed "Servants obey your masters!" If poverty was
widespread and seemingly inevitable, Christ was poor and alms praiseworthy.

There persisted the mud-sill theory of society that civilization not only 138
permitted but must have the poor, the diseased, the wretched, the criminal
upon which to build its temples of light. Western Europe did not and does
not want democracy, never believed in it, never practiced it and never
without fundamental and basic revolution will accept it. Not the keen, the
bold, the brave and the enlightened are the ones which modern individual
struggle throws to the fore but rather the lucky and the strong.

How now, not so much in the judgment of the common man, but in the 139
light of science, can the racial attitude of the white world be explained and
rationalized and removed from the harsh judgment put upon it by the
darker races today? Negroes in Africa, Indians in Asia, mulattoes and
mestizoes[26] in the West Indies, Central and South America, all explain the
attitude of the white world as sheer malevolence; while the white people of
the leading European countries honestly regard themselves as among the
great benefactors of mankind and especially of colored mankind.

In this dilemma sociologists of earlier years took refuge in inventing a 140
new entity, the group, which had action, guilt, praise and blame quite
apart from the persons composing the group. It was of course a metaphysical
hypothesis which had its uses in reasoning, but could not be regarded as
corresponding to exact truth. No such group over-soul has been proven to
exist.

The facts of the situation however as science today conceives it, are clear. 141
The individual may act consciously and rationally and be responsible for
what he does; but on the other hand many of his actions, and indeed, as we

---

[25] *Conference of Berlin:* This landmark meeting fueled the fires of European imperialism and
led to rapid recolonization of Africa. [Editors' notes.]

[26] *mestizoes:* persons of mixed racial heritage. [Editors' note.]

are coming to believe, most of his actions, are not rational and many of them arise from subconscious urges. It is our duty to assess praise and blame for the rational and conscious acts of men, but to regard the vast area of the subconscious and the irrational and especially of habit and convention which also produce significant action, as an area where we must apply other remedies and judgments if we would get justice and right to prevail in the world. Above all we must survey these vague and uncharted lands and measure their limits.

Looking at this whole matter of the white race as it confronts the world 142 today, what can be done to make its attitudes rational and consistent and calculated to advance the best interests of the whole world of men? The first point of attack is undoubtedly the economic. The progress of the white world must cease to rest upon the poverty and the ignorance of its own proletariat and of the colored world. Thus industrial imperialism must lose its reason for being and in that way alone can the great racial groups of the world come into normal and helpful relation to each other. The present attitude and action of the white world is not based solely upon rational, deliberate intent. It is a matter of conditioned reflexes; of long followed habits, customs and folkways; of subconscious trains of reasoning and unconscious nervous reflexes. To attack and better all this calls for more than appeal and argument. It needs carefully planned and scientific propaganda; the vision of a world of intelligent men with sufficient income to live decently and with the will to build a beautiful world. It will not be easy to accomplish all this, but the quickest way to bring the reason of the world face to face with this major problem of human progress is to listen to the complaint of those human beings today who are suffering most from white attitudes, from white habits, from the conscious and unconscious wrongs which white folk are today inflicting on their victims. The colored world therefore must be seen as existing not simply for itself but as a group whose insistent cry may yet become the warning which awakens the world to its truer self and its wider destiny.

Questions for Discussion and Writing

1. What is the rhetorical effect of DuBois's hypothetical dialogue with his hypothetical white supremacist, Robert Van Dieman? What are the advantages and disadvantages of such strategic devices?

2. Carefully retrace the steps of the argument in which DuBois moves his audience from the peace, good will, golden rule, liberty, and poverty of the "Christian" to the war, hate, suspicion, exploitation, and empire of the "White Man." Do you find this movement from the benign to the malign compelling? Why or why not?

3. Do you agree with DuBois that cultural superiority consists of "(1) Beauty and health of body. (2) Mental clearness and creative genius. (3) Spiritual goodness and receptivity. (4) Social adaptability and constructiveness" (paragraph 26)? Would you assemble a different list of qualifications? Would you seek to abolish such lists all together?

4. Write an argument—perhaps about a political or social issue important to you— in the dialogue form used by DuBois. Be sure that your opposition has a credible position to uphold and is not merely made of straw.

WALLACE STEVENS

(1879–1955)

peaking oxymoronically, Wallace Ste-
vens was an unconventional "square."
He was "square" in the sense that he
worked much of his adult life as an insurance attorney in Hartford, Connecticut.
What he is most remembered for, though, is not his business acumen but his
innovative, influential, and, yes, unconventional poetry, poetry that helped redefine
the American literary scene. But we are getting way ahead of the story.

Stevens, the son of a lawyer, was born in Reading, Pennsylvania. In 1897, he
entered Harvard with the intent of pursuing a literary career. He partook in literary
activities there and, much to his delight, produced a sonnet that earned him the
attention of poet and philosopher George Santayana. After three years at Harvard,
Stevens moved to New York City. A brief stint as a reporter for the New York
Herald Tribune *convinced him that he was unsuited for a career in journalism.*
Instead, he followed his father's lead and entered the New York University Law
School. (At that time, only three years of college were required by some law schools.)
On graduation in 1904, Stevens remained in New York City for a time, working
as an attorney and writing poems on the side. He struggled professionally, but he
moved in an exciting literary circle and befriended fellow poets such as William
Carlos Williams and Marianne Moore. In 1909, he married Elsie Kachel. His first
significant publication was featured in Poetry *in 1914, and from that time on he*
continued to publish steadily in small poetry magazines.

In 1916, Stevens joined the Hartford Accident and Indemnity Company and
moved to Hartford, where he lived for the rest of his life. He did very well with the
company and, as his professional life improved, associated less with his literary
friends. Still his interest in poetry endured. In 1923, he published Harmonium, *his*
first complete volume of poems. Although the book is now considered a classic of
American modernism, it was, like Whitman's first edition of Leaves of Grass,
initially unsuccessful. Fewer than 200 copies were sold, and Stevens was so depressed
over the perceived failure of the book that he virtually quit writing poetry for several
years.

Fortunately, Stevens's interest in composing verse returned. Although an expanded
version of Harmonium, *published in 1931, did not do marvelously well, Stevens*
maintained his commitment to his art. Other volumes of poems such as The Man
with the Blue Guitar *(1937),* Parts of a World *(1942), and* Notes Toward a
Supreme Fiction *(1942) were to follow. He also wrote about literary theory in* The
Necessary Angel *(1951) and* Opus Posthumous *(1957). Like—but very separate*
from—his career at the insurance company (where he became vice president in

1934), Stevens's reputation as a poet improved. Eventually, the greatness of his work was recognized by the literary establishment.

Despite his growing importance as a literary figure, though, Stevens continued to live the conventional life of the corporate vice president. Unlike such globetrotters as William James, he never traveled to Europe. He communicated with his literary friends and admirers by letter, and it is said that many of his business associates had no knowledge of his literary talents until he won the Bollingen Prize in 1950. His Collected Works, published the year before his death, won him his second National Book Award and the Pulitzer Prize.

The poetry of Wallace Stevens is particularly challenging. Although he is not afraid of feelings and often writes of them eloquently, his poems are not always immediately accessible at an emotional level. Very much a poet of ideas, Stevens requires the thoughtful attention of an undistracted mind. His examination of perception, point of view, objectivity, and subjectivity—concepts that were of special interest to intellectuals during the first part of the twentieth century—requires one to pause and ponder the subtle relationships among the persona, the implied author, the implied reader, and the objects presented in the poems. As you analyze "The Snow Man" and "The Idea of Order at Key West," both reprinted here, do not be deceived by the brevity of the work. Read carefully and often, or you may become the victim, rather than the master, of this complex presence.

THE SNOW MAN

One must have a mind of winter
To regard the frost and the boughs
Of the pine-trees crusted with snow;

And have been cold a long time
To behold the junipers shagged with ice,   5
The spruces rough in the distant glitter

Of the January sun; and not to think
Of any misery in the sound of the wind,
In the sound of a few leaves,

Which is the sound of the land   10
Full of the same wind
That is blowing in the same bare place

For the listener, who listens in the snow,
And, nothing himself, beholds
Nothing that is not there and the nothing that is.   15

THE IDEA OF ORDER AT KEY WEST

She sang beyond the genius of the sea.
The water never formed to mind or voice,
Like a body wholly body, fluttering
Its empty sleeves; and yet its mimic motion
Made constant cry, caused constantly a cry,   5
That was not ours although we understood,
Inhuman, of the veritable ocean.

The sea was not a mask. No more was she.
The song and water were not medleyed sound
Even if what she sang was what she heard,   10
Since what she sang was uttered word by word.
It may be that in all her phrases stirred
The grinding water and the gasping wind;
But it was she and not the sea we heard.

For she was the maker of the song she sang.   15
The ever-hooded, tragic-gestured sea
Was merely a place by which she walked to sing.
Whose spirit is this? we said, because we knew
It was the spirit we sought and knew
That we should ask this often as she sang.   20

If it was only the dark voice of the sea
That rose, or even colored by many waves;
If it was only the outer voice of sky
And cloud, of the sunken coral water-walled,
However clear, it would have been deep air,   25
The heaving speech of air, a summer sound
Repeated in a summer without end
And sound alone. But it was more than that,
More even than her voice, and ours, among

The meaningless plungings of the water and the wind,   30
Theatrical distances, bronze shadows heaped
On high horizons, mountainous atmospheres
Of sky and sea.

            It was her voice that made
The sky acutest at its vanishing.   35
She measured to the hour its solitude.
She was the single artificer of the world
In which she sang. And when she sang, the sea,
Whatever self it had, became the self
That was her song, for she was the maker. Then we,   40
As we beheld her striding there alone,
Knew that there never was a world for her
Except the one she sang and, singing, made.

Ramon Fernandez, tell me, if you know,
Why, when the singing ended and we turned   45
Toward the town, tell why the glassy lights,
The lights in the fishing boats at anchor there,
As the night descended, tilting in the air,
Mastered the night and portioned out the sea,
Fixing emblazoned zones and fiery poles,   50
Arranging, deepening, enchanting night.

Oh! Blessed rage for order, pale Ramon,
The maker's rage to order words of the sea,
Words of the fragrant portals, dimly-starred,
And of ourselves and of our origins,   55
In ghostlier demarcations, keener sounds.

Questions for Discussion and Writing

1. Who is the "one" in the opening stanza of "The Snow Man"? Who is the "listener" in the final stanza? In what ways might the speaker's ambiguity be strategic?

2. Why does the speaker in "The Idea of Order at Key West" strive so diligently to separate the song of the sea from the song of the entity referred to as "she"? Why, in this era preceding the Equal Rights Amendment, is it a "she" and not a "he" who sings? Why doesn't the speaker tell us more about this inspirational female presence?

3. Do the snow man and the female entity in "The Idea of Order at Key West" serve similar rhetorical functions? Why or why not?

4. Do Stevens's two poems present similar attitudes toward the natural world and its potential for inspiration? Where, according to Stevens, does reality seem to reside? In the object? In the person who examines the object? Write an essay that addresses one or more of these questions.

VIRGINIA WOOLF

(1882–1941)

Although in many circles she is remembered more for her novelistic accomplishments than her arguments about women's rights and gender equality, Virginia Woolf's impact on feminism has become an extremely important topic in recent years. She has assumed a central role in women's studies programs across the country and has inspired many to take a more careful look at the roles men and women play in society. An emotionally frail person, Woolf wrote courageously to expose the often unconscious sexism that crippled her society—and still hampers ours.

At first glance, perhaps, Woolf appears an unlikely heiress to the women's rights movement championed by such outspoken, hard-shelled warriors as Susan B. Anthony and Emmeline Pankhurst. Woolf, the second daughter of the famous English philosopher-scholar Sir Leslie Stephen, was born in the Kensington section of London. She lost both her parents early, and their deaths shook her deeply. Throughout her entire life, in fact, her psyche was fragile and subject to frequent collapse.

After the death of her father, Woolf moved with her sister and two brothers to Bloomsbury, a Bohemian section of London. There she formed a circle of brilliant young writers and thinkers including the historian Lytton Strachey, novelist E. M. Forster, economist John Maynard Keynes, and Leonard Woolf, whom she married in 1912. This collection of remarkable people, who stood in opposition to traditional Victorian mores and were an important part of the vanguard of modern thought in England, become known as the Bloomsbury Group.

In 1915, Woolf published her first novel, The Voyage Out. Along with Night and Day, published in 1919, this work demonstrated considerable talent, but it was not particularly innovative. In the twenties, however, Woolf began producing bold new fiction that featured the consciousness of her characters, rather than plot, setting, or human interaction as its fundamental subject. Novels such as Jacob's Ladder (1922), Mrs. Dalloway (1925), and To the Lighthouse (1927) forever altered the course of British literature. Waves, her most experimental novel, was published in 1931. Woolf also produced two important works of literary criticism and biography under the title The Common Reader.

Throughout their marriage, Leonard Woolf did his best to protect his wife from distress, but, sadly, the everyday stresses of life, when combined with the extraordinary pressures of writing, took an enormous toll. The strain of her final novel (Between the Acts) and the outbreak of World War II contributed to a depression that led to her suicide in 1941. Excerpts from her diaries, published posthumously in A Writer's Diary (1958), reveal both the subtlety of her mind and the enormity of her pain.

While Woolf was experimenting with novelistic form, she began to write about women's issues. In A Room of One's Own *(1927), excerpted here, she develops an elaborate argument about the systematic suppression of literarily minded women in British society. Although courageous women such as Pankhurst had cleared away some of the grossest inequities toward women that existed in British society, Woolf's generation still faced considerable discrimination toward the "weaker vessel." In much of her writing, Woolf sought to address some of the more covert, yet equally disturbing, elements of sexism. (In 1938, she produced* Three Guineas, *a brilliant antiwar essay that attempts to demonstrate the link between the male ego and violence.)*

Unfortunately, we are able to provide only a glimpse of the subtle argumentation that typifies A Room of One's Own. *In the bulk of the text, Woolf argues that without economic independence and "a room of one's own" in which to work with autonomy and detachment, women cannot be expected to produce great works of literature. She dramatizes the sorry state of women's education in the first part of the twentieth century, and she explains in considerable detail how many famous women writers in the past such as Charlotte Brontë and George Eliot have been limited artistically by their patriarchal times.*

To drive this fundamental point home, Woolf imagines that Shakespeare had a sister named Judith who equaled her brother in native literary talent, but was allowed none of the economic and social rights afforded males. While William reaches the pinnacle of British literature, Judith suffers for her brilliance and dies a wretched, anonymous death. (See the excerpt on pages 14–17 of this book.) After pleading the case for women's independence, Woolf closes her book by arguing for a more androgynous state of mind in both men and women. She suggests that when we think and write merely as men or merely as women, we cloud the objective perspective that is necessary for truly great expression.

FROM A ROOM OF ONE'S OWN

The scene, if I may ask you to follow me, was now changed. The leaves were still falling, but in London now, not Oxbridge;[1] and I must ask you to imagine a room, like many thousands, with a window looking across people's hats and vans and motorcars to other windows, and on the table

---

[1] *Oxbridge:* a word made by combining the names of England's two most prestigious universities, Oxford and Cambridge. The word usually pertains specifically to these schools. Woolf uses it here as the name of an imaginary university with the qualities of Oxford and Cambridge. In the first chapter of *A Room of One's Own*, the narrator Mary Beton visits this imaginary institution and is discouraged by its sexism. [Editors' note.]

inside the room a blank sheet of paper on which was written in large letters WOMEN AND FICTION, but no more. The inevitable sequel to lunching and dining at Oxbridge seemed, unfortunately, to be a visit to the British Museum.[2] One must strain off what was personal and accidental in all these impressions and so reach the pure fluid, the essential oil of truth. For that visit to Oxbridge and the luncheon and the dinner had started a swarm of questions. Why did men drink wine and women water? Why was one sex so prosperous and the other so poor? What effect has poverty on fiction? What conditions are necessary for the creation of works of art?—a thousand questions at once suggested themselves. But one needed answers, not questions; and an answer was only to be had by consulting the learned and the unprejudiced, who have removed themselves above the strife of tongue and the confusion of body and issued the result of their reasoning and research in books which are to be found in the British Museum. If truth is not to be found on the shelves of the British Museum, where, I asked myself, picking up a notebook and a pencil, is truth?

Thus provided, thus confident and enquiring, I set out in the pursuit of truth. The day, though not actually wet, was dismal, and the streets in the neighbourhood of the Museum were full of open coal-holes, down which sacks were showering; four-wheeled cabs were drawing up and depositing on the pavement corded boxes containing, presumably, the entire wardrobe of some Swiss or Italian family seeking fortune or refuge or some other desirable commodity which is to be found in the boarding-houses of Bloomsbury in the winter. The usual hoarse-voiced men paraded the streets with plants on barrows. Some shouted; others sang. London was like a workshop. London was like a machine. We were all being shot backwards and forwards on this plain foundation to make some pattern. The British Museum was another department of the factory. The swing-doors swung open; and there one stood under the vast dome, as if one were a thought in the huge bald forehead which is so splendidly encircled by a band of famous names. One went to the counter; one took a slip of paper; one opened a volume of the catalogue, and . . . . . the five dots here indicate five separate minutes of stupefaction, wonder and bewilderment. Have you any notion how many books are written about women in the course of one year? Have you any notion how many are written by men? Are you aware that you are, perhaps, the most discussed animal in the universe? Here had I come with a notebook and a pencil proposing to spend a morning reading, supposing that at the end of the morning I should have transferred the truth to my notebook. But I should need to be a herd of elephants, I thought, and a wilderness of spiders, desperately referring to the animals that are reputed longest lived and most multitudinously eyed, to cope with all this. I should

[margin: 2]

---

[2] *British Museum:* a museum in London that contains one of the world's largest libraries. [Editors' note.]

need claws of steel and beak of brass even to penetrate the husk. How shall I ever find the grains of truth embedded in all this mass of paper? I asked myself, and in despair began running my eye up and down the long list of titles. Even the names of the books gave me food for thought. Sex and its nature might well attract doctors and biologists; but what was surprising and difficult of explanation was the fact that sex—woman, that is to say— also attracts agreeable essayists, light-fingered novelists, young men who have taken the M.A. degree; men who have taken no degree; men who have no apparent qualification save that they are not women. Some of these books were, on the face of it, frivolous and facetious; but many, on the other hand, were serious and prophetic, moral and hortatory. Merely to read the titles suggested innumerable schoolmasters, innumerable clergymen mounting their platforms and pulpits and holding forth with a loquacity which far exceeded the hour usually allotted to such discourse on this one subject. It was a most strange phenomenon; and apparently—here I consulted the letter M—one confined to the male sex. Women do not write books about men—a fact that I could not help welcoming with relief, for if I had first to read all that men have written about women, then all that women have written about men, the aloe that flowers once in a hundred years would flower twice before I could set pen to paper. So, making a perfectly arbitrary choice of a dozen volumes or so, I sent my slips of paper to lie in the wire tray, and waited in my stall, among the other seekers for the essential oil of truth.

What could be the reason, then, of this curious disparity, I wondered, drawing cart-wheels on the slips of paper provided by the British taxpayer for other purposes. Why are women, judging from this catalogue, so much more interesting to men than men are to women? A very curious fact it seemed, and my mind wandered to picture the lives of men who spend their time in writing books about women; whether they were old or young, married or unmarried, red-nosed or hump-backed—anyhow, it was flatter- ing, vaguely, to feel oneself the object of such attention, provided that it was not entirely bestowed by the crippled and the infirm—so I pondered until all such frivolous thoughts were ended by an avalanche of books sliding down on to the desk in front of me. Now the trouble began. The student who has been trained in research at Oxbridge has no doubt some method of shepherding his question past all distractions till it runs into its answer as a sheep runs into its pen. The student by my side, for instance, who was copying assiduously from a scientific manual, was, I felt sure, extracting pure nuggets of the essential ore every ten minutes or so. His little grunts of satisfaction indicated so much. But if, unfortunately, one has had no training in a university, the question far from being shepherded to its pen flies like a frightened flock hither and thither, helter-skelter, pursued by a whole pack of hounds. Professors, schoolmasters, sociologists, clergymen, novelists, essayists, journalists, men who had no qualification save that they were not women, chased my simple and single question—

Why are women poor?—until it became fifty questions; until the fifty questions leapt frantically into mid-stream and were carried away. Every page in my notebook was scribbled over with notes. To show the state of mind I was in, I will read you a few of them, explaining that the page was headed quite simply, WOMEN AND POVERTY, in block letters; but what followed was something like this:

Condition in Middle Ages of,
Habits in the Fiji Islands of,
Worshipped as goddesses by,
Weaker in moral sense than,
Idealism of,
Great conscientiousness of,
South Sea Islanders, age of puberty among,
Attractiveness of,
Offered as sacrifice to,
Small size of brain of,
Profounder sub-consciousness of,
Less hair on the body of,
Mental, moral and physical inferiority of,
Love of children of,
Greater length of life of,
Weaker muscles of,
Strength of affections of,
Vanity of,
Higher education of,
Shakespeare's opinion of,
Lord Birkenhead's opinion of,
Dean Inge's opinion of,
La Bruyère's opinion of,
Dr. Johnson's opinion of,
Mr. Oscar Browning's opinion of, . . .

Here I drew breath and added, indeed, in the margin, Why does Samuel Butler[3] say, "Wise men never say what they think of women?" Wise men never say anything else apparently. But, I continued, leaning back in my chair and looking at the vast dome in which I was a single but by now somewhat harassed thought, what is so unfortunate is that wise men never think the same thing about women. Here is Pope:[4]

Most women have no character at all.

---

[3] *Samuel Butler:* an English novelist and satirist (1835–1902). [Editors' note.]
[4] *Pope:* Alexander Pope (1688–1744), an English poet. [Editors' note.]

And here is La Bruyère:[5]

> Les femmes sont extrêmes; elles sont meilleures ou pires que les hommes—[6]

a direct contradiction by keen observers who were contemporary. Are they capable of education or incapable? Napoleon thought them incapable. Dr. Johnson[7] thought the opposite.[8] Have they souls or have they not souls? Some savages say they have none. Others, on the contrary, maintain that women are half divine and worship them on that account.[9] Some sages hold that they are shallower in the brain; others that they are deeper in the consciousness. Goethe[10] honoured them; Mussolini despises them. Wherever one looked men thought about women and thought differently. It was impossible to make head or tail of it all, I decided, glancing with envy at the reader next door who was making the neatest abstracts, headed often with an A or a B or a C, while my own notebook rioted with the wildest scribble of contradictory jottings. It was distressing, it was bewildering, it was humiliating. Truth had run through my fingers. Every drop had escaped.

I could not possibly go home, I reflected, and add as a serious contribution to the study of women and fiction that women have less hair on their bodies than men, or that the age of puberty among the South Sea Islanders is nine—or is it ninety?—even the handwriting had become in its distraction indecipherable. It was disgraceful to have nothing more weighty or respectable to show after a whole morning's work. And if I could not grasp the truth about W. (as for brevity's sake I had come to call her) in the past, why bother about W. in the future? It seemed pure waste of time to consult all those gentlemen who specialise in woman and her effect on whatever it may be—politics, children, wages, morality—numerous and learned as they are. One might as well leave their books unopened.

---

[5] *La Bruyère:* Jean de La Bruyère (1645–1696), a French literary figure. [Editors' note.]

[6] *Les femmes . . . hommes—:* Women are extreme; they are either better or worse than men. [Editors' note.]

[7] *Dr. Johnson:* Samuel Johnson (1709–1784), an English man of letters. [Editors' note.]

[8] " 'Men know that women are an overmatch for them, and therefore they choose the weakest or the most ignorant. If they did not think so, they never could be afraid of women knowing as much as themselves.' . . . In justice to the sex, I think it but candid to acknowledge that, in a subsequent conversation, he told me that he was serious in what he said."—Boswell, *The Journal of a Tour to the Hebrides.* [Author's note.]

[9] "The ancient Germans believed that there was something holy in women, and accordingly consulted them as oracles."—Frazer, *Golden Bough.* [Author's note.]

[10] *Goethe:* Johann Wolfgang von Goethe (1749–1832), a German poet, dramatist, and philosopher. [Editors' note.]

But while I pondered I had unconsciously, in my listlessness, in my   5
desperation, been drawing a picture where I should, like my neighbour,
have been writing a conclusion. I had been drawing a face, a figure. It was
the face and the figure of Professor von X. engaged in writing his
monumental work entitled *The Mental, Moral, and Physical Inferiority of
the Female Sex*. He was not in my picture a man attractive to women. He
was heavily built; he had a great jowl; to balance that he had very small
eyes; he was very red in the face. His expression suggested that he was
labouring under some emotion that made him jab his pen on the paper as
if he were killing some noxious insect as he wrote, but even when he had
killed it that did not satisfy him; he must go on killing it; and even so,
some cause for anger and irritation remained. Could it be his wife, I asked,
looking at my picture? Was she in love with a cavalry officer? Was the
cavalry officer slim and elegant and dressed in astrachan? Had he been
laughed at, to adopt the Freudian theory, in his cradle by a pretty girl?
For even in his cradle the professor, I thought, could not have been an
attractive child. Whatever the reason, the professor was made to look very
angry and very ugly in my sketch, as he wrote his great book upon the
mental, moral and physical inferiority of women. Drawing pictures was an
idle way of finishing an unprofitable morning's work. Yet it is in our
idleness, in our dreams, that the submerged truth sometimes comes to the
top. A very elementary exercise in psychology, not to be dignified by the
name of psycho-analysis, showed me, on looking at my notebook, that the
sketch of the angry professor had been made in anger. Anger had snatched
my pencil while I dreamt. But what was anger doing there? Interest,
confusion, amusement, boredom—all these emotions I could trace and name
as they succeeded each other throughout the morning. Had anger, the black
snake, been lurking among them? Yes, said the sketch, anger had. It
referred me unmistakably to the one book, to the one phrase, which had
roused the demon; it was the professor's statement about the mental, moral
and physical inferiority of women. My heart had leapt. My cheeks had
burnt. I had flushed with anger. There was nothing specially remarkable,
however foolish, in that. One does not like to be told that one is naturally
the inferior of a little man—I looked at the student next me—who breathes
hard, wears a ready-made tie, and has not shaved this fortnight. One has
certain foolish vanities. It is only human nature, I reflected, and began
drawing cartwheels and circles over the angry professor's face till he looked
lika a burning bush or a flaming comet—anyhow, an apparition without
human semblance or significance. The professor was nothing now but a
faggot burning on the top of Hampstead Heath. Soon my own anger was
explained and done with; but curiosity remained. How explain the anger
of the professors? Why were they angry? For when it came to analysing the
impression left by these books there was always an element of heat. This
heat took many forms; it showed itself in satire, in sentiment, in curiosity,
in reprobation. But there was another element which was often present and

could not immediately be identified. Anger, I called it. But it was anger that had gone underground and mixed itself with all kinds of other emotions. To judge from its odd effects, it was anger disguised and complex, not anger simple and open.

Whatever the reason, all these books, I thought, surveying the pile on the desk, are worthless for my purposes. They were worthless scientifically, that is to say, though humanly they were full of instruction, interest, boredom, and very queer facts about the habits of the Fiji Islanders. They had been written in the red light of emotion and not in the white light of truth. Therefore they must be returned to the central desk and restored each to his own cell in the enormous honeycomb. All that I had retrieved from that morning's work had been the one fact of anger. The professors—I lumped them together thus—were angry. But why, I asked myself, having returned the books, why, I repeated, standing under the colonnade among the pigeons and the prehistoric canoes, why are they angry? And, asking myself this question, I strolled off to find a place for luncheon. What is the real nature of what I call for the moment their anger? I asked. Here was a puzzle that would last all the time that it takes to be served with food in a small restaurant somewhere near the British Museum. Some previous luncher had left the lunch edition of the evening paper on a chair, and, waiting to be served, I began idly reading the headlines. A ribbon of very large letters ran across the page. Somebody had made a big score in South Africa. Lesser ribbons announced that Sir Austen Chamberlain[11] was at Geneva. A meat axe with human hair on it had been found in a cellar. Mr. Justice ———— commented in the Divorce Courts upon the Shamelessness of Women. Sprinkled about the paper were other pieces of news. A film actress had been lowered from a peak in California and hung suspended in mid-air. The weather was going to be foggy. The most transient visitor to this planet, I thought, who picked up this paper could not fail to be aware, even from this scattered testimony, that England is under the rule of a patriarchy. Nobody in their senses could fail to detect the dominance of the professor. His was the power and the money and the influence. He was the proprietor of the paper and its editor and sub-editor. He was the Foreign Secretary and the Judge. He was the cricketer; he owned the racehorses and the yachts. He was the director of the company that pays two hundred per cent to its shareholders. He left millions to charities and colleges that were ruled by himself. He suspended the film actress in mid-air. He will decide if the hair on the meat axe is human; he it is who will acquit or convict the murderer, and hang him, or let him go free. With the exception of the fog he seemed to control everything. Yet he was angry. I knew that he was angry by this token. When I read what he wrote about women I

6

---

[11] *Sir Austen Chamberlain:* a British statesman (1863–1937). He won the Nobel Peace Prize in 1925. [Editors' note.]

thought, not of what he was saying, but of himself. When an arguer argues dispassionately he thinks only of the argument; and the reader cannot help thinking of the argument too. If he had written dispassionately about women, had used indisputable proofs to establish his argument and had shown no trace of wishing that the result should be one thing rather than another, one would not have been angry either. One would have accepted the fact, as one accepts the fact that a pea is green or a canary yellow. So be it, I should have said. But I had been angry because he was angry. Yet it seemed absurd, I thought, turning over the evening paper, that a man with all this power should be angry. Or is anger, I wondered, somehow, the familiar, the attendant sprite on power? Rich people, for example, are often angry because they suspect that the poor want to seize their wealth. The professors, or patriarchs, as it might be more accurate to call them, might be angry for that reason partly, but partly for one that lies a little less obviously on the surface. Possibly they were not "angry" at all; often, indeed, they were admiring, devoted, exemplary in the relations of private life. Possibly when the professor insisted a little too emphatically upon the inferiority of women, he was concerned not with their inferiority, but with his own superiority. That was what he was protecting rather hot-headedly and with too much emphasis, because it was a jewel to him of the rarest price. Life for both sexes—and I looked at them, shouldering their way along the pavement—is arduous, difficult, a perpetual struggle. It calls for gigantic courage and strength. More than anything, perhaps, creatures of illusion as we are, it calls for confidence in oneself. Without self-confidence we are as babes in the cradle. And how can we generate this imponderable quality, which is yet so invaluable, most quickly? By thinking that other people are inferior to oneself. By feeling that one has some innate superiority—it may be wealth, or rank, a straight nose, or the portrait of a grandfather by Romney[12]—for there is no end to the pathetic devices of the human imagination—over other people. Hence the enormous importance to a patriarch who has to conquer, who has to rule, of feeling that great numbers of people, half the human race indeed, are by nature inferior to himself. It must indeed be one of the chief sources of his power. But let me turn the light of this observation on to real life, I thought. Does it help to explain some of those psychological puzzles that one notes in the margin of daily life? Does it explain my astonishment the other day when Z, most humane, most modest of men, taking up some book by Rebecca West[13] and reading a passage in it, exclaimed, "The arrant feminist! She says that men are snobs!" The exclamation, to me so surprising—for why was Miss

---

[12] *Romney:* George Romney (1734–1802), an English painter who specialized in portraiture. [Editors' note.]

[13] *Rebecca West:* the pseudonym of Cicily Isabel Fairfield (1892–1983), a British novelist and critic. [Editors' note.]

West an arrant feminist for making a possibly true if uncomplimentary statement about the other sex?—was not merely the cry of wounded vanity; it was a protest against some infringement of his power to believe in himself. Women have served all these centuries as looking-glasses possessing the magic and delicious power of reflecting the figure of man at twice its natural size. Without that power probably the earth would still be swamp and jungle. The glories of all our wars would be unknown. We should still be scratching the outlines of deer on the remains of mutton bones and bartering flints for sheep skins or whatever simple ornament took our unsophisticated taste. Supermen and Fingers of Destiny would never have existed. The Czar and the Kaiser would never have worn crowns or lost them. Whatever may be their use in civilised societies, mirrors are essential to all violent and heroic action. That is why Napoleon and Mussolini both insist so emphatically upon the inferiority of women, for if they were not inferior, they would cease to enlarge. That serves to explain in part the necessity that women so often are to men. And it serves to explain how restless they are under her criticism; how impossible it is for her to say to them this book is bad, this picture is feeble, or whatever it may be, without giving far more pain and rousing far more anger than a man would do who gave the same criticism. For if she begins to tell the truth, the figure in the looking-glass shrinks; his fitness for life is diminished. How is he to go on giving judgement, civilising natives, making laws, writing books, dressing up and speechifying at banquets, unless he can see himself at breakfast and at dinner at least twice the size he really is? So I reflected, crumbling my bread and stirring my coffee and now and again looking at the people in the street. The looking-glass vision is of supreme importance because it charges the vitality; it stimulates the nervous system. Take it away and man may die, like the drug fiend deprived of his cocaine. Under the spell of that illusion, I thought, looking out of the window, half the people on the pavement are striding to work. They put on their hats and coats in the morning under its agreeable rays. They start the day confident, braced, believing themselves desired at Miss Smith's tea party; they say to themselves as they go into the room, I am the superior of half the people here, and it is thus that they speak with that self-confidence, that self-assurance, which have had such profound consequences in public life and lead to such curious notes in the margin of the private mind.

But these contributions to the dangerous and fascinating subject of the psychology of the other sex—it is one, I hope, that you will investigate when you have five hundred a year of your own—were interrupted by the necessity of paying the bill. It came to five shillings and ninepence. I gave the waiter a ten-shilling note and he went to bring me change. There was another ten-shilling note in my purse; I noticed it, because it is a fact that still takes my breath away—the power of my purse to breed ten-shilling notes automatically. I open it and there they are. Society gives me chicken and coffee, bed and lodging, in return for a certain number of pieces of

7

paper which were left me by an aunt, for no other reason than that I share her name.

My aunt, Mary Beton, I must tell you, died by a fall from her horse 8 when she was riding out to take the air in Bombay. The news of my legacy reached me one night about the same time that the act was passed that gave votes to women. A solicitor's letter fell into the post-box and when I opened it I found that she had left me five hundred pounds a year for ever. Of the two—the vote and the money—the money, I own, seemed infinitely the more important. Before that I had made my living by cadging odd jobs from newspapers, by reporting a donkey show here or a wedding there; I had earned a few pounds by addressing envelopes, reading to old ladies, making artificial flowers, teaching the alphabet to small children in a kindergarten. Such were the chief occupations that were open to women before 1918. I need not, I am afraid, describe in any detail the hardness of the work, for you know perhaps women who have done it; nor the difficulty of living on the money when it was earned, for you may have tried. But what still remains with me as a worse infliction than either was the poison of fear and bitterness which those days bred in me. To begin with, always to be doing work that one did not wish to do, and to do it like a slave, flattering and fawning, not always necessarily perhaps, but it seemed necessary and the stakes were too great to run risks; and then the thought of that one gift which it was death to hide—a small one but dear to the possessor—perishing and with it my self, my soul,—all this became like a rust eating away the bloom of the spring, destroying the tree at its heart. However, as I say, my aunt died; and whenever I change a ten-shilling note a little of that rust and corrosion is rubbed off; fear and bitterness go. Indeed, I thought, slipping the silver into my purse, it is remarkable, remembering the bitterness of those days, what a change of temper a fixed income will bring about. No force in the world can take from me my five hundred pounds. Food, house and clothing are mine for ever. Therefore not merely do effort and labour cease, but also hatred and bitterness. I need not hate any man; he cannot hurt me. I need not flatter any man; he has nothing to give me. So imperceptibly I found myself adopting a new attitude towards the other half of the human race. It was absurd to blame any class or any sex, as a whole. Great bodies of people are never responsible for what they do. They are driven by instincts which are not within their control. They too, the patriarchs, the professors, had endless difficulties, terrible drawbacks to contend with. Their education had been in some ways as faulty as my own. It had bred in them defects as great. True, they had money and power, but only at the cost of harbouring in their breasts an eagle, a vulture, for ever tearing the liver out and plucking at the lungs—the instinct for possession, the rage for acquisition which drives them to desire other people's fields and goods perpetually; to make frontiers and flags; battleships and poison gas; to offer up their own lives and their children's lives. Walk through the Admiralty Arch (I had reached that monument), or any other avenue given up to trophies and cannon, and reflect upon the kind of glory celebrated there. Or watch in the spring sunshine the stockbroker and the great barrister going indoors to make money and more money and more money when it is a fact that five hundred pounds a year will keep one alive in the sunshine. These are unpleasant instincts to harbour, I reflected. They are bred of the conditions of life; of the lack of civilisation, I thought, looking at the state of the Duke of Cambridge, and in particular at the feathers in his cocked hat, with a fixity that they have scarcely ever received before. And, as I realised these drawbacks, by degrees fear and bitterness modified themselves into pity and toleration; and then in a year or two, pity and toleration went, and the greatest release of all came, which is freedom to think of things in themselves. That building, for example, do I like it or not? Is that picture beautiful or not? Is that in my opinion a good book or a bad? Indeed my aunt's legacy unveiled the sky to me, and substituted for the large and imposing figure of a gentleman, which Milton[14] recommended for my perpetual adoration, a view of the open sky.

So thinking, so speculating I found my way back to my house by the river. Lamps were being lit and an indescribable change had come over London since the morning hour. It was as if the great machine after labouring all day had made with our help a few yards of something very exciting and beautiful—a fiery fabric flashing with red eyes, a tawny monster roaring with hot breath. Even the wind seemed flung like a flag as it lashed the houses and rattled the hoardings.   9

In my little street, however, domesticity prevailed. The house painter   10 was descending his ladder; the nursemaid was wheeling the perambulator carefully in and out back to nursery tea; the coal-heaver was folding his empty sacks on top of each other; the woman who keeps the greengrocer's shop was adding up the day's takings with her hands in red mittens. But so engrossed was I with the problem you have laid upon my shoulders that I could not see even these usual sights without referring them to one centre. I thought how much harder it is now than it must have been even a century ago to say which of these employments is the higher, the more necessary. Is it better to be a coal-heaver or a nursemaid; is the charwoman who has brought up eight children of less value to the world than the barrister who has made a hundred thousand pounds? It is useless to ask such questions; for nobody can answer them. Not only do the comparative values of charwomen and lawyers rise and fall from decade to decade, but we have no rods with which to measure them even as they are at the moment. I had been foolish to ask my professor to furnish me with "indisputable proofs" of this or that in his argument about women. Even if one could state the

---

[14] *Milton:* John Milton (1608–1674), an English poet and the author of *Paradise Lost.* [Editors' note.]

value of any one gift at the moment, those values will change; in a century's time very possibly they will have changed completely. Moreover, in a hundred years, I thought, reaching my own doorstep, women will have ceased to be the protected sex. Logically they will take part in all the activities and exertions that were once denied them. The nursemaid will heave coal. The shopwoman will drive an engine. All assumptions founded on the facts observed when women were the protected sex will have disappeared—as, for example (here a squad of soldiers marched down the street), that women and clergymen and gardeners live longer than other people. Remove that protection, expose them to the same exertions and activities, make them soldiers and sailors and engine-drivers and dock labourers, and will not women die off so much younger, so much quicker, than men that one will say, "I saw a woman to-day", as one used to say, "I saw an aeroplane". Anything may happen when womanhood has ceased to be a protected occupation, I thought, opening the door. But what bearing has all this upon the subject of my paper, Women and Fiction? I asked, going indoors.

Questions for Discussion and Writing

1. In presenting this narrative, Woolf employs a fictitious persona named "Mary Beton," an "I" that is, according to the narrator in her introduction, "a convenient term for somebody who has no real being." Based on the section of *A Room of One's Own* that you have read, how would you characterize the ethos of this artificial "I"? What are the rhetorical reasons for its presence? How would you go about comparing the ethos of this "I" with the ethos of the implied author?

2. In paragraph 6 of this excerpt, Mary Beton states, "When an arguer argues dispassionately he thinks only of the argument; and the reader cannot help thinking of the argument too." In a later section of the narrative (not reprinted here), the point is extended when Mary argues that "it is fatal for anyone who writes to think of their sex. . . . It is fatal for a woman to lay the least stress on any grievance; to plead even with justice any cause; in any way to speak consciously as a woman." Do you agree with Woolf's argument? Is dispassionate, gender-neutral prose rhetorically more effective than passionate, gender-specific writing? From the section you have read, does *A Room of One's Own* seem to help support or undermine Woolf's case?

3. In her introduction, Woolf argues that "when a subject is highly controversial—and any question about sex is that—one cannot hope to tell the truth." Is she right? Is "sex" still a controversial subject in the 1990s? Are Woolf's contentions about sex still valid in the contemporary scene?

4. Do not institutions of higher learning depend on the very hierarchy and competition that Woolf condemns? Do you believe that these traditionally male practices should be deemphasized? If we followed Woolf's advice, how would our colleges and universities be affected? Would the net change be positive? Write an essay that addresses the highly controversial issues broached in these questions.

WILLIAM CARLOS WILLIAMS

(1883–1963)

*L*ike fellow poet Wallace Stevens, William Carlos Williams lived a double life of sorts. Although he is now best known to the world for breaking new ground in the form and content of American poetry, to the people of Rutherford, New Jersey, he was simply Dr. Williams, town physician. Williams, in fact, was a native of Rutherford. Because his mother was from Puerto Rico, he grew up speaking both English and Spanish, and his cultured parents imbued him from an early age with an appreciation for art and literature. As a schoolboy, he visited Paris for several months and spent a year in Switzerland.

After high school, Williams entered the School of Medicine at the University of Pennsylvania as a dental student (at that time, a college degree was not required for some medical schools), but he soon switched his emphasis to medicine. While studying medicine, he met future literary figures such as H. D. (Hilda Doolittle), Marianne Moore, and Ezra Pound. With Pound he established an enduring friendship. He wrote poetry during this time and even self-published a book of verse, but it was derivative and relatively uninteresting. The poet himself described his early output as "bad Keats." Williams graduated from medical school in 1906 and received postgraduate pediatrics training in Europe before returning to his home town to begin his practice. He married his former sweetheart's younger sister and settled into domestic life and general medicine.

Despite the pressures and responsibilities of his growing new practice and family, Williams continued to hone his literary skills in Rutherford. Venturing into New York City, he associated with fellow poets such as Moore and Wallace Stevens and kept abreast of the changes in the art world brought about by the ferment of modernism, a movement in art and literature stressing a deliberate break with tradition and a search for new forms of expression. His second book of poetry, The Tempers, was published in 1913 with the help of Ezra Pound. Al Que Quiere! (1917) and Kora in Hell: Improvisations (1920) demonstrated Williams's experimental temperament, as did Sour Grapes (1921) and his breakthrough book Spring and All (1923). Williams continued to violate traditional expectations for poetic form as he emphasized distinctively American themes. Like Whitman, who presented nineteenth-century America in all its glorious confusion, he attempted to capture the pulse of the new twentieth-century American culture.

During the 1920s Williams continued to publish poetry, but he also produced some important prose works, including the historical and social commentary In the American Grain (1925). His "epic" poem, Paterson, an innovative attempt to use this New Jersey town to tell America's story, was published in five volumes during the 1940s and 1950s. Williams also wrote short stories—many about his unusual *experiences as a doctor—and collected some of them in* The Farmers' Daughters, *published in 1961. He even experimented with longer fiction, producing a trilogy of novels between 1937 and 1952. With the National Book Award for poetry in 1950 and the Bollingen Prize in 1953 came the literary recognition Williams had long deserved. He became a popular lecturer and an inspiration for many younger poets such as Allen Ginsberg, Robert Lowell, Kenneth Rexroth, and Denise Levertov. He was awarded the Pulitzer Prize posthumously for* Pictures from Brueghel, and Other Poems *(1962).*

On first glance, Williams's poetry appears relatively easy. After reading Stevens, we are tempted to view William Carlos Williams as a "quick fix" and then move on. This approach, however, would be a mistake. The surfaces of Williams's poetry may appear more sensual and less cerebral, less intellectually complex than those of a poet such as Stevens, but much is going on in poems such as "To Elsie" and "At the Ball Game" (both featured here) that requires our careful attention. Williams's lines are concise, but they require considerable unpacking.

TO ELSIE

The pure products of America
go crazy—
mountain folk from Kentucky

or the ribbed north end of
Jersey   5
with its isolate lakes and

valleys, its deaf-mutes, thieves
old names
and promiscuity between

devil-may-care men who have taken   10
to railroading
out of sheer lust of adventure—

and young slatterns, bathed
in filth
from Monday to Saturday   15

to be tricked out that night
with gauds
from imaginations which have no

peasant traditions to give them
character
but flutter and flaunt   20

sheer rags—succumbing without
emotion
save numbed terror

under some hedge of choke-cherry   25
or viburnum—
which they cannot express—

Unless it be that marriage
perhaps
with a dash of Indian blood   30

will throw up a girl so desolate
so hemmed round
with disease or murder

that she'll be rescued by an
agent—   35
reared by the state and

sent out at fifteen to work in
some hard-pressed
house in the suburbs—

some doctor's family, some Elsie—   40
voluptuous water
expressing with broken

brain the truth about us—
her great
ungainly hips and flopping breasts   45

addressed to cheap
jewelry
and rich young men with fine eyes

as if the earth under our feet
were   50
an excrement of some sky

and we degraded prisoners
destined
to hunger until we eat filth

while the imagination strains   55
after deer
going by fields of goldenrod in

the stifling heat of September
Somehow
it seems to destroy us   60

It is only in isolate flecks that
something
is given off

No one
to witness   65
and adjust, no one to drive the car

AT THE BALL GAME

The crowd at the ball game
is moved uniformly

by a spirit of uselessness
which delights them—

all the exciting detail   5
of the chase

and the escape, the error
the flash of genius—

all to no end save beauty
the eternal—   10

So in detail they, the crowd,
are beautiful

for this
to be warned against

saluted and defied—   15
It is alive, venomous

it smiles grimly
its words cut—

The flashy female with her
mother, gets it—   20

The Jew gets it straight—it
is deadly, terrifying—

It is the Inquisition, the
Revolution

It is beauty itself   25
that lives

day by day in them
idly—

This is
the power of their faces   30

It is summer, it is the solstice
the crowd is

cheering, the crowd is laughing
in detail

permanently, seriously   35
without thought

Questions for Discussion and Writing

1. In "To Elsie," not only do the "pure products of America go crazy," so do the
   images of the poem itself. This is especially true toward the end of the piece,
   when the persona moves from earth, to excrement, to prisoners, to deer, to
   "isolate flecks," to automobiles. What is the rhetorical function of such rapid
   movement? Is there method to this apparent madness?

2. Williams's depiction of our national pastime in "At the Ball Game" seems highly unorthodox. Is this poem about baseball, or is there a larger point to be made here?

3. If "To Elsie" were a freshman composition, the instructor might note with considerable disapproval the ambiguous "it" and "something" that complicate the final stanzas. In "At the Ball Game," as well, Williams makes great use of ambiguous references. A mysterious "it" is alive, venomous, smiling, and so on. To what do these ambiguous references refer? Why do you suppose Williams engages in such ambiguity? What is its rhetorical function?

4. In both poems, the speakers seem deeply disturbed by the potential for violence present in American culture. What seems to be the nature of this violence? What is its cause? Does Williams suggest or imply a solution? Is his analysis of American violence applicable today? Write an essay that addresses one or more of these questions.

ROLAND BARTHES

(1915–1980)

Roland Barthes, considered by many to be the most important French intellectual since Jean-Paul Sartre, was born in Cherbourg. Although recurring bouts of tuberculosis slowed his educational progress, he earned degrees from the University of Paris in classical letters (1939) and grammar and philosophy (1943). Barthes taught French in Romania and Egypt before he assumed the directorship of the social science section of the École Practique des Haut Études in Paris in 1960. By that time, he had already published two important works: Writing Degree Zero (1953), which discusses the merits of various prose styles, and Mythologies (1957), an analysis of French culture. Barthes remained at this job until 1977 and continued to produce provocative books on a wide variety of subjects. On Racine (1963), an innovative analysis of the seventeenth-century French playwright, shocked the world of "establishment" literary criticism. Criticism and Truth (1966) called for a new science of literary criticism based on linguistics. S/Z (1970), an interpretation of Balzac's short story "Sarrasine," set new standards for the "close reading" of literature. The Pleasures of the Text (1973) focused on the reader's role in literature, and Roland Barthes, a literary autobiography, emphasized his own role as a reader of texts. From 1977 till his death in a traffic accident, Barthes served as chair of literary semiology at the Collége de France.

To do full justice to Barthes's contributions to society and the complexity of his arguments, we should review some of the most important influences on his work. First, Barthes was fascinated by the twentieth-century intellectual movement known as Structuralism, which sought to uncover the fundamental organizing principles informing human behavior and cultural artifacts. Structuralism began in the early part of the century with Ferdinand de Saussure's study of linguistics. Early Structuralist linguists looked for the unstated but implicitly understood system of abstract rules and codes that lies behind any set of specific utterances. As Structuralism expanded to encompass anthropology, narrative analysis, and literary studies, its proponents searched for the ways that individual actions, artifacts, narratives, and literary works fit into more general systems of meaning. With an understanding of these larger patterns, they believed, a greater knowledge of human nature could be achieved.

Semiotics, a part of the Structuralist enterprise that focuses specifically on symbols (or "signs") and symbolic processes, was especially important to Barthes's work. Typical examples of Barthes's application of semiotics are The System of Fashion (1967), which explores how clothing functions as a symbolic code, and Empire of Signs (1970), which discusses the symbolic value of Japanese food, writing, dining rituals, movie images, and pinball games. In fact, one could argue that Barthes's most enduring accomplishment was to popularize this intriguing branch of Structuralism.

A second significant influence on Barthes was Marxism. He was concerned about issues of class structure and worked to reveal the ways in which the dominant class imposes its values on less advantaged, less powerful segments of society. Third, Barthes was drawn to Freud and sought to uncover the unconscious—often sexual—elements in the texts he analyzed. Both On Racine and S/Z exhibit a Freudian perspective. Finally, Barthes had an abiding interest in avant-garde French writers. Strongly influenced by Sartre's individualistic Existentialism, he questioned traditional, sacrosanct approaches to literature and life. Both The Pleasures of the Text and Roland Barthes emphasize the reader's right to read and then interpret a text as he or she pleases. It is, for Barthes, ultimately the interpreter, not the original creator, who gives the text its essential character and value.

It should come as no surprise that Barthes's work has caused considerable controversy. Consider, for example, two critics' comments about On Racine. Wrote Raymond Picard: "This work disregards the elementary rules of scientific, or quite simply articulate, thought." In contrast, Thomas Merton said: "It is a masterpiece of literary criticism. . . . The criticism goes far beyond Racine himself. It gets at the roots not only of French civilization, but of the entire culture of the Western world."

Mythologies, a wonderfully eclectic text, illustrates Barthes's leadership in interdisciplinary studies. It is semiotic and anthropological in its elucidation of the symbolic meanings of the "extra-linguistic languages" contained in French culture through analyses of toys, fashion, striptease, personality cults, literature, advertising campaigns, and sporting events. The text is Freudian in its quest to determine the unconscious meanings behind the cultural artifacts he analyzes. The influence of Marxism can be seen in the concept of "mythology" itself. Barthes argues that the symbolic meanings behind many components of French culture serve to reinforce the oppressive mythologies perpetuated by the dominant bourgeois class. To give you a taste of Barthes's interdisciplinary abilities, we have reprinted the opening essay from Mythologies. As you read "The World of Wrestling," focus special attention on the overall meanings Barthes ascribes to this extremely popular spectacle. Barthes's prose style is at times difficult to understand, but he is always provocative.

THE WORLD OF WRESTLING

The grandiloquent truth of gestures on life's great occasions.

Baudelaire[1]

The virtue of all-in wrestling is that it is the spectacle of excess. Here we   1
find a grandiloquence which must have been that of ancient theatres. And
in fact wrestling is an open-air spectacle, for what makes the circus or the
arena what they are is not the sky (a romantic value suited rather to
fashionable occasions), it is the drenching and vertical quality of the flood
of light. Even hidden in the most squalid Parisian halls, wrestling partakes
of the nature of the great solar spectacles, Greek drama and bullfights: in
both, a light without shadow generates an emotion without reserve.

There are people who think that wrestling is an ignoble sport. Wrestling   2
is not a sport, it is a spectacle, and it is no more ignoble to attend a wrestled
performance of Suffering than a performance of the sorrows of Arnolphe
or Andromaque.[2] Of course, there exists a false wrestling, in which the
participants unnecessarily go to great lengths to make a show of a fair fight;
this is of no interest. True wrestling, wrongly called amateur wrestling, is
performed in second-rate halls, where the public spontaneously attunes itself
to the spectacular nature of the contest, like the audience at a suburban
cinema. Then these same people wax indignant because wrestling is a stage-
managed sport (which ought, by the way, to mitigate its ignominy). The
public is completely uninterested in knowing whether the contest is rigged
or not, and rightly so; it abandons itself to the primary virtue of the
spectacle, which is to abolish all motives and all consequences: what matters
is not what it thinks but what it sees.

This public knows very well the distinction between wrestling and boxing;   3
it knows that boxing is a Jansenist[3] sport, based on a demonstration of
excellence. One can bet on the outcome of a boxing-match: with wrestling,
it would make no sense. A boxing-match is a story which is constructed
before the eyes of the spectator; in wrestling, on the contrary, it is each
moment which is intelligible, not the passage of time. The spectator is not
interested in the rise and fall of fortunes; he expects the transient image of
certain passions. Wrestling therefore demands an immediate reading of the
juxtaposed meanings, so that there is no need to connect them. The logical

---

[1] *Baudelaire:* Charles Pierre Baudelaire (1821–1867), a French poet and critic. [Editors'
note.]

[2] In Molière's *L'École des Femmes* and Racine's *Andromaque*. [Translator's note.]
Jean Baptiste Poquelin Molière (1622–1673) was a French actor and playwright. Jean
Baptiste Racine (1639–1699) was a French playwright. [Editors' note.]

[3] *Jansenist:* in the spirit of Cornelius Otto Jansen (1585–1638), a Dutch theologian who
emphasized preordained determinism over free will. [Editors' note.]

conclusion of the contest does not interest the wrestling-fan, while on the contrary a boxing-match always implies a science of the future. In other words, wrestling is a sum of spectacles, of which no single one is a function: each moment imposes the total knowledge of a passion which rises erect and alone, without ever extending to the crowning moment of a result.

Thus the function of the wrestler is not to win; it is to go exactly through 4 the motions which are expected of him. It is said that judo contains a hidden symbolic aspect; even in the midst of efficiency, its gestures are measured, precise but restricted, drawn accurately but by a stroke without volume. Wrestling, on the contrary, offers excessive gestures, exploited to the limit of their meaning. In judo, a man who is down is hardly down at all, he rolls over, he draws back, he eludes defeat, or, if the latter is obvious, he immediately disappears; in wrestling, a man who is down is exaggeratedly so, and completely fills the eyes of the spectators with the intolerable spectacle of his powerlessness.

This function of grandiloquence is indeed the same as that of ancient 5 theatre, whose principle, language and props (masks and buskins) concurred in the exaggeratedly visible explanation of a Necessity. The gesture of the vanquished wrestler signifying to the world a defeat which, far from disguising, he emphasizes and holds like a pause in music, corresponds to the mask of antiquity meant to signify the tragic mode of the spectacle. In wrestling, as on the stage in antiquity, one is not ashamed of one's suffering, one knows how to cry, one has a liking for tears.

Each sign in wrestling is therefore endowed with an absolute clarity, 6 since one must always understand everything on the spot. As soon as the adversaries are in the ring, the public is overwhelmed with the obviousness of the roles. As in the theatre, each physical type expresses to excess the part which has been assigned to the contestant. Thauvin, a fifty-year-old with an obese and sagging body, whose type of asexual hideousness always inspires feminine nicknames, displays in his flesh the characters of baseness, for his part is to represent what, in the classical concept of the *salaud*, the "bastard" (the key-concept of any wrestling-match), appears as organically repugnant. The nausea voluntarily provoked by Thauvin shows therefore a very extended use of signs: not only is ugliness used here in order to signify baseness, but in addition ugliness is wholly gathered into a particularly repulsive quality of matter: the pallid collapse of dead flesh (the public calls Thauvin *la barbaque*, "stinking meat"), so that the passionate condemnation of the crowd no longer stems from its judgment, but instead from the very depth of its humours. It will thereafter let itself be frenetically embroiled in an idea of Thauvin which will conform entirely with this physical origin: his actions will perfectly correspond to the essential viscosity of his personage.

It is therefore in the body of the wrestler that we find the first key to the 7 contest. I know from the start that all of Thauvin's actions, his treacheries, cruelties and acts of cowardice, will not fail to measure up to the first image of ignobility he gave me; I can trust him to carry out intelligently and to the last detail all the gestures of a kind of amorphous baseness, and thus fill to the brim the image of the most repugnant bastard there is: the bastard-octopus. Wrestlers therefore have a physique as peremptory as those of the characters of the *Commedia dell' Arte*,[4] who display in advance, in their costumes and attitudes, the future contents of their parts: just as Pantaloon can never be anything but a ridiculous cuckold, Harlequin an astute servant and the Doctor a stupid pedant, in the same way Thauvin will never be anything but an ignoble traitor, Reinières (a tall blond fellow with a limp body and unkempt hair) the moving image of passivity, Mazaud (short and arrogant like a cock) that of grotesque conceit, and Orsano (an effeminate teddy-boy first seen in a blue-and-pink dressing-gown) that, doubly humorous, of a vindictive *salope*, or bitch (for I do not think that the public of the Elysée-Montmartre,[5] like Littré,[6] believes the word *salope* to be a masculine).

The physique of the wrestlers therefore constitutes a basic sign, which like a seed contains the whole fight. But this seed proliferates, for it is at every turn during the fight, in each new situation, that the body of the wrestler casts to the public the magical entertainment of a temperament which finds its natural expression in a gesture. The different strata of meaning throw light on each other, and form the most intelligible of spectacles. Wrestling is like a diacritic writing: above the fundamental meaning of his body, the wrestler arranges comments which are episodic but always opportune, and constantly help the reading of the fight by means of gestures, attitudes and mimicry which make the intention utterly obvious. Sometimes the wrestler triumphs with a repulsive sneer while kneeling on the good sportsman; sometimes he gives the crowd a conceited smile which forebodes an early revenge; sometimes, pinned to the ground, he hits the floor ostentatiously to make evident to all the intolerable nature of his situation; and sometimes he erects a complicated set of signs meant to make the public understand that he legitimately personifies the ever-entertaining image of the grumbler, endlessly confabulating about his displeasure.

We are therefore dealing with a real Human Comedy, where the most socially inspired nuances of passion (conceit, rightfulness, refined cruelty, a sense of "paying one's debts") always felicitously find the clearest sign which can receive them, express them and triumphantly carry them to the confines of the hall. It is obvious that at such a pitch, it no longer matters whether the passion is genuine or not. What the public wants is the image

---

[4] *Commedia dell' Arte:* a genre of Italian popular comedy, which flourished from the sixteenth to the early eighteenth century, noted for its stock characters and situations. [Editors' note.]

[5] *Elysée-Montmartre:* two districts of Paris. Barthes may be attributing snobbish tendencies to the residents of these districts. [Editors' note.]

[6] *Littré:* Maximilien Paul Emile Littré (1801–1881), a French lexicographer. [Editors' note.]

of passion, not passion itself. There is no more a problem of truth in wrestling than in the theatre. In both, what is expected is the intelligible representation of moral situations which are usually private. This emptying out of interiority to the benefit of its exterior signs, this exhaustion of the content by the form, is the very principle of triumphant classical art. Wrestling is an immediate pantomime, infinitely more efficient than the dramatic pantomime, for the wrestler's gesture needs no anecdote, no decor, in short no transference in order to appear true.

Each moment in wrestling is therefore like an algebra which instanta-   10 neously unveils the relationship between a cause and its represented effect. Wrestling fans certainly experience a kind of intellectual pleasure in *seeing* the moral mechanism function so perfectly. Some wrestlers, who are great comedians, entertain as much as a Molière character, because they succeed in imposing an immediate reading of their inner nature: Armand Mazaud, a wrestler of an arrogant and ridiculous character (as one says that Harpagon[7] is a character), always delights the audience by the mathematical rigour of his transcriptions, carrying the form of his gestures to the furthest reaches of their meaning, and giving to his manner of fighting the kind of vehemence and precision found in a great scholastic disputation, in which what is at stake is at once the triumph of pride and the formal concern with truth.

What is thus displayed for the public is the great spectacle of Suffering,   11 Defeat, and Justice. Wrestling presents man's suffering with all the amplification of tragic masks. The wrestler who suffers in a hold which is reputedly cruel (an arm-lock, a twisted leg) offers an excessive portrayal of Suffering; like a primitive Pietà,[8] he exhibits for all to see his face, exaggeratedly contorted by an intolerable affliction. It is obvious, of course, that in wrestling reserve would be out of place, since it is opposed to the voluntary ostentation of the spectacle, to this Exhibition of Suffering which is the very aim of the fight. This is why all the actions which produce suffering are particularly spectacular, like the gesture of a conjuror who holds out his cards clearly to the public. Suffering which appeared without intelligible cause would not be understood; a concealed action that was actually cruel would transgress the unwritten rules of wrestling and would have no more sociological efficacy than a mad or parasitic gesture. On the contrary suffering appears as inflicted with emphasis and conviction, for everyone must not only see that the man suffers, but also and above all understand why he suffers. What wrestlers call a hold, that is, any figure which allows one to immobilize the adversary indefinitely and to have him at one's mercy, has precisely the function of preparing in a conventional, therefore intelligible, fashion the spectacle of suffering, of methodically

---

[7] In Molière's *L'Avare*. [Translator's note.]

[8] *Pietà:* a devotional representation of Mary, mother of Jesus, mourning over the body of her dead son. [Editors' note.]

establishing the conditions of suffering. The inertia of the vanquished allows the (temporary) victor to settle in his cruelty and to convey to the public this terrifying slowness of the torturer who is certain about the outcome of his actions; to grind the face of one's powerless adversary or to scrape his spine with one's fist with a deep and regular movement, or at least to produce the superficial appearance of such gestures: wrestling is the only sport which gives such an externalized image of torture. But here again, only the image is involved in the game, and the spectator does not wish for the actual suffering of the contestant; he only enjoys the perfection of an iconography.[9] It is not true that wrestling is a sadistic spectacle: it is only an intelligible spectacle.

There is another figure, more spectacular still than a hold; it is the   12
forearm smash, this loud slap of the forearm, this embryonic punch with which one clouts the chest of one's adversary, and which is accompanied by a dull noise and the exaggerated sagging of a vanquished body. In the forearm smash, catastrophe is brought to the point of maximum obviousness, so much so that ultimately the gesture appears as no more than a symbol; this is going too far, this is transgressing the moral rules of wrestling, where all signs must be excessively clear, but must not let the intention of clarity be seen. The public then shouts "He's laying it on!," not because it regrets the absence of real suffering, but because it condemns artifice: as in the theatre, one fails to put the part across as much by an excess of sincerity as by an excess of formalism.

We have already seen to what extent wrestlers exploit the resources of a   13
given physical style, developed and put to use in order to unfold before the eyes of the public a total image of Defeat. The flaccidity of tall white bodies which collapse with one blow or crash into the ropes with arms flailing, the inertia of massive wrestlers rebounding pitiably off all the elastic surfaces of the ring, nothing can signify more clearly and more passionately the exemplary abasement of the vanquished. Deprived of all resilience, the wrestler's flesh is no longer anything but an unspeakable heap spread out on the floor, where it solicits relentless reviling and jubilation. There is here a paroxysm of meaning in the style of antiquity, which can only recall the heavily underlined intentions in Roman triumphs. At other times, there is another ancient posture which appears in the coupling of the wrestlers, that of the suppliant who, at the mercy of his opponent, on bended knees, his arms raised above his head, is slowly brought down by the vertical pressure of the victor. In wrestling, unlike judo, Defeat is not a conventional sign, abandoned as soon as it is understood; it is not an outcome, but quite the contrary, it is a duration, a display, it takes up the ancient myths of public Suffering and Humiliation: the cross and the pillory. It is as if the wrestler is crucified in broad daylight and in the sight of all. I have heard

---

[9] *iconography:* in this context, a symbolic representation. [Editors' note.]

it said of a wrestler stretched on the ground: "He is dead, little Jesus, there, on the cross," and these ironic words revealed the hidden roots of a spectacle which enacts the exact gestures of the most ancient purifications.

But what wrestling is above all meant to portray is a purely moral   14
concept: that of justice. The idea of "paying" is essential to wrestling, and the crowd's "Give it to him" means above all else "Make him pay." This is therefore, needless to say, an immanent justice. The baser the action of the "bastard," the more delighted the public is by the blow which he justly receives in return. If the villain—who is of course a coward—takes refuge behind the ropes, claiming unfairly to have a right to do so by a brazen mimicry, he is inexorably pursued there and caught, and the crowd is jubilant at seeing the rules broken for the sake of a deserved punishment. Wrestlers know very well how to play up to the capacity for indignation of the public by presenting the very limit of the concept of Justice, this outermost zone of confrontation where it is enough to infringe the rules a little more to open the gates of a world without restraints. For a wrestling-fan, nothing is finer than the revengeful fury of a betrayed fighter who throws himself vehemently not on a successful opponent but on the smarting image of foul play. Naturally, it is the pattern of Justice which matters here, much more than its content: wrestling is above all a quantitative sequence of compensations (an eye for an eye, a tooth for a tooth). This explains why sudden changes of circumstances have in the eyes of wrestling habitués a sort of moral beauty: they enjoy them as they would enjoy an inspired episode in a novel, and the greater the contrast between the success of a move and the reversal of fortune, the nearer the good luck of a contestant to his downfall, the more sastisfying the dramatic mime is felt to be. Justice is therefore the embodiment of a possible transgression; it is from the fact that there is a Law that the spectacle of the passions which infringe it derives its value.

It is therefore easy to understand why out of five wrestling-matches, only   15
about one is fair. One must realize, let it be repeated, that "fairness" here is a role or a genre, as in the theatre: the rules do not at all constitute a real constraint; they are the conventional appearance of fairness. So that in actual fact a fair fight is nothing but an exaggeratedly polite one: the contestants confront each other with zeal, not rage; they can remain in control of their passions, they do not punish their beaten opponent relentlessly, they stop fighting as soon as they are ordered to do so, and congratulate each other at the end of a particularly arduous episode, during which, however, they have not ceased to be fair. One must of course understand here that all these polite actions are brought to the notice of the public by the most conventional gestures of fairness: shaking hands, raising the arms, ostensibly avoiding a fruitless hold which would detract from the perfection of the contest.

Conversely, foul play exists only in its excessive signs: administering a   16
big kick to one's beaten opponent, taking refuge behind the ropes while

ostensibly invoking a purely formal right, refusing to shake hands with one's opponent before or after the fight, taking advantage of the end of the round to rush treacherously at the adversary from behind, fouling him while the referee is not looking (a move which obviously only has any value or function because in fact half the audience can see it and get indignant about it). Since Evil is the natural climate of wrestling, a fair fight has chiefly the value of being an exception. It surprises the aficionado, who greets it when he sees it as an anachronism and a rather sentimental throwback to the sporting tradition ("Aren't they playing fair, those two"); he feels suddenly moved at the sight of the general kindness of the world, but would probably die of boredom and indifference if wrestlers did not quickly return to the orgy of evil which alone makes good wrestling.

    Extrapolated, fair wrestling could lead only to boxing or judo, whereas   17 true wrestling derives its originality from all the excesses which make it a spectacle and not a sport. The ending of a boxing-match or a judo-contest is abrupt, like the full-stop which closes a demonstration. The rhythm of wrestling is quite different, for its natural meaning is that of rhetorical amplification: the emotional magniloquence, the repeated paroxysms, the exasperation of the retorts can only find their natural outcome in the most baroque confusion. Some fights, among the most successful kind, are crowned by a final charivari,[10] a sort of unrestrained fantasia where the rules, the laws of the genre, the referee's censuring and the limits of the ring are abolished, swept away by a triumphant disorder which overflows into the hall and carries off pell-mell wrestlers, seconds, referee and spectators.

    It has already been noted that in America wrestling represents a sort of   18 mythological fight between Good and Evil (of a quasi-political nature, the "bad" wrestler always being supposed to be a Red). The process of creating heroes in French wrestling is very different, being based on ethics and not on politics. What the public is looking for here is the gradual construction of a highly moral image: that of the perfect "bastard." One comes to wrestling in order to attend the continuing adventures of a single major leading character, permanent and multiform like Punch or Scapino,[11] inventive in unexpected figures and yet always faithful to his role. The "bastard" is here revealed as a Molière character or a "portrait" by La Bruyère,[12] that is to say as a classical entity, an essence, whose acts are only significant epiphenomena arranged in time. This stylized character does not belong to any particular nation or party, and whether the wrestler is called Kuzchenko (nicknamed Moustache after Stalin), Yerpazian, Gaspardi, Jo

---

[10] *charivari:* a confusion of noises, a din. [Editors' note.]

[11] *Punch or Scapino:* Punch, an English adaptation of the *Commedia dell' Arte*'s Pulcinella character, a humpback and a buffoon. Scapino, also a stock character, was crafty, unprincipled, and cowardly. [Editors' note.]

[12] *La Bruyère:* Jean de La Bruyère (1645–1696), a French literary figure. [Editors' note.]

Vignola or Nollières, the aficionado does not attribute to him any country except "fairness"—observing the rules.

What then is a "bastard" for this audience composed in part, we are told, 19 of people who are themselves outside the rules of society? Essentially someone unstable, who accepts the rules only when they are useful to him and transgresses the formal continuity of attitudes. He is unpredictable, therefore asocial. He takes refuge behind the law when he considers that it is in his favour, and breaks it when he finds it useful to do so. Sometimes he rejects the formal boundaries of the ring and goes on hitting an adversary legally protected by the ropes, sometimes he reestablishes these boundaries and claims the protection of what he did not respect a few minutes earlier. This inconsistency, far more than treachery or cruelty, sends the audience beside itself with rage: offended not in its morality but in its logic, it considers the contradiction of arguments as the basest of crimes. The forbidden move becomes dirty only when it destroys a quantitative equilibrium and disturbs the rigorous reckoning of compensations; what is condemned by the audience is not at all the transgression of insipid official rules, it is the lack of revenge, the absence of a punishment. So that there is nothing more exciting for a crowd than the grandiloquent kick given to a vanquished "bastard"; the joy of punishing is at its climax when it is supported by a mathematical justification; contempt is then unrestrained. One is no longer dealing with a *salaud* but with a *salope*—the verbal gesture of the ultimate degradation.

Such a precise finality demands that wrestling should be exactly what the 20 public expects of it. Wrestlers, who are very experienced, know perfectly how to direct the spontaneous episodes of the fight so as to make them conform to the image which the public has of the great legendary themes of its mythology. A wrestler can irritate or disgust, he never disappoints, for he always accomplishes completely, by a progressive solidification of signs, what the public expects of him. In wrestling, nothing exists except in the absolute, there is no symbol, no allusion, everything is presented exhaustively. Leaving nothing in the shade, each action discards all parasitic meanings and ceremonially offers to the public a pure and full signification, rounded like Nature. This grandiloquence is nothing but the popular and age-old image of the perfect intelligibility of reality. What is portrayed by wrestling is therefore an ideal understanding of things; it is the euphoria of men raised for a while above the constitutive ambiguity of everyday situations and placed before the panoramic view of a univocal Nature, in which signs at last correspond to causes, without obstacle, without evasion, without contradiction.

When the hero or the villain of the drama, the man who was seen a few 21 minutes earlier possessed by moral rage, magnified into a sort of metaphysical sign, leaves the wrestling hall, impassive, anonymous, carrying a small suitcase and arm-in-arm with his wife, no one can doubt that wrestling holds that power of transmutation which is common to the Spectacle and to Religious Worship. In the ring, and even in the depths of their voluntary ignominy, wrestlers remain gods because they are, for a few moments, the key which opens Nature, the pure gesture which separates Good from Evil, and unveils the form of a Justice which is at last intelligible.

Questions for Discussion and Writing

1. How does Barthes use the comparison to theater to clarify and enhance his argument about professional wrestling? How might this same comparison be used to make an opposite point—for example, that professional wrestling is "ignoble"?

2. Do you accept Barthes's distinction between "spectacles" such as professional wrestling and "true" sports such as boxing? Is there a necessary element of spectacle in "true" sports as well? Are some sports more symbolic or mythic than others?

3. Consider the mythology of "Justice" Barthes describes. Is it a good one? How often do we find Barthes's mythology of "Justice" in the actual world around us? Is it present in everyday experience, or is it to be experienced only in the "purified" world of professional wrestling, theater, and art?

4. Choose a sport, spectacle (other than professional wrestling), or other cultural ritual, object, or image and analyze it in the manner of Barthes. What sort of spectacle is present? Are there comprehensible moral lessons (overt or covert) conveyed by the spectacle? Can you locate any broad cultural symbols or mythologies? If so, do these mythologies or symbols suggest or encourage the dominance of one class over another, or do they tend to project egalitarian values? Write an essay that specifically addresses these questions.

PAULO FREIRE

(b. 1921)

P aulo Freire is a Brazilian scholar and teacher who has dedicated his career to educational issues concerning the poor, iterate, and disenfranchised. He has been a professor of education at the Catholic University of São Paulo, Brazil, since 1981. He has also taught at Harvard University, and he has served as general coordinator of Brazil's National Plan of Adult Literacy and consultant to the UNESCO Institute of Research and Training in Agrarian Reform. Freire is especially interested in developing visual aids for communicating with illiterate peasants. His English publications include Cultural Action for Freedom (1970), The Pedagogy of the Oppressed (1970), Education for Critical Consciousness (1974), Education: The Practice of Freedom (1976), Pedagogy in Process: The Letters to Guinea-Bissau (1978), A Day with Paulo Freire (1980), The Politics of Education: Culture, Power, and Liberation (1985), Literacy: Reading the Word and the World (1987), A Pedagogy of Liberation: Dialogues on Transforming Education (1987), and Learning to Question: A Pedagogy of Liberation (with Antonio Faundez, 1989).

The following selection is a chapter from The Pedagogy of the Oppressed. Freire's central argument about knowledge, power, and critical thinking deeply enriches the debate over pedagogy and educational philosophy present in the selections from Hirsch, Wolfe, and Rodriguez. As a native Latin American who is intimately aware of the problems of Third World nations, Freire understands the dynamics and politics of education in ways that are not immediately obvious to American educators. As you read this selection, analyze the argument on its own terms, then consider its relationship to others you have read. How applicable is Freire's argument to contemporary conditions in the United States?

FROM THE PEDAGOGY OF THE OPPRESSED

A careful analysis of the teacher-student relationship at any level, inside or outside the school, reveals its fundamentally *narrative* character. This relationship involves a narrating Subject (the teacher) and patient, listening objects (the students). The contents, whether values or empirical dimensions of reality, tend in the process of being narrated to become lifeless and petrified. Education is suffering from narration sickness.

The teacher talks about reality as if it were motionless, static, compart-   2
mentalized, and predictable. Or else he expounds on a topic completely
alien to the existential experience of the students. His task is to "fill" the
students with the contents of his narration—contents which are detached
from reality, disconnected from the totality that engendered them and could
give them significance. Words are emptied of their concreteness and become
a hollow, alienated, and alienating verbosity.

The outstanding characteristic of this narrative education, then, is the   3
sonority of words, not their transforming power. "Four times four is
sixteen; the capital of Pará is Belém." The student records, memorizes, and
repeats these phrases without perceiving what four times four really means,
or realizing the true significance of "capital" in the affirmation "the capital
of Pará is Belém," that is, what Belém means for Pará and what Pará
means for Brazil.

Narration (with the teacher as narrator) leads the students to memorize   4
mechanically the narrated content. Worse yet, it turns them into "containers,"
into "receptacles" to be "filled" by the teacher. The more completely he
fills the receptacles, the better a teacher he is. The more meekly the
receptacles permit themselves to be filled, the better students they are.

Education thus becomes an act of depositing, in which the students are   5
the depositories and the teacher is the depositor. Instead of communicating,
the teacher issues communiqués and makes deposits which the students
patiently receive, memorize, and repeat. This is the "banking" concept of
education, in which the scope of action allowed to the students extends only
as far as receiving, filing, and storing the deposits. They do, it is true,
have the opportunity to become collectors or cataloguers of the things they
store. But in the last analysis, it is men themselves who are filed away
through the lack of creativity, transformation, and knowledge in this (at
best) misguided system. For apart from inquiry, apart from the praxis,
men cannot be truly human. Knowledge emerges only through invention
and re-invention, through the restless, impatient, continuing, hopeful
inquiry men pursue in the world, with the world, and with each other.

In the banking concept of education, knowledge is a gift bestowed by   6
those who consider themselves knowledgeable upon those whom they consider
to know nothing. Projecting an absolute ignorance onto others, a characteristic
of the ideology of oppression, negates education and knowledge as processes
of inquiry. The teacher presents himself to his students as their necessary
opposite; by considering their ignorance absolute, he justifies his own
existence. The students, alienated like the slave in the Hegelian dialectic,
accept their ignorance as justifying the teacher's existence—but, unlike the
slave, they never discover that they educate the teacher.

The *raison d'être*[1] of libertarian education, on the other hand, lies in its   7

---

[1] *raison d'être:* justification for existence. [Editors' note.]

drive towards reconciliation. Education must begin with the solution of the teacher-student contradiction, by reconciling the poles of the contradiction so that both are simultaneously teachers *and* students.

This solution is not (nor can it be) found in the banking concept. On 8 the contrary, banking education maintains and even stimulates the contradiction through the following attitudes and practices, which mirror oppressive society as a whole:

(a) the teacher teaches and the students are taught;
(b) the teacher knows everything and the students know nothing;
(c) the teacher thinks and the students are thought about;
(d) the teacher talks and the students listen—meekly;
(e) the teacher disciplines and the students are disciplined;
(f) the teacher chooses and enforces his choice, and the students comply;
(g) the teacher acts and the students have the illusion of acting through the action of the teacher;
(h) the teacher chooses the program content, and the students (who were not consulted) adapt to it;
(i) the teacher confuses the authority of knowledge with his own professional authority, which he sets in opposition to the freedom of the students;
(j) the teacher is the Subject of the learning process, while the pupils are mere objects.

It is not surprising that the banking concept of education regards men 9 as adaptable, manageable beings. The more students work at storing the deposits entrusted to them, the less they develop the critical consciousness which would result from their intervention in the world as transformers of that world. The more completely they accept the passive role imposed on them, the more they tend simply to adapt to the world as it is and to the fragmented view of reality deposited in them.

The capability of banking education to minimize or annul the students' 10 creative power and to stimulate their credulity serves the interests of the oppressors, who care neither to have the world revealed nor to see it transformed. The oppressors use their "humanitarianism" to preserve a profitable situation. Thus they react almost instinctively against any experiment in education which stimulates the critical faculties and is not content with a partial view of reality but always seeks out the ties which link one point to another and one problem to another.

Indeed, the interests of the oppressors lie in "changing the consciousness 11 of the oppressed, not the situation which oppresses them";[2] for the more the oppressed can be led to adapt to that situation, the more easily they can

---

[2] Simone de Beauvoir, *La Pensée de Droite, Aujord'hui* (Paris); ST, *El Pensamiento político de la Derecha* (Buenos Aires, 1963), p. 34. [Author's note.]

be dominated. To achieve this end, the oppressors use the banking concept of education in conjunction with a paternalistic social action apparatus, within which the oppressed receive the euphemistic title of "welfare recipients." They are treated as individual cases, as marginal men who deviate from the general configuration of a "good, organized, and just" society. The oppressed are regarded as the pathology of the healthy society, which must therefore adjust these "incompetent and lazy" folk to its own patterns by changing their mentality. These marginals need to be "integrated," "incorporated" into the healthy society that they have "forsaken."

The truth is, however, that the oppressed are not "marginals," are not   12 men living "outside" society. They have always been "inside"—inside the structure which made them "beings for others." The solution is not to "integrate" them into the structure of oppression, but to transform that structure so that they can become "beings for themselves." Such transformation, of course, would undermine the oppressors' purposes; hence their utilization of the banking concept of education to avoid the threat of student *conscientização*.[3]

The banking approach to adult education, for example, will never propose   13 to students that they critically consider reality. It will deal instead with such vital questions as whether Roger gave green grass to the goat, and insist upon the importance of learning that, on the contrary, *R*oger gave green grass to the *r*abbit. The "humanism" of the banking approach masks the effort to turn men into automatons—the very negation of their ontological vocation to be more fully human.

Those who use the banking approach, knowingly or unknowingly (for   14 there are innumerable well-intentioned bank-clerk teachers who do not realize that they are serving only to dehumanize), fail to perceive that the deposits themselves contain contradictions about reality. But, sooner or later, these contradictions may lead formerly passive students to turn against their domestication and the attempt to domesticate reality. They may discover through existential experience that their present way of life is irreconcilable with their vocation to become fully human. They may perceive through their relations with reality that reality is really a *process*, undergoing constant transformation. If men are searchers and their ontological vocation is humanization, sooner or later they may perceive the contradiction in which banking education seeks to maintain them, and then engage themselves in the struggle for their liberation.

But the humanist, revolutionary educator cannot wait for this possibility   15 to materialize. From the outset, his efforts must coincide with those of the students to engage in critical thinking and the quest for mutual humanization. His efforts must be imbued with a profound trust in men and their creative

---

[3] *conscientização:* becoming aware of social, political, and economic oppression. [Editors' note.]

power. To achieve this, he must be a partner of the students in his relations with them.

The banking concept does not admit to such partnership—and necessarily so. To resolve the teacher-student contradiction, to exchange the role of depositor, prescriber, domesticator, for the role of student among students would be to undermine the power of oppression and serve the cause of liberation. 16

Implicit in the banking concept is the assumption of a dichotomy between man and the world: man is merely *in* the world, not *with* the world or with others; man is spectator, not re-creator. In this view, man is not a conscious being (*corpo consciente*); he is rather the possessor of *a* consciousness: an empty "mind" passively open to the reception of deposits of reality from the world outside. For example, my desk, my books, my coffee cup, all the objects before me—as bits of the world which surrounds me—would be "inside" me, exactly as I am inside my study right now. This view makes no distinction between being accessible to consciousness and entering consciousness. The distinction, however, is essential: the objects which surround me are simply accessible to my consciousness, not located within it. I am aware of them, but they are not inside me. 17

It follows logically from the banking notion of consciousness that the educator's role is to regulate the way the world "enters into" the students. His task is to organize a process which already occurs spontaneously, to "fill" the students by making deposits of information which he considers to constitute true knowledge.[4] And since men "receive" the world as passive entities, education should make them more passive still, and adapt them to the world. The educated man is the adapted man, because he is better "fit" for the world. Translated into practice, this concept is well suited to the purposes of the oppressors, whose tranquility rests on how well men fit the world the oppressors have created, and how little they question it. 18

The more completely the majority adapt to the purposes which the dominant minority prescribe for them (thereby depriving them of the right to their own purposes), the more easily the minority can continue to prescribe. The theory and practice of banking education serve this end quite efficiently. Verbalistic lessons, reading requirements,[5] the methods for evaluating "knowledge," the distance between the teacher and the taught, the criteria for promotion: everything in this ready-to-wear approach serves to obviate thinking. 19

---

[4] This concept corresponds to what Sartre calls the "digestive" or "nutritive" concept of education, in which knowledge is "fed" by the teacher to the students to "fill them out." See Jean-Paul Sartre, "Une idée fondamentale de la phénomenologie de Husserl: L'intentionalité," *Situations I* (Paris, 1947). [Author's note.]

[5] For example, some professors specify in their reading lists that a book should be read from pages 10 to 15—and do this to "help" their students! [Author's note.]

The bank-clerk educator does not realize that there is no true security in 20 his hypertrophied role, that one must seek to live *with* others in solidarity. One cannot impose oneself, nor even merely co-exist with one's students. Solidarity requires true communication, and the concept by which such an educator is guided fears and proscribes communication.

Yet only through communication can human life hold meaning. The 21 teacher's thinking is authenticated only by the authenticity of the students' thinking. The teacher cannot think for his students, nor can he impose his thought on them. Authentic thinking, thinking that is concerned about *reality*, does not take place in ivory tower isolation, but only in communication. If it is true that thought has meaning only when generated by action upon the world, the subordination of students to teachers becomes impossible.

Because banking education begins with a false understanding of men as 22 objects, it cannot promote the development of what Fromm calls "biophily," but instead produces its opposite: "necrophily."

> While life is characterized by growth in a structured, functional manner, the necrophilous person loves all that does not grow, all that is mechanical. The necrophilous person is driven by the desire to transform the organic into the inorganic, to approach life mechanically, as if all living persons were things. . . . Memory, rather than experience; having, rather than being, is what counts. The necrophilous person can relate to an object— a flower or a person—only if he possesses it; hence a threat to his possession is a threat to himself; if he loses possession he loses contact with the world. . . . He loves control, and in the act of controlling he kills life.[6]

Oppression—overwhelming control—is necrophilic; it is nourished by 23 love of death, not life. The banking concept of education, which serves the interests of oppression, is also necrophilic. Based on a mechanistic, static, naturalistic, spatialized view of consciousness, it transforms students into receiving objects. It attempts to control thinking and action, leads men to adjust to the world, and inhibits their creative power.

When their efforts to act responsibly are frustrated, when they find 24 themselves unable to use their faculties, men suffer. "This suffering due to impotence is rooted in the very fact that the human equilibrium has been disturbed."[7] But the inability to act which causes men's anguish also causes them to reject their impotence, by attempting

> . . . to restore [their] capacity to act. But can [they], and how? One way is to submit to and identify with a person or group having power. By this symbolic participation in another person's life, [men have] the illusion of acting, when in reality [they] only submit to and become a part of those who act.[8]

---

[6] Eric Fromm, *The Heart of Man* (New York, 1966), p. 41. [Author's note.]

[7] Ibid., p. 31. [Author's note.]

[8] Ibid. [Author's note.]

Populist manifestations perhaps best exemplify this type of behavior by 25 the oppressed, who, by identifying with charismatic leaders, come to feel that they themselves are active and effective. The rebellion they express as they emerge in the historical process is motivated by that desire to act effectively. The dominant elites consider the remedy to be more domination and repression, carried out in the name of freedom, order, and social peace (that is, the peace of the elites). Thus they can condemn—logically, from their point of view—"the violence of a strike by workers and [can] call upon the state in the same breath to use violence in putting down the strike."⁹

Education as the exercise of domination stimulates the credulity of 26 students, with the ideological intent (often not perceived by educators) of indoctrinating them to adapt to the world of oppression. This accusation is not made in the naïve hope that the dominant elites will thereby simply abandon the practice. Its objective is to call the attention of true humanists to the fact that they cannot use banking educational methods in the pursuit of liberation, for they would only negate that very pursuit. Nor may a revolutionary society inherit these methods from an oppressor society. The revolutionary society which practices banking education is either misguided or mistrusting of men. In either event, it is threatened by the specter of reaction.

Unfortunately, those who espouse the cause of liberation are themselves 27 surrounded and influenced by the climate which generates the banking concept, and often do not perceive its true significance or its dehumanizing power. Paradoxically, then, they utilize this same instrument of alienation in what they consider an effort to liberate. Indeed, some "revolutionaries" brand as "innocents," "dreamers," or even "reactionaries" those who would challenge this educational practice. But one does not liberate men by alienating them. Authentic liberation—the process of humanization—is not another deposit to be made in men. Liberation is a praxis: the action and reflection of men upon their world in order to transform it. Those truly committed to the cause of liberation can accept neither the mechanistic concept of consciousness as an empty vessel to be filled, nor the use of banking methods of domination (propaganda, slogans—deposits) in the name of liberation.

Those truly committed to liberation must reject the banking concept in 28 its entirety, adopting instead a concept of men as conscious beings, and consciousness as consciousness intent upon the world. They must abandon the educational goal of deposit-making and replace it with the posing of the problems of men in their relations with the world. "Problem-posing" education, responding to the essence of consciousness—*intentionality*—rejects

---

⁹ Reinhold Niebuhr, *Moral Man and Immoral Society* (New York, 1960), p. 130. [Author's note.]

communiqués and embodies communication. It epitomizes the special characteristic of consciousness: being *conscious of*, not only as intent on objects but as turned in upon itself in a Jasperian[10] "split"—consciousness as consciousness *of* consciousness.

Liberating education consists in acts of cognition, not transferrals of information. It is a learning situation in which the cognizable object (far from being the end of the cognitive act) intermediates the cognitive actors— teacher on the one hand and students on the other. Accordingly, the practice of problem-posing education entails at the outset that the teacher-student contradiction be resolved. Dialogical relations—indispensable to the capacity of cognitive actors to cooperate in perceiving the same cognizable object— are otherwise impossible. 29

Indeed, problem-posing education, which breaks with the vertical patterns characteristic of banking education, can fulfill its function as the practice of freedom only if it can overcome the above contradiction. Through dialogue, the teacher-of-the-students and the students-of-the-teacher cease to exist and a new term emerges: teacher-student with students-teachers. The teacher is no longer merely the-one-who-teaches, but one who is himself taught in dialogue with the students, who in turn while being taught also teach. They become jointly responsible for a process in which all grow. In this process, arguments based on "authority" are no longer valid; in order to function, authority must be *on the side of* freedom, not *against* it. Here, no one teaches another, nor is anyone self-taught. Men teach each other, mediated by the world, by the cognizable objects which in banking education are "owned" by the teacher. 30

The banking concept (with its tendency to dichotomize everything) distinguishes two stages in the action of the educator. During the first, he cognizes a cognizable object while he prepares his lessons in his study or his laboratory; during the second, he expounds to his students about that object. The students are not called upon to know, but to memorize the contents narrated by the teacher. Nor do the students practice any act of cognition, since the object towards which that act should be directed is the property of the teacher rather than a medium evoking the critical reflection of both teacher and students. Hence in the name of the "preservation of culture and knowledge" we have a system which achieves neither true knowledge nor true culture. 31

The problem-posing method does not dichotomize the activity of the teacher-student: he is not "cognitive" at one point and "narrative" at another. He is always "cognitive," whether preparing a project or engaging in dialogue with the students. He does not regard cognizable objects as his private property, but as the object of reflection by himself and the students. 32

---

[10] *Jasperian:* relating to the philosophy of Karl Jaspers (1883–1969), a German Existentialist philosopher. [Editors' note.]

In this way, the problem-posing educator constantly re-forms his reflections in the reflection of the students. The students—no longer docile listeners— are now critical co-investigators in dialogue with the teacher. The teacher presents the material to the students for their consideration, and re-considers his earlier considerations as the students express their own. The role of the problem-posing educator is to create, together with the students, the conditions under which knowledge at the level of the *doxa* is superseded by true knowledge, at the level of the *logos*.

Whereas banking education anesthetizes and inhibits creative power, problem-posing education involves a constant unveiling of reality. The former attempts to maintain the *submersion* of consciousness; the latter strives for the *emergence* of consciousness and *critical intervention* in reality.   33

Students, as they are increasingly posed with problems relating to themselves in the world and with the world, will feel increasingly challenged and obliged to respond to that challenge. Because they apprehend the challenge as interrelated to other problems within a total context, not as a theoretical question, the resulting comprehension tends to be increasingly critical and thus constantly less alienated. Their response to the challenge evokes new challenges, followed by new understandings; and gradually the students come to regard themselves as committed.   34

Education as the practice of freedom—as opposed to education as the practice of domination—denies that man is abstract, isolated, independent, and unattached to the world; it also denies that the world exists as a reality apart from men. Authentic reflection considers neither abstract man nor the world without men, but men in their relations with the world. In these relations consciousness and world are simultaneous: consciousness neither precedes the world nor follows it.   35

> La conscience et le monde sont donnes d'un même coup: extérieur par essence à la conscience, le monde est, par essence relatif à elle.[11]

In one of our culture circles in Chile, the group was discussing (based on a codification[12]) the anthropological concept of culture. In the midst of the discussion, a peasant who by banking standards was completely ignorant said: "Now I see that without man there is no world." When the educator responded: "Let's say, for the sake of argument, that all the men on earth were to die, but that the earth itself remained, together with trees, birds, animals, rivers, seas, the stars . . . wouldn't all this be a world?" "Oh, no," the peasant replied emphatically. "There would be no one to say: 'This is a world'."

---

[11] Sartre, op cit., p. 32. [Author's note.] *"La conscience . . . elle"*: Consciousness and the world are given at a single stroke: essentially external to consciousness, the world is essentially relative to it. [Editors' note.]

[12] See Chapter 3. [Translator's note.]

The peasant wished to express the idea that there would be lacking the   36
consciousness of the world which necessarily implies the world of consciousness. *I* cannot exist without a *not-I*. In turn, the *not-I* depends on that
existence. The world which brings consciousness into existence becomes the
world *of* that consciousness. Hence, the previously cited affirmation of
Sartre: "*La conscience et le monde sont donnes d'un même coup.*"

As men, simultaneously reflecting on themselves and on the world,   37
increase the scope of their perception, they begin to direct their observations
towards previously inconspicuous phenomena:

> In perception properly so-called, as an explicit awareness [*Gewahren*], I
> am turned towards the object, to the paper, for instance. I apprehend it
> as being this here and now. The apprehension is a singling out, every
> object having a background in experience. Around and about the paper
> lie books, pencils, ink-well, and so forth, and these in a certain sense are
> also "perceived," perceptually there, in the "field of intuition"; but whilst
> I was turned towards the paper there was no turning in their direction,
> nor any apprehending of them, not even in a secondary sense. They
> appeared and yet were not singled out, were not posited on their own
> account. Every perception of a thing has such a zone of background
> intuitions or background awareness, if "intuiting" already includes the
> state of being turned towards, and this also is a "conscious experience,"
> or more briefly a "consciousness of" all indeed that in point of fact lies in
> the co-perceived objective background.[13]

That which had existed objectively but had not been perceived in its deeper
implications (if indeed it was perceived at all) begins to "stand out,"
assuming the character of a problem and therefore of challenge. Thus, men
begin to single out elements from their "background awarenesses" and to
reflect upon them. These elements are now objects of men's consideration,
and, as such, objects of their action and cognition.

In problem-posing education, men develop their power to perceive   38
critically *the way they exist* in the world *with which* and *in which* they find
themselves; they come to see the world not as a static reality, but as a reality
in process, in transformation. Although the dialectical relations of men with
the world exist independently of how these relations are perceived (or
whether or not they are perceived at all), it is also true that the form of
action men adopt is to a large extent a function of how they perceive
themselves in the world. Hence, the teacher-student and the students-
teachers reflect simultaneously on themselves and the world without dichot-
omizing this reflection from action, and thus establish an authentic form of
thought and action.

---

[13] Edmund Husserl, *Ideas—General Introduction to Pure Phenomenology* (London, 1969),
pp. 105–106. [Author's note.]

Once again, the two educational concepts and practices under analysis   39
come into conflict. Banking education (for obvious reasons) attempts, by
mythicizing reality, to conceal certain facts which explain the way men exist
in the world; problem-posing education sets itself the task of demytholo-
gizing. Banking education resists dialogue; problem-posing education
regards dialogue as indispensable to the act of cognition which unveils
reality. Banking education treats students as objects of assistance; problem-
posing education makes them critical thinkers. Banking education inhibits
creativity and domesticates (although it cannot completely destroy) the
intentionality of consciousness by isolating consciousness from the world,
thereby denying men their ontological and historical vocation of becoming
more fully human. Problem-posing education bases itself on creativity and
stimulates true reflection and action upon reality, thereby responding to the
vocation of men as beings who are authentic only when engaged in inquiry
and creative transformation. In sum: banking theory and practice, as
immobilizing and fixating forces, fail to acknowledge men as historical
beings; problem-posing theory and practice take man's historicity as their
starting point.

Problem-posing education affirms men as beings in the process of   40
becoming—as unfinished, uncompleted beings in and with a likewise unfinished reality. Indeed, in contrast to other animals who are unfinished, but
not historical, men know themselves to be unfinished; they are aware of
their incompletion. In this incompletion and this awareness lie the very
roots of education as an exclusively human manifestation. The unfinished
character of men and the transformational character of reality necessitate
that education be an ongoing activity.

Education is thus constantly remade in the praxis. In order to *be*, it must   41
become. Its "duration" (in the Bergsonian[14] meaning of the word) is found
in the interplay of the opposites *permanence* and *change*. The banking method
emphasizes permanence and becomes reactionary; problem-posing education—which accepts neither a "well-behaved" present nor a predetermined
future—roots itself in the dynamic present and becomes revolutionary.

Problem-posing education is revolutionary futurity. Hence it is prophetic   42
(and, as such, hopeful). Hence, it corresponds to the historical nature of
man. Hence, it affirms men as beings who transcend themselves, who move
forward and look ahead, for whom immobility represents a fatal threat, for
whom looking at the past must only be a means of understanding more
clearly what and who they are so that they can more wisely build the future.
Hence, it identifies with the movement which engages men as beings aware
of their incompletion—an historical movement which has its point of
departure, its Subjects and its objective.

---

[14] *Bergsonian:* from Henri Bergson (1859–1941), a French philosopher. In Bergson's
philosophy, "duration" refers to time as psychologically experienced, as opposed to time as
measured by the clock. [Editors' note.]

The point of departure of the movement lies in men themselves. But 43 since men do not exist apart from the world, apart from reality, the movement must begin with the men-world relationship. Accordingly, the point of departure must always be with men in the "here and now," which constitutes the situation within which they are submerged, from which they emerge, and in which they intervene. Only by starting from this situation—which determines their perception of it—can they begin to move. To do this authentically they must perceive their state not as fated and unalterable, but merely as limiting—and therefore challenging.

Whereas the banking method directly or indirectly reinforces men's 44 fatalistic perception of their situation, the problem-posing method presents this very situation to them as a problem. As the situation becomes the object of their cognition, the naïve or magical perception which produced their fatalism gives way to perception which is able to perceive itself even as it perceives reality, and can thus be critically objective about that reality.

A deepened consciousness of their situation leads men to apprehend that 45 situation as an historical reality susceptible of transformation. Resignation gives way to the drive for transformation and inquiry, over which men feel themselves to be in control. If men, as historical beings necessarily engaged with other men in a movement of inquiry, did not control that movement, it would be (and is) a violation of men's humanity. Any situation in which some men prevent others from engaging in the process of inquiry is one of violence. The means used are not important; to alienate men from their own decision-making is to change them into objects.

This movement of inquiry must be directed towards humanization— 46 man's historical vocation. The pursuit of full humanity, however, cannot be carried out in isolation or individualism, but only in fellowship and solidarity; therefore it cannot unfold in the antagonistic relations between oppressors and oppressed. No one can be authentically human while he prevents others from being so. Attempting *to be more* human, individual-istically, leads to *having more*, egotistically: a form of dehumanization. Not that it is not fundamental *to have* in order *to be* human. Precisely because it *is* necessary, some men's *having* must not be allowed to constitute an obstacle to others' *having*, must not consolidate the power of the former to crush the latter.

Problem-posing education, as a humanist and liberating praxis, posits as 47 fundamental that men subjected to domination must fight for their eman-cipation. To that end, it enables teachers and students to become Subjects of the educational process by overcoming authoritarianism and an alienating intellectualism; it also enables men to overcome their false perception of reality. The world—no longer something to be described with deceptive words—becomes the object of that transforming action by men which results in their humanization.

Problem-posing education does not and cannot serve the interests of the 48 oppressor. No oppressive order could permit the oppressed to begin to question: Why? While only a revolutionary society can carry out this education in systematic terms, the revolutionary leaders need not take full power before they can employ the method. In the revolutionary process, the leaders cannot utilize the banking method as an interim measure, justified on grounds of expediency, with the intention of *later* behaving in a genuinely revolutionary fashion. They must be revolutionary—that is to say, dialogical—from the outset.

Questions for Discussion and Writing

1. What is the principal rhetorical effect of Freire's banking metaphor and his portrayal of students as containers (paragraph 4)? What does his decision to cast his argument in terms of oppression, emancipators, oppressors, and the oppressed tell us about his intended audience?

2. What basic cultural knowledge (i.e., banked knowledge) is necessary to understand Freire's discourse? Does his argument sufficiently consider the potential need for this kind of knowledge? Under Freire's program, how would such knowledge be attained?

3. In terms of our concept of ethos, how would you describe the rhetorical effect of Freire's discussion of authority in paragraphs 29–30 (see also paragraphs 1–8)? To what extent can the teacher-student relationship free itself from the potentially oppressive bonds of authority?

4. How does Freire's analysis apply to this anthology? Keeping Freire's argument in mind, write an evaluation of the pedagogical usefulness of *Investigating Arguments*. What are the text's strengths and weaknesses? In the final analysis, does it liberate or oppress its readers?

STEPHEN TOULMIN

(b. 1922)

LOREN R. GRAHAM

(b. 1933)

*S*tephen Edelston Toulmin is a well-respected English philosopher who has dedicated most of his scholarly career to studying the history of ideas and the philosophy of science. Like William Winslade and Judith Wilson Ross, he is an interdisciplinary thinker with a strong interest in ethical questions, particularly as they apply to scientific questions.

Toulmin earned his B.A. from Cambridge University in 1943, while he was working as a junior scientific officer for the British Ministry of Aircraft Production. He received his M.A. from Cambridge in 1946, and his Ph.D. two years later. After serving as a lecturer in the philosophy of science at Oxford, he became a professor of philosophy at the University of Leeds, a position he held until 1959, when he moved to the directorship of the Unit for the History of Ideas. In the mid-1960s he crossed the Atlantic to teach at various universities in the United States. Since 1986, he has been the Avalon Professor of the Humanities at Northwestern University.

Not surprisingly, even a short list of Toulmin's publications covers a wide variety of topics: An Examination of the Place of Reason in Ethics (1950), The Philosophy of Science: An Introduction (1953), Physical Reality: Philosophical Essays on Twentieth-Century Physics (1970), An Introduction to Reasoning (with Allan Janik and Richard Rieke, 1979), The Return of Cosmology: Postmodern Science and the Theology of Nature (1982), The Abuse of Casuistry: A History of Moral Reasoning (1988). Ironically, Toulmin is perhaps most famous for his contributions to rhetoric, a field in which he was not formally trained. In The Uses of Argument (1958), Toulmin outlines a system for analyzing arguments and classifying forms of argumentative support and backing that has been of great interest to rhetoricians. In the last twenty years, Toulmin's model has ranked with the enthymeme (the basic form of argument, according to Aristotle's Rhetoric; see the Glossary of Rhetorical Terms) as one of the most popular and successful means of teaching argument.

Loren R. Graham has a strong interest in many of the same issues that concern Toulmin, yet he comes to science and ethics from a rather different direction. Graham earned his B.S. from Purdue in 1955 and worked as a research engineer before receiving his M.A. from Columbia University in 1960. After some graduate study in Moscow, he received his Ph.D. in 1964, also from Columbia University. Since

1978, he has been professor of the history of science at Massachusetts Institute of Technology.

Although Graham's publications reflect a strong interest in Soviet studies, he, too, is an eclectic scholar. A partial listing of his work includes: The Soviet Academy of Sciences and the Communist Party, 1927–32 *(1967),* Science and Philosophy in the Soviet Union *(1972),* Between Science and Values *(1981),* Function and Uses of Disciplinary Histories *(1983),* Science, Philosophy, and Human Behavior in the Soviet Union *(1987).*

The basic kind of argument in which Toulmin and Graham engage is not new to the twentieth century. The perceived split between value and fact, or opinion and observable objective truth has been the subject of considerable debate during the last hundred years. William James's "The Will to Believe," reprinted earlier, demonstrates the importance of this controversy to the intellectual thought of the late nineteenth century. Perhaps we can even see the embryo of the controversial dichotomy in René Descartes's seventeenth-century writings, also reprinted here. In the last thirty years, two noted rhetoricians, Chaim Perelman and Wayne Booth, have considered the fact/value split in great depth in The New Rhetoric *(1958 in French, 1969 in English) and* Modern Dogma and the Rhetoric of Assent *(1974), respectively. In the following exchange, which appeared in the* Hastings Center Report *in 1979, Toulmin and Graham focus specifically on the perceived tension between science and ethics. Graham gives a fuller treatment of these questions in his* Between Science and Values, *Columbia University Press, New York, 1981.*

CAN SCIENCE AND ETHICS BE RECONNECTED?

STEPHEN TOULMIN

Anyone familiar with the contemporary literature on the philosophical foundations of ethics—say, from John Rawls's *Theory of Justice* (1972) up to Alan Donagan's *Theory of Morality* (1977) and Ronald Dworkin's *Taking Rights Seriously* (1977)—will know how little attention such books give to "science," or at least to "the natural and social sciences," as they are conceived of at the present time in the English-speaking world.[1]

The question is, "How far does this lack of attention reflect some immutable verities about the *essential* relations between science and ethics? And how far is it, rather, a temporary—even, transient—fact about their *actual* relation in our own day?" At other times, certainly, both "science" and "ethics" have been conceived of in other ways, and their interactions have been both more obvious and more vigorous. By recognizing how those interactions have been minimized over the last 100 or 150 years, we should be able to recognize also how they might be reestablished and reactivated. Even to agree on that diagnosis would be to achieve something substantial. The arguments in this paper will therefore be partly historical and partly diagnostic.

THE PURIST VIEW OF SCIENCE

From a strict philosophical point of view, all attempts to insulate the sciences   3
from ethics can easily be undercut. This is true whether our focus of discussion is intellectual, sociological, or psychological: the basic concepts of the sciences, the institutions and collective conduct of the scientific profession, or the personal motives of individual scientists.

As to the concept of science: so long as we restrict ourselves to the physi-   4
cochemical sciences, our basic notions and hypotheses (e.g., hadron, field gradient, and amino acid) may have no obvious evaluative implications. But the physiological, to say nothing of the psychological and social sciences, employ whole families of concepts, for instance, those associated with functionality and adaptedness, and their cognates, which raise evaluative issues directly, both within the relevant scientific theories and in their broader implications.[2]

As to the scientific profession: the codes of good intellectual practice, and   5
the criteria of professional judgment in the sciences, may once upon a time have looked to the needs of effective inquiry alone, rather than to broader "ethical" considerations. But it is by now no longer possible to draw so clear or sharp a line between the intellectual demands of good science and the ethical demands of the good life. The increasingly close links between basic science and its practical applications expose working scientists more and more to ethical problems and public accountability of sorts that are commonplace in service professions such as medicine and law.[3] A strong case can also be made for seeing the professional enterprises of natural science as creating, and even defining, certain basic ethical modes of life and conduct having their own characteristic virtues, duties, and obligations.[4]

Finally, as to the individual motives that operate for scientists in their   6
work: though the "ideal" spring of action for scientific inquiry may be a pure respect for the rationality of the inquiry itself, such a "pure respect" is at best an aspiration, and a *moral* aspiration at that. Furthermore, it is something that can be developed in the course of any individual's lifetime, only as a somewhat refined product of moral education.[5]

Yet, despite these powerful objections, the notion that the intellectual   7
activities of science are carried on at a level that sets them, if not above, then at any rate beside and on a par with the moral law, continues to have its charms; and we must try to understand its seductive power. One potent source, I suggest, has been scientists' fear of relativism. During a period when exploration and anthropology were encouraging a sense of *pluralism* in human affairs, and so generating a kind of moral relativism and

subjectivism that put the very foundation of ethics in doubt,* it was understandable that scientists should have resisted the intrusion of ethics into the business of science; and that, in return, they should have insisted that the concerns of science—unlike those of ethics—were entirely objective, and in no sense "matters of taste or feeling." Furthermore, the fact that scientific issues could plausibly be depicted as public and intersubjective (rational) made it possible, also, to define the intellectual demands of the scientific life in a similarly objective way. So, both the collective conduct of the scientific profession and the personal choices of individual scientists were apparently freed from the existential arbitrariness and ambiguity of the ethical realm.

At this point, it might have been better if philosophers and scientists 8 alike had emphasized the similarities between science and ethics, and had used the "rational objectivity" of science as a model in seeking to reestablish the claims of moral objectivity, as well. The argument that ethical issues are, in their own proper ways, as public and intersubjective as scientific issues (and so equally "rational") was thus abandoned too quickly and lightly. But many scientists, lacking any sense of joint intellectual responsibility and interest with the moral philosophers, were happy enough to disown relativism in science and bolt for cover on their own. For so long as relativism and subjectivism remained viable options in philosophical ethics, most scientists understandably felt that it was more important to emphasize the distinctively intellectual—and so, presumably, "value-neutral"—character of their own enterprises. Provided they could preserve the autonomy of the scientific community against all outsiders, they did not mind letting the moral philosophers sink or swim by themselves.

By now, however, the "rationality" of science—the objectivity of scientific 9 issues, the autonomy of the scientific professions, and the categorical claims of the scientific life—can no longer be used to differentiate science entirely from the rest of thought and morality. We are faced, on every level, not by a hard and fast distinction, but by a spectrum.

---

* In discussion, Paul Ramsey queried whether the natural sciences have in fact been affected by the debate about subjectivism and relativism carried on *within philosophy* over the last fifty or one hundred years. That, of course, would be highly questionable. The point of my present argument is that the recognition of anthropological diversity led, by around 1800, to a widespread sense—not by any means confined to philosophers—that ethical beliefs and practices vary arbitrarily from culture to culture. Earlier in the eighteenth century it had still been possible for Voltaire to declare, "There is only one morality, as there is only one geometry"; but, from 1800 on, cultural relativism became a force to reckon with in general thinking about ethical matters. The corresponding doubts about "objectivity" in natural science did not become serious until the present century: first, following the collapse of the classical Newtonian/Euclidean synthesis on which Kant had rested his case, and more recently with the widespread adoption of Thomas Kuhn's theory of "paradigms" as justifying a similar diversity in "views of Nature." [Author's note.]

- The basic concepts of the sciences range along a spectrum from the effectively "value-free" to the irretrievably "value-laden";
- The goals of the scientific enterprise range along a spectrum from a purely abstract interest in theoretical speculations to a direct concern with human good and ill;
- The professional responsibilities of the scientific community range along a spectrum from the strictly internal and intellectual to the most public and practical.

Nonetheless, as recently as the 1930s, when I first acquired my ideas about "science," the most characteristic mark of the scientific attitude and the scientific task was to select as one's preferred center of attention the purest, the most intellectual, the most autonomous, and the least ethically implicated extreme on each of these different spectrums.

No doubt this "puristic" view of science was an extreme one, and by no means universally shared by working scientists, to say nothing of the outside social commentators who wrote about the scientific scene. Yet it is a view that had, and continues to have, great attractions for many professional scientists. Since "rational objectivity" is an indispensable part of the scientific mission, and the intrusion of "values" into science had come to be regarded as incompatible with such objectivity, all concern with values (or other arbitrary, personal preferences) had to be foresworn in the higher interest of rationality. Certainly, the professional institutions of science tended to be organized on this basis. The memberships of scientific academies, for instance, have for the last 75 or 100 years been increasingly recruited on the basis of the narrowly defined intellectual contributions of candidates alone,* without regard to their social perceptiveness, ethical sensitivity, or political wisdom. Indeed, the puristic view is still powerful today: consider, for instance, Arthur Kantrowitz's current proposals for a Science Court, whose duty would be to pronounce on the "factual implications" of science and technology for issues of public policy, without reference to the "values" at stake in each case.[6]

Accordingly, the purism of the views about science into which I was initiated was not merely a feature of the particular culture and time of my youth: one more local and temporary characteristic (so to say) of the factual, unemotional, antiphilosophical, class-structured, and role-oriented attitudes of the English professional classes between the two world wars. In part, the nature of that culture may have accentuated the larger tendency toward purism. Perhaps, if I had grown up in the United States rather than Britain

---

* Even in the second half of the nineteenth century, it was still accepted as a matter of common form that a poet such as Alfred Tennyson should be a Fellow of the Royal Society, and sit on important Royal Society committees. The restriction of membership in National Academies of Science to expert, full-time working scientists is thus largely a twentieth-century development. [Author's note.]

(or even in Britain thirty years later) I would have acquired different views, both about science itself, and about its ethical significance. Certainly, there have not always been the kinds of barriers between ethics and science that I grew up with; nor need there always be such barriers in the future. Still, I seriously doubt whether this attitude was solely a local and temporary oddity of twentieth-century English upper-middle-class life and social structure. For many of the considerations advanced to explain and justify scientific purism have a force that carries them across national boundaries. These considerations—the intellectual reaction against ethical relativism, the collective desire for professional autonomy, the personal charms of an ethically unambiguous life plan—may have been felt with a special strength in the England of my youth, but they were by no means confined to it.

The Professionalization of Science

What deeper explanation should we look for, then, to account for the emergence of this puristic view of science? Granted that, by the early twentieth century, relativism and subjectivism were beginning to pose an implicit threat to the objectivity of science as well as to ethics, how was it that scientists perceived and defined their own collective interests and self-image so clearly? How did they come to suppose that they could see science as capable of being the stronghold of reason by itself and on its own, in contradistinction to ethics, which had seemingly been unmasked as the plaything of emotion? 12

In part, these questions are issues for the history of ideas: in part, they will carry us deeper into the sociology and philosophy of science. Certainly, the distinction between an objective science and a subjective ethics may be traced back at least as far as the scientific positivism of Comte,* in the early nineteenth century; and the same contrast helped to encourage the revival of scientific positivism in Vienna in the 1920s. But why was scientific positivism itself able to carry conviction from the early nineteenth century on, in a way that it had not done earlier? At this point, we should go behind the history of ideas, and consider these changes in "ideas" against their larger human background. 13

For our present purposes, I believe, the crucial development in the history of nineteenth-century science was the establishment of distinct scientific disciplines, professions and roles: that is, the process by which individual, sharply delimited special sciences began to crystallize from the larger and less-defined matrix of eighteenth-century natural philosophy. As a result of this change, scientific workers divided themselves up into new and self-organized collectivities, and acquired a collective consciousness of their specialized intellectual tasks, as contrasted with the broader concerns 14

---

* *Comte:* Auguste Comte (1798–1857), a French mathematician and philosopher. [Editors' note.]

of philosophical, literary, and theological discussion more generally. In this way, it at last became possible to define the new individual role of "scientist." (This familiar word was coined as recently as 1840 by William Whewell, on the model of the much older term "artist," for his Presidential address to the British Association for the Advancement of Science.)

In all these respects, scientific roles and writings, organizations and 15 arguments dating from before 1830 differ sharply from anything to be found after around 1890. In the hands of the most distinguished eighteenth-century authors, scientific issues were always expanding into, and merging with, broader intellectual questions. In the writings of a John Ray* or a Joseph Priestley,† the doors between science, ethics, and religion are always open. "And why not?" they would have asked; "for natural philosophy must surely embrace within itself, not just mathematical and experimental philosophy, but also natural theology and natural morality." (Their sentiments were also those of Isaac Newton himself, for whom "to discourse of God" from a study of His Creation "does certainly belong to natural philosophy."[7]) Indeed, it took a series of deliberate and collective decisions to restrict the scope of scientific debate before these larger issues of philosophy and theology were effectively excluded from the professional debate about scientific issues. One such example was the resolution adopted by the Geological Society of London in 1807 to exclude from its Proceedings all arguments about the origin, antiquity, and creation of the earth, as being merely speculative, and to confine the Proceedings to papers based on direct observations of the earth's crust.[8] This is simply one early illustration of a trend that rapidly became general. During the rest of the nineteenth century, the intellectual concerns of the different special sciences were identified and defined in progressively sharper terms, setting them apart from the broader interests of philosophers, theologians, and the general reading public.

At this point, it would be helpful to develop a fuller understanding of 16 the manner in which natural philosophy, as conceived in the seventeenth and eighteenth centuries, fell apart into its component elements, and the sciences (and scientists) were led to set up shop on their own. Even as late as the 1820s, Joseph Townsend could still present significant contributions to geological science in the guise of an argument vindicating *The Veracity of Moses as an Historian*.[9] By the end of the century, Biblical history and geochronology had become entirely distinct disciplines, pursued by quite separate communities of scholars. Yet, even in this case, the transitions involved were protracted, hard-fought, and painful. Similarly, one major reason for the hostile reception that greeted Darwin's *Origin of Species* was the threat it seemingly posed to the traditional association between natural history and sacred history. Acknowledging a presentation copy of the book,

---

* *John Ray:* an English naturalist (1627?–1705). [Editors' note.]

† *Joseph Priestley:* an English theologian and chemist (1733–1804). [Editors' note.]

Darwin's teacher Adam Sedgwick expressed sorrow and alarm at Darwin's disregard of the "essential link" between the moral and material order of the world. If natural historians no longer showed us how the hand of the Creator was exemplified in the living creatures that were His handiwork, how then could the human race be expected to retain its confidence in divine wisdom and providence?

In addition, it would be helpful to have more detailed studies of the institutional changes during the nineteenth century by the leading scientific academies and societies that had originally been founded from 1650 on. How did they move from being general associations of scholars, clerics, and gentlemen to being specialized organizations of professional experts, with a narrowly defined scope and strict entrance qualifications? Before 1830, the Royal Society of London was still largely an association for the general discussion of issues in natural philosophy. By the 1890s, it had become the mode to pursue, not just art for art's sake, but also science for science's sake: even, electrical theory for electrical theory's sake, organic chemistry for organic chemistry's sake, botanical taxonomy for botanical taxonomy's sake. This was so because, by 1890, the self-defining disciplines and autonomous professions with which we are familiar today—each of them devoted to the special aims of one or another science—had finally established an existence independent of each other. 17

Once again, however, these institutional changes did not come automatically or easily. On the contrary, the intellectual and institutional claims of the special sciences faced continued resistance from the churches and elsewhere. So the collective experience, interests, and self-perceptions of, for example, cell physiologists, historical geologists, and electromagnetic theorists led them to defend their newly won territories with some real jealousy, to act protectively toward the intellectual goals of their disciplines, and to resist any countermoves aimed at reabsorbing them into some larger system of philosophy or theology. Ernst Haeckel, the German zoologist and a leader of the German Monistic Alliance, is an interesting figure in this respect. He was perhaps the last representative of the older tradition, comprised of scientists who could maintain an acceptable balance between generalism and specialism, combining genuine expertise in a restricted field of study with a talent for larger-scale philosophical synthesis and exposition. 18

In short, if we are to understand how science came to part company from the foundations of ethics, we need to focus attention on the history of scientific specialization. It was the development of specialization and professionalization that was responsible for excluding ethical issues from the foundations of science, and so, though inadvertently, destroyed most of the links between science and the foundations of ethics, as well. During the hundred or so years beginning around 1840, the concepts and methods, collective organization, and individual roles of science were progressively sharpened and defined, in ways designed to insulate truly "scientific" issues and investigations from all external distractions. So defined, the task of 19 "positive science" was to reveal how and in what respects, regardless of whether we like them or not, discoverable regularities, connections, and mechanisms are manifest in, or responsible for, the phenomena of the natural world.

This "positive" program for science was sometimes associated, but was   20 never identical, with the philosophy of scientific positivism. It rested on a number of significant assumptions, which are worth spelling out here.

A scientific picture of the world differs radically from a metaphysico-   21 religious picture. The former is realistically confined to demonstrable facts about the natural world: the latter embeds those demonstrable facts within a larger conceptual system, structured according to prejudices that are (from the scientific standpoint) arbitrary, externally motivated, and presumably wish-fulfilling.

A realistic view of the natural world is one that is kept free of irrelevant   22 preferences and evaluations, and so depicts Nature as it is, "whether we like it or not."

If scientific work is to be effectively organized and prosecuted, questions   23 of "demonstrable fact" must be investigated quite separately from all arbitrary, external, wish-fulfilling notions. Only in this way can we carry forward the technical inquiries of science proper, without being sidetracked into fruitless and inconclusive debates about rival values or *Weltanschauungen** to which individual scientists may happen (like anyone else) to be attracted for personal reasons, external to science, but which are not part of the collective agenda of science.

Thus, the deeper reasons for defining the scope and procedures of the   24 special sciences in ways that keep ethical issues out of their foundations were connected with the basic methodological program of the modern scientific movement. In particular, they reflect the steps which have been taken over the last 100 years to give institutional expression to the maxims and ambitions of the founders of the Royal Society, through the professionalization of the scientific enterprise. Given the care and effort that the community of professional scientists has taken in this way to insulate the foundations of science from ethics, we should not therefore be surprised if they have made it that much the harder to preserve clear and significant connections between science and the foundations of ethics, as well.

---

* *Weltanschauungen:* world views. [Editors' note.]

Philosophical Justifications for Separating
Ethics and Science

My argument* is aimed at showing how natural scientists worked to keep   25
ethical considerations and preferences from operating within "the foundations
of science"; so that, for instance, the tests for deciding whether one scientific
theory or concept was "better" or "worse" than its rivals, from the scientific
point of view, should be wholly divorced from issues about what was
ethically "better" or "worse." It was a matter of great importance for
scientists to be able to make the choice between alternative theories or
concepts turn solely on "objective" or "factual" considerations: they hoped
to avoid having to face the question whether one theory or concept is morally
preferable to, or more objectionable than, rival theories or concepts. (Can
this divorce be preserved absolutely in psychiatry, for example? May it not
be legitimate to raise moral objections to one or another theoretical
formulation in the psychiatric field? Leaving aside all questions about their
other rights and wrongs, we may still approve of Thomas Szasz's arguments
for simply raising that issue.)

That kind of value neutrality is, of course, quite compatible with   26
particular scientists adopting all sorts of ethical views and positions on their
own responsibility. It is even compatible with one rather more general,
collective view: namely, that we must begin by drawing a sharp line between
matters of pure or real science and matters of applied science or—more
precisely—of technology, after which it will become clear that questions of
ethical desirability can arise only in the latter, technological area. (To put
it crudely, anatomy is value-free, clinical medicine value-laden.) Above all,
it is compatible with all sorts of philosophical discussions, as professional
scientists seek to rationalize or justify their particular ethical positions, and
square their personal views about ethics with their scientific interests and
methodologies.

That is what seems to me to be happening in most of the cases that Loren   27
Graham discusses in his commentary (see pp. 425–435). His exemplary
scientists are not people who went out of their way to bring ethical
considerations into their scientific work, to the detriment of the intellectual
detachment at which professional scientists had aimed for so long. Rather,
they were people with idiosyncratic views about the philosophical relevance
of science to ethics, and vice versa. And, interestingly enough, several of

---

* Against this background, it will be easier to analyze and deal with the points of difference
between my own position in this paper and Loren Graham's, as presented in his commentary
on my argument. For Professor Graham claims to find a far livelier and healthier interaction
between science and ethics during the last hundred years than I here allow. Yet on closer
examination (I believe) even his best and most carefully expanded example—that of the
English astrophysicist and cosmologist, A. S. Eddington—will be found to support my
conclusion. [Author's note.]

them are people whose philosophical positions are ones that justify divorcing science from other realms of experience.

In this respect, Arthur Eddington in Britain resembles Pierre Duhem   28 in France. Duhem combined a scientific expertise in the field of thermodynamics with a religious commitment to Roman Catholicism. He was anxious not merely to avoid, but actually to prevent, any conflict between those two parts of his thinking. So, he adopted early in his career a "phenomenalist" attitude toward scientific theories and ideas. In his view, it is not the business of scientists to aim at discovering the nature of reality, but only to formulate mathematical schematisms capable in practice of "saving the phenomena": this posture allowed him to reserve questions about reality to the pronouncements of the metaphysicians and theologians. For instance: when J. J. Thomson first argued for the existence of "electrons" less than 1/1000 as massive as the lightest chemical atoms, Duhem was very scornful. To publish speculative arguments of that sort was to take the pretensions of the atomistic manner of talking far more seriously than they deserved. (Thermodynamics was, of course, almost totally "phenomenalistic" in its methods of analysis.) And he went on to pursue his learned and classic researches into the history of astronomy—researches whose motto might well have been, *Osiander was right*. Finally, he published an essay in which he made his underlying program entirely clear, with the revealing title, *Physique d'un Croyant*, or *The Physics of a Believer*.

Both Duhem and Eddington were thus seeking to provide philosophical   29 justifications for keeping science and ethics, or science and theology, at arm's length. Far from their example refuting my position, it tends only to confirm it. Both of them were in this respect people of their time, armed with a program for defining and pursuing the proper work of science in separation from ethical or religious thought. If they differed from the majority of their colleagues of the time, it was only in being more than wholly devout in their personal commitments to Catholicism or Quakerism. But their other commitments played their part in other areas of their lives, not within their science. They were, in short, both professional scientists and also religiously devout; not "religiously devout" in their actual ways of thinking about scientific issues. And, if that is a correct diagnosis, they were concerned to scrutinize the relations between science and ethics only for the sake of keeping them more securely apart.

THE LIMITS OF POSITIVISM

In our own day, the accumulated successes of the "positive" methodology   30 have carried science—and scientists—up against the limits of that program's validity, and in some places across them. As a preparation for answering my central question—"How can we set about reconnecting the sciences with the foundations of ethics?"—I can usefully begin by identifying certain points at which, during the last few years, the location of those limits has become apparent.

    To begin with, the positive program for science normally took for granted 31
a sentimental view of ethics: this was used to justify excluding ethics—which was assumed to deal with labile and subjective matters of taste or feeling— from the systematic investigation of "demonstrable facts." It was assumed, in other words, that human values, valuations and preferences have no place within the world of nature that is the scientist's object of study.

During the twentieth century, by contrast, science has expanded into the 32
realms of physiology and psychology, and in so doing has shown the limits of that assumption. As physiology and psychology have succeeded in securing their own position as sciences, human beings have ceased to be onlookers contemplating a natural world to which they themselves are foreign and have become parts of (or participants within) that world. As a result, the makeup, operations, and activities of human beings themselves have become legitimate issues for scientific investigation. At the very least, the biochemical and physiological preconditions of *normal* functioning, and so of *good* health, can accordingly be discussed nowadays as problems for science, as well as for ethics.* With this crucial incursion by science into the foundations of ethics, we can recognize that not all *human* evaluations must necessarily be regarded, from the scientific point of view, as *irrelevant* evaluations. On the contrary, some of the processes and phenomena studied by natural sciences carry with them certain immediate evaluative implications for the "good and ill" of human life. With this example before us, we are ready to take the first step in the direction hinted at earlier in this paper: that of using the "rational objectivity" of science as a model for reestablishing the claims of moral objectivity, as well.

    Given the increasingly close involvement of basic science with its applications 33
to human welfare, notably in the area of medical research, it is meanwhile becoming clear that the professional organization and priorities of scientific work can no longer be concerned solely *with considerations of intellectual content and merit, as contrasted with the ethical acceptability and social value, either of the research process itself, or of its practical consequences.*

The very existence of the bioethics movement generally, is one indication 34
of this change. The work of the National Commission for the Protection

---

* Notice, in this connection, John Stuart Mill's remark early on in *Utilitarianism* about the "goodness" of health. Health is in fact, for Mill, one of those paradigmatic "goods" about which utilitarian questions do not have to arise: it is "desirable," just because there would be something clearly paradoxical about people's not "desiring" it. (It should not have to be underlined that Mill was *not* committing G. E. Moore's "naturalistic fallacy" by this association of the "desirable" with "what is actually desired": on the contrary, what Mill sees is that any ethical system must rest on the existence of *some* things that anybody *may be presumed to* regard as "desirable," since they are the prerequisites—like health—for all other potentially "good" human experiences.) [Author's note.]

of Human Subjects, and of institutional review boards to review research involving human subjects, is another.

This being the case, the doors between science and the foundations of ethics can no longer be kept bolted from the scientific side, as they were in the heyday of positive science. Neither the disciplinary aspects of the sciences, their basic concepts and intellectual methods, nor the professional aspects of scientific work, the collective organization of science, and its criteria of professional judgment, can ever again be insulated against the "extraneous and irrelevant" influence of ethics, values, and preferences. 35

On what conditions, then, can we set about reestablishing the frayed links between science and ethics? 36

1. We should not attempt to reestablish these links by reviving outworn styles of natural theology. The kind of syncretistic cosmology to be found in Teilhard de Chardin, for example, is no improvement on its predecessors: this is indeed an area in which "demonstrable facts" are in real danger of being obscured by a larger wish-fulfilling framework of theological fantasies.[10] Instead, we should embark on a critical scientific and philosophical reexamination of humanity's place in nature, with special reference to the use of such terms as "function" and "adaptation," by which the ethical aspects of our involvement in the natural world are too easily obscured. 37

2. We should not attempt to force the pace, and insist on seeing ethical significance in all of science, let alone require that every piece of scientific investigation should have a demonstrable human relevance. Though the enthusiasms of the 1960s "counterculture" were intelligible enough in their historical context, that would be going too far in the opposite direction, and would land us in worse trouble than the positivist program itself.[11] Instead, we should pay critical attention to the respects in which, and the points at which, ethical issues enter into the conduct of scientific work, including its immediate practical consequences. The ethical aspects of human experimentation, and of such enterprises as sex research, are only samples, from a much larger group of possible issues. 38

3. We should not see this renewed interaction between science and ethics as threatening, or justifying, any attack on the proper autonomy of scientists within their own specific professional domains. The recent debate about recombinant DNA research generated rhetoric of two contrary kinds: both from scientists who saw the whole affair as a pretext for outside interference in the proper affairs of the scientific professions, and from laypersons who genuinely believed that those affairs were being carried on irresponsibly.[12] Instead, we should reconsider, in a more selective way, just what the proper scope and limits of professional autonomy are, and at what points scientists cross the line separating legitimate professional issues from matters of proper public concern, whether political or ethical. 39

4. We should not suppose that renewing diplomatic relations between   40
science and ethics will do anything to throw doubt on the virtues, duties,
and obligations of the scientific role or station. During the last decade, the
antiscientific excesses of the radicals have sometimes made it appear necessary
to apologize for being a scientist; and, as a reaction against this radical
rhetoric, some professional scientists have developed, in turn, a kind of
resentful truculence toward public discussions about the ethical and political
involvements of the scientific life. Instead, we need to set about understanding
better, both how the line between the narrowly professional and broader
social responsibilities of scientists runs in the collective sphere, and also
how individual scientists can balance their obligations within the overall
demands of a morally acceptable life, as between their chosen professional
roles as neurophysiologists, for example, and the other obligations to which
they are subject in other capacities as citizens, colleagues, lovers, parents,
religious believers, or whatever.

RENEGOTIATING THE CONNECTION BETWEEN SCIENCE AND ETHICS

I have suggested that changes in the social and historical context of science   41
could easily end the divorce of science from the foundations of ethics; and
even that such changes may, already, in fact, be underway. There is indeed
some evidence that this is already happening. During the last few years,
the "purist" view of science—as a strictly autonomous intellectual enterprise,
insulated against the influence of all merely human needs, wishes, and
preferences—has lost its last shreds of plausibility. Whether we consider
the basic concepts of the sciences, the collective enterprises of professional
science, or the personal commitments and motivations of individual scientists,
we can maintain a strictly value-free (or rather, ethics-free) position only
by sticking arbitrarily to one extreme end of a long spectrum.

From that extreme point of view, the ideally scientific investigation would   42
be a piece of strictly academic research on some application-proof project
in theoretical physics, conducted by a friendless and stateless bachelor of
independent means. There may have been a substantial body of science
approximating this idea as recently as the 1880s and 1890s, but that is
certainly not the case any longer. On the contrary, we can learn something
about the foundations of ethics by reconsidering the character and content
of the scientific enterprise on all three levels.

1.   As a collective activity, any science is of significance for ethics on
     account of the ways in which it serves as an embodiment or exemplar
     of applied rationality. In this respect, the very objectivity of the goals
     at which scientists aim, both collectively and individually, provides us
     with the starting point for a counterattack against relativism and

subjectivism in ethics, too; while the manner in which the sciences themselves, considered as "forms of life," define individual roles, with their own specific virtues, can also be taken as a starting point for a much broader reconstruction of ethics.[13]

2. Correspondingly, the moral character of the scientist's personal motivation, particularly the way in which the Kantian "pure respect for rationality as such" grows out of the wider life of affect or "inclination"—what I have elsewhere called "the moral psychology of science"[14]—can teach us something about the nature of personal virtue and commitment in other areas of life as well.

3. Finally, the actual content of the sciences is at last contributing to a better understanding of the human locus within the natural world. This fact is well recognized in the physiological sciences, where the links between *normal* functioning and *good* health are comparatively unproblematic. But it is a matter of active dispute in several areas just at this time: for example, in the conflict over the relations between social psychology and sociobiology. And there are some other fields in which it should be the topic of much more active debate than it is: for example, in connection with the rivalry between psychotherapeutic and psychopharmacological modes of treatment in psychiatry.

This done, it should not be hard to indicate the points at which issues [43] originating in the natural sciences can give rise to, and grow together with, evaluative issues—and not merely with issues that involve the values "intrinsic to" the scientific enterprise itself, but also larger human values of a more strictly ethical kind. For as we saw, the new phase of scientific development into which we are now moving requires us to reinsert human observers into the world of nature, so that we become not merely onlookers, but also participants in many of the natural phenomena and processes that are the subject matter of our scientific investigations. This is true across the whole spectrum of late twentieth-century science: all the way from quantum mechanics, where Heisenberg's Principle requires us to acknowledge the interdependence of the observer and the observed, to ecology, where the conduct of human beings is one crucial factor in any causal analysis of the condition of, say, Lake Erie, or to psychiatry, where the two-way interaction between the psychatrist and his client is in sharp contrast to the one-way influence of nature on the human observer (but not *vice versa*) presupposed in classical nineteenth-century science.[15]

One likely outcome of this novel phase of science could well be the [44] revival of interest in quasi-Stoic systems of ethics and philosophy, not to say, natural theology. The purist, or positivist, conception of science discussed earlier has a certain significant analogy with the Epicurean philosophy of late antiquity: both attempted to justify equanimity, or *ataraxia*, by pointing to the essential indifference ("value neutrality") of natural phenomena toward human affairs, and vice versa. By contrast, any improved understanding of the human locus *within* the natural world will presumably undercut this assumption of mutual indifference, and encourage people to move in a neo-Stoic direction—seeing human conduct as subject to ethical principles that must harmonize with the principles of the natural world.[16] Just as good health and physiological functioning are intrinsically linked together, so too human beings can presumably contribute to, or impair, the welfare of the natural ecosystems, or chains, within which they are links or elements.

45   Recognizing the interconnectedness of human conduct and natural phenomena may not by itself, of course, determine the direction in which those interconnections should point us. Acknowledging the need to establish some harmony between human conduct and natural processes is one thing: agreeing on what constitutes such a harmony is another, harder task. There was, for instance, a disagreement between Thomas Henry Huxley and his grandson, Julian, about the relations between human ethics and organic evolution.[17] (T.H. saw it a basic human obligation to fight against the cruelty and destructiveness of natural selection, whereas Julian saw the direction of human progress as a simple continuation of the direction of organic evolution.) What both Huxleys agreed about, however, was the need to see human ethics as having a place in the world of nature, and to arrive at a rational understanding of what that is.

46   It was with this need in mind that I referred, at the outset, to such concepts as function and adaptation as requiring particular scrutiny at the present time. For the question, "What is the true *function* of human beings?", is potentially as much a topic of debate today as it was in classical Athens, when Plato had Socrates raise it in the *Republic*. Likewise, the question, "How should our ways of acting change, in order to become *better adapted* to the novel situations in which we are finding ourselves?" is a question that also invites answers—sometimes, overly simple answers—based on a reading of contemporary biology and ecology. We are probably ripe for a revival of the organic theory of society and the state. And, though this is a topic that must be taken seriously, it is also one that is going to need to be handled with great caution and subtlety, if we are to avoid the crudely conservative emphases of earlier versions of the theory.[18] Starting from where we do, the answers we give to such questions will certainly need to be richer and more complex than those available in Plato's time; but, sharing Plato's questions, we are evidently back in a situation where our view of ethics and our view of nature are coming back together again.

47   To conclude: if there is one major field of discussion within which we should most urgently renegotiate the relations between the sciences and the foundations of ethics, that has to do with the concept of responsibility. There is a certain tension in all the sciences of human behavior at the present time, which I have discussed elsewhere under the heading of Townes's Paradox.[19] In thinking about the behavior of their research subjects, as objects of scientific study, psychologists and psychiatrists,

neurophysiologists and the rest, are inclined to interpret their observations in a systematically *causal* manner. In thinking about their own behavior, as psychologists, psychiatrists, neurophysiologists or whatever, they are inclined to do so always in *rational* terms. They are prepared, that is, to take credit on their own behalf for a kind of rationality—a freedom to think, act, and write as they do for good reasons—that is missing from their accounts of the thoughts, actions, and expressions of their research subjects. And, since the human capacity to act "for good reasons" is a basic presupposition of all ethics (just as it is of any truly rational science) arriving at a satisfactory resolution of this tension between the causal and rational way of interpreting human conduct is a matter of some urgency, both for science and for the foundations of ethics.

REFERENCES

1. The point cannot be stated quite so crisply in French or German: Dworkin, at any rate, is certainly contributing to *Rechtswissenschaft*, or *les sciences du droit*. But the differences in scope and sense between the English "science," French *science*, German *Wissenschaft*, Greek *episteme*, Arabic *'ilm* etc., provide too large and complex a topic to pursue here.

2. See, for instance, my paper, "Concepts of Function and Mechanism in Medicine and Medical Science," in *Evaluation and Explanation in the Biomedical Sciences*, H.T. Engelhardt, Jr. and S.F. Spicker, eds. (Dordrecht: 1975), pp. 51–66.

3. See, for instance, my paper, "The Meaning of Professionalism," in *Knowledge, Value and Belief*, Vol. II of "The Foundations of Ethics and Its Relationship to Science," H.T. Engelhardt, Jr. and Daniel Callahan, eds. (Hastings-on-Hudson, N.Y.: Institute of Society, Ethics and the Life Sciences, 1977), pp. 25ff.

4. Cf. Alasdair MacIntyre, "Objectivity in Morality and Objectivity in Science," in *Morals, Science, and Sociality*, Vol. III of "The Foundations of Ethics and Its Relationship to Science," H.T. Engelhardt, Jr., and Daniel Callahan, eds. (Hastings-on-Hudson, N.Y.: Institute of Society, Ethics and the Life Sciences, 1978), pp. 21–39.

5. See, for instance, my paper, "The Moral Psychology of Science," in *Morals, Science and Sociality*, pp. 48–67.

6. Arthur Kantrowitz, "The Science Court Experiment: An Interim Report," *Science*, 193 (1976), pp. 653 ff.

7. Cf: John Ray, *The Wisdom of God*, which is an indispensable source for the early history of botanical and zoological systematics; Joseph Priestley, *Disquisitions concerning Spirit and Matter*; and Isaac Newton, particularly his *Four Letters to Richard Bentley*.

8. Charles Gillispie's fascinating book, *Genesis and Geology* (New York: Harper & Row, 1959), is the classic source for this episode in the relations between geological science and natural theology.

9. See Gillispie, *Genesis and Geology*.

10. I have discussed this topic at greater length in an article about Teilhard de Chardin in *Commentary*, 39 (1965), 50 ff.

11. See for instance, my paper, "The historical background to the anti-science movement," in *Civilization and Science*, a Ciba Foundation Symposium, Amsterdam, 1972, pp. 23–32.

12. Cf. the National Academy of Science report on recombinant DNA research in February 1977.

13. Cf. Alasdair MacIntyre, "Objectivity in Morality and Morality in Science," and his forthcoming book, *Beyond Virtue*.

14. Cf. Toulmin, "The Moral Psychology of Science."

15. Cf. Karl Popper's striking arguments in *On Clouds and Clocks* (St. Louis: Washington University, 1966).

16. It is interesting to consider Arthur Koestler's scientific writings as a kind of neo-Stoic reaction against the supposed Epicureanism of behaviorist psychology, neo-Darwinist biology etc. See, e.g., his *Janus* (London and New York: 1978).

17. The contributions of both men to this topic are conveniently printed together in the book, *Evolution and Ethics 1893–1943* (London: 1947), which comprises T.H. Huxley's original Romanes Lecture together with Julian's subsequent Herbert Spencer lecture.

18. See, for instance, my paper, "Ethics and Social Functioning," in *Science, Ethics and Medicine*, Vol. I of "The Foundations of Ethics and Its Relationship to Science," H.T. Engelhardt, Jr. and Daniel Callahan, eds. N.Y.: Institute of Society, Ethics and the Life Sciences, (Hastings-on-Hudson: 1976), which discusses the role of physiological analogies in the writings of such social theorists as Emile Durkheim and Talcott Parsons.

19. See my paper on "Reasons and Causes," in *Explanation in the Behavioural Sciences*, R. Borger and F. Cioffi, eds. (Cambridge, England: 1970). Hans Jonas has recently drawn my attention to similar arguments in his own writings: see, e.g., *The Phenomenon of Life* (New York: 1966), pp. 124–25, and his earlier paper in *Social Research* 20 (1953).

THE MULTIPLE CONNECTIONS BETWEEN SCIENCE AND ETHICS

LOREN R. GRAHAM

Stephen Toulmin's attempt to answer the question, "How can we reconnect the sciences with the foundations of ethics?" contains a great many observations with which I entirely agree. His belief that we have recently passed through a period (a generation or two) in which an extreme and historically conditioned effort was made to achieve a complete divorce between science and values is, in my opinion, correct. His observation (and prediction) that this era is now coming to an end, and will not soon be repeated, is supported by current controversies in many scientific fields. Equally helpful is his suggested alternative of a "series of spectra" to the "value-free" picture of science that has reigned in much of Western Europe and America in past decades.

He drew our attention to several points on these spectra which he thinks we should study more carefully, such as the scientific terms "function," "adaptation," the ethical aspects of human experimentation, the proper scope and limits of "professional autonomy," and the concept of "responsibility." Finally, Toulmin issued several crucial warnings about how *not* to go about the effort to investigate links between science and ethics: do not try to revive outworn styles of natural theology; do not insist on seeing ethical significance in all of science; and do not engage in such examinations in order to attack or defend the professional autonomy of scientists within their own specific domains.

With all of the above points I am in agreement. And yet, I must admit that I am troubled by what I see as a striking discrepancy between the actual, historical interaction of science and ethical values during our century and the relationship which he described. Is the century described by Toulmin the one in which I have been living? While he sees few connections between science and ethics in past decades, I see a multiplicity of such contacts. Indeed, I maintain that the interaction of science and ethics has been particularly intense through this century and that, at the present moment, it is probably greater than at any time in history.

Part of the explanation of this paradox can be found in the distinction between ethics as an academic discipline and ethics as the principles of conduct of an individual or a group. Toulmin is undoubtedly correct when he says that ethics as an academic discipline has recently been little affected by science. He began his essay by referring to the works of John Rawls, Alan Donagan, and Ronald Dworkin; he correctly noted that these works give scant attention to science. It would be a mistake, however, to consider ethics only as an academic field; our dictionaries give us various definitions of "ethics," and several of the main definitions place ethics squarely in a broad social rather than a narrow academic context. An example would be "the rules of conduct recognized in respect to a particular class of human actions or a particular group, culture. . . ."

I maintain that within the framework of this definition of ethics there 5 has been during recent decades a massive influence of science upon ethics and *vice versa*. If the leading academic writers on the foundations of ethics have not wrestled adequately with this vigorous interaction, then an appropriate response would be "Why not?" instead of "Why are there so few contacts between science and ethics?" Or, returning to Toulmin's essay, it seems to me that a more helpful title would be, "How can we analyze the existing connections between the sciences and the foundations of ethics?" The problem we face is not in creating connections that earlier did not exist, but in recognizing and interpreting connections that have been there all along.

Ideally, an analysis of the connections of science and ethics or values 6 should be broad enough to include most of the interactions we have observed in the history of modern science. Only in that way can we hope to understand how science has influenced our values and how values have influenced science. It is true that by casting our net so widely we will include within our analysis instances in which the concepts of science are connected with ethics and values by processes of poor reasoning and bad logic, but if these historical events had actual effects, they must be considered in order to meet our goal of understanding how society has been affected by science-value interactions. We cannot dismiss these cases by maintaining that individual authors were guilty of committing the "naturalistic fallacy." Scientific theories have often interacted with ethical and value systems at moments when a rigorous philosophical examination might result in the conclusion that the interaction was illegitimate. But just as illegitimate children need to be taken seriously by those who conceive them, so also must the interactions of the supposedly aloof systems of science and values be taken seriously by those who wish to understand history.

Throughout the history of science a great many attempts have been made 7 to draw conclusions about ethical or sociopolitical values on the basis of science, and these attempts have differed greatly in approach and in quality of argument. Without attempting to classify exhaustively all of these efforts, I would like to point to two distinctly different classes of arguments about the relationship of science and values which I will call Expansionism and Restrictionism.

THE EXPANSIONIST APPROACH

By Expansionism I mean that type of argument which cites evidence within 8 the body of scientific theories and findings which can supposedly be used, either directly or indirectly, to support conclusions about ethical, sociopolitical, or religious values. I call this approach Expansionism because its result is to expand the boundaries of science in such a way that they include, at least by implication, value questions. A historically well-known type of interpretation in this category is an "argument by design" for the existence of God; the architecture of the universe, the structure of organisms, or the form of individual organs may be cited as evidence for the existence of some sort of a Supreme Architect. Numerous examples could easily be given, from Newton to Paley. A critic of religion who argues in the opposite direction—as, say, Clemence Royer did in the introduction to her French translation of Darwin's *Origin of Species*—is also using an Expansionist approach, for evidence found in the body of science is brought to bear on value questions.

Within Expansionism several different types of subclasses of arguments 9
exist, which I will not be able to discuss in detail here. I will merely mention that the linkage between science and values constructed by Expansionist authors can be either direct or indirect. A direct linkage is one where the science is supposed to relate to values in a way that is not merely by suggestion or implication, but in a logical, confirming or denying fashion. Charles Gillispie's *Genesis and Geology* contains much discussion of this sort of argument. If a person is a Biblical literalist who takes the Genesis story as factually true—or even merely its main assumption of a historically describable divine creation—then the sciences of geology and biology should speak to that person in a direct way. On a more sophisticated and contemporary level, psychological behaviorists who believe that values are environmentally formed and can be created and controlled at will— once science is refined—are clearly Expansionists who are making direct linkages between science and values. An example of such a linkage is this statement of B.F. Skinner's:

> When we say that a value judgement is a matter not of fact but of how someone feels about a fact, we are simply distinguishing between a thing and its reinforcing effect. . . . Reinforcing effects of things are the province of behavioral science, which to the extent that it is concerned with operant reinforcement, is a science of values.[1]

E.O. Wilson in his *Sociobiology* opened the door leading to direct 10
Expansionist linkages when he called for a "biologicization of ethics" but one remarkable aspect of that book was that, by and large, Wilson did not walk through the door; he only opened it and pointed through it. The reason, however, that the fields of sociobiology and animal behavior have excited interest among the educated lay public is that the members of that public correctly see these academic fields as efforts to expand natural science further into at least a partial explanation of human behavior, including ethics.

Expansionist authors may belong to a second subclass, that of indirect 11
linkages. These are people who do not try to bring a particular piece of scientific evidence into immediate logical relationship with values, but

instead work indirectly with the instruments of analogy, simile or metaphor. Social Darwinists who made apologies for industrial capitalism by pointing to the analogy between the struggle for existence in the biological world and competition in the economic world were following the line of argument of indirect linkage within the Expansionist approach. So was Friedrich Engels when he pointed to similar dialectical laws in chemistry and economics in his *Anti-Dühring*. And the astronomer James Jeans playfully pursued a similar type of argument in his popular writings when he spoke of the "finger of God" that started the planets in their orbits.

THE RESTRICTIONIST APPROACH

The logical alternative to Expansionism is Restrictionism, an approach that 12 confines science to a particular realm or a particular methodology and leaves values outside its boundaries. Although there are many types of values other than religious ones, Restrictionism is best known in debates about religion; Restrictionists often say "science and religion cannot possibly conflict, because they talk about entirely different things."

A strict adherence to this approach would mean that the relationship of 13 science to ethical, sociopolitical, and religious values is neutral. Science can be used to support neither human selfishness nor human altruism, nor can it affirm or deny either religious belief or atheism. Science is simply neutral with respect to values.

Returning now to the analysis of recent attitudes toward science-value 14 interactions given by Stephen Toulmin, we see that the view of science that he described as the attempt "to choose the purest, the most intellectual, the most autonomous, and the least ethically implicated extreme" on the spectra of science-value interactions was simply an unusually vigorous Restrictionism. Toulmin implies (and I agree) that the main error of this Restrictionism was not that it *never* is correct, but that it ignored almost everything that was happening at the other ends of the spectra, those topics in science, particularly in the biological and social sciences, where the basic concepts are irrevocably value-laden.

Before discussing why this view of science is now breaking down, I 15 would like to examine one of its paradoxical features. As we have seen, strictly speaking, the adherence to Restrictionism that reigned in the thirties and forties should not have supported any particular value system, for it was based on the assumption that science and values belong to separate realms. But in order to understand the function of Restrictionism, we need to turn from abstract analysis to chronological and social analysis. Historically, the Restrictionism of those decades had a considerable impact on values, for its actual function was to protect two systems of values: the professional values of scientists and the predominant nonscientific ethical and sociopolitical values of society. For if science and values could not interact, then scientists were safe from incursions by critics who tried to submit scientific ideas and the scientific profession to social criticism; and ethicists and spokesmen for political or religious values were safe from attempts by scientists to show the relevance of science for their concerns. With the realms of science and values effectively insulated from each other, the historical effect of this demarcation of boundaries was to support existing institutional expressions of positions on science and values. Since I am a supporter of the scientific enterprise and also believe that society cannot exist without value systems, I believe that at least some of the effects of this demarcation were positive, but I also agree with Toulmin that it was a temporary historical product based on assumptions no longer tenable. Indeed, the negative effects of this compromise are now increasingly clear.

Let us look briefly at one well-known scientist who wrote extensively in   16 the middle of the period between the two world wars, the generation upon which Toulmin concentrated in his description of the "value-free" era of science. The great British astrophysicist Arthur Stanley Eddington supported Restrictionism strongly and yet, simultaneously, he found it a useful foundation on which to support existing social values. He was well aware of the naturalistic fallacy and—contrary to the opinions of several of his critics—he never tried to support religion directly with the findings of science. He wrote:

> I repudiate the idea of proving the distinctive beliefs of religion either from the data of physical science or by the methods of physical science.[2]

Eddington realized that to give scientific arguments in favor of ethics or religion was simultaneously to provide the theoretical base for scientific arguments pointed in the opposite direction. Thus, he affirmed that "The religious person may well be content that I have not offered him a God revealed by the quantum theory, and therefore liable to be swept away in the next scientific revolution."[3] Eddington found Restrictionism a source of great security, for it left his religious preferences undisturbed.

His motivation for relying on Restrictionism emerges in the following   17 quotation:

> . . . If you want to fill a vessel with anything you must make it hollow. . . . Any of the young theoretical physicists of today will tell you that what he is dragging to light on the basis of all the phenomena that come within his province is a scheme of symbols connected by mathematical equa-tions. . . . Now a skeleton scheme of symbols is hollow enough to hold anything. It can be—nay, it cries out to be—filled with something to transform it from skeleton into being, from shadow into actuality, from symbols into the interpretation of symbols.[4]

Eddington was trying to create a thirst in his readers for values derived   18 from nonscientific realms, and he was accomplishing that purpose by maintaining that science was merely a system of symbols with no relevance to the major questions of human existence. Far too sophisticated and subtle a person to engage in proselytizing for his own religion of Quakerism, he nonetheless pointed out that "Quakerism in dispensing with creeds holds out a hand to the scientist." Eddington confined science to a small realm of man's concerns and he then invited his readers to fill the remaining space with value systems based on religion. We thus see that in Eddington's hands Restrictionism was turned in on itself and became a justification for certain kinds of values.

It is my opinion that Eddington is only one example of a number of writers on science during the twenties and thirties who found the principle that science is value-free useful in defending their own value preferences. If science tells us nothing about values, then every person is free to defend values without fearing that science will interfere. I should add, of course, that the use of the value-free principle in this "value-laden" way says nothing about the particular values being defended, because the principle could be used to justify any values at all. In historical reality, however, the principle tended to support societal values already dominant. 19

In his paper Toulmin tends to discount the relevance of people such as Eddington for an understanding of the relationship between science and values in the last generation or two. Eddington, he says, was a person "with idiosyncratic views about the philosophical relevance of science to ethics, and *vice versa*." For the moment I will leave aside the fact that Eddington was probably the most influential and popular writer on physics (for the educated English-speaking public, not for professional philosophers) of the middle decades of this century, and I will agree with Toulmin that Eddington was indeed idiosyncratic. However, I think that the example of Eddington is still instructive for us in our effort to understand the relationship between science and values in recent generations. Eddington made explicit in a specific and idiosyncratic way the social relevance of Restrictionism that was, in a more general and less idiosyncratic fashion, widely accepted elsewhere. That view can be summarized as follows: if you insist that science and values do not mix, then the antecedent values of society are protected. 20

This position can be defended until that point in time when the relevance of new scientific knowledge to antecedent social values becomes so overwhelming that their separation becomes obviously artificial. After several generations of brave efforts to keep the two realms separate we have now reached that point of artificiality and the whole question of the relationship of science to values has to be raised anew. 21

I agree with Toulmin that a historical reconstruction or reinterpretation of the ways in which science came to part company with ethics "needs to focus attention on the history of scientific specialization." However, too narrow a concentration on professionalization and specialization could be misleading, for they are merely the *modes* by which science was separated from ethics, they are not the *reasons*, or, as a biologist might say, they do not reveal the "adaptive value" of the separation. Restrictionism (a term I prefer to "Separationism," since a pure separation was never possible) 22 protected science, but not only science. Restrictionism also protected society by making its values imperturbable by science.

LINKS OF SCIENCE TO VALUES

The move toward Restrictionism came not because of specialization but 23 because the relevance of science to values seemed to be changing in a way that made such protection desirable. In the eighteenth century, science could be rather easily used as an apologia or justification of the values most widely accepted in society at large. "Arguments by design" were essentially the employment of science for the buttressing of orthodox value positions. When this kind of argument was readily available and fairly persuasive, it was in the interests of scientists (natural philosophers) to advance such views in an explicit fashion. However, when science began to undermine existing values (for example, historical geology versus Creationism; Darwinian evolution versus *a priori* moral systems), the motivation for being explicit about links between science and values disappeared. Professional societies restricted their memberships increasingly to working scientists who avoided value questions because it was much safer that way. However, implicit links between science and values continued to pile up, as in some secret bank account, as science continued to develop. One day the dimensions of the reserve would demand discussion. Twentieth-century science moved heavily into the fields of behavioral psychology, human genetics, biomedicine, and ethology; the impossibility of keeping the links between science and values outside the concerns of scientists and their institutions became increasingly apparent. We now must reckon with the account that was gradually accumulated, as well as define our position on its future growth. Viewing the situation from this standpoint, I think the need is not so much to "reconnect" the links of science to values as it is to evaluate the links that have been multiplying for decades.

The exaggeration of the value-free nature of science which reigned in 24 the interwar period (1918–39) had many causes, both intellectual and social, and a full analysis of them will not be possible here. One important intellectual stimulus, however, was the revolutionary developments in physics in the first thirty years of this century. Physics was seen in these decades as the science *par excellence*; when many scientists and philosophers talked about "science" they often meant "physics." And one of the important effects of the crisis in physics leading to the emergence of relativity theory was the stress on the extreme value-free and assumption-free end of the spectrum of science-value interactions that Toulmin described. Not only did most people agree, then and now, that the concepts of physics are far from value considerations, but even *within physics* the effect of the advent of relativity was to push thinkers back to the absolute minimum of assumptions about the natural world. Einstein had insisted that each physical quantity be defined as the result of certain operations of measurement, and he showed that by examining these operations more closely than anyone before had done a logical opening appeared through which a new concept of time, or simultaneity, could be drawn. Scientists and philosophers of science were understandably impressed by the fruitfulness of this approach, and a generation of writing followed in which physics was the major influence in the philosophy of science, driving it toward an analogous minimum of value-free assumptions.

Our more recent concerns about the relationship of science and values   25
have been shaped by events in scientific disciplines on the other end of the spectra of science-value interactions, those where the connections between science and values seem unavoidable, probably intrinsic. Increasingly the attempt in the interwar years to build a value-free concept of science based on physics seems constricted, even quaint, to our ears. The areas of science that have treaded most closely on human values in the last decades are not ones in which quantitative approaches or measurement theory are crucially important. To take one example, the science of animal behavior, recognized by the award of Nobel Prizes to three of its leading practitioners in 1973, attempts to explain animal and human behavior in ways that have obvious value significance. What would Konrad Lorenz—who rarely made measurements, once boasted that he had never drawn a graph in his life, and found mathematics largely incomprehensible—say to the assertions of a number of scientists and philosophers of the interwar years that the division between scientific and extrascientific realms is the same as the cleavage between the metrical and the nonmetrical? And in other areas where science-value interactions are currently important, as in behavioral psychology, human genetics, neurophysiology, the concepts of philosophy of science, which came largely from physics, are not very helpful in solving our problems.

We are obviously now in a new era in our understanding of science-   26
value relationships, and this new period brings with it both novel opportunities and novel dangers. We must live in the middle range of the science-value spectra, recognizing the erroneousness of the value-free conception of science so prevalent in the previous generation, and the equal erroneousness of the countering view that "all of science" is value-laden.

We now recognize more openly than before that at least some of the   27
concepts of science, especially those of the social and behavioral sciences, contain value elements. We also know that scientific theories and findings in areas such as psychology, genetics, neurophysiology, and animal behavior can have important value effects. It seems, furthermore, increasingly likely that some of the aspects of human behavior that were previously assigned to the ethical realm are influenced by genetic and physiological bases. As we learn more about what sociobiologists and others have called the "emotive centers of the hypothalamic-limbic system" we will probably see more clearly that genetics and physiology are relevant to discussions of ethics.

And as our knowledge of these areas increases, our power of intervention often grows.

In chronological terms the most dangerous period of the development of a science is when enough is known to advance the first fruitful speculations and to try a few interventions, but not enough is known to bring discipline to those speculations or to predict the possible side effects or aftereffects of intervention. When the science of human genetics first began to develop at the end of the nineteenth century and the first decades of the twentieth it was so inexact and contained so many flawed conceptions, such as beliefs in single-gene determination of behavioral and psychological characteristics, that it allowed room for a rash of pseudo-scientific eugenic theories and practices in which social and political prejudices played important roles. As we move into the newer areas of science-value interactions on the basis of such still fairly recent sciences as sociobiology a little conservatism about accepting all the claims advanced by advocates is entirely warranted. 28

As we learn that aspects of our behavior which earlier seemed to be based solely on nonscientific ethical values are actually conditioned genetically, we should be cautious about shifting the entire weight of our attention to that sort of explanation. Some important part of our ethical values may not be well-explained genetically, and these cultural aspects of ethics may play valuable roles of which we are still unaware. Just as we wish to preserve our genetic reserves, so we should preserve our cultural ones as well. Human beings are probably wiser than they know; *both* the genetic bases of their behavior and the cultural, ethical bases of their behavior have been selectively tested throughout the evolution of civilization. This cultural and biological evolution has been successful (in the sense of reproductive success and its surrogates), but its mechanisms are not fully understood. 29

Anthropologists tell us that the beliefs and superstitions of primitive peoples, at first glance irrational, often serve very practical goals in preserving the security of the particular primitive society although the society itself may not be aware of the value of their customs. Our traditional value systems, hopelessly nonscientific, may still work in some similar ways. Despite the injustices of contemporary civilization, it works fairly well, and we should not attempt to change its underlying assumptions in a wholesale way when we are operating on the basis of very partial scientific knowledge. There is an argument for gradualism even when irrationality is being replaced by rationality. 30

Perhaps a somewhat simple analogy will help a bit here. A grade-school child is often superb at riding a bicycle even though he or she knows nothing of the principles of physics that permit one to ride a bicycle and that govern what can be done with it. Later he or she may learn the necessary physics at school. If the youth would on some fine day decide to relearn how to ride a bicycle on a scientific basis, applying these principles, his riding would at first gain nothing, and he might even have a wreck. 31

Accumulated experience is more important here than science. In a similar way, it is quite likely that some of the values necessary for the continuation of civilization were learned on a nonscientific basis and are now encased in nonscientific or even irrational beliefs; as we learn what the scientific explanations for some of these values and ethical systems are, we should be intelligently cautious about attempting a sudden new way of keeping our equilibrium. Indeed, we are so far from having a scientific explanation of ethics that genuine skepticism about a "biologicization of ethics" is warranted.

We have left behind the view that science is value-free. We recognize 32 the links that exist between many areas of science and our values and ethics. We are ready to benefit from the insights that science can bring to our understanding of these values. We know that we must live in the middle range of science-value interactions, seeing that the pure poles of "value-free science" and "science-free values" are diminishing in strength. But living on this particular slippery slope will require extreme caution. The major flaw in the view of the past generation described by Toulmin was to refuse to see where science was affected by values; we should guard against a possible future period in which we might fall into one of two possible different errors: the attempt to explain values exhaustively in terms of a science that is always incomplete, or the attempt to attack all science as being intrinsically value-laden.

Avoiding these extremes, much valuable work remains to be done. We 33 need to examine the internal concepts of science, as Toulmin has suggested, to find how we might analyze the connections of the sciences with the foundations of ethics. We need to study more thoroughly the importance of genetic evolution for understanding our social behavior. We also need to re-examine the history of science to see where science-value interactions have occurred with important social effects, even though some of the concepts were, from our present point of view, faulty (the history of eugenics, the attempts to link quantum mechanical indeterminacy with concepts of free will, the relationship between Marxism and science, the relationship between religion and science). And of course we need to explore the ethical dimensions of present scientific research procedures and technological practices. By pursuing these different approaches we will learn much more about the great variety of ways in which science and values can interact.

REFERENCES

1. B.F. Skinner, *Beyond Freedom and Dignity* (New York: Alfred A. Knopf, 1971), p. 104.

2. A.S. Eddington, *The Nature of the Physical World* (Cambridge: Cambridge University Press, 1928), p. 333.

3. Eddington, *The Nature of the Physical World*, p. 353.

4. A.S. Eddington, *Science and Religion* (London: Friends Home Service Committee, 1931), pp. 9–10.

Questions for Discussion and Writing

1. What, according to Toulmin, is Townes's Paradox? How important is it to Toulmin's overall argument?

2. One of the key elements in debate is accurately establishing the principal bones of contention between your opponent and yourself. Part of this process includes assessing the strengths and weaknesses of your opponent's case. Do you believe that Graham, in the process of sizing up Toulmin's argument, accurately evaluates its merits and demerits?

3. How do specialization and professionalization fit into Toulmin's argument? Does Graham have a reasonable response to Toulmin's claim? How do you feel about the issue?

4. Toward the end of his argument, Toulmin calls for "reestablishing the frayed links between science and ethics" (paragraph 36). "We should not," he argues, "see this renewed interaction between science and ethics as threatening, or justifying, any attack on the proper autonomy of scientists within their own specific professional domains" (paragraph 39). In a somewhat similar manner, Graham closes his discussion by urging the scholarly community to "explore the ethical dimensions of present scientific research procedures and technological practices" (paragraph 33). What do you believe about the interface of science and ethics? Keeping Toulmin and Graham's debate in mind, write an essay in which you develop a position concerning the "interaction" between ethics and scientific endeavor. Focus your response on a current form of scientific research that contains possible ethical implications (for example, genetic engineering, the use of animals in research, space technology for military purposes, Pentagon funding for basic research at universities, and so on).

E. D. HIRSCH, JR.

(b. 1928)

Edward Donald Hirsch, Jr., has enjoyed two distinct careers as a scholar, teacher, and writer. Born in Memphis, Tennessee, and raised in the South, Hirsch moved to the Northeast for his college education. He received his B.A. from Cornell University (1950) and his M.A. (1955) and Ph.D. (1957) from Yale University. From 1957 to 1966, he taught English at Yale; in 1966, he returned to the South and assumed a professorship in English at the University of Virginia, Charlottesville. In 1973, he was appointed as William R. Kenan Professor of English.

Hirsch's first academic career focused primarily on literary interpretation. His first two major publications, Wordsworth and Schelling: A Typological Study of Romanticism (1960) and Innocence and Experience: An Introduction to Blake (1964), considered interpretative questions about specific Romantic poets. His next two important works, Validity in Interpretation (1967) and The Aims of Interpretation (1976), took up the subject of literary interpretation in general. With these scholarly contributions to the field, Hirsch had formed for himself a solid reputation as a literary critic.

In The Philosophy of Composition (1977), Hirsch argued that student writers should be steeped in the standard grammatical and stylistic conventions of the written language that dominates their culture. In making this argument, Hirsch launched what could be considered his second career, in which he stressed the importance of shared cultural knowledge to general education. This second career came to full bloom in 1987, when Hirsch published his best-known and most controversial book, Cultural Literacy: What Every American Needs to Know. Seeking to answer the age-old question, "What is the knowledge most worth having?" Hirsch compares the merits of educational philosophies that stress general skills such as critical thinking with a pedagogical program that inculcates students with a standardized body of cultural knowledge.

Along with Allan Bloom's The Closing of the American Mind (1987), Hirsch's Cultural Literacy and its supplement, The Dictionary of Cultural Literacy (1988), have inspired one of the most heated academic debates in years. The first chapter of Hirsch's work, excerpted here, presents the essence of his argument. Although there is no need to rehearse his entire line of reasoning, we will augment your reading by providing one quote from the concluding chapter that specifically addresses the skills approach to teaching (also called "educational formalism" by Hirsch):

> The skills model of education is illusory, because it overlooks the fact that reading and thinking skills alike depend upon a wide range of specific, quickly

available information. Every citizen needs to have immediately at hand a critical mass of specific information in order to possess that skill of skills which is literacy.

As you read Hirsch's argument, give careful consideration to his criticism of the American educational system. Based on your experience, is his criticism on the mark?

LITERACY AND CULTURAL LITERACY

The Decline of Literate Knowledge

This books explains why we need to make some very specific educational changes in order to achieve a higher level of national literacy. It does not anatomize the literacy crisis or devote many pages to Scholastic Aptitude Test scores. It does not document at length what has already been established, that Americans do not read as well as they should. It takes no position about methods of initial reading instruction beyond insisting that content must receive as much emphasis as "skill." It does not discuss teacher training or educational funding or school governance. In fact, one of its major purposes is to break away entirely from what Jeanne S. Chall has called "the great debate" about methods of reading instruction. It focuses on what I conceive to be the great hidden problem in American education, and I hope that it reveals this problem so compellingly that anyone who is concerned about American education will be persuaded by the book's argument and act upon it.

The standard of literacy required by modern society has been rising throughout the developed world, but American literacy rates have not risen to meet this standard. What seemed an acceptable level in the 1950s is no longer acceptable in the late 1980s, when only highly literate societies can prosper economically. Much of Japan's industrial efficiency has been credited to its almost universally high level of literacy. But in the United States, only two thirds of our citizens are literate, and even among those the average level is too low and should be raised. The remaining third of our citizens need to be brought as close to true literacy as possible. Ultimately our aim should be to attain universal literacy at a very high level, to achieve not only greater economic prosperity but also greater social justice and more effective democracy. We Americans have long accepted literacy as a paramount aim of schooling, but only recently have some of us who have done research in the field begun to realize that literacy is far more than a skill and that it requires large amounts of specific information. That new insight is central to this book.

Professor Chall is one of several reading specialists who have observed   3
that "world knowledge" is essential to the development of reading and
writing skills.[1] What she calls world knowledge I call cultural literacy,
namely, the network of information that all competent readers possess. It
is the background information, stored in their minds, that enables them to
take up a newspaper and read it with an adequate level of comprehension,
getting the point, grasping the implications, relating what they read to the
unstated context which alone gives meaning to what they read. In describing
the contents of this neglected domain of background information, I try to
direct attention to a new opening that can help our schools make the
significant improvement in education that has so far eluded us. The
achievement of high universal literacy is the key to all other fundamental
improvements in American education.

Why is literacy so important in the modern world? Some of the reasons,   4
like the need to fill out forms or get a good job, are so obvious that they
needn't be discussed. But the chief reason is broader. The complex undertakings of modern life depend on the cooperation of many people with
different specialties in different places. Where communications fail, so do
the undertakings. (That is the moral of the story of the Tower of Babel.)
The function of national literacy is to foster effective nationwide communications. Our chief instrument of communication over time and space
is the standard national language, which is sustained by national literacy. Mature literacy alone enables the tower to be built, the business to be
well managed, and the airplane to fly without crashing. All nationwide
communications, whether by telephone, radio, TV, or writing are fundamentally dependent upon literacy, for the essence of literacy is not simply
reading and writing but also the effective use of the standard literate
language. In Spain and most of Latin America the literate language is
standard written Spanish. In Japan it is standard written Japanese. In our
country it is standard written English.

Linguists have used the term "standard written English" to describe both   5
our written and spoken language, because they want to remind us that
standard spoken English is based upon forms that have been fixed in
dictionaries and grammars and are adhered to in books, magazines, and
newspapers. Although standard written English has no intrinsic superiority
to other languages and dialects, its stable written forms have now standardized
the oral forms of the language spoken by educated Americans.[2] The chief
function of literacy is to make us masters of this standard instrument of
knowledge and communication, thereby enabling us to give and receive
complex information orally and in writing over time and space. Advancing
technology, with its constant need for fast and complex communications, has
made literacy ever more essential to commerce and domestic life. The
literate language is more, not less, central in our society now than it was
in the days before television and the silicon chip.

The recently rediscovered insight that literacy is more than a skill is   6 based upon knowledge that all of us unconsciously have about language. We know instinctively that to understand what somebody is saying, we must understand more than the surface meanings of words; we have to understand the context as well. The need for background information applies all the more to reading and writing. To grasp the words on a page we have to know a lot of information that isn't set down on the page.

Consider the implications of the following experiment described in an 7 article in *Scientific American*.³ A researcher goes to Harvard Square in Cambridge, Massachusetts, with a tape recorder hidden in his coat pocket. Putting a copy of the *Boston Globe* under his arm, he pretends to be a native. He says to passers-by, "How do you get to Central Square?" The passers-by, thinking they are addressing a fellow Bostonian, don't even break their stride when they give their replies, which consist of a few words like "First stop on the subway."

The next day the researcher goes to the same spot, but this time he 8 presents himself as a tourist, obviously unfamiliar with the city. "I'm from out of town," he says. "Can you tell me how to get to Central Square?" This time the tapes show that people's answers are much longer and more rudimentary. A typical one goes, "Yes, well you go down on the subway. You can see the entrance over there, and when you get downstairs you buy a token, put it in the slot, and you go over to the side that says Quincy. You take the train headed for Quincy, but you get off very soon, just the first stop is Central Square, and be sure you get off there. You'll know it because there's a big sign on the wall. It says Central Square." And so on.

Passers-by were intuitively aware that communication between strang- 9 ers requires an estimate of how much relevant information can be taken for granted in the other person. If they can take a lot for granted, their communications can be short and efficient, subtle and complex. But if strangers share very little knowledge, their communications must be long and relatively rudimentary.

In order to put in perspective the importance of background knowledge 10 in language, I want to connect the lack of it with out recent lack of success in teaching mature literacy to all students. The most broadly based evidence about our teaching of literacy comes from the National Assessment of Educational Progress (NAEP). This nationwide measurement, mandated by Congress, shows that between 1970 and 1980 seventeen-year-olds declined in their ability to understand written materials, and the decline was especially striking in the top group, those able to read at an "advanced" level.⁴ Although these scores have now begun to rise, they remain alarmingly low. Still more precise quantitative data have come from the scores of the verbal Scholastic Aptitude Test (SAT). According to John B. Carroll, a distinguished psychometrician, the verbal SAT is essentially a test of "advanced vocabulary knowledge," which makes it a fairly sensitive instrument for measuring levels of literacy.⁵ It is well known that verbal SAT scores have declined dramatically in the past fifteen years, and though recent reports have shown them rising again, it is from a very low base. Moreover, performance on the verbal SAT has been slipping steadily *at the top*. Ever fewer numbers of our best and brightest students are making high scores on the test.

Before the College Board disclosed the full statistics in 1984, antialarmists could argue that the fall in average verbal scores could be explained by the rise in the number of disadvantaged students taking the SATs. That argument can no longer be made. It's now clear that not only our disadvantaged but also our best educated and most talented young people are showing diminished verbal skills. To be precise, out of a constant pool of about a million test takers each year, 56 percent more students scored above 600 in 1972 than did so in 1984. More startling yet, the percentage drop was even greater for those scoring above 650—73 percent.[6]

In the mid 1980s American business leaders have become alarmed by the lack of communication skills in the young people they employ. Recently, top executives of some large U.S. companies, including CBS and Exxon, met to discuss the fact that their younger middle-level executives could no longer communicate their ideas effectively in speech or writing. This group of companies has made a grant to the American Academy of Arts and Sciences to analyze the causes of this growing problem. They want to know why, despite breathtaking advances in the technology of communication, the effectiveness of business communication has been slipping, to the detriment of our competitiveness in the world. The figures from NAEP surveys and the scores on the verbal SAT are solid evidence that literacy has been declining in this country just when our need for effective literacy has been sharply rising.

I now want to juxtapose some evidence for another kind of educational decline, one that is related to the drop in literacy. During the period 1970–1985, the amount of shared knowledge that we have been able to take for granted in communicating with our fellow citizens has also been declining. More and more of our young people don't know things we used to assume they knew.

A side effect of the diminution in shared information has been a noticeable increase in the number of articles in such publications as *Newsweek* and the *Wall Street Journal* about the surprising ignorance of the young. My son John, who recently taught Latin in high school and eighth grade, often told me of experiences which indicate that these articles are not exaggerated. In one of his classes he mentioned to his students that Latin, the language they were studying, is a dead language that is no longer spoken. After his pupils had struggled for several weeks with Latin grammar and vocabulary, this news was hard for some of them to accept. One girl raised her hand to challenge my son's claim. "What do they speak in Latin America?" she demanded.

At least she had heard of Latin America. Another day my son asked his Latin class if they knew the name of an epic poem by Homer. One pupil

11

12

13

14

15

shot up his hand and eagerly said, "The Alamo!" Was it just a slip for *The Iliad?* No, he didn't know what the Alamo was, either. To judge from other stories about information gaps in the young, many American school-children are less well informed than this pupil. The following, by Benjamin J. Stein, is an excerpt from one of the most evocative recent accounts of youthful ignorance.

> I spend a lot of time with teen agers. Besides employing three of them part-time, I frequently conduct focus groups at Los Angeles area high schools to learn about teen agers' attitudes towards movies or television shows or nuclear arms or politicians. . . .
>
> I have not yet found one single student in Los Angeles, in either college or high school, who could tell me the years when World War II was fought. Nor have I found one who could tell me the years when World War I was fought. Nor have I found one who knew when the American Civil War was fought. . . .
>
> A few have known how many U.S. senators California has, but none has known how many Nevada or Oregon has. ("Really? Even though they're so small?") . . . Only two could tell me where Chicago is, even in the vaguest terms. (My particular favorite geography lesson was the junior at the University of California at Los Angeles who thought that Toronto must be in Italy. My second-favorite geography lesson is the junior at USC, a pre-law student, who thought that Washington, D.C. was in Washington State.) . . .
>
> Only two could even approximately identify Thomas Jefferson. Only one could place the date of the Declaration of Independence. None could name even one of the first ten amendments to the Constitution or connect them with the Bill of Rights. . . .
>
> On and on it went. On and on it goes. I have mixed up episodes of ignorance of facts with ignorance of concepts because it seems to me that there is a connection. . . . The kids I saw (and there may be lots of others who are different) are not mentally prepared to continue the society because they basically do not understand the society well enough to value it.[7]

My son assures me that his pupils are not ignorant. They know a great deal. Like every other human group they share a tremendous amount of knowledge among themselves, much of it learned in school. The trouble is that, from the standpoint of their literacy and their ability to communicate with others in our culture, what they know is ephemeral and narrowly confined to their own generation. Many young people strikingly lack the information that writers of American books and newspapers have traditionally taken for granted among their readers from all generations. For reasons explained in this book, our children's lack of intergenerational information is a serious problem for the nation. The decline of literacy and the decline of shared knowledge are closely related, interdependent facts. 16

The evidence for the decline of shared knowledge is not just anecdotal. 17

In 1978 NAEP issued a report which analyzed a large quantity of data showing that our children's knowledge of American civics had dropped significantly between 1969 and 1976.[8] The performance of thirteen-year-olds had dropped an alarming 11 percentage points. That the drop has continued since 1976 was confirmed by preliminary results from a NAEP study conducted in late 1985. It was undertaken both because of concern about declining knowledge and because of the growing evidence of a causal connection between the drop in shared information and in literacy. The Foundations of Literacy project is measuring some of the specific information about history and literature that American seventeen-year-olds possess.

Although the full report will not be published until 1987, the preliminary field tests are disturbing.[9] If these samplings hold up, and there is no reason to think they will not, then the results we will be reading in 1987 will show that two thirds of our seventeen-year-olds do not know that the Civil War occurred between 1850 and 1900. Three quarters do not know what *reconstruction* means. Half do not know the meaning of *Brown decision* and cannot identify either Stalin or Churchill. Three quarters are unfamiliar with the names of standard American and British authors. Moreover, our seventeen-year-olds have little sense of geography or the relative chronology of major events. Reports of youthful ignorance can no longer be considered merely impressionistic.[10]   18

My encounter in the seventies with this widening knowledge gap first caused me to recognize the connection between specific background knowledge and mature literacy. The research I was doing on the reading and writing abilities of college students made me realize two things.[11] First, we cannot assume that young people today know things that were known in the past by almost every literate person in the culture. For instance, in one experiment conducted in Richmond, Virginia, our seventeen- and eighteen-year-old subjects did not know who Grant and Lee were. Second, our results caused me to realize that we cannot treat reading and writing as empty skills, independent of specific knowledge. The reading skill of a person may vary greatly from task to task. The level of literacy exhibited in each task depends on the relevant background information that the person possesses.   19

The lack of wide-ranging background information among young men and women now in their twenties and thirties is an important cause of the illiteracy that large corporations are finding in their middle-level executives. In former days, when business people wrote and spoke to one another, they could be confident that they and their colleagues had studied many similar things in school. They could talk to one another with an efficiency similar to that of native Bostonians who speak to each other in the streets of Cambridge. But today's high school graduates do not reliably share much common information, even when they graduate from the same school. If young people meet as strangers, their communications resemble the uncertain,   20 rudimentary explanations recorded in the second part of the Cambridge experiment.

My father used to write business letters that alluded to Shakespeare. 21 These allusions were effective for conveying complex messages to his associates, because, in his day, business people could make such allusions with every expectation of being understood. For instance, in my father's commodity business, the timing of sales and purchases was all-important, and he would sometimes write or say to his colleagues, "There is a tide," without further elaboration, Those four words carried not only a lot of complex information, but also the persuasive force of a proverb. In addition to the basic practical meaning, "Act now!" what came across was a lot of implicit reasons why immediate action was important.

For some of my younger readers who may not recognize the allusion, 22 the passage from *Julius Caesar* is:

> There is a tide in the affairs of men
> Which taken at the flood leads on to fortune;
> Omitted, all the voyage of their life
> Is bound in shallows and in miseries.
> On such a full sea are we now afloat,
> And we must take the current when it serves,
> Or lose our ventures.

To say "There is a tide" is better than saying "Buy (or sell) now and you'll cover expenses for the whole year, but if you fail to act right away, you may regret it the rest of your life." That would be twenty-seven words instead of four, and while the bare message of the longer statement would be conveyed, the persuasive force wouldn't. Think of the demands of such a business communication. To persuade somebody that your recommendation is wise and well-founded, you have to give lots of reasons and cite known examples and authorities. My father accomplished that and more in four words, which made quoting Shakespeare as effective as any efficiency consultant could wish. The moral of this tale is not that reading Shakespeare will help one rise in the business world. My point is a broader one. The fact that middle-level executives no longer share literate background knowledge is a chief cause of their inability to communicate effectively.

THE NATURE AND USE OF CULTURAL LITERACY

The documented decline in shared knowledge carries implications that go 23 far beyond the shortcomings of executives and extend to larger questions of educational policy and social justice in our country. Mina Shaughnessy was a great English teacher who devoted her professional life to helping disadvantaged students become literate. At the 1980 conference dedicated to her memory, one of the speakers who followed me to the podium was the

Harvard historian and sociologist Orlando Patterson. To my delight he departed from his prepared talk to mention mine. He seconded my argument that shared information is a necessary background to true literacy. Then he extended and deepened the ideas I had presented. Here is what Professor Patterson said, as recorded in the *Proceedings* of the conference.

> Industrialized civilization [imposes] a growing cultural and structural complexity which requires persons to have a broad grasp of what Professor Hirsch has called cultural literacy: a deep understanding of mainstream culture, which no longer has much to do with white Anglo-Saxon Protestants, but with the imperatives of industrial civilization. It is the need for cultural literacy, a profound conception of the whole civilization, which is often neglected in talk about literacy.

Patterson continued by drawning a connection between background information and the ability to hold positions of responsibility and power. He was particularly concerned with the importance for blacks and other minorities of possessing this information, which is essential for improving their social and economic status.

> The people who run society at the macro-level must be literate in this culture. For this reason, it is dangerous to overemphasize the problems of basic literacy or the relevancy of literacy to specific tasks, and more constructive to emphasize that blacks will be condemned in perpetuity to oversimplified, low-level tasks and will never gain their rightful place in controlling the levers of power unless they also acquire literacy in this wider cultural sense.

Although Patterson focused his remarks on the importance of cultural literacy for minorities, his observations hold for every culturally illiterate person in our nation. Indeed, as he observed, cultural literacy is not the property of any group or class.

> To assume that this wider culture is static is an error; in fact it is not. It's not a WASP culture; it doesn't belong to any group. It is essentially and constantly changing, and it is open. What is needed is recognition that the accurate metaphor or model for this wider literacy is not domination, but dialectic; each group participates and contributes, transforms and is transformed, as much as any other group. . . . The English language no longer belongs to any single group or nation. The same goes for any other area of the wider culture.[12]

As Professor Patterson suggested, being taught to decode elementary 24 reading materials and specific, job-related texts cannot constitute true literacy. Such basic training does not make a person literate with respect to newspapers or other writings addressed to a general public. Moreover, a directly practical drawback of such narrow training is that it does not prepare anyone for technological change. Narrow vocational training in one state of a technology will not enable a person to read manuals that explain new developments in the same technology. In modern life we need general knowledge that enables us to deal with new ideas, events, and challenges. In today's world, general cultural literacy is more useful than what Professor Patterson terms "literacy to a specific task," because general literate information is the basis for many changing tasks.

Cultural literacy is even more important in the social sphere. The aim 25 of universal literacy has never been a socially neutral mission in our country. Our traditional social goals were unforgettably renewed for us by Martin Luther King, Jr., in his "I Have a Dream" speech. King envisioned a country where the children of former slaves sit down at the table of equality with the children of former slave owners, where men and women deal with each other as equals and judge each other on their characters and achievements rather than their origins. Like Thomas Jefferson, he had a dream of a society founded not on race or class but on personal merit.

In the present day, that dream depends on mature literacy. No modern 26 society can hope to become a just society without a high level of universal literacy. Putting aside for the moment the practical arguments about the economic uses of literacy, we can contemplate the even more basic principle that underlies our national system of education in the first place—that people in a democracy can be entrusted to decide all important matters for themselves because they can deliberate and communicate with one another. Universal literacy is inseparable from democracy and is the canvas for Martin Luther King's picture as well as for Thomas Jefferson's.

Both of these leaders understood that just having the right to vote is 27 meaningless if a citizen is disenfranchised by illiteracy or semiliteracy. Illiterate and semiliterate Americans are condemned not only to poverty, but also to the powerlessness of incomprehension. Knowing that they do not understand the issues, and feeling prey to manipulative oversimplifications, they do not trust the system of which they are supposed to be the masters. They do not feel themselves to be active participants in our republic, and they often do not turn out to vote. The civic importance of cultural literacy lies in the fact that true enfranchisement depends upon knowledge, knowledge upon literacy, and literacy upon cultural literacy.

To be truly literate, citizens must be able to grasp the meaning of any 28 piece of writing addressed to the general reader. All citizens should be able, for instance, to read newspapers of substance, about which Jefferson made the following famous remark:

> Were it left to me to decide whether we should have a government without newspapers, or newspapers without a government, I should not hesitate a moment to prefer the latter. But I should mean that every man should receive those papers and be capable of reading them.[13]

Jefferson's last comment is often omitted when the passage is quoted, but it's the crucial one.

Books and newspapers assume a "common reader," that is, a person who   29
knows the things known by other literate persons in the culture. Obviously,
such assumptions are never identical from writer to writer, but they show
a remarkable consistency. Those who write for a mass public are always
making judgments about what their readers can be assumed to know, and
the judgments are closely similar. Any reader who doesn't possess the
knowledge assumed in a piece he or she reads will in fact be illiterate with
respect to that particular piece of writing.

Here, for instance, is a rather typical excerpt from the *Washington Post*   30
of December 29, 1983.

> A federal appeals panel today upheld an order barring foreclosure on a
> Missouri farm, saying that U.S. Agriculture Secretary John R. Block
> has reneged on his responsibilities to some debt ridden farmers. The
> appeals panel directed the USDA to create a system of processing loan
> deferments and of publicizing them as it said Congress had intended. The
> panel said that it is the responsibility of the agriculture secretary to carry
> out this intent "not as a private banker, but as a public broker."

Imagine that item being read by people who are well trained in phonics,   31
word recognition, and other decoding skills but are culturally illiterate.
They might know words like *foreclosure*, but they would not understand
what the piece means. Who gave the order that the federal panel upheld?
What is a federal appeals panel? Where is Missouri, and what about
Missouri is relevant to the issue? Why are many farmers debt ridden? What
is the USDA? What is a public broker? Even if culturally illiterate readers
bothered to look up individual words, they would have little idea of the
reality being referred to. The explicit words are just surface pointers to
textual meaning in reading and writing. The comprehending reader must
bring to the text appropriate background information that includes knowledge
not only about the topic but also the shared attitudes and conventions that
color a piece of writing.

Our children can learn this information only by being taught it. Shared   32
literate information is deliberately sustained by national systems of education
in many countries because they recognize the importance of giving their
children a common basis for communication. Some decades ago a charming
book called *1066 and All That* appeared in Britain.[14] It dealt with facts of
British history that all educated Britons had been taught as children but
remembered only dimly as adults. The book caricatured those recollections,
purposely getting the "facts" just wrong enough to make them ridiculous
on their face. Readers instantly recognized that the book was mistaken in its
theory about what Ethelred-the-Unready was unready for, but on the other
hand, they couldn't say precisely what he *was* unready for. The book was
hilarious to literate Britons as a satire of their own vague and confused
memories. But even if their schoolchild knowledge had become vague with

the passage of time, it was still functional, because the information essential to literacy is rarely detailed or precise.

This haziness is a key characteristic of literacy and cultural literacy. To 33 understand the *Washington Post* extract literate readers have to know only vaguely, in the backs of their minds, that the American legal system permits a court decision to be reversed by a higher court. They would need to know only that a judge is empowered to tell the executive branch what it can or cannot do to farmers and other citizens. (The secretary of agriculture was barred from foreclosing a Missouri farm.) Readers would need to know only vaguely what and where Missouri is, and how the department and the secretary of agriculture fit into the scheme of things. None of this knowledge would have to be precise. Readers wouldn't have to know whether an appeals panel is the final judicial level before the U.S. Supreme Court. Any practiced writer who feels it is important for a reader to know such details always provides them.

Much in verbal communication is necessarily vague, whether we are 34 conversing or reading. What counts is our ability to grasp the general shape of what we are reading and to tie it to what we already know. If we need details, we rely on the writer or speaker to develop them. Or if we intend to ponder matters in detail for ourselves, we do so later, at our leisure. For instance, it is probably true that many people do not know what a beanball is in baseball. So in an article on the subject the author conveniently sets forth as much as the culturally literate reader must know.

> Described variously as the knockdown pitch, the beanball, the duster and purpose pitch—the Pentagon would call it the peacekeeper—this delightful strategem has graced the scene for most of the 109 years the major leagues have existed. It starts fights. It creates lingering grudges. It sends people to the hospital. . . . "You put my guy in the dirt, I put your guy in the dirt."[15]

To understand this text, we don't have to know much about the particular topic in advance, but we do require quite a lot of vague knowledge about baseball to give us a sense of the whole meaning, whether our knowledge happens to be vague or precise.

The superficiality of the knowledge we need for reading and writing may 35 be unwelcome news to those who deplore superficial learning and praise critical thinking over mere information. But one of the sharpest critical thinkers of our day, Dr. Hilary Putnam, a Harvard philosopher, has provided us with a profound insight into the importance of vague knowledge in verbal communication.[16]

> Suppose you are like me and cannot tell an elm from a beech tree. . . . [I can nonetheless use the word "elm" because] *there is a division of linguistic labor.* . . . It is not at all necessary or efficient that everyone

who wears a gold ring (or a gold cufflink, etc.) be able to tell with any reliability whether or not something is really gold. . . . Everyone to whom the word "gold" is important for any reason has to *acquire* the word "gold"; but he does not have to acquire the *method of recognizing* if something is or is not gold.

Putnam does acknowledge a limit on the degrees of ignorance and vagueness that are acceptable in discourse. "Significant communication," he observes," requires that people know something of what they are talking about." Nonetheless, what is required for communication is often so vague and superficial that we can properly understand and use the word *elm* without being able to distinguish an elm tree from a beech tree. What we need to know in order to use and understand a word is an initial stereotype that has a few vague traits. 36

> Speakers are *required* to know something about (stereotypic) tigers in order to count as having acquired the word "tiger"; something about elm trees (or anyway about the stereotype thereof) to count as having acquired the word "elm," etc. . . . The nature of the required minimum level of competence depends heavily upon both the culture and the topic, however. In our culture speakers are not . . . required to know the fine details (such as leaf shape) of what an elm tree looks like. English speakers are *required by their linguistic community* to be able to tell tigers from leopards; they are not required to be able to tell beech trees from elm trees.

When Putnam says that Americans can be depended on to distinguish tigers and leopards but not elms and beeches, he assumes that his readers will agree with him because they are culturally literate. He takes for granted that one literate person knows approximately the same things as another and is aware of the probable limits of the other person's knowledge. That second level of awareness—knowing what others probably know—is crucial for effective communication. In order to speak effectively to people we must have a reliable sense of what they do and do not know. For instance, if Putnam is right in his example, we should not have to tell a stranger that a leopard has spots or a tiger stripes, but we would have to explain than an elm has rough bark and a beech smooth bark if we wanted that particular piece of information conveyed. To know what educated people know about tigers but don't know about elm trees is the sort of cultural knowledge, limited in extent but possessed by all literate people, that must be brought into the open and taught to our children. 37

Besides being limited in extent, cultural literacy has another trait that is important for educational policy—its national character. It's true that literate English is an international language, but only so long as the topics it deals with are international. The background knowledge of people from other English-speaking nations is often inadequate for complex and subtle communications within our nation. The knowledge required for national literacy differs from country to country, even when their national language 38 is the same. It is no doubt true that one layer of cultural literacy is the same for all English-speaking nations. Australians, South Africans, Britons, and Americans share a lot of knowledge by virtue of their common language. But much of the knowledge required for literacy in, say, Australia is specific to that country, just as much of ours is specific to the United States.

For instance, a literate Australian can typically understand American 39 newspaper articles on international events or the weather but not one on a federal appeals panel. The same holds true for Americans who read Australian newspapers. Many of us have heard "Waltzing Matilda," a song known to every Australian, but few Americans understand or need to understand what the words mean.

> Once a jolly swagman camped by a billy-bong,
> Under the shade of a kulibar tree,
> And he sang as he sat and waited for his billy-boil,
> "You'll come a-waltzing, Matilda, with me."

Waltzing Matilda doesn't mean dancing with a girl; it means walking with a kind of knapsack. A *swagman* is a hobo, a *billy-bong* is a brook or pond, a *kulibar* is a eucalyptus, and *billy-boil* is coffee.

The national character of the knowledge needed in reading and writing 40 was strikingly revealed in an experiment conducted by Richard C. Anderson and others at the Center for the Study of Reading at the University of Illinois. They assembled two paired groups of readers, all highly similar in sexual balance, educational background, age, and social class.[17] The only difference between the groups was that one was in India, the other in the United States. Both were given the same two letters to read. The texts were similar in overall length, word-frequency distribution, sentence length and complexity, and number of explicit propositions. Both letters were on the same topic, a wedding, but one described an Indian wedding, the other an American wedding. The reading performances of the two groups—their speed and accuracy of comprehension—split along national lines. The Indians performed well in reading about the Indian wedding but poorly in reading about the American one, and the Americans did the opposite. This experiment not only reconfirmed the dependence of reading skill on cultural literacy, it also demonstrated its national character.

Although nationalism may be regrettable in some of its worldwide political 41 effects, a mastery of national culture is essential to mastery of the standard language in every modern nation. This point is important for educational policy, because educators often stress the virtues of multicultural education. Such study is indeed valuable in itself; it inculcates tolerance and provides a perspective on our own traditions and values. But however laudable it is, it should not be the primary focus of national education. It should not be allowed to supplant or interfere with our schools' responsibility to ensure our children's mastery of American literature culture. The acculturative responsibility of the schools is primary and fundamental. To teach the ways of one's own community has always been and still remains the essence of the education of our children, who enter neither a narrow tribal culture nor a transcendent world culture but a national literate culture. For profound historical reasons, this is the way of the modern world.[18] It will not change soon, and it will certainly not be changed by educational policy alone.

THE DECLINE OF TEACHING CULTURAL LITERACY

Why have our schools failed to fulfill their fundamental acculturative responsibility? In view of the immense importance of cultural literacy for speaking, listening, reading, and writing, why has the need for a definite, shared body of information been so rarely mentioned in discussions of education? In the educational writings of the past decade, I find almost nothing on this topic, which is not arcane. People who are introduced to the subject quickly understand why oral or written communication requires a lot of shared background knowledge. It's not the difficulty or novelty of the idea that has caused it to receive so little attention.   42

Let me hazard a guess about one reason for our neglect of the subject. We have ignored cultural literacy in thinking about education—certainly I as a researcher also ignored it until recently—precisely because it was something we have been able to take for granted. We ignore the air we breathe until it is thin or foul. Cultural literacy is the oxygen of social intercourse. Only when we run into cultural illiteracy are we shocked into recognizing the importance of the information that we had unconsciously assumed.   43

To be sure, a minimal level of information is possessed by any normal person who lives in the United States and speaks elementary English. Almost everybody knows what is meant by *dollar* and that cars must travel on the right-hand side of the road. But this elementary level of information is not sufficient for a modern democracy. It isn't sufficient to read newspapers (a sin against Jeffersonian democracy), and it isn't sufficient to achieve economic fairness and high productivity. Cultural literacy lies *above* the everyday levels of knowledge that everyone possess and *below* the expert level known only to specialists. It is that middle ground of cultural knowledge possessed by the "common reader." It includes information that we have traditionally expected our children to receive in school, but which they no longer do.   44

During recent decades Americans have hesitated to make a decision about the specific knowledge that children need to learn in school. Our elementary schools are not only dominated by the content-neutral ideas of Rousseau and Dewey,* they are also governed by approximately sixteen thousand   45

Rousseau and Dewey: Jean Jacques Rousseau (1712–1778), a French philosopher, educational theorist, and writer; John Dewey (1859–1952), an American philosopher and educational theorist. Both men's theories of education emphasize process, critical thinking, and experiential learning over content. [Editors' note.]

independent school districts. We have viewed this dispersion of educational authority as an insurmountable obstacle to altering the fragmentation of the school curriculum even when we have questioned that fragmentation. We have permitted school policies that have shrunk the body of information that Americans share, and these policies have caused our national literacy to decline.

At the same time we have searched with some eagerness for causes such 46 as television that lie outside the schools. But we should direct our attention undeviatingly toward what the schools teach rather than toward family structure, social class, or TV programming. No doubt, reforms outside the schools are important, but they are harder to accomplish. Moreover, we have accumulated a great deal of evidence that faulty policy in the schools is the chief cause of deficient literacy. Researchers who have studied the factors influencing educational outcomes have found that the school curriculum is the most important controllable influence on what our children know and don't know about our literate culture.[19]

It will not do to blame television for the state of our literacy. Television watching does reduce reading and often encroaches on homework. Much of it is admittedly the intellectual equivalent of junk food. But in some respects, such as its use of standard written English, television watching is acculturative.[20] Moreover, as Herbert Walberg points out, the schools themselves must be held partly responsible for excessive television watching, because they have not firmly insisted that students complete significant amounts of homework, an obvious way to increase time spent on reading and writing.[21] Nor should our schools be excused by an appeal to the effects of the decline of the family or the vicious circle of poverty, important as these factors are. Schools have, or should have, children for six or seven hours a day, five days a week, nine months a year, for thirteen years or more. To assert that they are powerless to make a significant impact on what their students learn would be to make a claim about American education that few parents, teachers, or students would find it easy to accept.

Just how fragmented the American public school curriculum has become 48 is described in *The Shopping Mall High School*, a report on five years of firsthand study inside public and private secondary schools. The authors report that our high schools offer courses of so many kinds that "the word 'curriculum' does not do justice to this astonishing variety." The offerings include not only academic courses of great diversity, but also courses in sports and hobbies and a "services curriculum" addressing emotional or social problems. All these courses are deemed "educationally valid" and carry course credit. Moreover, among academic offerings are numerous versions of each subject, corresponding to different levels of student interest and ability. Needless to say, the material covered in these "content area" courses is highly varied.[22]

Cafeteria-style education, combined with the unwillingness of our schools 49 to place demands on students, has resulted in a steady diminishment of commonly shared information between generations and between young people themselves. Those who graduate from the same school have often studied different subjects, and those who graduate from different schools have often studied different material even when their courses have carried the same titles. The inevitable consequence of the shopping mall high school is a lack of shared knowledge across and within schools. It would be hard to invent a more effective recipe for cultural fragmentation.

The formalistic educational theory behind the shopping mall school (the theory that any suitable content will inculcate reading, writing, and thinking skills) has had certain political advantages for school administrators. It has allowed them to stay scrupulously neutral with regard to content.[23] Educational formalism enables them to regard the indiscriminate variety of school offerings as a positive virtue, on the grounds that such variety can accommodate the different interests and abilities of different students. Educational formalism has also conveniently allowed school administrators to meet objections to the traditional literate materials that used to be taught in the schools. Objectors have said that traditional materials are class-bound, white, Anglo-Saxon, and Protestant, not to mention racist, sexist, and excessively Western. Our schools have tried to offer enough diversity to meet these objections from liberals and enough Shakespeare to satisfy conservatives. Caught between ideological parties, the schools have been attracted irresistibly to a quantitative and formal approach to curriculum making rather than one based on sound judgments about what should be taught.

Some have objected that teaching the traditional literate culture means teaching conservative material. Orlando Patterson answered that objection when he pointed out that mainstream culture is not the province of any single social group and is constantly changing by assimilating new elements and expelling old ones.[24] Although mainstream culture is tied to the written word and may therefore seem more formal and elitist than other elements of culture, that is an illusion. Literate culture is the most democratic culture in our land: it excludes nobody; it cuts across generations and social groups and classes; it is not usually one's first culture, but it should be everyone's second, existing as it does beyond the narrow spheres of family, neighborhood, and region.

As the universal second culture, literate culture has become the common currency for social and economic exchange in our democracy, and the only available ticket to full citizenship. Getting one's membership card is not tied to class or race. Membership is automatic if one learns the background information and the linguistic conventions that are needed to read, write, and speak effectively. Although everyone is literate in some local, regional, or ethnic culture, the connection between mainstream culture and the national written language justifies calling mainstream culture *the* basic culture of the nation.

The claim that universal cultural literacy would have the effect of 53 preserving the political and social status quo is paradoxical because in fact the traditional forms of literate culture are precisely the most effective instruments for political and social change. All political discourse at the national level must use the stable forms of the national language and its associated culture. Take the example of *The Black Panther*, a radical and revolutionary newspaper if ever this country had one. Yet the *Panther* was highly conservative in its language and cultural assumptions, as it had to be in order to communicate effectively. What could be more radical in sentiment but more conservative in language and assumed knowledge than the following passages from that paper?

> The present period reveals the criminal growth of bourgeois democracy since the betrayal of those who died that this nation might live "free and indivisible." It exposes through the trial of the Chicago Seven, and its law and order edicts, its desperate turn toward the establishment of a police state. (January 17, 1970)

> In this land of "milk and honey," the "almightly dollar" rules supreme and is being upheld by the faithful troops who move without question in the name of "law and order." Only in this garden of hypocrisy and inequality can a murderer not be considered a murderer—only here can innocent people be charged with a crime and be taken to court with the confessed criminal testifying against them. Incredible? (March 28, 1970)

> In the United States, the world's most technologically advanced country, one million youths from 12 to 17 years of age are illiterate—unable to read as well as the average fourth grader, says a new government report. Why so much illiteracy in a land of so much knowledge? The answer is because there is racism. Blacks and other Nonwhites receive the worst education. (May 18, 1974)

The last item of the Black Panther Party platform, issued March 29, 1972, begins

> 10. WE WANT LAND, BREAD, HOUSING, EDUCATION, CLOTHING, JUSTICE, PEACE AND PEOPLE'S CONTROL OF MODERN TECHNOLOGY.
>
> When in the course of human events it becomes necessary for one people to dissolve the political bands which have connected them with another, and to assume among the powers of the earth the separate and equal station to which the laws of nature and nature's God entitle them, a decent respect to the opinions of mankind requires that they should declare the causes which impel them to the separation.

And so on for the first five hundred of Jefferson's words without the least hint, or need of one, that this is a verbatim repetition of an earlier revolutionary declaration. The writers for *The Black Panther* had clearly received a rigorous traditional education in American history, in the Declaration of Independence, the Pledge of Allegiance to the Flag, the Gettysburg Address, and the Bible, to mention only some of the direct quotations and allusions in these passages. They also received rigorous traditional instruction in reading, writing, and spelling. I have not found a single misspelled word in the many pages of radical sentiment I have examined in that newspaper. Radicalism in politics, but conservatism in literate knowledge and spelling: to be a conservative in the *means* of communication is the road to effectiveness in modern life, in whatever direction one wishes to be effective.

To withhold traditional culture from the school curriculum, and therefore   54
from students, in the name of progressive ideas is in fact an unprogressive action that helps preserve the political and economic status quo. Middle-class children acquire mainstream literate culture by daily encounters with other literate persons. But less privileged children are denied consistent interchanges with literate persons and fail to receive this information in school. The most straightforward antidote to their deprivation is to make the essential information more readily available inside the schools.

Providing our children with traditional information by no means indoctri-   55
nates them in a conservative point of view. Conservatives who wish to preserve traditional values will find that these are not necessarily inculcated by a traditional education, which can in fact be subversive of the status quo. As a child of eleven, I turned against the conservative views of my family and the Southern community in which I grew up, precisely because I had been given a traditional education and was therefore literate enough to read Gunnar Myrdal's *An American Dilemma*, an epoch-making book in my life.

Although teaching children national mainstream culture doesn't mean   56
forcing them to accept its values uncritically, it does enable them to understand those values in order to predict the typical attitudes of other Americans. The writers for *The Black Panther* clearly understood this when they quoted the Declaration of Independence. George Washington, for instance, is a name in our received culture that we associate with the truthfulness of the hero of the story of the cherry tree. Americans should be taught that value association, whether or not they believe the story. Far from accepting the cherry-tree tale or its implications, Oscar Wilde in "The Decay of Lying" used it ironically, in a way that is probably funnier to Americans than to the British audience he was addressing.

> [Truth telling is] vulgarizing mankind. The crude commercialism of America, its materializing spirit, its indifference to the poetical side of things, and its lack of imagination and of high unattainable ideals, are entirely due to that country having adopted for its national hero a man who, according to his own confession, was incapable of telling a lie, and

> it is not too much to say that the story of George Washington and the cherry tree has done more harm, and in a shorter space of time, than any other moral tale in the whole of literature. . . . And the amusing part of the whole thing is that the story of the cherry tree is an absolute myth.[25]

For us no less than for Wilde, the values affirmed in traditional literature culture can serve a whole spectrum of value attitudes. Unquestionably, decisions about techniques of conveying traditions to our children are among the most sensitive and important decisions of a pluralistic nation. But the complex problem of how to teach values in American schools mustn't distract attention from our fundamental duty to teach shared content.

The failure of our schools to create a literate society is sometimes excused on the grounds that the schools have been asked to do too much. They are asked, for example, to pay due regard to the demands of both local and national acculturation. They are asked to teach not only American history but also state and city history, driving, cardiopulmonary resuscitation, consumerism, carpentry, cooking, and other special subjects. They are given the task of teaching information that is sometimes too rudimentary and sometimes too specialized. If the schools did not undertake this instruction, much of the information so provided would no doubt go unlearned. In some of our national moods we would like the schools to teach everything, but they cannot. There is a pressing need for clarity about our educational priorities.

As an example of the priorities we need to set, consider the teaching of local history in the Commonwealth of Virginia. Suppose Virginians had to choose between learning about its native son Jeb Stuart and Abraham Lincoln. The example is arbitrary, but since choices have to be made in education, we might consider the two names emblematic of the kind of priority decision that has to be made. Educational policy always involves choices between degrees of worthiness.

The concept of cultural literacy helps us to make such decisions because it places a higher value on national than on local information. We want to make our children competent to communicate with Americans throughout the land. Therefore, if Virginians did have to decide between Stuart and Lincoln they ought to favor the man from Illinois over the one from Virginia. All literate Americans know traditional information about Abraham Lincoln but relatively few know about Jeb Stuart. To become literate it's therefore more important to know about Lincoln than about Stuart. The priority has nothing to do with inherent merit, only with the accidents of culture. Stuart certainly had more merit than Benedict Arnold did, but Arnold also should be given educational priority over Stuart. Why? Because Benedict Arnold is as much a part of our national language as is, say, Judas.

To describe Benedict Arnold and Abraham Lincoln as belonging to the national language discloses another way of conceiving cultural literacy—as a vocabulary that we are able to use throughout the land because we share associations with others in our society. A universally shared national

455

vocabulary is analogous to a universal currency like the dollar. Of course the vocabulary consists of more than just words. *Benedict Arnold* is part of national cultural literacy; *eggs Benedict* isn't.

THE CRITICAL IMPORTANCE OF EARLY SCHOOLING

Once we become aware of the inherent connection between literacy and cultural literacy, we have a duty to those who lack cultural literacy to determine and disclose its contents. To someone who is unaware of the things a literate person is expected to know, a writer's assumption that readers possess cultural literacy could appear to be a conspiracy of the literate against the illiterate, for the purpose of keeping them out of the club. But there is no conspiracy. Writers *must* make assumptions about the body of information their readers know. Unfortunately for the disadvantaged, no one ever spells out what the information is. But, as the Appendix illustrates, the total quantity of commonly shared information that the schools need to impart is less daunting than one might think, for the crucial background knowledge possessed by literate people is, as I have pointed out, telegraphic, vague, and limited in extent. 61

Preschool is not too early for starting earnest instruction in literate national culture. Fifth grade is almost too late. Tenth grade usually *is* too late. Anyone who is skeptical of this assertion should take a look at a heterogeneous class of fifth-graders engaged in summarizing a piece they have read. There are predictable differences between the summaries given by children with culturally adequate backgrounds and those given by children without. Although disadvantaged children often show an acceptable ability to decode and pronounce individual words, they are frequently unable to gain an integrated sense of a piece as a whole. They miss central implications and associations because they don't possess the background knowledge necessary to put the text in context. Hearing they hear not, and seeing they do not understand.[26] 62

Yet if you observe a kindergarten or first-grade class in which pupils have the same diversity of family background, you will *not* find a similar spread in the reading performances of pupils from different social classes. Disadvantaged first-graders do as well as middle class ones in sounding out letters and simple words.[27] What happens between first grade and fifth grade to change the equality of performance? The impression that something significant has occurred or has failed to occur in these early grades is confirmed by international comparisons of reading attainment at early ages in different countries. Before grade three, when reading skills are more mechanical than interpretive, the United States stands in the top group of countries. Later, when reading requires an understanding of more complex content, our comparative ranking drops.[28] Although our schools do comparatively well in teaching elementary decoding skills, they do less well 63 than schools in some other countries in teaching the background knowledge that pupils must possess to succeed at mature reading tasks.

The importance of this evidence for improving our national literacy can scarcely be overemphasized. If in the early grades our children were taught texts with cultural content rather than "developmental" texts that develop abstract skills, much of the specific knowledge deficit of disadvantaged children could be overcome. For it is clear that one critical difference in the reading performances of disadvantaged fifth-graders as compared with advantaged pupils is the difference in their cultural knowledge. Background knowledge does not take care of itself. Reading and writing are cumulative skills; the more we read the more necessary knowledge we gain for further reading. 64

Around grade four, those who lack the initial knowledge required for significant reading begin to be left behind permanently. Having all too slowly built up their cultural knowledge, they find reading and learning increasingly toilsome, unproductive, and humiliating. It follows that teaching cultural information in the early grades would do more than just improve the reading performance of all our children. By removing one of the causes of failure, it would especially enhance the motivation, self-esteem, and performance of disadvantaged children. 65

Really effective reforms in the teaching of cultural literacy must therefore begin with the earliest grades. Every improvement made in teaching very young children literate background information will have a multiplier effect on later learning, not just by virtue of the information they will gain but also by virtue of the greater motivation for reading and learning they will feel when they actually understand what they have read. 66

Young children enjoy absorbing formulaic knowledge. Even if they did not, our society would still find it essential to teach them all sorts of traditions and facts. Critical thinking and basic skills, two areas of current focus in education, do not enable children to create out of their own imaginations the essential names and concepts that have arisen by historical accident. The Rio Grande, the Mason-Dixon line, "The Night Before Christmas," and *Star Wars* are not products of basic skills or critical thought. Many items of literate culture are arbitrary, but that does not make them dispensable. Facts are essential components of the basic skills that a child entering a culture must have. 67

I'm not suggesting that we teach our children exactly what our grandparents learned. We should teach children current mainstream culture. It's obvious that the content of cultural literacy changes over the years. Today the term "Brown decision"* belongs to cultural literacy, but in 1945 there hadn't 68

---

* *Brown decision:* the 1954 U.S. Supreme Court decision in the *Brown v. the Topeka Board of Education* case that paved the way for the desegregation of the American school system by ruling that racial segregation in public elementary schools is unconstitutional. [Editors' note.]

been any Brown decision. The name Harold Ickes* was current in 1945 but no longer is. Such mutability is the fate of most names and events of recent history. Other changes come through the contributions of various subnational cultures. Ethnic words (like *pizza*) and art forms (like *jazz*) are constantly entering and departing from mainstream culture. Other subnational cultures, including those of science and technology, also cause changes in the mainstream culture. DNA and quarks, now part of cultural literacy, were unknown in 1945. In short, terms that literate people know in the 1980s are different from those they knew in 1945, and forty years hence the literate culture will again be different.

The flux in mainstream culture is obvious to all. But stability, not change, is the chief characteristic of cultural literacy. Although historical and technical terms may follow the ebb and flow of events, the more stable elements of our national vocabulary, like George Washington, the tooth fairy, the Gettysburg Address, Hamlet, and the Declaration of Independence, have persisted for a long time. These stable elements of the national vocabulary are at the core of cultural literacy, and for that reason are the most important contents of schooling. Although the terms that ebb and flow are tremendously important at a given time, they belong, from an educational standpoint, at the periphery of literate culture. The persistent, stable elements belong at the educational core. 69

Let me give some concrete examples of the kinds of core information I mean. American readers are assumed to have a general knowledge of the following people (I give just the beginning of a list): John Adams, Susan B. Anthony, Benedict Arnold, Daniel Boone, John Brown, Aaron Burr, John C. Calhoun, Henry Clay, James Fenimore Cooper, Lord Cornwallis, Davy Crockett, Emily Dickinson, Stephen A. Douglas, Frederick Douglass, Jonathan Edwards, Ralph Waldo Emerson, Benjamin Franklin, Robert Fulton, Ulysses S. Grant, Alexander Hamilton, and Nathaniel Hawthorne. Most of us know rather little about these people, but that little is of crucial importance, because it enables writers and speakers to assume a starting point from which they can treat in detail what they wish to focus on. 70

Here is another alphabetical list that no course in critical thinking skills, however masterful, could ever generate: Antarctic Ocean, Arctic Ocean, Atlantic Ocean, Baltic Sea, Black Sea, Caribbean Sea, Gulf of Mexico, North Sea, Pacific Ocean, Red Sea. It has a companion list: Alps, Appalachians, Himalayas, Matterhorn, Mount Everest, Mount Vesuvius, Rocky Mountains. Because literate people mention such names in passing, usually without explanation, children should acquire them as part of their intellectual equipment. 71

Children also need to understand elements of our literary and mythic 72

---

* *Harold Ickes:* an American lawyer and statesman (1874–1952) who resigned from Truman's cabinet. [Editor's note.]

heritage that are often alluded to without explanation, for example, Adam and Eve, Cain and Abel, Noah and the Flood, David and Goliath, the Twenty-third Psalm, Humpty Dumpty, Jack Sprat, Jack and Jill, Little Jack Horner, Cinderella, Jack and the Beanstalk, Mary had a little lamb, Peter Pan, and Pinocchio. Also Achilles, Adonis, Aeneas, Agamemnon, Antigone, and Apollo, as well as Robin Hood, Paul Bunyan, Satan, Sleeping Beauty, Sodom and Gomorrah, the Ten Commandments, and Tweedledum and Tweedledee.

Our current distaste for memorization is more pious than realistic. At 73 an early age when their memories are most retentive, children have an almost instinctive urge to learn specific tribal traditions. At that age they seem to be fascinated by catalogues of information and are eager to master the materials that authenticate their membership in adult society. Observe for example how they memorize the rather complex materials of football, baseball, and basketball, even without benefit of formal avenues by which that information is inculcated.

The weight of human tradition across many cultures supports the view 74 that basic acculturation should largely be completed by age thirteen. At that age Catholics are confirmed, Jews bar or bat mitzvahed, and tribal boys and girls undergo the rites of passage into the tribe. According to the anthropological record, all cultures whose educational methods have been reported in the *Human Relations Area Files* (a standard source for anthropological data) have used early memorization to carry on their traditions.[29]

In Korea, "numerous books must be memorized, including the five 75 *Kyung*, and the four *Su*." In Tibet, "from eight to ten years of age, the boy spends most of his time reading aloud and memorizing the scriptures." In Chile, the Araucanian Indians use the memorization of songs as an educational technique to teach "the subtleties of the native tongue, and an insight into the customs and traditions of their tribe." In southern Africa, the children of the Kung bushmen listen for hours to discussions of which they understand very little until they "know the history of every object, every exchange between their families, before they are ten or twelve years old." In Indonesia, "memorization is the method commonly used." In Thailand, children "repeat their lessons until they know them by heart." In Arizona, the Papago Indians take children through the lengthy rituals "as many times as needed for the learner to say it all through, which may take a year."[30]

The new kind of teaching espoused by Rousseau and Dewey, which 76 avoids rote learning and encourages the natural development of the child on analogy with the development of an acorn into an oak, has one virtue certainly: it encourages independence of mind. But the theory also has its drawbacks, one of which is that a child is not in fact like an acorn. Left to itself, a child will not grow into a thriving creature; Tarzan is pure fantasy. To thrive, a child needs to learn the traditions of the particular human society and culture it is born into.[31] Like children everywhere, American children need traditional information at a very early age.

A great deal is at stake in understanding and acting on this essential   77
perception as soon as possible. The opportunity of acquiring cultural literacy,
once lost in the early grades is usually lost for good. That is most likely to
be true for children of parents who were not themselves taught the literate
national culture.

In the technological age, Washington and the cherry tree, Scrooge and   78
Christmas, the fights historical, the oceans geographical, the "beings
animalculus," and all the other shared materials of literate culture have
become more, not less, important. The more computers we have, the more
we need shared fairy tales, Greek myths, historical images, and so on. That
is not really the paradox it seems to be. The more specialized and technical
our civilization becomes, the harder it is for nonspecialists to participate in
the decisions that deeply affect their lives. If we do not achieve a literate
society, the technicians, with their arcane specialties, will not be able to
communicate with us nor we with them. That would contradict basic
principles of democracy and must not be allowed to happen.

The antidote to growing specialization is to reinvigorate the unspecialized   79
domain of literate discourse, where all can meet on common ground. That
this ideal *can* be achieved is proved by such admirable writers as Theodore
H. White, John Kenneth Galbraith, Lewis Thomas, Peter Medawar, and
Richard Feynman, who are able to communicate their complex expertise to
a wide audience of educated people. We will be able to achieve a just and
prosperous society only when our schools ensure that everyone commands
enough shared background knowledge to be able to communicate effectively
with everyone else.

NOTES

1. For rising standards of literacy, see R. L. Thorndike, *Reading Comprehension
    Education in Fifteen Countries: An Empirical Study* (New York: Wiley, 1973).
    On the connection between high literacy and Japan's economic performance, see
    Thomas P. Rohlen, "Japanese Education: If They Can Do It, Should We?"
    American Scholar 55, 1 (Winter 1985–86): 29–44. For American literacy rates
    see Jeanne Chall, "Afterword," in R. C. Anderson et al., *Becoming a Nation of
    Readers: The Report of the Commission on Reading* (Washington, D. C.: National
    Institute of Education, 1985), 123–24. On "world knowledge" in literacy, see
    Jeanne S. Chall, *Stages of Reading Development* (New York: McGraw-Hill,
    1983), 8.

2. The two classical discussions of the stabilizing effects of mass literacy on oral
    speech are Henry Bradley, *The Making of English*, revised edition by Simeon
    Potter (London: Macmillan, 1968), and Otto Jespersen, *Mankind, Nation, and
    Individual from a Linguistic Point of View*, Midland edition (Bloomington:
    Indiana University Press, 1964). Wider bibliographical references to this subject
    may be found in the first two chapters of my *Philosophy of Composition* (Chicago:
    University of Chicago Press, 1977).

3. The experiment is described in R. M. Krauss and S. Glucksberg, "Social and Nonsocial Speech," *Scientific American* 236 (February 1977): 100–105.

4. National Assessment of Educational Progress, *Three National Assessments of Reading: Changes in Performance, 1970–1980* (Report 11-R-01) (Denver: Education Commission of the States, 1981). The percentage of students scoring at the "advanced" level (4.9 percent) has climbed back to the very low levels of 1970. See *The Reading Report Card: Progress Toward Excellence in Our Schools, Trends in Reading Over Four National Assessments, 1971–1984* (Princeton, N.J.: Educational Testing Service No. 15-R-01, 1986).

5. John B. Carroll, "Psychometric Approaches to the Study of Language Abilities," in C. J. Fillmore, D. Kempler, and S.-Y. Wang, eds., *Individual Differences in Language Abilities and Language Behavior* (New York: Academic Press, 1979), 29.

6. The College Board, *College-Bound Seniors: Eleven Years of National Data from the College Board's Admission Testing Program, 1973–83* (New York, 1984). The College Board has sent me further details from an unpublished report that shows the breakdown of scores over 600 between 1972 and 1984. The percentage of students who scored over 600 was 7.3 percent in 1984 and 11.4 percent in 1972. The percentage scoring over 650 was 3.0 percent in 1984 and 5.29 percent in 1972.

7. Benjamin J. Stein, "The Cheerful Ignorance of the Young in L.A.," *Washington Post*, October 3, 1983. Reprinted with the kind permission of the author.

8. *Changes in Poltical Knowledge and Attitudes, 1969–76: Selected Results from the Second National Assessments of Citizenship and Social Studies* (Denver: National Assessment of Educational Progress, 1978).

9. The Foundations of Literacy Project under a grant from the National Endowment for the Humanities, has commissioned NAEP, now conducted by the Educational Testing Service of Princeton, to probe the literary and historical knowledge of American seventeen-year-olds.

10. I am breaking no confidences as a member of the NAEP panel in revealing these pretest figures. They were made public on October 8, 1985, in a press release by NEH Chairman John Agresto, which stated in part: "Preliminary findings indicate that two-thirds of the seventeen-year-old students tested could not place the Civil War in the correct half century; a third did not know that the Declaration of Independence was signed between 1750 and 1800; half could not locate the half century in which the First World War occurred; a third did not know that Columbus sailed for the New World 'before 1750'; three-fourths could not identify Walt Whitman or Thoreau or E. E. Cummings or Carl Sandburg. And one-half of our high school seniors did not recognize the names of Winston Churchill or Joseph Stalin."

11. See Chapter 2, pages 42–47.

12. Orlando Patterson, "Language, Ethnicity, and Change," in S. G. D'Eloia, ed., *Toward a Literate Democracy: Proceedings of the First Shaughnessy Memorial Conference, April 3, 1980,* special number of *The Journal of Basic Writing,* III (1980): 72–73.

13. Letter to Colonel Edward Carrington, January 16, 1787, taken from *The Life and Selected Writings of Thomas Jefferson,* ed. A. Koch and W. Peden (New York: Random House, 1944), 411–12.

14. W. C. Sellar and R. J. Yeatman, *1066 and All That: A Memorable History of England, Comprising All the Parts You Can Remember, Including 103 Good Things, 5 Bad Kings, and 2 Genuine Dates* (London: Methuen, 1947).

15. Melvin Durslag, "To Ban the Beanball," *TV Guide,* June 8–14, 1985, 9.

16. H. Putnam, "The Meaning of Meaning," in *Philosophical Papers, Volume 2: Mind, Language and Reality* (Cambridge: Cambridge University Press, 1975), 227–48.

17. See M. S. Steffensen, C. Joag-Des, and R. C. Anderson, "A Cross-Cultural Perspective on Reading Comprehension," *Reading Research Quarterly* 15, 1 (1979): 10–29.

18. This is fully discussed in Chapter 3.

19. See H. J. Walberg and T. Shanahan, "High School Effects on Individual Students," *Educational Researcher* 12 (August–September 1983): 4–9.

20. "Up to about ten hours a week, there is actually a slight positive relationship between the amount of time children spend watching TV and their school achievement, including reading achievement. Beyond this point, the relationship turns negative and, as the number of hours per week climbs, achievement declines sharply." R. C. Anderson et al., *Becoming a Nation of Readers,* 27.

21. Walberg and Shanahan, "High School Effects on Individual Students," 4–9.

22. Arthur G. Powell, Eleanor Farrar, and David K. Cohen, *The Shopping Mall High School: Winners and Losers in the Educational Marketplace* (Boston: Houghton Mifflin, 1985), 1–8.

23. The neutrality and avoidance of the schools are described in detail in *The Shopping Mall High School.*

24. Patterson, "Language, Ethnicity, and Change," 72–73.

25. Oscar Wilde, "The Decay of Lying" (1889).

26. Jeanne S. Chall, "Afterword," in R. C. Anderson et al., *Becoming a Nation of Readers*, 123–25.

27. J. S. Chall, C. Snow, et al., *Families and Literacy*, Final Report to the National Institute of Education, 1982.

28. R. L. Thorndike, *Reading Comprehension Education in Fifteen Countries: An Empirical Study* (New York: Wiley, 1973). There is also recent evidence that advanced reading skills have declined in the United States while elementary skills have risen. See J. S. Chall, "Literacy: Trends and Explanations," *Educational Researcher* 12 (1983): 3–8, and R. C. Anderson et al., *Becoming a Nation of Readers*, 2.

29. *Human Relations Area Files*, microfiches (New Haven: Human Relations Area Files, 1899–1956).

30. Ibid. My examples are from more than two hundred entries, stretching from 1899 to 1949, under the topics "Educational Theories and Methods" and "Transmission of Beliefs."

31. L. A. Cremin, *The Transformation of the American School: Progressivism in American Education, 1876–1957* (New York: Knopf, 1964).

Questions for Discussion and Writing

1. How would you evaluate Hirsch's definition of "cultural literacy"? What does he seem to mean by this term? Precisely how *much* knowledge of a specific subject is adequate? Who decides how much is enough? How else might one define cultural literacy?

2. Who do you suppose is Hirsch's intended audience? What degree of cultural literacy is required to read this chapter?

3. How would you evaluate Hirsch's proof of cultural illiteracy among the youth of our culture? Do you find his examples and statistics convincing?

4. Write a comparison of Hirsch's approach to education with a skills approach such as critical thinking. Be sure to consider the strengths and weaknesses of both sides of the issue. Ultimately, which approach would you favor? Why?

TOM WOLFE

(b. 1931)

L ike Joan Didion, Thomas Kennerly Wolfe, Jr., better known as Tom Wolfe, is considered one of the foremost practitioners of "New Journalism." (For further discussion of New Journalism, see pages 479–480.) Also like Didion, Wolfe is a sophisticated writer whose views are hard to fix in simple categories such as liberal, conservative, progressive, radical, and so on. Unlike Didion, however, Wolfe has made a career of shocking his readers by taking highly controversial—and often unpopular—positions on a wide variety of contemporary subjects. A journalistic bad boy with an exceptionally keen eye and ear for detail, Wolfe has been attacked—and admired—by both the left and the right, both of which he has attacked and, occasionally, admired. He has been called everything from a fraud to a genius, but few call him boring.

Wolfe received his B.A. from Washington and Lee University in 1951, and his Ph.D. in American Studies from Yale University in 1957. Beginning as a reporter for the Springfield, Massachusetts, Union, Wolfe wrote for papers such as the Washington Post and the New York Herald Tribune before establishing his national reputation with lively articles in magazines such as Esquire and Harper's. In provocatively titled books such as The Kandy-Colored Tangerine-Flake Streamlined Baby (1965), The Electric Kool-Aid Acid Test (1968), The Pump House Gang (1968), Radical Chic and Mau Mauing the Flak Catchers (1970), The Painted Word (1975), Mauve Gloves & Madmen, Clutter & Vine, and Other Stories, Sketches, and Essays (1976), Marie Cosindas, Color Photographs (1978), The Right Stuff (1979, which won the American Book Award and the National Book Critics Circle Award), In Our Time (1980), From Bauhaus to Our House (1981), and The Purple Decades: A Reader (1982), Wolfe takes on contemporary American subjects such as the customized car industry, Las Vegas, fashion, the LSD culture of novelist Ken Kesey, surfers, cruisers, strippers, celebrities such as conductor/composer Leonard Bernstein and boxer Muhammad Ali, the New York art scene, the space program, the college lecture circuit, and modern architecture. His novel, The Bonfire of the Vanities, was published serially in Rolling Stone in 1984–85. An artist himself, Wolfe has illustrated several of his books. He is also cofounder of the literary quarterly Shenandoah.

Controversial in person as well as in print, Wolfe has garnered nearly as much attention for his distinctive wardrobe as he has for his often-imitated prose style. In "The Intelligent Coed's Guide to America," reproduced here, see if it is possible to discern the method operating amid Wolfe's flamboyance.

THE INTELLIGENT COED'S
GUIDE TO AMERICA

1. O'HARE!

O Mother O'Hare, big bosom for our hungry poets, pelvic saddle for our   1
sexologists and Open Classroom theorists—O houri O'Hare, who keeps
her Perm-O-Pour Stone-glow thighs ajar to receive a generation of frustrated
and unreadable novelists—

But wait a minute. It may be too early for the odes. Has it even been   2
duly noted that O'Hare, which is an airport outside Chicago, is now the
intellectual center of the United States?

Curious, but true. There at O'Hare, on any day, Monday through   3
Friday, from September to June, they sit . . . in row after Mies van der
row[1] of black vinyl and stainless steel sling chairs . . . amid soaring walls
of plate glass . . . from one tenth to one third of the literary notables of
the United States. In October and April, the peak months, the figure goes
up to one half.

Masters and Johnson and Erica Jong, Kozol and Rifkin and Hacker and   4
Kael, Steinem and Nader, Marks, Hayden and Mailer, Galbraith and
Heilbroner, and your bear-market brothers in the PopEco business,
Lekachman & Others[2]—which of you has not hunkered down lately in the
prodigious lap of Mother O'Hare!

And why? Because they're heading out into the land to give lectures.   5
They are giving lectures at the colleges and universities of America's
heartland, which runs from Fort Lee, New Jersey, on the east to the
Hollywood Freeway on the west. Giving lectures in the heartland is one of
the lucrative dividends of being a noted writer in America. It is the writer's
faint approximation of, say, Joe Cocker's[3] $25,000 one-night stand at the
West Springfield Fair. All the skyways to Lecture-land lead through O'Hare
Airport. In short, up to one half of our intellectual establishment sits outside
of Chicago between planes.

At a literary conference at Notre Dame, I (no stranger to bountiful   6
O'Hare myself) ran into a poet who is noted for his verse celebrating the
ecology, née Nature. He lives in a dramatic house nailed together completely
from uncut pieces of hickory driftwood, perched on a bluff overlooking

---

[1] *Mies van der row:* a pun on Mies Van Der Rohe, a German-born American architect
(1886–1969). [Editors' note.]

[2] *Masters and Johnson . . . Others:* influences on post–World War II American society. See
the Editors' Note on page 477 for more detail. [Editors' note.]

[3] *Joe Cocker:* an American rock-and-roll musician (b. 1944). [Editors' note.]

the crashing ocean, a spot so remote that you can drive no closer than five miles to it by conventional automobile and barely within a mile and a half by Jeep. The last 7,500 feet it's hand over hand up rocks, vines, and lengths of hemp. I remarked that this must be the ideal setting in which to write about the ecological wonders.

"I wouldn't know," he said. "I do all my writing in O'Hare."   7

And what is the message that the bards and sages of O'Hare bring to   8
millions of college students in the vast fodderlands of the nation? I'm afraid I must report that it is a gloomy message; morose, even, heading for gangrene.

2. THE FRISBEE ION

If you happen to attend a conference at which whole contingents of the   9
O'Hare philosophers assemble, you can get the message in all its varieties in a short time. Picture, if you will, a university on the Great Plains . . . a new Student Activities Center the color of butter-almond ice cream . . . a huge interior space with tracks in the floor, along which janitors in green twill pull Expando-Flex accordion walls to create meeting rooms of any size. The conference is about to begin. The students come surging in like hormones. You've heard of rosy cheeks? They *have* them! Here they come, rosy-cheeked, laughing, with Shasta and 7-Up pumping through their veins, talking chipsy, flashing weatherproof smiles, bursting out of their down-filled Squaw Valley jackets and their blue jeans—O immortal denim mons veneris!—looking, all of them, boys and girls, Jocks & Buds & Freaks, as if they spent the day hang-gliding and then made a Miller commercial at dusk and are now going to taper off with a little Culture before returning to the coed dorm. They grow quiet. The conference begins. The keynote speaker, a historian wearing a calfskin jacket and hair like Felix Mendelssohn's,[4] informs them that the United States is "a leaden, life-denying society."

Over the next thirty-six hours, other O'Hare regulars fill in the rest: 10

Sixty families control one half the private wealth of America, and two   11
hundred corporations own two thirds of the means of production. "A small group of nameless, faceless men" who avoid publicity the way a werewolf avoids the dawn now dominates American life. In America a man's home is not his castle but merely "a gigantic listening device with a mortgage"— a reference to eavesdropping by the FBI and the CIA. America's foreign policy has been and continues to be based upon war, assassination, bribery,

---

[4] *Felix Mendelssohn:* a German performing musician and composer (1809–1847). [Editors' note.]

genocide, and the sabotage of democratic governments. "The new Mc-Carthyism" (Joe's,[5] not Gene's[6]) is already upon us. Following a brief charade of free speech, the "gagging of the press" has resumed. Racism in America has not diminished; it is merely more subtle now. The gulf between rich and poor widens daily, creating "permanent ghetto-colonial populations." The decline in economic growth is causing a crisis in capitalism, which will lead shortly to authoritarian rule and to a new America in which everyone waits, in horror, for the knock on the door in the dead of the night, the descent of the knout on the nape of the neck—

How other people attending this conference felt by now, I didn't dare 12 ask. As for myself, I was beginning to feel like Job or Miss Cunégonde.[7] What further devastations or humiliations could possibly be in store, short of the sacking of Kansas City? It was in that frame of mind that I attended the final panel discussion, which was entitled "The United States in the Year 2000."

The prognosis was not good, as you can imagine. But I was totally 13 unprepared for the astounding news brought by an ecologist.

"I'm not sure I want to be alive in the year 2000," he said, although he 14 certainly looked lively enough at the moment. He was about thirty-eight, and he wore a Madras plaid cotton jacket and a Disco Magenta turtleneck jersey.

It seemed that recent studies showed that, due to the rape of the atmosphere 15 by aerosol spray users, by 2000 a certain ion would no longer be coming our way from the sun. I can't remember which one . . . the aluminum ion, the magnesium ion, the neon ion, the gadolinium ion, the calcium ion . . . the calcium ion perhaps; in any event, it was crucial for the formation of bones, and by 2000 it would be no more. Could such a thing be? Somehow this went beyond any of the horrors I was already imagining. I began free-associating . . . Suddenly I could see Lexington Avenue, near where I live in Manhattan. The presence of the storm troopers was the least of it. It was the look of ordinary citizens that was so horrible. Their bones were going. They were dissolving. Women who had once been clicking and clogging down the avenue up on five-inch platform soles, with their pants seams smartly cleaving their declivities, were now mere denim & patent-leather blobs . . . oozing and inching and suppurating along the

---

[5] *Joe:* Joseph R. McCarthy (1908–1957), the American politician for whom McCarthyism, the practice of making accusations and conducting investigations unfairly to suppress opposition, is named. [Editors' note.]

[6] *Gene:* Eugene McCarthy (b. 1916), a senator from Minnesota who in 1968 ran unsuccessfully for the U.S. presidency as a peace candidate. [Editors' note.]

[7] *Miss Cunégonde:* the heroine of Voltaire's *Candide* (see pp. 141–147). [Editors' note.]

sidewalk like amoebas or ticks . . . A cab driver puts his arm out the window . . . and it just dribbles down the yellow door like hot Mazola . . . A blind news dealer tries to give change to a notions buyer for Bloomingdale's, and their fingers run together like fettucine over a stack of *New York Posts* . . . It's horrible . . . it's obscene . . . it's the end—

I was so dazed, I was no longer wondering what the assembled students 16 thought of all this. But just at that moment one of them raised his hand. He was a tall boy with a lot of curly hair and a Fu Manchu mustache.

"Yes?" said the ecologist. 17

"There's one thing I can't understand," said the boy. 18

"What's that?" said the ecologist. 19

"Well," said the boy. "I'm a senior, and for four years we've been told 20 by people like yourself and the other gentlemen that everything's in terrible shape, and it's all going to hell, and I'm willing to take your word for it, because you're all experts in your fields. But around here, at this school, for the past four years, the biggest problem, as far as I can see, has been finding a parking place near the campus."

Dead silence. The panelists looked at this poor turkey to try to size him 21 up. Was he trying to be funny? Or was this the native bray of the heartland? The ecologist struck a note of forbearance as he said:

"I'm sure that's true, and that illustrates one of the biggest difficulties 22 we have in making realistic assessments. A university like this, after all, is a middle-class institution, and middle-class life is calculated precisely to create a screen—"

"I understand all that," said the boy. "What I want to know is—how 23 old are you, usually, when it all hits you?"

And suddenly the situation became clear. The kid was no wiseacre! He 24 was genuinely perplexed! . . . For four years he had been squinting at the horizon . . . looking for the grim horrors which he knew—on faith—to be all around him . . . and had been utterly unable to find them . . . and now he was afraid they might descend on him all at once when he least expected it. He might be walking down the street in Omaha one day, minding his own business, when—whop! whop! whop! whop!—War! Fascism! Repression! Corruption!—they'd squash him like bowling balls rolling off a roof!

Who was that lost lad? What was his name? Without knowing it, he was 25 playing the xylophone in a boneyard. He was the unique new creature of the 1970's. He was Candide in reverse. Candide and Miss Cunégonde, one will recall, are taught by an all-knowing savant, Dr. Pangloss. He keeps assuring them that this is "the best of all possible worlds," and they believe him implicitly—even though their lives are one catastrophe after another. Now something much weirder was happening. The Jocks & Buds & Freaks of the heartland have their all-knowing savants of O'Hare, who keep warning them that this is "the worst of all possible worlds," and they

know it must be true—and yet life keeps getting easier, sunnier, happier
. . . *Frisbee!*

How can such things be?   26

3. S-s-s-s-s-s-s-ssssssss

One Saturday night in 1965 I found myself on a stage at Princeton   27
University with Günter Grass, Allen Ginsberg,[8] Paul Krassner, and an
avant-garde filmmaker named Gregory Markopoulos. We were supposed
to talk about "the style of the sixties." The auditorium had a big balcony
and a lot of moldings. It reminded me of the National Opera House in
San José, Costa Rica. The place was packed with about twelve hundred
Princeton students and their dates. Before things got started, it was hard to
figure out just what they expected. Somebody up in the balcony kept making
a sound like a baby crying. Somebody on the main floor always responded
with a strange sound he was able to make with his mouth and his cupped
hands. It sounded like a raccoon trapped in a garbage can. The baby . . .
the raccoon in a can . . . Every time they did it the whole place cracked
up, twelve hundred Princeton students and their dates. "Dates" . . . yes
. . . this was back before the era of "Our eyes met, our lips met, our
bodies met, and then we were introduced."

Anyway, the format was that each man on the stage would make an   28
opening statement about the 1960's, and then the panel discussion would
begin. Günter Grass, as Germany's new giant of the novel, the new Thomas
Mann,[9] went first. He understood English but didn't feel confident speaking
in English, and so he made his statement in German. I doubt that there
were ten people in the place who knew what he was saying, but he seemed
to speak with gravity and passion. When he finished, there was tremendous
applause. Then an interpreter named Albert Harrison (as I recall) delivered
Mr. Grass's remarks in English. Sure enough, they were grave and
passionate. They were about the responsibility of the artist in a time of
struggle and crisis. The applause was even greater than before. Some of
the students rose to their feet. Some of the dates rose, too.

The moderator was Paul Krassner, editor of *The Realist* magazine. I   29
remember looking over at Krassner. He looked like one of the trolls that
live under the bridge in Norse tales and sit there stroking their molting
noses and waiting for hotshots to swagger over the span. Krassner had to
wait for about two minutes for the applause to die down enough to make
himself heard. Then he leaned into his microphone and said quite solemnly:

---

[8] *Allen Ginsberg:* a counterculture American poet (b. 1926) best known for his contributions
to "Beat" poetry. [Editors' note.]

[9] Thomas Mann: a German novelist (1875–1955) and winner of the Nobel Prize for
literature in 1929. [Editors' note.]

"Thank you, Günter Grass. And thank you, Albert Harrison, for   30
translating . . . Mr. Grass's bar mitzvah speech."

Stunned—like twelve hundred veal calves entering the abattoir. Then   31
came the hissing. Twelve hundred Princeton students & dates started
hissing. I had never heard such a sound before . . . an entire hall consumed
in hisses . . .

"S-s-s-s-s-s-s-s-s-sssssss!"   32

You couldn't hear yourself talk. You could only hear that sibilant storm.   33
Krassner just sat there with his manic-troll look on, waiting for it to die
down. It seemed to take forever. When the storm began to subside a bit,
he leaned into the microphone again and said:

"For two years I've been hearing that God is dead. I'm very much   34
relieved to see he only sprung a leak."

For some reason, that stopped the hissing. The kid up in the balcony   35
made a sound like a baby crying. The kid on the main floor made a sound
like a raccoon in a garbage can. The crowd laughed and booed, and people
tried out new noises. The gyroscope was now gone from the control panel
. . . Our trajectory was end over end . . .

The next thing I knew, the discussion was onto the subject of fascism in   36
America. Everybody was talking about police repression and the anxiety
and paranoia as good folks waited for the knock on the door and the descent
of the knout on the nape of the neck. I couldn't make any sense out of it.
I had just made a tour of the country to write a series called "The New
Life Out There" for *New York* magazine. This was the mid-1960's. The
post–World War II boom had by now pumped money into every level of
the population on a scale unparalleled in any nation in history. Not only
that, the folks were running wilder and freer than any people in history.
For that matter, Krassner himself, in one of the strokes of exuberance for
which he was well known, was soon to publish a slight hoax: an account of
how Lyndon Johnson was so overjoyed about becoming President that he
had buggered a wound in the neck of John F. Kennedy on Air Force One
as Kennedy's body was being flown back from Dallas. Krassner presented
this as a suppressed chapter from William Manchester's book *Death of a
President*. Johnson, of course, was still President when it came out. Yet the
merciless gestapo dragnet missed Krassner, who cleverly hid out onstage at
Princeton on Saturday nights.

Suddenly I heard myself blurting out over my microphone: "My God,   37
what are you talking about? We're in the middle of a . . . Happiness
Explosion!"

That merely sounded idiotic. The kid up in the balcony did the crying   38
baby. The kid down below did the raccoon . . . *Krakatoa, East of Java*
. . . I disappeared in a tidal wave of the rude sounds . . . Back to the goon
squads, search-and-seize and roust-a-daddy . . .

Support came from a quarter I hadn't counted on. It was Grass, speaking   39
in English.

"For the past hour I have my eyes fixed on the doors here," he said. 40
"You talk about fascism and police repression. In Germany when I was a
student, they come through those doors long ago. Here they must be very
slow."

Grass was enjoying himself for the first time all evening. He was not 41
simply saying, "You really don't have so much to worry about." He was
indulging his sense of the absurd. He was saying: "You American
intellectuals—you want so desperately to feel besieged and persecuted!"

He sounded like Jean-François Revel, a French socialist writer who talks 42
about one of the great unexplained phenomena of modern astronomy:
namely, that the dark night of fascism is always descending in the United
States and yet lands only in Europe.

Not very nice, Günter! Not very nice, Jean-François! A bit supercilious, 43
wouldn't you say!

In fact, during the 1960's American intellectuals seldom seemed to realize 44
just how patronizing their European brethren were being. To the Europeans,
American intellectuals were struggling so hard (yet once again) to be correct
in ideology and in attitude . . . and they were *being* correct . . . impeccable,
even—which was precisely what prompted the sniggers and the knowing
looks. European intellectuals looked upon American intellectuals much the
way English colonial officials used to look upon the swarthy locals who
came forward with their Calcutta Toff Oxford accents or their Lagos
Mayfair tailored clothes. It was so touching (*then why are you laughing?*) to
see the natives try to *do it right*.

I happened to have been in a room in Washington in 1961 when a 45
member of Nigeria's first Cabinet (after independence) went into a long
lament about the insidious and seductive techniques the British had used
over the years to domesticate his people.

"Just look at *me*!" he said, looking down at his own torso and flipping 46
his hands toward his chest. "Look at this *suit*! A worsted suit on an African—
and a *double-breasted waistcoat*!"

He said "double-breasted waistcoat" with the most shriveling self-contempt 47
you can imagine.

"This is what they've done to me," he said softly. "I can't even do the 48
High Life any more."

The High Life was a Low Rent Nigerian dance. He continued to stare 49
down at the offending waistcoat, wondering where he'd left his soul, or his
Soul, in any event.

Perhaps someday, if Mr. Bob Silvers's *Confessions* are published, we will 50
read something similar. Silvers is co-editor of *The New York Review of
Books*. His accent arrived mysteriously one day in a box from London.
Intrigued, he slapped it into his mouth like a set of teeth. It seemed . . .
right. He began signing up so many English dons to write for *The New
York Review of Books* that wags began calling it *The London Review of Bores*
and *Don & Grub Street*. He seemed to take this good-naturedly. But

perhaps someday we will learn that Mr. Bob Silvers, too, suffered blue moods of the soul and stood in front of a mirror wiggling his knees, trying to jiggle his roots, wondering if his feet could ever renegotiate the Lindy or the Fish or the Hokey-Pokey.

4. HELL'S ANGELS

O how faithfully our native intelligentsia has tried to . . . *do it right!* The [51] model has not always been England. Not at all. Just as frequently it has been Germany or France or Italy or even (on the religious fringe) the Orient. In the old days—seventy-five-or-so years ago—the well-brought-up young intellectual was likely to be treated to a tour of Europe . . . we find Jane Addams recuperating from her malaise in London and Dresden . . . Lincoln Steffens going to college in Heidelberg and Munich . . . Mabel Dodge setting up house in Florence . . . Randolph Bourne discovering Germany's "charming villages" and returning to Bloomfield, New Jersey—*Bloomfield, New Jersey?*—which now "seemed almost too grotesquely squalid and frowsy to be true." The business of being an intellectual and the urge to set oneself apart from provincial life began to be indistinguishable. In July 1921 Harold Stearns[10] completed his anthology called *Civilization in the United States*—a contradiction in terms, he hastened to note—and set sail for Europe. The "Lost Generation" adventure began. But what was the Lost Generation really? It was a post–Great War discount tour in which middle-class Americans, too, not just Bournes and Steffenses, could learn how to become European intellectuals; preferably French.

The European intellectual! What a marvelous figure! A brilliant cynic, [52] dazzling, in fact, set like one of those Gustave Miklos[11] Art Deco sculptures of polished bronze and gold against the smoking rubble of Europe after the Great War. The American intellectual did the best he could. He could position himself against a backdrop of . . . well, not exactly rubble . . . but of the booboisie, the Herd State, the United States of Puritanism, Philistinism, Boosterism, Greed, and the great Hog Wallow. It was certainly a *psychological* wasteland. For the next fifty years, from that time to this, with ever-increasing skill, the American intellectual would perform this difficult feat, which might be described as the Adjectival Catch Up. The European intellectuals have a real wasteland? Well, we have a psychological wasteland. They have real fascism? Well, we have social fascism (a favorite phrase of the 1930's, amended to "liberal fascism" in the 1960's). They

---

[10] *Jane Addams, Lincoln Steffens, Mabel Dodge, Randolph Bourne, Harold Stearns:* early twentieth-century New York intellectuals interested in social reform and artistic innovation. [Editors' note.]

[11] *Gustave Miklos:* a Hungarian painter and sculptor. [Editors' note.]

have real poverty? Well, we have relative poverty (Michael Harrington's[12] great Adjectival Catch Up of 1963). They have real genocide? Well, we have cultural genocide (i.e., what universities were guilty of in the late 1960's if they didn't have open-admissions policies for minority groups).

Well—all right! They were difficult, these one-and-a-half gainers in 53 logic. But they were worth it. What had become important above all was to be that polished figure amid the rubble, a vision of sweetness and light in the smoking tar pit of hell. The intellectual had become not so much an occupational type as a status type. He was like the medieval cleric, most of whose energies were devoted to separating himself from the mob—which in modern times, in Revel's[13] phrase, goes under the name of the middle class.

Did he want to analyze the world systematically? Did he want to add to 54 the store of human knowledge? He not only didn't want to, he belittled the notion, quoting Rosa Luxemburg's[14] statement that the "pot-bellied academics" and their interminable monographs and lectures, their intellectual nerve gas, were sophisticated extensions of police repression. Did he even want to change the world? Not particularly; it was much more elegant to back exotic, impossible causes such as the Black Panthers'. Moral indignation was the main thing; that, and a certain pattern of consumption. In fact, by the 1960's it was no longer necessary to produce literature, scholarship, or art—or even to be involved in such matters, except as a consumer—in order to qualify as an intellectual. It was only necessary to live *la vie intellectuelle*.[15] A little brown bread in the bread box, a lapsed pledge card to CORE,[16] a stereo and a record rack full of Coltrane[17] and all the Beatles albums from *Revolver* on, white walls, a huge *Dracaena marginata* plant, which is there because all the furniture is so clean-lined and spare that without this piece of frondose tropical Victoriana the room looks empty, a stack of unread *New York Review of Books* rising up in a surly mound of subscription guilt, the conviction that America is materialistic, repressive, bloated, and deadened by its Silent Majority, which resides in the heartland,

---

[12] *Michael Harrington:* an American socialist (1928–1989), perhaps best known for his disturbing study of America's poor, *The Other America: Poverty in the United States,* published in 1963. [Editors' note.]

[13] *Revel:* Jean-François Revel (b. 1924), a French social philosopher and champion of American culture. [Editors' note.]

[14] *Rosa Luxemburg:* a German socialist, feminist, and pacifist (1870–1919). [Editors' note.]

[15] *la vie intellectuelle:* the intellectual life. [Editors' note.]

[16] *CORE:* Congress of Racial Equality, an American civil rights organization. [Editors' note.]

[17] *Coltrane:* John Coltrane (1926–1967), an African-American jazz saxophonist. [Editors' note.]

three grocery boxes full of pop bottles wedged in behind the refrigerator and destined (one of these days) for the Recycling Center, a small, uncomfortable European car—that pretty well got the job done. By the late 1960's it seemed as if American intellectuals had at last . . . Caught Up. There were riots on the campuses and in the slums. The war in Vietnam had developed into a full-sized hell. War! Revolution! Imperialism! Poverty! I can still remember the ghastly delight with which literary people in New York embraced the Four Horsemen.[18] The dark night was about to descend. All agreed on that; but there were certain ugly, troublesome facts that the native intellectuals, unlike their European mentors, had a hard time ignoring.

By 1967 Lyndon Johnson may have been the very generalissimo of [55] American imperialism in Southeast Asia—but back here in the U.S. the citizens were enjoying freedom of expression and freedom of dissent to a rather astonishing degree. For example, the only major Western country that allowed public showings of *MacBird*—a play that had Lyndon Johnson murdering John F. Kennedy in order to become President—was the United States (Lyndon Johnson, President). The citizens of this fascist bastion, the United States, unaccountably had, and exercised, the most extraordinary political freedom and civil rights in all history. In fact, the government, under the same Johnson, had begun the novel experiment of sending organizers into the slums—in the Community Action phase of the poverty program—to mobilize minority groups to rise up against the government and demand a bigger slice of the pie. (They obliged.) Colored peoples were much farther along the road to equality—whether in the area of rights, jobs, income, or social acceptance—in the United States than were the North Africans, Portuguese, Senegalese, Pakistanis, and Jamaicans of Europe. In 1966 England congratulated herself over the appointment of her first colored policeman (a Pakistani in Coventry). Meanwhile, young people in the U.S.—in the form of the Psychedelic or Flower Generation— were helping themselves to wild times that were the envy of children all over the world.

In short, freedom was in the air like a flock of birds. Just how fascist [56] could it be? This problem led to perhaps the greatest Adjectival Catch Up of all times: Herbert Marcuse's[19] doctrine of "repressive tolerance." Other countries had real repression? Well, we had the obverse, repressive tolerance. This was an insidious system through which the government granted meaningless personal freedoms in order to narcotize the pain of class repression, which only socialism could cure. Beautiful! Well-nigh flawless!

Yet even at the moment of such exquisite refinements—things have a [57] way of going wrong. Another troublesome fact has cropped up, gravely

---

[18] *Four Horsemen:* apocalyptic figures described in the New Testment Book of Revelation. [Editors' note.]

[19] *Herbert Marcuse:* American social and political philosopher (1898–1979). [Editors' note.]

complicating the longtime dream of socialism. That troublesome fact may be best summed up in a name: Solzhenitsyn.

5. BLAMING THE MESSENGER

With the Hungarian uprising of 1956 and the invasion of Czechoslovakia in 1968 it had become clear to Mannerist Marxists such as Sartre[20] that the Soviet Union was now an embarrassment. The fault, however, as *tout le monde*[21] knew, was not with socialism but with Stalinism. Stalin was a madman and had taken socialism on a wrong turn. (Mistakes happen.) Solzhenitsyn began speaking out as a dissident inside the Soviet Union in 1967. His complaints, his revelations, his struggles with Soviet authorities— they merely underscored just how wrong the Stalinist turn had been. 58

The publication of *The Gulag Archipelago* in 1973, however, was a wholly unexpected blow. No one was ready for the obscene horror and grotesque scale of what Solzhenitsyn called "Our Sewage Disposal System"—in which *tens of millions* were shipped in boxcars to concentration camps all over the country, in which tens of millions died, in which entire races and national groups were liquidated, insofar as they had existed in the Soviet Union. Moreover, said Solzhenitsyn, the system had not begun with Stalin but with Lenin, who had immediately exterminated non-Bolshevik opponents of the old regime and especially the student factions. It was impossible any longer to distinguish the Communist liquidation apparatus from the Nazi. 59

Yet Solzhenitsyn went still further. He said that not only Stalinism, not only Leninism, not only Communism—but socialism itself led to the concentration camps; and not only socialism, but Marxism; and not only Marxism but any ideology that sought to reorganize morality on an *a priori* basis. Sadder still, it was impossible to say that Soviet socialism was not "real socialism." On the contrary—it was socialism done by experts! 60

Intellectuals in Europe and America were willing to forgive Solzhenitsyn a great deal. After all, he had been born and raised in the Soviet Union as a Marxist, he had fought in combat for his country, he was a great novelist, he had been in the camps for eight years, he had suffered. But for his insistence that the *isms* themselves led to the death camps—for this he was not likely to be forgiven soon. And in fact the campaign of antisepsis began soon after he was expelled from the Soviet Union in 1974. ("He suffered *too* much—he's crazy." "He's a Christian zealot with a Christ complex." "He's an agrarian reactionary." "He's an egotist and a publicity junkie.") 61

Solzhenitsyn's tour of the United States in 1975 was like an enormous funeral procession that no one wanted to see. The White House wanted no part of him. *The New York Times* sought to bury his two major speeches, 62

---

[20] *Sartre:* Jean-Paul Sartre (1905–1980), a French philosopher and author. [Editors' note.]

[21] *tout le monde:* everyone. [Editors' note.]

and only the moral pressure of a lone *Times* writer, Hilton Kramer, brought them any appreciable coverage at all. The major television networks declined to run the Solzhenitsyn interview that created such a stir in England earlier this year (it ran on some of the educational channels).

And the literary world in general ignored him completely. In the huge   63
unseen coffin that Solzhenitsyn towed behind him were not only the souls of the *zeks* who died in the Archipelago. No, the heartless bastard had also chucked in one of the last great visions: the intellectual as the Stainless Steel Socialist glistening against the bone heap of capitalism in its final, brutal, fascist phase. There was a bone heap, all right, and it was grisly beyond belief, but socialism had created it.

In 1974, in one of his last speeches, the late Lionel Trilling, who was   64
probably the most prestigious literary critic in the country and had been a professor of English at Columbia for thirty-five years, made what falls under the heading of "a modest proposal." He suggested that the liberal-arts curriculum in the universities be abandoned for one generation.

His argument ran as follows: Children come to the university today, and   65
they register, and they get the student-activity card and the map of the campus and the university health booklet, and just about as automatically they get a packet of cultural and political attitudes. That these attitudes are negative or cynical didn't seem to be what worried Trilling. It was more that they are dispensed and accepted with such an air of conformity and inevitability. The student emerges from the university with a set of ready-mades, intact, untouched by direct experience. What was the solution? Well—why not turn off the packaging apparatus for a while? In time there might develop a generation of intelligent people who had experienced American life directly and "earned" their opinions.

Whether his proposal was serious or not, I couldn't say. But somehow   66
he made me think once more of the Lost Lad of the Great Plains, the Candide in Reverse,

> Who asked how old you had to be
> Before the O'Hare curse
> Coldcocked you like the freight train
> Of history—
> Tell me, are you willing,
> Lost Lad, to pick yourself some
> Intelligent lost coed Cunégonde
> And head out shank-to-flank in Trilling's
> Curriculum?
> Will you hector *tout le monde*?
> Will you sermonize
> On how perceiving
> Is believing
> The heresy of your own eyes?

EDITORS' NOTE

Masters and Johnson: William H. Masters and Virginia E. Johnson, a husband-and-wife team of researchers who wrote a widely read, controversial study of human sexuality in 1966 entitled *Human Sexual Response.*

Erica Jong: a feminist writer (b. 1942).

Kozol: Jonathan Kozol (b. 1936), a liberal author who has focused primarily on educational issues.

Rifkin: Jeremy Rifkin (b. 1945), a radical social activist and author interested in issues such as genetic engineering and economics.

Hacker: Andrew Hacker (b. 1929), a political scientist.

Kael: Pauline Kael (b. 1919), a film critic for the *New Yorker.*

Steinem: Gloria Steinem (b. 1935), a feminist writer and editor of *Ms.*

Nader: Ralph Nader (b. 1934), a consumer rights advocate and environmentalist.

Hayden: Tom Hayden (b. 1940), a 1960s radical who became a Democratic politician.

Mailer: Norman Mailer (b. 1923), a novelist and essayist, and one of the leading representatives of the New Journalism.

Galbraith: John Kenneth Galbraith (b. 1908), a liberal economist.

Heilbroner: Robert Heilbroner (b. 1919), a leftist-leaning economist and author.

bear-market brothers in the PopEco business: a bear market is a declining stock market; PopEco is a nickname for the field of popular economics.

Lekachman: Robert Lekachman (b. 1920), a liberal economist, educator, and author.

Questions for Discussion and Writing

1. How would you describe Wolfe's prose style? How does it contribute to his ethos and to the persuasiveness of his prose? Use specific examples from the text to support your claims.

2. What, overall, seems to be Wolfe's rhetorical intention in this essay? In an essay of your own, analyze Wolfe's essential argument and its main sources of persuasion. Be sure to provide plenty of textual evidence in support of your argument about his intention.

3. Does this essay seem to have a carefully arranged structure? Do the five small sections fit together to create a greater whole? Do you notice any transitions at work here? What rhetorical purpose does Wolfe's structure serve?

4. Writing for an audience that has read Wolfe's essay, develop your own argument in response to one of the issues Wolfe addresses—such as the validity of liberal critiques of American society or the value of skepticism in education.

JOAN DIDION

(b. 1934)

Joan Didion is one of the most intriguing—and difficult to characterize—contributors to contemporary American writing. She was born in Sacramento, California, where her family roots are deep; some of her ancestors had pursued the American Dream across the continent to the Pacific in the middle of the nineteenth century. It should not be surprising, therefore, that California culture has been one of her favorite subjects as a writer.

Didion began creative writing at the request of her mother, who sought a positive medium of self-expression for her frustrated child. In the 1950s, she attended the University of California at Berkeley, where she studied English literature and wrote for the campus literary magazine. On graduation in 1956, she moved to New York to work for Vogue, where she began as a promotional copy writer. By the time she quit the magazine to move back to her native California eight years later, she had advanced to associate feature editor. She married writer John Gregory Dunne in 1964, and they settled in Los Angeles.

Didion's career as a freelance writer had begun to take shape during her New York years. In 1963, she published Run River, a novel set in the Sacramento River Valley. On her return to the West Coast, both Didion and her husband became full-time writers. With the publication of Slouching Towards Bethlehem (1968), a collection of essays about life in California in the 1960s, Didion's reputation as a major journalist was established.

The literary allusion that informs the book is to William Butler Yeats's apocalyptic "The Second Coming." At the conclusion of this unsettling poem, the speaker asks, "And what rough beast, its hour come round at last, / Slouches towards Bethlehem to be born?" The speaker also says, "Things fall apart; the center cannot hold." Indeed, in this collection of essays Didion portrays a society that is falling apart because it has failed to pass along its basic values from generation to generation. Her title essay is a shocking account of the hippie movement that engulfed San Francisco's Haight-Ashbury District in the mid-1960s. The opening essay, "Some Dreamers of the Golden Dream," is reprinted here.

With the publication of Slouching Towards Bethlehem, Didion joined the ranks of a popular new literary movement known as "New Journalism." "New Journalism" investigates and reports the "news," but it allows the journalist greater freedom than previously to interject his or her own feelings about the subject and thus renders problematic the journalistic doctrine of objectivity. "New Journalists" have been known actually to participate in the events about which they write. Furthermore, "New Journalism" tends to be less rigid formally than traditional reporting, often

479

following a stream-of-consciousness structure while exhibiting a well-developed sense of prose style.

Since Slouching Towards Bethlehem, Didion has written slowly but steadily, and her work has received considerable critical acclaim. She has produced three more novels: Play It as It Lays (1970), A Book of Common Prayer (1977), and Democracy (1984). In 1979, she published a second collection of essays entitled The White Album, and in 1983, she came out with Salvador, a book-length essay based on her 1982 visit to El Salvador. Gradually, she has shifted her emphasis away from personal reflections about California and has focused increasingly on Central American issues. She has also written columns, short stories, and screenplays, often in collaboration with her husband.

In evaluating Didion's work, many have admired her careful prose. She writes slowly, painstakingly reworking her pieces until they satisfy her; her ultimate goal is "total control" over the language. This great concern for the fine points of style is nothing new for Didion, however. As a student, she reworked passages from the canon of English and American literature, striving to understand the stylistic choices of the masters.

In an essay entitled "Why I Write," Didion states: "In many ways writing is the act of saying I, of imposing oneself upon other people, of saying listen to me, see it my way, change your mind." Of course, for Didion, writing is other things as well: a process of self-discovery, a way of understanding the world, and an exploration of the almost infinite possibilities of language for inventing and shaping meaning. But the goal of all this exploration, understanding, and discovery is to make a new meaning happen in someone else's mind, to persuade. Didion is thus committed to the social use of writing as an instrument of social commentary and change.

In terms of her specific argumentative intentions, though, Didion is a difficult writer to pin down. Unlike many of the figures presented in this anthology, she has not sided consistently with any particular camp or political movement. Although, for example, she has questioned the feminist movement in print, she is by no means a reactionary. While reading "Some Dreamers of the Golden Dream," try to avoid facile categorization of her message.

SOME DREAMERS OF THE GOLDEN DREAM

This is a story about love and death in the golden land, and begins with the country. The San Bernardino Valley lies only an hour east of Los Angeles by the San Bernardino Freeway but is in certain ways an alien place: not the coastal California of the subtropical twilights and the soft westerlies off the Pacific but a harsher California, haunted by the Mojave just beyond the mountains, devastated by the hot dry Santa Ana wind that

1

comes down through the passes at 100 miles an hour and whines through the eucalyptus windbreaks and works on the nerves. October is the bad month for the wind, the month when breathing is difficult and the hills blaze up spontaneously. There has been no rain since April. Every voice seems a scream. It is the season of suicide and divorce and prickly dread, wherever the wind blows.

The Mormons settled this ominous country, and then they abandoned it, but by the time they left the first orange tree had been planted and for the next hundred years the San Bernardino Valley would draw a kind of people who imagined they might live among the talismanic fruit and prosper in the dry air, people who brought with them Midwestern ways of building and cooking and praying and who tried to graft those ways upon the land. The graft took in curious ways. This is the California where it is possible to live and die without ever eating an artichoke, without ever meeting a Catholic or a Jew. This is the California where it is easy to Dial-A-Devotion, but hard to buy a book. This is the country in which a belief in the literal interpretation of Genesis has slipped imperceptibly into a belief in the literal interpretation of *Double Indemnity*,[1] the country of the teased hair and the Capris and the girls for whom all life's promise comes down to a waltz-length white wedding dress and the birth of a Kimberly or a Sherry or a Debbi and a Tijuana divorce[2] and a return to hairdressers' school. "We were just crazy kids," they say without regret, and look to the future. The future always looks good in the golden land, because no one remembers the past. Here is where the hot wind blows and the old ways do not seem relevant, where the divorce rate is double the national average and where one person in every thirty-eight lives in a trailer. Here is the last stop for all those who come from somewhere else, for all those who drifted away from the cold and the past and the old ways. Here is where they are trying to find a new life style, trying to find it in the only places they know to look: the movies and the newspapers. The case of Lucille Marie Maxwell Miller is a tabloid monument to that new life style.

Imagine Banyan Street first, because Banyan is where it happened. The way to Banyan is to drive west from San Bernardino out Foothill Boulevard, Route 66: past the Santa Fe switching yards, the Forty Winks Motel. Past the motel that is nineteen stucco tepees: "SLEEP IN A WIGWAM—GET MORE FOR YOUR WAMPUM." Past Fontana Drag City and the Fontana Church of

2

3

---

[1] *Double Indemnity:* Double indemnity is a provision often written into life insurance policies stipulating that the provider will pay twice the value of the policy if the holder's death is accidental. This provision was the inspiration for the 1944 American film *Double Indemnity*, from the novel by James M. Cain, about a man who exploits his mistress's husband's generous insurance policy. [Editors' note]

[2] *Tijuana divorce:* an uncomplicated divorce that can be obtained quickly in Tijuana, Mexico. [Editor's note.]

the Nazarene and the Pit Stop A Go-Go; past Kaiser Steel, through Cucamonga, out to the Kapu Kai Restaurant-Bar and Coffee Shop, at the corner of Route 66 and Carnelian Avenue. Up Carnelian Avenue from the Kapu Kai, which means "Forbidden Seas," the subdivision flags whip in the harsh wind. "HALF-ACRES RANCHES! SNACK BARS! TRAVERTINE ENTRIES! $95 DOWN." It is the trail of an intention gone haywire, the flotsam of the New California. But after a while the signs thin out on Carnelian Avenue, and the houses are no longer the bright pastels of the Springtime Home owners but the faded bungalows of the people who grow a few grapes and keep a few chickens out here, and then the hill gets steeper and the road climbs and even the bungalows are few, and here—desolate, roughly surfaced, lined with eucalyptus and lemon groves—is Banyan Street.

Like so much of this country, Banyan suggests something curious and   4
unnatural. The lemon groves are sunken, down a three- or four-foot retaining wall, so that one looks directly into their dense foliage, too lush, unsettlingly glossy, the greenery of nightmare; the fallen eucalyptus bark is too dusty, a place for snakes to breed. The stones look not like natural stones but like the rubble of some unmentioned upheaval. There are smudge pots, and a closed cistern. To one side of Banyan there is the flat valley, and to the other the San Bernardino Mountains, a dark mass looming too high, too fast, nine, ten, eleven thousand feet, right there above the lemon groves. At midnight on Banyan Street there is no light at all, and no sound except the wind in the eucalyptus and a muffled barking of dogs. There may be a kennel somewhere, or the dogs may be coyotes.

Banyan Street was the route Lucille Miller took home from the twenty-   5
four-hour Mayfair Market on the night of October 7, 1964, a night when the moon was dark and the wind was blowing and she was out of milk, and Banyan Street was where, at about 12:30 a.m., her 1964 Volkswagen came to a sudden stop, caught fire, and began to burn. For an hour and fifteen minutes Lucille Miller ran up and down Banyan calling for help, but no cars passed and no help came. At three o'clock that morning, when the fire had been put out and the California Highway Patrol officers were completing their report, Lucille Miller was still sobbing and incoherent, for her husband had been asleep in the Volkswagen. "What will I tell the children, when there's nothing left, nothing left in the casket," she cried to the friend called to comfort her. "How can I tell them there's nothing left?"

In fact there was something left, and a week later it lay in the Draper   6
Mortuary Chapel in a closed bronze coffin blanketed with pink carnations. Some 200 mourners heard Elder Robert E. Denton of the Seventh-Day Adventist Church of Ontario speak of "the temper of fury that has broken out among us." For Gordon Miller, he said, there would be "no more death, no more heartaches, no more misunderstandings." Elder Ansel Bristol mentioned the "peculiar" grief of the hour. Elder Fred Jensen asked "what shall it profit a man, if he shall gain the whole world, and lose his own

soul?" A light rain fell, a blessing in a dry season, and a female vocalist sang "Safe in the Arms of Jesus." A tape recording of the service was made for the widow, who was being held without bail in the San Bernardino County Jail on a charge of first-degree murder.

Of course she came from somewhere else, came off the prairie in search of   7
something she had seen in a movie or heard on the radio, for this is a Southern California story. She was born on January 17, 1930, in Winnipeg, Manitoba, the only child of Gordon and Lily Maxwell, both schoolteachers and both dedicated to the Seventh-Day Adventist Church, whose members observe the Sabbath on Saturday, believe in an apocalyptic Second Coming, have a strong missionary tendency, and, if they are strict, do not smoke, drink, eat meat, use makeup, or wear jewelry, including wedding rings. By the time Lucille Maxwell enrolled at Walla Walla College in College Place, Washington, the Adventist school where her parents then taught, she was an eighteen-year-old possessed of unremarkable good looks and remarkable high spirits. "Lucille wanted to see the world," her father would say in retrospect, "and I guess she found out."

The high spirits did not seem to lend themselves to an extended course   8
of study at Walla Walla College, and in the spring of 1949 Lucille Maxwell met and married Gordon ("Cork") Miller, a twenty-four-year-old graduate of Walla Walla and of the University of Oregon dental school, then stationed at Fort Lewis as a medical officer. "Maybe you could say it was love at first sight," Mr. Maxwell recalls. "Before they were ever formally introduced, he sent Lucille a dozen and a half roses with a card that said even if she didn't come out on a date with him, he hoped she'd find the roses pretty anyway." The Maxwells remember their daughter as a "radiant" bride.

Unhappy marriages so resemble one another that we do not need to know   9
too much about the course of this one. There may or may not have been trouble on Guam, where Cork and Lucille Miller lived while he finished his Army duty. There may or may not have been problems in the small Oregon town where he first set up private practice. There appears to have been some disappointment about their move to California: Cork Miller had told friends that he wanted to become a doctor, that he was unhappy as a dentist and planned to enter the Seventh-Day Adventist College of Medical Evangelists at Loma Linda, a few miles south of San Bernardino. Instead he bought a dental practice in the west end of San Bernardino County, and the family settled there, in a modest house on the kind of street where there are always tricycles and revolving credit and dreams about bigger houses, better streets. That was 1957. By the summer of 1964 they had achieved the bigger house on the better street and the familiar accouterments of a family on its way up: the $30,000 a year, the three children for the Christmas card, the picture window, the family room, the newspaper photographs that showed "Mrs. Gordon Miller, Ontario Heart Fund Chair-

man. . . ." They were paying the familiar price for it. And they had reached the familiar season of divorce.

It might have been anyone's bad summer, anyone's siege of heat and   10
nerves and migraine and money worries, but this one began particularly early and particularly badly. On April 24 an old friend, Elaine Hayton, died suddenly; Lucille Miller had seen her only the night before. During the month of May, Cork Miller was hospitalized briefly with a bleeding ulcer, and his usual reserve deepened into depression. He told his accountant that he was "sick of looking at open mouths," and threatened suicide. By July 8, the conventional tensions of love and money had reached the conventional impasse in the new house on the acre lot of 8488 Bella Vista, and Lucille Miller filed for divorce. Within a month, however, the Millers seemed reconciled. They saw a marriage counselor. They talked about a fourth child. It seemed that the marriage had reached the traditional truce, the point at which so many resign themselves to cutting both their losses and their hopes.

But the Millers' season of trouble was not to end that easily. October 7   11
began as a commonplace enough day, one of those days that sets the teeth on edge with its tedium, its small frustrations. The temperature reached 102° in San Bernardino that afternoon, and the Miller children were home from school because of Teachers' Institute. There was ironing to be dropped off. There was a trip to pick up a prescription for Nembutal,[3] a trip to a self-service dry cleaner. In the early evening, an unpleasant accident with the Volkswagen: Cork Miller hit and killed a German shepherd, and afterward said that his head felt "like it had a Mack truck on it." It was something he often said. As of that evening Cork Miller was $63,479 in debt, including the $29,637 mortgage on the new house, a debt load which seemed oppressive to him. He was a man who wore his responsibilities uneasily, and complained of migraine headaches almost constantly.

He ate alone that night, from a TV tray in the living room. Later the   12
Millers watched John Forsythe and Senta Berger in *See How They Run*, and when the movie ended, about eleven, Cork Miller suggested that they go out for milk. He wanted some hot chocolate. He took a blanket and pillow from the couch and climbed into the passenger seat of the Volkswagen. Lucille Miller remembers reaching over to lock his door as she backed down the driveway. By the time she left the Mayfair Market, and long before they reached Banyan Street, Cork Miller appeared to be asleep.

There is some confusion in Lucille Miller's mind about what happened   13
between 12:30 a.m., when the fire broke out, and 1:50 a.m., when it was reported. She says that she was driving east on Banyan Street at about 35 m.p.h. when she felt the Volkswagen pull sharply to the right. The next thing she knew the car was on the embankment, quite near the edge of the

---

[3] *Nembutal:* a commonly prescribed barbituate. [Editors' note.]

retaining wall, and flames were shooting up behind her. She does not remember jumping out. She does remember prying up a stone with which she broke the window next to her husband, and then scrambling down the retaining wall to try to find a stick. "I don't know how I was going to push him out," she says. "I just thought if I had a stick, I'd push him out." She could not, and after a while she ran to the intersection of Banyan and Carnelian Avenue. There are no houses at that corner, and almost no traffic. After one car had passed without stopping, Lucille Miller ran back down Banyan toward the burning Volkswagen. She did not stop, but she slowed down, and in the flames she could see her husband. He was, she said, "just black."

At the first house up Sapphire Avenue, half a mile from the Volkswagen, 14 Lucille Miller finally found help. There Mrs. Robert Swenson called the sheriff, and then, at Lucille Miller's request, she called Harold Lance, the Millers' lawyer and their close friend. When Harold Lance arrived he took Lucille Miller home to his wife, Joan. Twice Harold Lance and Lucille Miller returned to Banyan Street and talked to the Highway Patrol officers. A third time Harold Lance returned alone, and when he came back he said to Lucille Miller, "O.K. . . . you don't talk any more."

When Lucille Miller was arrested the next afternoon, Sandy Slagle was 15 with her. Sandy Slagle was the intense, relentlessly loyal medical student who used to baby-sit for the Millers, and had been living as a member of the family since she graduated from high school in 1959. The Millers took her away from a difficult home situation, and she thinks of Lucille Miller not only as "more or less a mother or a sister" but as "the most wonderful character" she has ever known. On the night of the accident, Sandy Slagle was in her dormitory at Loma Linda University, but Lucille Miller called her early in the morning and asked her to come home. The doctor was there when Sandy Slagle arrived, giving Lucille Miller an injection of Nembutal. "She was crying as she was going under," Sandy Slagle recalls. "Over and over she'd say, 'Sandy, all the hours I spent trying to save him and now what are they trying to *do* to me?' "

At 1:30 that afternoon, Sergeant William Paterson and Detectives Charles 16 Callahan and Joseph Karr of the Central Homicide Division arrived at 8488 Bella Vista. "One of them appeared at the bedroom door," Sandy Slagle remembers, "and said to Lucille, 'You've got ten minutes to get dressed or we'll take you as you are.' She was in her nightgown, you know, so I tried to get her dressed."

Sandy Slagle tells the story now as if by rote, and her eyes do not waver. 17 "So I had her panties and bra on her and they opened the door again, so I got some Capris on her, you know, and a scarf." Her voice drops. "And then they just took her."

The arrest took place just twelve hours after the first report that there 18 had been an accident on Banyan Street, a rapidity which would later prompt Lucille Miller's attorney to say that the entire case was an instance of trying to justify a reckless arrest. Actually what first caused the detectives who arrived on Banyan Street toward dawn that morning to give the accident more than routine attention were certain apparent physical inconsistencies. While Lucille Miller had said that she was driving about 35 m.p.h. when the car swerved to a stop, an examination of the cooling Volkswagen showed that it was in low gear, and that the parking rather than the driving lights were on. The front wheels, moreover, did not seem to be in exactly the position that Lucille Miller's description of the accident would suggest, and the right rear wheel was dug in deep, as if it had been spun in place. It seemed curious to the detectives, too, that a sudden stop from 35 m.p.h.—the same jolt which was presumed to have knocked over a gasoline can in the back seat and somehow started the fire—should have left two milk cartoons upright on the back floorboard, and the remains of a Polaroid camera box lying apparently undisturbed on the back seat.

No one, however, could be expected to give a precise account of what [19] did and did not happen in a moment of terror, and none of these inconsistencies seemed in themselves incontrovertible evidence of criminal intent. But they did interest the Sheriff's Office, as did Gordon Miller's apparent unconsciousness at the time of the accident, and the length of time it had taken Lucille Miller to get help. Something, moreover, struck the investigators as wrong about Harold Lance's attitude when he came back to Banyan Street the third time and found the investigation by no means over. "The way Lance was acting," the prosecuting attorney said later, "they thought maybe they'd hit a nerve."

And so it was that on the morning of October 8, even before the doctor [20] had come to give Lucille Miller an injection to calm her, the San Bernardino County Sheriff's Office was trying to construct another version of what might have happened between 12:30 and 1:50 a.m. The hypothesis they would eventually present was based on the somewhat tortuous premise that Lucille Miller had undertaken a plan which failed: a plan to stop the car on the lonely road, spread gasoline over her presumably drugged husband, and, with a stick on the accelerator, gently "walk" the Volkswagen over the embankment, where it would tumble four feet down the retaining wall into the lemon grove and almost certainly explode. If this happened, Lucille Miller might then have somehow negotiated the two miles up Carnelian to Bella Vista in time to be home when the accident was discovered. This plan went awry, according to the Sheriff's Office hypothesis, when the car would not go over the rise of the embankment. Lucille Miller might have panicked then—after she had killed the engine the third or fourth time, say, out there on the dark road with the gasoline already spread and the dogs baying and the wind blowing and the unspeakable apprehension that a pair of headlights would suddenly light up Banyan Street and expose her there—and set the fire herself.

Although this version accounted for some of the physical evidence—the [21] car in low because it had been started from a dead stop, the parking lights on because she could not do what needed doing without some light, a rear wheel spun in repeated attempts to get the car over the embankment, the milk cartons upright because there had been no sudden stop—it did not seem on its own any more or less credible than Lucille Miller's own story. Moreover, some of the physical evidence did seem to support her story: a nail in a front tire, a nine-pound rock found in the car, presumably the one with which she had broken the window in an attempt to save her husband. Within a few days an autopsy had established that Gordon Miller was alive when he burned, which did not particularly help the State's case, and that he had enough Nembutal and Sandoptal in his blood to put the average person to sleep, which did: on the other hand Gordon Miller habitually took both Nembutal and Fiorinal (a common headache prescription which contains Sandoptal), and had been ill besides.

It was a spotty case, and to make it work at all the State was going to have to find a motive. There was talk of unhappiness, talk of another man. That kind of motive, during the next few weeks, was what they set out to establish. They set out to find it in accountants' ledgers and double-indemnity clauses and motel registers, set out to determine what might move a woman who believed in all the promises of the middle class—a woman who had been chairman of the Heart Fund and who always knew a reasonable little dressmaker and who had come out of the bleak wild of prairie fundamentalism to find what she imagined to be the good life—what should drive such a woman to sit on a street called Bella Vista and look out her new picture window into the empty California sun and calculate how to burn her husband alive in a Volkswagen. They found the wedge they wanted closer at hand than they might have at first expected, for, as testimony would reveal later at the trial, it seemed that in December of 1963 Lucille Miller had begun an affair with the husband of one of her friends, a man whose daughter called her "Auntie Lucille," a man who might have seemed to have the gift for people and money and the good life that Cork Miller so noticeably lacked. The man was Arthwell Hayton, a well-known San Bernardino attorney and at one time a member of the district attorney's staff.

In some ways it was the conventional clandestine affair in a place like San Bernardino, a place where little is bright or graceful, where it is routine to misplace the future and easy to start looking for it in bed. Over the seven weeks that it would take to try Lucille Miller for murder, Assistant District Attorney Don A. Turner and defense attorney Edward P. Foley would between them unfold a curiously predictable story. There were the falsified motel registrations. There were the lunch dates, the afternoon drives in Arthwell Hayton's red Cadillac convertible. There were the interminable discussions of the wronged partners. There were the confidantes ("I knew everything," Sandy Slagle would insist fiercely later. "I knew every time, places, everything") and there were the words remembered from bad magazine stories ("Don't kiss me, it will trigger things," Lucille

Miller remembered telling Arthwell Hayton in the parking lot of Harold's Club in Fontana after lunch one day) and there were the notes, the sweet exchanges: "Hi Sweetie Pie! You are my cup of tea!! Happy Birthday—you don't look a day over 29!! Your baby, Arthwell."

And, toward the end, there was the acrimony. It was April 24, 1964,   24 when Arthwell Hayton's wife, Elaine, died suddenly, and nothing good happened after that. Arthwell Hayton had taken his cruiser, *Captain's Lady,* over to Catalina that weekend; he called home at nine o'clock Friday night, but did not talk to his wife because Lucille Miller answered the telephone and said that Elaine was showering. The next morning the Haytons' daughter found her mother in bed, dead. The newspapers reported the death as accidental, perhaps the result of an allergy to hair spray. When Arthwell Hayton flew home from Catalina that weekend, Lucille Miller met him at the airport, but the finish had already been written.

It was in the breakup that the affair ceased to be in the conventional   25 mode and began to resemble instead the novels of James M. Cain,[4] the movies of the late 1930's, all the dreams in which violence and threats and blackmail are made to seem commonplaces of middle-class life. What was most startling about the case that the State of California was preparing against Lucille Miller was something that had nothing to do with law at all, something that never appeared in the eight-column afternoon headlines but was always there between them: the revelation that the dream was teaching the dreamers how to live. Here is Lucille Miller talking to her lover sometime in the early summer of 1964, after he had indicated that, on the advice of his minister, he did not intend to see her any more: "First, I'm going to go to that dear pastor of yours and tell him a few things. . . . When I do tell him that, you won't be in the Redlands Church any more. . . . Look, Sonny Boy, if you think your reputation is going to be ruined, your life won't be worth two cents." Here is Arthwell Hayton, to Lucille Miller: "I'll go to Sheriff Frank Bland and tell him some things that I know about you until you'll wish you'd never heard of Arthwell Hayton." For an affair between a Seventh-Day Adventist dentist's wife and a Seventh-Day Adventist personal-injury lawyer, it seems a curious kind of dialogue.

"Boy, I could get that little boy coming and going," Lucille Miller later   26 confided to Erwin Sprengle, a Riverside contractor who was a business partner of Arthwell Hayton's and a friend to both the lovers. (Friend or no, on this occasion he happened to have an induction coil attached to his telephone in order to tape Lucille Miller's call.) "And he hasn't got one thing on me that he can prove. I mean, I've got concrete—he has nothing concrete." In the same taped conversation with Erwin Sprengle, Lucille Miller mentioned a tape that she herself had surreptitiously made, months before, in Arthwell Hayton's car.

---

[4] *James M. Cain:* an American writer (1892–1977). See note 1. [Editors' note.]

"I said to him, I said 'Arthwell, I just feel like I'm being used.' . . .   27
He started sucking his thumb and he said 'I love you. . . . This isn't
something that happened yesterday. I'd marry you tomorrow if I could. I
don't love Elaine.' He'd love to hear that played back, wouldn't he?"

"Yeah," drawled Sprengle's voice on the tape. "That would be just a   28
little incriminating, wouldn't it?"

"Just a *little* incriminating," Lucille Miller agreed. "It really *is*."   29

Later on the tape, Sprengle asked where Cork Miller was.   30

"He took the children down to the church."   31

"You didn't go?"   32

"No."   33

"You're naughty."   34

It was all, moreover, in the name of "love"; everyone involved placed a   35
magical faith in the efficacy of the very word. There was the significance
that Lucille Miller saw in Arthwell's saying that he "loved" her, that he
did not "love" Elaine. There was Arthwell insisting, later, at the trial, that
he had never said it, that he may have "whispered sweet nothings in her
ear" (as her defense hinted that he had whispered in many ears), but he
did not remember bestowing upon her the special seal, saying the word,
declaring "love." There was the summer evening when Lucille Miller and
Sandy Slagle followed Arthwell Hayton down to his new boat in its mooring
at Newport Beach and untied the lines with Arthwell aboard, Arthwell and
a girl with whom he later testified he was drinking hot chocolate and
watching television. "I did that on purpose," Lucille Miller told Erwin
Sprengle later, "to save myself from letting my heart do something crazy."

January 11, 1965, was a bright warm day in Southern California, the kind   36
of day when Catalina[5] floats on the Pacific horizon and the air smells of
orange blossoms and it is a long way from the bleak and difficult East, a
long way from the cold, a long way from the past. A woman in Hollywood
staged an all-night sit-in on the hood of her car to prevent repossession by
a finance company. A seventy-year-old pensioner drove his station wagon
at five miles an hour past three Gardena poker parlors and emptied three
pistols and a twelve-gauge shotgun through their windows, wounding
twenty-nine people. "Many young women become prostitutes just to have
enough money to play cards," he explained in a note. Mrs. Nick Adams
said that she was "not surprised" to hear her husband announce his divorce
plans on the Les Crane Show, and, farther north, a sixteen-year-old jumped
off the Golden Gate Bridge and lived.

And, in the San Bernardino County Courthouse, the Miller trial opened.   37
The crowds were so bad that the glass courtroom doors were shattered in
the crush, and from then on identification disks were issued to the first

---

[5] *Catalina:* Santa Catalina, an island off the coast of Southern California. [Editors' note.]

forty-three spectators in line. The line began forming at 6 a.m. and college girls camped at the courthouse all night, with stores of graham crackers and No-Cal.

All they were doing was picking a jury, those first few days, but the 38 sensational nature of the case had already suggested itself. Early in December there had been an abortive first trial, a trial at which no evidence was ever presented because on the day the jury was seated the San Bernardino *Sun-Telegram* ran an "inside" story quoting Assistant District Attorney Don Turner, the prosecutor, as saying, "We are looking into the circumstances of Mrs. Hayton's death. In view of the current trial concerning the death of Dr. Miller, I do not feel I should comment on Mrs. Hayton's death." It seemed that there had been barbituates in Elaine Hayton's blood, and there had seemed some irregularity about the way she was dressed on that morning when she was found under the covers, dead. Any doubts about the death at the time, however, had never gotten as far as the Sheriff's Office. "I guess somebody didn't want to rock the boat," Turner said later. "These were prominent people."

Although all of that had not been in the *Sun-Telegram*'s story, an 39 immediate mistrial had been declared. Almost as immediately, there had been another development: Arthwell Hayton had asked newspapermen to an 11 a.m. Sunday morning press conference in his office. There had been television cameras, and flash bulbs popping. "As you gentlemen may know," Hayton had said, striking a note of stiff bonhomie, "there are very often women who become amorous toward their doctor or lawyer. This does not mean on the physician's or lawyer's part that there is any romance toward the patient or client."

"Would you deny that you were having an affair with Mrs. Miller?" a 40 reporter had asked.

"I would deny that there was any romance on my part whatsoever." 41

It was a distinction he would maintain through all the wearing weeks to 42 come.

So they had come to see Arthwell, these crowds who now milled beneath 43 the dusty palms outside the courthouse, and they had also come to see Lucille, who appeared as a slight, intermittently pretty woman, already pale from lack of sun, a woman who would turn thirty-five before the trial was over and whose tendency toward haggardness was beginning to show, a meticulous woman who insisted, against her lawyer's advice, on coming to court with her hair piled high and lacquered. "I would've been happy if she'd come in with it hanging loose, but Lucille wouldn't do that," her lawyer said. He was Edward P. Foley, a small, emotional Irish Catholic who several times wept in the courtroom. "She has a great honesty, this woman," he added, "but this honesty about her appearance always worked against her."

By the time the trial opened, Lucille Miller's appearance included 44 maternity clothes, for an official examination on December 18 had revealed that she was then three and a half months pregnant, a fact which made picking a jury even more difficult than usual, for Turner was asking the death penalty. "It's unfortunate but there it is," he would say of the pregnancy to each juror in turn, and finally twelve were seated, seven of them women, the youngest forty-one, an assembly of the very peers—housewives, a machinist, a truck driver, a grocery-store manager, a filing clerk—above whom Lucille Miller had wanted so badly to rise.

That was the sin, more than the adultery, which tended to reinforce the one for which she was being tried. It was implicit in both the defense and the prosecution that Lucille Miller was an erring woman, a woman who perhaps wanted too much. But to the prosecution she was not merely a woman who would want a new house and want to go to parties and run up high telephone bills ($1,152 in ten months), but a woman who would go so far as to murder her husband for his $80,000 in insurance, making it appear an accident in order to collect another $40,000 in double indemnity and straight accident policies. To Turner she was a woman who did not want simply her freedom and a reasonable alimony (she could have had that, the defense contended, by going through with her divorce suit), but wanted everything, a woman motivated by "love and greed." She was a "manipulator." She was a "user of people."

To Edward Foley, on the other hand, she was an impulsive woman who "couldn't control her foolish little heart." Where Turner skirted the pregnancy, Foley dwelt upon it, even calling the dead man's mother down from Washington to testify that her son had told her they were going to have another baby because Lucille felt that it would "do much to weld our home again in the pleasant relations that we used to have." Where the prosecution saw a "calculator," the defense saw a "blabbermouth," and in fact Lucille Miller did emerge as an ingenuous conversationalist. Just as, before her husband's death, she had confided in her friends about her love affair, so she chatted about it after his death, with the arresting sergeant. "Of course Cork lived with it for years, you know," her voice was heard to tell Sergeant Paterson on a tape made the morning after her arrest. "After Elaine died, he pushed the panic button one night and just asked me right out, and that, I think, was when he really—the first time he really faced it." When the sergeant asked why she had agreed to talk to him, against the specific instructions of her lawyers, Lucille Miller said airily, "Oh, I've always been basically quite an honest person. . . . I mean I can put a hat in the cupboard and say it cost ten dollars less, but basically I've always kind of just lived my life the way I wanted to, and if you don't like it you can take off."

The prosecution hinted at men other than Arthwell, and even, over Foley's objections, managed to name one. The defense called Miller suicidal. The prosecution produced experts who said that the Volkswagen fire could not have been accidental. Foley produced witnesses who said that it could have been. Lucille's father, now a junior-high-school teacher in Oregon, quoted Isaiah to reporters: *"Every tongue that shall rise against thee in judgment thou shalt condemn."* "Lucille did wrong, her affair," her mother said judiciously. "With her it was love. But with some I guess it's just passion." There was Debbie, the Millers' fourteen-year-old, testifying in a steady voice about how she and her mother had gone to a supermarket to buy the gasoline can the week before the accident. There was Sandy Slagle, in the courtroom every day, declaring that on at least one occasion Lucille Miller had prevented her husband not only from committing suicide but from committing suicide in such a way that it would appear an accident and ensure the double-indemnity payment. There was Wenche Berg, the pretty twenty-seven-year-old Norwegian governess to Arthwell Hayton's children, testifying that Arthwell had instructed her not to allow Lucille Miller to see or talk to the children.

Two months dragged by, and the headlines never stopped. Southern   48
California's crime reporters were headquartered in San Bernardino for the duration: Howard Hertel from the *Times*, Jim Bennett and Eddy Jo Bernal from the *Herald-Examiner*. Two months in which the Miller trial was pushed off the *Examiner*'s front page only by the Academy Award nominations and Stan Laurel's death. And finally, on March 2, after Turner had reiterated that it was a case of "love and greed," and Foley had protested that his client was being tried for adultery, the case went to the jury.

They brought in the verdict, guilty of murder in the first degree, at 4:50   49
p.m. on March 5. "She didn't do it," Debbie Miller cried, jumping up from the spectators' section. "She didn't *do* it." Sandy Slagle collapsed in her seat and began to scream. "Sandy, for God's sake please *don't*," Lucille Miller said in a voice that carried across the courtroom, and Sandy Slagle was momentarily subdued. But as the jurors left the courtroom she screamed again: "You're murderers. . . . Every last one of you is a *murderer*." Sheriff's deputies moved in then, each wearing a string tie that read "1965 SHERIFF'S RODEO," and Lucille Miller's father, that sad-faced junior-high-school teacher who believed in the word of Christ and the dangers of wanting to see the world, blew her a kiss off his fingertips.

The California Institution for Women at Frontera, where Lucille Miller   50
is now, lies down where Euclid Avenue turns into country road, not too many miles from where she once lived and shopped and organized the Heart Fund Ball. Cattle graze across the road, and Rainbirds sprinkle the alfalfa. Frontera has a softball field and tennis courts, and looks as if it might be a California junior college, except that the trees are not yet high enough to conceal the concertina wire around the top of the Cyclone fence. On visitors' day there are big cars in the parking area, big Buicks and Pontiacs that belong to grandparents and sisters and fathers (not many of them belong to husbands), and some of them have bumper stickers that say "SUPPORT YOUR LOCAL POLICE."

A lot of California murderesses live here, a lot of girls who somehow   51 misunderstood the promise. Don Turner put Sandra Garner here (and her husband in the gas chamber at San Quentin) after the 1959 desert killings known to crime reporters as "the soda-pop murders." Carole Tregoff is here, and has been ever since she was convicted of conspiring to murder Dr. Finch's wife in West Covina, which is not too far from San Bernardino. Carole Tregoff is in fact a nurse's aide in the prison hospital, and might have attended Lucille Miller had her baby been born at Frontera; Lucille Miller chose instead to have it outside, and paid for the guard who stood outside the delivery room in St. Bernardine's Hospital. Debbie Miller came to take the baby home from the hospital, in a white dress with pink ribbons, and Debbie was allowed to choose a name. She named the baby Kimi Kai. The children live with Harold and Joan Lance now, because Lucille Miller will probably spend ten years at Frontera. Don Turner waived his original request for the death penalty (it was generally agreed that he had demanded it only, in Edward Foley's words, "to get anybody with the slightest trace of human kindness in their veins off the jury"), and settled for life imprisonment with the possibility of parole. Lucille Miller does not like it at Frontera, and has had trouble adjusting. "She's going to have to learn humility," Turner says. "She's going to have to use her ability to charm, to manipulate."

The new house is empty now, the house on the street with the sign that says

PRIVATE ROAD

BELLA VISTA

DEAD END

The Millers never did get it landscaped, and weeds grow up around the fieldstone siding. The television aerial has toppled on the roof, and a trash can is stuffed with the debris of family life: a cheap suitcase, a child's game called "Lie Detector." There is a sign on what would have been the lawn, and the sign reads "ESTATE SALE." Edward Foley is trying to get Lucille Miller's case appealed, but there have been delays. "A trial always comes down to a matter of sympathy," Foley says wearily now. "I couldn't create sympathy for her." Everyone is a little weary now, weary and resigned, everyone except Sandy Slagle, whose bitterness is still raw. She lives in an apartment near the medical school in Loma Linda, and studies reports of the case in *True Police Cases* and *Official Detective Stories*. "I'd much rather we not talk about the Hayton business too much," she tells visitors, and she keeps a tape recorder running. "I'd rather talk about Lucille and what a wonderful person she is and how her rights were violated." Harold Lance does not talk to visitors at all. "We don't want to give away what we can sell," he explains pleasantly; an attempt was made to sell Lucille Miller's personal story to *Life*, but *Life* did not want to buy it. In the district attorney's offices they are prosecuting other murders now, and do not see why the Miller trial attracted so much attention. "It wasn't a very interesting

493

murder as murders go," Don Turner says laconically. Elaine Hayton's death is no longer under investigtion. "We know everything we want to know," Turner says.

Arthwell Hayton's office is directly below Edward Foley's. Some people 53 around San Bernardino say that Arthwell Hayton suffered; others say that he did not suffer at all. Perhaps he did not, for time past is not believed to have any bearing upon time present or future, out in the golden land where every day the world is born anew. In any case, on October 17, 1965, Arthwell Hayton married again, married his children's pretty governess, Wenche Berg, at a service in the Chapel of the Roses at a retirement village near Riverside. Later the newlyweds were feted at a reception for seventy-five in the dining room of Rose Garden Village. The bridegroom was in black tie, with a white carnation in his buttonhole. The bride wore a long white *peau de soie* dress and carried a shower bouquet of sweetheart roses with stephanotis streamers. A coronet of seed pearls held her illusion veil.

Questions for Discussion and Writing

1. Structurally, what is particularly notable about paragraph 6 of the essay? How would you describe the effect of the passage on the reader? Analyze other paragraphs in the essay, paying particular attention to how Didion develops her argument by exploiting the conventional expectations of her audience.

2. As mentioned in the headnote, Joan Didion is considered one of the leading practitioners of the literary movement known as "New Journalism." Compare "Some Dreamers of the Golden Dream" to more conventional news stories from magazines such as *Time*, *Newsweek*, or *U.S. News and World Report*. How does Didion's approach to "news" differ from other approaches?

3. What is the "golden dream" portrayed in Didion's essay, who dreams it, and how is the reader meant to evaluate it? Are Didion's impressions about life in San Bernardino in 1966 meant to be applied more generally to life in California, life in America, or perhaps even life in the modern world? Are Didion's impressions applicable to the dreams and dreamers of today?

4. As observed in the headnote, "New Journalism" is highly subjective in nature. How might a different writer marshal the same set of "facts" presented in this essay to make a very different impression on the reader and to argue for an alternative interpretation of the tale? Write one such alternative account. Noting that Didion makes the most of even the smallest details, pay careful attention to elements of setting, dress, speech, and so on.

MARGARET ATWOOD

(b. 1939)

In the 1970s and 1980s, Margaret At-wood emerged as an important North American writer. Born in Ottawa, Ontario, Atwood studied with the great literary critic Northrop Frye at the University of Toronto. After earning her B.A. from Toronto in 1961 and her A.M. from Radcliffe College in 1962, she continued her graduate studies at Harvard. Although she never finished her doctorate, she conducted research that influenced her own writing. Since then, as an instructor and a writer in residence, she has been affiliated with many universities in Canada and the United States. She has published over ten books of poetry and eight novels, including The Edible Woman (1969), Surfacing (1972), Lady Oracle (1976), Life Before Man (1977), The Handmaid's Tale (1985), and Cat's Eye (1988). The Handmaid's Tale, her best known book, presents a dystopic (unutopian) vision of life in the twenty-first century when the triumph of fundamentalism reduces women to the status of breeders. The novel has been compared favorably to masterpieces such as Aldous Huxley's Brave New World and George Orwell's 1984. Atwood has also published three collections of short stories and two children's books. She has won numerous awards for her work.

As a strong supporter of her native culture, Atwood has worked diligently to promote Canadian literature. Together with her husband Graeme Gibson, who is also a writer, she has served the Writer's Union of Canada. She has edited two anthologies of Canadian literature, The New Oxford Book of Canadian Verse in English (1982) and The Oxford Book of Canadian Short Stories in English (1986), and she has written a study of Canadian literature entitled Survival: A Thematic Guide to Canadian Literature (1972). In fact, while her fiction and poetry have earned Atwood an international reputation as a writer, her nationalistic spirit has won her a heroine's status in her native country. She has become a Canadian media figure of sorts and a popular guest on radio and television programs. Not afraid to tackle political issues, she has spoken out on controversial concerns such as Canada's political and economic ties with the United States.

Feminism, as well, is an important issue for Atwood; both her novels and her stories emphasize women's concerns. Like Alice Walker, Atwood is unsatisfied with clichéd characterizations of women or knee-jerk responses to gender problems. Although she often focuses on the suffering experienced by women, she is also known for her keen sense of humor. Bluebeard's Egg and Other Stories (1986), Atwood's most recent collection of short stories, features some of the stereotypes that have evolved about femininity. Typical of Atwood's work, it is not without a sense of humor. A selection from this collection, "Significant Moments in the Life of My Mother," follows.

SIGNIFICANT MOMENTS IN
THE LIFE OF MY MOTHER

When my mother was very small, someone gave her a basket of baby chicks   1
for Easter. They all died.

"I didn't know you weren't supposed to pick them up," says my mother.   2
"Poor little things. I laid them out in a row on a board, with their little
legs sticking out straight as pokers, and wept over them. I'd loved them to
death."

Possibly this story is meant by my mother to illustrate her own stupidity,   3
and also her sentimentality. We are to understand she wouldn't do such a
thing now.

Possibly it's a commentary on the nature of love; though, knowing my   4
mother, this is unlikely.

My mother's father was a country doctor. In the days before cars he drove   5
a team of horses and a buggy around his territory, and in the days before
snow ploughs he drove a team and a sleigh, through blizzards and rainstorms
and in the middle of the night, to arrive at houses lit with oil lamps where
water would be boiling on the wood range and flannel sheets warming on
the plate rack, to deliver babies who would subsequently be named after
him. His office was in the house, and as a child my mother would witness
people arriving at the office door, which was reached through the front
porch, clutching parts of themselves—thumbs, fingers, toes, ears, noses—
which had accidentally been cut off, pressing these severed parts to the raw
stumps of their bodies as if they could be stuck there like dough, in the
mostly vain hope that my grandfather would be able to sew them back on,
heal the gashes made in them by axes, saws, knives, and fate.

My mother and her younger sister would loiter near the closed office   6
door until shooed away. From behind it would come groans, muffled
screams, cries for help. For my mother, hospitals have never been glamorous
places, and illness offers no respite or holiday. "Never get sick," she says,
and means it. She hardly ever does.

Once, though, she almost died. It was when her appendix burst. My   7
grandfather had to do the operation. He said later that he shouldn't have
been the person to do it: his hands were shaking too much. This is one of
the few admissions of weakness on his part that my mother has ever reported.
Mostly he is portrayed as severe and in charge of things. "We all respected
him, though," she says. "He was widely respected." (This is a word which
has slipped a little in the scale since my mother's youth. It used to outrank
love.)

It was someone else who told me the story of my grandfather's muskrat   8
farm: how he and one of my mother's uncles fenced in the swamp at the
back of their property and invested my mother's maiden aunt's savings in

muskrats. The idea was that these muskrats would multiply and eventually be made into muskrat coats, but an adjoining apple farmer washed his spraying equipment upstream, and the muskrats were all killed by the poison, as dead as doornails. This was during the Depression, and it was no joke.

When they were young—this can cover almost anything these days, but   9
I put it at seven or eight—my mother and her sister had a tree house, where they spent some of their time playing dolls' tea parties and so forth. One day they found a box of sweet little bottles outside my grandfather's dispensary. The bottles were being thrown out, and my mother (who has always hated waste) appropriated them for use in their dolls' house. The bottles were full of yellow liquid, which they left in because it looked so pretty. It turned out that these were urine samples.

"We got Hail Columbia for that," says my mother. "But what did we   10
know?"

My mother's family lived in a large white house near an apple orchard, in   11
Nova Scotia. There was a barn and a carriage-house; in the kitchen there was a pantry. My mother can remember the days before commercial bakeries, when flour came in barrels and all the bread was made at home. She can remember the first radio broadcast she ever heard, which was a singing commercial about socks.

In this house there were many rooms. Although I have been there,   12
although I have seen the house with my own eyes, I still don't know how many. Parts of it were closed off, or so it seemed; there were back staircases. Passages led elsewhere. Five children lived in it, two parents, a hired man and a hired girl, whose names and faces kept changing. The structure of the house was hierarchical, with my grandfather at the top, but its secret life—the life of pie crusts, clean sheets, the box of rags in the linen closet, the loaves in the oven—was female. The house, and all the objects in it, crackled with static electricity; undertows washed through it, the air was heavy with things that were known but not spoken. Like a hollow log, a drum, a church, it amplified, so that conversations whispered in it sixty years ago can be half-heard even today.

In this house you had to stay at the table until you had eaten everything   13
on your plate. " 'Think of the starving Armenians,' mother used to say," says my mother. "I didn't see how eating my bread crusts was going to help them out one jot."

It was in this house that I first saw a stalk of oats in a vase, each oat   14
wrapped in the precious silver paper which had been carefully saved from a chocolate box. I thought it was the most wonderful thing I had ever seen, and began saving silver paper myself. But I never got around to wrapping the oats, and in any case I didn't know how. Like many other art forms of vanished civilizations, the techniques for this one have been lost and cannot quite be duplicated.

"We had oranges at Christmas," says my mother. "They came all the 15
way from Florida; they were very expensive. That was the big treat: to find
an orange in the toe of your stocking. It's funny to remember how good
they tasted, now."

When she was sixteen, my mother had hair so long she could sit on it. 16
Women were bobbing their hair by then; it was getting to be the twenties.
My mother's hair was giving her headaches, she says, but my grandfather,
who was very strict, forbade her to cut it. She waited until one Saturday
when she knew he had an appointment with the dentist.

"In those days there was no freezing," says my mother. "The drill was 17
worked with a foot pedal, and it went *grind, grind, grind.* The dentist
himself had brown teeth: he chewed tobacco, and he would spit the tobacco
juice into a spittoon while he was working on your teeth."

Here my mother, who is good mimic, imitates the sounds of the drill 18
and the tobacco juice: "*Rrrrr! Rrrrr! Rrrrr! Phtt! Rrrrr! Rrrrr! Rrrrr!
Phtt!* It was always sheer agony. It was a heaven-sent salvation when gas
came in."

My mother went into the dentist's office, where my grandfather was 19
sitting in the chair, white with pain. She asked him if she could have her
hair cut. He said she could do anything in tarnation as long as she would
get out of there and stop pestering him.

"So I went out straight away and had it all chopped off," says my mother 20
jauntily. "He was furious afterwards, but what could he do? He'd given
his word."

My own hair reposes in a cardboard box in a steamer trunk in my 21
mother's cellar, where I picture it becoming duller and more brittle with
each passing year, and possibly moth-eaten; by now it will look like the
faded wreaths of hair in Victorian funeral jewellery. Or it may have
developed a dry mildew; inside its tissue-paper wrappings it glows faintly,
in the darkness of the trunk. I suspect my mother has forgotten it's in
there. It was cut off, much to my relief, when I was twelve and my sister
was born. Before that it was in long curls: "Otherwise," says my mother,
"it would have been just one big snarl." My mother combed it by winding
it around her index finger every morning, but when she was in the hospital
my father couldn't cope. "He couldn't get it around his stubby fingers,"
says my mother. My father looks down at his fingers. They are indeed
broad compared with my mother's long elegant ones, which she calls boney.
He smiles a pussy-cat smile.

So it was that my hair was sheared off. I sat in the chair in my first 22
beauty parlour and watched it falling, like handfuls of cobwebs, down over
my shoulders. From within it my head began to emerge, smaller, denser,
my face more angular. I aged five years in fifteen minutes. I knew I could
go home now and try out lipstick.

"Your father was upset about it," says my mother, with an air of 23
collusion. She doesn't say this when my father is present. We smile, over
the odd reactions of men to hair.

I used to think that my mother, in her earlier days, led a life of sustained 24
hilarity and hair-raising adventure. (That was before I realized that she
never put in the long stretches of uneventful time that must have made up
much of her life: the stories were just the punctuation.) Horses ran away
with her, men offered to, she was continually falling out of trees or off the
ridgepoles of barns, or nearly being swept out to sea in rip-tides; or, in a
more minor vein, suffering acute embarrassment in trying circumstances.

Churches were especially dangerous. "There was a guest preacher one 25
Sunday," she says. "Of course we had to go to church every Sunday. There
he was, in full career, preaching hellfire and damnation"—she pounds an
invisible pulpit—"and his full set of false teeth shot out of his mouth—
phoop—just like that. Well, he didn't miss a stride. He stuck his hand up
and caught them and popped them back into his mouth, and he kept right
on, condemning us all to eternal torment. The pew was shaking! The tears
were rolling down our faces, and the worst of it was, we were in the front
pew, he was looking right at us. But of course we couldn't laugh out loud:
father would have given us Hail Columbia."

Other people's parlours were booby-trapped for her; so were any and all 26
formal social occasions. Zippers sprang apart on her clothes in strategic
places, hats were unreliable. The shortage of real elastic during the war
demanded constant alertness: underpants then had buttons, and were more
taboo and therefore more significant than they are now. "There you would
be," she says, "right on the street, and before you knew it they'd be down
around your galoshes. The way to do was to step out of them with one foot,
then kick them up with your other foot and whip them into your purse. I
got quite good at it."

This particular story is told only to a few, but other stories are for general 27
consumption. When she tells them, my mother's face turns to rubber. She
takes all the parts, adds the sound effects, waves her hands around in the
air. Her eyes gleam, sometimes a little wickedly, for although my mother
is sweet and old and a lady, she avoids being a sweet old lady. When people
are in danger of mistaking her for one, she flings in something from left
field; she refuses to be taken for granted.

But my mother cannot be duped into telling stories when she doesn't 28
want to. If you prompt her, she becomes self-conscious and clams up. Or
she will laugh and go out into the kitchen, and shortly after that you will
hear the whir of the Mixmaster. Long ago I gave up attemping to make
her do tricks at parties. In gatherings of unknown people, she merely listens
intently, her head tilted a little, smiling a smile of glazed politeness. The
secret is to wait and see what she will say afterwards.

499

At the age of seventeen my mother went to the Normal School in Truro.   29
This name—"Normal School"—once held a certain magic for me. I thought
it had something to do with learning to be normal, which possibly it did,
because really it was where you used to go to learn how to be a schoolteacher.
Subsequently my mother taught in a one-room school house not far from
her home. She rode her horse to and from the school house every day, and
saved up the money she earned and sent herself to university with it. My
grandfather wouldn't send her: he said she was too frivolous-minded. She
liked ice-skating and dancing too much for his taste.

At Normal School my mother boarded with a family that contained   30
several sons in more or less the same age group as the girl boarders. They
all ate around a huge dining-room table (which I pictured as being of dark
wood, with heavy carved legs, but covered always with a white linen
tablecoth), with the mother and father presiding, one at each end. I saw
them both as large and pink and beaming.

"The boys were great jokers," says my mother. "They were always up   31
to something." This was desirable in boys: to be great jokers, to be always
up to something. My mother adds a key sentence: "We had a lot of fun."

Having fun has always been high on my mother's agenda. She has as   32
much fun as possible, but what she means by this phrase cannot be understood
without making an adjustment, an allowance for the great gulf across which
this phrase must travel before it reaches us. It comes from another world,
which, like the stars that originally sent out the light we see hesitating in
the sky above us these nights, may be or is already gone. It is possible to
reconstruct the facts of this world—the furniture, the clothing, the ornaments
on the mantelpiece, the jugs and basins and even the chamber pots in the
bedrooms, but not the emotions, not with the same exactness. So much that
is now known and felt must be excluded.

This was a world in which guileless flirtation was possible, because there   33
were many things that were simply not done by nice girls, and more girls
were nice then. To fall from niceness was to fall not only from grace:
sexual acts, by girls at any rate, had financial consequences. Life was more
joyful and innocent then, and at the same time permeated with guilt and
terror, or at least the occasions for them, on the most daily level. It was
like the Japanese haiku: a limited form, rigid in its perimeters, within
which an astonishing freedom was possible.

There are photographs of my mother at this time, taken with three or   34
four other girls, linked arm in arm or with their arms thrown jestingly
around each other's necks. Behind them, beyond the sea or the hills or
whatever is in the background, is a world already hurtling towards ruin,
unknown to them: the theory of relativity has been discovered, acid is
accumulating at the roots of trees, the bull-frogs are doomed. But they
smile with something that from this distance you could almost call gallantry,
their right legs thrust forward in parody of a chorus line.

One of the great amusements for the girl boarders and the sons of the   35 family was amateur theatre. Young people—they were called "young people"—frequently performed in plays, which were put on in the church basement. My mother was a regular actor. (I have a stack of the scripts somewhere about the house, yellowing little booklets with my mother's parts checked in pencil. They are all comedies, and all impenetrable.) "There was no television then," says my mother. "You made your own fun."

For one of these plays a cat was required, and my mother and one of the   36
sons borrowed the family cat. They put it into a canvas bag and drove to the rehearsal (there were cars by then), with my mother holding the cat on her lap. The cat, which must have been frightened, wet itself copiously, through the canvas bag and all over my mother's skirt. At the same time it made the most astonishingly bad smell.

"I was ready to sink through the floorboards," says my mother. "But   37
what could I do? All I could do was sit there. In those days things like that"—she means cat pee, or pee of any sort—"were not mentioned." She means in mixed company.

I think of my mother driven through the night, skirts dripping, overcome   38
with shame, the young man beside her staring straight ahead, pretending not to notice anything. They both feel that this act of unmentionable urination has been done, not by the cat, but by my mother. And so they continue, in a straight line that takes them over the Atlantic and past the curvature of the earth, out through the moon's orbit and into the dark reaches beyond.

Meanwhile, back on earth, my mother says: "I had to throw the skirt   39
out. It was a good skirt, too, but nothing could get rid of the smell."

"I only heard your father swear once," says my mother. My mother herself   40
never swears. When she comes to a place in a story in which swearing is called for, she says "dad-ratted" or "blankety-blank."

"It was when he mashed his thumb, when he was sinking the well, for   41
the pump." This story, I know, takes place before I was born, up north, where there is nothing underneath the trees and their sheddings but sand and bedrock. The well was for a hand pump, which in turn was for the first of the many cabins and houses my parents built together. But since I witnessed later wells being sunk and later hand pumps being installed, I know how it's done. There's a pipe with a point at one end. You pound it into the ground with a sledge hammer, and as it goes down you screw other lengths of pipe onto it, until you hit drinkable water. To keep from ruining the thread on the top end, you hold a block of wood between the sledge hammer and the pipe. Better, you get someone else to hold it for you. This is how my father mashed his thumb: he was doing both the holding and the hammering himself.

"It swelled up like a radish," says my mother. "He had to make a hole   42
in the nail, with his toad-sticker, to ease the pressure. The blood spurted out like pips from a lemon. Later on the whole nail turned purple and

black and dropped off. Luckily he grew another one. They say you only get two chances. When he did it though, he turned the air blue for yards around. I didn't even know he knew those words. I don't know where he picked them up." She speaks as if these words are a minor contagious disease, like chicken pox.

Here my father looks modestly down at his plate. For him, there are   43
two worlds: one containing ladies, in which you do not use certain expressions, and another one—consisting of logging camps and other haunts of his youth, and of gatherings of acceptable sorts of men—in which you do. To let the men's world slip over verbally into the ladies' would reveal you as a mannerless boor, but to carry the ladies' world over into the men's brands you a prig and maybe even a pansy. This is the word for it. All of this is well understood between them.

This story illustrates several things: that my father is no pansy, for one;   44
and that my mother behaved properly by being suitably shocked. But my mother's eyes shine with delight while she tells this story. Secretly, she thinks it funny that my father got caught out, even if only once. The thumbnail that fell off is, in any significant way, long forgotten.

There are some stories which my mother does not tell when there are men   45
present: never at dinner, never at parties. She tells them to women only, usually in the kitchen, when they or we are helping with the dishes or shelling peas, or taking the tops and tails off the string beans, or husking corn. She tells them in a lowered voice, without moving her hands around in the air, and they contain no sound effects. These are stories of romantic betrayals, unwanted pregnancies, illnesses of various horrible kinds, marital infidelities, mental breakdowns, tragic suicides, unpleasant lingering deaths. They are not rich in detail or embroidered with incident: they are stark and factual. The women, their own hands moving among the dirty dishes or the husks of vegetables, nod solemnly.

Some of these stories, it is understood, are not to be passed on to my   46
father, because they would upset him. It is well known that women can deal with this sort of thing better than men can. Men are not to be told anything they might find too painful; the secret depths of human nature, the sordid physicalities, might overwhelm or damage them. For instance, men often faint at the sight of their own blood, to which they are not accustomed. For this reason you should never stand behind one in the line at the Red Cross donor clinic. Men, for some mysterious reason, find life more difficult than women do. (My mother believes this, despite the female bodies, trapped, diseased, disappearing, or abandoned, that litter her stories.) Men must be allowed to play in the sandbox of their choice, as happily as they can, without disturbance; otherwise they get cranky and won't eat their dinners. There are all kinds of things that men are simply not equipped to understand, so why expect it of them? Not everyone shares this belief about men; nevertheless, it has its uses.

"She dug up the shrubs from around the house," says my mother. This   47
story is about a shattered marriage: serious business. My mother's eyes
widen. The other women lean forward. "All she left him were the shower
curtains." There is a collective sigh, an expelling of breath. My father
enters the kitchen, wondering when the tea will be ready, and the women
close ranks, turning to him their deceptive blankly smiling faces. Soon
afterwards, my mother emerges from the kitchen, carrying the tea pot, and
sets it down on the table in its ritual place.

"I remember the time we almost died," says my mother. Many of her   48
stories begin this way. When she is in a certain mood, we are to understand
that our lives have been preserved only by a series of amazing coincidences
and strokes of luck; otherwise the entire family, individually or collectively,
would be dead as doornails. These stories, in addition to producing adrenalin,
serve to reinforce our sense of gratitude. There is the time we almost went
over a waterfall, in a canoe, in a fog; the time we almost got caught in a
forest fire; the time my father almost got squashed, before my mother's
very eyes, by a ridgepole he was lifting into place; the time my brother
almost got struck by a bolt of lightning, which went by him so close it
knocked him down. "You could hear it sizzle," says my mother.

This is the story of the hay wagon. "Your father was driving," says my   49
mother, "at the speed he usually goes." We read between the lines: *too fast*.
"You kids were in the back." I can remember this day, so I can remember
how old I was, how old my brother was. We were old enough to think it
was funny to annoy my father by singing popular songs of a type he
disliked, such as "Mockingbird Hill"; or perhaps we were imitating bagpipe
music by holding our noses and humming, while hitting our Adam's apples
with the edges of our hands. When we became too irritating my father
would say, "Pipe down." We weren't old enough to know that his irritation
could be real: we thought it was part of the game.

"We were going down a steep hill," my mother continues, "when a hay   50
wagon pulled out right across the road, at the bottom. Your father put on
the brakes, but nothing happened. The brakes were gone! I thought our
last moment had come." Luckily the hay wagon continued across the road,
and we shot past it, missing it by at least a foot. "My heart was in my
mouth," says my mother.

I didn't know until afterwards what had really happened. I was in the   51
back seat, making bagpipe music, oblivious. The scenery was the same as
it always was on car trips: my parents' heads, seen from behind, sticking
up above the front seat. My father had his hat on, the one he wore to keep
things from falling off the trees into his hair. My mother's hand was placed
lightly on the back of his neck.

"You had such an acute sense of smell when you were younger," says my   52
mother.

Now we are on more dangerous ground: my mother's childhood is one   53
thing, my own quite another. This is the moment at which I start rattling
the silverware, or ask for another cup of tea. "You used to march into
houses that were strange to you, and you would say in a loud voice, 'What's
that funny smell?'" If there are guests present, they shift a little away from
me, conscious of their own emanations, trying not to look at my nose.

"I used to be so embarrassed," says my mother absent-mindedly. Then   54
she shifts gears. "You were such an easy child. You used to get up at six
in the morning and play by yourself in the play room, singing away. . . ."
There is a pause. A distant voice, mine, high and silvery, drifts over the
space between us. "You used to talk a blue streak. Chatter, chatter, chatter,
from morning to night." My mother sighs imperceptibly, as if wondering
why I have become so silent, and gets up to poke the fire.

Hoping to change the subject, I ask whether or not the crocuses have   55
come up yet, but she is not to be diverted. "I never had to spank you," she
says. "A harsh word, and you would be completely reduced." She looks at
me sideways; she isn't sure what I have turned into, or how. "There were
just one or two times. Once, when I had to go out and I left your father
in charge." (This may be the real point of the story: the inability of men
to second-guess small children.) "I came back along the street, and there
were you and your brother, throwing mud balls at an old man out of the
upstairs window."

We both know whose idea this was. For my mother, the proper   56
construction to be put on this event is that my brother was a hell-raiser and
I was his shadow, "easily influenced," as my mother puts it. "You were
just putty in his hands."

"Of course, I had to punish both of you equally," she says. Of course.   57
I smile a forgiving smile. The real truth is that I was sneakier than my
brother, and got caught less often. No front-line charges into enemy
machine-gun nests for me, if they could be at all avoided. My own solitary
acts of wickedness were devious and well concealed; it was only in partnership
with my brother that I would throw caution to the winds.

"He could wind you around his little finger," says my mother. "Your   58
father made each of you a toy box, and the rule was—" (My mother is
good at the devising of rules "—the rule was that neither of you could take
the toys out of the other one's toy box without permission. Otherwise he
would have got all your toys away from you. But he got them anyway,
mind you. He used to talk you into playing house, and he would pretend
to be the baby. Then he would pretend to cry, and when you asked what
he wanted, he'd demand whatever it was out of your toy box that he wanted
to play with at the moment. You always gave it to him."

I don't remember this, though I do remember staging World War Two   59
on the living-room floor, with armies of stuffed bears and rabbits; but
surely some primal patterns were laid down. Have these early toy-box

experiences—and "toy box" itself, as a concept, reeks with implications—have they made me suspicious of men who wish to be mothered, yet susceptible to them at the same time? Have I been conditioned to believe that if I am not solicitous, if I am not forthcoming, if I am not a never-ending cornucopia of entertaining delights, they will take their collections of milk-bottle tops and their mangy one-eared teddy bears and go away into the woods by themselves to play snipers? Probably. What my mother thinks was merely cute may have been lethal.

But this is not her only story about my suckiness and gullibility. She 60 follows up with the *coup de grâce*, the tale of the bunny-rabbit cookies.

"It was in Ottawa. I was invited to a government tea," says my mother, 61 and this fact alone should signal an element of horror: my mother hated official functions, to which however she was obliged to go because she was the wife of a civil servant. "I had to drag you kids along; we couldn't afford a lot of babysitters in those days." The hostess had made a whole plateful of decorated cookies for whatever children might be present, and my mother proceeds to describe these: wonderful cookies shaped like bunny rabbits, with faces and clothes of coloured icing, little skirts for the little girl bunny rabbits, little pants for the little boy bunny rabbits.

"You chose one," says my mother. "You went off to a corner with it, by 62 yourself. Mrs. X noticed you and went over. 'Aren't you going to eat your cookie?' she said. 'Oh, no,' you said. 'I'll just sit here and talk to it.' And there you sat, as happy as a clam. But someone had made the mistake of leaving the plate near your brother. When they looked again, there wasn't a single cookie left. He'd eaten every one. He was very sick that night, I can tell you."

Some of my mother's stories defy analysis. What is the moral of this 63 one? That I was a simp is clear enough, but on the other hand it was my brother who got the stomach ache. Is it better to eat your food, in a straight-forward materialistic way, and as much of it as possible, or go off into the corner and talk to it? This used to be a favourite of my mother's before I was married, when I would bring what my father referred to as "swains" home for dinner. Along with the dessert, out would come the bunny-rabbit cookie story, and I would cringe and twiddle my spoon while my mother forged blithely on with it. What were the swains supposed to make of it? Were my kindliness and essential femininity being trotted out for their inspection? Were they being told in a roundabout way that I was harmless, that they could expect to be talked to by me, but not devoured? Or was she, in some way, warning them off? Because there is something faintly crazed about my behaviour, some tinge of the kind of person who might be expected to leap up suddenly from the dinner table and shout, "Don't eat that! It's alive!"

There is, however, a difference between symbolism and anecdote. 64 Listening to my mother, I sometimes remember this.

"In my next incarnation," my mother said once, "I'm going to be an   65
archaeologist and go around digging things up." We were sitting on the
bed that had once been my brother's, then mine, then my sister's; we were
sorting out things from one of the trunks, deciding what could now be
given away or thrown out. My mother believes that what you save from
the past is mostly a matter of choice.

At that time something wasn't right in the family; someone wasn't happy.   66
My mother was angry: her good cheer was not paying off.

This statement of hers startled me. It was the first time I'd ever heard   67
my mother say that she might have wanted to be something other that what
she was. I must have been thirty-five at the time, but it was still shocking
and slightly offensive to me to learn that my mother might not have been
totally contented fulfilling the role in which fate had cast her: that of being
my mother. What thumbsuckers we all are, I thought, when it comes to
mothers.

Shortly after this I became a mother myself, and this moment altered   68
for me.

While she was combing my next-to-impossible hair, winding it around her   69
long index finger, yanking out the snarls, my mother used to read me
stories. Most of them are still in the house somewhere, but one has vanished.
It may have been a library book. It was about a little girl who was so poor
she had only one potato left for her supper, and while she was roasting it
the potato got up and ran away. There was the usual chase, but I can't
remember the ending: a significant lapse.

"That story was one of your favourites," says my mother. She is probably   70
still under the impression that I identified with the little girl, with her
hunger and her sense of loss; whereas in reality I identified with the potato.

Early influences are important. It took that one a while to come out;   71
probably until after I went to university and started wearing black stockings
and pulling my hair back into a bun, and having pretentions. Gloom set
in. Our next-door neighbour, who was interested in wardrobes, tackled my
mother: " 'If she would only *do* something about herself,' " my mother
quotes, " 'she could be *quite attractive.*' "

"You always kept yourself busy," my mother says charitably, referring   72
to this time. "You always had something cooking. Some project or other."

It is part of my mother's mythology that I am as cheerful and productive   73
as she is, though she admits that these qualities may be occasionally and
temporarily concealed. I wasn't allowed much angst around the house. I
had to indulge it in the cellar, where my mother wouldn't come upon me
brooding and suggest I should go out for a walk, to improve my circulation.
This was her answer to any sign, however slight, of creeping despondency.
There wasn't a lot that a brisk sprint through dead leaves, howling winds,
or sleet couldn't cure.

It was, I knew, the *zeitgeist*[1] that was afflicting me, and against it such 74 simple remedies were powerless. Like smog I wafted through her days, dankness spreading out from around me. I read modern poetry and histories of Nazi atrocities, and took to drinking coffee. Off in the distance, my mother vacuumed around my feet while I sat in chairs, studying, with car rugs tucked around me, for suddenly I was always cold.

My mother has few stories to tell about these times. What I remember 75 from them is the odd look I would sometimes catch in her eyes. It struck me, for the first time in my life, that my mother might be afraid of me. I could not even reassure her, because I was only dimly aware of the nature of her distress, but there must have been something going on in me that was beyond her: at any time I might open my mouth and out would come a language she had never heard before. I had become a visitant from outer space, a time-traveller come back from the future, bearing news of a great disaster.

Questions for Discussion and Writing

1. On what sorts of events has Atwood focused the reader's attention? Are the "moments" in this story truly "significant"? What intention or intentions does this focus seem to serve?

2. What stereotypical attitudes about girls, women, and the relationships between them seem to be operating within this story? Is Atwood able to use stereotypes to address more complex issues? In the headnote, we mentioned that Atwood is concerned with feminist issues. Would you label this story "feminist"? Why or why not?

3. Does the intended audience of this story include a male reader? Construct a hypothetical male reader and discuss his probable responses. How, for example, is he to view the "swains" the daughter brings home? How is he to view the storyteller and her mother?

4. Using Atwood's story as a springboard, write an essay that analyzes stereotypical attitudes about gender roles and the relationship between parents and children. Consider carefully the audience you wish to address, and what specific issue(s) you plan to feature.

---

[1] *zeitgeist:* the spirit of the era. [Editors' note.]

STEPHEN JAY GOULD

(b. 1941)

A native of New York City, Stephen Jay Gould ranks among America's most prominent writers about science. After earning his A.B. at Antioch College in 1963 and his Ph.D. at Columbia University in 1967, Gould joined the faculty of Harvard University. He is currently Alexander Agassiz Professor of Zoology and director of Harvard's Museum of Comparative Zoology. A man of great energy and wide-ranging intellectual interests, Gould remains active in field research, teaching, writing, and lecturing. In all his endeavors, he continues to dazzle.

Like Carl Sagan in the field of astronomy, Gould has been a leading popularizer of evolution and paleontology. Gould's ability to express complex scientific concepts in prose accessible to the layperson is virtually unmatched. His explanations of the difference between the "gradual" evolution suggested by Darwin and the more sudden, "punctuated" evolution advocated by more recent theorists (including Gould himself) have become particularly well known. Drawing on an extremely broad range of knowledge, Gould relates science to such diverse aspects of the human condition as literature and sports. These relationships serve both to vivify his descriptions and to demonstrate the interdisciplinary, synthetic nature of his thought.

Gould's published works include Ever Since Darwin: Reflections in Natural History (1977), Ontogeny and Phylogeny (1977), The Panda's Thumb: More Reflections in Natural History (1980), The Mismeasure of Man (1981), Hen's Teeth and Horse's Toes: Further Reflections in Natural History (1983), Darwin's Legacy (1983), The Flamingo's Smile: Reflections in Natural History (1985), Illuminations: A Bestiary (1986), Time's Arrow, Time's Cycle: Myth and Metaphor in the Discovery of Geological Time (1987), and Wonderful Life: The Burgess Shale and the Nature of History (1989). In addition, he has edited numerous scientific collections. His column in Natural History has enchanted readers for many years. Not surprisingly, Gould has won many different awards for his writing, including the National Book Critics Award for general nonfiction for The Mismeasure of Man and the American Book Award in Science for The Panda's Thumb.

"Measuring Heads," the selection we present here, is Chapter 3 of The Mismeasure of Man. As Gould states in his introductory chapter,

> This book, then, is about the abstraction of intelligence as a single entity, its location within the brain, its quantification as one number for each individual, and the use of these numbers to rank people in a single series of worthiness, invariably to find that oppressed and disadvantaged groups—races, classes, or

sexes—are innately inferior and deserve their status. In short, this book is about the Mismeasure of Man.

Gould reviews both nineteenth-century efforts to measure brain size and the twentieth-century "science" of IQ testing. As he points out, the early IQ tests were the forerunners of "aptitude" tests currently administered in the United States—such as the Scholastic Aptitude Test. Gould believes that all these endeavors suffer from the same basic problem. As you read the selection, carefully consider Gould's central argument and what it suggests about the nature of science itself.

MEASURING HEADS

Paul Broca and the Heyday of Craniology

No rational man, cognisant of the facts, believes that the average negro is the equal, still less the superior, of the average white man. And, if this be true, it is simply incredible that, when all his disabilities are removed, and our prognathous relative has a fair field and no favor, as well as no oppressor, he will be able to compete successfully with his bigger-brained and smaller-jawed rival, in a contest which is to be carried on by thoughts and not by bites.

T. H. Huxley

THE ALLURE OF NUMBERS

INTRODUCTION

Evolutionary theory swept away the creationist rug that had supported the intense debate between monogenists and polygenists, but it satisfied both sides by presenting an even better rationale for their shared racism. The monogenists continued to construct linear hierarchies of races according to mental and moral worth; the polygenists now admitted a common ancestry in the prehistoric mists, but affirmed that races had been separate long enough to evolve major inherited differences in talent and intelligence. As historian of anthropology George Stocking writes (1973, p. lxx): "The resulting intellectual tensions were resolved after 1859 by a comprehensive evolutionism which was at once monogenist and racist, which affirmed human unity even as it relegated the dark-skinned savage to a status very near the ape."

The second half of the nineteenth century was not only the era of evolution in anthropology. Another trend, equally irresistible, swept through the human sciences—the allure of numbers, the faith that rigorous measurement could guarantee irrefutable precision, and might mark the transition between subjective speculation and a true science as worthy as Newtonian physics. Evolution and quantification formed an unholy alliance; in a sense, their union forged the first powerful theory of "scientific" racism—if we define "science" as many do who misunderstand it most profoundly: as any claim apparently backed by copious numbers. Anthropologists had presented numbers before Darwin, but the crudity of Morton's analysis (Chapter 2 [in *The Mismeasure of Man*]) belies any claim to rigor. By the end of Darwin's century, standardized procedures and a developing body of statistical knowledge had generated a deluge of more truthworthy numerical data.

This chapter is the story of numbers once regarded as surpassing all   3
others in importance—the data of craniometry, or measurement of the skull and its contents. The leaders of craniometry were not conscious political ideologues. They regarded themselves as servants of their numbers, apostles of objectivity. And they confirmed all the common prejudices of comfortable white males—that blacks, women, and poor people occupy their subordinate roles by the harsh dictates of nature.

Science is rooted in creative interpretation. Numbers suggest, constrain,   4
and refute; they do not, by themselves, specify the content of scientific theories. Theories are built upon the interpretation of numbers, and interpreters are often trapped by their own rhetoric. They believe in their own objectivity, and fail to discern the prejudice that leads them to one interpretation among many consistent with their numbers. Paul Broca is now distant enough. We can stand back and show that he used numbers not to generate new theories but to illustrate a priori conclusions. Shall we believe that science is different today simply because we share the cultural context of most practicing scientists and mistake its influence for objective truth? Broca was an exemplary scientist; no one has ever surpassed him in meticulous care and accuracy of measurement. By what right, other than our own biases, can we identify his prejudice and hold that science now operates independently of culture and class?

FRANCIS GALTON—APOSTLE OF QUANTIFICATION

No man expressed his era's fascination with numbers so well as Darwin's   5
celebrated cousin, Francis Galton (1822–1911). Independently wealthy, Galton had the rare freedom to devote his considerable energy and intelligence to his favorite subject of measurement. Galton, a pioneer of modern statistics, believed that, with sufficient labor and ingenuity, anything might be measured, and that measurement is the primary criterion of a scientific study. He even proposed and began to carry out a statistical inquiry into the efficacy of prayer! Galton coined the term "eugenics" in 1883 and advocated the regulation of marriage and family size according to hereditary endowment of parents.

Galton backed his faith in measurement with all the ingenuity of his
idiosyncratic methods. He sought, for example, to construct a "beauty map"
of the British Isles in the following manner (1909, pp. 315–316):

> Whenever I have occasion to classify the persons I meet into three classes,
> "good, medium, bad," I use a needle mounted as a pricker, wherewith
> to prick holes, unseen, in a piece of paper, torn rudely into a cross with
> a long leg. I use its upper end for "good," the cross arm for "medium,"
> the lower end for "bad." The prick holes keep distinct, and are easily
> read off at leisure. The object, place, and date are written on the paper.
> I used this plan for my beauty data, classifying the girls I passed in streets
> or elsewhere as attractive, indifferent, or repellent. Of course this was a
> purely individual estimate, but it was consistent, judging from the
> conformity of different attempts in the same population. I found London
> to rank highest for beauty; Aberdeen lowest.

With good humor, he suggested the following method for quantifying
boredom (1909, p. 278):

> Many mental processes admit of being roughly measured. For instance,
> the degree to which people are bored, by counting the number of their
> fidgets. I not infrequently tried this method at the meetings of the Royal
> Geographical Society, for even there dull memoirs are occasionally
> read. . . . The use of a watch attracts attention, so I reckon time by the
> number of my breathings, of which there are 15 in a minute. They are
> not counted mentally, but are punctuated by pressing with 15 fingers
> successively. The counting is reserved for the fidgets. These observations
> should be confined to persons of middle age. Children are rarely still,
> while elderly philosophers will sometimes remain rigid for minutes
> altogether.

Quantification was Galton's god, and a strong belief in the inheritance
of nearly everything he could measure stood at the right hand. Galton
believed that even the most socially embedded behaviors had strong innate
components: "As many members of our House of Lords marry the daughters
of millionaires," he wrote (1909, pp. 314–315), "it is quite conceivable
that our Senate may in time become characterized by a more than common
share of shrewd business capacity, possibly also by a lower standard of
commercial probity than at present." Constantly seeking new and ingenious
ways to measure the relative worth of peoples, he proposed to rate blacks
and whites by studying the history of encounters between black chiefs and
white travelers (1884, pp. 338–339):

> The latter, no doubt, bring with them the knowledge current in civilized
> lands, but that is an advantage of less importance than we are apt to
> suppose. A native chief has as good an education in the art of ruling men,
> as can be desired; he is continually exercised in personal government, and
> usually maintains his place by the ascendancy of his character shown every

day over his subjects and rivals. A traveller in wild countries also fills, to a certain degree, the position of a commander, and has to confront native chiefs at every inhabited place. The result is familiar enough—the white traveller almost invariably holds his own in their presence. It is seldom that we hear of a white traveller meeting with a black chief whom he feels to be the better man.

Galton's major work on the inheritance of intelligence (*Hereditary Genius*, 8 1869) included anthropometry among its criteria, but his interest in measuring skulls and bodies peaked later when he established a laboratory at the International Exposition of 1884. There, for threepence, people moved through his assembly line of tests and measures, and received his assessment at the end. After the Exposition, he maintained the lab for six years at a London museum. The laboratory became famous and attracted many notables, including Gladstone:[1]

> Mr. Gladstone was amusingly insistent about the size of his head, saying that hatters often told him that he had an Aberdeenshire head—"a fact which you may be sure I do not forget to tell my Scotch constituents." It was a beautifully shaped head, though rather low, but after all it was not so very large in circumference (1909, pp. 249–250).

Lest this be mistaken for the harmless musings of some dotty Victorian 9 eccentric, I point out that Sir Francis was taken quite seriously as a leading intellect of his time. The American hereditarian Lewis Terman, the man most responsible for instituting IQ tests in America, retrospectively calculated Galton's IQ at above 200, but accorded only 135 to Darwin and a mere 100–110 to Copernicus (see pp. 183–188 [in *The Mismeasure of Man*] on this ludicrous incident in the history of mental testing). Darwin, who approached hereditarian arguments with strong suspicion, wrote after reading *Hereditary Genius:* "You have made a convert of an opponent in one sense, for I have always maintained that, excepting fools, men did not differ much in intellect, only in zeal and hard work" (in Galton, 1909, p. 290). Galton responded: "The rejoinder that might be made to his remark about hard work, is that character, including the aptitude for work, is heritable like every other faculty."

A CURTAIN-RAISER WITH A MORAL:
NUMBERS DO NOT GUARANTEE TRUTH

In 1906, a Virginia physician, Robert Bennett Bean, published a long, 10 technical article comparing the brains of American blacks and whites. With a kind of neurological green thumb, he found meaningful differences

---

[1] *Gladstone:* William Ewart Gladstone (1809–1898), a British statesman and prime minister. [Editors' note.]

wherever he looked—meaningful, that is, in his favored sense of expressing black inferiority in hard numbers.

Bean took special pride in his data on the corpus callosum, a structure within the brain that contains fibers connecting the right and left hemispheres. Following a cardinal tenet of craniometry, that higher mental functions reside in the front of the brain and sensorimotor capacities toward the rear, Bean reasoned that he might rank races by the relative sizes of parts within the corpus callosum. So he measured the length of the genu, the front part of the corpus callosum, and compared it with the length of the splenium, the back part. He plotted genu vs. splenium (Fig. 3.1) and obtained, for a respectably large sample, virtually complete separation between black and white brains. Whites have a relatively large genu, hence more brain up front in the seat of intelligence. All the more remarkable, Bean exclaimed (1906, p. 390) because the genu contains fibers both for olfaction and for intelligence! Bean continued: We all know that blacks have a keener sense of smell than whites; hence we might have expected larger genus in blacks if intelligence did not differ substantially between races. Yet black genus are smaller despite their olfactory predominance; hence, blacks must really suffer from a paucity of intelligence. Moreover, Bean did not neglect to push the corresponding conclusion for sexes. Within each race, women have relatively smaller genus than men.

Bean then continued his discourse on the relatively greater size of frontal vs. parietal and occipital (side and back) parts of the brain in whites. In the relative size of their frontal areas, he proclaimed, blacks are intermediate between "man [*sic*] and the ourang-outang" (1906, p. 380).

Throughout this long monograph, one common measure is conspicuous by its absence: Bean says nothing about the size of the brain itself, the favored criterion of classical craniometry. The reason for this neglect lies buried in an addendum: black and white brains did not differ in overall size. Bean temporized: "So many factors enter into brain weight that it is questionable whether discussion of the subject is profitable here." Still, he found a way out. His brains came from unclaimed bodies given to medical schools. We all know that blacks have less respect for their dead than whites. Only the lowest classes of whites—prostitutes and the depraved—would be found among abandoned bodies, "while among Negroes it is known that even the better classes neglect their dead." Thus, even an absence of measured difference might indicate white superiority, for the data "do perhaps show that the low class Caucasian has a larger brain than a better class Negro" (1906, p. 409).

Bean's general conclusion, expressed in a summary paragraph before the troublesome addendum, proclaimed a common prejudice as the conclusion of science:

> The Negro is primarily affectionate, immensely emotional, then sensual
> and under stimulation passionate. There is love of ostentation, and capacity
> for melodious articulation; there is undeveloped artistic power and taste—

3.1   *Bean's plot of the genu on the y-axis vs. the splenium on the x-axis. White circles are, unsurprisingly, for white brains; black squares for black brains. Whites seem to have a larger genu, hence more up front, and presumably more intelligence.*

Negroes make good artisans, handicraftsmen—and there is instability of character incident to lack of self-control, especially in connection with the sexual relation; and there is lack of orientation, or recognition of position and condition of self and environment, evidenced by a peculiar bumptiousness, so called, that is particularly noticeable. One would naturally expect some such character for the Negro, because the whole posterior part of the brain is large, and the whole anterior portion is small.

Bean did not confine his opinions to technical journals. He published 15 two articles in popular magazines during 1906, and attracted sufficient attention to become the subject of an editorial in *American Medicine* for April 1907 (cited in Chase, 1977, p. 179). Bean had provided, the editorial proclaimed, "the anatomical basis for the complete failure of the negro schools to impart the higher studies—the brain cannot comprehend them any more than a horse can understand the rule of three. . . . Leaders in all political parties now acknowledge the error of human equality. . . . It may be practicable to rectify the error and remove a menace to our prosperity— a large electorate without brains."

But Franklin P. Mall, Bean's mentor at Johns Hopkins, became 16 suspicious: Bean's data were too good. He repeated Bean's work, but with an important difference in procedure—he made sure that he did not know which brains were from blacks and which from whites until *after* he had measured them (Mall, 1909). For a sample of 106 brains, using Bean's method of measurement, he found no difference between whites and blacks in the relative sizes of genu and splenium (Fig. 3.2). This sample included 18 brains from Bean's original sample, 10 from whites, 8 from blacks. Bean's measure of the genu was larger than Mall's for 7 whites, but for only a single black. Bean's measure of the splenium was larger than Mall's for 7 of the 8 blacks.

I use this small tale of zealotry as a curtain-raiser because it illustrates so 17 well the major contentions of this chapter and book:

1. Scientific racists and sexists often confine their label of inferiority to 18 a single disadvantaged group; but race, sex, and class go together, and each acts as a surrogate for the others. Individual studies may be limited in scope, but the general philosophy of biological determinism pervades— hierarchies of advantage and disadvantage follow the dictates of nature; stratification reflects biology. Bean studied races, but he extended his most important conclusion to women, and also invoked differences of social class to argue that equality of size between black and white brains really reflects the inferiority of blacks.

2. Prior prejudice, not copious numerical documentation, dictates con- 19 clusions. We can scarcely doubt that Bean's statement about black bumptiousness reflected a prior belief that he set out to objectify, not an induction from data about fronts and backs of brains. And the special pleading that

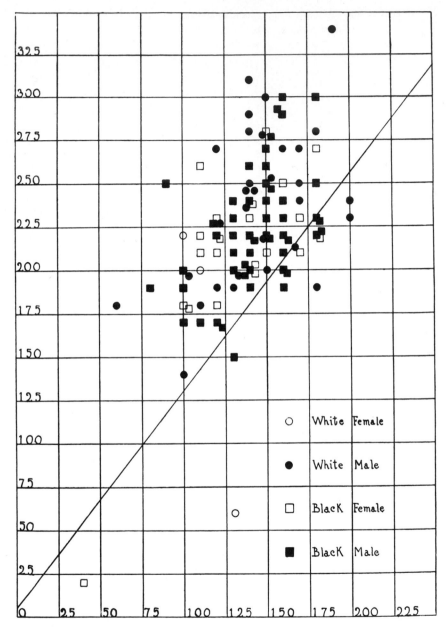

3.2   *Mall's plot of genu vs. splenium. Mall measured the brains without knowing whether they came from whites or blacks. He found no difference between the races. The line represents Bean's separation between whites and blacks.*

yielded black inferiority from equality of brain size is ludicrous outside a shared context of a priori belief in the inferiority of blacks.

3. Numbers and graphs do not gain authority from increasing precision [20] of measurement, sample size, or complexity in manipulation. Basic experimental designs may be flawed and not subject to correction by extended repetition. Prior commitment to one among many potential conclusions often guarantees a serious flaw in design.

4. Craniometry was not just a plaything of academicians, a subject [21] confined to technical journals. Conclusions flooded the popular press. Once entrenched, they often embarked on a life of their own, endlessly copied from secondary source to secondary source, refractory to disproof because no one examined the fragility of primary documentation. In this case, Mall nipped a dogma in the bud, but not before a leading journal had recommended that blacks be barred from voting as a consequence of their innate stupidity.

But I also note an important difference between Bean and the great European craniometricians. Bean committed either conscious fraud or extraordinary self-delusion. He was a poor scientist following an absurd experimental design. The great craniometricians, on the other hand, were fine scientists by the criteria of their time. Their numbers, unlike Bean's, were generally sound. Their prejudices played a more subtle role in specifying interpretations and in suggesting what numbers might be gathered in the first place. Their work was more refractory to exposure, but equally invalid for the same reason: prejudices led through data in a circle back to the same prejudices—an unbeatable system that gained authority because it seemed to arise from meticulous measurement.

Bean's story has been told several times (Myrdal, 1944; Haller, 1971; [23] Chase, 1977), if not with all its details. But Bean was a marginal figure on a temporary and provincial stage. I have found no modern analysis of the main drama, the data of Paul Broca and his school.

Masters of Craniometry: Paul Broca and His School

The Great Circle Route

In 1861 a fierce debate extended over several meetings of a young association [24] still experiencing its birth pangs. Paul Broca (1824–1880), professor of clinical surgery in the faculty of medicine, had founded the Anthropological Society of Paris in 1859. At a meeting of the society two years later, Louis Pierre Gratiolet read a paper that challenged Broca's most precious belief: Gratiolet dared to argue that the size of a brain bore no relationship to its degree of intelligence.

Broca rose in his own defense, arguing that "the study of the brains of [25] human races would lose most of its interest and utility" if variation in size counted for nothing (1861, p. 141). Why had anthropologists spent so much time measuring skulls, unless their results could delineate human groups and assess their relative worth?

> Among the questions heretofore discussed within the Anthropological Society, none is equal in interest and importance to the question before us now. . . . The great importance of craniology has struck anthropologists with such force that many among us have neglected the other parts of our science in order to devote ourselves almost exclusively to the study of skulls. . . . In such data, we hoped to find some information relevant to the intellectual value of the various human races (1861, p. 139).

Broca then unleashed his data and poor Gratiolet was routed. His final contribution to the debate must rank among the most oblique, yet abject concession speeches ever offered by a scientist. He did not abjure his errors; he argued instead that no one had appreciated the subtlety of his position. (Gratiolet, by the way, was a royalist, not an egalitarian. He merely sought other measures to affirm the inferiority of blacks and women—earlier closure of the skull sutures, for example.)

Broca concluded triumphantly: 26

> In general, the brain is larger in mature adults than in the elderly, in men than in women, in eminent men than in men of mediocre talent, in superior races than in inferior races (1861, p. 304). . . . Other things equal, there is a remarkable relationship between the development of intelligence and the volume of the brain (p. 188).

Five years later, in an encyclopedia article on anthropology, Broca expressed himself more forcefully:

> A prognathous [forward-jutting] face, more or less black color of the skin, wooly hair and intellectual and social inferiority are often associated, while more or less white skin, straight hair and an orthognathous [straight] face are the ordinary equipment of the highest groups in the human series (1866, p. 280). . . . A group with black skin, woolly hair and a prognathous face has never been able to raise itself spontaneously to civilization (pp. 295–296).

These are harsh words, and Broca himself regretted that nature had 27 fashioned such a system (1866, p. 296). But what could he do? Facts are facts. "There is no faith, however respectable, no interest, however legitimate, which must not accommodate itself to the progress of human knowledge and bend before truth" (in Count, 1950, p. 72). Paul Topinard, Broca's leading disciple and successor, took as his motto (1882, p. 748): *"J'ai horreur des systèmes et surtout des systèmes a priori"* (I abhor systems, especially a priori systems).

Broca singled out the few egalitarian scientists of his century for particularly 28 harsh treatment because they had debased their calling by allowing an ethical hope or political dream to cloud their judgment and distort objective truth.

"The intervention of political and social considerations has not been less injurious to anthropology than the religious element" (1855, in Count, 1950, p. 73). The great German anatomist Friedrich Tiedemann, for example, had argued that blacks and whites did not differ in cranial capacity. Broca nailed Tiedemann for the same error I uncovered in Morton's work (see pp. 50–69 [in *The Mismeasure of Man*]). When Morton used a subjective and imprecise method of reckoning, he calculated systematically lower capacities for blacks than when he measured the same skulls with a precise technique. Tiedemann, using an even more imprecise method, calculated a black average 45 cc above the mean value recorded by other scientists. Yet his measures for white skulls were no larger than those reported by colleagues. (For all his delight in exposing Tiedemann, Broca apparently never checked Morton's figures, though Morton was his hero and model. Broca once published a one-hundred-page paper analyzing Morton's techniques in the most minute detail—Broca, 1873b.)

Why had Tiedemann gone astray? "Unhappily," Broca wrote (1873b, p. 12), "he was dominated by a preconceived idea. He set out to prove that the cranial capacity of all human races is the same." But "it is an axiom of all observational sciences that facts must precede theories" (1868, p. 4). Broca believed, sincerely I assume, that facts were his only constraint and that his success in affirming traditional rankings arose from the precision of his measures and his care in establishing repeatable procedures.

Indeed, one cannot read Broca without gaining enormous respect for his care in generating data. I believe his numbers and doubt that any better have ever been obtained. Broca made an exhaustive study of all previous methods used to determine cranial capacity. He decided that lead shot, as advocated by "le célèbre Morton" (1861, p. 183), gave the best results, but he spent months refining the technique, taking into account such factors as the form and height of the cylinder used to receive the shot after it is poured from the skull, the speed of pouring shot into the skull, and the mode of shaking and tapping the skull to pack the shot and to determine whether or not more will fit in (Broca, 1873b). Broca finally developed an objective method for measuring cranial capacity. In most of his work, however, he preferred to weigh the brain directly after autopsies performed by his own hands.

I spent a month reading all of Broca's major work, concentrating on his statistical procedures. I found a definite pattern in his methods. He traversed the gap between fact and conclusion by what may be the usual route—predominantly in reverse. Conclusions came first and Broca's conclusions were the shared assumptions of most successful white males during his time—themselves on top by the good fortune of nature, and women, blacks, and poor people below. His facts were reliable (unlike Morton's), but they were gathered selectively and then manipulated unconsciously in the service of prior conclusions. By this route, the conclusions achieved not only the blessing of science, but the prestige of numbers. Broca and his school used facts as illustrations, not as constraining documents. They began with conclusions, peered through their facts, and came back in a circle to the same conclusions. Their example repays a closer study, for unlike Morton (who manipulated data, however unconsciously), they reflected their prejudices by another, and probably more common, route: advocacy masquerading as objectivity.

Selecting Characters

When the "Hottentot Venus" died in Paris, Georges Cuvier, the greatest 32
scientist and, as Broca would later discover to his delight, the largest brain of France, remembered this African woman as he had seen her in the flesh.

> She had a way of pouting her lips exactly like what we have observed in the orang-utan. Her movements had something abrupt and fantastical about them, reminding one of those of the ape. Her lips were monstrously large [those of apes are thin and small as Cuvier apparently forgot]. Her ear was like that of many apes, being small, the tragus weak, and the external border almost obliterated behind. These are animal characters. I have never seen a human head more like an ape than that of this woman (in Topinard, 1878, pp. 493–494).

The human body can be measured in a thousand ways. Any investigator, 33
convinced beforehand of a group's inferiority, can select a small set of measures to illustrate its greater affinity with apes. (This procedure, of course, would work equally well for white males, though no one made the attempt. White people, for example, have thin lips—a property shared with chimpanzees—while most black Africans have thicker, consequently more "human," lips.)

Broca's cardinal bias lay in his assumption that human races could be 34
ranked in a linear scale of mental worth. In enumerating the aims of ethnology, Broca included: "to determine the relative position of races in the human series" (in Topinard, 1878, p. 660). It did not occur to him that human variation might be ramified and random, rather than linear and hierarchical. And since he knew the order beforehand, anthropometry became a search for characters that would display the correct ranking, not a numerical exercise in raw empiricism.

Thus Broca began his search for "meaningful" characters—those that 35
would display the established ranks. In 1862, for example, he tried the ratio of radius (lower arm bone) to humerus (upper arm bone), reasoning that a higher ratio marks a longer forearm—a character of apes. All began well: blacks yielded a ratio of .794, whites .739. But then Broca ran into trouble. An Eskimo skeleton yielded .703, an Australian aborigine .709, while the Hottentot Venus, Cuvier's near ape (her skeleton had been preserved in Paris), measured a mere .703. Broca now had two choices. He could either admit that, on this criterion, whites ranked lower than several dark-skinned

groups, or he could abandon the criterion. Since he knew (1862a, p. 10) that Hottentots, Eskimos, and Australian aborigines ranked below most African blacks, he chose the second course: "After this, it seems difficult to me to continue to say that elongation of the forearm is a character of degradation or inferiority, because, on this account, the European occupies a place between Negroes on the one hand, and Hottentots, Australians, and eskimos on the other" (1862, p. 11).

Later, he almost abandoned his cardinal criterion of brain size because 36 inferior yellow people scored so well:

> A table on which races were arranged by order of their cranial capacities would not represent the degrees of their superiority or inferiority, because size represents only one element of the problem [of ranking races]. On such a table, Eskimos, Lapps, Malays, Tartars and several other peoples of the Mongolian type would surpass the most civilized people of Europe. A lowly race may therefore have a big brain (1873a, p. 38).

But Broca felt that he could salvage much of value from his crude measure of overall brain size. It may fail at the upper end because some inferior groups have big brains, but it works at the lower end because small brains belong exclusively to people of low intelligence. Broca continued:

> But this does not destroy the value of small brain size as a mark of inferiority. The table shows that West African blacks have a cranial capacity about 100 cc less than that of European races. To this figure, we may add the following: Caffirs, Nubians, Tasmanians, Hottentots, Australians. These examples are sufficient to prove that if the volume of the brain does not play a decisive role in the intellectual ranking of races, it nevertheless has a very real importance (1873a, p. 38).

An unbeatable argument. Deny it at one end where conclusions are uncongenial; affirm it by the same criterion at the other. Broca did not fudge numbers; he merely selected among them or interpreted his way around them to favored conclusions.

In choosing among measures, Broca did not just drift passively in the sway 37 of a preconceived idea. He advocated selection among characters as a stated goal with explicit criteria. Topinard, his chief disciple, distinguished between "empirical" characters "having no apparent design," and "rational" characters "related to some physiological opinion" (1878, p. 221). How then to determine which characters are "rational"? Topinard answered: "Other characteristics are looked upon, whether rightly or wrongly, as dominant. They have an affinity in negroes to those which they exhibit in apes, and establish the transition between these and Europeans" (1878, p. 221). Broca had also considered this issue in the midst of his debate with Gratiolet, and had reached the same conclusion (1861, p. 176):

> We surmount the problem easily by choosing, for our comparison of brains, races whose intellectual inequalities are completely clear. Thus,

the superiority of Europeans compared with African Negroes, American Indians, Hottentots, Australians and the Negroes of Oceania, is sufficiently certain to serve as a point of departure for the comparison of brains.

Particularly outrageous examples abound in the selection of individuals to represent groups in illustrations. Thirty years ago, when I was a child, the Hall of Man in the American Museum of Natural History still displayed the characters of human races by linear arrays running from apes to whites. Standard anatomical illustrations, until this generation, depicted a chimp, a Negro, and a white, part by part in that order—even though variation among whites and blacks is always large enough to generate a different order with other individuals: chimp, white, black. In 1903, for example, the American anatomist E. A. Spitzka published a long treatise on brain size and form in "men of eminence." He printed the following figure (Fig. 3.3) with a comment: "The jump from a Cuvier or a Thackeray[2] to a Zulu or a Bushman is not greater than from the latter to the gorilla or the orang" (1903, p. 604). But he also published a similar figure (Fig. 3.4) illustrating variation in brain size among eminent whites apparently never realizing that he had destroyed his own argument. As F. P. Mall, the man who exposed Bean, wrote of these figures (1909, p. 24): "Comparing [them], it appears that Gambetta's brain resembles the gorilla's more than it does that of Gauss."[3] 38

AVERTING ANOMALIES

Inevitably, since Broca amassed so much disparate and honest data, he generated numerous anomalies and apparent exceptions to his guiding generality—that size of brain records intelligence and that comfortable white males have larger brains than women, poor people, and lower races. In noting how he worked around each apparent exception, we obtain our clearest insight into Broca's methods of argument and inference. We also understand why data could never overthrow his assumptions. 39

BIG-BRAINED GERMANS

Gratiolet, in his last desperate attempt, pulled out all the stops. He dared to claim that, on average, German brains are 100 grams heavier than French brains. Clearly, Gratiolet argued, brain size has nothing to do with intelligence! Broca responded disdainfully: "Monsieur Gratiolet has almost appealed to our patriotic sentiments. But it will be easy for me to show him 40

---

[2] *Thackeray:* William Makepeace Thackeray (1811–1863), an English novelist. [Editors' note.]

[3] *Gauss:* Karl Friedrich Gauss (1777–1855), a German mathematician and astronomer. [Editors' note.]

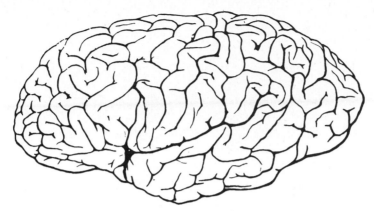

The brain of the great mathematician K. F. Gauss

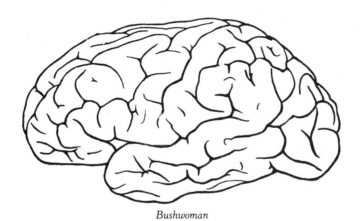

Bushwoman

Gorilla

3.3   *Spitzka's chain of being according to brain size.*

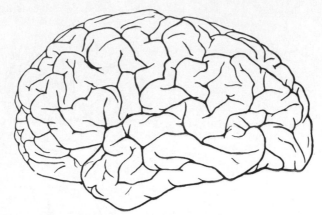

The brain of General Skobeleff

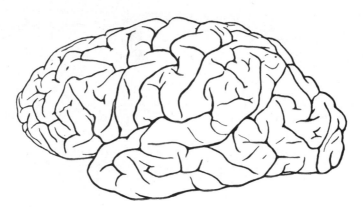

Professor Altmann, famous anatomist

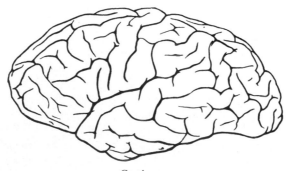

Gambetta

3.4   *Spitzka's depiction of variation in brain size among white men of eminence.*

that he can grant some value to the size of the brain without ceasing, for that, to be a good Frenchman" (1861, pp. 441–442).

Broca then worked his way systematically through the data. First of all, Gratiolet's figure of 100 grams came from unsupported claims of the German scientist E. Huschke. When Broca collated all the actual data he could find, the difference in size between German and French brains fell from 100 to 48 grams. Broca then applied a series of corrections for nonintellectual factors that also affect brain size. He argued, quite correctly, that brain size increases with body size, decreases with age, and decreases during long periods of poor health (thus explaining why executed criminals often have larger brains than honest folk who die of degenerative diseases in hospitals). Broca noted a mean French age of fifty-six and a half years in his sample, while the Germans averaged only fifty-one. He estimated that this difference would account for 16 grams of the disparity between French and Germans, cutting the German advantage to 32 grams. He then removed from the German sample all individuals who had died by violence or execution. The mean brain weight of twenty Germans, dead from natural causes, now stood at 1,320 grams, already *below* the French average of 1,333 grams. And Broca had not even yet corrected for the larger average body size of Germans. *Vive la France*. 41

Broca's colleague de Jouvencel, speaking on his behalf against the unfortunate Gratiolet, argued that greater German brawn accounted for all the apparent difference in brain and then some. Of the average German, he wrote (1861, p. 466): 42

> He ingests a quantity of solid food and drink far greater than that which satisfies us. This, joined with his consumption of beer, which is pervasive even in areas where wine is made, makes the German much more fleshy [*charnu*] than the Frenchman—so much so that their relation of brain size to total mass, far from being superior to ours, appears to me, on the contrary, to be inferior.

I do not challenge Broca's use of corrections but I do note his skill in wielding them when his own position was threatened. Bear this in mind when I discuss how deftly he avoided them when they might have challenged a congenial conclusion—the small brains of women. 43

SMALL-BRAINED MEN OF EMINENCE

The American anatomist E. A. Spitzka urged men of eminence to donate their brains to science after their death. "To me the thought of an autopsy is certainly less repugnant than I imagine the process of cadaveric decomposition in the grave to be" (1907, p. 235). The dissection of dead colleagues became something of a cottage industry among nineteenth-century craniometricians. Brains exerted their customary fascination, and lists were proudly touted, accompanied by the usual invidious comparisons. (The leading American anthropologists J. W. Powell and W. J. McGee even made a 44 wager over who carried the larger brain. As Ko-Ko told Nanki-Poo[4] about the fireworks that would follow his execution, "You won't see them, but they'll be there all the same.")

Some men of genius did very well indeed. Against a European average of 1,300 to 1,400 grams, the great Cuvier stood out with his topheavy, 1,830 grams. Cuvier headed the charts until Turgenev[5] finally broke the 2,000 gram barrier in 1883. (Other potential occupants of this stratosphere, Cromwell[6] and Swift,[7] lay in limbo for insufficiency of record.)

The other end was a bit more confusing and embarrassing. Walt Whitman managed to hear America singing with only 1,282 grams. As a crowning indignity, Franz Josef Gall, one of the two founders of phrenology—the original "science" of judging various mental capacities by the size of localized brain areas—weighed in at a meager 1,198 grams. (His colleague J. K. Spurzheim yielded a quite respectable 1,559 grams.) And, though Broca didn't know it, his own brain weighed only 1,424 grams, a bit above average to be sure, but nothing to crow about. Anatole France[8] extended the range of famous authors to more than 1,000 grams when, in 1924, he opted for the other end of Turgenev's fame and clocked in at a mere 1,017 grams.

The small brains were troublesome, but Broca, undaunted, managed to account for all of them. Their possessors either died very old, were very short and slightly built, or had suffered poor preservation. Broca's reaction to a study by his German colleague Rudolf Wagner was typical. Wagner had obtained a real prize in 1855, the brain of the great mathematician Karl Friedrich Gauss. It weighed a modestly overaverage 1,492 grams, but was more richly convoluted than any brain previously dissected (Fig. 3.5). Encouraged, Wagner went on to weigh the brains of all dead and willing professors at Göttingen, in an attempt to plot the distribution of brain size among men of eminence. By the time Broca was battling with Gratiolet in 1861, Wagner had four more measurements. None posed any challenge to Cuvier, and two were distinctly puzzling—Hermann, the professor of philosophy at 1,368 grams, and Hausmann, the professor of mineralogy, at 1,226 grams. Broca corrected Hermann's brain for his age and raised it by 16 grams to 1.19 percent above average—"not much for a professor of linguistics," Broca admitted, "but still something" (1861, p.

---

[4] *Ko-Ko and Nanki-Poo:* characters from *The Mikado*, an operetta by William Gilbert and Arthur Sullivan. [Editors' note.]

[5] *Turgenev:* Ivan Sergeyevich Turgenev (1818–1883), a Russian novelist. [Editors' note.]

[6] *Cromwell:* Oliver Cromwell (1599–1658), an English general and statesman. [Editors' note.]

[7] *Swift:* Jonathan Swift (1667–1745), an English poet and satirist. [Editors' note.]

[8] *Anatole France:* a French novelist and satirist (1844–1924). [Editors' note.]

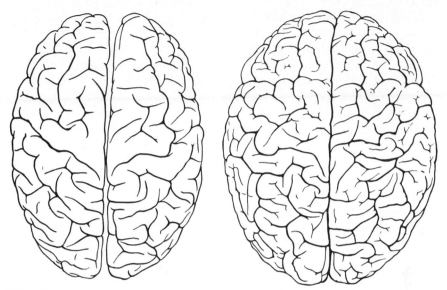

3.5   *The brain of the great mathematician K. F. Gauss (right) proved to be something of an embarrassment since, at 1,492 grams, it was only slightly larger than average. But other criteria came to the rescue. Here, E. A. Spitzka demonstrates that Gauss's brain is much more richly convoluted than that of a Papuan (left).*

167). No correction could raise Hausmann to the mean of ordinary folks, but considering his venerable seventy-seven years, Broca speculated that his brain may have undergone more than the usual amount of senile degeneration: "The degree of decadence that old age can impose upon a brain is very variable and cannot be calculated."

But Broca was still bothered. He could get around the low values, but he couldn't raise them to unusual weights. Consequently, to clinch an unbeatable conclusion, he suggested with a touch of irony that Wagner's post-Gaussian subjects may not have been so eminent after all:

> It is not very probable that 5 men of genius should have died within five years at the University of Göttingen. . . . A professorial robe is not necessarily a certificate of genius; there may be, even at Göttingen, some chairs occupied by not very remarkable men (1861, pp. 165–166).

At this point, Broca desisted: "The subject is delicate," he wrote (1861, p. 169), "and I must not insist upon it any longer."

LARGE-BRAINED CRIMINALS

The large size of many criminal brains was a constant source of bother to craniometricians and criminal anthropologists. Broca tended to dismiss it with his claim that sudden death by execution precluded the diminution that long bouts of disease produced in many honest men. In addition, death by hanging tended to engorge the brain and lead to spuriously high weights.

In the year of Broca's death, T. Bischoff published his study on the brains of 119 assassins, murderers, and thieves. Their average exceeded the mean of honest men by 11 grams, while 14 of them topped 1,500 grams, and 5 exceeded 1,600 grams. By contrast, only three men of genius could boast more than 1,600 grams, while the assassin Le Pelley, at 1,809 grams, must have given pause to the shade of Cuvier. The largest female brain ever weighed (1,565 grams) belonged to a woman who had killed her husband. [50]

Broca's successor Paul Topinard puzzled over the data and finally decided that too much of a good thing is bad for some people. Truly inspired criminality may require as much upstairs as professorial virtuosity; who shall decide between Moriarty and Holmes? Topinard concluded: "It seems established that a certain proportion of criminals are pushed to depart from present social rules by an exuberance of cerebral activity and, consequently, by the fact of a large or heavy brain" (1888, p. 15). [51]

FLAWS IN A PATTERN OF INCREASE THROUGH TIME

Of all Broca's studies, with the exception of his work on differences between men and women, none won more respect or attention than his supposed demonstration of steady increase in brain size as European civilization advanced from medieval to modern times (Broca, 1862b). [52]

This study merits close analysis because it probably represents the best case of hope dictating conclusion that I have ever encountered. Broca viewed himself as a liberal in the sense that he did not condemn groups to permanent inferiority based on their current status. Women's brains had degenerated through time thanks to a socially enforced underusage; they might increase again under different social conditions. Primitive races had not been sufficiently challenged, while European brains grew steadily with the march of civilization. [53]

Broca obtained large samples from each of three Parisian cemeteries, from the twelfth, the eighteenth, and the nineteenth centuries. Their average cranial capacities were, respectively, 1,426, 1,409, and 1,462 cc—not exactly the stuff for a firm conclusion of steady increase through time. (I have not been able to find Broca's raw data for statistical testing, but with a 3.5 percent mean difference between smallest and largest sample, it is likely that no statistically significant differences exist at all among the three samples.) [54]

But how did these limited data—only three sites with no information on ranges of variation at a given time and no clear pattern through time—lead [55]

Broca to his hopeful conclusion? Broca himself admitted an initial disappointment: he had expected to find intermediate values in the eighteenth-century site (1862b, p. 106). Social class, he argued, must hold the answer, for successful groups within a culture owe at least part of their status to superior wits. The twelfth-century sample came from a churchyard and must represent gentry. A common grave provided the eighteenth-century skulls. But the nineteenth-century sample was a mixture, ninety skulls from individual graves with a mean of 1484 cc, and thirty-five from a common grave with an average of 1403 cc. Broca claimed that if differences in social class do not explain why calculated values fail to meet expectations, then the data was unintelligible. Intelligible, to Broca, meant steadily increasing through time—the proposition that the data were meant to prove, not rest upon. Again, Broca travels in a circle:

> Without this [difference in social class], we would have to believe that the cranial capacity of Parisians has really diminished during centuries following the 12th. Now during this period . . . intellectual and social progress has been considerable, and even if we are not yet certain that the development of civilization makes the brain grow as a consequence, no one, without doubt, would want to consider this cause as capable of making the brain decrease in size (1862b, p. 106).

But Broca's division of the nineteenth-century sample by social class also brought trouble as well as relief—for he now had two samples from common graves and the earlier one had a larger mean capacity, 1,409 for the eighteenth century vs. 1,403 for the nineteenth. But Broca was not to be defeated; he argued that the eighteenth-century common grave included a better class of people. In these prerevolutionary times, a man had to be really rich or noble to rest in a churchyard. The dregs of the poor measured 1,403 in the nineteenth century; the dregs leavened by good stock yielded about the same value one hundred years before.

Each solution brought Broca new trouble. Now that he was committed to a partition by social class within cemeteries, he had to admit that an additional seventeen skulls from the morgue's grave at the nineteenth-century site yielded a higher value than skulls of middle- and upper-class people from individual graves—1,517 vs. 1,484 cc. How could unclaimed bodies, abandoned to the state, surpass the cream of society? Broca reasoned in a chain of surpassingly weak inference: morgues stood on river borders; they probably housed a large number of drowned people; many drowned are suicides; many suicides are insane; many insane people, like criminals, have surprisingly large brains. With a bit of imagination, nothing can be truly anomalous.

FRONT AND BACK

*Tell me about this new young surgeon, Mr. Lydgate. I am told he is wonderfully
clever; he certainly looks it—a fine brow indeed.*

George Eliot,[9] Middlemarch (1872)

Size of the whole, however useful and decisive in general terms, did not
begin to exhaust the content of craniometry. Ever since the heyday of
phrenology, specific parts of the brain and skull had been assigned definite
status, thus providing a set of subsidiary criteria for the ranking of groups.
(Broca, in his other career as a medical man, made his most important
discovery in this area. In 1861 he developed the concept of cortical
localization of function when he discovered that an aphasic patient had a
lesion in the left inferior frontal gyrus, now called Broca's convolution.) [58]

Most of these subsidiary criteria can be reduced to a single formula:
front is better. Broca and his colleagues believed that higher mental functions
were localized in anterior regions of the cortex, and that posterior areas
busied themselves with the more mundane, though crucial, roles of
involuntary movement, sensation, and emotion. Superior people should
have more in front, less behind. We have already seen how Bean followed
this assumption in generating his spurious data on front and back parts of
the corpus callosum in whites and blacks. [59]

Broca often used the distinction of front and back, particularly to extract
himself from uncomfortable situations imposed by his data. He accepted
Gratiolet's classification of human groups into *"races frontales"* (whites with
anterior and frontal lobes most highly developed), *"races pariétales"* (Mon-
golians with parietal or mid lobes most prominent), and *"races occipitales"*
(blacks with most in the back). He often unleashed the double whammy
against inferior groups—small size and posterior prominence: "Negroes,
and especially Hottentots, have a simpler brain than ours, and the relative
poverty of their convolutions can be found primarily on their frontal lobes"
(1873a, p. 32). As more direct evidence, he argued that Tahitians artificially
deformed the frontal areas of certain male children in order to make the
back portions bulge. These men became courageous warriors, but could
never match white heroes for style: "Frontal deformation produced blind
passions, ferocious instincts, and animal courage, all of which I would
willingly call occipital courage. We must not confound it with true courage,
frontal courage, which we may call Caucasian courage" (1861, pp. 202–
203). [60]

Broca also went beyond size to assess the quality of frontal vs. occipital
regions in various races. Here, and not only to placate his adversary, he [61]

---

[9] *George Eliot:* pseudonym of Mary Ann Evans (1819–1880), an English novelist. [Editors'
note.]

accepted Gratiolet's favorite argument that the sutures between skull bones close earlier in inferior races, thus trapping the brain within a rigid vault and limiting the effectiveness of further education. Not only do white sutures close later; they close in a different order—guess how? In blacks and other inferior people, the front sutures close first, the back sutures later; in whites, the front sutures close last. Extensive modern studies of cranial closure show no difference of timing or pattern among races (Todd and Lyon, 1924 and 1925).

Broca used this argument to extricate himself from a serious problem. He had described a sample of skulls from the earliest populations of *Homo sapiens* (Cro-Magnon type) and found that they exceeded modern Frenchmen in cranial capacity. Fortunately, however, their anterior sutures closed first and these progenitors must have been inferior after all: "These are signs of inferiority. We find them in all races in which the material life draws all cerebral activity to it. As intellectual life develops among a people, the anterior sutures become more complicated and stay open for a longer time" (1873a, p. 19).

The argument of front and back,[10] so flexible and far-ranging, served as a powerful tool for rationalizing prejudice in the face of apparently contradictory fact. Consider the following two examples.

THE CRANIAL INDEX

Beyond brain size itself, the two most hoary and misused measures of craniometry were surely the facial angle (jutting forward of face and jaws—the less the better), and the cranial index. The cranial index never had much going for it beyond ease of measurement. It was calculated as the ratio of maximum width to maximum length of the skull. Relatively long skulls (ratio of .75 or less) were called dolichocephalic; relatively short skulls (over .8), brachycephalic. Anders Retzius, the Swedish scientist who popularized the cranial index, constructed a theory of civilization upon it. He believed that Stone Age peoples of Europe were brachycephalic, and that progressive Bronze Age elements (Indo-European, or Aryan dolichocephalics) later invaded and replaced the original and more primitive inhabitants. Some original brachycephalic stocks survive among such benighted people as Basques, Finns, and Lapps.

Broca disproved this popular tale conclusively by discovering dolichocephalics both among Stone Age skulls and within modern remnants of "primitive" stocks. Indeed, Broca had good reason to be suspicious of

---

[10] Broca did not confine his arguments on the relative worth of brain parts to the distinction between front and back. Virtually any measured difference between peoples could be given a value in terms of prior conviction about relative worth. Broca once claimed, for example (1861, p. 187), that blacks probably had larger cranial nerves than whites, hence a larger nonintellectual portion of the brain. [Author's note.]

attempts by Nordic and Teutonic scientists to enshrine dolichocephaly as a mark of higher capability. Most Frenchmen, including Broca himself (Manouvrier, 1903), were brachycephalic. In a passage that recalls his dismissal of Tiedemann's claims for equality between black and white brains, Broca labeled Retzius's doctrine as self-serving gratification rather than empirical truth. Did he ever consider the possibility that he might fall prey to similar motivations?

> Since the work of Mr. Retzius, scientists have generally held, without sufficient study, that dolichocephaly is a mark of superiority. Perhaps so; but we must also not forget that the characters of dolichocephaly and brachycephaly were studied first in Sweden, then in England, the United States and Germany—and that in all these countries, particularly in Sweden, the dolichocephalic type clearly predominates. It is a natural tendency of men, even among those most free of prejudice, to attach an idea of superiority to the dominant characteristics of their race (1861, p. 513).

Obviously, Broca declined to equate brachycephaly with inherent stupidity. Still, the prestige of dolichocephaly was so great that Broca felt more than a little uncomfortable when clearly inferior people turned up longheaded—uncomfortable enough to invent one of his most striking, unbeatable arguments. The cranial index had run into a stunning difficulty: not only were African blacks and Australian aborigines dolichocephalic, but they turned out to be the world's most longheaded peoples. Adding insult to this injury, the fossil Cro-Magnon skulls were not only larger than those of modern Frenchmen; they were more dolichocephalic as well. 66

Dolichocephaly, Broca reasoned, could be attained in several ways. The longheadedness that served as a mark of Teutonic genius obviously arose by frontal elongation. Dolichocephalics among people known to be inferior must have evolved by lengthening the back—occipital dolichocephaly in Broca's terms. With one sweep, Broca encompassed both the superior cranial capacity and the dolichocephaly of his Cro-Magnon fossils: "It is by the greater development of their posterior cranium that their general cranial capacity is rendered greater than ours" (1873a, p. 41). As for blacks, they had acquired both a posterior elongation and a diminution in frontal width, thus giving them both a smaller brain in general and a longheadedness (not to be confused with the Teutonic style) exceeded by no human group. As to the brachycephaly of Frenchmen, it is no failure of frontal elongation (as the Teutonic supremacists claimed), but an addition of width to a skull already admirable. 67

THE CASE OF THE FORAMEN MAGNUM

The foramen magnum is the hole in the base of our skull. The spinal cord passes through it and the vertebral column articulates to the bone around its edge (the occipital condyle). In the embryology of all mammals, the 68 foramen magnum begins under the skull, but migrates back to a position behind the skull at birth. In humans, the foramen magnum migrates only slightly and remains under the skull in adults. The foramen magnum of adult great apes occupies an intermediate position, not so far forward as in humans, not so far back as in other mammals. The functional significance of these orientations is clear. An upright animal like *Homo sapiens* must have its skull mounted *on top* of its vertebral column in order to look forward when standing erect; fourfooted animals mount their vertebral column *behind* their skull and look forward in their usual posture.

These differences provided an irresistible source for invidious comparison. 69 Inferior peoples should have a more posterior foramen magnum, as in apes and lower mammals. In 1862 Broca entered an existing squabble on this issue. Relative egalitarians like James Cowles Pritchard had been arguing that the foramen magnum lies exactly in the center of the skull in both whites and blacks. Racists like J. Virey had discovered graded variation, the higher the race, the more forward the foramen magnum. Neither side, Broca noted, had much in the way of data. With characteristic objectivity, he set out to resolve this vexatious, if minor, issue.

Broca amassed a sample of sixty whites and thirty-five blacks and measured 70 the length of their skulls both before and behind the anterior border of the foramen magnum. Both races had the same amount of skull behind—100.385 mm for whites, 100.857 mm for blacks (note precision to third decimal place). But whites had much less in front (90.736 vs. 100.304 mm) and their foramen magnum therefore lay in a more anterior position (see Table 3.1). Broca concluded: "In orang-utans, the posterior projection [the part of the skull behind the foramen magnum] is shorter. It is therefore incontestable . . . that the conformation of the Negro, in this respect as in many others, tends to approach that of the monkey" (1862c, p. 16).

But Broca then began to worry. The standard argument about the foramen 71 magnum referred only to its relative position on the cranium itself, not to the face projecting in front of the cranium. Yet Broca had included the face in his anterior measure. Now everyone knows, he wrote, that blacks have longer faces than whites. This is an apelike sign of inferiority in its own right, but it should not be confused with the relative position of the foramen

Table 3.1 *Broca's measurements on the relative position of the foramen magnum*

	WHITES	BLACKS	DIFFERENCE IN FAVOR OF BLACKS
ANTERIOR	90.736	100.304	+ 9.568
Facial	12.385	27.676	+15.291
Cranial	78.351	72.628	− 5.723
POSTERIOR	100.385	100.857	+ 0.472

magnum within the cranium. Thus Broca set out to subtract the facial influence from his measures. He found that blacks did, indeed, have longer faces—white faces accounted for only 12.385 mm of their anterior measure, black faces for 27.676 mm (see Table 3.1). Subtracting facial length, Broca obtained the following figures for anterior cranium: 78.351 for whites, 72.628 for blacks. In other words, based on the cranium alone, the foramen magnum of blacks lay *farther forward* (the ratio of front to back, calculated from Broca's data, is .781 for whites, and .720 for blacks). Clearly, by criteria explicitly accepted before the study, blacks are superior to whites. Or so it must be, unless the criteria suddenly shift, as they did forthwith.

The venerable argument of front and back appeared to rescue Broca and the threatened people he represented. The more forward position of the foramen magnum in blacks does not record their superiority after all; it only reflects their lack of anterior brain power. Relative to whites, blacks have lost a great deal of brain in front. But they have added some brain behind, thus reducing the front/back ratio of the foramen magnum and providing a spurious appearance of black advantage. But they have not added to these inferior back regions as much as they lost in the anterior realm. Thus blacks have smaller and more poorly proportioned brains than whites:

> The anterior cranial projection of whites . . . surpasses that of Negroes by 4.9 percent. . . . Thus, while the foramen magnum of Negroes is further back with respect to their incisors [Broca's most forward point in his anterior measure that included the face], it is, on the contrary, further forward with respect to the anterior edge of their brain. To change the cranium of a white into that of a Negro, we would have not only to move the jaws forward, but also to reduce the front of the cranium—that is, to make the anterior brain atrophy and to give, as insufficient compensation, part of the material we extracted to the posterior cranium. In other words, in Negroes, the facial and occipital regions are developed to the detriment of the frontal region (1862c, p. 18).

This was a small incident in Broca's career, but I can imagine no better illustration of his method—shifting criteria to work through good data toward desired conclusions. Heads I'm superior; tails, you're inferior.

And old arguments never seem to die. Walter Freeman, dean of American lobotomists (he performed or supervised thirty-five hundred lesions of frontal portions of the brain before his retirement in 1970), admitted late in his career (cited in Chorover, 1979):

> What the investigator misses most in the more highly intelligent individuals is their ability to introspect, to speculate, to philosophize, especially in regard to oneself. . . . On the whole, psychosurgery reduces creativity, sometimes to the vanishing point.

Freeman then added that "women respond better than men, Negroes better than whites." In other words, people who didn't have as much up front in the first place, don't miss it as badly.

Women's Brains

Of all his comparisons between groups, Broca collected most information   74
on the brains of women vs. men—presumably because it was more accessible, not because he held any special animus toward women. "Inferior" groups are interchangeable in the general theory of biological determinism. They are continually juxtaposed, and one is made to serve as a surrogate for all— for the general proposition holds that society follows nature, and that social rank reflects innate worth. Thus, E. Huschke, a German anthropologist, wrote in 1854: "The Negro brain possesses a spinal cord of the type found in children and women and, beyond this, approaches the type of brain found in higher apes" (in Mall, 1909, pp. 1–2). The celebrated German anatomist Carl Vogt wrote in 1864:

> By its rounded apex and less developed posterior lobe the Negro brain resembles that of our children, and by the protuberance of the parietal lobe, that of our females. . . . The grown-up Negro partakes, as regards his intellectual faculties, of the nature of the child, the female, and the senile white. . . . Some tribes have founded states, possessing a peculiar organization; but, as to the rest, we may boldly assert that the whole race has, neither in the past nor in the present, performed anything tending to the progress of humanity or worthy of preservation (1864, pp. 183–192).

G. Hervé, a colleague of Broca, wrote in 1881: "Men of the black races   75
have a brain scarcely heavier than that of white women" (1881, p. 692). I do not regard as empty rhetoric a claim that the battles of one group are for all of us.

Broca centered his argument about the biological status of modern women   76
upon two sets of data: the larger brains of men in modern societies and a supposed widening through time of the disparity in size between male and female brains. He based his most extensive study upon autopsies he performed in four Parisian hospitals. For 292 male brains, he calculated a mean weight of 1,325 grams; 140 females brains averaged 1,144 grams for a difference of 181 grams, or 14 percent of the male weight. Broca understood, of course, that part of this difference must be attributed to the larger size of males. He had used such a correction to rescue Frenchmen from a claim of German superiority (p. 89). In that case, he knew how to make the correction in exquisite detail. But now he made no attempt to measure the effect of size alone, and actually stated that he didn't need to do so. Size,

after all, cannot account for the entire difference because we know that women are not as intelligent as men.

> We might ask if the small size of the female brain depends exclusively upon the small size of her body. Tiedemann has proposed this explanation. But we must not forget that women are, on the average, a little less intelligent than men, a difference which we should not exaggerate but which is, nonetheless, real. We are therefore permitted to suppose that the relatively small size of the female brain depends in part upon her physical inferiority and in part upon her intellectual inferiority (1861, p. 153).

To record the supposed widening of the gap through time, Broca 77 measured the cranial capacities of prehistoric skulls from L'Homme Mort cave. Here he found a difference of only 99.5 cc between males and females, while modern populations range from 129.5 to 220.7 cc. Topinard, Broca's chief disciple, explained the increasing discrepancy through time as a result of differing evolutionary pressures upon dominant men and passive women:

> The man who fights for two or more in the struggle for existence, who has all the responsibility and the cares of tomorrow, who is constantly active in combatting the environment and human rivals, needs more brain than the woman whom he must protect and nourish, than the sedentary woman, lacking any interior occupations, whose role is to raise children, love, and be passive (1888, p. 22).

In 1879 Gustave Le Bon, chief misogynist of Broca's school, used these 78 data to publish what must be the most vicious attack upon women in modern scientific literature (it will take some doing to beat Aristotle). Le Bon was no marginal hate-monger. He was a founder of social psychology and wrote a study of crowd behavior still cited and respected today (*La psychologie des foules*, 1895). His writings also had a strong influence upon Mussolini. Le Bon concluded:

> In the most intelligent races, as among the Parisians, there are a large number of women whose brains are closer in size to those of gorillas than to the most developed male brains. This inferiority is so obvious that no one can contest it for a moment; only its degree is worth discussion. All psychologists who have studied the intelligence of women, as well as poets and novelists, recognize today that they represent the most inferior forms of human evolution and that they are closer to children and savages than to an adult, civilized man. They excel in fickleness, inconstancy, absence of thought and logic, and incapacity to reason. Without doubt there exist some distinguished women, very superior to the average man, but they are as exceptional as the birth of any monstrosity, as, for example, of a gorilla with two heads; consequently, we may neglect them entirely (1879, pp. 60–61).

Nor did Le Bon shrink from the social implications of his views. He was horrified by the proposal of some American reformers to grant women higher education on the same basis as men:

> A desire to give them the same education, and, as a consequence, to propose the same goals for them, is a dangerous chimera. . . . The day when, misunderstanding the inferior occupations which nature has given her, women leave the home and take part in our battles; on this day a social revolution will begin, and everything that maintains the sacred ties of the family will disappear (1879, p. 62).

Sound familiar?[11]

I have reexamined Broca's data, the basis for all this derivative pronouncement, and I find the numbers sound but Broca's interpretation, to say the least, ill founded. The claim for increasing difference through time is easily dismissed. Broca based this contention on the sample from L'Homme Mort alone. It consists of seven male, and six female, skulls. Never has so much been coaxed from so little!

In 1888 Topinard published Broca's more extensive data on Parisian hospitals. Since Broca recorded height and age as well as brain size, we may use modern statistical procedures to remove their effect. Brain weight decreases with age, and Broca's women were, on average, considerably older than his men at death. Brain weight increases with height, and his average man was almost half a foot taller than his average woman. I used multiple regression, a technique that permits simultaneous assessment of the influence of height and age upon brain size. In an analysis of the data for women, I found that, at average male height and age, a woman's brain would weigh 1,212 grams.[12] Correction for height and age reduces the 181 gram difference by more than a third to 113 grams.

It is difficult to assess this remaining difference because Broca's data contain no information about other factors known to influence brain size in a major way. Cause of death has an important effect, as degenerative disease often entails a substantial diminution of brain size. Eugene Schreider (1966), also working with Broca's data, found that men killed in accidents had brains weighing, on average, 60 grams more than men dying of infectious

---

[11] Ten years later, America's leading evolutionary biologist, E. D. Cope, dreaded the result if "a spirit of revolt became general among women." "Should the nation have an attack of this kind," he wrote (1890, p. 2071), "like a disease, it would leave its traces in many after-generations." He detected the beginnings of such anarchy in pressures exerted by women "to prevent men from drinking wine and smoking tobacco in moderation," and in the carriage of misguided men who supported female suffrage: "Some of these men are effeminate and long-haired." [Author's note.]

[12] I calculate, where y is brain size in grams, x_1 age in years, and x_2 body height in cm: $y = 764.5 - 2.55x_1 + 3.47x_2$. [Author's note.]

diseases. The best modern data that I can find (from American hospitals) records a full 100 gram difference between death by degenerative heart disease and by accident or violence. Since so many of Broca's subjects were elderly women, we may assume that lengthy degenerative disease was more common among them than among the men.

More importantly, modern students of brain size have still not agreed $\quad$ 82 on a proper measure to eliminate the powerful effect of body size (Jerison, 1973; Gould, 1977). Height is partly adequate, but men and women of the same height do not share the same body build. Weight is even worse then height, because most of its variation reflects nutrition rather than intrinsic size—and fat vs. skinny exerts little influence upon the brain. Léonce Manouvrier took up this subject in the 1880s and argued that muscular mass and force should be used. He tried to measure this elusive property in various ways and found a marked difference in favor of men, even in men and women of the same height. When he corrected for what he called "sexual mass," women came out slightly ahead in brain size.

Thus, the corrected 113 gram difference is surely too large; the true $\quad$ 83 figure is probably close to zero and may as well favor women as men. One hundred thirteen grams, by the way, is exactly the average difference between a five-foot-four-inch and a six-foot-four-inch male in Broca's data[13] —and we would not want to ascribe greater intelligence to tall men. In short, Broca's data do not permit any confident claim that men have bigger brains than women.

Maria Montessori did not confine her activities to educational reform for $\quad$ 84 young children. She lectured on anthropology for several years at the University of Rome and wrote an influential book entitled *Pedagogical Anthropology* (English edition, 1913). She was, to say the least, no egalitarian. She supported most of Broca's work and the theory of innate criminality proposed by her compatriot Cesare Lombroso (next chapter). She measured the circumference of children's heads in her schools and inferred that the best prospects had bigger brains. But she had no use for Broca's conclusions about women. She discussed Manouvrier's work at length and made much of his tentative claim that women have slightly larger brains when proper corrections are made. Women, she concluded, are intellectually superior to men, but men have prevailed heretofore by dint of physical force. Since technology has abolished force as an instrument of power, the era of women may soon by upon us: "In such an epoch there will really be superior human beings, there will really be men strong in morality and in sentiment. Perhaps in this way the reign of woman is approaching, when the enigma

---

[13] For his largest sample of males, and using the favored power function for bivariate analysis of brain allometry, I calculate, where y is brain weight in grams and x is body height in cm: $y = 121.6x^{0.47}$. [Author's note.]

of her anthropological superiority will be deciphered. Woman was always the custodian of human sentiment, morality and honor" (1913, p. 259).

Montessori's argument represents one possible antidote to "scientific" 85 claims for the constitutional inferiority of certain groups. One may affirm the validity of biological distinctions, but argue that the data have been misinterpreted by prejudiced men with a stake in the outcome, and that disadvantaged groups are truly superior. In recent years, Elaine Morgan has followed this strategy in her *Descent of Woman*, a speculative reconstruction of human prehistory from the woman's point of view—and as farcical as more famous tall tales by and for men.

I dedicate this book to a different position. Montessori and Morgan 86 follow Broca's method to reach a more congenial conclusion. I would rather label the whole enterprise of setting a biological value upon groups for what it is: irrelevant, intellectually unsound, and highly injurious.

POSTSCRIPT

Craniometric arguments lost much of their luster in our century, as 87 determinists switched their allegiance to intelligence testing—a more "direct" path to the same invalid goal of ranking groups by mental worth—and as scientists exposed the prejudiced nonsense that dominated most literature on form and size of the head. The American anthropologist Franz Boas, for example, made short work of the fabled cranial index by showing that it varied widely both among adults of a single group and within the life of an individual (Boas, 1899). Moreover, he found significant differences in cranial index between immigrant parents and their American-born children. The immutable obtuseness of the brachycephalic southern European might veer toward the dolichocephalic Nordic norm in a single generation of altered environment (Boas, 1911).

Yet the supposed intellectual advantage of bigger heads refuses to disappear 88 entirely as an argument for assessing human worth. We still encounter it occasionally at all levels of determinist contention.

1. Variation within the general population: Arthur Jensen (1979, pp. 89 361–362) supports the value of IQ as a measure of innate intelligence by claiming that the correlation between brain size and IQ is about 0.30. He doesn't doubt that the correlation is meaningful and that "there has been a direct causal effect, through natural selection in the course of human evolution, between intelligence and brain size." Undaunted by the low value of the correlation, he proclaims that it would be even higher if so much of the brain were not "devoted to noncognitive functions."

On the same page, Jensen cites an average correlation of 0.25 between 90 IQ and physical stature. Although this value is effectively the same as the IQ vs. brain size correlation, Jensen switches ground and holds that "this correlation almost certainly involves no causal or functional relationship between stature and intelligence." Both height and intelligence, he argues, are perceived as desirable traits, and people lucky enough to possess more than the average of both are drawn to each other. But is it not more likely that height vs. brain size represents the primary causal correlation for the obvious reason that tall people tend to have large body parts? Brain size would then be an imperfect measure of height, and IQ might correlate with it (at the low value of 0.3) for the primarily envionmental reason that poverty and poor nutrition can lead both to reduced stature and poor IQ scores.

2. Variation among social classes and occupational groups: In a book   91
dedicated to putting educators in touch with latest advances in the brain sciences, H. T. Epstein (in Chall and Mirsky, 1978) states (pp. 349–350):

> First we shall ask if there is any indication of a linkage of any kind between brain and intelligence. It is generally stated that there is no such linkage. . . . But the one set of data I have found seems to show clearly that there is a substantial connection. Hooton studied the head circumferences of white Bostonians as part of his massive study of criminals. The following table shows that the ordering of people according to head size yields an entirely plausible ordering according to vocational status. It is not at all clear how the impression has been spread that there is no such correlation.

Epstein's chart, reproduced as he presents it in Table 3.2, seems to   92
support the notion that people in more prestigious jobs have larger heads. But a bit of probing and checking in original sources exposes the chart as a shoddy bit of finagling (not by Epstein who, I suspect, copied it from another secondary source that I have not been able to identify).

i) Epstein's reported standard deviations are so low, and therefore imply   93
such a small range of variation within each occupational class, that the differences in mean head size must be significant even though they are so

Table 3.2   *Mean and standard deviation of head circumference for people of varied vocational statuses*

VOCATIONAL STATUS	N	MEAN (IN MM)	S.D.
Professional	25	569.9	1.9
Semiprofessional	61	566.5	1.5
Clerical	107	566.2	1.1
Trades	194	565.7	0.8
Public service	25	564.1	2.5
Skilled trades	351	562.9	0.6
Personal services	262	562.7	0.7
Laborers	647	560.7	0.3

Source: *Ernest A. Hooton,* The American Criminal, *vol. 1 (Cambridge, Mass.: Harvard University Press, 1939), Table VIII-17.*

small. But a glance at Hooton's original table (1939, Table VIII-17) reveals that the wrong column (standard errors of the mean) has been copied and called standard deviation. The true standard deviations, given in another column of Hooton's table, run from 14.4 to 18.6—large enough to render most mean differences between occupational groups statistically insignificant.

ii) The chart arranges occupational groups by mean head size, but does 94 not include Hooton's ranked assessments of vocational status based upon years of education (1939, p. 150). In fact, since the column is labeled "vocational status," we are led to assume that the jobs have been listed in their proper order of prestige and that a perfect correlation therefore exists between status and head size. But the professions are arranged only by head size. Several professions do not fit the pattern; personal services and skilled trades (Hooton's status 5 and 6) rank just above the bottom in head size but at the middle in prestige.

iii) As a much worse, and entirely inexcusable omission, my consultation 95 of Hooton's original chart shows that data for three trades have been expunged without comment in Table 3.2. Guess why? All three rank at or near the bottom of Hooton's list of status—factory workers at rank 7 (of 11), transportation employees at rank 8, and "extractive" trades (farming and mining) at the lowest rank 11. All three have mean head circumferences (564.7, 564.9, and 564.7, respectively) *above* the grand average for all professions (563.9)!

I do not know the source of this disgracefully fudged chart. Jensen 96 (1979, p. 361) reproduces it in Epstein's version with the three trades omitted. But he correctly labels the standard error (though he also omits the standard deviation) and properly denotes the professions as "occupational category" rather than "vocational status." Yet Jensen's version includes the same minor numerical error as Epstein's (standard error of 0.3 for laborers, miscopied as the correct value from the omitted line of "extractive" workers placed just above laborers in Hooton's chart). Since I doubt that the same insignificant error would have been made twice independently, and since Jensen's book and Epstein's article appeared at virtually the same time, I assume that both took the information from an unidentified secondary source (neither cite anyone but Hooton).

iv) Since Epstein and Jensen make so much of Hooton's data, they might 97 have consulted his own opinion about it. Hooton was no do-gooding environmentalist liberal. He was a strong eugenicist and biological determinist who ended his study of American criminals with these chilling words: "The elimination of crime can be effected only by the extirpation of the physically, mentally, and morally unfit, or by their complete segregation in a socially aseptic environment" (1939, p. 309). Yet Hooton himself thought that his chart of head sizes and professions had proved nothing (1939, p. 154). He noted that only one vocational group, laborers, departed significantly from the average of all groups. And he stated explicitly that his sample for the only profession with noticeably larger than average heads—the professionals—was "wholly inadequate" (p. 153) as a result of its small size.

v) The primary environmental hypothesis for correlations of head size 98 with social class holds that they are artifacts of a causal correlation between body size and status. Large bodies tend to carry large heads, and proper nutrition and freedom from poverty fosters better growth in childhood. Hooton's data provide tentative support for both parts of this argument, though Epstein doesn't mention these data on stature at all. Hooton provides information on both height and weight (both inadequate measures of stature—see p. 537). Most significant deviations from the grand average support the environmental hypothesis. For weight, two groups departed significantly: professionals (status 1) heavier than average, and laborers (status 10) lighter than average. For height, three groups were deficient and none significantly taller than average: laborers (status 10), personal service (status 5), and clerical (status 2—and contrary to the environmentalist hypothesis). I also computed correlation coefficients for head circumference vs. stature from Hooton's data. I found no correlation for total height, but significant correlations for both sitting height (0.605) and weight (0.741).

3. Variation among races: In its eighteenth edition of 1964, the 99 *Encyclopaedia Britannica* was still listing "a small brain in relation to their size" along with woolly hair as characteristic of black people.

In 1970 the South African anthropologist P. V. Tobias wrote a courageous 100 article exposing the myth that group differences in brain size bear any relationship to intelligence—indeed, he argued, group differences in brain size, independent of body size and other biasing factors, have never been demonstrated at all.

This conclusion may strike readers as strange, especially since it comes 101 from a famous scientist well acquainted with the reams of published data on brain size. After all, what can be simpler than weighing a brain?—Take it out, and put it on the scale. Not so. Tobias lists fourteen important biasing factors. One set refers to problems of measurement itself: at what level is the brain severed from the spinal cord; are the meninges removed or not (meninges are the brain's covering membranes, and the dura mater, or thick outer covering, weighs 50 to 60 grams); how much time elapsed after death; was the brain preserved in any fluid before weighing and, if so, for how long; at what temperature was the brain preserved after death. Most literature does not specify these factors adequately, and studies made by different scientists usually cannot be compared. Even when we can be sure that the same object has been measured in the same way under the same conditions, a second set of biases intervenes—influences upon brain size with no direct tie to the desired properties of intelligence or racial affiliation: sex, body size, age, nutrition, nonnutritional environment, occupation, and cause of death. Thus, despite thousands of published pages, and tens of thousands of subjects, Tobias concludes that we do not know— as if it mattered at all—whether blacks, on the average, have larger or smaller brains than whites. Yet the larger size of white brains was an unquestioned "fact" among white scientists until quite recently.

Many investigators have devoted an extraordinary amount of attention to 102 the subject of group differences in human brain size. They have gotten nowhere, not because there are no answers, but because the answers are so difficult to get and because the a priori convictions are so clear and controlling. In the heat of Broca's debate with Gratiolet, one of Broca's defenders, admittedly as a nasty debating point, made a remark that admirably epitomizes the motivations implicit in the entire craniometric tradition: "I have noticed for a long time," stated de Jouvencel (1861, p. 465), "that, in general, those who deny the intellectual importance of the brain's volume have small heads." Self-interest, for whatever reason, has been the wellspring of opinon on this heady issue from the start.

References

Bean, Robert Bennett. 1906. Some racial peculiarities of the Negro brain. *American Journal of Anatomy* 5: 353–432.

Boas, F. 1899. The cephalic index. *American Anthropology* 1:448–461.

———. 1911. Changes in the bodily form of descendants of immigrants. Senate Document 208, 61st Congress, 2nd Session.

Broca, P. 1861. Sur le volume et la forme du cerveau suivant les individus et suivant les races. *Bulletin Société d'Anthropologie Paris* 2: 139–207, 301–321, 441–446.

———. 1862a. Sur les proportions relatives du bras, de l'avant bras et de la clavicule chez les nègres et les européens. *Bulletin Société d'Anthropologie Paris*, vol. 3, part 2, 13pp.

———. 1862b. Sur la capacité des crânes parisiens des diverses époques. *Bulletin Société d'Anthropologie Paris* 3: 102–116.

———. 1862c. Sur les projections de la tête et sur un nouveau procédé de céphalométrie. *Bulletin Société d'Anthropologie Paris* 3: 32pp.

———. 1866. Anthropologie. In *Dictionnaire encyclopédique des sciences médicales*, ed. A. Dechambre. Paris: Masson, pp. 276–300.

———. 1868. *Mémoire sur les crânes des Basques*. Paris: Masson, 79pp.

———. 1873a. Sur les crânes de la caverne de l'Homme-Mort (Lozère). *Revue d'Anthropologie* 2: 1–53.

———. 1873b. Sur la mensuration de la capacité du crâne. *Memoire Société Anthropologie*, 2nd series, vol. 1, 92pp.

Chase, A. 1977. *The legacy of Malthus*. New York: A. Knopf, 686pp.

Chorover, S. L. 1979. *From genesis to genocide*. Cambridge, MA: Massachusetts Institute of Technology Press.

Cope, E. D. 1890. Two perils of the Indo-European. *The Open Court* 3: 2052–2054 and 2070–2071.

Count, E. W. 1950. *This is race*. New York: Henry Schuman, 747pp.

Epstein, H. T. 1978. Growth spurts during brain development: implications for educational policy and practice. In *Education and the brain*, pp. 343–370, eds. J. S. Chall and A. F. Mirsky. 77th Yearbook, National Society for the Study of Education. Chicago: University of Chicago Press.

Galton, F. 1884. *Hereditary genius*. New York: D. Appleton, 390pp.

————. 1909. *Memories of my life*. London: Methuen.

Gould, S. J. 1977. *Ever since Darwin*. New York: W. W. Norton.

Haller, J. S., Jr. 1971. *Outcasts from evolution: scientific attitudes of racial inferiority, 1859–1900*. Urbana, Ill.: University of Illinois Press, 228pp.

Hervé, G. 1881. Du poids de l'encéphale. *Revue d'Anthropologie*, 2nd séries, vol. 4, pp. 681–698.

Jensen, A. R. 1979. *Bias in mental testing*. New York: Free Press.

Jerison, J. J. 1973. *The evolution of the brain and intelligence*. New York: Academic Press.

Jouvencel, M. de. 1861. Discussion sur le cerveau. *Bulletin Société d'Anthropologie Paris* 2: 464–474.

LeBon, G. 1879. Recherches anatomiques et mathématiques sur les lois des variations du volume du cerveau et sur leurs relations avec l'intelligence. *Revue d'Anthropologie*, 2nd series, vol. 2, pp. 27–104.

Mall, F. P. 1909. On several anatomical characters of the human brain, said to vary according to race and sex, with especial reference to the weight of the frontal lobe. *American Journal of Anatomy* 9: 1–32.

Manouvrier, L. 1903. Conclusions générales sur l'anthropologie des sexes et applications sociales. *Revue de l'École d'Anthropologie* 13: 405–423.

Montessori, M. 1913. *Pedagogical anthropology*. New York: F. A. Stokes Company, 508pp.

Myrdal, G. 1944. An American dilemma: the Negro problem and modern democracy. New York: Harper and Brothers, 2 vols., 1483pp.

Schreider, E. 1966. Brain weight correlations calculated from original results of Paul Broca. *American Journal of Physical Anthropology* 25: 153–158.

Spitzka, E. A. 1903. A study of the brain of the late Major J. W. Powell. *American Anthropology*. 5: 585–643.

————. 1907. A study of the brains of six eminent scientists and scholars belonging to the American Anthropometric Society, together with a description of the skull of Professor E. D. Cope. *Transactions of the American Philosophical Society* 21: 175–308.

Stocking, G. 1973. *From chronology to ethnology. James Cowles Prichard and British Antropology 1800–1850*. In facsimile of 1813 ed. of J. C. Prichard, Researches into the physical history of man. Chicago: University of Chicago Press, pp. ix–cxvii.

Tobias, P. V. 1970. Brain-size, grey matter, and race—fact or fiction? *American Journal of Physical Anthropology* 32: 3–26.

Todd, T. W., and Lyon, D. W., Jr. 1924. Endocranial suture closure. Its progress and age relationship. Part 1. Adult males of white stock. *American Journal of Physical Anthropology* 7: 325–384.

———. 1925a. Cranial suture closure. II. Ectocranial closure in adult males of white stock. *American Journal of Physical Anthropology* 8: 23–40.

———. 1925b. Cranial suture closure. III. Endocranial closure in adult males of Negro stock. *American Journal of Physical Anthropology* 8: 47–71.

Topinard, P. 1878. *Anthropology*. London: Chapman and Hall, 548pp.

———. 1888. Le poids de l'encéphale d'après les registres de Paul Broca. *Mémoires Société d'Anthropologie Paris*, 2nd series, vol. 3, pp. 1–41.

Vogt, Carl. 1864. *Lectures on man*. London: Longman, Green, Longman, and Roberts, 475pp.

Questions for Discussion and Writing

1. Identify Gould's central argument. On what form of proof does it primarily rely? What assumptions? Assess the strengths and weaknesses of his method of proof.

2. Paul Broca is generally considered one of the great pioneers of modern brain research. Do you think that Gould treats him fairly? Why or why not?

3. Can you identify any hidden agendas in Gould's argument? Is he using the data to prove preconceived notions of his own?

4. What does Gould's argument suggest about the objectivity of science? Is it reasonable to believe that a scientist such as Broca could have avoided his errors? Is it probable that he could have been sufficiently objective so as to have escaped his cultural assumptions? In what ways could modern science be affected by general cultural values and beliefs? Focusing on a specific area of modern scientific inquiry, discuss, develop, and write an argument in response to these questions.

WILLIAM J. WINSLADE
(b. 1941)

JUDITH WILSON ROSS
(b. 1937)

William Joseph Winslade is an inter-disciplinary scholar whose education and writing cross many fields. After earning his B.A. from Monmouth College in 1963 and his Ph.D. in philosophy from Northwestern in 1966, he taught philosophy for a few years and then studied law at the University of California, Los Angeles. On graduation in 1972, he returned briefly to the philosophy classroom, worked as an attorney in Los Angeles for two years, and then began a twelve-year stint with the program in Law, Medicine, and Human Values at UCLA. While serving in this capacity, he earned a second Ph.D., this time in psychoanalysis, from the Southern California Psychoanalytic Institute. Since 1984, he has served as an associate professor of medical humanities at the University of Texas Medical Branch at Galveston.

Judith Wilson Ross earned her A.B. from St. Lawrence University in 1958 and her M.A. from UCLA in 1961. She has worked as a researcher and writer for the U.S. House of Representatives; as an administrator and writer for the Advisory for Open Education in Cambridge, Massachusetts; and with the program in Medicine, Law, and Human Values at UCLA. In 1984, she became an ethicist for the St. Joseph Health System, Orange, California. In this capacity, she works in hospitals, helping to resolve ethical dilemmas that arise in health care situations.

Together with Albert R. Jonsen and Mark Siegler, Winslade published Clinical Ethics: A Practical Approach to Ethical Decisions in Clinical Medicine (1982). Winslade and Ross collaborated on The Insanity Plea (1983) and Choosing Life or Death: A Guide for Patients, Families, and Professionals (1986). As these titles show, Winslade and Ross's publications demonstrate a strong concern for the ethical and legal dimensions of medical practice.

The Insanity Plea, a series of essays covering individual legal cases in which insanity pleas were argued, begins with Dan White—who murdered Harvey Milk and San Francisco Mayor George Moscone in 1978—and concludes with the case of John Hinckley, which we have excerpted here. As you read this account of the attempted assassination of President Ronald Reagan and the trial of his would-be assassin that followed, pay particular attention to the manner in which Winslade and Ross seek to make connections across traditional disciplines. Study, as well, Winslade and Ross's means of proof.

JOHN HINCKLEY

The Shooting of the President

Two weeks after a Washington, D.C., jury found John Hinckley not guilty   1
by reason of insanity for the attempted assassination of President Reagan
and the shooting of three other men, Hinckley sent a letter to a *New York
Times* reporter. The letter purported to be the speech Hinckley would have
made had the June 21, 1982, verdict been guilty, as many—perhaps
including Hinckley himself—believed it would be. In the letter, he pointed
out that "my actions on March 30, 1981, have given special meaning to
my life and no amount of imprisonment or hospitalization can tarnish my
historical deed." He continued, alluding to his long-distance infatuation
with movie actress Jodie Foster, "I . . . committed the ultimate crime in
hopes of winning the heart of a girl. It was an unprecedented demonstration
of love. But does the American public appreciate what I've done?"

Love has frequently been the justification for deeds more disastrous and   2
more far-ranging in consequences than an attempted presidential assassination, and thus we may disagree with Hinckley's description of his action as
"unprecedented." Surely these are the words of a callow young man putting
on airs. However, as to the American public's failure to appreciate his
"historical deed," he is quite right. We did not appreciate it at all if by
"appreciate" Hinckley means "approve." Nor did we appreciate the jury's
verdict of not guilty by reason of insanity. On the other hand, if "appreciate"
is taken to mean "to understand," then perhaps the jury did appreciate
Hinckley's historic act. And the American public appreciated the verdict.
The jury's appreciation of Hinckley's act offered understanding infused
with sympathy, while the public's appreciation of the verdict displayed
understanding filled with alarm. A young man had shot the president and
only by chance had not killed him. That he should be exonerated, and pronounced not guilty, when anyone could see him fire the gun time and time
again on television replays, was itself some kind of crime and some
perversion of justice. The American public fully appreciated the meaning
of this verdict.

Thousands of letters have been written to newspapers and magazines   3
since then, decrying the shamefulness and outrageousness of the verdict;
accusing lawmakers, psychiatrists, and go-easy-on-criminals judges of making this travesty possible. And thousands of those letters have been considered important enough to be printed. Voters have bombarded legislatures across the country with requests to eliminate the insanity defense
or to introduce a guilty but insane plea, and legislators have started to draw
up new legislation. The U.S. Senate, in midsummer and at the height of
the Washington, D.C., tourist season, was able to gear up for subcommittee
hearings on federal insanity laws within days of the Hinckley verdict. If

anything in this series of events was unprecedented, it was the speed with which these hearings were convened.

The public response suggested that John Hinckley had single-handedly   4
created an immense new judicial problem. But the problems inherent in the insanity defense have been with us for a long time. For all of recorded history, we have been troubled by the question of mental illness and the mentally ill: who—and perhaps what—are they? How are we to regard them? To treat them? For more than a hundred years, the insanity defense has grown increasingly more incoherent as courts and legislatures have reinterpreted and broadened it to encompass diminished capacity, irresistible impulse, temporary insanity, and all the other causal descriptions of inexplicable actions. For more than fifty years, we have had the problem of the psychologizing of the public and of juries being ever more sympathetic to the deterministic, explanatory views of psychology. For the past thirty years the problem of psychiatric expert testimony has mushroomed because psychological theories have multiplied in number, complexity, and contradictions while psychiatric knowledge has grown at a snail's pace. For twenty years, we have had the problem of the successful insanity defense coupled with the use of modern psychotropic drugs that make it possible to release patients with mental disturbances who would once have faced life-long institutionalization.

The problems inherent in the insanity defense were made evident in the   5
Hinckley trial:

1. The philosophical problem of allocating responsibility for human actions
2. The legal problem of defining states of mind that mitigate or eliminate imposition of moral guilt
3. The psychological problem of jurors' identifying with the defendant, being unable to imagine how a fellow human could have performed certain acts unless he was crazy, and thus excusing and forgiving him
4. The medical problem of treatment that does not cure but can reduce symptoms so that imprisonment achieved under the name of institutionalization can no longer be justified because of civil rights.

The facts of the John Hinckley case are straightforward. The youngest   6
child of a wealthy Colorado couple, Hinckley had been withdrawn and depressed for a number of years. His life had little consistent direction; he was in and out of college and periodically planned to go to Hollywood and become a musician. His family feared he was becoming dependent on Valium, which had been prescribed by a physician for anxiety. At his family's urging, John began seeing a psychiatrist who treated him with a combination of verbal therapy and behavior modification. The psychiatrist did not think the Valium was a problem, nor did he think Hinckley had a serious mental illness. He diagnosed Hinckley as an immature young man who needed help in establishing a life independent from his parents. The

goal of the therapy was to get Hinckley out of his parent's home and into a job. Hinckley was never hospitalized for mental illness, nor had he ever been diagnosed as having any major mental illness.

During the months that this therapy took place, Hinckley was trailing back and forth across the United States, travels that were not known to the therapist. He wrote letters, poems, and short stories, frequently with violent and death-oriented themes. He pursued Jodie Foster, a student at Yale University, wrote her notes, called her on the phone, and, on the Yale campus, once asked her for directions.

By March 1981 John Hinckley had made an agreement with his parents and his therapist to get a job and move out of the family home. The plan didn't work. Hours after leaving a note at Jodie Foster's door, he called his father from New York and asked for help to get back to Colorado. His father reluctantly provided a plane ticket and John flew to Colorado. His parents gave him money, wished him well, but though they felt badly, told him that he could not return to the family home. The next word they had of him was the radio news a few weeks later that he had been arrested for attempting to assassinate the president of the United States.

In his writings, filled with fantasies and ramblings, Hinckley spoke of great events, his place in history, his death, his love for Jodie, and the death of others. He planned airplane hijackings and he wrote a short story about a young man who viciously murders his father. These are not the writings of the typical twenty-year-old. He had no friends and scarcely any acquaintances. His only girl friend turned out to be a story he had made up for his parents' benefit. His older brother and sister had not had much to do with him for years. Although he periodically planned a career as a musician, his parents had never heard him play or sing. He was a loner, he was alienated, he was insecure, he was confused. But was he responsible for his actions? Did he know what he was doing and that it was wrong?

It was established at the trial that Hinckley had purchased a handgun, had engaged in a considerable amount of target practice, and had been in suspicious proximity to both Reagan and Carter on several occasions prior to the shooting of President Reagan.

The philosophical question of the nature of individual responsibility permeates all aspects of John Hinckley's trial. Was it chance, for example, that he loaded his gun with the six devastator (exploding) bullets rather than with any of the relatively less damaging bullets that he possessed? Or did he intend to maximize injury? Was he infatuated with Jodie Foster or obsessed with Jodie Foster? Did his parents' unwillingness to let him come home in March 1981 inevitably lead him to the attempted killing, as Hinckley's father seemed to believe when, on the witness stand, he said it was all his fault? Almost every witness testified—either directly or indirectly—to two questions: Could he choose and did he choose?

Perhaps the most peculiar instance of this was the defense's contention that Hinckley's actions had been delineated and determined by the movie

7

8

9

10

11

12

Taxi Driver, which starred Jodie Foster as a twelve-year-old prostitute. The movie's hero, Travis Bickel, is a taxi driver, a loner who is rejected by a girl, stalks a presidential candidate, and, to rescue the prostitute, shoots up a screenful of extras in a particularly blood-drenched scene. At the end of the movie, Bickel is seen as a hero. The defense contended that Hinckley had so identified with Travis Bickel that he had been obliged to reenact the events in his own life.

Surely there was a correlation. Hinckley had reportedly seen the movie   13
fifteen times, although his devotion to Jodie Foster alone might account for that. He did stalk presidential candidates: testimony showed that he had tracked both Carter and Reagan at earlier times. He had certainly been rejected by his fantasy love, Jodie Foster. Although the climactic shooting of President Reagan and three others at the Washington Hilton could hardly be said to have rescued anybody from anything, it was sufficiently bloody and violent to be equal to the movie's conclusion. And, if the shooting did not make him a hero, it certainly made him famous. The defense convinced the judge that the parallels between the movie and Hinckley's actions were potentially meaningful, and the movie was shown to the jury during the trial, to make sure that they got the point.

But what, exactly, was the point? That life imitates art? Hardly news.   14
That the immature are easily influenced? Yes, but that is a well-known fact and probably a normal and necessary stage in human development. How can we conclude an absence of personal responsibility from the fact that the young and inexperienced frequently model their lives on others who appear to be more in control?

Heroes and hero-worship were once an ordinary part of growing up.   15
Young people were expected to idolize some figure—a parent or older sibling, a community or religious leader, a president or some historical personage. They dreamed about growing up and being like the hero. They imitated actions and laid out goals in conscious simulation of the hero's behavior, style, and achievements. It was a culturally endorsed and accepted way of growing up and finding direction. But the belief in heroes lost favor when the heroes whom the young chose no longer reflected the traditional values of adult society. When fast-living movie and television stars, or outrageous, rebellious musicians began to be the kind of people that the young looked up to as heroes, hero-worship seemed less appropriate. When their heroes were noble and good, we believed that such behavior on the part of the young was natural, wise, and virtuous. But when their heroes are bad do we believe that choosing such a hero is unwise and foolish, or do we now think that such choices are unnatural and crazy, the act of an insane person?

John Hinckley's defenders argued that he was beyond choice, that he was   16
the captive of a bad hero. But the only evidence of his captivity is that the choice was a poor one. The reasoning seems to go like this: Travis Bickel is a bad person. No rational person would freely choose to model his life

on the life of a bad person. John Hinckley modeled his life on Travis Bickel's. Therefore, John Hinckley is not a rational person. If we believe that rational people make only rational (or desirable) choices, then it is a short journey from that conclusion to a verdict of not guilty by reason of insanity.

At the trial, some of the testimony focused on whether Hinckley had   17 planned the killing. The evidence is persuasive: he had purchased a gun and bullets, had learned how to shoot, and had found out where President Reagan was to be that day. He had taken himself and the gun and bullets to the Hilton at the appropriate time. He had written a note explaining how the "historical deed" would convince Jodie Foster of his sincerity. It is clear that John Hinckley had planned to shoot the president. In many insanity trials, the question of planning is central. In Dan White's trial, for example, there was much made about whether, when he pocketed his police revolver on the way to meet Mayor Moscone, the act proved planning or only proved that he often carried a gun. In this trial, there could be no such debate. Hinckley had surely planned the shooting.

But the defense lawyers bypassed the question of planning and premed-   18 itation by using the movie as the planning force. Not Hinckley at work here, they said. It was a movie script. No need for him to be responsible. No need for the movie maker to be responsible either, probably. Nobody was responsible. Following this line of thinking, a mind that is influenced by the outside world is a mind out of control and beyond responsibility.

There must be something about all this that is vaguely plausible since   19 the jury bought the story. But if we were to change the events somewhat the foolishness of it becomes apparent. Suppose a lonely, misunderstood, isolated girl in Montana sees an extremely effective movie about a woman who gives up all the traditional rewards of life and instead works in miserable conditions, sacrificing her own health working with poor, abandoned children in some fetid city slum. And suppose the young girl is so impressed with the power and love that this woman has gathered unto her that she decides to emulate all the heroine's actions and goals.

If the young girl were to succeed and, as did Mother Theresa, eventually   20 receive a Noble Peace Prize, would the forensic psychiatrists of the world stand up and testify that she should receive no rewards for her deeds because she was not responsible for the good she had done? Would they swear under oath that she was merely under the sway of a powerful movie and that, when young and immature, her neurotic need for love and power had sent her in these directions?

We cannot have it both ways. It cannot be that good choices are our   21 responsibility and bad choices are not. But the Hinckley defense argued that the good John Hinckley might have done was to his credit, while the evil belonged to something or someone else. And the jury agreed.

The legal problem of defining insanity was not limited to the usual   22 questions in this trial. It is difficult enough to provide jurors with any precision about what the law means when its says that they must decide whether the defendant had, for example, the capacity or ability to understand that his contemplated act was wrong, or that he even had the capacity to contemplate the act. The problem of how much capacity or how much understanding is always present and essentially insoluble. But in this case, because it was tried under federal rules, there was an added problem. To obtain a guilty verdict, the prosecution had to prove that John Hinckley was sane and the legal standard of proof was "beyond a reasonable doubt." Federal courts require the prosecution to prove sanity; most states place the burden of proof on the defense, so that to gain an acquittal they must prove the defendant insane.

Burden and standard of proof are complex legal issues and many 23 commentators on this trial have suggested that the jurors paid no attention to these issues because they did not understand what they meant. On the other hand, jurors were quoted as saying that they had handed down the verdict that the law required, implying that the legal constraints had forced them to make a decision of which they personally disapproved. But these statements might as easily be the result of the jurors attempting to absolve themselves of responsibility for a verdict that proved extremely unpopular.

It is, however, hard to imagine how any prosecutor could prove John 24 Hinckley, or anyone else, for that matter, sane beyond a reasonable doubt. Sanity and insanity are, of course, legal, not psychiatric, terms. The law has been notoriously unsuccessful in defining insanity. It does not even attempt to define sanity. It is certainly not obvious that sanity is simply the absence of insanity, whatever that may be. A juror, representing the lay public, probably interprets insanity to be a condition of varying degrees, depending on the extent of abnormal behavior or the seriousness of the apparent mental illness. Thus, a defendant might evidence some small mental disorder or an extremely serious mental disorder, or be anywhere in between. Correspondingly, he might be somewhat insane or extremely insane, or anywhere in the middle. It is hard to imagine any defendant on trial for a serious crime who could not be seen as abnormal. The crime itself is abnormal behavior in the society, and to be a criminal is to be deviant. If he is abnormal and deviant, then he is surely also mentally disordered and thus at least somewhat insane.

Proving sanity is as difficult as proving good physical health. A doctor 25 can poke, prod, look, listen, and test to find illness but if he finds no evidence of it, he cannot be certain that the patient is well. There may be no detectable, empirical evidence of disease, but that does not prove the patient is well. Our knowledge of the body's functioning is not good enough for us to be able to assure "wellness." And our knowledge of the mind's functioning is microscopic compared to our knowledge of physical health. It is factually impossible to prove anyone sane or mentally healthy, although we might suppose they are sane unless proven otherwise, as is customary in most state courts.

When jurors are impaneled for a trial, the attorneys or judges often ask 26
during the preliminary questioning whether the prospective juror understands what is meant by "preponderance of evidence" and "beyond reasonable
doubt" standards of proof. They stress that the "beyond reasonable doubt"
standard—which tends to prevail in criminal trials—means that no other
reasonable explanation would account for the events that have transpired.
They suggest that other explanations—irrational, fanciful, or far-fetched
ones—are possible. But the jury need not be concerned with these. Only
reasonable explanations need apply. By applying the "beyond reasonable
doubt" standard of proof of sanity, the Hinckley jury was asked if there
was any reasonable explanation for the assassination attempt other than the
premeditated, thoughtful plan of a competent, rational human to kill
President Reagan? The question must inevitably be answered affirmatively.
That Hinckley was crazy is a reasonable explanation. That half a dozen or
so psychiatrists and psychologists believed and testified that Hinckley was
seriously mentally ill and incapable of controlling his actions certainly
underscores the reasonableness of that explanation.

Placing the burden of proving sanity on the prosecution and then 27
requiring that the standard of proof be "beyond a reasonable doubt" should
have assured a not guilty by reason of insanity verdict for John Hinckley.
The possibility that the jurors didn't understand burden and standard does
not mitigate the law's foolishness for placing such a burden and standard.
If one disinterested, qualified, expert forensic psychiatrist had testified to
Hinckley's insanity, the prosecution could not have logically met the burden
or standard of proof. And John Hinckley had enough peculiarities of mind
and behavior that it was not difficult to find psychiatrists to testify to his
incapacities, his confusion, his delusions, and his weakness.

The legal problem of the insanity defense in this trial was this: all the 28
questionable mental states were placed in the not guilty by reason of insanity
category. "If you are not absolutely sure of sanity," said the law, "rule
insane."

"When in doubt," it counseled the jury, "make a finding of not guilty, 29
even though you know the defendant committed the act. "When we speak
of guilt," said the law, "we are talking about something else." We may
well ask, exactly what is it that the law was talking about?

The expert witnesses in the Hinckley trial provided the usual panoply of 30
conflicting definitions, variant diagnoses (four different kinds of schizophrenia from the defense alone), and wide-ranging role interpretations.
Was killing Reagan an act of aggression toward Hinckley's father? Or was
it identification with the Travis Bickel character? Was Jodie Foster an
idealized mother or a fantasy child-princess in need of rescue? Was John
spoiled and manipulating or helpless and driven?

As in the legal issues, this trial produced an unusual twist in the area of 31
expertise when the defense sought to introduce the results of a CAT scan—
a kind of X-ray of the brain using computerized axial tomography—to

bolster the assertion that Hinckley was schizophrenic. It has been noted that the great weakness of the insanity defense (particularly from the defense's point of view) is its amorphousness. Unlike chemistry, pathology, or fingerprint expertise, psychiatric expertise tends to lack measurements, physical evidence, and quantifiable statements. When such evidence is available (for example, the machine-scored tests in Leonard Smith's second trial), juries seem very favorably disposed toward it and for good reason. After the vagaries of most psychiatric testimony—complicated sentences, judgments that need endless qualifications, abstract concepts defined in even less specific terms—numbers must seem a blessing. They can be counted, remembered, talked about, compared. Unfortunately, the numbers that psychiatric expertise occasionally provide only *appear* to be factual information. Under cross-examination or serious thought, they become as amorphous as the rest of the psychiatric testimony.

The Hinckley lawyers tried to introduce CAT scan results to provide   32
genuine hard evidence—visual, physiological findings—to strengthen their contention that Hinckley had a serious mental disorder. The prosecution opposed the CAT scan results on the grounds that the scientific aspects of CAT scan technology would make the jury apply undue importance to the photos that showed shrunken brain tissue. They contended there was no evidence, either diagnostic or causal, to link reduced brain tissue to schizophrenia. Initially, the judge ruled the CAT scan evidence inadmissable. Later, he reversed his decision and permitted the testimony on the grounds that it might possibly be relevant.

This disputed testimony was a new but nonetheless typical example of   33
the problem of psychiatric expert testimony. A jury of twelve very ordinary people were left to decide whether group A of highly trained medical specialists was correct in thinking that there was some relationship between Hinckley's brain quantity and his behavior, or whether group B of highly trained medical specialists was correct in saying that there was no known link between Hinckley's brain quantity and his behavior. Any sensible juror would surely wash his hands of the entire question. How could he possibly make such a decision? If experts are to be of use to jurors, they must bring them information, not more questions. If the doctors couldn't agree about CAT scans and schizophrenia, there is no reason to ask already burdened jurors to pass judgment on that dispute, too. They had their hands full already.

After the jurors announced the decision, there was the customary clamor   34
by news media for inside information about what the jury really thought, how they really came to their decisions. The published accounts of the process certainly do not bolster one's faith in the jury system. But the trial did not bolster one's faith in the legal system or the psychiatric profession, either. Reports of jurors succumbing to pressure, anxiety, nervousness, and loneliness at being away from their families and reports of their willingness to vote certain ways in order to gain their own release from the ordeal all

sound less noble, sincere, hard-working, and vigilant than we might have hoped. Posttrial interviews with jurors who allege they had always thought he was guilty but just didn't vote that way are a sad commentary on human weakness.

But these jurors also told enough about how they did make their decision to suggest that technical legal questions and technical medical questions were the last thing on their minds. They didn't talk to interviewers or Senate Committee members about shrunken brain tissue or burden and standard of proof. They talked about whether poetry was fact or fiction, they wondered why Hinckley didn't have any friends, and they puzzled over why he'd been traveling all over the country, spending money on fares and then not staying in any one place. They thought his ideas, writings, and behavior were weird. Their verdict seems to be an attempt to explain that weirdness.

The jurors seemed to focus on a narrow view of life, a view that seemed reasonable to them. John Hinckley certainly didn't seem reasonable to them. Here he was, writing all these poems and stories and letters that didn't make much sense. The defense psychiatrists had used Hinckley's bizarre writings as a basis for their diagnosis of severe mental illness and a prosecution psychiatrist had argued that such a practice was nonsense. "Poetry is fiction," he argued, and "a writer's writings are not that useful in determining the mental state of the writer." The jurors apparently took the question of whether or not poetry is true in a quite literal way. Did it actually represent Hinckley's true state of mind or had he just made it up, as a writer makes up the things he writes? This difficult question seemed to be resolvable by getting an official definition of poetry and, at one point, the jurors requested the judge's assistance in determining whether poetry was fiction or fact. The judge refused to provide a definition.

Although this conflict over the writings was surely only one of many issues the jury struggled with, most of their public comments have the same quality. When they could not understand on a personal level what Hinckley was doing or why he was doing it, they were inclined to see the behavior as evidence of mental illness and then of insanity. It wasn't natural not to have friends, said one juror. Another juror couldn't imagine why anyone would spend all that money on plane fares and then not stay put. That lack of understanding may evidence a man who knows how difficult money is to come by and how carefully it ought to be used. But John Hinckley obtained money easily and, if he had no sense of money, it was not because he was insane.

There are some suggestions in interviews with jurors that the group saw him as a young man who had everything going for him. The jurors— primarily lower middle class, blue-collar or clerical blacks living in Washington, D.C.—must have seen Hinckley as a privileged member of America's elite, which he was. There should be no excuse for his coming to such a bad end. He had everything. If someone with everything going for him has attempted to murder the president, then he must be crazy.

In the Washington, D.C., federal court where Hinckley was tried, those   39
who are found not guilty by reason of insanity are sent to St. Elizabeth's
Hospital and, after fifty days, the individual may request release in a court
hearing. If he is found to be a danger to society no longer, he will be
released. John Hinckley spent those fifty days in St. Elizabeth's undergoing
yet further psychiatric evaluation. In spite of the hundreds of hours of
examination prior to his trial—examinations that led to opposite conclusions
by various psychiatrists—the St. Elizabeth's staff retested and made their
decision. They did not, of course, have to decide whether he was legally
insane; their job was simply to decide whether he continued to be a danger
to himself or to others.

Hinckley's attorneys rushed to announce that they would not request his   40
release until *they* were convinced that he was no longer a danger to society.
This peculiar announcement suggested that they were somehow trying to
apologize for having gotten Hinckley off and to demonstrate their basically
responsible nature. But it is no concern of the courts whether Hinckley's
lawyers (or his parents) thought he was dangerous. That expertise is the
property of institutional psychiatrists. And the institutional psychiatrists
concluded that he *was* dangerous.

Such a conclusion was likely, given public reaction to the verdict. But   41
it is not always the case. When Robert Torsney was sent for evaluation, the
institutional psychiatrists refused to be responsible for the courtroom
conclusion and recommended Torsney's immediate release. In April 1982,
just prior to the beginning of the Hinckley trial, Simon Karoly, who had
threatened to kill the president, was released after he had been found not
guilty by reason of insanity, in July 1981. The federal district court and
the St. Elizabeth's psychiatrists believed that Mr. Karoly was no longer dangerous, although they released him with a diagnosis of paranoid schizophrenia. Psychiatrists were in a better position to recommend release in
these less well-known instances. The Hinckley case, on the other hand,
was a media event that led to widespread and severe criticism of both
psychiatrists and psychiatry. Although many of the doctors who examined
Hinckley before the trial believed he had no serious mental illness, the
after-trial hysteria made a quick release most unlikely. What psychiatrist
would want to be identified with that decision in the face of an enraged
public?

Hinckley himself is reported to have said that if the psychiatrists concluded   42
he was no longer dangerous, he was "going to walk out the door, whether
the public likes it or not."

The public wouldn't have liked it. But even though he remains in St.   43
Elizabeth's, he is eligible for review. Every six months the question of
John Hinckley's dangerousness will be considered. Two weeks after he was
returned to St. Elizabeth's, Hinckley sent the public a message about the
insanity defense and his actions, speculating that "perhaps the uproar is for

the belief that a person can shoot the President of the United States and not be punished for it." But, he counseled, the public should understand that "[s]ending a John Hinckley to a mental hospital instead of prison is the American Way." The American Way of what?

The long-term effects of the Hinckley trial are not difficult to imagine. 44 The U.S. Senate subcommittee has held hearings and many notable lawyers and psychiatrists have been heard. After the Hinckley decision, nine bills were introduced in the House of Representatives and four in the Senate, adding to those that had already collected there to revise the insanity defense. President Reagan sent the Congress an "anti-crime package" that included reform, though not elimination, of the insanity defense.

At the state level, numerous proposals have been made, although no bill 45 was rushed through in the months immediately following the Hinckley trial. But the impetus for revision clearly exists, and a number of states will probably adopt guilty but mentally ill pleas. Psychiatrists are conducting hand-wringing discussions in their professional newsletters about their role in the judicial process. The American Psychiatric Association will surely appoint a committee to study the question. Criminal lawyers have pointed out that the issue is being blown out of proportion because relatively few insanity pleas are successful. Eminent jurists have counseled caution, for "the principle behind the insanity defense . . . should not be abandoned thoughtlessly." Newspapers around the country received letters from mental health workers who made compassionate pleas for those seriously ill individuals who have no control over their actions, and from ordinary citizens who were angry at such misplaced compassion. Forensic psychiatrists who indulge themselves in this line of work continue to claim that they alone have the expertise to know whether or not they have expertise. The public will have difficulty knowing how to balance these claims against their own vital sense that something in all this is very wrong. After a while, they will forget the issue as it fades from the headlines. New laws will be in place, but the legal system will grind on inexorably in its customary way, allowing psychiatrists to testify to the same old vagaries but in the slightly different form required by new legislation.

One day, another case will spread across the newspapers and the public 46 will again be outraged, unable to understand why there is still this problem.

"Didn't we get that straightened out after the Hinckley trial?" they will ask. 47

It will not be straightened out with quick-fix publicity appealing solutions. 48 The guilty but insane and the guilty but mentally ill pleas are not panaceas for the problem, though they *sound* good. Untangling the puzzle will demand a broader and politically more difficult solution. Psychiatrists must not be allowed to testify to mental states but must testify to treatment possibilities. Jurors must not be allowed to make decisions about disposition without understanding whether treatment is possible or advisable. Decisions about guilt must be separated from decisions about disposition. The insanity defense must be eliminated to keep lawyers and juries from replacing responsibility for actions with explanations of behavior.

Questions for Discussion and Writing

1. What kind of response is the opening paragraph meant to elicit from the reader? What is the reader's immediate impression of Hinckley's guilt? His sanity? How do Winslade and Ross use this initial response to launch their argument?

2. How important are the characters themselves in the drama Winslade unfolds for the reader? Is the reader meant to identify with Hinckley, Reagan, Jodie Foster, the jurors, the attorneys, or the judge as people, or are they introduced as objective components in a sociological argument? In short, what is the rhetorical effect of Winslade and Ross's characterizations?

3. In paragraph 34, Winslade and Ross express doubt about the jury system, the legal system, the psychiatric profession, the jury in the Hinckley trial, and human nature itself. They question psychiatry's ability to determine sanity, but they also seem disturbed about the responsibility given to the layperson. What, ultimately, do Winslade and Ross appear to affirm? Do you agree with their conclusions?

4. On the whole, do Winslade and Ross seem to give their opposition equal time? Having read Winslade and Ross's argument, do you feel that the insanity plea is *ever* appropriate? Should it be stricken from our legal system? Write an essay that addresses one or more of these questions.

RICHARD RODRIGUEZ

(b. 1944)

Just as W. E. B. DuBois and Alice Walker write eloquently of the African-American experience, so Richard Rodriguez tells a moving story of the victories and the losses he experiences living as a Mexican American in a white world. The son of immigrant Mexicans, Rodriguez grew up in a middle-class neighborhood in Sacramento, California. Speaking almost entirely Spanish at home, he entered Catholic school with a weak understanding of English. Bright and eager to learn, he overcame the initial language barrier and excelled in his studies. He earned his B.A. from Stanford in 1967, then pursued graduate study in English literature at Columbia University. After earning his M.A. in 1969, he enrolled in the Ph.D. program in English at the University of California, Berkeley. For several years, Rodriquez made steady progress toward his degree. Awarded a Fulbright fellowship, he traveled to England to engage in advanced literary research at the Warburg Institute in London. The stage was set for a triumphant conclusion to Rodriguez's career as a student.

It was just then, as he engaged in research for his dissertation on English Renaissance literature, that Rodriguez began to waver. He realized that he had labored, not truly for the love of his subject, but because he craved the praise and respect of his white teachers. He came to understand that he had been encouraged and rewarded not only for the excellence of his work, but because he was a Mexican American striving to succeed in a traditionally white profession. In short, he came to the conclusion that he and his teachers had so internalized the principle of affirmative action that they had been swept up in its momentum unconsciously.

As a result of this realization, Rodriguez never filed his dissertation, and he was never awarded his Ph.D. Nor did he accept any of the prestigious university teaching jobs he was offered. Instead, he decided to earn his living as a writer. Proud of his accomplishments yet troubled by the price he paid for his successful assimilation into mainstream American culture, Rodriguez felt compelled to tell the story of his life.

With the publication of his spiritual autobiography, Hunger of Memory: The Education of Richard Rodriguez (1982), he achieved this goal. The book records its author's progress from the non–English-speaking child to the assimilated adult. While telling his story, Rodriguez expresses controversial opinions about important topics such as affirmative action, bilingual education, ethnic studies, and bilingual ballots. Like Alice Walker, Rodriguez's courageous expression of unpopular ideas has earned him both praise and criticism from his own ethnic group. We have excerpted here the first chapter of Hunger of Memory.

ARIA

I

I remember to start with that day in Sacramento—a California now nearly thirty years past—when I first entered a classroom, able to understand some fifty stray English words.

The third of four children, I had been preceded to a neighborhood Roman Catholic school by an older brother and sister. But neither of them had revealed very much about their classroom experiences. Each afternoon they returned, as they left in the morning, always together, speaking in Spanish as they climbed the five steps of the porch. And their mysterious books, wrapped in shopping-bag paper, remained on the table next to the door, closed firmly behind them.

An accident of geography sent me to a school where all my classmates were white, many the children of doctors and lawyers and business executives. All my classmates certainly must have been uneasy on that first day of school—as most children are uneasy—to find themselves apart from their families in the first institution of their lives. But I was astonished.

The nun said, in a friendly but oddly impersonal voice, 'Boys and girls, this is Richard Rodriguez.' (I heard her sound out: *Rich-heard Road-ree-guess.*) It was the first time I had heard anyone name me in English. 'Richard,' the nun repeated more slowly, writing my name down in her black leather book. Quickly I turned to see my mother's face dissolve in a watery blur behind the pebbled glass door.

Many years later there is something called bilingual education—a scheme proposed in the late 1960s by Hispanic-American social activists, later endorsed by a congressional vote. It is a program that seeks to permit non-English-speaking children, many from lower-class homes, to use their family language as the language of school. (Such is the goal its supporters announce.) I hear them and am forced to say no: It is not possible for a child—any child—ever to use his family's language in school. Not to understand this is to misunderstand the public uses of schooling and to trivialize the nature of intimate life—a family's 'language.'

Memory teaches me what I know of these matters; the boy reminds the adult. I was a bilingual child, a certain kind—socially disadvantaged—the son of working-class parents, both Mexican immigrants.

In the early years of my boyhood, my parents coped very well in America. My father had steady work. My mother managed at home. They were nobody's victims. Optimism and ambition led them to a house (our home) many blocks from the Mexican south side of town. We lived among *gringos*[1]

---

[1] *gringos:* Mexican slang for strangers, foreigners, Americans. [Editors' note.]

and only a block from the biggest, whitest houses. It never occurred to my parents that they couldn't live wherever they chose. Nor was the Sacramento of the fifties bent on teaching them a contrary lesson. My mother and father were more annoyed than intimidated by those two or three neighbors who tried initially to make us unwelcome. ('Keep your brats away from my sidewalk!') But despite all they achieved, perhaps because they had so much to achieve, any deep feeling of ease, the confidence of 'belonging' in public was withheld from them both. They regarded the people at work, the faces in crowds, as very distant from us. They were the others, *los gringos*. That term was interchangeable in their speech with another, even more telling, *los americanos*.

I grew up in a house where the only regular guests were my relations.   8
For one day, enormous families of relatives would visit and there would be so many people that the noise and the bodies would spill out to the backyard and front porch. Then for weeks, no one came by. (It was usually a salesman who rang the doorbell.) Our house stood apart. A gaudy yellow in a row of white bungalows. We were the people with the noisy dog. The people who raised pigeons and chickens. We were the foreigners on the block. A few neighbors smiled and waved. We waved back. But no one in the family knew the names of the old couple who lived next door; until I was seven years old, I did not know the names of the kids who lived across the street.

In public, my father and mother spoke a hesitant, accented, not always   9
grammatical English. And they would have to strain—their bodies tense—to catch the sense of what was rapidly said by *los gringos*. At home they spoke Spanish. The language of their Mexican past sounded in counterpoint to the English of public society. The words would come quickly, with ease. Conveyed through those sounds was the pleasing, soothing, consoling reminder of being at home.

During those years when I was first conscious of hearing, my mother   10
and father addressed me only in Spanish; in Spanish I learned to reply. By contrast, English (*inglés*), rarely heard in the house, was the language I came to associate with *gringos*. I learned my first words of English overhearing my parents speak to strangers. At five years of age, I knew just enough English for my mother to trust me on errands to stores one block away. No more.

I was a listening child, careful to hear the very different sounds of   11
Spanish and English. Wide-eyed with hearing, I'd listen to sounds more than words. First, there were English (*gringo*) sounds. So many words were still unknown that when the butcher or the lady at the drugstore said something to me, exotic polysyllabic sounds would bloom in the midst of their sentences. Often, the speech of people in public seemed to me very loud, booming with confidence. The man behind the counter would literally ask, 'What can I do for you?' But by being so firm and so clear, the sound of his voice said that he was a *gringo*; he belonged in public society.

I would also hear then the high nasal notes of middle-class American   12
speech. The air stirred with sound. Sometimes, even now, when I have
been traveling abroad for several weeks, I will hear what I heard as a boy.
In hotel lobbies or airports, in Turkey or Brazil, some Americans will
pass, and suddenly I will hear it again—the high sound of American voices.
For a few seconds I will hear it with pleasure, for it is now the sound of
my society—a reminder of home. But inevitably—already on the flight
headed for home—the sound fades with repetition. I will be unable to hear
it anymore.

When I was a boy, things were different. The accent of *los gringos* was   13
never pleasing nor was it hard to hear. Crowds at Safeway or at bus stops
would be noisy with sound. And I would be forced to edge away from the
chirping chatter above me.

I was unable to hear my own sounds, but I knew very well that I spoke   14
English poorly. My words could not stretch far enough to form complete
thoughts. And the words I did speak I didn't know well enough to make
into distinct sounds. (Listeners would usually lower their heads, better to
hear what I was trying to say.) But it was one thing for *me* to speak English
with difficulty. It was more troubling for me to hear my parents speak in
public: their high-whining vowels and guttural consonants; their sentences
that got stuck with 'eh' and 'ah' sounds; the confused syntax; the hesitant
rhythm of sounds so different from the way *gringos* spoke. I'd notice,
moreover, that my parents' voices were softer than those of *gringos* we'd
meet.

I am tempted now to say that none of this mattered. In adulthood I am   15
embarrassed by childhood fears. And, in a way, it didn't matter very much
that my parents could not speak English with ease. Their linguistic difficulties
had no serious consequences. My mother and father made themselves
understood at the county hospital clinic and at government offices. And yet,
in another way, it mattered very much—it was unsettling to hear my parents
struggle with English. Hearing them, I'd grow nervous, my clutching
trust in their protection and power weakened.

There were many times like the night at a brightly lit gasoline station (a   16
blaring white memory) when I stood uneasily, hearing my father. He was
talking to a teenaged attendant. I do not recall what they were saying, but
I cannot forget the sounds my father made as he spoke. At one point his
words slid together to form one word—sounds as confused as the threads
of blue and green oil in the puddle next to my shoes. His voice rushed
through what he had left to say. And, toward the end, reached falsetto
notes, appealing to his listener's understanding. I looked away to the lights
of passing automobiles. I tried not to hear anymore. But I heard only too
well the calm, easy tones in the attendant's reply. Shortly afterward, walking
toward home with my father, I shivered when he put his hand on my
shoulder. The very first chance that I got, I evaded his grasp and ran on
ahead into the dark, skipping with feigned boyish exuberance.

But then there was Spanish. *Español*: my family's language. *Español*: the 17
language that seemed to me a private language. I'd hear strangers on the
radio and in the Mexican Catholic church across town speaking in Spanish,
but I couldn't really believe that Spanish was a public language, like
English. Spanish speakers, rather, seemed related to me, for I sensed that
we shared—through our language—the experience of feeling apart from
los gringos. It was thus a ghetto Spanish that I heard and I spoke. Like
those whose lives are bound by a barrio, I was reminded by Spanish of my
separateness from *los otros*,[2] *los gringos* in power. But more intensely than
for most barrio children—because I did not live in a barrio—Spanish
seemed to me the language of home. (Most days it was only at home that
I'd hear it.) It became the language of joyful return.

A family member would say something to me and I would feel myself 18
specially recognized. My parents would say something to me and I would
feel embraced by the sounds of their words. Those sounds said: *I am
speaking with ease in Spanish. I am addressing you in words I never use with*
los gringos. *I recognize you as someone special, close, like no one outside. You
belong with us. In the family.*

(*Ricardo.*) 19

At the age of five, six, well past the time when most other children no 20
longer easily notice the difference between sounds uttered at home and
words spoken in public, I had a different experience. I lived in a world
magically compounded of sounds. I remained a child longer than most; I
lingered too long, poised at the edge of language—often frightened by the
sounds of *los gringos*, delighted by the sounds of Spanish at home. I shared
with my family a language that was startlingly different from that used in
the great city around us.

For me there were none of the gradations between public and private 21
society so normal to a maturing child. Outside the house was public society;
inside the house was private. Just opening or closing the screen door behind
me was an important experience. I'd rarely leave home all alone or without
reluctance. Walking down the sidewalk, under the canopy of tall trees, I'd
warily notice the—suddenly—silent neighborhood kids who stood warily
watching me. Nervously, I'd arrive at the grocery store to hear there the
sounds of the *gringo*—foreign to me—reminding me that in this world so
big, I was a foreigner. But then I'd return. Walking back toward our
house, climbing the steps from the sidewalk, when the front door was open
in summer, I'd hear voices beyond the screen door talking in Spanish. For
a second or two, I'd stay, linger there, listening. Smiling, I'd hear my
mother call out, saying in Spanish (words): 'Is that you, Richard?' All the
while her sounds would assure me: *You are home now; come closer; inside.
With us.*

---

[2] *los otros:* the others. [Editors' note.]

'*Sí*,' I'd reply.   22

Once more inside the house I would resume (assume) my place in the   23
family. The sounds would dim, grow harder to hear. Once more at home,
I would grow less aware of that fact. It required, however, no more than
the blurt of the doorbell to alert me to listen to sounds all over again. The
house would turn instantly still while my mother went to the door. I'd hear
her hard English sounds. I'd wait to hear her voice return to soft-sounding
Spanish, which assured me, as surely as did the clicking tongue of the lock
on the door, that the stranger was gone.

Plainly, it is not healthy to hear such sounds so often. It is not healthy   24
to distinguish public words from private sounds so easily. I remained
cloistered by sounds, timid and shy in public, too dependent on voices at
home. And yet it needs to be emphasized: I was an extremely happy child
at home. I remember many nights when my father would come back from
work, and I'd hear him call out to my mother in Spanish, sounding relieved.
In Spanish, he'd sound light and free notes he never could manage in English. Some nights I'd jump up just at hearing his voice. With *mis hermanos*[3]
I would come running into the room where he was with my mother.
Our laughing (so deep was the pleasure!) became screaming. Like others
who know the pain of public alienation, we transformed the knowledge of
our public separateness and made it consoling—the reminder of intimacy.
Excited, we joined our voices in a celebration of sounds. *We are speaking
now the way we never speak out in public. We are alone—together*, voices
sounded, surrounded to tell me. Some nights, no one seemed willing to
loosen the hold sounds had on us. At dinner, we invented new words.
(Ours sounded Spanish, but made sense only to us.) We pieced together
new words by taking, say, an English verb and giving it Spanish endings.
My mother's instructions at bedtime would be lacquered with mock-urgent
tones. Or a word like *sí* would become, in several notes, able to convey
added measures of feeling. Tongues explored the edges of words, especially
the fat vowels. And we happily sounded that military drum roll, the twirling
roar of the Spanish *r*. Family language: my family's sounds. The voices of
my parents and sisters and brother. Their voices insisting: *You belong here.
We are family members. Related. Special to one another. Listen!* Voices singing
and sighing, rising, straining, then surging, teeming with pleasure that
burst syllables into fragments of laughter. At times it seemed there was
steady quiet only when, from another room, the rustling whispers of my
parents faded and I moved closer to sleep.

2

Supporters of bilingual education today imply that students like me miss   25
a great deal by not being taught in their family's language. What they seem

---

[3] *mis hermanos:* my siblings. [Editors' note.]

not to recognize is that, as a socially disadvantaged child, I considered Spanish to be a private language. What I needed to learn in school was that I had the right—and the obligation—to speak the public language of *los gringos*. The odd truth is that my first-grade classmates could have become bilingual, in the conventional sense of that word, more easily than I. Had they been taught (as upper-middle-class children are often taught early) a second language like Spanish or French, they could have regarded it simply as that: another public language. In my case such bilingualism could not have been so quickly achieved. What I did not believe was that I could speak a single public language.

Without question, it would have pleased me to hear my teachers address me in Spanish when I entered the classroom. I would have felt much less afraid. I would have trusted them and responded with ease. But I would have delayed—for how long postponed?—having to learn the language of public society. I would have evaded—and for how long could I have afforded to delay?—learning the great lesson of school, that I had a public identity. 26

Fortunately, my teachers were unsentimental about their responsibility. What they understood was that I needed to speak a public language. So their voices would search me out, asking me questions. Each time I'd hear them, I'd look up in surprise to see a nun's face frowning at me. I'd mumble, not really meaning to answer. The nun would persist, 'Richard, stand up. Don't look at the floor. Speak up. Speak to the entire class, not just to me!' But I couldn't believe that the English language was mine to use. (In part, I did not want to believe it.) I continued to mumble. I resisted the teacher's demands. (Did I somehow suspect that once I learned public language my pleasing family life would be changed?) Silent, waiting for the bell to sound, I remained dazed, diffident, afraid. 27

Because I wrongly imagined that English was intrinsically a public language and Spanish an intrinsically private one, I easily noted the difference between classroom language and the language of home. At school, words were directed to a general audience of listeners. ('Boys and girls.') Words were meaningfully ordered. And the point was not self-expression alone but to make oneself understood by many others. The teacher quizzed: 'Boys and girls, why do we use that word in this sentence? Could we think of a better word to use there? Would the sentence change its meaning if the words were differently arranged? And wasn't there a better way of saying much the same thing?' (I couldn't say. I wouldn't try to say.) 28

Three months. Five. Half a year passed. Unsmiling, ever watchful, my teachers noted my silence. They began to connect my behavior with the difficult progress my older sister and brother were making. Until one Saturday morning three nuns arrived at the house to talk to our parents. Stiffly, they sat on the blue living room sofa. From the doorway of another room, spying the visitors, I noted the incongruity—the clash of two worlds, the faces and voices of school intruding upon the familiar setting of home. 29

I overheard one voice gently wondering, 'Do your children speak only Spanish at home, Mrs. Rodriguez?' While another voice added, 'That Richard especially seems so timid and shy.'

That Rich-heard! 30

With great tact the visitors continued, 'Is it possible for you and your 31
husband to encourage your children to practice their English when they are home?' Of course, my parents complied. What would they not do for their children's well-being? And how could they have questioned the Church's authority which those women represented? In an instant, they agreed to give up the language (the sounds) that had revealed and accentuated our family's closeness. The moment after the visitors left, the change was observed. '*Ahora*, speak to us *en inglés*,' my father and mother united to tell us.

At first, it seemed a kind of game. After dinner each night, the family 32
gathered to practice 'our' English. (It was still then *inglés*, a language foreign to us, so we felt drawn as strangers to it.) Laughing, we would try to define words we could not pronounce. We played with strange English sounds, often overanglicizing our pronunciations. And we filled the smiling gaps of our sentences with familiar Spanish sounds. But that was cheating, somebody shouted. Everyone laughed. In school, meanwhile, like my brother and sister, I was required to attend a daily tutoring session. I needed a full year of special attention. I also needed my teachers to keep my attention from straying in class by calling out, *Rich-heard*—their English voices slowly prying loose my ties to my other name, its three notes, *Ri-car-do*. Most of all I needed to hear my mother and father speak to me in a moment of seriousness in broken—suddenly heartbreaking—English. The scene was inevitable: One Saturday morning I entered the kitchen where my parents were talking in Spanish. I did not realize that they were talking in Spanish however until, at the moment they saw me, I heard their voices change to speak English. Those *gringo* sounds they uttered startled me. Pushed me away. In that moment of trivial misunderstanding and profound insight, I felt my throat twisted by unsounded grief. I turned quickly and left the room. But I had no place to escape to with Spanish. (The spell was broken.) My brother and sisters were speaking English in another part of the house.

Again and again in the days following, increasingly angry, I was obliged 33
to hear my mother and father: 'Speak to us *en inglés*.' (*Speak*.) Only then did I determine to learn classroom English. Weeks after, it happened: One day in school I raised my hand to volunteer an answer. I spoke out in a loud voice. And I did not think it remarkable when the entire class understood. That day, I moved very far from the disadvantaged child I had been only days earlier. The belief, the calming assurance that I belonged in public, had at last taken hold.

Shortly after, I stopped hearing the high and loud sounds of *los gringos*. 34
A more and more confident speaker of English, I didn't trouble to listen to *how* strangers sounded, speaking to me. And there simply were too many

English-speaking people in my day for me to hear American accents anymore. Conversations quickened. Listening to persons who sounded eccentrically pitched voices, I usually noted their sounds for an initial few seconds before I concentrated on *what* they were saying. Conversations became content-full. Transparent. Hearing someone's *tone* of voice—angry or questioning or sarcastic or happy or sad—I didn't distinguish it from the words it expressed. Sound and word were thus tightly wedded. At the end of a day, I was often bemused, always relieved, to realize how 'silent,' though crowded with words, my day in public had been. (This public silence measured and quickened the change in my life.)

At last, seven years old, I came to believe what had been technically true 35
since my birth: I was an American citizen.

But the special feeling of closeness at home was diminished by then. 36
Gone was the desperate, urgent, intense feeling of being at home; rare was the experience of feeling myself individualized by family intimates. We remained a loving family, but one greatly changed. No longer so close; no longer bound tight by the pleasing and troubling knowledge of our public separateness. Neither my older brother nor sister rushed home after school anymore. Nor did I. When I arrived home there would often be neighborhood kids in the house. Or the house would be empty of sounds.

Following the dramatic Americanization of their children, even my par- 37
ents grew more publicly confident. Especially my mother. She learned the names of all the people on our block. And she decided we needed to have a telephone installed in the house. My father continued to use the word *gringo*. But it was no longer charged with the old bitterness or distrust. (Stripped of any emotional content, the word simply became a name for those Americans not of Hispanic descent.) Hearing him, sometimes, I wasn't sure if he was pronouncing the Spanish word *gringo* or saying gringo in English.

Matching the silence I started hearing in public was a new quiet at home. 38
The family's quiet was partly due to the fact that, as we children learned more and more English, we shared fewer and fewer words with our parents. Sentences needed to be spoken slowly when a child addressed his mother or father. (Often the parent wouldn't understand.) The child would need to repeat himself. (Still the parent misunderstood.) The young voice, frustrated, would end up saying, 'Never mind'—the subject was closed. Dinners would be noisy with the clinking of knives and forks against dishes. My mother would smile softly between her remarks; my father at the other end of the table would chew and chew at his food, while he stared over the heads of his children.

My *mother!* My *father!* After English became my primary language, I 39
no longer knew what words to use in addressing my parents. The old Spanish words (those tender accents of sound) I had used earlier—*mamá* and *papá*—I couldn't use anymore. They would have been too painful reminders of how much had changed in my life. On the other hand, the

words I heard neighborhood kids call *their* parents seemed equally unsatisfactory. *Mother* and *Father*; *Ma, Papa, Pa, Dad, Pop* (how I hated the all-American sound of that last word especially)—all these terms I felt were unsuitable, not really terms of address for *my* parents. As a result, I never used them at home. Whenever I'd speak to my parents, I would try to get their attention with eye contact alone. In public conversations, I'd refer to 'my parents' or 'my mother and father.'

My mother and father, for their part, responded differently, as their 40 children spoke to them less. She grew restless, seemed troubled and anxious at the scarcity of words exchanged in the house. It was she who would question me about my day when I came home from school. She smiled at small talk. She pried at the edges of my sentences to get me to say something more. (What?) She'd join conversations she overheard, but her intrusions often stopped her children's talking. By contrast, my father seemed reconciled to the new quiet. Though his English improved somewhat, he retired into silence. At dinner he spoke very little. One night his children and even his wife helplessly giggled at his garbled English pronunciation of the Catholic Grace before Meals. Thereafter he made his wife recite the prayer at the start of each meal, even on formal occasions, when there were guests in the house. Hers became the public voice of the family. On official business, it was she, not my father, one would usually hear on the phone or in stores, talking to strangers. His children grew so accustomed to his silence that, years later, they would speak routinely of his shyness. (My mother would often try to explain: Both his parents died when he was eight. He was raised by an uncle who treated him like little more than a menial servant. He was never encouraged to speak. He grew up alone. A man of few words.) But my father was not shy, I realized, when I'd watch him speaking Spanish with relatives. Using Spanish, he was quickly effusive. Especially when talking with other men, his voice would spark, flicker, flare alive with sounds. In Spanish, he expressed ideas and feelings he rarely revealed in English. With firm Spanish sounds, he conveyed confidence and authority English would never allow him.

The silence at home, however, was finally more than a literal silence. 41 Fewer words passed between parent and child, but more profound was the silence that resulted from my inattention to sounds. At about the time I no longer bothered to listen with care to the sounds of English in public, I grew careless about listening to the sounds family members made when they spoke. Most of the time I heard someone speaking at home and didn't distinguish his sounds from the words people uttered in public. I didn't even pay much attention to my parents' accented and ungrammatical speech. At least not at home. Only when I was with them in public would I grow alert to their accents. Though, even then, their sounds caused me less and less concern. For I was increasingly confident of my own public identity.

I would have been happier about my public success had I not sometimes 42 recalled what it had been like earlier, when my family had conveyed its intimacy through a set of conveniently private sounds. Sometimes in public, hearing a stranger, I'd hark back to my past. A Mexican farmworker approached me downtown to ask directions to somewhere. '¿*Hijito*[4]. . . ?' he said. And his voice summoned deep longing. Another time, standing beside my mother in the visiting room of a Carmelite convent, before the dense screen which rendered the nuns shadowy figures, I heard several Spanish-speaking nuns—their busy, singsong overlapping voices—assure us that yes, yes, we were remembered, all our family was remembered in their prayers. (Their voices echoed faraway family sounds.) Another day, a dark-faced old woman—her hand light on my shoulder—steadied herself against me as she boarded a bus. She murmured something I couldn't quite comprehend. Her Spanish voice came near, like the face of a never-before-seen relative in the instant before I was kissed. Her voice, like so many of the Spanish voices I'd hear in public, recalled the golden age of my youth. Hearing Spanish then, I continued to be a careful, if sad, listener to sounds. Hearing a Spanish-speaking family walking behind me, I turned to look. I smiled for an instant, before my glance found the Hispanic-looking faces of strangers in the crowd going by.

Today I hear bilingual educators say that children lose a degree of 'individuality' by becoming assimilated into public society. (Bilingual schooling was popularized in the seventies, that decade when middle-class ethnics began to resist the process of assimilation—the American melting pot.) But the bilingualists simplistically scorn the value and necessity of assimilation. They do not seem to realize that there are *two* ways a person is individualized. So they do not realize that while one suffers a diminished sense of *private* individuality by becoming assimilated into public society, such assimilation makes possible the achievement of *public* individuality. 43

The bilingualists insist that a student should be reminded of his difference from others in mass society, his heritage. But they equate mere separateness with individuality. The fact is that only in private—with intimates—is separateness from the crowd a prerequisite for individuality. (An intimate draws me apart, tells me that I am unique, unlike all others.) In public, by contrast, full individuality is achieved, paradoxically, by those who are able to consider themselves members of the crowd. Thus it happened for me: Only when I was able to think of myself as an American, no longer an alien in *gringo* society, could I seek the rights and opportunities necessary for full public individuality. The social and political advantages I enjoy as a man result from the day that I came to believe that my name, indeed, is *Rich-heard Road-ree-guess*. It is true that my public society today is often impersonal. (My public society is usually mass society.) Yet despite the anonymity of the crowd and despite the fact that the individuality I achieve 44

---

[4] *Hijito:* Son. [Editors' note.]

in public is often tenuous—because it depends on my being one in a crowd—I celebrate the day I acquired my new name. Those middle-class ethnics who scorn assimilation seem to me filled with decadent self-pity, obsessed by the burden of public life. Dangerously, they romanticize public separateness and they trivialize the dilemma of the socially disadvantaged.

My awkward childhood does not prove the necessity of bilingual education. My story discloses instead an essential myth of childhood—inevitable pain. If I rehearse here the changes in my private life after my Americanization, it is finally to emphasize the public gain. The loss implies the gain: The house I returned to each afternoon was quiet. Intimate sounds no longer rushed to the door to greet me. There were other noises inside. The telephone rang. Neighborhood kids ran past the door of the bedroom where I was reading my schoolbooks—covered with shopping-bag paper. Once I learned public language, it would never again be easy for me to hear intimate family voices. More and more of my day was spent hearing words. But that may only be a way of saying that the day I raised my hand in class and spoke loudly to an entire roomful of faces, my childhood started to end. 45

3

I grew up victim to a disabling confusion. As I grew fluent in English, I no longer could speak Spanish with confidence. I continued to understand spoken Spanish. And in high school, I learned how to read and write Spanish. But for many years I could not pronounce it. A powerful guilt blocked my spoken words; an essential glue was missing whenever I'd try to connect words to form sentences. I would be unable to break a barrier of sound, to speak freely. I would speak, or try to speak, Spanish, and I would manage to utter halting, hiccuping sounds that betrayed my unease. 46

When relatives and Spanish-speaking friends of my parents came to the house, my brother and sisters seemed reticent to use Spanish, but at least they managed to say a few necessary words before being excused. I never managed so gracefully. I was cursed with guilt. Each time I'd hear myself addressed in Spanish, I would be unable to respond with any success. I'd know the words I wanted to say, but I couldn't manage to say them. I would try to speak, but everything I said seemed to me horribly anglicized. My mouth would not form the words right. My jaw would tremble. After a phrase or two, I'd cough up a warm, silvery sound. And stop. 47

It surprised my listeners to hear me. They'd lower their heads, better to grasp what I was trying to say. They would repeat their questions in gentle, affectionate voices. But by then I would answer in English. No, no, they would say, we want you to speak to us in Spanish. ('. . . *en español*.') But I couldn't do it. *Pocho* then they called me. Sometimes playfully, teasingly, using the tender diminutive—*mi pochito*. Sometimes not so playfully, mockingly, *Pocho*. (A Spanish dictionary defines that word as an adjective 48

570

meaning 'colorless' or 'bland.' But I heard it as a noun, naming the Mexican-American who, in becoming an American, forgets his native society.) '¡*Pocho*!' the lady in the Mexican food store muttered, shaking her head. I looked up to the counter where red and green peppers were strung like Christmas tree lights and saw the frowning face of the stranger. My mother laughed somewhere behind me. (She said that her children didn't want to practice 'our Spanish' after they started going to school.) My mother's smiling voice made me suspect that the lady who faced me was not really angry at me. But, searching her face, I couldn't find the hint of a smile.

Embarrassed, my parents would regularly need to explain their children's   49 inability to speak flowing Spanish during those years. My mother met the wrath of her brother, her only brother, when he came up from Mexico one summer with his family. He saw his nieces and nephews for the very first time. After listening to me, he looked away and said what a disgrace it was that I couldn't speak Spanish, '*su proprio idioma*.'[5] He made that remark to my mother; I noticed, however, that he stared at my father.

I clearly remember one other visitor from those years. A long-time friend   50 of my father from San Francisco would come to stay with us for several days in late August. He took great interest in me after he realized that I couldn't answer his questions in Spanish. He would grab me as I started to leave the kitchen. He would ask me something. Usually he wouldn't bother to wait for my mumbled response. Knowingly, he'd murmur: '¿*Ay Pocho, Pocho, adónde vas?*'[6] And he would press his thumbs into the upper part of my arms, making me squirm with currents of pain. Dumbly, I'd stand there, waiting for his wife to notice us, for her to call him off with a benign smile. I'd giggle, hoping to deflate the tension between us, pretending that I hadn't seen the glittering scorn in his glance.

I remember that man now, but seek no revenge in this telling. I recount   51 such incidents only because they suggest the fierce power Spanish had for many people I met at home; the way Spanish was associated with closeness. Most of those people who called me a *pocho* could have spoken English to me. But they would not. They seemed to think that Spanish was the only language we could use, that Spanish alone permitted our close association. (Such persons are vulnerable always to the ghetto merchant and the politician who have learned the value of speaking their clients' family language to gain immediate trust.) For my part, I felt that I had somehow committed a sin of betrayal by learning English. But betrayal against whom? Not against visitors to the house exactly. No, I felt that I had betrayed my immediate family. I *knew* that my parents had encouraged me to learn English. I *knew* that I had turned to English only with angry reluctance.

---

[5] *su proprio idioma:* his own language. [Editors' note.]

[6] ¿*Ay Pocho . . . vas?:* Hey Pocho, Pocho, where are you going? [Editors' note.]

But once I spoke English with ease, I came to *feel* guilty. (This guilt defied logic.) I felt that I had shattered the intimate bond that had once held the family close. This original sin against my family told whenever anyone addressed me in Spanish and I responded, confounded.

But even during those years of guilt, I was coming to sense certain consoling truths about language and intimacy. I remember playing with a friend in the backyard one day, when my grandmother appeared at the window. Her face was stern with suspicion when she saw the boy (the *gringo*) I was with. In Spanish she called out to me, sounding the whistle of her ancient breath. My companion looked up and watched her intently as she lowered the window and moved, still visible, behind the light curtain, watching us both. He wanted to know what she had said. I started to tell him, to say—to translate her Spanish words into English. The problem was, however, that though I knew how to translate exactly *what* she had told me, I realized that any translation would distort the deepest meaning of her message: It had been directed only to me. This message of intimacy could never be translated because it was not *in* the words she had used but passed *through* them. So any translation would have seemed wrong; her words would have been stripped of an essential meaning. Finally, I decided not to tell my friend anything. I told him that I didn't hear all she had said. 52

This insight unfolded in time. Making more and more friends outside my house, I began to distinguish intimate voices speaking through *English*. I'd listen at times to a close friend's confidential tone or secretive whisper. Even more remarkable were those instances when, for no special reason apparently, I'd become conscious of the fact that my companion was speaking only to me. I'd marvel just hearing his voice. It was a stunning event: to be able to break through his words, to be able to hear this voice of the other, to realize that it was directed only to me. After such moments of intimacy outside the house, I began to trust hearing intimacy conveyed through my family's English. Voices at home at last punctured sad confusion. I'd hear myself addressed as an intimate at home once again. Such moments were never as raucous with sound as past times had been when we had had 'private' Spanish to use. (Our English-sounding house was never to be as noisy as our Spanish-speaking house had been.) Intimate moments were usually soft moments of sound. My mother was in the dining room while I did my homework nearby. And she looked over at me. Smiled. Said something—her words said nothing very important. But her voice sounded to tell me (*We are together*) I was her son. 53

(*Richard!*) 54

Intimacy thus continued at home; intimacy was not stilled by English. It is true that I would never forget the great change of my life, the diminished occasions of intimacy. But there would also be times when I sensed the deepest truth about language and intimacy: *Intimacy is not created by a particular language; it is created by intimates.* The great change in my 55 life was not linguistic but social. If, after becoming a successful student, I no longer heard intimate voices as often as I had earlier, it was not because I spoke English rather than Spanish. It was because I used public language for most of the day. I moved easily at last, a citizen in a crowded city of words.

4

This boy became a man. In private now, alone, I brood over language 56 and intimacy—the great themes of my past. In public I expect most of the faces I meet to be the faces of strangers. (How do you do?) If meetings are quick and impersonal, they have been efficiently managed. I rush past the sounds of voices attending only to the words addressed to me. Voices seem planed to an even surface of sound, soundless. A business associate speaks in a deep baritone, but I pass through the timbre to attend to his words. The crazy man who sells me a newspaper every night mumbles something crazy, but I have time only to pretend that I have heard him say hello. Accented versions of English make little impression on me. In the rush-hour crowd a Japanese tourist asks me a question, and I inch past his accent to concentrate on what he is saying. The Eastern European immigrant in a neighborhood delicatessen speaks to me through a marinade of sounds, but I respond to his words. I note for only a second the Texas accent of the telephone operator or the Mississippi accent of the man who lives in the apartment below me.

My city seems silent until some ghetto black teenagers board the bus I 57 am on. Because I do not take their presence for granted, I listen to the sounds of their voices. Of all the accented versions of English I hear in a day, I hear theirs most intently. They are *the* sounds of the outsider. They annoy me for being loud—so self-sufficient and unconcerned by my presence. Yet for the same reason they seem to me glamorous. (A romantic gesture against public acceptance.) Listening to their shouted laughter, I realize my own quiet. Their voices enclose my isolation. I feel envious, envious of their brazen intimacy.

I warn myself away from such envy, however. I remember the black 58 political activists who have argued in favor of using black English in schools. (Their argument varies only slightly from that made by foreign-language bilingualists.) I have heard 'radical' linguists make the point that black English is a complex and intricate version of English. And I do not doubt it. But neither do I think that black English should be a language of public instruction. What makes black English inappropriate in classrooms is not something *in* the language. It is rather what lower-class speakers make of it. Just as Spanish would have been a dangerous language for me to have used at the start of my education, so black English would be a dangerous language to use in the schooling of teenagers for whom it reenforces feelings of public separateness.

573

This seems to me an obvious point. But one that needs to be made. In 59
recent years there have been attempts to make the language of the alien
public language. 'Bilingual education, two ways to understand . . . ,'
television and radio commercials glibly announce. Proponents of bilingual
education are careful to say that they want students to acquire good schooling.
Their argument goes something like this: Children permitted to use their
family language in school will not be so alienated and will be better able
to match the progress of English-speaking children in the crucial first
months of instruction. (Increasingly confident of their abilities, such children
will be more inclined to apply themselves to their studies in the future.)
But then the bilingualists claim another, very different goal. They say that
children who use their family language in school will retain a sense of their
individuality—their ethnic heritage and cultural ties. Supporters of bilingual
education thus want it both ways. They propose bilingual schooling as a
way of helping students acquire the skills of the classroom crucial for public
success. But they likewise insist that bilingual instruction will give students
a sense of their identity apart from the public.

Behind this screen there gleams an astonishing promise: One can become 60
a public person while still remaining a private person. At the very same
time one can be both! There need be no tension between the self in the
crowd and the self apart from the crowd! Who would not want to believe
such an idea? Who can be surprised that the scheme has won the support
of many middle-class Americans? If the barrio or ghetto child can retain
his separateness even while being publicly educated, then it is almost possible
to believe that there is no private cost to be paid for public success. Such
is the consolation offered by any of the current bilingual schemes. Consider,
for example, the bilingual voters' ballot. In some American cities one can
cast a ballot printed in several langugages. Such a document implies that a
person can exercise that most public of rights—the right to vote—while
still keeping apart, unassimilated from public life.

It is not enough to say that these schemes are foolish and certainly doomed. 61
Middle-class supporters of public bilingualism toy with the confusion of
those Americans who cannot speak standard English as well as they can.
Bilingual enthusiasts, moreover, sin against intimacy. An Hispanic-American writer tells me, 'I will never give up my family language; I would as
soon give up my soul.' Thus he holds to his chest a skein of words, as
though it were the source of his family ties. He credits to language what
he should credit to family members. A convenient mistake. For as long as
he holds on to words, he can ignore how much else has changed in his life.

It has happened before. In earlier decades, persons newly successful and 62
ambitious for social mobility similarly seized upon certain 'family words.'
Working-class men attempting political power took to calling one another
'brother.' By so doing they escaped oppressive public isolation and were
able to unite with many others like themselves. But they paid a price for

this union. It was a public union they forged. The word they coined to address one another could never be the sound (*brother*) exchanged by two in intimate greeting. In the union hall the word 'brother' became a vague metaphor; with repetition a weak echo of the intimate sound. Context forced the change. Context could not be overruled. Context will always guard the realm of the intimate from public misuse.

Today nonwhite Americans call 'brother' to strangers. And white feminists   63
refer to their mass union of 'sisters.' And white middle-class teenagers continue to prove the importance of context as they try to ignore it. They seize upon the idioms of the black ghetto. But their attempt to appropriate such expressions invariably changes the words. As it becomes a public expression, the ghetto idiom loses its sound—its message of public separateness and strident intimacy. It becomes with public repetition a series of words, increasingly lifeless.

The mystery remains: intimate utterance. The communication of intimacy   64
passes through the word to enliven its sound. But it cannot be held by the word. Cannot be clutched or ever quoted. It is too fluid. It depends not on word but on person.

My grandmother!   65

She stood among my other relations mocking me when I no longer spoke   66
Spanish. '*Pocho*,' she said. But then it made no difference. (She'd laugh.) Our relationship continued. Language was never its source. She was a woman in her eighties during the first decade of my life. A mysterious woman to me, my only living grandparent. A woman of Mexico. The woman in long black dresses that reached down to her shoes. My one relative who spoke no word of English. She had no interest in *gringo* society. She remained completely aloof from the public. Protected by her daughters. Protected even by me when we went to Safeway together and I acted as her translator. Eccentric woman. Soft. Hard.

When my family visited my aunt's house in San Francisco, my grand-   67
mother searched for me among my many cousins. She'd chase them away. Pinching her granddaughters, she'd warn them all away from me. Then she'd take me to her room, where she had prepared for my coming. There would be a chair next to the bed. A dusty jellied candy nearby. And a copy of *Life en Español* for me to examine. 'There,' she'd say. I'd sit there content. A boy of eight. *Pocho*. Her favorite. I'd sift through the pictures of earthquake-destroyed Latin American cities and blond-wigged Mexican movie stars. And all the while I'd listen to the sound of my grandmother's voice. She'd pace round the room, searching through closets and drawers, telling me stories of her life. Her past. They were stories so familiar to me that I couldn't remember the first time I'd heard them. I'd look up sometimes to listen. Other times she'd look over at me. But she never seemed to expect a response. Sometimes I'd smile or nod. (I understood exactly what she was saying.) But it never seemed to matter to her one way

or another. It was enough I was there. The words she spoke were almost irrelevant to the fact—the sounds she made. Content.

The mystery remained: intimate utterance.   68

I learn little about language and intimacy listening to those social activists   69
who propose using one's family language in public life. Listening to songs
on the radio, or hearing a great voice at the opera, or overhearing the
woman downstairs singing to herself at an open window, I learn much
more. Singers celebrate the human voice. Their lyrics are words. But
animated by voice those words are subsumed into sounds. I listen with
excitement as the words yield their enormous power to sound—though the
words are never totally obliterated. In most songs the drama or tension
results from the fact that the singer moves between word (sense) and note
(song). At one moment the song simply 'says' something. At another moment
the voice stretches out the words—the heart cannot contain!— and the voice
moves toward pure sound. Words take flight.

Singing out words, the singer suggests an experience of sound most   70
intensely mine at intimate moments. Literally, most songs are about love.
(Lost love; celebrations of loving; pleas.) By simply being occasions when
sound escapes word, however, songs put me in mind of the most intimate
moments of my life.

Finally, among all types of song, it is the song created by lyric poets   71
that I find most compelling. There is no other public occasion of sound so
important for me. Written poems exist on a page, at first glance, as a mere
collection of words. And yet, despite this, without musical accompaniment,
the poet leads me to hear the sounds of the words that I read. As song, the
poem passes between sound and sense, never belonging for long to one
realm or the other. As public artifact, the poem can never duplicate intimate
sound. But by imitating such sound, the poem helps me recall the intimate
times of my life. I read in my room—alone—and grow conscious of being
alone, sounding my voice, in search of another. The poem serves then as
a memory device. It forces remembrance. And refreshes. It reminds me of
the possibility of escaping public words, the possibility that awaits me in
meeting the intimate.

The poems I read are not nonsense poems. But I read them for reasons   72
which, I imagine, are similar to those that make children play with
meaningless rhyme. I have watched them before: I have noticed the way
children create private languages to keep away the adult; I have heard their
chanting riddles that go nowhere in logic but harken back to some kingdom
of sound; I have watched them listen to intricate nonsense rhymes, and I
have noted their wonder. I was never such a child. Until I was six years
old, I remained in a magical realm of sound. I didn't need to remember
that realm because it was present to me. But then the screen door shut
behind me as I left home for school. At last I began my movement toward

words. On the other side of initial sadness would come the realization that intimacy cannot be held. With time would come the knowledge that intimacy must finally pass.

I would dishonor those I have loved and those I love now to claim 73 anything else. I would dishonor our closeness by holding on to a particular language and calling it my family language. Intimacy is not trapped within words. It passes through words. It passes. The truth is that intimates leave the room. Doors close. Faces move away from the window. Time passes. Voices recede into the dark. Death finally quiets the voice. And there is no way to deny it. No way to stand in the crowd, uttering one's family language.

The last time I saw my grandmother I was nine years old. I can tell you 74 some of the things she said to me as I stood by her bed. I cannot, however, quote the message of intimacy she conveyed with her voice. She laughed, holding my hand. Her voice illumined disjointed memories as it passed them again. She remembered her husband, his green eyes, the magic name of Narciso. His early death. She remembered the farm in Mexico. The eucalyptus nearby. (Its scent, she remembered, like incense.) She remembered the family cow, the bell round its neck heard miles away. A dog. She remembered working as a seamstress. How she'd leave her daughters and son for long hours to go into Guadalajara to work. And how my mother would come running toward her in the sun—her bright yellow dress—to see her return. '*Mmmaaammmmááááá*,' the old lady mimicked her daughter (my mother) to her son. She laughed. There was the snap of a cough. An aunt came into the room and told me it was time I should leave. 'You can see her tomorrow,' she promised. And so I kissed my grandmother's cracked face. And the last thing I saw was her thin, oddly youthful thigh, as my aunt rearranged the sheet on the bed.

At the funeral parlor a few days after, I knelt with my relatives during 75 the rosary. Among their voices but silent, I traced, then lost, the sounds of individual aunts in the surge of the common prayer. And I heard at that moment what I have since heard often again—the sounds the women in my family make when they are praying in sadness. When I went up to look at my grandmother, I saw her through the haze of a veil draped over the open lid of the casket. Her face appeared calm—but distant and unyielding to love. It was not the face I remembered seeing most often. It was the face she made in public when the clerk at Safeway asked her some question and I would have to respond. It was her public face the mortician had designed with his dubious art.

Questions for Discussion and Writing

1. Why is this chapter entitled "Aria"? What is the rhetorical effect of this title?

2. For what purpose does Rodriguez move back and forth between his personal

experiences growing up in Sacramento and the general question of bilingual education? Do you find the overall structure of the chapter effective?

3. How does Rodriguez establish the overall tone of this essay, and how does he want his audience to feel about his childhood? In its entirety, is the piece meant to be optimistic or pessimistic? How does the title of the book, *Hunger of Memory*, relate to the emotional character of this essay? What kind of evidence can you marshal to answer these questions?

4. Interview someone you know who grew up in a non–English-speaking household or who immigrated to the United States from a non–English-speaking country. How do his or her experiences compare to Rodriguez's? What possible conclusions could be drawn from your comparison? Write an essay in which you develop an argument in support of one or more of these conclusions.

ALICE WALKER

(b. 1944)

lice Walker, who occupies a place in the first rank of contemporary American writers, has dedicated her formidable talents to expressing the complex combination of frustration and the hope that characterizes the twentieth-century African-American experience. Like her predecessor W. E. B. DuBois, who died just as she began her career as a writer, Walker fearlessly voices her opinion, even if it means ruffling the feathers of the white or the African-American establishments.

Walker, the youngest of eight children, was born into a sharecropping family in the small town of Eatonton, Georgia. She cut her teeth on poverty, overcrowded living conditions, and institutionalized racism. As she attended segregated public schools, she could not help but notice how the white children she knew received favorable treatment over her African-American siblings and friends. She witnessed the oppressive conditions under which her parents labored. Her escape from the drudgery and despair of this life was found in books and reading.

Because she excelled in high school, Walker earned the privilege of attending Spelman College in Atlanta, the oldest African-American women's college in the nation. Later she transferred to Sarah Lawrence College in New York, a women's college attended mostly by the upper middle class. During her college career, she began to write poetry. The work of these years was published in her first book, Once (1968).

After completing her bachelor's degree in 1965, she turned to public service and civil rights issues. After a stint with New York City's welfare department, she returned to the South, where she worked with voter registration in Georgia and "Head Start" in Mississippi. These jobs further exposed her to the problems of the Southern African American and provided valuable experience for her literary career. In 1967, she challenged laws against interracial marriage by marrying Melvyn Laventhal, a white civil rights lawyer. In the process, she angered many male African-American civil rights activists, some of whom, in fact, had married white women themselves. Later, the sexism and hypocrisy reflected in this anger was to become an important theme in Walker's message.

After her work in civil rights, Walker moved into college teaching. She has taught at Jackson State College and Tougaloo College in Mississippi; Wellesley College in Massachusetts; the University of Massachusetts, Boston; the University of California, Berkeley; and Brandeis University. As her reputation has grown, Walker has dedicated her time more to writing than to teaching. Since her first book of poems, she has published two collections of short stories—In Love and Trouble: Stories of Black Women (1967) and You Can't Keep a Good Woman Down (1971)—

579

three books of poetry—Revolutionary Petunias *(1973),* Goodnight Willie Lee *(1979), and* Horses Make a Landscape Look More Beautiful *(1985)—four novels*—The Third Life of Grange Copeland *(1970),* Meridian *(1976),* The Color Purple *(1982), and* The Temple of My Familiar *(1989)—two collections of essays*—In Search of Our Mothers' Gardens *(1984) and* Living by the Word: Selected Writings, 1973–1987 *(1988)—and two books for young people*—Langston Hughes, A Poet *(1973) and* To Hell with Dying *(1988).* The Color Purple, *her best-known work, won her the Pulitzer Prize and the National Book Award in 1983.*

Not surprisingly, Walker has written most poignantly of the fate of the African American. What distinguishes her from the vast majority of writers, though, and what places her with other African-American women writers such as Toni Morrison and Maya Angelou, is her commitment to confront the most difficult, complex, and troubling aspects of the African-American experience. One finds few easy answers in Walker's writing, and in many instances Walker implicates her fellow African Americans. Speaking courageously for the African-American woman, Walker discusses racism, but she also focuses on a persistent sexism within her own community. Her effort to identify problems within, as well as without, the African-American community has brought her much criticism. Some, in fact, have labeled her a twentieth-century "Uncle Tom." Still, Walker persistently delivers her strong message, and even though she is determined to tell of the injustices that have been and remain in our society, she nonetheless strives to rise above them. She offers inspiration and hope as well as lamentation. It is just this approach to writing and to issues of race and gender that Walker herself has come to call "womanist."

The piece that follows, "In Search of Our Mothers' Gardens," is reprinted from her collection of essays of the same name.

IN SEARCH OF OUR MOTHERS' GARDENS

I described her own nature and temperament. Told how they needed a larger life for
their expression. . . . I pointed out that in lieu of proper channels, her emotions had
overflowed into paths that dissipated them. I talked, beautifully I thought, about an
art that would be born, an art that would open the way for women the likes of her.
I asked her to hope, and build up an inner life against the coming of that day. . . .
I sang, with a strange quiver in my voice, a promise song.

Jean Toomer   "Avey"
Cane

The poet speaking to a prostitute who falls asleep while he's talking—

When the poet Jean Toomer[1] walked through the South in the early twenties,   1
he discovered a curious thing: black women whose spirituality was so
intense, so deep, so *unconscious*, that they were themselves unaware of the
richness they held. They stumbled blindly through their lives: creatures so
abused and mutilated in body, so dimmed and confused by pain, that they
considered themselves unworthy even of hope. In the selfless abstractions their
bodies became to the men who used them, they became more than "sexual
objects," more even than mere women: they became "Saints." Instead of being perceived as whole persons, their bodies became shrines: what
was thought to be their minds became temples suitable for worship. These
crazy Saints stared out at the world, wildly, like lunatics—or quietly, like
suicides; and the "God" that was in their gaze was as mute as a great stone.

Who were these Saints? These crazy, loony, pitiful women?   2

Some of them, without a doubt, were our mothers and grandmothers.   3

In the still heat of the post-Reconstruction South, this is how they seemed   4
to Jean Toomer: exquisite butterflies trapped in an evil honey, toiling away
their lives in an era, a century, that did not acknowledge them, except as
"the *mule* of the world." They dreamed dreams that no one knew—not even
themselves, in any coherent fashion—and saw visions no one could understand. They wandered or sat about the countryside crooning lullabies
to ghosts, and drawing the mother of Christ in charcoal on courthouse
walls.

They forced their minds to desert their bodies and their striving spirits   5
sought to rise, like frail whirlwinds from the hard red clay. And when
those frail whirlwinds fell, in scattered particles, upon the ground, no one
mourned. Instead, men lit candles to celebrate the emptiness that remained,
as people do who enter a beautiful but vacant space to resurrect a God.

---

[1] *Jean Toomer:* an African-American author (1894–1967) whose best-known work, *Cane*,
was a major achievement of the Harlem Renaissance. [Editors' note.]

581

Our mothers and grandmothers, some of them: moving to music not yet written. And they waited. 6

They waited for a day when the unknown thing that was in them would be made known; but guessed, somehow in their darkness, that on the day of their revelation they would be long dead. Therefore to Toomer they walked, and even ran, in slow motion. For they were going nowhere immediate, and the future was not yet within their grasp. And men took our mothers and grandmothers, "but got no pleasure from it." So complex was their passion and their calm. 7

To Toomer, they lay vacant and fallow as autumn fields, with harvest time never in sight: and he saw them enter loveless marriages, without joy; and become prostitutes, without resistance; and become mothers of children, without fulfillment. 8

For these grandmothers and mothers of ours were not Saints, but Artists; driven to a numb and bleeding madness by the springs of creativity in them for which there was no release. They were Creators, who lived lives of spiritual waste, because they were so rich in spirituality—which is the basis of Art—that the strain of enduring their unused and unwanted talent drove them insane. Throwing away this spirituality was their pathetic attempt to lighten the soul to a weight their work-worn, sexually abused bodies could bear. 9

What did it mean for a black woman to be an artist in our grandmothers' time? In our great-grandmothers' day? It is a question with an answer cruel enough to stop the blood. 10

Did you have a genius of a great-great-grandmother who died under some ignorant and depraved white overseer's lash? Or was she required to bake biscuits for a lazy backwater tramp, when she cried out in her soul to paint watercolors of sunsets, or the rain falling on the green and peaceful pasturelands? Or was her body broken and forced to bear children (who were more often than not sold away from her)—eight, ten, fifteen, twenty children—when her one joy was the thought of modeling heroic figures of rebellion, in stone or clay? 11

How was the creativity of the black woman kept alive, year after year and century after century, when for most of the years black people have been in America, it was a punishable crime for a black person to read or write? And the freedom to paint, to sculpt, to expand the mind with action did not exist. Consider, if you can bear to imagine it, what might have been the result if singing, too, had been forbidden by law. Listen to the voices of Bessie Smith, Billie Holiday, Nina Simone, Roberta Flack, and Aretha Franklin,[2] among others, and imagine those voices muzzled for life. Then you may begin to comprehend the lives of our "crazy," "Sainted" 12

---

[2] *Bessie Smith, Billie Holiday, Nina Simone, Roberta Flack, Aretha Franklin:* twentieth-century African-American female vocalists. [Editors' note.]

mothers and grandmothers. The agony of the lives of women who might have been Poets, Novelists, Essayists, and Short-Story Writers (over a period of centuries), who died with their real gifts stifled within them.

And, if this were the end of the story, we would have cause to cry out   13
in my paraphrase of Okot p'Bitek's[3] great poem:

> O, my clanswomen
> Let us all cry together!
> Come,
> Let us mourn the death of our mother,
> The death of a Queen
> The ash that was produced
> By a great fire!
> O, this homestead is utterly dead
> Close the gates
> With *lacari* thorns,
> For our mother
> The creator of the Stool is lost!
> And all the young women
> Have perished in the wilderness!

But this is not the end of the story, for all the young women—our   14
mothers and grandmothers, *ourselves*—have not perished in the wilderness. And if we ask ourselves why, and search for and find the answer, we will know beyond all efforts to erase it from our minds, just exactly who, and of what, we black American women are.

One example, perhaps the most pathetic, most misunderstood one, can   15
provide a backdrop for our mothers' work: Phillis Wheatley, a slave in the 1700s.

Virginia Woolf, in her book *A Room of One's Own*, wrote that in order   16
for a woman to write fiction she must have two things, certainly: a room of her own (with key and lock) and enough money to support herself.

What then are we to make of Phillis Wheatley, a slave, who owned not   17
even herself? This sickly, frail black girl who required a servant of her own at times—her health was so precarious—and who, had she been white, would have been easily considered the intellectual superior of all the women and most of the men in the society of her day.

Virginia Woolf wrote further, speaking of course not of our Phillis, that   18
"any woman born with a great gift in the sixteenth century [insert "eighteenth century," insert "black woman," insert "born or made a slave"] would certainly have gone crazed, shot herself, or ended her days in some lonely cottage outside the village, half witch, half wizard [insert "Saint"], feared and mocked at. For it needs little skill and psychology to be sure that a

---

[3] *Okot p'Bitek:* a Ugandan poet, anthropologist, and social critic (b. 1930). [Editors' note.]

highly gifted girl who had tried to use her gift for poetry would have been so thwarted and hindered by contrary instincts [add "chains, guns, the lash, the ownership of one's body by someone else, submission to an alien religion"], that she must have lost her health and sanity to a certainty."

The key words, as they relate to Phillis, are "contrary instincts." For 19 when we read the poetry of Phillis Wheatley—as when we read the novels of Nella Larsen[4] or the oddly false-sounding autobiography of that freest of all black women writers, Zora Hurston[5]—evidence of "contrary instincts" is everywhere. Her loyalties were completely divided, as was, without question, her mind.

But how could this be otherwise? Captured at seven, a slave of wealthy, 20 doting whites who instilled in her the "savagery" of the Africa they "rescued" her from . . . one wonders if she was even able to remember her homeland as she had known it, or as it really was.

Yet, because she did try to use her gift for poetry in a world that made 21 her a slave, she was "so thwarted and hindered by . . . contrary instincts, that she . . . lost her health. . . ." In the last years of her brief life, burdened not only with the need to express her gift but also with a penniless, friendless "freedom" and several small children for whom she was forced to do strenuous work to feed, she lost her health, certainly. Suffering from malnutrition and neglect and who knows what mental agonies, Phillis Wheatley died.

So torn by "contrary instincts" was black, kidnapped, enslaved Phillis 22 that her description of "the Goddess"—as she poetically called the Liberty she did not have—is ironically, cruelly humorous. And, in fact, has held Phillis up to ridicule for more than a century. It is usually read prior to hanging Phillis's memory as that of a fool. She wrote:

> The Goddess comes, she moves divinely fair,
> Olive and laurel binds her *golden* hair.
> Wherever shines this native of the skies,
> Unnumber'd charms and recent graces rise. [My italics]

It is obvious that Phillis, the slave, combed the "Goddess's" hair every 23 morning; prior, perhaps, to bringing in the milk, or fixing her mistress's lunch. She took her imagery from the one thing she saw elevated above all others.

With the benefit of hindsight we ask, "How could she?" 24

But at last, Phillis, we understand. No more snickering when your stiff, 25 struggling, ambivalent lines are forced on us. We know now that you

---

[4] *Nella Larsen:* an African-American author (1893–1963) active in the Harlem Renaissance. [Editors' note.]

[5] *Zora Neale Hurston:* an African-American author (1901?–1960) prominent in the Harlem Renaissance. [Editors' note.]

were not an idiot or a traitor; only a sickly little black girl, snatched from your home and country and made a slave; a woman who still struggled to sing the song that was your gift, although in a land of barbarians who praised you for your bewildered tongue. It is not so much what you sang, as that you kept alive, in so many of our ancestors, *the notion of song.*

Black women are called, in the folklore that so aptly identifies one's status 26 in society, "the *mule* of the world," because we have been handed the burdens that everyone else—*everyone* else—refused to carry. We have also been called "Matriarchs," "Superwomen," and "Mean and Evil Bitches." Not to mention "Castraters" and "Sapphire's Mama." When we have pleaded for understanding, our character has been distorted; when we have asked for simple caring, we have been handed empty inspirational appellations, then stuck in the farthest corner. When we have asked for love, we have been given children. In short, even our plainer gifts, our labors of fidelity and love, have been knocked down our throats. To be an artist and a black woman, even today, lowers our status in many respects, rather than raises it: and yet, artists we will be.

Therefore we must fearlessly pull out of ourselves and look at and identify 27 with our lives the living creativity some of our great-grandmothers were not allowed to know. I stress *some* of them because it is well known that the majority of our great-grandmothers knew, even without "knowing" it, the reality of their spirituality, even if they didn't recognize it beyond what happened in the singing at church—and they never had any intention of giving it up.

How they did it—those millions of black women who were not Phillis 28 Wheatley, or Lucy Terry[6] or Frances Harper[7] or Zora Hurston or Nella Larsen or Bessie Smith; or Elizabeth Catlett,[8] or Katherine Dunham,[9] either—brings me to the title of this essay, "In Search of Our Mothers' Gardens," which is a personal account that is yet shared, in its theme and its meaning, by all of us. I found, while thinking about the far-reaching world of the creative black woman, that often the truest answer to a question that really matters can be found very close.

In the late 1920s my mother ran away from home to marry my father. 29 Marriage, if not running away, was expected of seventeen-year-old girls.

---

[6] *Lucy Terry:* Lucy Terry Prince (1730?–1821), who has been called the first African-American woman poet. [Editors' note.]

[7] *Frances Harper:* an African-American poet (1825–1911) who has been called the first major African-American woman poet of the nineteenth century. [Editors' note.]

[8] *Elizabeth Catlett:* an African-American sculptor and painter (b. 1919). [Editors' note.]

[9] *Katherine Dunham:* an African-American dancer, choreographer, anthropologist, and author (b. 1910). [Editors' note.]

By the time she was twenty, she had two children and was pregnant with a third. Five children later, I was born. And this is how I came to know my mother: she seemed a large, soft, loving-eyed woman who was rarely impatient in our home. Her quick, violent temper was on view only a few times a year, when she battled with the white landlord who had the misfortune to suggest to her that her children did not need to go to school.

She made all the clothes we wore, even my brothers' overalls. She made all the towels and sheets we used. She spent the summers canning vegetables and fruits. She spent the winter evenings making quilts enough to cover all our beds. 30

During the "working" day, she labored beside—not behind—my father in the fields. Her day began before sunup, and did not end until late at night. There was never a moment for her to sit down, undisturbed, to unravel her own private thoughts; never a time free from interruption— by work or the noisy inquiries of her many children. And yet, it is to my mother—and all our mothers who were not famous—that I went in search of the secret of what has fed that muzzled and often mutilated, but vibrant, creative spirit that the black woman has inherited, and that pops out in wild and unlikely places to this day. 31

But when, you will ask, did my overworked mother have time to know or care about feeding the creative spirit? 32

The answer is so simple that many of us have spent years discovering it. We have constantly looked high, when we should have looked high—and low. 33

For example: in the Smithsonian Institution in Washington, D.C., there hangs a quilt unlike any other in the world. In fanciful, inspired, and yet simple and identifiable figures, it portrays the story of the Crucifixion. It is considered rare, beyond price. Though it follows no known pattern of quilt-making, and though it is made of bits and pieces of worthless rags, it is obviously the work of a person of powerful imagination and deep spiritual feeling. Below this quilt I saw a note that says it was made by "an anonymous Black woman in Alabama, a hundred years ago." 34

If we could locate this "anonymous" black woman from Alabama, she would turn out to be one of our grandmothers—an artist who left her mark in the only materials she could afford, and in the only medium her position in society allowed her to use. 35

As Virginia Woolf wrote further, in *A Room of One's Own*: 36

> Yet genius of a sort must have existed among women as it must have existed among the working class. [Change this to "slaves" and "the wives and daughters of sharecroppers."] Now and again an Emily Brontë[10] or

[10] *Emily Brontë:* an English novelist (1818–1848). [Editors' note.]

a Robert Burns[11] [change this to "a Zora Hurston or a Richard Wright"[12]] blazes out and proves its presence. But certainly it never got itself on to paper. When, however, one reads of a witch being ducked, of a woman possessed by devils [or "Sainthood"], of a wise woman selling herbs [our root workers], or even a very remarkable man who had a mother, then I think we are on the track of a lost novelist, a suppressed poet, of some mute and inglorious Jane Austen. . . . Indeed, I would venture to guess that Anon, who wrote so many poems without signing them, was often a woman. . . .

And so our mothers and grandmothers have, more often than not   37 anonymously, handed on the creative spark, the seed of the flower they themselves never hoped to see: or like a sealed letter they could not plainly read.

And so it is, certainly, with my own mother. Unlike "Ma" Rainey's[13] songs,   38 which retained their creator's name even while blasting forth from Bessie Smith's mouth, no song or poem will bear my mother's name. Yet so many of the stories that I write, that we all write, are my mother's stories. Only recently did I fully realize this: that through years of listening to my mother's stories of her life, I have absorbed not only the stories themselves, but something of the manner in which she spoke, something of the urgency that involves the knowledge that her stories—like her life—must be recorded. It is probably for this reason that so much of what I have written is about characters whose counterparts in real life are so much older than I am.

But the telling of these stories, which came from my mother's lips as   39 naturally as breathing, was not the only way my mother showed herself as an artist. For stories, too, were subject to being distracted, to dying without conclusion. Dinners must be started, and cotton must be gathered before the big rains. The artist that was and is my mother showed itself to me only after many years. This is what I finally noticed:

Like Mem, a character in *The Third Life of Grange Copeland*, my   40 mother adorned with flowers whatever shabby house we were forced to live in. And not just your typical straggly country stand of zinnias, either. She planted ambitious gardens—and still does—with over fifty different varieties of plants that bloom profusely from early March until late November. Before she left home for the fields, she watered her flowers, chopped up the grass, and laid out new beds. When she returned from

---

[11] *Robert Burns:* a Scottish poet (1759–1796). [Editors' note.]

[12] *Richard Wright:* an African-American writer (1908–1960). [Editors' note.]

[13] *Ma Rainey:* Gertrude Malissa Rainey (1886–1939), an African-American blues singer who was a major influence on Bessie Smith and succeeding blues singers. [Editors' note.]

the fields she might divide clumps of bulbs, dig a cold pit, uproot and replant roses, or prune branches from her taller bushes or trees—until night came and it was too dark to see.

Whatever she planted grew as if by magic, and her fame as a grower of 41 flowers spread over three counties. Because of her creativity with her flowers, even my memories of poverty are seen through a screen of blooms— sunflowers, petunias, roses, dahlias, forsythia, spirea, delphiniums, verbena . . . and on and on.

And I remember people coming to my mother's yard to be given cuttings 42 from her flowers; I hear again the praise showered on her because whatever rocky soil she landed on, she turned into a garden. A garden so brilliant with colors, so original in its design, so magnificent with life and creativity, that to this day people drive by our house in Georgia—perfect strangers and imperfect strangers—and ask to stand or walk among my mother's art.

I notice that it is only when my mother is working in her flowers that 43 she is radiant, almost to the point of being invisible—except as Creator: hand and eye. She is involved in work her soul must have. Ordering the universe in the image of her personal conception of Beauty.

Her face, as she prepares the Art that is her gift, is a legacy of respect 44 she leaves to me, for all that illuminates and cherishes life. She has handed down respect for the possibilities—and the will to grasp them.

For her, so hindered and intruded upon in so many ways, being an artist 45 has still been a daily part of her life. This ability to hold on, even in very simple ways, is work black women have done for a very long time.

This poem is not enough, but it is something, for the woman who 46 literally covered the holes in our walls with sunflowers:

> They were women then
> My mama's generation
> Husky of voice—Stout of
> Step
> With fists as well as
> Hands
> How they battered down
> Doors
> And ironed
> Starched white
> Shirts
> How they led
> Armies
> Headragged Generals
> Across mined
> Fields
> Booby-trapped
> Kitchens

To discover books
Desks
A place for us
How they knew what we
Must know
Without knowing a page
Of it
Themselves.

Guided by my heritage of a love of beauty and a respect for strength— 47 in search of my mother's garden, I found my own.

And perhaps in Africa over two hundred years ago, there was just such 48 a mother; perhaps she painted vivid and daring decorations in oranges and yellows and greens on the walls of her hut; perhaps she sang—in a voice like Roberta Flack's—*sweetly* over the compounds of her village; perhaps she wove the most stunning mats or told the most ingenious stories of all the village storytellers. Perhaps she was herself a poet—though only her daughter's name is signed to the poems that we know.

Perhaps Phillis Wheatley's mother was also an artist. 49

Perhaps in more than Phillis Wheatley's biological life is her mother's 50 signature made clear.

Questions for Discussion and Writing

1. Who is the audience for this piece? Does it speak primarily to African Americans? To women? To African-American women? Does it have something to say to whites? To white males? What different effects could this piece have on these different audiences?

2. How does Walker marshal the life of Phillis Wheatley to "set the stage" for her discussion of her own mother?

3. Precisely what is Alice Walker's garden? How does it relate to her mother's? Do you find the connection credible?

4. In an essay, describe the spiritual or intellectual ties between an older relative or friend and yourself. Think carefully about implicit values that are featured in your account of this relation and how you can most convincingly communicate them. Who is your audience? What strategies will help you to reach them? What sorts of intellectual or emotional tensions do you wish to emphasize? You may wish to portray, as does Walker, how patterns of human behavior tend to repeat themselves from generation to generation. You may wish to show, as well, how you have come to assess your links or ties with your past.

EXTENSIONS

*I*n the Introduction of this book and in the Questions for Discussion and Writing *that accompany each reading, we have asked you to focus intensively on single texts. Here, however, we ask for a more extensive kind of critical reading—to consider various texts in relation to each other and to consider the various perspectives they offer on a question or set of questions. These questions fall into three main categories: General Issues, which ask you to examine relatively broad matters of belief and value; Rhetorical Issues, which concentrate on matters of rhetorical principle and strategy; and Comparisons, which focus on the arguments or strategies of just two or three texts. In each extension, the questions we pose are meant primarily as discussion starters. Beyond these starting points, the issues that arise— and that you may choose to write about—will depend on the way the discussion itself unfolds as you and your classmates respond to (and critically examine) one another's claims.*

GENERAL ISSUES

MYTHOLOGIES WE LIVE BY

Roland Barthes, "The World of Wrestling" pages 385–393

Tom Wolfe, "The Intelligent Coed's Guide to America" pages 465–477

Joan Didion, "Some Dreamers of the Golden Dream" pages 480–494

Stephen Jay Gould, "Measuring Heads" pages 509–543

Basically, "mythologies" are stories that are deeply woven into the fabric of a culture. How much do we live according to such stories? How much do we believe in them? How much do they shape or control our thoughts and actions without our being consciously aware of their influence? Is there a clear boundary between fiction and reality?

How would the four writers included in this extension answer these questions? Briefly describe the roles that believed-in mythologies play—or are shown to play—in the "spectacle" of professional wrestling (Barthes), in the lifestyle of American intellectuals (Wolfe), in the life of a woman convicted of murdering her husband (Didion), and in the work of scientists attempting to measure intelligence (Gould).

As you discuss these portrayals in class, you might consider one or more of the following questions: Is the influence of mythologies necessarily harmful? To what extent do they make reality intelligible, and livable? Is it possible for a mythology to be true, or beneficial (even if false)? Is it possible to live without mythologies? Is it possible to step outside the mythologies we live by and critically examine them? Or do we just step into another mythology? We suggest you focus your group discussion, and the argument you develop in response to it, by selecting a particular mythology (or set of mythologies) you find people living by today.

NATURE

When we speak of "nature," or "getting in touch with nature," what do we mean? What is the relation between "nature" and "human nature"? Why, for example, are national parks important? (Or are they?) How important is the protection of endangered species, such as whales or condors, if their extinction has no significant impact on the prospects for human survival? List and discuss, in class, the ways such questions might be answered today.

Then examine (and be prepared to discuss) the ways that each of these six writers seems to view nature, or the significance of nature in human experience. How would each writer be likely to respond to these questions? In what ways might their responses be similar, in what ways different? How might they respond to each other's answers? To the contemporary answers you and your discussion partners have surveyed?

Taking your group discussion into account, develop an argument for the view of nature you find most persuasive. Be sure to clearly focus the question at issue and to consider what the alternative arguments on this question may be. If you wish, you can speak from the position of one of the six writers, in response to another writer's position or a contemporary position; or invent and develop an argument for a contemporary audience that is aware of these writers' views and the views you have discussed in class.

POLITICS

Aristotle once described humankind as a "political animal": By nature we organize ourselves into communities, cities, nations, the structure of which we invent. As we do so, and as this structure becomes larger and more complex, inevitable questions arise about the proper distribution of decision-making power among its members, and about balancing the needs and rights of individuals and groups. Who should have control over the material resources of society? Who should make and enforce the laws? How much should power be concentrated in the hands of an elite, and how much should it be equally spread among individual citizens? How much (or in what way) should the average citizen participate in the processes of government?

This extension starts from Thomas Paine's *Common Sense*, the political pamphlet that sparked the American Revolution, and then proceeds through three alternative views. In class discussion, carefully analyze each of these four arguments and consider its relations to the others. According to each argument, what is the ideal distribution of power (and wealth) within a society, and why? What assumptions does each argument depend on? Whose interests does each argument appear to serve? What are the points of agreement and difference between these arguments? How valid does each argument seem today?

We suggest you focus your discussion on a specific aspect of contemporary American society or politics, or on a specific issue. How much, for example, should a congressional representative be the "servant" of his or her constituencies? How much influence should the wealthier segments of society have in politics? Should members of Congress be allowed to stay in office as long as they can keep getting reelected (as now), or should their terms be limited (like the President's)? How much responsibility should government take for the correction of social and economic injustices? How should the disparity between rich and poor be judged? And so on.

Working from the perspective of one of the four arguments included in this extension or from a fifth perspective of your own devising, develop and write an essay in response to issues raised in class discussion. Remember that the focus you choose should be relevant (or at least arguably so) to the interests of your discussion group or to current public issues—and that your invention process should take into account not only what might be said from the perspective you have taken, but also what responses, counterarguments, *and agreements* might come from the other perspectives you have encountered in your reading and discussion.

AMERICAN DREAMS

Thomas Paine, *Common Sense* pages 150–181

Alexis de Tocqueville, "In What Spirit the Americans Cultivate the Arts" pages 205–208

Walt Whitman, "Passage to India" pages 241–249

W. E. B. DuBois, "The White World" pages 335–357

William Carlos Williams, "To Elsie" and "At the Ball
Game" pages 378–381

Joan Didion, "Some Dreamers of the Golden Dream" pages 480–494

What is the "American Dream," and how good a dream is it? Consider,
first, what contemporary answers might be given to such a question; list
and discuss these in class. Then consider what sorts of answers each of these
six writers might give (or do give), and how they might respond (or do
respond) to the contemporary answers and to each other. How persuasive
do these answers and responses seem? Finally, when you and your discussion
partners have had sufficient opportunity to explore and discuss these writers'
positions, develop an essay in which you do one of the following things:

1. Speaking from the perspective of one writer's position, argue in
    response to one of the others: Whitman in response to Tocqueville,
    DuBois to Whitman, Williams to DuBois (and/or Tocqueville), Paine
    to Didion, and so on. As you do this, you should assume an audience
    that is also aware of all six writers' views, of contemporary versions of
    the American Dream, and of relevant points that have been raised in
    class discussion.
2. Develop an argument concerning a contemporary version of the
    American Dream—or concerning what you think the American Dream
    "really" is or should be. You could speak from the perspective of one
    of these six writers or from your own perspective. Again, however,
    you should assume an audience that is aware of all the views that you
    and your discussion partners have encountered in the readings for this
    extension and in class discussion.

EXCLUSION AND EMPOWERMENT

Karl Marx and Frederick Engels, *Manifesto of the Communist
Party* pages 212–238

Susan B. Anthony, "On Women's Right to Suffrage," and Emmeline Pankhurst,
"Militant Suffragists" pages 252–255

W. E. B. DuBois, "The White World" pages 335–357

Virginia Woolf, from *A Room of One's Own* pages 365–376

Richard Rodriguez, "Aria" pages 560–577

In the United States, as elsewhere in the world, the rights of full citizenship—
to fully participate, as an equal, in all domains of public life (political,
economic, professional, cultural, and so on)—or even to be recognized as
a "person" endowed with basic human rights—have traditionally been

denied to women and to members of racial or ethnic minorities. What is the basis of such exclusion, and how is it to be overcome? Can social change be brought about through rational discussion? What explains the resistance to reform? What must members of excluded groups do, and at what cost, to gain admission to the public realm? How can the powerless become empowered?

Consider (and discuss in class) how the writers included in this extension would answer such questions. What would be their points of agreement and disagreement? How persuasive does each argument seem? How applicable are these arguments to contemporary conditions? (What *are* "contemporary conditions"? Here you may need to do some research.) As the group discussion proceeds and as you develop your argument, we suggest you focus on a single problem—such as barriers to advancement in the professions, economic discrimination, "white flight" and the formation of an urban "underclass," the impoverishment of women, and the like—and on the possible solutions. What solutions have been proposed? What solutions seem to have worked in the past? What would the writers included in this extension say about those solutions (past and/or proposed)? What solutions would they propose? What solutions would *you* propose? Or which available proposals would you support or resist? Argue either for or against a solution to specific problems faced by women and/or minorities.

CRIME AND PUNISHMENT

Gorgias of Leontini, "Encomium of Helen" pages 61–64

Lysias, "On the Murder of Eratosthenes" pages 67–73

Roland Barthes, "The World of Wrestling" pages 385–393

Joan Didion, "Some Dreamers of the Golden Dream" pages 480–494

William J. Winslade and Judith Wilson Ross, "John Hinckley: The Shooting of the President" pages 547–558

On what basis can a person justly be held responsible for his or her wrongdoing? How much should justice be a matter of "an eye for an eye," and how much should it be merciful? How much should justice be an expression of community morality? What, for example, should be proper treatment for convicted terrorists? Muggers? Burglars? Rapists? Kidnappers? Swindlers? Drunk drivers? Drug dealers? Corporations that violate environmental laws or that cause harm to others through negligence? Answers to such questions tend to focus on a number of concerns, including debt to society, the rights of victims, revenge, protection of moral standards, deterrence, rehabilitation, the psychology of the criminal, the circumstances of the crime, the social causes of crime, and the definition of "criminality" itself.

Identify the concepts of justice that are either implied or presented by the five writers included in this extension. Consider how each writer's argument might apply to questions about responsibility, blame, and punishment; and consider also how each might respond to the arguments of the others. We suggest you focus your discussion by concentrating on a single type of wrongdoing (such as one of the examples listed or a current example)—or on a specific case discussed by one of the writers. How, for example, would Lysias, Barthes, Didion, and Winslade and Ross respond to Gorgias' defense of Helen? How would Gorgias respond to the case of Lucille Miller (in Didion's "Some Dreamers")? How would Lysias respond to Gorgias' response? And so on.

Ultimately, the question is: *How would you respond?* As you and your discussion partners explore the ideas of justice presented by these six writers, develop your own argument about what constitutes justice for the offense or type of offense that you have chosen to focus on. As you develop your argument, remember that your audience is aware of what these writers say and of all that has been said in class discussion also.

ENGINEERING THE GOOD SOCIETY

Voltaire, from *Candide* pages 141–147

T. H. Huxley, "Evolution and Ethics" pages 259–279

Sigmund Freud, from *Civilization and Its Discontents* pages 329–332

Stephen Toulmin, "Can Science and Ethics Be Reconnected?" pages 408–419

Stephen Jay Gould, "Measuring Heads" pages 509–545

To what degree (or in what ways) can science or technology provide solutions to social problems, or contribute to the creation of a "good" society? To what degree (or in what ways) do they actually *threaten* or impede such a project? What are the social consequences of specific scientific and technological developments? List and review, in group discussion, what some of the contemporary answers to these questions would be, focusing as much as possible on selected scientific or technological developments.

Next, consider (and discuss in class) how the writers included in this extension might answer (or do answer) such questions, noting the reasoning each would (or does) present and the assumptions each depends on. What possibilities and problems do they see? Where do they agree with each other and where do they differ? How would they respond to the contemporary answers? How persuasive do you find them?

Develop the argument you find most persuasive, with respect to a particular development or developments; assume an audience aware of the positions taken by these five writers and by the participants in your class discussion. Note that, in your argument, a great deal will depend on how you (and your audience) define "good society."

Values and Belief

Our willingness to act on our ideas of right and wrong depends, in no small part, on the degree to which we *believe in* them or feel them to be *true*. But how do we know that our beliefs are true? When is our belief justified, and when is it blind faith? What should be the limits of our skepticism? This extension includes a range of philosophical perspectives on such questions, perspectives spread over a very wide historical span.

Start by comparing the radical skepticism of the ancient Sophist Gorgias with the Platonic idealism embodied in "Socrates' Second Speech." As you read, and in class discussion, consider the arguments these writers would present (or do present) concerning the nature of truth, values, and belief. What assumptions do their arguments depend on? What implications follow from their arguments? What would they say to each other? Here you might wish to construct a hypothetical dialogue between these two writers, either in writing or in class discussion (with different persons, or groups, speaking from the position of Gorgias or Plato/Socrates).

Descartes, speaking in the early Enlightenment, reflects and responds to the centuries of Christian faith (in the Middle Ages) that followed the collapse of the ancient world, as well as a new spirit of rational skepticism and scientific investigation that he himself is partly responsible for. As you read and discuss Descartes's arguments and the assumptions those arguments depend on, carefully consider his own relation to the debate between Gorgias and Plato. How much does Descartes resemble each? On what points does he differ? How much, for example, does his method of "seeking truth in the sciences" depend on a religious faith in a world designed by God? If we were to construct a hypothetical, three-way conversation among Gorgias, Plato, and Descartes, how might it proceed?

Next examine the arguments presented by Huxley, James, Nietzsche, and Toulmin. All four belong to the modern period, in which many seemingly stable truths, and faiths, have been steadily eroded or have broken down. All four, significantly, inherit the Darwinian revolution in thought about nature, a revolution that prompted early modern thinkers to view the world around them as an essentially meaningless, random process—a world not designed by God or anyone (or anything) else. (Nietzsche, in particular, is famous for announcing the "death of God," in the selection we have included here.) In such a world, how does one justify belief, especially belief concerning right and wrong? Consider carefully the kinds of arguments each of these four writers might offer (or does offer) in response to the modern problem of values and belief and in response to one another's arguments. Further, how would each respond to Gorgias, Plato, and Descartes?

And finally, how should *we* respond? What arguments should we, in this year, find most persuasive? On what should we base our beliefs and values, and why? In group discussion and in writing, develop your best argument on this fundamental issue.

EDUCATION

Plato, from *Phaedrus*, "Socrates' Second Speech" pages 87–99

Paolo Freire, from *The Pedagogy of the Oppressed* pages 394–406

E. D. Hirsch, "Literacy and Cultural Literacy" pages 437–463

Tom Wolfe, "The Intelligent Coed's Guide to America" pages 465–477

Richard Rodriguez, "Aria" pages 560–577

What are schools for? What is the knowledge most worth having, and what form of education best imparts it? What education best prepares the student for life beyond school, for life in the public world? What sort of education is most conducive to the development of a "good" society?

Consider, in your reading and class discussion, how the five writers included in this extension would (or do) answer such questions—from Plato's poetic descriptions of the soul, true love, and the philosophic life; to Freire's argument for "libertarian" education; to Hirsch's emphasis on cultural knowledge; to Wolfe's satiric portrait of the American college scene; to Rodriguez's reflections on bilingualism and the effects of public education on minorities. What seems to be at stake in each writer's argument? What interests would each have education serve? Are there any areas of general agreement? What seem to be the principal points of controversy? What arguments—including those devised by you and your classmates as well as those offered by these five writers—seem most persuasive, and why?

As in the preceding extensions, we suggest you focus the issues for your discussion—and for the argument you develop and write—by concentrating on a specific aspect (or aspects) of contemporary education. You could, for example, debate and write about the emphasis on "skills" that Hirsch attacks, or the kinds of educational programs (such as bilingual education or Hispanic studies) that Rodriguez criticizes, or any other aspect of education that seems relevant to the interests of your group and the general issues under discussion.

RHETORICAL ISSUES

The Grounds of Argument

Gorgias of Leontini, "Encomium of Helen" pages 61–64

Sappho, Fragments pages 53–58

Plato, from *Phaedrus* pages 75–99

Andrew Marvell, "To His Coy Mistress," and Lady Mary Whortley Montagu, "The Lover" pages 136–139

Gorgias, in his "defense" of Helen of Troy, portrays love in a particular way. In class discussion, describe what love is according to Gorgias and what role it plays in his argument. How crucial is Gorgias' account of love to his defense of Helen, and how persuasive does it seem? What would his audience have to believe *in advance* about love to be persuaded by him? Then consider what love is according to Sappho and how it functions in the argumentation of her poems (note, in particular, the poem "Some say a cavalry corps"): How much are Gorgias and Sappho in agreement? Are there any points of major disagreement? Has Gorgias significantly modified the idea of love that Sappho presents? Or has he simply used a traditional, well-established idea (of love) as the basis for overturning another traditional idea (of Helen's guilt)? As you discuss these questions, remember that Sappho lived and wrote approximately two centuries before Gorgias and was still revered as a great poet in Gorgias' time.

Next, consider the notion of love that Plato's Socrates opposes to the notion of love presented by the Sophist Lysias (as Plato portrays him), in the extract from *Phaedrus*. Is this notion of love significantly different from the one(s) that Gorgias and Sappho work with, or has Plato used more or less the *same* traditional idea to serve his own antisophistical purposes and to make Socrates seem morally superior? (Remember that Plato lived and wrote about a generation later than Gorgias.)

Finally, consider the rhetorical roles that preexisting ideas of love play in the poems of Marvell and Montagu. Both wrote for educated audiences aware of Plato, Sappho, and other writers of the ancient world. In what ways has Marvell used ideas of love like those we find in Plato or Sappho to shape the reader's responses to the witty speaker portrayed in his poem? Or has he modified those ideas? How has Montagu used and/or modified those ideas to shape the reader's responses to *her* speaker?

It is often said that persuasion works by relating an idea that seems initially doubtful (the claim or thesis one has to prove) to ideas with which the audience strongly identifies already. Develop an essay in which you show how such a statement applies (or does not apply) to the use of love in the rhetoric of at least two of these five writers.

INTRODUCTIONS

How should a piece of discourse start? In Lewis Carroll's *Alice in Wonderland*, the King of Hearts gives the White Rabbit some advice: "Begin at the beginning and go on till you come to the end: then stop." The point, of course, is that such a prescription is ridiculous.

Most writers have, at one time or another, experienced great difficulty with introductions. Many, in fact, write them last. The problem is understandable: The opening of a piece of discourse must bring to focus the issue or issues at hand, establish the writer's ethos, and persuade the audience to continue reading (or to continue listening, in the case of oratory). Introductions have the difficult job of justifying the existence, and the importance—or even the urgency—of the text.

For each of the writers included in this extension, identify the introductory segment of the discourse: Where does it end, and where does the "body" of the discourse begin? (How can you tell?) Then examine the way each writer handles the task of introducing an argument; in class, discuss and compare the various strategies you find employed. How do the relationships among writer (or speaker), audience, and issue affect the construction of an introduction? Develop an essay in which you answer this question by explaining the *differences* in strategy between at least two introductions.

Argument Through Time: Structure and Transitions

Thomas Paine, *Common Sense* pages 150–181

Roland Barthes, "The World of Wrestling" pages 385–393

Stephen Toulmin, "Can Science and Ethics Be Reconnected?" pages 408–419

Richard Rodriguez, "Aria" pages 560–577

Alice Walker, "In Search of Our Mothers' Gardens" pages 581–589

The simple design of the five-part essay, although a staple of writing textbooks for generations, has little resemblance to what we find in most real world argumentation. For each of the writers included in this extension, identify and analyze the major steps or movements in the progression of the argument from its opening to its close. Where does each step seem to begin and end? (Is it always clear?) How are transitions signaled? What rhetorical function does each step perform? How does the writer link the steps in the argument together to form a coherent (and persuasive) whole? Where does the writer's thesis first appear? (And why at this particular place?) How and why are supporting arguments and premises repeated? In what ways do a writer's structural choices seem rhetorically effective or appropriate for the writer's purposes, and in what ways do they seem unhelpful? Discuss and compare, in class, the different structural strategies employed by these five writers, and develop an essay in which you explain the structural differences between at least two arguments.

Orality and Rhetoric

Lysias, "On the Murder of Eratosthenes" pages 67–73

Alexander Hamilton, from *Debates* pages 184–186

Susan B. Anthony, "On Women's Right to Suffrage," and Emmeline Pankhurst, "Militant Suffragists" pages 252–255

The ancient Greek words *rhetoric* and *rhetor*—as well as their Latin (and modern) derivatives, *oratory* and *orator*—originally meant "speech" and "speaker." Rhetoric began as an art of the spoken word, of *oral argument* in public assemblies. As writing and print media overtook the oral tradition in European culture, however, the formal study of rhetoric gradually expanded to consider a wide variety of discourses, written as well as spoken, private as well as public. And yet the oral aspect of rhetoric—the presence of a speaking voice, or the *illusion* of it—has always seemed somehow central to the art. Moreover, oratory or "public speaking" is still, as always, an essential medium of argument.

This extension includes the texts of four actual orations: one ancient courtoom speech, one political speech from the late eighteenth century, and two early modern speeches on political topics. As you analyze and discuss the rhetoric of these four orations, consider how the rhetorical situation of oratory (in which the speaker and audience are physically present to each other) differs from that of writing (in which writer and reader are not present to each other). In what ways does the design of each text seem to reflect or respond to the special needs of the speaking situation? What are the distinctive advantages and disadvantages of oratory as a medium of argument? What features of oral rhetoric seem "lost in translation" when the text of an oration is put in writing? To supplement your discussion, we strongly recommend that you also consider tape recordings—or better, videotapes or films—of actual contemporary speeches. (Your college library should have a wealth of material available.)

To further supplement your discussion of oral rhetoric and to provide a basis for comparison, we suggest you consider one or more *written* arguments as well: for example, Hamilton and Madison's *The Federalist* (pp. 187–196), or Winslade and Ross's "John Hinckley: The Shooting of the President" (pp. 547–558), which offer argumentation on political and legal issues; or Toulmin's "Can Science and Ethics be Reconnected?" (pp. 408–419), which is a good contemporary example of "academic" scholarly writing; or Woolf's chapter from *A Room of One's Own* (pp. 365–376), which is a literary imitation of a speech. In what ways does written argumentation seem to differ from oral argumentation? In what ways does the preservation of oral qualities enhance or impede the effectiveness of written arguments?

Develop and write an argument on the distinctive qualities of oral rhetoric and its advantages or disadvantages or on the role that "oral" qualities may play in written rhetoric, using the texts (and tapes, videotapes and/or films) you have discussed in class as your examples. *Or* develop and present a speech—for an audience of "colleagues," as represented by your class—in which you advance your argument on this subject.

POETIC RHETORIC

The word "poetry" comes from the ancient Greek word *poiein*, which means
make, *invent*, *create*—and, originally, all poetic discourse was "made" in
the form of verse, song, or rhythmic chant. By means of artful, rhythmic
language, poetry tells stories (some made up, some "true"), presents speaking
characters (who are living in stories), makes arguments (some direct, some
indirect), offers ways of understanding and judging human experience, and
aims to speak both eloquently and memorably. As such, it is the oldest and
most enduring form of rhetoric there is.

What is distinctive about poetic rhetoric? Examine (and discuss, in class)
the ways the seven poets included here seek to persuade their audiences.
How do they resemble and differ from each other in their rhetorical
methods? How do their texts differ, rhetorically, from the varieties of
nonpoetic discourse we find included in this anthology? What are the
similarities? What seem to be the advantages and limitations of poetic
discourse as a medium of argument? Do different forms of verse have
different argumentational possibilities? What roles might poetic qualities
play in the rhetoric of nonpoetic discourse?

To supplement your discussion and for purposes of comparison, we
suggest you also examine the "practical" rhetoric of political and legal
argument, for example in Lysias (pp. 67–73), Paine (pp. 150–181),
Hamilton and Madison (pp. 184–196), Marx and Engels (pp. 212–238),
or Anthony and Pankhurst (pp. 252–255); or the "academic," scholarly
prose of Toulmin and Graham (pp. 408–435); or the more "literary"prose
rhetoric of Tocqueville (pp. 205–208), Wolfe (pp. 465–477), or Didion
(pp. 480–494).

Develop and write an argument concerning the distinctive qualities of
poetic rhetoric, and its advantages or limits as a medium of argument, or
concerning the uses of poetic rhetoric in nonpoetic discourse. If you are
really daring, try writing this argument in verse; you could use one of the
seven poets included here as a model for your versification.

THE ETHICS OF RHETORIC

In the part of Plato's *Phaedrus* we have included in this book, Plato presents three speeches: the first is purportedly by the Sophist Lysias; the second and third are put in the mouth of Socrates. As the dialogue proceeds, Plato has Socrates reveal that the speech of Lysias is technically and morally "bad"—bad not only for what it says, but also for the way it operates. How much should we agree with Plato?

First, carefully examine the three speeches presented by Plato. What are the major differences between the ways that Lysias and Socrates unfold their arguments? What main sources of appeal do they depend on? On what basis might we find one way more "honest" or more ethical than the other? Prepare a statement for class discussion.

After examining and discussing the differences between the speeches of Socrates and Lysias in Plato's dialogue, analyze (and be prepared to discuss in class) the ways that Anthony, Pankhurst, Barthes, Toulmin, Rodriguez, and Walker unfold an argument. In what ways do the methods of these more modern writers resemble or differ from the methods of Plato's Socrates and Lysias? In what ways do they confirm or refute a distinction between the "badness" and "goodness" of those methods? When you and your discussion partners have examined these comparisons, consider again the grounds on which a writer's rhetoric should be considered "good" or not. Develop an argument in response to Plato, using one or more of the modern writers (or any other writers you wish to bring up) as examples.

COMPARISONS

PLATO, LYSIAS, AND GORGIAS

In the extract from *Phaedrus*, Plato presents the "Speech of Lysias" as an example of the kind of rhetoric taught and practiced by his competitors, the Sophists; this speech is shown to be "bad," and in the rest of the dialogue (not included in this book) the teachings of the Sophists are demolished. (The main arguments used in that demolition are summarized in the "Rhetoric and/or Philosophy" section of the Introduction, pp. 3–7.)

The "Speech of Lysias," however, is in all probability not an actual speech by Lysias but was created by Plato himself. How fairly has Plato represented actual sophistic practices?

First, carefully examine the rhetoric of the "Speech of Lysias" in the extract from *Phaedrus* as compared to the rhetoric of the "better" speeches Plato has put in the mouth of Socrates. Then examine the two actual speeches by Lysias and Gorgias. How much do these speeches resemble Plato's "Speech of Lysias," and how much do they resemble the speeches Plato has Socrates produce? Write a brief description of this comparison, and be ready to discuss it in class.

In group discussion, consider this: Gorgias, on reading a dialogue by Plato in which he himself was portrayed (the dialogue entitled *Gorgias*), once said, "How well Plato knows to satirize!" In "Helen," Gorgias also says "All who . . . persuade people of things do so by molding a false argument." In what ways do these statements apply to Plato's representation of sophistic rhetoric in the "Speech of Lysias"? How much should we trust the rhetoric of Plato? After discussing possible answers to these questions— both negative and positive—develop and write an argument for the position you find most persuasive.

Wordsworth and Montagu

William Wordsworth, "Lines" pages 199–203

Lady Mary Wortley Montagu, "The Lover" pages 137–139

"Lines," Wordsworth's great ode to nature, is addressed to his sister Dorothy. How is Dorothy portrayed? What role does Wordsworth give his sister in the poem, and what role in relation to himself? What does Dorothy's essential nature as a woman seem to be? How is it related to "nature" (as Wordsworth defines it) in general?

When you have examined and discussed (in class) Wordworth's portrayal of womanly nature and nature in general, compare (and discuss) Lady Montagu's portrayal of these things—and of herself. What are the chief differences? Are there any points of agreement, any shared assumptions? How might Montagu respond to Wordworth's treatment of his sister? To his poems as a whole?

Taking Montagu's perspective, write an answer to Wordsworth on behalf of his sister Dorothy—or on your own behalf.

Woolf and DuBois

W. E. B. DuBois, "The White World" pages 335–357

Virginia Woolf, from *A Room of One's Own* pages 365–376

Both W. E. B. DuBois and Virginia Woolf offer analyses of the mind set of a white male culture that has traditionally discriminated against women and racial (or ethnic) minorities. How do these two analyses differ? Are there any points of similarity? How might DuBois and Woolf respond to one another?

When you have discussed these questions in class, next consider the argumentational methods of these two writers and your responses to them. Which seems to you most persuasive, and why? Is it a matter of ethos or style? Of evidence or reasoning? At what points during your reading did you or your classmates feel resistant (especially during the first reading)? At what points were you especially receptive? What was the basis of such receptiveness or resistancy? To what degree did these responses actually exemplify the analysis each writer offers?

Finally, consider the problems each writer faces when speaking to a white and/or male audience. How much (and how successfully) is each writer's rhetoric adapted to such an audience? How much *can* each writer adapt, without fatally compromising his or her position? Compare and assess the argumentational methods of Woolf and DuBois.

WALKER AND ATWOOD

Margaret Atwood, "Significant Moments in the Life of
My Mother" pages 496–507

Alice Walker, "In Search of Our Mothers' Gardens" pages 581–589

First, make a list of conventional or standard things that might be said about the mother-daughter relationship. Then examine the portrayal of this relationship offered by these two writers. In what ways do their rhetorical intentions differ? Their methods of persuasion? How do their strategies correspond with their intentions? How effective do those strategies seem?

Prepare an initial statement about the relation between intention and method in these two essays, and be ready to discuss it in class; after the discussion, revise and develop your statement in a short written argument (for example, approximately 750–1000 words).

As a further step, and with these two essays in view, consider how you might portray the mother-daughter (or father-son) relationship. In what ways would your image of that relation differ from the conventional things that might be said about it? (Or in what ways would it affirm them?) What strategies would best serve to make your portrayal seem persuasive? Write an initial brief statement of your intentions and probable strategies, and be prepared to discuss it in class; afterward, revise and write your argument, in a more fully developed essay (for example, approximately 1000–2000 words).

(Note: you need not approach this portrayal as a matter of personal autobiography; it could also be a fictionalized image of the mother-daughter or father-son relation, or an image based on relationships you know of.)

CARNEGIE AND HUXLEY

T. H. Huxley, "Evolution and Ethics" pages 259–279

Andrew Carnegie, from *The Gospel of Wealth* pages 282–291

Social Darwinism, a philosophy born in the late nineteenth and early twentieth centuries, was an effort to apply the Darwinian notions of "survival of the fittest" and "struggle for survival" to theories of society and politics: If we wish to organize society according to objective scientific principles, shouldn't that organization be consistent with the laws of nature? How do Huxley and Carnegie answer that question? How would you?

Compare the ways that Huxley and Carnegie adapt and use the Darwinian ideas. Where do they agree, and where do they differ? More specifically, how do their *argumentational strategies* differ? What assumptions (stated or unstated) do their arguments depend on? Which argument seems most persuasive, and why? Write an essay in which you compare the rhetoric of these two pieces.

Or, after discussing and comparing the rhetoric of these two essays, go further to develop an argument about the application of Social Darwinist ideas today: Where do we find such ideas being expressed, and how should they be responded to?

TOULMIN, GRAHAM, AND GOULD

Stephen Toulmin, "Can Science and Ethics Be Reconnected?" and Loren R. Graham, "The Multiple Connections Between Science and Ethics" pages 408–435

Stephen Jay Gould, "Measuring Heads" pages 509–545

Stephen Toulmin argues, in the selection included here, that "science is of significance for ethics on account of the ways in which it serves as an exemplar of applied rationality." Loren R. Graham, in his response, is friendly but skeptical toward such a view. What grounds does Toulmin present for his claim, and what grounds does Graham present for his skepticism? What seem to be the strengths and weaknesses of these two arguments? Who do you find most persuasive, and why?

When you have examined and discussed in class the debate between Toulmin and Graham, consider Stephen Jay Gould's analysis of the early history of intelligence measurement. Does Gould's analysis provide support for Toulmin or for Graham? What is his central argument? Taking Gould's perspective, how would you respond to Toulmin's or Graham's argument? Taking their perspectives, how would you respond to Gould? Discuss, in class, the relevance of Gould's argument (and his examples) to the Toulmin-Graham debate and develop a written argument either supporting or opposing Toulmin's claim about the significance of scientific rationality for ethics.

NIETZSCHE AND JAMES

Friedrich Nietzsche, from *The Gay Science* pages 315–325

William James, "The Will to Believe" pages 294–312

Friedrich Nietzsche, who also gave us the concepts of the "superman" and life "beyond good and evil," presents in the selection included here his famous and troubling discourse on the "death of God." James, in a public lecture written about twenty years later, presents an argument in defense of religious faith. Examine, and discuss in class, the rhetoric of these two discourses. What are the most notable differences between them? In what ways are each writer's methods of persuasion appropriate to his purposes and to the nature of his argument? Are there any points of shared agreement or any shared assumptions? Is James's argument an adequate response to Nietzsche's? Which argument seems most effective, and why? Develop an essay in which you compare and assess the rhetoric of these two philosophers.

GLOSSARY OF TERMS

*N*ote: *We include here a number of informal terms, as they are used in this book, as well as a number of common rhetorical terms that we have not actually used but that students may encounter. Some of these terms are roughly equivalent or have large areas of overlap. The italicized terms that appear in any definition are themselves defined elsewhere in this Glossary.*

aesthetic criterion: The criterion of beauty, perfection, or pleasure; one of the three main criteria (the other two being the *ethical* and the *pragmatic*) on which evaluative *judgments* can be based. Using the aesthetic criterion, one may judge something to be "good" because it is (or seems) beautiful or gives pleasure—or "bad" if ugly or unpleasant. See also: *evaluative issue.*

amplification: A general term for enlarging or "amplifying" the presence of a concept in the *audience's* mind. Amplification includes a wide assortment of strategies, such as repetition, restating the concept through a series of variations, climactic variation, accumulation of details and/or related ideas, or simply "dwelling on the subject" at some length—plus (when appropriate) the use of emotive expression and/or *figures of speech* to heighten the psychological impact and memorability of the concept. See also: *stance figure.*

analytic issue: The question of how the known or accepted facts most probably fit together, and/or what other facts the known, accepted facts make probable; one of the two subissues (the other being the *descriptive* issue) involved in "What is the case?" arguments. For example: "How was the eminent neurologist Paul Broca's belief in scientific objectivity related to the racist conclusions reached by his experiments with intelligence measurement?" (see Stephen Jay Gould, pp. 509–545); "Does a breakdown in shared cultural knowledge reduce the possibilities for a democratic society?" (see E. D. Hirsch, Jr., pp. 437–463). Such questions can generally be resolved by means of *consequential* and/or *comparative arguments* that ultimately rest on *assumptions* about the structure of reality. See also: *issue.*

appeal: A traditional name for the *reason* or *proof* to which one "appeals" in order to support a *thesis.* Traditional rhetoric recognizes three main kinds of appeal: the appeal to *ethos* or "ethical appeal," in which the *speaker's* character functions as a reason for belief; the appeal to *logos* or "logical appeal," in which the speaker's statements function as a reason for belief; and the appeal to *pathos* or "pathetic appeal," in which the *audience's* feelings function as a reason for belief. To these, some ancient and modern rhetorical theories would probably add the formal appeal created sheerly through *style* and *structure.* See also: *enthymeme.*

argument: A structure of ideas, consisting of a *thesis*, the *reason* or reasons for believing that thesis, and the underlying *assumptions* or general concepts on which the link between reason and thesis depends. Example:
- Thesis: Helen cannot be blamed for her treasonous adultery.
- Reason: She was compelled to do it by a divine force.
- Assumption: A person acting under divine compulsion cannot be held responsible for what she does. (See Gorgias of Leontini, pp. 61–64.)

Note that the actual presentation of an argument to an audience can be developed in any number of ways. See also: *enthymeme; syllogism; Toulmin argument.*

argumentation: The process by which a writer or speaker's *discourse* establishes relationships between ideas, guiding an audience's thinking toward particular *infer-*

ences and *judgments;* the persuasive strategy involved in the actual unfolding of an *argument;* argumentative discourse.

arrangement: The traditional name for what is called *structure* in this book. Classical treatments of arrangement usually take up, in order, the constituent parts of a piece of *argumentation*—the *introduction, middle* (or "body," which can itself be divided into parts), and *conclusion*—with a detailed discussion of the distinctive functions and possible ways of handling each part in different types of argumentation. The main parts recognized by classical rhetoric are: the "exordium" (introduction); the "narratio" or narration (preliminary statements); the "confirmatio" (presentation of proofs); the "reprehensio" (refutation of objections and summing up); and the "peroratio" or peroration (conclusion). See also: *formal appeal.*

assumption: Any idea or set of ideas that a writer or speaker takes as a "given," requiring no proof or explanation, and that functions as the basis or *grounds* for drawing an *inference* or *judgment* from a piece of *evidence;* the conceptual basis on which an *argument* depends. The assumption or assumptions that underlie a given piece of *argumentation* may be stated or (more usually) unstated; in either case, it is the audience's ability or willingness to accept those assumptions that will tend to make the argumentation seem "reasonable" or persuasive (or not). See also: *warrant.*

audience: See *intended audience.*

author: See *implied author.*

claim: The term used in Stephen Toulmin's model of argument for what this book generally refers to as *thesis.* See also: *argument; Toulmin argument.*

comparative argument: *Argument* based on perceived relations of comparability— similarities and/or differences between two things—as understood or accepted by the audience. Examples:

♦ From analogy (what is true for X is true for Y): "Like the founders of our nation, those who engage in civil disobedience today embody the American commitment to freedom of thought and conscience."

♦ From comparative degree (what is true for X is more true for Y): "If City Hall can be corrupted by someone with a few thousand dollars—and we have seen that it can—just imagine what someone with millions could do."

♦ From antithesis/opposition (the opposite of what is true for X is true for Y): "If a criminal is someone who violates the rights of others, then we who are not criminals must defend them."

♦ From contrast (what is true for X is not true for Y): "The modern televangelist, unlike the great founders of his own religion, is marketing his creed for personal profit and has his eyes very much on the kingdom of this world—whereas they devoted themselves to saving souls, accepted poverty, and sought the kingdom of Heaven."

See also: *analytic issue; evaluative issue.*

conclusion: Often used loosely to mean the *thesis* of an *argument,* as in "the conclusion that follows from this *evidence*"; in a more technical sense, however, "conclusion" means an element of *structure,* namely the closing passage(s) in a piece of *argumentation.* The functions traditionally ascribed to conclusions are: reasserting one's thesis and/or reflecting on its *implications* (*logos* function); foregrounding or reemphasizing one's *stance* (*ethos* function); and/or moving the audience to take action (*pathos* function). See also: *arrangement.*

consequential argument: *Argument* based on perceived relations of consequential-ity—how one thing causes (or is caused by) another or how one idea logically "follows" from another—as understood or accepted by the audience. Examples:

+ From causality (X causes Y, or has certain effects on Y): "This policy will increase social tensions because it favors the rich at the expense of disadvantaged minorities"; "This writer's ethos undermines his credibility because the attitudes he displays reveal a lack of interest in fair and careful reasoning as well as a lack of respect for his audience's intelligence—and no one who lacks these things is credible"; "Thomas Paine joined revolutionary causes in both America and France because of his earlier personal experiences with governmental injustice in England."
+ From logical entailment (X implies Y): "If we assume that education is merely a matter of filling up students' heads with information, then it seems we must also assume that those heads are essentially empty—since only what is empty can be filled—and that, therefore, our students lack the distinguishing characteristic of human beings, namely the possession of a mind."

See also: *analytic issue; evaluative issue; policy issue.*

critical reading: The process of reading analytically (as opposed to casually or passively), by which one tries to form a clear perception of the writer or speaker's *argument*, and of the *assumptions* on which that argument depends. Further, critical reading involves a careful assessment of the argument's quality or strength, the *implications* that it seems to raise, and its relation to other possible (or available) arguments on the *issue* or issues involved, as the reader begins to formulate a reasoned response. See also: *enthymeme; Toulmin argument.*

decorum: Appropriateness. In classical rhetoric, decorum is often treated as a matter of what is "opportune" at any given moment in a particular situation, rather than a matter of fixed rules. See also: *kairos.*

definitional criteria: Basically, the characteristics by which a certain thing can be identified, and that can be used (if the audience accepts them) as the basis for resolving a *definitional issue,* including:
+ Genus (generic identity) and distinctive feature(s): "Democracy is government [genus] based on the consent of the governed [distinctive feature]."
+ Constituents: "A school has students, teachers, a formalized process of instruction, places where students and teachers meet, textbooks, grades, exams, administrators, offices, administrative staff . . . [etc.]."
+ Function(s): "Education is whatever prepares one for effective and responsible participation in the life of one's society."
+ Form: "Anything that can meaningfully be called a city is always organized around a central business and administrative area, a downtown."
+ Origin: "A genuine community is always the product of a natural evolution, a history, as people drawn together by mutual needs and interests gradually work out a complex network of relationships and create for themselves a shared code of values and behavior; a 'planned community' created out of nothing by some designer, a mere collection of people housed in a collection of buildings, is not really a community at all in any meaningful sense."

See also: *evaluative issue; issue.*

definitional issue: The question of what something should be called; one of the two subissues (the other being the *evaluative* issue) involved in "How should we judge it?" arguments. Examples: "Is professional wrestling a phony sport, as some say, or is it a form of ritualistic drama?" (see Roland Barthes, pp. 385–393.); note that, as in this example, definition can be used as a mode of evaluation since calling something "ritualistic drama" rather than "phony sport" suggests a better opinion of it. *Arguments* resolving definitional issues ultimately depend on *assumptions* regarding the *definitional criteria* by which things may be identified—as "sport," "phony sport," "ritualistic drama," and so on. See also: *issue*.

descriptive issue: The question of what the facts are; one of the two subissues (the other being the *analytic* issue) involved in "What is the case?" arguments. Examples: "What subjects did René Descartes study when he was in school?"; "Under what conditions did Elizabethan women live?"; "How frequently does William James use argument from examples?" All such questions can generally be resolved by means of *documentary evidence* acquired either by direct observation or by the collection of information from reliable sources. Generally, the persuasiveness of such evidence will depend on the audience's perception of its reliability or the reliability of the means by which it was collected. See also: *issue*.

dialectic: A classical method of philosophical debate (as illustrated in the dialogues of Plato and later codified by Aristotle) in which two disputants carry on a formalized dialogue, usually by means of question and answer and governed by the rules of *syllogisms*. The German philosopher Georg W. F. Hegel developed a somewhat different concept of "dialectic"—as a process in which a "thesis" generates its own "antithesis," leading to a new "synthesis" of the opposed positions; Hegel's concept (or a modified version of it) underlies the "dialectical" view of history found in Marxist thought.

diction: The traditional name for the aspect of *style* that is concerned with word choice. One can, for example, choose a diction that is formal or informal, simple or elaborate, plain or figured, comic or serious, and so forth, to talk about any given subject. The main prescription for diction given by classical rhetoric is the principle of *decorum*: one's diction should be appropriate to the subject, the audience, and the occasion. See also: *figure of speech; trope*.

discourse: Any continuous and meaningful stream of language; in linguistics (most specifically, in the branch of linguistics known as "discourse analysis"), "discourse" refers to language in units larger than the single sentence or to an extended series of utterances. Thus, we can speak of either an oration or a written essay as "a discourse" (which is the primary usage in this book). Further, however, the term is sometimes used for any nonformalized stream of language with no definite beginning or end, including casual conversation and even the "mental speech" by which one thinks or talks to oneself. See also: *logos*.

discourse community: The community of all participants—as writer/speaker and/ or *audience*—in a given *discourse*, or a specific mode of discourse or field of inquiry. Examples: those persons concerned with environmental issues; those concerned with public school policy in your hometown; astrophysicists; and so on. See also: *rhetorical situation*.

documentary evidence: What is typically called "inartistic proof" in classical rhetoric: *evidence* drawn from external sources, or "data" one has collected, as opposed to the evidence created by one's own *invention* process (*enthymemes* and *examples*). Documentary evidence includes testimony by witnesses (or responses to a survey-questionnaire), quotation from printed materials (books, articles, letters, memos, etc.), reports of studies undertaken by others, citation of opinions from authorities, presentation of statistics, exhibition of physical objects (e.g., showing the murder weapon during a courtroom trial), display of photographs, and the like. The persuasiveness of documentary evidence depends on the audience's perception either of its reliability or of the reliability of the means by which it was collected and/or the source from which it comes. See also: *descriptive issue.*

drafting: That aspect of the *writing process* (as opposed to *planning* and *revising*) devoted to the actual generation of *text*—or, more specifically, of a "draft" or version of the *discourse* (an essay, story, etc.) one intends to produce.

enthymeme: According to Aristotelian rhetorical theory, the basic form of *argument* in *rhetoric:* in essence, any combination of a *thesis* with a *reason* (or reasons) for believing it, as in "Euphiletus' killing of Eratosthenes should not be judged as a criminal murder, because it was, in fact, a fulfillment of the requirements of Athenian law, which none of us would want to abandon by convicting him" (see Lysias, pp. 67–73). Because Aristotle described the enthymeme as a "rhetorical counterpart" of the *syllogism,* subsequent theorists have tended to consider it an incomplete syllogism (i.e., with one of its *premises* left unstated) or as a syllogism based on the *assumptions* of the audience concerning what is probable. Others have pointed out that the enthymeme need not be confined to the realm of *logos,* since one can also include *pathos* and *ethos* among the reasons employed by enthymematic argument: The syllogism is the mode of *reasoning* preferred in classical *dialectic,* and the enthymeme is its "rhetorical counterpart" simply because it is the looser, more fluid and intuitive kind of reasoning employed in real-world argumentation. See also: *appeal; Toulmin argument.*

ethical criterion: The criterion of morality or honor; one of the three main criteria (the other two being the *aesthetic* and the *pragmatic*), on which evaluative *judgments* can be based. Using the ethical criterion, one may judge something to be "good" because it is (or seems) honorable—or "bad" because it is (or seems) the opposite. Example: "Building a shelter for the homeless won't bring the city any financial advantages, and it won't do anything, really, to beautify the city, but it's the right thing to do." See also: *evaluative issue.*

ethos: The character of the speaker or writer, as perceived by the audience; the basis of the writer/speaker's credibility. In classical rhetoric, one of the three main *appeals* or sources of persuasion (along with *logos* and *pathos*). Ethos functions as a *reason* for accepting a *thesis* when the speaker or writer seems well intentioned and reliable (i.e., informed and rational). Audience perception of one's ethos depends partly on what reputation (if any) one may have already, but it is mainly created through: "credentials" or qualifications (such as knowledge of the subject) directly presented or revealed in what one says; one's directly stated attitudes and values; and attitudes and values indirectly communicated by one's *style* or *tone.* See also: *enthymeme; persona.*

evaluative issue: The question of whether something is good or bad, or desirable or undesirable; one of the two subissues (the other being the *definitional* issue) involved in "How should we judge it?" arguments. For example: "Were Professor Quirk's studies of language processes in the human brain good or bad science?" *Arguments* resolving evaluative issues depend on *assumptions* about the criteria by which things are valued: *ethical criteria* ("the studies were good because they were honest"); *aesthetic criteria* ("the studies were good because they were elegantly done"); and *pragmatic criteria* ("the studies were good because they performed a useful sociopolitical function"). See also: *issue.*

evidence: As employed in this book, a general term for any information presented as a *reason* for considering a given *thesis* persuasive, including *documentary evidence, reasoning,* and *examples.* See also: *appeal; argument; logos; proof.*

example: One of the main forms of *evidence* employed in *argument*. The basic function of the example is to represent or illustrate a typical pattern in "the way things happen" in order to provide a basis for a *thesis:* "The insanity plea, as currently used, subverts the basic principles of our justice system, as we can see in the case of John Hinckley . . ." (see Winslade and Ross, pp. 547–558). Examples can be real or hypothetical, brief or extended; an argument can be based on one example or on many. The persuasiveness of examples depends on the audience's perception of their typicality. In consequence, they are a relatively weak form of proof because it is almost always possible to cite a counterexample. Examples are most effective when used to supplement and confirm a line of *reasoning*.

exigence: What this book generally refers to as *issue*. See also: *rhetorical situation*.

figure of speech: According to most recent theory, any distinctive patterning of *discourse*—or a distinctive, deliberate disruption of expected patterns—used to create an emphasis. The distinctive turn of phrase "stands out" in the audience's perception and has greater psychological impact than whatever the audience would consider ordinary or "neutral" in a given context. According to classical rhetoric, figures of speech can be divided into two main types: *schemes* (which alter the arrangement of words) and *tropes* (which alter the meaning of words). See also: *amplification; formal appeal; style*.

formal appeal: According to the rhetorical theories of the ancient Sophists, persuasion created through the sheer "charm" of formal patternings, especially the musical and rhythmic effects of *prosody* (see Gorgias of Leontini, pp. 61–64). In the twentieth century, the American rhetorician Kenneth Burke has drawn attention to the psychological effects of form, including both stylistic form and larger discursive forms such as "syllogistic" (logical) progression, "qualitative" (emotional or associative) progression, repetitive form, and even conventional form. See also: *appeal; figure of speech; scheme; structure; style*.

ground(s): A common term for the *reasons* and/or *assumptions* on which an *argument* is based.

implication: As employed in this book, logical *inferences* that go beyond a writer's (or speaker's) stated *argument(s)*—whether "invited" (intentionally) by the writer's arguments or discovered by the reader on his or her own. The latter type of inference arises from two main sources: connections between the writer's statements and the reader's own knowledge (which includes experiences, ideas, and beliefs the writer could not have anticipated); and connections between two or more statements presented but not actually linked by the writer (usually because they are given at disparate places in the text). Frequently, the implications perceived by the reader raise new *issues* and provide the starting points for a reasoned response. See also: *critical reading*.

implied author: The image of the author of a *text*, as conveyed by that text and perceived by the reader. This image may be supplemented by whatever information about the author the reader may have from other sources (biographies, etc.), but it is always separable from the actual author—who may, in fact, be a very different person than the figure the reader imagines and who for all practical purposes remains beyond the reader's knowing. References to the "author" or "writer" of a text generally mean the implied author. See also: *ethos*.

inference: The mostly intuitive act of recognizing what "follows" from a perceived relation between any two (or more) pieces of information; the idea(s) produced by the act of inferring. Example: Given the two statements, "Jones's research methods have gained disapproval from his fellow psychologists" and "Americans tend to find restriction of liberty morally objectionable"—and assuming that the two statements are reliable and related to each other—one might infer, among other things, that Jones's research methods involve the restriction of liberty in some way, and/or (depending on one's own attitudes) that his methods may be morally dubious, though neither idea has been explicitly stated. See also: *argumentation; enthymeme; judgment.*

intended audience: The audience for which a *text* apparently has been designed; the audience of all those to whom the text "speaks" because (1) they have an interest in the *issues* it deals with, and/or (2) they can accept a sufficient number of the text's *assumptions* to be responsive to its *argument(s);* sometimes also called "implied audience." According to this definition, it is possible for both ancient and modern readers of a dialogue by Plato to belong, in varying degrees, to its intended audience. Likewise, the intended audience of a text is not necessarily the same as the original audience to which it was actually presented or to the person who happens to read it now. References to the "audience" or "reader" of a text generally mean the intended audience.

intention: In general, the speaker or writer's rhetorical purpose; the particular perception(s), belief(s) and/or response(s) the speaker or writer seeks to create in the reader's mind by means of *discourse* or *argumentation;* the overall effect on an *intended audience* the speaker or writer's discourse has been designed to create.

introduction: The element of *structure* that serves to begin a piece of *argumentation.* The basic functions of the introduction are: to focus the *issue* or issues that the *argument* to be presented will deal with (*logos* function); to make the audience wish to continue listening or reading, usually by creating a sense of the issue's importance or relevance to the audience's interests (*pathos* function); and to make the audience feel well disposed toward the writer or speaker, mainly by establishing the speaker or writer's reliability (*ethos* function). See also: *arrangement.*

invention: The aspect of *rhetoric* concerned with the creation and development of persuasive *arguments.* Invention can proceed by means of *stasis,* that is, by considering the topics relevant to each type of *issue* and to the specific issue in hand in order to discover what might be said; or by means of a "dialogic" process of testing possible arguments against each other (or against the counterarguments and objections they may provoke) until the strongest available argument is discovered; or by both methods combined. See also: *kairos; rhetorical situation.*

irony: In "verbal irony," an intentional contrast or contradiction between what is said and what is meant, often for purposes of sarcasm or wit; in "situational irony," an observable contrast or contradiction between what seems and what is, usually at someone's expense. See also: *figure of speech; style; tone.*

issue: Basically, the question that an *argument* is designed to resolve. For a question to be genuinely "at issue," however, both the writer (or speaker) and audience must perceive it as a question that needs to be answered and that has no obvious or generally agreed-on answer. As both ancient and modern rhetorical theories have recognized, there are different general types of questions, each with its own requirements, about which people argue. The three main types of issue considered in this book are: "What is the case?" (including *descriptive* and *analytic* issues); "How should it be judged?" (including *definitional* and *evaluative* issues); and

"What should we do?" (or *policy* issues). Note that these three basic issues are closely interrelated and that all three could be involved in a single argument (though one will predominate). See also: *invention; rhetorical situation; stasis.*

judgment: A term employed informally, in this book, to refer to *inference* with a specifically evaluative component. "Judgment," in this sense, may take the form of an attitude (approval or disapproval, etc.) or emotional response as well as overt statement. See also: *definitional issue; evaluative issue; pathos.*

kairos: In Greek, "the opportune." A central concept in the rhetorical theories of the Sophists: What is "best" in any *argument* is always a function of the situation; the best *rhetor* is the one who can swiftly recognize and exploit the argumentational possibilities available at any given moment. The concept of *kairos* implies that fixed formulas and mechanical recipes for writing (or oratory) will always be inadequate because they do not take into account the flexibility, variability, and unpredictability of situations. See also: *invention; rhetorical situation.*

logos: In Greek, "word(s)" or "utterance(s)" or "what is said"; the actual statements given in the writer's (or speaker's) *discourse.* In classical rhetoric, one of the three main *appeals* or sources of persuasion (along with *ethos* and *pathos*), and indeed the central one. What tradition calls (somewhat misleadingly) the "logical" appeal or *proof* occurs whenever a statement is presented as the rational basis for believing another statement (a *claim* or *thesis*). The basic forms of "logical" proof recognized by classical (and modern) rhetoric are: *enthymemes* (or what this book refers to, informally, as *reasonings*); *examples*; and *documentary evidence.* See also: *argument; syllogism; Toulmin argument.*

metaphor: A term often used to refer loosely to any *figure of speech,* or to what classical rhetoric refers to as a *trope;* more technically, a particular type of trope based on analogy. See also: *diction; style.*

middle: What is often called the "body" of an argumentative *discourse,* or everything that comes between the *introduction* and *conclusion.* The structural possibilities of middles are quite fluid, but they generally consist of three main functions that tend to be worked out in distinct steps or "movements": "setting up" whatever basic information, definitions, and/or assumptions must be shared before the *argument* can proceed; "proof," or presentation and discussion of the argument's main *reasons,* including response to whatever significant questions or objections those reasons might provoke (if any); and (if needed) a "summation" that briefly and concisely pulls the overall argument together for the audience. See also: *arrangement; structure.*

occasion: See *issue; rhetorical situation.*

pathos: The feelings—emotions, attitudes, desires—of the *audience;* in classical rhetoric, one of the three main *appeals* or sources of persuasion (along with *ethos* and *logos*). Pathos is aroused primarily by: presenting images that make strong impact on the audience's imagination; emphasizing emotionally resonant concepts by means of *figures of speech* or *amplification;* using emotive language to intensify the feelings provoked by images and/or concepts. Once pathos is aroused, it can then function as a *reason* for accepting a given *thesis* (or for being more willing to accept it), particularly when the thesis is a call to action. Pathos is "logical" or rational in the sense that emotional response depends on the audience's deep *assumptions* concerning what is sad, laughable, frightening, admirable, pitiable, and so on. See also: *argument; enthymeme; judgment.*

persona: A term often used as an equivalent for *ethos.* Persona differs from ethos, however, in that (1) it suggests a fictional identity or "mask" that a speaker or writer puts on in order to play a particular role (the term is derived from the Latin name for the masks worn by actors in classical drama), and (2) unlike ethos, persona has no necessary reference to the ethical quality of the speaker's character. We thus can say that the same writer could adopt the persona of (or speak in the role of) "a corporate manager" or "a concerned citizen" (note Woolf's adoption of "Mary Beton," pp. 14–17 and 365–376)—or that two writers could share the same persona (note Hamilton and Madison's "Publius," pp. 187–196)—but the ethos of any of these personae could be good or bad. See also: *speaker*.

planning: That aspect of the *writing process* (as opposed to *drafting* and *revising*) devoted mainly to working out the *argument* and *structure* of the *text* one intends to produce; sometimes also called "prewriting." Planning, however, may involve such writing activities as making lists, writing notes to oneself, exploratory writing or "freewriting," outlining, and the like.

policy issue: Basically, the question of "What should we do?" In general, *arguments* resolving policy issues must propose a solution to a perceived problem and show that the proposed policy (1) probably will have desirable results, and (2) is feasible. Policy arguments, then, are largely matters of *consequential argument*, though they must also connect with *evaluative criteria* (because the consequences must be desirable for the policy to be worth pursuing, and the problem must be perceived as a problem by the audience) and may involve all other types of issues and arguments as well. See also: *issue; pragmatic criterion*.

pragmatic criterion: The criterion of practical benefit or profit; one of the three main criteria (the other two being the *aesthetic* and the *ethical*) on which evaluative *judgments* can be based. Using the pragmatic criterion, one may judge something to be "good" because it confers some practical advantage—such as wealth, power, success, security, health—or "bad" if it does the opposite. Examples: "Expanding the state prison facilities will enable us to protect society from dangerous criminals who are now simply released because there is no place to put them" (security); "The proposal to expand prison facilities is not feasible because we cannot possibly create enough cells to house all dangerous criminals with our present resources, and indeed we cannot even come close" (success). See also: *evaluative issue; issue; policy issue*.

premise: Used informally, a term for any *reason* or *assumption* employed in an *argument*; more technically, one of the parts of a *syllogism*. See also: *ground(s)*.

proof: A traditional (if somewhat misleading) term for any *reason* or *appeal* employed in *argument*; it is generally recognized that, in rhetoric, a "proof" need not establish absolute certainty to be persuasive and need only establish a sufficient degree of probability. See also: *evidence*.

prose rhythm: The rhythm or cadence created by the lengths (and forms) of successive phrases and sentences. Prose rhythm resembles poetic rhythm but is looser and more flexible, using variations on a basic pattern to create emphasis and interest. Controlling prose rhythm is largely a matter of controlling and manipulating sentence structure, and thus it requires fluency with the range of syntactical possibilities afforded by one's language. See also: *formal appeal; prosody; syntax; voice*.

prosody: The sound quality or "music" of language. The chief elements of prosody are: the phonetic textures of the consonants and vowels composing syllables; the patterns of linguistic stress (emphasis) within words, phrases, and sentences; rhythm; and the rising and falling pitch of the voice. See also: *formal appeal; prose rhythm; style; voice*.

reason: As used in this book, an informal term for any idea (whether "logical" or "emotional") that is employed as a means of persuading an *audience* to accept or believe a given *thesis*. See also: *appeal; argument; enthymeme.*

reasonings: A term employed in this book to refer, informally, to what classical rhetoric calls *enthymemes;* in general, any explicit statement and/or explanation of the reason(s) for believing a given *thesis,* as opposed to the use of *examples* or *documentary evidence.* Example: "The proposed renovation of the old waterfront district will help revive the downtown economy because it will attract large numbers of affluent spenders and will create several thousand new jobs" (the "because" in this reasoning could, of course, be supported by examples, documentary evidence, and/or further reasonings). "Reasonings" or enthymemes work by establishing (and bringing into focus) relationships between ideas, specifically between the thesis that needs to be proven and *assumptions* the audience believes in or identifies with already. See also: *argument; evidence; logos; syllogism; Toulmin argument.*

refutation: *Argument* designed to render an opposed argument unpersuasive or ineffective. "Logical" refutation—generally the most reliable kind—works by exposing inconsistencies or inadequacies in reasoning: a *comparative argument,* for example, may be refuted by showing that the things being compared are not really comparable; a *consequential argument* by showing that neglected factors make a claimed cause-effect relation unlikely or by showing that the argument depends on unrealistic or improbable *assumptions;* a *policy* argument by showing that it is infeasible or by showing that a different policy would have better results or would accomplish the same results more efficiently; and so on. Refutation from *ethos* works by casting doubts on the opponent's reliability or credibility; from *pathos,* by arguing that the opponent's argument has undesirable *implications,* even if probable and well intentioned. The latter two kinds of refutation can be quite effective, but they can also degenerate into mere slander (or can be perceived as such by one's *audience*) and so are risky. See also: *inference; judgment.*

revising: That aspect of the *writing process* (as opposed to *planning* and *drafting*) devoted mainly to reworking the *text* one has already developed. Revising is more than a matter of merely "fixing mistakes" or reworking one's *style* (activities generally referred to as "proofreading" or "editing"), and can involve both major and minor changes in one's *argument* and/or *structure.*

rhetor: Originally, in Greek, an orator; in modern usage, any practitioner of the art of *rhetoric,* whether spoken or written. See also: *rhetorician.*

rhetoric: Originally, in Greek, "rhetoric" meant oratory, particularly in political, legal, and ceremonial contexts; in later classical and modern usage, the art of persuasion or of persuasive *discourse* whether spoken or written; or (in Aristotle's influential definition) the art of "observing the available means of persuasion in any given case." The latter definition applies to rhetoric as: (1) the practical skill of generating effective *argumentation* (in speaking or writing) from the materials afforded by one's *rhetorical situation,* (2) *critical reading* or analysis of the argumentation of others, and (3) a theory of the principles and methods of persuasive argumentation. The main aspects of rhetorical art, as classically defined, are *invention, structure,* and *style;* ancient (and some modern) treatises also include memory (recollection of a memorized speech or of the materials needed for the extemporaneous creation of effective arguments in the course of a debate) and delivery (oral performance and gesture). These so-called "parts of rhetoric" have sometimes been misinterpreted as a five-step (or three-step) sequence, but in most classical rhetorics they are actually presented as simultaneous or parallel functions, with the focus of the *rhetor's* attention shifting back and forth from one function to another as necessary. See also: *writing process*.

rhetorical situation: The situation for which, or in response to which, a piece of *argumentation* has been created; the scene or context of argumentation. The constituents of any rhetorical situation are: the perceived existence of a state of affairs about which there are (or can be) differences of opinion and about which something needs to be said; a writer or speaker and an *audience* drawn together by the felt need to establish agreement; an available body of knowledge and shared *assumptions* on which the writer or speaker's *arguments* can be based; and the specific forum in which the argumentation is presented (e.g., an editorial, an article in a scholarly journal, a televised speech, a presentation in a conference room, etc.). See also: *discourse community; issue; kairos*.

rhetorician: A practitioner and/or theorist of *rhetoric*. See also: *rhetor*.

scheme: The classical term for any striking (emphatic, memorable) arrangement of language, such as: parallel or repeated structures ("of the people, by the people, for the people"); disrupted or inserted structures ("he told me—and I believe it—that he was innocent"); elliptical structures ("our friends need help, our enemies chastisement"); inverted structures ("insist I most certainly will"); linked structures ("power breeds arrogance, arrogance ignorance, ignorance humiliation"); and so on. See also: *amplification; figure of speech; formal appeal; style*.

speaker: As applied to written *discourse*, the "speaker" is an invented identity, embodied in the *text* primarily as a *voice*, and is in principle distinguishable from the *author* of the text; the speaker can be the author's "self-portrait" or an entirely fictive character (or something in between). See also: *persona*.

stance: The general attitude of the writer (or speaker) toward the subject or *issue* under discussion, as communicated by direct statement and/or *tone*. See also: *ethos; stance figure*.

stance figure: Any argumentational gambit that serves to dramatize the *stance* of the writer or speaker. Classical stance figures include: "apostrophe" ("turning aside" to utter a declaration to someone or something other than the main *audience*, such as an absent person, God, or the scenery, as in, "They're going to ban this book. . . . Well, Thomas Jefferson, are you turning in your grave yet?"); "erotema" (the famous "rhetorical question" that is really an assertion, as in, "Isn't your refusal to answer this question a confession of your guilt?"); "praeteritio" (drawing attention to something by pretending to omit it, as in, "I won't even mention my opponent's questionable financial dealings"); "aposiopesis" (breaking off as if unable to continue, as in, "If you fail to control the national debt, you will destroy the economy, you will blight the future of your children, you will—but let's turn to another point"); "aporia" (talking about being unable to talk about something, as in, "Words cannot describe the beauty of the scene"); and "praecisio" (eloquent silence or pointed omission, as in, "Concerning that point, all know what I believe"). See also: *amplification; style; tone*.

stasis: The classical (Latin) term for what is referred to informally, in this book, as *issue*. Literally, the "stasis" is the place where agreement between discussants stops or breaks down and where *argumentation* must begin; the precise point of disagreement. Argumentation not focused on the essential stasis in a dispute risks irrelevance.

structure: The aspect of *rhetoric* concerned primarily with sequencing the materials or parts of an *argument* by a step-by-step progression (as opposed to a mere list of "points") that will (1) sustain the reader's feeling of forward movement (or the feeling that the argument is "going somewhere"), and (2) effectively guide the reader's thinking toward agreement with the writer's *thesis*. An argument can usually be structured in several possible ways; the central principle for developing the most effective structure, however, is that what comes first conditions the *audience's* response to what comes after—the writer needs to consider what ideas or feelings need to be established or "set up" in the audience's mind before any given point can have the desired impact. As traditionally recognized, the basic parts of an argumentative *discourse* are the *introduction*, *middle* (or "body"), and *conclusion*. See also: *argumentation; arrangement; formal appeal*.

style: The aspect of *rhetoric* concerned with the actual language—sentence by sentence, word by word—of *argumentation;* the sum total of the writer's (or speaker's) linguistic choices. The basic function of style is to establish the writer or speaker's *tone* and to emphasize key concepts in the *argument;* the basic elements of style include *diction, prosody, figures of speech,* and *stance figures.* In general, an effective style (1) makes use of rhythm, variety, and emphasis to embody the writer's *ethos* as a believable *voice*, and (2) is reasonably clear and appropriate to the situation. See also: *amplification; decorum; formal appeal; kairos; prose rhythm; syntax.*

syllogism: Originally, in ancient Greek, "joined statements" or *reasoning*. Technically, a formal mode of stating and analyzing *arguments* first developed in Aristotelian logic and *dialectic.* Logicians recognize many kinds of syllogisms and many rules governing their forms, but in general a "valid" (correctly formed) syllogism consists of two *premises*, containing three and only three *terms*, from which a *conclusion* necessarily follows, as in this standard example:

- Major premise [all A are B]:   All men are mortal.
- Minor premise [C is A]:   Socrates is a man.
- Conclusion [C is B]:   Therefore, Socrates is mortal.

If the premises of a valid syllogism are true, the conclusion must be true. Note, however, that a valid syllogism can still be false if its premises are false, as in, "All Martians speak medieval Latin; George Washington was a Martian; therefore, George Washington spoke medieval Latin." In contrast, an invalid syllogism or "logical fallacy" is an error in reasoning not because its premises are false but because it is incorrectly formed, as in, "All men are mortal; all turtles are mortal; therefore, all men are turtles." See also: *enthymeme; Toulmin argument.*

syntax: Sentence structure; or the rules governing the possible ways that grammatical elements can be composed and rearranged to form sentences in any given language. See also: *prose rhythm; scheme.*

term: In logic, "terms" are the basic concepts contained in the subjects and predicates of the *premises* used in logical reasoning. Thus, the premise "All men are mortal" contains two logical terms: [A] the category of things called "man" (in the subject) and [B] the category of mortal things (in the predicate). The premise "All A are B" asserts, then, that all members of the first category are members of the second category. Likewise, the premise "Socrates is a man" asserts that the thing called "Socrates" belongs to the category of things called "man"—"C is A." See also: *syllogism.*

text: As used in this book, a term for any written *discourse.*

tone: The writer or speaker's attitude toward the subject under discussion, or a general mood or atmosphere surrounding it, as created by the writer or speaker's *style*. For example, the two sentences, "The government made some bad choices" and "The beltway bureaucrats blew it," may both be communicating the same basic information, but each has a very different tone. See also: *ethos; stance.*

Toulmin argument: A model of the informal logic used in practical reasoning and real-world argument developed by the contemporary British philosopher Stephen Toulmin in a book entitled *The Uses of Argument* (1958). In Toulmin's basic model, an argument consists of: a "datum" or piece of *evidence*; a *claim* that one can make on the basis of that datum; and a *warrant* that makes the link between datum and claim seem valid. In this basic model, arguments take the form "[datum] SO [claim] SINCE [warrant]" as in Toulmin's example, "George was born in Jamaica [datum] SO George is probably a British citizen [claim] SINCE persons born in Jamaica are entitled by law to British citizenship [warrant]." To this basic model, Toulmin adds "restrictions" or qualifications to the claim ("George is a British citizen unless . . . "), and "backing" for the warrant if it is disputed or potentially disputable ("Jamaicans are entitled by law to British citizenship because . . . "). See also: *argument; enthymeme; syllogism.*

thesis: As used in this book, a general term for the main idea proposed by an *argument* as the resolution of the *issue* in dispute; the point the argument is meant to prove (or make persuasive). See also: *claim; enthymeme; syllogism; Toulmin argument.*

trope: The classical term for any *figure of speech* based on the distortion or "turning" of word meanings, generally on the basis of some logical relationship between the figure employed and the concept or thing it applies to. Some basic types of trope are:
- Metaphor (comparison): "The mayor *piloted* the city through difficult straits."
- Metonymy (consequence/cause): "The tobacco industry wants to sell you *cancer*."
- Synechdoche (part/whole, container/contained): "Look at all these *business suits* walking by."
- Catachresis (loose association): "This *plastic* music bores me."

Tropes can be regarded as miniature *arguments* because they implicitly assert that qualities associated with the figural term are to be applied to the base concept. See also: *diction; enthymeme; inference; irony; judgment; metaphor; style; tone.*

voice: The feeling or illusion of actual speech, or of the presence of an actual speaking person, as created by the *style* of a written *text*; it is thus possible to speak of a written style as "voiced" or "voiceless," or to speak of the specific qualities of a writer's voice. See also: *ethos; persona; prosody; speaker.*

warrant: The term used in Stephen Toulmin's model of argument for what this book generally refers to as *assumption*. See also: *argument; Toulmin argument.*

writing process: A general term for the range of activities involved in the production of a written *text*; sometimes also referred to as the "composing process." The basic aspects of the writing process, as conventionally defined, are *planning, drafting,* and *revising*. These activites should not be thought of as a mechanical three-step sequence; the writing process of skilled writers tends to be recursive, as they shift back and forth from one kind of activity to another. See also: *rhetoric.*

FRIEDRICH NIETZSCHE
From *The Gay Science* by Friedrich Nietzsche, translated by Walter Kaufmann. Copyright © 1974 by Random House, Inc. Reprinted by permission of the publisher.

SIGMUND FREUD
Reprinted from CIVILIZATION AND ITS DISCONTENTS by Sigmund Freud, Translated and Edited by James Strachey, by permission of W. W. Norton & Company, Inc. Copyright © 1961 by James Strachey. Copyright renewed 1989. Reprinted from the *Standard Edition of the Complete Psychological Works of Sigmund Freud*, tr. and ed. by James Strachey, by permission of Sigmund Freud Copyrights, The Institute of Psycho-Analysis, and The Hogarth Press.

W. E. B. DU BOIS
Excerpt from W. E. B. Du Bois, *Dusk of Dawn*. Copyright 1940 by Harcourt, Brace & World, Inc. Copyright © 1968 by Shirley Graham Du Bois. Reprinted by permission of David G. Du Bois.

WALLACE STEVENS
"The Snow Man": Copyright 1923 and renewed 1951 by Wallace Stevens. "The Idea of Order at Key West": Copyright 1936 by Wallace Stevens and renewed 1964 by Holly Stevens. Reprinted from *The Collected Poems of Wallace Stevens*, by permission of Alfred A. Knopf Inc.

VIRGINIA WOOLF
Excerpt from *A Room of One's Own* by Virginia Woolf, copyright 1929 by Harcourt Brace Jovanovich, Inc. and renewed 1957 by Leonard Woolf, reprinted by permission of the publisher. Reprinted by permission of the Executors of the Virginia Woolf Estate and The Hogarth Press as publisher.

WILLIAM CARLOS WILLIAMS
"To Elsie" and "At the Ball Game": William Carlos Williams: *Collected Poems, volume 1, 1909–1939*. Copyright 1938 by New Directions Publishing Corporation. Reprinted by permission of New Directions Publishing Corporation. U.S. and Canadian rights.

ROLAND BARTHES
"The World of Wrestling" from *Mythologies* by Roland Barthes. Translation copyright © 1972 by Jonathan Cape Ltd. Reprinted by permission of Hill and Wang, a division of Farrar, Straus and Giroux, Inc. Reprinted by permission of the Estate of Roland Barthes; the translator, Annette Lavers; and Jonathan Cape. Ltd.

PAULO FREIRE
From *Pedagogy of the Oppressed* by Paulo Freire, tr. by Myra Bergman Ramos. Copyright © 1970 by Paulo Freire. Reprinted by permission of the Continuum Publishing Company.

STEVEN TOULMIN
"Can Science and Ethics Be Reconnected?" by Steven Toulmin, Ph.D. *The Hastings Center Report*, June 1979. Reprinted by permission of the author and publisher.

LOREN GRAHAM
"The Multiple Connections Between Science and Ethics" by Loren Graham, Ph.D. *The Hastings Center Report*, June 1979. Reprinted by permission of the author and publisher. The author gives a fuller treatment of these questions in his *Between Science and Values*, Columbia University Press, New York, 1981.

E. D. HIRSCH
Excerpts from *Cultural Literacy* by E. D. Hirsch, Jr. Copyright © 1987 by Houghton Mifflin Company. Reprinted by permission of Houghton Mifflin Co.

INDEX OF AUTHORS AND TITLES